International Business Research

International Business Research

James P. Neelankavil

M.E.Sharpe
Armonk, New York
London, England

Library of Congress Cataloging-in-Publication Data

Neelankavil, James P.
International business research / by James P. Neelankavil.
   p. cm.
   Includes bibliographical references and index.
   ISBN 978-0-7656-1772-9 (pbk. : alk. paper)

   1. International business enterprises—Management—Research. 2. Business enterprises, Foreign—Research.
3. International trade—Research. 4. Business—Research. I. Title.

HD62.4.N434 2007
338.8'8072--dc22   2006020667

To Angel, Prince, Erica, and Salve

With all my love

Contents

Preface   xvii

1. Introduction and Overview of Research   **3**
Research Issues   7
    Costs   7
    Availability of Secondary Data   8
    Quality of Data Collected   8
    Time Pressures   8
    Lead Time   9
    Complexity of International Research   9
    Coordinating Multicountry Research   9
Nature of Research   10
General Definition of International Research   10
Uses of Research   11
    Evaluating Countries   11
    Determining Market Potential   12
    Financial Decisions   12
    Production Location Decisions   13
    Formalizing Strategies   13
Appendix 1.1. Country Risk Analysis   14
Notes   17
Additional Reading   17

2. Organizational Considerations in International Research   **19**
Divisional Structures   21
Product Structures   22
Geographically Based Structures   24
Function-Based Structures   25
Matrix Structures   25

Organizing for International Research   27
    Centralization   27
    Decentralization   30
    Outside Research Suppliers   32
    Syndicated Services   34
    Standardized Services   34
    Customized Services   34
    Research Needs of the Firm   35
    Cost of International Research   35
Chapter Summary   37
Chapter Review   38
Notes   39
Additional Reading   39

3. Research Process and Research Proposal   **41**
Research Process   42
    Preliminary Phase   42
    Problem Definition   44
    Level of Management   48
    Scope of Decision   48
    Identifying Information Needs   49
    Data Sources   49
    Data Analysis   53
    Presentation of Research Findings   53
    Integration of Recommendations into Decision Making 54
    Storage and Retrieval of Research Reports   54
    Research Proposal   55
Chapter Summary   57
Chapter Review   57
Notes   58
Additional Reading   58

4. Secondary Data   **59**
Advantages of Secondary Data   60
Disadvantages of Secondary Data   60
Criteria for Evaluating Secondary Data   61
International Business Environment   62
Description of the International Business Environment   64
    Competitive Environment   64
    Economic Environment   65
    Financial Environment   67
    Political Environment   68
    Legal Environment   69
    Infrastructure   69
    Technology   70

Demographic Environment 70
Sociocultural Environment 70
Geography 71
Types of Secondary Data 71
Internal Secondary Sources 72
External Secondary Information Sources 73
Uses and Applications of Secondary Data 81
Selecting Countries for Entry 82
Deciding on an Entry Strategy 83
Deciding on Plant Location 83
Making Financial Decisions 84
Making Marketing Decisions 84
Chapter Summary 85
Chapter Review 85
Notes 86
Additional Reading 86

5. Databases and Management Information Systems in International Research **88**
What Is a Database? 89
Advantages of Databases 90
Management Information Systems 92
Development of an MIS 93
Uses of MIS 94
MIS Subsystems 95
Developing a Database 96
Uses of External Databases 99
Problems in International Databases 100
Chapter Summary 101
Chapter Review 102
Notes 102
Additional Reading 103

6. Primary Data Collection: Exploratory Research **104**
Uses of Exploratory Research 105
Qualitative Research Techniques 107
Focus Groups 107
Depth Interviews 116
Indirect or Disguised Exploratory Techniques 118
Word Association 119
Sentence Completion 120
Expressive Techniques 121
Thematic Apperception Test 121
Advantages of Projective Techniques 122
Disadvantages of Projective Techniques 122

New Directions in Exploratory Research 123
Chapter Summary 124
Chapter Review 125
Notes 126
Additional Reading 126

7. Primary Data Collection: An Introduction to Conclusive Research **128**
Factors Influencing Primary Data Collection 129
    Comparability of Data 129
    Cultural Bias 129
    Equivalence of Data 130
Conclusive Research 133
Types of Conclusive Research 134
Descriptive Research Techniques 134
    Surveys 135
    Longitudinal Studies 136
    Observation Techniques 137
    Other Classifications of Observation Techniques 141
    Benefits of Using Observation Methods 142
    Problems Associated with Observation Methods 143
Chapter Summary 143
Chapter Review 144
Notes 144
Additional Reading 145

8. Experimental Research **146**
Key Terms in Experimental Research 147
Extraneous Variables in Experiments 147
Experimental Designs 148
    After-Only Design 149
    One Group Pre-Post Test Design 149
    After-Only with Control or Static Group Design 150
    Before-After with Control Group Design (or Pre-Post Test
      with Control Group Design) 150
    After-Only with Control Group or Posttest with Control Group Design 151
    Time Series Design 152
    Randomized Block Design 153
    Factorial Design 154
Validity in Experimentation 154
Preconditions for Conducting Experiments 155
    Concomitant Variation 155
    Time Order of Occurrence of Variables 155
    Absence of Other Possible Causal Factors 156
Problems in Conducting Experiments 156
    Time 156

        Cost   156
        Execution   156
    Chapter Summary   157
    Chapter Review   157
    Notes   158
    Additional Reading   158

9. Questionnaire Design   **159**
    Basic Requirements of a Questionnaire   160
    Questionnaire Design   161
        Descriptions of Questionnaire Design   161
        Developing Questions   164
        Things to Avoid in Questionnaire Development   166
        Question Structure   171
        Reevaluating the Wording of the Questions   173
        Translation of Questionnaires into Other Languages   174
        Developing the Range of Answers for Each Question   175
        Reworking the Questions   177
        Arranging the Questions   180
        Style and Presentation   183
        Pretesting the Questionnaire   184
    Chapter Summary   184
    Chapter Review   185
    Appendix 9.1. Sample Questionnaire   186
    Notes   191

10. Scale Measurements   **193**
    Characteristics of Scales   194
    Types of Scales   195
        Nominal Scale   195
        Ordinal Scale   196
        Interval Scale   197
        Ratio Scale   197
    Scale Question Forms   198
        Likert Scale   199
        Semantic Differential Scale   200
    Issues in the Use of Scales   202
    Scaled-Response Question Formats   202
        Graphic Rating Scale   202
        Itemized Rating Scale   203
        Percentage Scale   204
        Staple Scale   204
    Reliability Measurements in Scaled Responses   204
    Validity of Measurements in Scaled Responses   206
    International Considerations in Scale Development   207

Chapter Summary 208
Chapter Review 208
Notes 209

11. Questionnaire Administration 210
Mail Interviews 211
    Advantages of Mail Interviews 211
    Disadvantages of Mail Interviews 212
    Steps in Conducting Mail Interviews 213
Telephone Interviews 214
    Advantages of Telephone Interviews 215
    Disadvantages of Telephone Interviews 216
Personal Interviews 217
    Advantages of Personal Interviews 217
    Disadvantages of Personal Interviews 218
Technology-Driven Approaches to Interviewing 219
Selecting an Interviewing Approach 222
Chapter Summary 223
Chapter Review 224
Notes 224
Additional Reading 225

12. Sampling 227
Types of Samples 229
    Nonprobability Sampling Procedures 230
    Probability Samples 231
Sampling Process 233
    Define the Target Population 234
    Obtain an Accurate List of the Population 235
    Determine an Appropriate Sampling Method 236
    Plan the Procedure for Selecting Sampling Units 237
    Determine the Sample Size 237
    Draw the Sample 238
Chapter Summary 240
Chapter Review 241
Notes 241
Additional Reading 241

13. Sample Size Determination Using Statistics 243
Frequency Distribution 244
Central Tendency 246
    The Arithmetic Mean 246
    Median 247
    Mode 248
Measures of Dispersion 248

Variability in Data   250
   Standard Deviation   250
   Coefficient of Variation   252
Distributions   253
Sample Size to Estimate the Mean (μ)   255
Unknown Population Standard Deviation   257
Sample Size to Estimate the Proportion   258
Summary of Steps in Determining Sample Size for Means and Proportions   259
Sample Size Estimation for Measuring Multiple Parameters   259
Adjustments to Sample Size   260
Response Problems in Sampling   261
Chapter Summary   262
Chapter Review   263
Note   264
Additional Reading   264

14. Data Analysis: Fundamentals   **266**
Establishing Categories   266
Editing   267
Coding   268
Computerized Data Entry   271
Data Analysis   272
Classification of Data-Analysis Techniques   272
   Simple Data Analysis   272
   Hypothesis Testing   276
   Hypothesis Testing with Unknown Standard Deviation ($\sigma2$)
      Using Student T Distribution   289
   Chi-square Distribution   293
   Chi-square Distribution and Contingency Tables   296
   Interpreting Chi-square Results   299
Chapter Summary   299
Chapter Review   301
Notes   303
Additional Reading   303

15. Data Analysis: Tests of Differences   **304**
Goodness-of-Fit Tests   305
   Goodness-of-Fit Tests: Steps   305
Analysis of Variance (ANOVA)   308
   Basic Steps in ANOVA   308
   Between-Column Variation   311
   Between-Row Variation   312
   Number of Degrees of Freedom (df)   312
   Sums of Squares   313
Two-way Analysis of Variance (ANOVA)   316

Chapter Summary 317
Chapter Exercises 317
Appendix 15.1. Solved ANOVA Problem Using SAS 320
Additional Reading 322

16. Regression Analysis **323**
Simple Linear Regression 324
Slope and the Intercept 324
Standard Error of the Estimate 327
Using Computer Programs to Determine Linear Regression 328
    Interpreting the SAS Printout 330
Evaluating the Regression Model 330
Analyzing the Slope (b) 330
    Interpreting the SAS Printout 334
Coefficient of Correlation in Regression Analysis 334
Coefficient of Determination 335
Multiple Regression 336
    Interpreting the SAS Printout 341
Chapter Summary 342
Chapter Review and Exercises 342
Appendix 16.1. SAS Program to Solve Simple Regression Problems 347
Appendix 16.2. SAS Program to Solve Multiple Regression Problems 350
Note 352
Additional Reading 352

17. Multivariate Analysis **354**
Factor Analysis 355
    Considerations in Factor Analysis 355
    Uses of Factor Analysis 356
    Terms Used in Factor Analysis 357
    Factor Analysis Model 358
    Factor Scores 359
Cluster Analysis 360
Discriminant Analysis 360
Multidimensional Scaling 362
Chapter Summary 363
Chapter Review 364
Notes 365
Additional Reading 365

18. Research Reports **367**
Written Report 367
Outline of a Written Report 368
Guidelines for Writing a Comprehensive Report 369
Oral Report 370

Guidelines for a Successful Oral Presentation 371
Storage and Retrieval of Research Reports 374
Chapter Summary 375
Chapter Review 375
Additional Reading 375

Appendix A. Questionnaires 377
A1. Detergent Questionnaire 377
A2. Managerial Questionnaire (in English) 382
A3. Managerial Questionnaire (in German) 385

Appendix B. Selected Secondary Sources 389
Data for Asian-Pacific Countries 389
Data for Developing Countries 390
Data for European Countries 390
Data for Latin American Countries 391
International Data (General) 392
National Data (General) 394
Economic Data 396
Financial and Investment Data 399
Marketing Data 402
Political Data and Government Information 404
Statistical Information Sources 406

Appendix C. Statistical Tables 410
C1. Random Numbers 410
C2. Area under the Normal Distribution 412
C3. t Distribution 413
C4. Chi-square Test 414
C5. F Distribution, $\alpha = 0.05$ 415
C6. F Distribution, $\alpha = 0.01$ 416

Appendix D. Statistical Software Packages 417
D1. An Introduction to SPSS 417
D2. A Brief Introduction to the SAS System 423

Appendix E. Country Statistics 436

Glossary 445
Name Index 453
Subject Index 457
About the Author 469

Preface

As the globalization process continues and more companies enter international markets, it is critical that they be able to collect relevant information specific to their industry and the country that they wish to enter. Strategic decisions in the international environment are based on accurate, timely, and appropriate information. Information gathering and analysis are part of the research process—a process with which every student of international business should be familiar.

This introductory text in international business research is aimed at the students who wish to learn and work in the field of international business. Well-planned and well-organized international business research provides information that can be used by decision makers.

The research process discussed here begins by defining a research problem, and then proceeds with identifying information requirements, explaining research methodology, discussing analytical techniques, and, finally, writing a report that highlights the important findings of the research.

In writing this book, I have drawn from my own experiences in teaching marketing and international business research courses. My philosophy in developing this text has been shaped by many authors, especially research textbook authors, whose explanations and insights I have used over the years to formulate my own approach. The authors who have influenced me and to whom I am indebted include Harper W. Boyd and Ralph Westfall (*Marketing Research*); Gilbert A. Churchill Jr. (*Marketing Research: Methodological Foundations*); Susan P. Douglas and C. Samuel Craig (*International Marketing Research*); Paul E. Green and Donald S. Tull (*Research for Marketing Decisions*); V. Kumar (*International Marketing Research*); Naresh K. Malhotra (*Marketing Research: An Applied Orientation*); A. Parasuraman (*Marketing Research*); Donald S. Tull and Del I. Hawkins (*Marketing Research: Measurement and Method*); George P. Tsetsekos (*Research Methods in Finance*); and William G. Zikmund (*Business Research Methods*).

In preparing and writing this textbook I received assistance from many people who have contributed their time and effort in suggesting revisions, compiling data, writing programs, and being cheerleaders. To them I owe a great debt of gratitude. Of the many individuals who helped in the development of this text, the following went out of their way to assist me: Dennis Wesley, who took the time to design the statistical programs, format the text, and organize the charts and tables; my friend Professor Tao Gao of Northeastern University for his comments and suggestions; my colleagues Mahesh Chandra, Andrew Forman, William James, Anil Mathur, Rusty Moore, Shawn Thelen, Yong Zhang, and Boonghee Yoo for their inputs on specific chapters.

I am greatly indebted to Dr. Naresh Malhotra, academic editor, and Harry M. Briggs, executive editor of M.E. Sharpe, for their interest and enthusiasm in supporting the publication of this text. Also, thanks to all the staff at M.E. Sharpe, especially Angela Piliouras, the Managing Editor and Elizabeth Granda, the Associate Editor for their help during the production process of this text. I would like extend my sincere thanks to the late Wolfgang Plumhoff for his help in translating the managerial questionnaire from English to German.

Finally, I would like to thank my family, Angel, Prince, Erica, and Salve, for being there for me throughout this process and encouraging me during times of frustration and setback; to them, I am eternally indebted.

International Business Research

1 Introduction and Overview of Research

International business research is the process of gathering, analyzing, and disseminating information for management decision making in an international context.

LEARNING OBJECTIVES

After reading this chapter, students should be able to

- Understand the growth and importance of international business
- Understand the nature and scope of international business research
- Understand the role of organizational structures in international business research
- Identify the critical factors in international business research
- Identify the types of external research suppliers

Global management, also called international management, is a complex multidimensional field. Intense competition for world markets, global expansion, and dramatic changes in technology have made the task of managing a global firm increasingly challenging. Phenomenal growth in Asian and Latin American countries such as Brazil, Chile, China, India, South Korea, Malaysia, Mexico, Peru, Thailand, and Singapore is shifting the world economic order from the West to other parts of the world. These emerging countries are recording very high annual economic growth rates and present a vast, untapped market for goods and services. This growth coupled with stagnant and saturated markets in most industrialized nations is forcing many companies to seek growth in these emerging markets.

Rising input costs in industrialized countries are another motivation for companies to expand their operations into overseas markets. An assembly-line worker in the Volkswagen plant in Wolfsburg, Germany, earns $25 an hour and works for 33–35 hours per week compared to a factory worker in China, who earns $2 an hour and works for 45–48 hours a week. Availability of low-cost resources such as labor and raw materials in foreign markets makes global expansion attractive to international firms. For example, Motorola, a U.S.-based electronics company, has set up two large manufacturing plants in China to tap into the low-cost but highly trained workforce.

Most businesses are adopting a global philosophy. Globalization proposes that companies view the world as one single market to assemble, produce, and market goods and services. *Globalization* is defined as sourcing, manufacturing, and marketing goods and services that consciously address global customers, markets, and competition in formulating a business strategy. From the simple across-the-border transactions of a few decades ago, international business has grown to encompass a vast network of countries, installations, individuals, resources, and organizations. Table 1.1 presents the world's 10 largest international corporations ranked by foreign assets.

The dynamic changes occurring in the economic, political, and social climate in many countries represent a new challenge to businesses. Western Europe has dismantled internal barriers to form a unified region with a single currency and a vast market made up of 500 million consumers. The former Soviet Union has spawned 18 new countries. Eastern Europe and Russia have acknowledged the failure of centrally managed economies and have adapted free market economic structures and privatization. Indeed, the world has changed profoundly over the past decade. On the one hand, these dynamic shifts are seen as problem areas, but on the other hand these changes provide rare opportunities that didn't exist before. Higher economic growth among emerging countries coupled with stagnant economic growth in Europe and Japan in the last decade has shifted the balance and direction in investments. Since the 1950s, growth in international investments has been substantially larger than the growth in the U.S. economy. Large multinational companies such as Boeing, BP, Citicorp, Coca-Cola, Ford, Gillette, Heineken, Mitsubishi, Philips, Sony, Toyota, and Unilever derive more than half their revenues and profits from international operations.

As businesses venture outside their own countries, the need to know and understand the market conditions in foreign countries is becoming more and more critical. Business research, like all business activity, has become increasingly global. Firms that conduct business in overseas markets must understand the unique features of these markets and determine whether they need to develop customized strategies to be successful. For example, to tap into the vast Chinese market, international companies are dispatching legions of researchers to China in order to get a sense of consumers' tastes.[1] Before 1990, there was only 1 professional marketing research firm in the whole of China; today there are more than 300 professional firms.[2] It is no longer sufficient to know what Chinese consumers want by simply possessing lists of how much individuals earn and what they own. Companies need to understand what motivates Chinese consumers and what products they desire and can use.

To further its research capabilities globally, ACNielsen, a marketing research information company based in the United States, is planning to invest more than $1 million in India during the next five years.[3] Similarly, Market Research Institute of Germany has formed subsidiaries in Poland, Hungary, Czechoslovakia, and Russia to assist international companies in learning about these markets.[4]

Information about environments, customers, market forces, and competition is essential in planning entry into an overseas market. Generally, business executives

Table 1.1   **The World's 10 Largest International Corporations Ranked by Foreign Assets**

Company	Country	Revenues ($ billion)		Assets ($ billion)		Employment (000)	
		Total	Foreign (%)	Total	Foreign (%)	Total	Foreign (%)
1 General Electric	United States	111.6	30	405.2	35	310.0	46
2 Exxon/Mobil	United States	144.5	72	144.5	69	107.0	64
3 Royal Dutch Shell	Netherlands/ United Kingdom	105.4	51	113.9	59	99.3	58
4 General Motors	United States	176.6	26	274.7	25	398.0	41
5 Ford Motors	United States	162.6	31	273.4	—	364.6	53
6 Toyota Motors	Japan	119.7	50	154.9	36	214.6	63
7 Daimler Chrysler	Germany	151.0	74	175.9	32	466.9	48
8 Total Fina	France	39.6	80	77.6	—	74.4	68
9 IBM	United States	87.6	58	87.5	51	307.4	53
10 British Petroleum	United Kingdom	83.5	69	52.6	75	80.4	77

Source: United Nations Conference on Trade and Development, *World Investment Report.* New York: United Nations, 2001.

lack detailed knowledge of overseas market conditions. Compounding the problem is the unpredictability of the foreign markets compared to markets in many of the industrialized countries. For example, the economic turmoil in countries such as Indonesia, Malaysia, and Thailand in July of 1997 came as a surprise to most business leaders and economists, as these countries were projected to continue their strong growth into the twenty-first century. The home market presents a known environment for business executives, whereas a foreign market appears to be a big black box for many of these same executives. Availability of accurate information is most often the equalizer in this equation. That is why many of the large international companies spend millions of dollars on information. For example, Hitachi Corporation of Japan spends a major portion of its $4 billion research and development (R&D) budget on understanding its target customers.[5]

Information is essential to business decision making. Information gathered through research is useful in defining problems, resolving critical issues, identifying opportunities, and fundamentally improving the strategic decision-making process in an organization. Specifically, in international business, research may be used to identify countries with the greatest potential to market goods and services, to predict changes in the political environment of a country, to decide on a location for a manufacturing plant, to identify sources of capital, or to select a target market. In addition, information may also be used to evaluate the effectiveness of a business plan.

In the international context, the need for useful information is even greater. As mentioned earlier, international business operates in an unknown and more volatile environment than that of a business's home country. Many of the external variables that have little effect on businesses in domestic markets play a more critical role in international operations. For example, political stability, exchange rate volatility, and sudden surges in inflation do not ordinarily take place in Japan, the United States, and other industrialized countries. Therefore, for companies and their executives operating in these countries, managing is much easier than, say, running a subsidiary in Bolivia, Ghana, or Indonesia. In the aforementioned countries you may have to deal with the sudden collapse of governments, unpredicted devaluation of local currencies, and an unexplained jump in the consumer price index. Outside the industrialized group of countries, the business environment tends to be unpredictable.

Many international business and marketing failures result from neglecting to recognize cultural and other consumer differences. Consider the following examples in which research would have not only helped the international company avoid an embarrassing situation but also saved the firm from losing market share and/or profits. When a furniture polish firm introduced its aerosol spray polish and advertised its time-saving attribute in Portugal, the product failed miserably as the housewives in Portugal were reluctant to buy such a labor-saving device for their maids. A comprehensive consumer study might have revealed the cleaning habits of households and helped the firm avoid this costly mistake. In a similar case, when General Mills introduced its breakfast cereal in the United Kingdom, its package showed a freckled, redheaded, grinning kid with a crew cut saying, "See kids, it's great." The campaign failed to recognize that in the United Kingdom, family is not as child oriented as in the United States; hence, mothers seldom turn over the decision of which foods to buy to their kids. Depicting a typical American kid on the package was not very helpful either. Research into food-buying habits in the United Kingdom could have saved General Mills time and money without significantly delaying their cereal entry into the UK market.[6]

Following are a few more examples demonstrating the importance of research in international business:

- When Campbell Soup Company attempted its introduction of canned soup in Italy, it used the ad slogan "An instant soup that's as good as home cooked." The product failed, as the message did not appeal to Italian consumers, who place great emphasis on home cooking.
- Cummins, an engine company, ventured into Europe seeking to establish itself in the truck diesel engine market. But it failed to notice that European truck manufacturers, such as Berbiet, Fiat, and Mercedes Benz, manufacture their own diesel engines. As a result, Cummins encountered tremendous obstacles and was unable to develop the market it sought.
- An American firm secured sales for its offset duplicating machines in a developing country. This country had its own paper-manufacturing facilities, which were a source of national pride. Unfortunately, the local paper manufacturers could not produce the highly standardized paper needed for these duplicating machines. Since importing the standard paper was not feasible because of the existence of a paper industry, the machines already sold remained idle and the market was closed to the American firm.

Appropriate research prior to making the decision to enter the above markets could have saved these companies considerable costs and embarrassment.

Most international executives recognize the need for and usefulness of information, but quite often, time and competitive pressures force them to act quickly—with no research. A systematic approach to business research is a critical first step in exploring international markets. Gathering information through research is not confined just to marketing anymore. More and more financial institutions, manufacturing firms, and even human resources departments of international firms are using business research to be more efficient and effective in their decision making. For example, as the competitive landscape for financial services became crowded, investment companies and brokerage houses rushed to grab consumer deposits. This meant that these institutions needed information. Today, financial service companies in many parts of the world use an array of qualitative and quantitative research techniques to guide their decisions, both strategic and tactical.[7] Similarly, sophisticated new techniques in cognitive mapping are now being used to assess managers' mental models in some of today's firms.[8]

Answers to the following questions provide a synopsis of the international research process.

- What are the key research issues?
- What is the nature of research?
- How is international research defined?
- What are the uses of research?
- What are organizational considerations in international research?
- How does a company organize for international research?

RESEARCH ISSUES

Conducting international research is challenging, expensive, and time-consuming. Many factors affect its outcome, including the cost of conducting research, availability of secondary data, quality of data collected, time pressure, lead time (time that it takes to complete an international research study), complexity of the study, and whether a multicountry study is necessary.

COSTS

International research is expensive, and the cost of conducting research varies considerably from country to country. However, information is essential in reducing costs through improved decision making. Research should be viewed as an investment, not an expense. One of the reasons for the higher costs in international research is the dearth of uniformly qualified staff. This requires additional training of the local research staff, which adds to the overall cost of conducting research. Second, there is a lack of research infrastructure (focus group facilities, training facilities, computing skills, etc.) in many developing countries. Therefore, international companies have to either not use the local research setup or develop the necessary infrastructure on their own. The lack of research infrastructure leads foreign companies to incur costs in the areas of training, research facilities, and computing systems. In some industrialized countries, the costs are higher due to higher salaries. Even among industrialized countries, costs vary considerably. For example, focus group research may cost as little as $5,000 in the United States, and the same research would cost about $10,000 in Japan.

AVAILABILITY OF SECONDARY DATA

Secondary data is the backbone of international research. It is cost-efficient and easily gathered. Secondary data is sometimes the only information available for international executives making critical decisions. But in many countries, secondary data is sparse or nonexistent. Local governments do not have the resources or people to collect data; therefore, economic, financial, and other relevant information is often outdated or unavailable. Researchers in the United States, Japan, and other industrialized countries who are accustomed to an abundance of government-provided secondary data find their forays into other countries shockingly disappointing.

In some instances when secondary data is available, it is often inaccurate or unreliable. In Middle Eastern and African countries, where there are large nomadic tribes, the size of a regional population might vary depending on the season. Similarly, population figures would be less accurate where estimates are drawn from village elders, who sometimes exaggerate the number of villagers residing in a village, not only to enhance their own power base, but also to receive government assistance which may be based on population figures. In countries where national income statistics are compiled from tax returns, the figures tend to be notoriously understated.

QUALITY OF DATA COLLECTED

International research suffers from inconsistency in quality. In some countries, such as the United States, the United Kingdom, and Germany, the quality and the reliability of the data collected are high. In other countries, especially the less developed ones, the quality and reliability of data collected may be questionable. This problem applies to both secondary data as well as primary data. In many countries of Africa, Asia, and Latin America, commonly used secondary data such as population census, industrial output, and national incomes are often two to three years old, and in some cases, not available at all.

As mentioned earlier, quality of primary research suffers from poorly trained research personnel, difficulties in obtaining sampling statistics, and cultural values and customs that result in low response rates.

TIME PRESSURES

Quite often the decision to enter an overseas market is made under considerable time pressure. Decisions have to be made fast to allow the firm to be the first in the market place and to attain a certain competitive advantage. In some instances, competitors are already in the market, and there is a rush to follow. At other times, the necessary negotiations with host government agencies dictate the need for quick action. These conditions lead to a very small window of opportunity for an international company, forcing executives to arrive at a decision much sooner than appropriate, leading to actions based on very little information.

LEAD TIME

Generally, it takes a firm a much longer time to obtain research information from overseas markets than from domestic markets. Some of the problems associated with data collection abroad have already been identified. In addition, the international executive's lack of complete knowledge of overseas markets makes the task of compiling data even harder. Sometimes an international firm will rely on local research suppliers or local staff to collect and process data to overcome the firm's lack of knowledge in the target country. Other factors that contribute to requiring a long lead time in international research are the lack of sophistication in data-collection techniques, the unavailability of databases to gather up-to-date information, and the lack of single-source data (from retail scanners).

COMPLEXITY OF INTERNATIONAL RESEARCH

Conducting a successful research project in one's own country is challenging in itself. When the project is international, the dynamics are even more complex. When working internationally, firms must recognize that even the basic research steps have their own twists. Schedules tend to be longer, vendor selection is more difficult, and depth of analysis is weak. Even more difficult is controlling the exact design and methodology for each country in a multicountry study.[9] The factors that contribute to the complexity in international research are the following: different levels of market development, vast differences in government policies toward foreign firms, unique sets of external variables in foreign markets, and the unfamiliarity of international managers with consumers and markets in foreign countries.

COORDINATING MULTICOUNTRY RESEARCH

By definition, international research is conducted across many countries. The differences in language, cultures, business practices, and customs make the coordination of research activities across these markets all the more challenging. Difficulties in establishing comparability and equivalency in data collection and analysis can make research across countries problematic and unusable.

International operations encompass a multitude of activities from a simple export operation to management of a wholly owned subsidiary. Depending on the level of international activity, the information requirements for decision makers vary from situation to situation.

By nature, the operations of international firms are far-flung. Diverse operations located, in some instances, thousands of miles away complicate the management of an international firm. For instance, for a Japanese multinational, managing one of its subsidiaries in Guangdong Province in China, just three hours away by air, is much easier than managing one of its operations in Munich, Germany, which is more than twelve hours away and across several time zones.

The issues discussed in the previous section reinforce the importance of research in international business. At the same time, they also spell out the difficulties of conducting international research. In conducting research internationally, the extent and the method of research vary from situation to situation. In other words, information required to develop an export strategy will be quite different and less involved from that needed when a firm is planning to set up a wholly owned subsidiary.

NATURE OF RESEARCH

The task of research is to provide managers with information that is accurate, timely, relevant, and valid. Decisions made in an environment of uncertainty carry a certain amount of risk in terms of revenue loss, competitive disadvantage, and loss of customers. As the marketplace becomes increasingly competitive with the emergence of large global firms, the goal is to obtain good and relevant information for use in strategic decision making. As international business operations become the mainstay of many firms, decision making has to be precise.

Whereas intuition, judgment, and experience carried the day for most managers a few years back, these same managers need to be much more informed to operate a modern globally oriented company. Information alone becomes the critical difference between success and failure. International businesses have to deal with an ever-changing environment with limited resources, increased competition, and a sophisticated and knowledgeable consumer. International firms must have a very well-thought-out and effective strategic action plan to be successful in a global marketplace.

GENERAL DEFINITION OF INTERNATIONAL RESEARCH

For our purposes, *international research* may be defined as a scientific and objective method to collect, analyze, and disseminate information for the purpose of assisting management in decision making and problem solving in an international context. There are several important concepts to be derived from the above definition.

- First, the research is *scientific*; in other words, it follows sound methodology, it is planned and well documented, it tests a priori hypotheses, and the results can be validated.
- Second, the research is *objective*; that is, the research is unbiased and tries to provide the true state of a given situation. This objectivity assures that the information gathered is accurate. Information collected has to be independent of any biases related to respondents, sampling, questionnaires, and researchers. Many new product entries have failed in the marketplace because of the subjective interpretation of data by managers.
- Third, research involves not only collection of data but also *analysis*. Analysis converts raw data into meaningful information. This step allows researchers to

interpret the data. Analysis includes simple calculations of means, proportions, and frequencies as well as more thorough statistical research procedures, such as regression, factor analysis, and conjoint analysis.
- Fourth, research information needs to be *disseminated.* The information gathered has to be distributed to relevant executives and staff for action.
- Fifth, research is used for *decision making.* All information collected needs to be put to use, whether it is to solve a problem faced by the company or to make a major investment for a new venture. Information is not gathered for posterity but used as a basis for decision making.

USES OF RESEARCH

International research is used for many purposes, ranging from evaluating countries to making multimillion-dollar investments in a production facility in a foreign country. Following is a list of some of the uses of international research:

- Evaluating countries or markets
- Determining market potential
- Assisting financial decision making
- Selecting plant locations
- Formalizing specific strategies

EVALUATING COUNTRIES

Country selection is fundamental to international business. Evaluating the market potential of a group of countries to select one with the best opportunity is critical to the long-term success of an international firm. International companies are faced with many options, and an incorrect decision might close the firm out of a potentially lucrative market for a long time. In evaluating countries (also called *country risk analysis*), companies seek broad-based country information as well as specific market and target consumer information. Some of the macro information that is required to assess a country's market potential is as follows:

- *Competitor information* (number of competitors, their strengths, their market position)
- *Economic factors* (GDP, per capita GDP, economic growth rate, inflation rate, interest rate, balance of payments, national income, production)
- *Political conditions* (political stability, political risk in terms of ownership, political philosophy)
- *Government regulations* (export controls, ownership restrictions, repatriation of profits, marketing regulations, exchange rate controls)
- *Banking and finance* (availability of capital, banking facilities, country's credit standing, external debt)
- *Technical considerations* (availability of technology, government support for technology, technical competence of the population)

- *Infrastructure capabilities* (transportation facilities, telecommunication facilities, power supply, distribution and warehousing facilities)
- *Sociocultural factors* (traditions, values, mores, social institutions)

In addition, market-based information on population (census), demographic breakdown, literacy rate, urbanization, rate of unemployment, life expectancy, family or household size, and personal or household incomes are all necessary in assessing foreign markets.

Larger companies tend to do their own (internal) country risk analysis. For medium-size companies, outside research suppliers provide this type of research. For smaller companies, secondary data through government publications or through periodic reports published by business presses could be used to assess country risk. A few research studies are available for free or at a reasonable cost that could be used by companies that do not have the personnel or capabilities to conduct country risk analysis. Appendix 1.1 discusses a few such studies that are useful for international companies in assessing foreign markets.

DETERMINING MARKET POTENTIAL

As domestic markets get saturated, companies branch out to foreign markets to seek newer, as-yet-untapped markets to maintain a steady flow of income and profits. Market potential is the upper limit of market demand. Market potential is the basis for selecting a country for entry. In estimating a country's market potential, companies consider factors such as total demand, size of the target market, total sales potential, size of the subsegment, buying power of the target segment, frequency of purchase, volume of purchase per shopping trip, and share of market by individual competitors.

FINANCIAL DECISIONS

Financial decisions in the international field are complex and risky. Exchange rate fluctuations, different accounting systems, and government intervention often complicate financial decisions. Appropriate information assists financial planners in making objective decisions about financing and investment choices. As technology and computers play a key role in financial decisions, the need for a faster turnaround of information becomes a necessity. Thus, to compete in a complex global financial market, international companies need to invest in information systems. International companies have more options for acquiring funds than do domestic firms. International companies can borrow euro-based currencies, make use of offshore banking facilities, and borrow from financial institutions in the countries where they have operations.

The many options available to international companies also force them to obtain the most current information to minimize their cost of capital and be efficient in the management of their funds. Some of the factors that affect financial decisions are unpredictable and may undergo dynamic shifts. A case in point is the recent exchange rate volatility observed in Latin America, Russia, and Southeast Asian countries.

Exchange rate fluctuations along with a rise in inflation increase both the cost and the risk of financial decisions.

PRODUCTION LOCATION DECISIONS

Production facilities are located to take advantage of such factors as inexpensive and technically qualified labor forces, abundant supply of raw materials, qualified supplier sources, efficient transportation systems, and proximity to markets. If raw material and adequate parts suppliers are available near major markets, then a production facility can be located near the source as well as the market, completing the value chain. However, for many multinational firms, inputs come from around the world and markets may or may not be located close to supply sources.

In addition to production facility location, international companies also have to decide on the size of the plant (capacity) of each of the manufacturing facilities. Some companies adopt a concentrated production approach, that is, a small number of large plants in a few locations. Other companies have set up a dispersed strategy, in other words, a large number of small plants in many locations. Matsushita of Japan has just a few manufacturing facilities, most of them concentrated around Asia and servicing the entire world market. In contrast, Phillips of the Netherlands has hundreds of plants located in many countries servicing one or two markets at a time.

FORMALIZING STRATEGIES

Information is useful for executives who are developing strategies. By understanding competitors' strengths and weaknesses and through a thorough internal analysis, firms are in a position to develop winning strategies in the marketplace. These strategies may be any one of the aforementioned plant decisions or other decisions that affect the revenues of the firm. For example, Sharp, the large consumer electronics company based in Japan, was able to use market research information, called "town watching," to increase its operating income by 25 percent in fiscal year 1994 alone.[10]

As international companies develop their manufacturing strategy, they need to be aware of the highly competitive environment in which they operate. Many factors affect manufacturing strategies. Some, like costs, are easier to control; others, such as quality, are affected by a combination of variables and tend to be difficult to manage. Efficiency, reliability, and flexibility are the other factors that need to be managed well for a firm to gain competitive advantage in international operations. Competitive information and information on sources of materials and suppliers can therefore help companies to have an effective manufacturing strategy. As the globalization process continues, the need for information on business-related areas also grows.

Most companies realize that going global is more important than ever before and that they can no longer avoid it. In developing a global strategy, these companies must assess global opportunities and also set up a tracking system to evaluate their efforts. International research is the key to the development of global strategy.[11] International business research has definitely grown in the last decade. Many large international firms make use of research to chart their strategies. Under scarce resources, it is suggested that these global companies concentrate on the data that is most important—the data that is essential in conducting their overseas operations.[12] The size of the non-U.S. market for research is now larger than it was in the past.[13] Additionally, some small exporters are using research to explore foreign markets. These exporters do not make use of traditional research approaches but rely on personal contact with distributors, agents, customers, and even competitors to gather information concerning markets they serve.[14]

APPENDIX 1.1. COUNTRY RISK ANALYSIS

In selecting a country for entry, companies conduct risk analysis. In conducting country risk analysis, international companies consider those factors that expose them to various types of risks, including financial losses. Factors considered in conducting country risk analysis include political, economic, banking and finance, regulatory, and cultural.

Political risk is one the key factors that all international companies consider in assessing countries.[15] Political risk is the fear of losses incurred by international companies through sudden and unexpected changes in the political environment of the host country. Many of the political risk analyses conducted by external agencies use a combination of factors in assessing a country's political risk. *Political Risk Services,* a Rochester, NY–based publication, periodically ranks countries on political risk using 12 different factors. These factors include government stability, socioeconomic conditions, internal conflicts, external conflicts, and corruption (see Table 1.2 for the 12 factors used by the PRS Group). The scores are based on a rating scale that uses various internal and external sources to assess the risk for each factor. Table 1.2 lists the 10 least politically risky countries ranked by the PRS Group.

Similarly, in conducting an overall country risk analysis, researchers consider factors that may impact the operations of an international company. As mentioned earlier, some of the common factors considered in assessing countries include economic and political climate, culture, regulatory environment, banking and finance, quality of infrastructure, level of technology, and the country's external debt. Depending on the industry, some factors may be more important than others. For example, for a fast-food company, the cultural and infrastructure variables might be more critical than the technology factor. On the other hand, for a telecommunications company, the technology factor might be more critical than many others. In most instances, researchers believe that the economic and political factors are the most important in assessing a country's risk. In most cases, researchers assign weights to each factor and then rank the risk element for each country. For example, *Euromoney,* a UK publication, in its semiannual country risk rankings assigns a weight of 25 percent each to the economic and political factors.

Euromoney polls economists, political analysts, and insurance brokers and combines these data with quantitative data collected from the World Bank, International Monetary Fund, and credit agencies such as Moody's and Standard & Poor's to arrive at a score for each country. Table 1.3 lists the nine variables considered by *Euromoney* in its ranking of countries and the respective weights assigned to each variable.

Table 1.2   **10 Least Politically Risky Countries**

Country	F1	F2	F3	F4	F5	F6	F7	F8	F9	F10	F11	F12	Total
Netherlands	10	10	12	11	12	6	6	6	6	6	6	4	95.5
Luxembourg	11	11	12	12	12	5	6	6	6	5	5	4	95.0
Finland	9	9	12	12	11	6	6	6	6	6	6	4	94.5
Denmark	10	10	12	11	11	5	6	6	6	6	6	4	93.5
Switzerland	10	10	12	12	12	11	4	6	6	5	6	4	93.0
Sweden	9	10	12	11	11	6	5	6	6	5	6	4	92.5
Norway	8	10	12	11	11	5	6	5	6	5	6	4	91.0
New Zealand	9	10	12	11	12	5	6	6	6	4	6	4	91.0
Canada	10	9	12	12	10	6	6	6	6	3	6	4	90.5
Ireland	10	11	12	11	10	2	6	5	6	6	6	4	90.0

Source: PRS Group, Political Risk Services (November 2003).
Factors: F1 = Government stability; F2 = Socioeconomic conditions; F3 = Investment profile; F4 = Internal conflicts; F5 = External conflicts; F6 = Corruption; F7 = Military in politics; F8 = Religion in politics; F9 = Law and order; F10 = Ethnic tensions; F11 = Democratic accountability; F12 = Bureaucracy quality.

Table 1.3   **Variables Used in *Euromoney*'s Country Rankings**

	Variable	Weight (%)
1	Economic performance	25
2	Political risk	25
3	Debt indicators	10
4	Debt in default	10
5	Credit ratings	10
6	Access to bank financing	5
7	Access to short-term finance	5
8	Access to capital markets	5
9	Forfeiting (discount rate on letter of credit)	5

Using the above variables, *Euromoney* ranks 185 countries of the world every six months. Table 1.4 lists the 10 least risky and Table 1.5 lists the 10 most risky countries to invest in based on *Euromoney*'s September 2006 rankings.

Some large international companies do not rely on rankings published by the business press, but conduct their own country risk analysis. Most of the factors considered by these companies are similar to the ones published by the business journals. For example, the U.S.-based American Can Company assigns the most weight to economic and political risk factors in developing its own country risk ranking lists. Table 1.6 lists a few of the key factors used by American Can in its country risk analysis and the respective weights assigned to each factor.

In a recent study of global competitiveness ranking by the World Economic Forum, Finland was ranked as the most attractive economy to invest in, the United States was second, and three other Nordic countries—Sweden, Denmark, and Norway—were third, fifth, and sixth, respectively. Similarly, in the "Doing Business" report released by the World Bank, Denmark, Finland, Norway, and Sweden were ranked near the top as well. The United States was again ranked second. These rankings by various

Table 1.4   **The 10 Least Risky Countries of the World—September 2006 *Euromoney* Rankings**

	Country	V1*	V2	V3	V4	V5	V6	V7	V8	V9	Totals
1	Luxembourg	25.00	24.81	10.00	10.00	10.00	5.00	5.00	5.00	4.97	99.78
2	Norway	24.85	24.88	10.00	10.00	10.00	5.00	5.00	5.00	4.97	99.70
3	Switzerland	22.72	25.00	10.00	10.00	10.00	5.00	5.00	5.00	4.97	97.69
4	United States	23.01	24.88	10.00	10.00	10.00	5.00	5.00	5.00	5.00	97.49
5	Denmark	21.85	24.15	10.00	10.00	9.79	5.00	5.00	5.00	4.97	95.97
6	Sweden	20.78	24.57	10.00	10.00	9.17	5.00	5.00	5.00	4.97	95.32
7	United Kingdom	19.87	24.64	10.00	10.00	10.00	5.00	5.00	5.00	4.97	94.48
8	Ireland	19.74	24.32	10.00	10.00	10.00	5.00	5.00	5.00	4.97	94.03
9	Finland	19.66	24.30	10.00	10.00	10.00	5.00	5.00	5.00	4.97	93.93
10	Netherlands	19.37	24.54	10.00	10.00	10.00	5.00	5.00	5.00	4.97	93.88

*V = Variable.

Table 1.5   **The 10 Most Risky Countries of the World—September 2006 *Euromoney* Rankings**

	Country	V1*	V2	V3	V4	V5	V6	V7	V8	V9	Total
176	Liberia	6.53	0.75	4.05	10.00	0.00	0.00	0.83	0.00	0.00	22.16
177	Zimbabwe	0.00	1.39	9.64	10.00	0.00	0.00	0.83	1.00	0.00	21.87
178	Marshall Islands	10.66	8.05	0.00	0.00	0.00	0.00	1.50	0.00	0.00	20.21
179	Somalia	6.41	1.33	0.00	10.00	0.00	0.00	1.17	0.00	0.00	18.91
180	Tajikistan	5.90	1.84	8.51	0.48	0.00	0.00	1.17	0.00	0.00	17.90
181	Cuba	10.11	3.06	0.00	10.00	0.00	0.00	2.83	0.00	0.00	16.00
182	Congo	7.29	2.73	0.00	0.00	0.00	0.00	1.17	0.00	0.00	11.19
183	Iraq	5.28	1.02	0.00	10.00	0.00	0.00	0.83	0.00	0.00	7.13
184	North Korea	5.38	0.00	0.00	0.00	0.00	0.00	1.17	0.00	0.00	6.55
185	Afghanistan	4.24	1.32	0.00	0.00	0.00	0.00	0.83	0.00	0.00	6.39

*V = Variable.

Table 1.6   **Relative Factor Weights Used by American Can for Analyzing Country Risks**

Factor	Weight (%)
Political stability	26.0
Political freedom	7.0
Quality of infrastructure	6.7
Inflation	3.6
Currency stability	3.3
Balance of payments	3.3

agencies show that there is some uniformity in all rankings and their lists are quite reliable.[16]

NOTES

1. Fara Warner, "Marketing Army Hits China: Researchers Track the Changing Patterns and Tastes of Chinese Consumers," *Asian Wall Street Journal,* March 31, 1997, p. 1.

2. Barton Lee, Tony Zhao, and David Tatterson, "Emerging Trends in China's Marketing Research Industry," *Quirk's Marketing Research Review* (November 1998), p. 1.

3. "AC Nielsen Plans $1 Million Investments," *Financial Express,* July 11, 1998, p. 5.

4. "Deutsche Marken in Osteuropa Populaer," *Frankfurter-Allgemeine,* September 15, 1991, p. 19.

5. Liz Brooks, "Inspiring, the C-level Audience," *Adweek,* February 2002, p. 17.

6. A. Ricks David, *Big Business Blunders.* Homewood, IL: Irwin, 1983.

7. Sheila Reily, "Using Market Research to Survive and Thrive in Financial Service," *Marketing Review* (December 1996), pp. 7–8.

8. Kevin Daniels, Leslie De Chernatony, and Gerry Johnson, "Validating a Method for Mapping Managers' Mental Models of Competitive Industry Structures," *Human Relations* (September 1995), pp. 975–991.

9. The Client/Market Research Group, JP Morgan, "The Do's and Don'ts of International Market Research," *Marketing Review* (December 1996), pp. 18–20.

10. Kathleen Morris, "The Town Watcher," *Financial World,* July 19, 1994, pp. 42–44.

11. Paula Kephart, "Think Globally," *American Demographics* (November–December 1994), pp. 76ff.

12. Abdalla F. Hayajneh and Sammy G. Amin, "The Utilization of International Information for Global Marketing Competitiveness: An Empirical Investigation," *Journal of Applied Business Research* 11, no. 2 (1995), pp. 29–37.

13. Peter Bartram, "The Challenge for Research Internationally in the Decade of the 1990's," *Journal of Advertising Research* 30, no. 6 (1991), pp. RC3–RC6.

14. Susan J. Hart, John R. Webb, and Marian V. Jones, "Export Marketing Research and the Effects of Export Experience in Industrial SME's," *International Marketing Review* 11, no. 6 (1994), pp. 4–22.

15. Jerry Rogers, ed., *Global Risk Assessments: Issues Concepts, and Applications.* Riverside, CA: GRA Publications, June 1988.

16. Elizabeth Becker, "Nordic Countries Come out Near Top in Two Business Surveys," *New York Times,* October 14, 2004, p. C3.

ADDITIONAL READING

BOOKS

Churchill, Gilbert A., Jr., and Tom J. Brown. *Basic Marketing Research.* 5th ed. Mason, OH: Thomson Publishing, 2004.

Douglas, Susan P., and C. Samuel Craig. *International Marketing Research.* Upper Saddle River, NJ: Prentice Hall, 2000.

Green, Paul E., and Donald Tull. *Research for Marketing Decisions.* Upper Saddle River, NJ: Prentice Hall, 1978.

Kumar, V. *International Marketing Research.* Upper Saddle River, NJ: Prentice Hall, 2000.

Malhotra, Naresh K. *Marketing Research: An Applied Orientation.* 4th ed. Upper Saddle River, NJ: Pearson Publishing, 2003.

Tull, Donald S., and Del I. Hawkins. *Marketing Research: Measurement and Method.* 4th ed. New York: Macmillan, 1987.

Zikmund, William G. *Exploring Marketing Research.* 8th ed. Mason, OH: Thomson Publishing, 2003.

ARTICLES

Bangert, David C. (1994) "Hungary: Exploring New European Management Challenges." *International Studies of Management and Organization* 24 (1), pp. 209–230.

Barson, Donna C. (2002) "Research: It's Not Just for School Reports Anymore." *Global Cosmetic Industry* (December), p. 23.

Czinkota, Michael R., and Ilkka A. Ronkainen (1994) "Market Research for Your Export Operations." *International Trade Forum* (3), pp. 22–33.

Czinkota, Michael R., and Ilkka A. Ronkainen (1995) "Market Research for Your Export Operations: Conducting Primary Market Research." *International Trade Forum* (1), pp. 16–21ff.

Gallup, George Jr. (1988) "Survey Research: Current Problems and Future Opportunities." *The Journal of Consumer Marketing* 5 (1), pp. 27–30.

Gendall, Philip, and Don Esselmont (1992) "Market Research: What It Can and Can't Do." *Marketing Bulletin* 3 (May), pp. 63–66.

Ian, Murphy P. (1996) "Surveying a Decade of Surveys in Germany." *Marketing News* (September 23), p. 33.

Johansson, Johny K., and Ikujiro Nonaka (1987) "Market Research the Japanese Way." *Harvard Business Review* (May–June), pp. 16–22.

Macht, Joshua (1998) "The New Marketing Research." *Inc.* 20 (10), pp. 86–94.

Malhotra, Naresh K., Jane Agarwal, and Mark Peterson (1996) "Methodological Issues in Cross-Cultural Marketing Research: A State-of-the-Art Review." *International Marketing Review* 13 (5), p. 7.

Malhotra, Naresh K., Mark Peterson, and Susan Kleiser (1999) "Marketing Research: A State-of-the-Art Review and Directions for the Twenty-first Century." *Academy of Marketing Science Journal* 27 (2), pp. 160–183.

Mohan, Carroll N. (1994) "Pacific Rim Prices." *Marketing Research: A Magazine of Management and Application* 6 (1), pp. 22–27.

Ricks, David A., Brian Toyne, and Zaida Martinez (1990) "Recent Developments in International Management Research." *Journal of Management* 16 (2), pp. 219–253.

Solomon, Mary Beth (1996) "Targeting Trendsetters." *Marketing Research: A Magazine of Management and Applications* 8 (2), pp. 9–11.

2 Organizational Considerations in International Research

Organizational structures dictate the workforce divisions and distribution of roles to facilitate the orderly functioning of a firm.

LEARNING OBJECTIVES

After reading this chapter, students should be able to

- Distinguish and describe different types of organizational structures
- Discuss factors that affect organizational decision making in an international firm
- Understand the role of divisional and departmental setups in organizing for international business
- Understand the importance of coordination in organizing for international business research

Organizational structures and human resources functions are key elements in organizing for an effective information system. Most international business failures are caused by three key factors: *people*—managers making poor decisions; *organizational structures*—inadequate structures creating communication and control problems; and *management information systems*—inaccurate or untimely information.

International research departments are generally part of overall corporate structures. Therefore, to understand international research structures, we need to first discuss international business structures.

Effective and efficient organizational structures help international companies achieve the necessary control and coordination of their far-flung operations. The global design adopted by any firm must deal with the need to integrate three types of knowledge to compete effectively—*area knowledge, product knowledge,* and *functional knowledge.*[1] In addition, they aid in improving communications between headquarters and subsidiaries. In the international arena, these factors loom even bigger in importance.

By nature, international operations are spread across many national borders, and it becomes difficult for international executives to control and coordinate these multiple operations. Furthermore, the differences in business practices, culture, language, and time zones make the coordination of their activities even more problematic. For example, if an executive in Tokyo wants to speak to the corporate planning group in New York, which is 12 hours behind Tokyo time, the discussion has to take place during the day in one country and at night in the other.

International operations are also set up differently from domestic operations. An international firm may be an exporter, a licensee, a joint-venture operator, or a wholly owned subsidiary. Each of these operations has unique aspects that make the organizational setup different for different types of operations. To compound the problem even further, some large international companies may be involved in all these activities.

Control is the ability of the parent company to ensure the quality of its offerings, and the ability to coordinate the activities of all its units to meet corporate objectives is a critical factor in international operations. On the one hand, excessive control by the home office might endanger the subsidiary decision-making process, resulting in slower reactions to competitors' strategies. On the other hand, a lack of control might lead to duplication of effort, especially in areas such as research and development, sourcing, financing, and promotional campaigns. Duplication leads not only to inefficiencies in decision making but also to increases in the cost of operations.

There is no single approach to developing an organization for international operations. Depending on a corporation's philosophy, its culture, its past experiences, the industry it is in, and the number of personnel it has, different organizational structures might be needed. International firms have developed structures according to the level of their international involvement. In early stages of internationalization, autonomous units that report directly to top management are set up. As they expand their product and geographic scope, regional structures may be developed, and, as they really attain globalization, a global structure might be necessary.

Organizational structures normally reflect where the level of authority and control is vested. When decision making is concentrated at headquarters and the structure exerts tight control, the system is called *centralization.* If subsidiaries are granted a high degree of autonomy with loose controls, the structure is referred to as *decentralization.* In the present business climate, with dynamic shifts in the external environment, companies are usually neither totally centralized nor totally decentralized. Some functions, such as R & D, might be centralized, but media planning and pricing might be left to local managers.

Another area of concern in international operations is whether all international activities should be grouped together under an international division or should be organized around functional areas. The intensity of competition also influences the choice of structures in international operations. The overall goal of any structure is to have the diverse operations of an international company work in harmony to provide the basis for achieving preset performance objectives.

In those organizations where international activities are handled by a separate division, the management of international operations might be left in the hands of specialists. Because the problems encountered by foreign managers are unique to the international arena, this setup has some merit to it. Foreign exchange transactions, for example, are uniquely international, and therefore the person dealing with this function needs to be a specialist in that area.

In the final analysis, organizational structures are developed to plan and execute strategies to achieve company goals. The structure defines how individuals communicate and interact in carrying out their responsibilities and how individual units within a company are grouped to carry out the various tasks. The most commonly used international organizational structures are *divisional* structures, *product* structures, *geographic* structures, *functional* structures, and *hybrid* or *matrix* structures.

DIVISIONAL STRUCTURES

Companies that start their international operations by first exporting and then, as sales increase, forming overseas operations either in the form of an overseas sales office or by setting up production facilities normally go through changes in their organizational structures to reflect this intensified involvement. Most of the earlier firms that expanded into overseas markets formed organizations with an international division that was responsible for the overseas operations. The international division centralizes in one entity all the responsibility for international activities. From information gathering to setting up subsidiary operations, all activities were undertaken by this unit. Divisional structures are simple and easy to set up.

The separation of domestic from international operations is normally the first step in recognizing the importance of foreign activities for a firm. This separation permits firms to assign specialized staff to various activities within the international division. These specialists then allocate and coordinate resources for international activities under a single unit, providing a better overall direction and enhancing the firm's ability to respond quickly to market opportunities.

In those firms that had international divisional structures (Ford Motor Company and IBM are good examples of large international firms that operated for many years under the divisional structure), staff was able to focus the firm's undivided attention on exploring the international market.[2] This autonomy allowed the division to be recognized as a profit center and eliminated possible bias against international activities that may have existed with international sales when they were handled within a division that had the sole responsibility of developing the domestic market. Companies that desire to differentiate their operations between domestic and foreign businesses would normally set up a separate international division. The new arrangement allows the firm to independently serve international customers.

As a firm evolved into a multitiered, product-oriented company, the international division was often viewed as restrictive and perceived as an impedance to the growth of the company. As foreign operations increased in importance and scope, the divisional structure was viewed as inefficient and cumbersome. Many firms found it necessary to establish worldwide organizations that focused more on the product, function, or region. At present, there are very few international firms that still use the international division structure.[3] The few global firms that do use international divisional structures

Figure 2.1　**International Division-Based Structure**

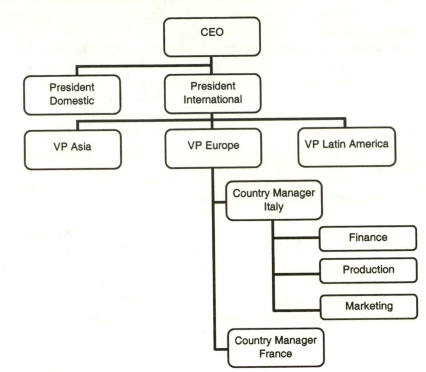

tend to be in industries that have limited product offerings, such as petroleum or mining, or are very small companies with, again, limited product offerings.

Under a divisional structure, the activities of gathering information and coordinating research are normally entrusted to a research department or a few designated staff who are part of the international division. Figure 2.1 is a good example of an organizational structure with an international division.

PRODUCT STRUCTURES

Many international organizations operate through product-based structures. These companies focus on their product offerings as the basis for organizing into various units. For example, both Procter & Gamble and Kimberly-Clark, two diversified consumer packaged goods U.S. companies, have recently adopted product-oriented organizational structures from a geographic setup. Procter & Gamble was reorganized from four geographic units into seven global business units responsible for each of its product areas worldwide. In this setup, the various domestic product divisions are given the responsibility for international line and staff functions. Because the global product design forces managers to think globally, it facilitates geocentric corporate philosophies. This is a useful mind-set as firms work to develop greater international skills internally.[4]

Companies that operate with a product structure may have regional experts to assist the product group. This type of structure is best suited for coordination of domestic and international activities related to a product category. The goal here is to reduce duplication in such areas as product research, systems development, and package design. In this form of organization, the key individual is the head of the domestic product division. All the international activities are coordinated from a product point of view. The international activities are secondary to the product.

Product-based structures are set for greater control of international operations, and feedback from various countries is used to develop a strong overall product strategy. For example, in 1991 IBM restructured its organization from a geographically based structure to an industry/product-based structure to better serve the needs of its global customers. The new structure is based on specific industries such as banking, insurance, government, retail, and utilities. Since adapting the industry-based structure, IBM has improved its bottom line performance and its customers are equally pleased with the improved services that they have been receiving. Though this structure avoids duplication in product development, it can create confusion for regional or country managers, as they have to report to as many product heads as there are product divisions. Figure 2.2 is an example of a product-based structure.

Figure 2.2   **Product-Based Structure**

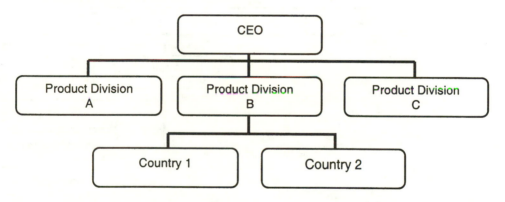

In the product structure shown in Figure 2.2, specialists with some country or regional expertise are assigned to assist the chief executive office (CEO). These specialists may be recruited from each of the regions or may come from the parent organization. The divisional head of each product exercises a greater role in the function and management of the unit. Country managers are mostly administrators who coordinate the activities of the various functional departments.

Research in product-based organizations may be centralized at the headquarters, with each region or country assigned the task of conducting the research with assistance from the central office. In some companies the research function is totally decentralized, with each country undertaking its own research and some coordination taking place at the regional or central level.

Geographically Based Structures

In the geographically based structure, the responsibility for all international activities is in the hands of a regional or country manager reporting directly to the CEO or an international divisional head. This type of organization simplifies the task of directing worldwide operations, as the individual in charge is directly in contact with a very senior officer at the firm's headquarters. In this case, the country operations become just another division of the company for allocation of resources. Geographically based structures ensure that sufficient funds are made available to the country operations.

Besides the advantage of the allocation of resources, this structure helps local managers to contribute considerably more to the decision-making process. With their knowledge of local market conditions, they are able to direct the company's efforts more effectively than if they were managed directly from the headquarters. In addition, this type of organizational structure enables international companies to develop a pool of local managers, adding diversity to the management ranks.

Figure 2.3   **Geographically Based Structure**

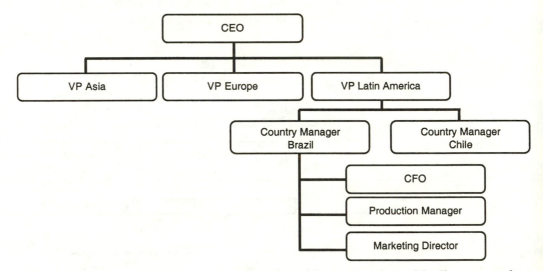

Geographic structures are most often found in companies with diverse product categories requiring a strong marketing approach. These structures also tend to be used more by packaged goods companies such as Coca-Cola, Campbell Soup, and the Altria Group . The companies in these categories face intense competition, require constant modifications to their strategies, and come under foreign government scrutiny. For local governments, especially those in developing countries, some of these products are not high-priority items (soft drinks, packaged foods, and tobacco) and therefore do not help in their economic development programs.

As each foreign operation needs both product and functional specialists, a geographically based international organization necessarily requires more staff in the international division to provide support to the geographic units. It also creates problems in terms of coordination of the activities of the various product offerings. Figure 2.3 is a good example of a typical geographically based organization.

In the above setup, the functional managers report to country heads. These country managers are directly under regional managers. The regional managers report either to the company CEO or to a high-ranking executive at corporate headquarters.

FUNCTION-BASED STRUCTURES

The philosophy behind the function-based structure is that it is more efficient to have functional expertise than to have product or country/regional expertise. In this type of structure, the senior executive responsible for each functional area—production, finance, or marketing—is responsible for the same functions at the country level. Function-based organizations are most often found among companies with a limited product line, such as industrial product companies (office equipment) or those whose products are highly technical (robotics).

On the one hand, function-based organizations are able to manage individual departments very well. On the other hand, the coordination of activities between functions both at headquarters and at the country level is problematic. The coordination between various functional divisions is either left to the CEO at the country level or handled by a senior executive at headquarters. Figure 2.4 is a good example of a function-based structure.

Figure 2.4   **Function-Based Structure**

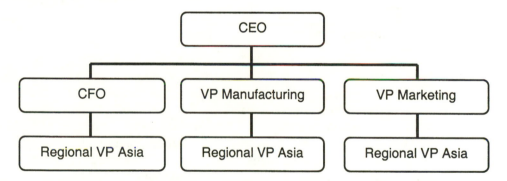

As can be seen in Figure 2.4, the marketing executive coordinates the same activities in every country in which the company has operations. This is true for the other company functions also.

MATRIX STRUCTURES

The previously identified organizational structures, though useful in specific situations, have deficiencies in coordinating and implementing the various activities of an international firm. To reduce these problems, some international firms have tried to combine the structures. Called a matrix organization, this type of structure blends the product, geographic, and functional elements while maintaining clear lines of authority. The large Anglo-Dutch consumer goods company Unilever is a good example of a company that uses the matrix structure.

Figure 2.5   **Matrix Organizational Structure**

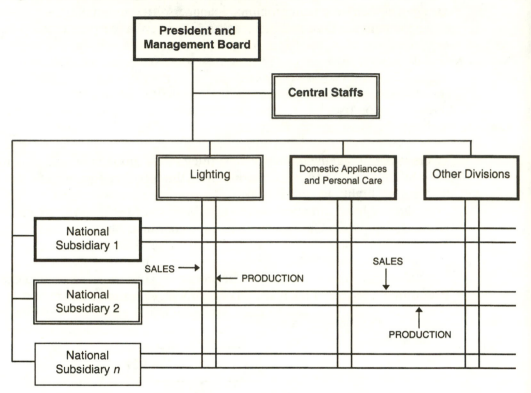

In the matrix organizational structure, a subsidiary reports to more than one group (functional, product, or geographic). This design is based on the theory that because each group shares responsibility over foreign operations, the groups will become more interdependent, exchange information, and exchange resources with one another.[5] In matrix organizations, both the area and product managers have overlapping responsibilities. A manufacturing manager in Japan will report not only to the vice president of manufacturing but also to the regional manager for Asia at world headquarters. In this case, the lines of responsibility and resultant flow of communication occur both horizontally and vertically across the main dimensions. Generally, in a matrix organizational structure, it is customary to have staff personnel coordinate the various lines of authority and communications, including the research function.

Many international managers agree that the matrix structure is the most complex form of international organizational design.[6] Although matrix structures were meant to take advantage of the merits of product, geographic, and functional forms, in practice they create new problems of their own. Since matrix structures form managerial teams with no single person in charge, the focus is on building team consensus. This slows the decision-making process. Also, in instances of a lack of consensus, top management has to step in to resolve the conflicts, taking up valuable time of these senior executives. ING Group, a large Dutch-based financial institution, recently reorganized itself from a matrix structure to a product-based structure because of difficulties in attaining coordination under the matrix structure. Figure 2.5 is a typical matrix organizational structure.

As can be seen in Figure 2.5, the lines of communication tend to be quite complex, but they do help in opening multiple channels of communications.

So far we have discussed general organizational structures found in international organizations. Now we focus on specific structures developed to organize international research departments. International research departments are part of the overall organizational structures discussed earlier. In the following section we try to address the organizational issues in setting up research departments.

ORGANIZING FOR INTERNATIONAL RESEARCH

In the previous section we introduced the various forms of organizational structures used by international firms. In some cases the functional areas were the foundation for forming an organizational setup. As research is considered a function within an organization, it would seem prudent to apply the functional structure to set up the research departments in international organizations. As in the case of the corporate organizational structures, we find many variations in the setup of research departments among international firms.

For openers, not all international firms have their own internal research departments. In addition, the size of the research department, experience and expertise of research personnel, complexity of the research project, and extent to which the company's operations are international are important variables that influence the research department structure within an organization. In those instances when an international firm does not have its own research department, the respective functional departments might undertake the information gathering, or it might be handled by outside research suppliers, or both.

The major issues to be considered in developing international research for a multinational firm are

- The degree of centralization to be exercised in conducting and coordinating the research activities of the firm
- The degree of decentralization in international research
- The reasons for and the extent to which outside research suppliers should be utilized to fulfill or complement the research needs of an international firm
- The type of research needed
- The cost of international research

CENTRALIZATION

Centralized research structures in international organizations are an output of the manner in which the various business units are organized within a company. The governing criterion normally found in centralized structures is the functional efficiency of the key departments, such as production, finance, and marketing. The research department structure is considered last. Among Japanese companies, the research function is scattered across the organization. Twenty percent of Japanese international companies have centralized research departments; 10 percent have decentralized research departments.[7]

In a centralized organizational structure, the direction, control, and execution of research for all divisions and every country are located at world headquarters. The research department establishes specifications and develops the design of the research, with the execution handled at the country level. In developing the research, headquarters staff reviews existing information at the head office as well as all the country offices to avoid duplication of effort. Centralized coordination helps the international firm in all aspects of research, including the secondary and primary data-collection phases. Whatever the research approach, in a centralized structure, headquarters research staff outlines the details of research design, collection methods, and analytical framework.

The degree of centralization in research is dependent on the extent of the firm's operations—the number of product offerings and the number of countries in which it has operations. The degree of centralization among international firms can vary from company to company. Some international companies follow a very rigid structure in which all research needs for all the countries are coordinated centrally at world headquarters. This may include applying a common research design and sending research staff from headquarters to individual country operations to direct the research. Other companies follow a loosely held centralized structure with a basic research design that is applied locally with some modifications. In either case, headquarters exercises greater control on the type of research conducted in all its overseas operations than it would with a decentralized approach.

In addition, in a centralized approach, duplication of research efforts among local markets is vastly reduced. The home office provides local managers with information gathered in the home office and other countries to ensure that no new research is conducted if information already exists in some form within the organization. It also appears that a centralized research department allows the firm to exert stronger control over its operations, enabling it to develop a standardized decision-making process.

The other benefits associated with centralized research structures are:

- *Cost efficiency.* Since in a centralized setup all research is coordinated from company headquarters, there are considerable savings in the number of staff needed at the individual country level. Savings are also derived from avoiding duplication of research efforts.
- *Comparability.* Since all research is coordinated at one location, the research staff can work on the comparability of data from country to country. They are also able to use common measures and standards to administer and evaluate research.
- *Quality of information.* Because the centralized research organization can be the depository of data and information from a wide variety of sources and locations, it is in a very good position to identify and select the best available information for dissemination to all its units. The centralized organizational structure enables local managers to use information of the highest quality in most instances.

- *Power of negotiations.* Because of the volume of research undertaken by the centralized research group at company headquarters, it is in a much better position to exact the best possible terms when using outside research suppliers. This negotiating position might result in cost efficiencies as well as the acquisition of the services of the most qualified research experts.

Centralized research structures are not without their share of problems. Some of the critical problems associated with centralized organizational structures are

- *Lack of input from local managers.* Since the headquarters staff conducts its research far from local markets, the talents and creative ideas of local managers are omitted. This mode of research not only ignores an important source of input but also creates morale problems at the local unit level, as the local staff feels left out. Centralized research departments also do not benefit from the target country personnel's know-how and understanding of unique local market conditions. Both of these factors might lead to poor execution of research by the local managers, negating some of the efficiencies derived through centralized structures.
- *Reaction time.* When sudden shifts in environmental variables require local managers to act, the centralized structure slows the process. Since local managers have to wait for input and direction from headquarters, their reactions to strategic changes are slower. This delay in taking corrective action could be catastrophic in some instances.
- *Environmental diversity.* Uniform research designs neglect to recognize the diversity among different countries. Factors such as the size of the market, strength of local competitors, government influence, and local industry structure are ignored, undermining the effectiveness of the uniform research design under a centralized structure.
- *Cultural biases.* In a centralized structure, vast cultural differences are basically ignored, but cultural factors influence many aspects of research, including perceptions, values, and the social interactions of a society. The resulting response bias distorts the research findings, contributing to an ethnocentric cultural bias.

Figure 2.6 is an organizational chart for an international company with a centralized research department.

In the company structure shown in Figure 2.6, the individual country research managers report to a research manager or coordinator at headquarters. Companies with a centralized research department undertake those functions that can be easily managed from headquarters, such as secondary research collection, country analysis, exploratory research, and simple primary studies. The more detailed and country-specific research studies are usually allocated to the research staff in individual countries.

Figure 2.6 **Centralized Research Department Structure**

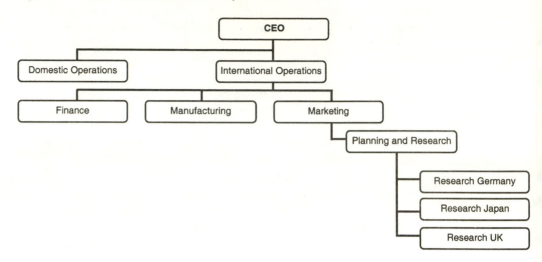

DECENTRALIZATION

In a decentralized structure, headquarters takes a hands-off approach when dealing with the various country units in terms of research. In this type of structure, an international company may be organized into divisions by product, geography, or functional area, with the research personnel assigned to the various divisions. Generally, the research personnel report to a division manager. Since these research managers are much closer to the local markets, they use their market knowledge in designing research to suit local conditions. When a firm uses a decentralized structure, strategic control is not as logically connected as it is in a centralized design.[8]

In a decentralized setup, the role of the headquarters research staff is to establish general objectives and guidelines and to give a free hand to local managers to design and execute the research. The decisions made by local research managers include whether to conduct the research in-house or to have outside suppliers.

The primary advantage of a decentralized structure is the culture-specific research conducted by the local managers—a polycentric approach. This approach minimizes cultural biases, a major problem with research undertaken in a centralized structure. The decentralized system provides for a good fit between local market conditions and the research capabilities of the research staff in each country.

The other major advantages of a decentralized system are:

- *Use of local talents.* The decentralized structure makes use of the talents of local country staff and gets their cooperation and involvement in both the research design and execution. This involvement enhances the morale of local staff and provides a vehicle for developing local talent.
- *Reaction time.* In a decentralized structure, local managers can more quickly and easily react to changes in local competitive or environmental conditions. In a

highly competitive market, timing of response may spell the difference between success and failure.

- *Environmental diversity.* Diversity of country factors is better understood when the research decisions are made at the country level. This arrangement negates a major disadvantage in the centralized structure in which the headquarters research staff has difficulty tracking the diverse economic, cultural, political, and other environmental differences among various countries.

- *Collection of information.* Because each country collects its own set of data, an international firm now has the luxury of a vast database compiled from a wide variety of sources and locations. This database tends to be more thorough and complete compared to one collected in centralized structures.

Decentralized research departments, though very practical, have some drawbacks. The major problems associated with decentralized structures are:

- *Duplication of efforts.* Since each individual country unit has its own research department, coordination between countries is more difficult under a decentralized setup. This lack of coordination quite often leads to duplication of research activities, which results in higher costs and wasted resources.

- *Comparability.* As each country develops its own research design with locally developed instruments and measurements, comparing and evaluating data across countries becomes difficult. Researchers at different units are not likely to employ uniform standards and measurement techniques. This lack of common standards creates difficulties in sharing the information among the various countries. Lack of standardized procedures for coding and categorizing data, the use of different analytical techniques by individual countries, and the different languages used in writing reports all contribute to comparability problems.

Culturally, there are differences in classifying data across societies. For example, Rena Bartos observed that women are classified differently with regard to their age in different countries. To be called a woman in Germany you have to be 14 years of age, whereas in Australia the age is 18.

- *Adherence to overall corporate goals.* As country managers direct their own research and develop strategies for local markets, there is a tendency to lose sight of the overall goals of the international firm. Each country unit might try to set its own objectives, which might not be compatible with the goals of the firm. For example, a country unit might seek a large market share in its own market by producing locally, but headquarters may have plans to service the market by importing from a neighboring manufacturing facility that has excess capacity. Producing locally can lead to underutilization of the firm's resources.

Figure 2.7 is an example of a decentralized research organizational structure. In this organizational structure, a local research department reports directly to the

Figure 2.7   **Decentralized Research Department Structure**

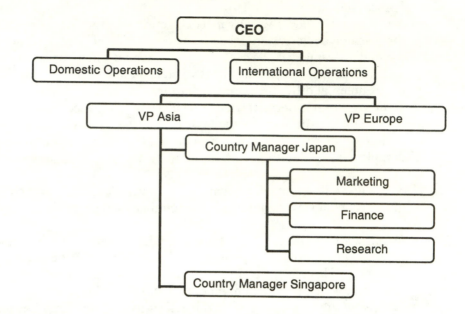

country manager. Activities of the research department are coordinated locally, and the research meets the specific needs of the country unit.

Because both centralization and decentralization offer attractive benefits to the global company, most firms constantly tinker with a blend of the two to achieve the best outcome in terms of overall strategy.[9]

OUTSIDE RESEARCH SUPPLIERS

Not all international firms have internal research departments to design and coordinate research activities. These international companies turn to independent research companies when in need of specific information. VNU, IMS Health, and the Kantar Group are among the largest research companies, with subsidiaries in many parts of the world. For example, VNU operates in 81 countries and derives 99 percent of its revenues from global operations. The top 10 research companies are presented in Table 2.1.[10] These companies set up various country operations to service their worldwide clients. Even when an international firm has its own internal research department, it may still seek outside research suppliers for specialized expertise. Outside suppliers may also be called in when a research project is too involved or too big for a firm's internal research department.

The external suppliers who specialize in conducting various types of research for a fee form the *research industry*. These suppliers range from one-person shops with limited clients to large companies that employ thousands of people and generate billions of dollars in revenues. The industry collectively is capable of conducting almost any type of research, from a feasibility study for a manufacturing plant to a test market for a new product. For example, Information Resources Inc. (IRI), a

Table 2.1 **The Top 10 Research Companies Worldwide**

Rank 2004	Company	Headquarters	No. of countries	Revenue ($ million)	International revenue	% of Revenue from international activities
1	VNU	Netherlands and United States	100	3,400.0	3,366.0	99.0
2	Taylor Nelson Sofres	United Kingdom	70	1,720.6	1,430.6	83.2
3	IMS Health	United States	100	1,600.0	998.0	63.6
4	Kantar Group	United States	61	1,140.0	770.6	68.3
5	GfK Group	Germany	59	835.5	541.5	64.8
6	Ipsos Group	France	41	753.2	633.8	84.2
7	Information Resources	United States	8	572.8	193.2	33.7
8	Synovate	United Kingdom	46	499.3	407.7	81.7
9	NOP World	United Kingdom	7	407.1	297.3	73.0
10	Westat	United States	1	397.8	NA	NA

Source: Anne Ryman, "Global Top 25 2005," *Marketing News*, August 15, 2003, p. H4.
NA, not applicable.

large U.S.-based research supplier, used its Infoscan Census system to refocus the product offerings of the troubled diet foods maker Estee. By conducting a detailed store-by-store sales study through its scanners, IRI was able help Estee eliminate a few products and introduce 18 new ones, resulting in a 70 percent sales increase in less than a year.[11]

Research suppliers can be classified as full-service suppliers or limited-service suppliers. A full-service supplier provides an extensive array of services from simple one-country analysis of markets to sophisticated computer-based large-scale studies involving many countries. These companies generally have a large client base and have offices in many countries. In contrast, limited-service companies focus in one or two specialized services such as conducting focus group studies or fielding question-naires. Generally, these limited-service providers do not have the staff or expertise to conduct a wider range of, or very sophisticated, research studies.

The services provided by a full-service research company may be further classified as *syndicated services, standardized services,* and *customized services.*

SYNDICATED SERVICES

These research suppliers collect information on a regular basis with no particular client in mind. Their studies are then sold to a limited number of subscribers. These research studies tend to be industry specific. For example, the Yankee Group tracks the telecommunications industry and provides periodic reports to subscribers (generally companies involved in telecommunications or related services). Forrester Research compiles data on Internet-related companies. Another good example of a syndicated service in the United States is the scanner volume-tracking data (referred to as single-source data). Scanner data are generated through electronic scanning at checkout counters in supermarkets. U.S.-based ACNielsen compiles scanner data for the use of its clients.

Syndicated service companies make use of both primary and secondary research to compile their reports. Since these studies are not developed for the express use of a single firm, they are considered secondary sources.

STANDARDIZED SERVICES

Research suppliers who provide standardized services have a structured way of collecting and analyzing data for the use of different clients. In this regard there is only a slight difference between syndicated-service companies and standardized-service companies. The users of these services are able to compare and evaluate data across studies. An example of a standardized service is the Starch Readership Survey, conducted by Starch INRA Hopper, Inc., which evaluates print advertising.

CUSTOMIZED SERVICES

Suppliers of customized services conduct specific studies at the request of a client. Each study may be different from the previous one. Suppliers of customized services offer a wide variety of research services, and each study is custom-made to suit a client's need. Each study is treated as unique, and therein lies the difference between customized services and the others. International companies that have their own research departments sometimes use customized services to avail themselves of expertise that their own departments do not possess.

RESEARCH NEEDS OF THE FIRM

International companies generally face a multitude of issues in managing their dispersed operations. These issues are affected by a wide variety of factors. Firm size, number of foreign operations, product mix, customer base, and home-office location are some of the factors that affect the operations of an international firm. These factors affect information needs and hence research requirements. For example, a small firm involved in exporting needs a different set of information than a firm that is planning a multicountry new product introduction. In the case of the small exporter, a review of secondary sources might be sufficient. In contrast, for the new product introduction, the international firm may have to conduct a sophisticated market study to determine demand. For the latter, research may involve using both syndicated services and customized services.

COST OF INTERNATIONAL RESEARCH

The final critical issue in organizing for international research is the cost of doing one's own research as opposed to the cost of contracting outside suppliers to do it. Research can be expensive when it involves many countries under varying conditions. International companies try to obtain the most appropriate information at the lowest possible price. An international firm has to evaluate whether doing research in-house will produce the desired quality of information at the lowest cost or whether contracting an outside supplier is most cost-effective. A related issue is the question of how much to spend for research. Even ardent supporters of research concede that there is no sure way of setting budgets for research. Some form of cost-benefit analysis needs to be done in allocating research funds. In a business where perfect information is hard to find or is cost prohibitive, caution is the mantra to be adopted.

In addition, there is the philosophical issue of how to treat research expenditures. Should they be an investment, considered from a long-term point of view, or should they be an expense, considered from a short-term point of view? This investment/expense issue is of serious concern to international executives, as costs are generally higher in international research, and the results obtained may not be implemented immediately. In addition, in some countries the tax laws may not allow writing off research costs as an investment.

The major reasons for the differences in international research costs stem from the varying research capabilities available in different countries. In some countries, especially some of the industrialized countries, such as the United States, Japan, and Germany, local research suppliers are superior and able to handle any type of study a company wishes. In contrast, in some developing countries, that same level of research capability might not be available. Furthermore, the number of qualified suppliers is limited in developing countries. Consequently, the few available research suppliers in developing countries charge higher fees. An international firm may have to pay dearly for good-quality research in some of these developing countries. The availability of suppliers, their experience, and their capabilities contribute to the higher costs of international research.

Costs may also be higher in some countries due to the difficulties of collecting both secondary and primary data. A focus-group study for an analgesic product conducted in Argentina will cost 50 percent more than the same study in the United States. The difficulties in recruiting subjects, finding an appropriate site for conducting the focus group, locating a qualified moderator, and transcribing and analyzing the discussion contribute to the higher cost in Argentina and other nonindustrialized countries.

Often the higher costs associated with conducting research internationally have meant that decisions are sometimes made without the benefit of research and information. Even though this is not a prudent approach, international managers justify their decision to skip research on the grounds of the higher costs in conducting international research and the time it takes to complete a research study. Smaller companies are more prone to making decisions without research because of limited resources. Larger companies tend to conduct extensive research before undertaking major investment decisions, as they have a much greater risk exposure.

Interestingly, a major portion of the world's research expenditures is accounted for by a small number of industrialized countries. Nearly 92 percent of all research expenditures for the year 2003 were spent in Canada, the United States, Asian Pacific, and Western European countries. Paradoxically, where the volatility of conditions is the greatest, requiring constant and accurate information, hardly any research is done.

As the markets in many of the developing countries of Asia, Eastern Europe, Latin America, and the Middle East are attracting attention, there is a need to research and study these markets more thoroughly. Up to this point, research efforts and expenditures to study these markets have been minimal. Some of the worst international blunders in business have taken place in many of the developing countries, whose economic, political, and cultural factors have been alien to international firms from the United States and Europe. For example, in setting up a manufacturing plant in Mexico, an American international firm adopted the team management concept, which it had found to be extremely useful at its American plant. The Mexican labor force did not respond positively to the team management concept, and productivity and quality of output suffered. The Mexican labor force did not want to take on management responsibilities, and they perceived the team management concept as an imposition of those responsibilities on them. For the Mexican workforce, management responsibilities are the domain of management, and the status and pay scales of managers reflect this. If factory workers had to participate in the management of the company, they needed to be compensated accordingly. Prior research on Mexican culture and labor practices could have helped the company to avoid this predicament.

An equally important factor contributing to higher international research costs is the lack of research infrastructure in many countries of the world. Research infrastructure includes technically qualified research staff, telephone service, mail service, computers, and facilities for conducting focus-group studies. For example, in the United States, the use of WATS lines (wide area telephone service, which is based on a flat rate) can considerably lower telephone-interviewing costs. The lack of such services in countries that have high rates for basic telephone service results in higher costs for telephone interviews. In many industrialized countries, computers are linked to telephones so that as each respondent answers questions on a survey, the computer automatically tabulates and analyzes the information. In many developing countries, computers are not readily available, and, therefore, most of the data entry and analysis are done manually.

Finally, exchange rate fluctuations and high inflation rates in some countries contribute to higher costs for international research. Any fluctuations in exchange rates may alter the overall costs of research. In some instances the change in rates may favor the international firm, but quite often it has the opposite effect. For example, a Dutch firm plans to enter the U.S. market and commissions a local research firm to conduct a consumer demand study. At the time of the commission of the research, the cost was determined to be $10,000. At an exchange rate of $1 = €0.80 the cost of research for the Dutch company is €8,000. By the time the research was completed, the U.S. dollar had appreciated in value by 10 percent, resulting in a new exchange rate of $1= €0.88. At the new rate, the Dutch firm will have to convert €8,800 to pay the U.S. research firm the equivalent of $10,000, whereas it would have paid only €8,000 at the old rate. Similarly, changes in inflation rate also affect the cost of international research.

Additionally, when the political climate in a developing country shifts, there may be additional pressures on the country's exchange rate. The recent upheavals in Indonesia are a good example of how quickly the political climate can change, affecting exchange rates. Between July 1997 and December 1997, Suharto, who ruled the country for more than 30 years, suddenly resigned under pressure from opposition forces. This affected the local currency, which dropped in value by 65 percent. As recently as 1994, countries such as Bolivia, Brazil, Israel, and Russia were grappling with triple-digit inflation rates. In countries with high rates of inflation, the cost of research can escalate from one day to the next. Issues of cost in conducting research are definitely a major concern of international managers, especially when they have to deal with many countries and evaluate a variety of projects.

CHAPTER SUMMARY

This chapter provided an overview of international research. Many more companies are venturing into foreign markets than were in the past. As these firms try to establish a presence in a foreign country, there appears to be a definite need for more information. The informational needs of international managers are diverse, and they draw data from a wide variety of sources. At the same time, international research is very complex, with constant and dynamic shifts in the nature and scope of the environment in which international managers have to function. This complexity, coupled with a wide discrepancy in the quality and availability of research personnel, makes the task of collecting international information very difficult and costly.

Research should be viewed as an investment to maximize the benefits it can provide. However, some companies view research as an expense. As a means of reducing costly mistakes, research should be viewed from a long-term point of view.

Diversity in many of the key environmental variables, such as the wide variances in economic conditions or the diversity in cultures and languages, contributes to the difficulties of conducting research in foreign markets. Organizing and designing international research must be undertaken with care to maximize the benefits of research.

This chapter dealt with the scope and nature of international research. In a simplistic sense, research is the process of gathering, analyzing, and disseminating information through the use of objective and scientific techniques. International managers use the resulting information to make decisions, to select between options, or to clarify problems.

This chapter also presented the uses of research in an international context. Specifically, international research is used to select countries for market entry, to identify locations for setting up production plants, to evaluate funding sources, to identify target markets, and to determine market potential.

As international firms search for information, they need to organize their research departments. Various forms of organizational structures were discussed. For research departments, the two most commonly used structures are either a centralized approach, with strong control exerted by the headquarters staff, or a decentralized structure, with each country manager deciding on the design and execution of research. Each structure has advantages and disadvantages. The specific structure adopted by a firm is dependent on its size, its product mix, its market diversity, its corporate philosophy, and the industry in which it operates. The ultimate goal in embracing a particular structure is to have an efficient organization capable of making good decisions.

Finally, we looked at some key decision criteria to be considered in conducting international research. Besides the organizational considerations, an international firm has to consider the type of research it needs to undertake, whether to use outside suppliers or depend on its own research department, and the total costs associated with its informational needs.

CHAPTER REVIEW

1. Identify those factors that have led to the growth of international business.
2. What role does information play in decision making?
3. Identify some of the major issues in international research.
4. Define international business research.
5. What are some of the uses of international research?
6. What makes international research complex?
7. Identify the various organizational structures used in international business.
8. Discuss the differences between centralized and decentralized structures in international research.
9. How are outside research suppliers classified? What are the major differences between the various research suppliers?

10. If a local small business owner asks your help in selecting a country for exporting his or her products, how will you help this entrepreneur?

NOTES

1. Anil Gupta and Vijay Govindarajan, "Knowledge Flows within Multinational Corporations," *Strategic Management Journal* 21, no. 4 (2000), pp. 473–496.

2. "Building a Competitive Organization for the 1990's," *Business International,* June 11, 1990, p. 190.

3. "Corporate Networking Increases Organizational Choices," *Business International,* July 9, 1990, p. 225.

4. Tarun Khana and Krishna Palepu, "The Right Way to Restructure Conglomerates in Emerging Markets," *Harvard Business Review* (July–August 1999), pp. 125–134.

5. John W. Hunt, "Is Matrix Management a Recipe for Chaos?" *Wall Street Journal,* January 12, 1998, p. 10.

6. Christopher A. Bartlett and Sumantra Ghoshal, "Matrix Management: Not a Structure, a Frame of Mind," *Harvard Business Review* (July–August 1990), pp. 138–145.

7. Kazuo Kobayashi and Peter Draper, "Reviews of Market Research in Japan," *Journal of Advertising Research* 30, no. 2 (1990), pp. 13–18.

8. Michael Goold, "Strategic Control in the Decentralized Firm," *Sloan Management Review* (Winter 1991), pp. 69–81.

9. C.K. Prahalad and Jan P. Oosterveld, "Transforming Internal Governance: The Challenge for Multinationals," *Sloan Management Review* (Spring 1999), pp. 31–41.

10. ESOMAR Annual Study of the Market Research Industry 2001, as reported in *Marketing News,* August 19, 2002.

11. Shermach Kelly, "Techniques to Help Convert Marketing Liabilities into Assets," *Marketing News,* August 29, 1994, p. 11.

ADDITIONAL READING

BOOKS

Daft, R.A. *Essentials of Organization Theory and Design.* New York: Thomson Publishing, 2000.
Jones, Gareth. *Organizational Theory.* 3rd ed. Upper Saddle River, NJ: Prentice-Hall, 2001.

ARTICLES

Bartlett, Christopher A. (1983) "MNCs: Get Off the Reorganization Merry-Go-Around." *Harvard Business Review* (March–April), p. 138.
Brooks, Liz (2002) "Inspiring, the C-level Audience." *Adweek Magazine* (February), p. 17.
Conference Board (1995) "Organizing for Global Competitiveness: The Business Unit Design." Report #1110–95-RR.
Czinkota, Michael R., and Ilkka A. Ronkainen (1995) "Market Research for Your Export Operations: Conducting Primary Market Research." *International Trade Forum* (1), pp. 16–21ff.
Martinez, Jon I., and J. Carlos Jarillo (1989) "The Evolution of Research on Coordination Mechanisms in Multinational Corporations." *Journal of International Business Studies* 20 (3), pp. 489–514.
Morton, Michael Scott (1995) "Emerging Organizational Forms: Work and Organization in the 21st Century." *European Management Journal* 13 (4), pp. 339–345.
O'Donnell, Watson S. (2000) "Managing Foreign Subsidiaries: Agents of Headquarters, or an Interdependent Network?" *Strategic Management Journal* 20 (5), pp. 525–548.

Sundaram, Anant K., and J. Stewart Black (1992) "The Environment and Internal Organization of Multinational Enterprises." *Academy of Management Review* 17 (4), pp. 729–757.

Taggart, James H. (1998) "Strategy Shifts in MNC Subsidiaries." *Strategic Management Journal* 19, pp. 663–681.

3 Research Process and Research Proposal

The international research process assures the successful completion of a research project from problem definition to implementation of the research findings. A research proposal is a written statement of the research design and a formal plan of action.

LEARNING OBJECTIVES

After reading this chapter, students should be able to

- Identify and describe the research process
- Understand problem definition
- Understand the role of secondary and primary data
- Understand the environmental variables affecting international research
- Understand the role of international business research in the broader context of information systems
- Be able to determine the type of information to be researched
- Understand the decision-making process once research has been completed
- Understand and know the uses of a research proposal
- Learn how to develop and evaluate a proposal

Every business faces an external environment over which it has limited control. Environmental factors affect how businesses operate. Both domestic and international companies face some of the same external factors. The external environment confronting international companies is more complex than the one surrounding domestic business operations. External factors confronted by international companies tend to be more dynamic, less predictable, and often totally unfamiliar to the international manager. In this volatile environment, decisions are made in an environment of uncertainty. Reliable information can reduce the uncertainty and improve decision making. At the same time, in many multinational situations either time is insufficient or the budget inadequate to conduct research.[1]

International operations require managers to make many decisions. The first decision typically made in international business is the selection of a country for entry. Because of the difficulties involved in gathering international information and because of other problems associated with international research, screening many prospective countries based on general information first and then subjecting a favored subset of those countries to a more rigorous process is the customary approach for selecting a country for market entry.

As multinational firms operate in a large number of countries (for example, Coca Cola markets its products in 197 countries), the network of local, regional, and corporate offices in planning and coordinating international research becomes challenging. When undertaking a research project, an international researcher first has to determine whether the particular information he or she is seeking is available in other units of the company. It is best to learn from the experiences of other local units in preparing to enter a new market. Information from many local units also allows international firms to compare data across countries, to make use of a common methodology, and to validate their findings. If a company is venturing for the first time into a foreign market, it does not have the luxury of tapping into previous experiences. The company relies solely on its own research. In this case, using an outside supplier who has the necessary expertise to provide the critical information may be appropriate.

RESEARCH PROCESS

Designing a valid research project means thinking through research needs first, and then using the research techniques that most directly meet the needs.[2] Research design involves a series of steps that provides a systems approach to research. These steps are referred to as the research process. The *research process* consists of a series of activities planned by management in conducting international research. A research process is made up of the steps shown in Figure 3.1.

The international research process follows the same sequence as the process for domestic research situations. The differences tend to be in the complexity and difficulty in completing each of these steps. The research process assumes that these steps are undertaken sequentially.

In practice, international companies may not follow all the steps shown in Figure 3.1. Depending on the circumstances, a firm might decide to stop the process early if it finds that the country it is exploring is not a viable market. It might also skip some of the intermediate steps to speed up the process due to competitive pressures or cost factors.

Researchers must complete some procedures in the research process before moving on to the next step. Problem definition must precede identification of information sources. Similarly, it is recommended that all secondary sources be fully exhausted before primary research is attempted.

Following is a brief description of the steps in the research process.

PRELIMINARY PHASE

The preliminary phase precedes the problem-formulation stage. Often, the problem is not clearly defined for the international executive, so he or she needs additional input

Figure 3.1 **International Research Process**

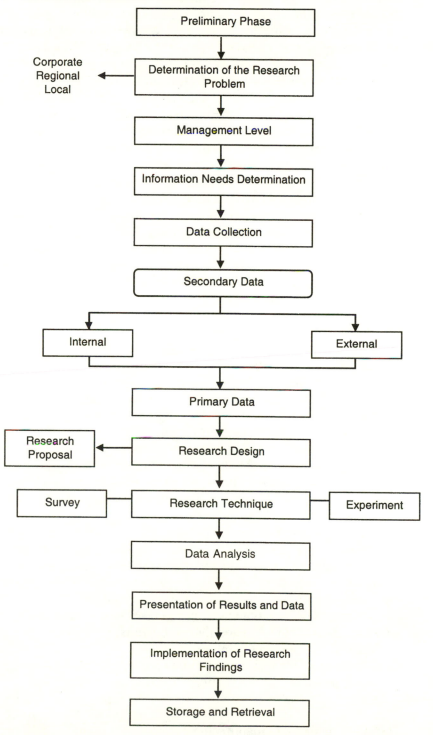

to clearly identify or formulate the key issues. This preliminary investigation is not a formalized approach and takes on various forms. It might be as simple as talking to other managers at headquarters or questioning country managers, or it may involve review of internal reports. For example, the headquarters accounting staff, in reviewing country financial reports, may observe very high expenditures for after-sales service in one of the overseas markets. Before deciding on a full-fledged research effort, the headquarters staff might review the historic data for after-sales service for different countries to determine the seriousness of the problem. Using sales volume or sales by customer as a base, the expenditures for after-sales services may be compared to those for similar markets to determine whether there are any unusual patterns that might shed light on the increase in these costs. The headquarters staff may also contact local managers to find out whether there is a need to conduct further research.

The preliminary phase of research is purely an exploratory investigation that narrows the scope of issues to be dealt with and provides a direction for further research. Though there is disagreement among both practitioners and academicians as to whether the research process starts with a preliminary investigation or problem definition, there is evidence to suggest that this step might be useful when the researcher is faced with a problem that is not clearly defined.

Problem Definition

In the conduct of any decision process, the most important step is problem definition. Stating the problem clearly provides the direction for the entire research process. Unless the problem is properly defined, the information produced by the research is unlikely to be useful. Problem definition spells out the issues to be investigated and becomes the starting point for the design phase of research. A clear and well-defined problem specifies the types of information that are needed by management. Incorrect problem definition is a leading cause of failures in research.

In identifying the problem, researchers may contact and discuss the situation with the managers concerned. This step ensures that the decision maker's initial description of the management decision is accurate and reflects the appropriate area of concern for research.

A management problem can be understood only within the context of the decisional situation. This requires the researcher to explore the factors that may have contributed to the present situation. Conducting a situational analysis focuses on the variables that have produced the stated management problem. This analysis helps isolate the specific variables that need to be further studied.

The output of the problem definition process is a clear statement of the information required to assist the decision maker. Defining the research problem is more difficult in international research. Unfamiliarity with the external factors and the difficulties encountered in conducting a thorough situational analysis make it difficult to define research problems for international research.

From a business standpoint, a problem may not necessarily mean something negative; it may also provide an opportunity for the firm. For example, both European and Japanese automobile manufacturers responded to higher gasoline prices and narrow roads in their countries as an opportunity to develop smaller and more fuel-efficient cars.

A research problem may be defined in the context of a business environment, a strategic position, a tactical point, or all of the above. Research cannot provide solutions. Solutions require executive judgment. Research provides information that may be used to make decisions.

Figure 3.2 presents a helpful scheme that may be used to identify research problems. Factors that may contribute to a problem may be classified as environmental, strategic, or tactical. Environmental factors are competition, industry type, economic, legal, and political factors, technology, geography, and sociocultural issues. Strategic variables are growth objectives, choice of country, entry strategy, target market selection, financing, sourcing and supply links, and organizational issues. Tactical variables are type of manufacturing and manufacturing process, type of product, pricing issues, distribution channels, promotional vehicles, research and development efforts, and product positioning.

Problem definition that encompasses the above factors assures management that all possible areas of the problem have been considered. This approach helps the researcher to develop a commonly understood and agreed-upon definition of the management problem.

General Motors in the early 1970s is a good example of a company faced with a variety of environmental issues. GM's market share declines during this period could be traced to effects of environmental factors. Imported Japanese cars were superior in quality (competitive). Japanese manufacturers had a cost advantage due to use of modern technology, including robots employed in assembly of cars (technology). The Ministry of International Trade and Industry (MITI) provided assistance to Japanese automobile manufacturers (government). Finally, American consumers switched from buying large cars to buying smaller ones (consumers). General Motors in this case had to define its problem in terms of multiple environmental variables.

Problems faced in the strategic area may include variables such as how and where to expand (growth). International companies also have to decide how to enter a new market—through exports, by joint venture, or via a wholly owned subsidiary. Because these areas entail reviewing the allocation of company resources in order to position the firm strategically, the issues raised have to be defined accordingly. Strategic issues transcend many functional areas, and the problem definition for research is more complex in these instances.

Problem definition in the area of strategic decisions is more often governed by internal considerations. A problem definition in the strategic area may be stated as "how to expand our market in countries that provide us with the greatest potential in making use of our competitive advantage in product quality, and which target group is most likely to be attracted to this attribute?" To respond to this problem, an international company will have to conduct research to gather comparative data on countries to determine the market demand and will also have to conduct a market study to identify the most likely target group for its product.

Tactics are specific action plans that are devised from strategic options. Problems that occur in this category are different from environmental and strategic factors.

Figure 3.2   **Identification of Research Problem**

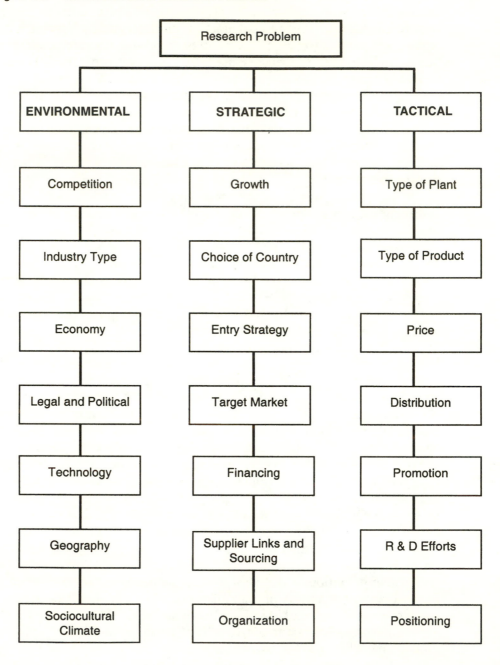

Execution of a promotion program by an international company in a new country may entail developing a media plan. To develop a media plan, a marketing manager may require information on the media habits of its target group. A problem definition that focuses on information about media habits of consumers would differ greatly from the one outlined earlier for gathering information on target market selection.

The more precise and accurate the problem definition, the easier it is to design the research methodology. Research issues should be limited in scope and measurable (observable) in order for a researcher to proceed with the study. As explained earlier, it is difficult to define international research problems, and international executives often make mistakes in defining research problems.

Following are some of the commonly observed mistakes made in defining international research problems:

- Sometimes researchers define the problem too broadly. For example, "How should we expand our market?" is too broad a problem definition to be of any use to the researcher. A better statement is "Which countries in Latin America have the greatest market potential for our services?"
- In some instances, researchers define the problem too narrowly. For example, "How should we respond to increased price competition?" This company would be better off defining the problem in terms of its competitive position within the marketplace rather than focusing on price alone.

Knowing the difficulties in defining problems, some researchers have suggested a more systematic approach to defining research problems. They suggest approaching problem definition in two stages. In the first stage, the problem is defined in the broadest terms, and the various components of the problem are identified. In the second phase, the components of the problem are prioritized, from the most critical to the least critical. After the components are prioritized, the lower-order components are eliminated and the problem is restated. For example, an American fast-food chain in South Korea has difficulty attracting customers to its outlets. To determine the reasons for this lack of interest, the company undertakes a market research study. The fast-food company defines its problem as "lack of interest for American type of fast food among South Korean consumers." This problem is broken into several elements, such as "What type of food do local consumers prefer? What are the specific eating-out habits of local people?" "What are the types of outlets frequented by the locals?" and "What are the consumption habits of local consumers?" During the second stage of problem definition, the fast-food company identifies the key components (prioritizes). In this example, the fast-food company may identify "types of food preferred by the locals" and "patterns of eating outside the home" as the two key elements and define the problem through these elements.

Another approach to defining a problem has two components. In the first phase, a researcher should first formulate an explicit single-sentence research objective statement to guide the research effort. In the second phase, a series of research questions are developed. Answers to these research questions, individually and in total, result in the achievement of the research objective.[3]

Level of Management

International research may be initiated by the headquarters staff, the regional office staff, or country managers. Therefore, identifying the level at which the research decisions are made is critical to understanding the focus of the research. Though in both domestic and international situations there are similarities in the levels of decision making, the decision-making structure is far more complex at the international level. The great distances between the various units of an international company combined with the differences in country conditions and lack of local market knowledge compound the difficulties in decision making for international research.

As mentioned previously, international research can be initiated at the country, regional, international, or corporate level. The differences between the research initiated at various levels lie in the scope of the research and the funds allocated for such research. At the country level, the research design considers only issues pertaining to the local market, and limited funds are allocated to these studies. At the divisional level, the research study might consider multiple countries, and a far greater number of issues may be researched. The budget allocated at this level is greater than that allocated to studies at the country level. For example, when the international division of Unilever, the giant British-Dutch conglomerate, evaluates plant location sites, it usually evaluates six or seven countries. The research for this task would be entrusted to the international division of the company located in the Netherlands and may require a substantial budget. On the other hand, if Unilever's subsidiary in the United States is planning a media study, it may not want the headquarters staff to get involved in formulating and executing this research, and this study could be completed by spending a significantly smaller amount than is invested in the country evaluation study.

Research at different levels of an international company may sometimes lead to duplication of efforts, which would increase costs unnecessarily. To avoid these problems, international research is quite often tightly controlled at the headquarters level. Since the organizational framework in international companies requires greater linkages than are required in domestic firms between the various functional and country-level managers, there is a greater need to coordinate the research function. This coordination is critical when considering the level of management in a research process.

Scope of Decision

Research provides information relevant to the decisions faced by executives. Therefore, the type of decisions to be made, that is, the information used for strategic purposes or for tactical reasons, would affect the research. Whereas strategy looks at an appropriate course of action to achieve company objectives, the tactical aspects of the strategy attempt to develop specific tasks or steps to be performed to execute the strategies. Information gathered to make prespecified planning decisions falls under the strategic category, and information generated to identify sources of funding is considered tactical.

IDENTIFYING INFORMATION NEEDS

The previously identified research problem and the stated research objectives should be used to identify the specific information needs of the research project. By focusing on each element of the problem, research questions that need to be answered, and the hypotheses that have to be tested, the researcher can determine what information should be obtained. The information could be about customers, competitors, suppliers, or even employees. It is recommended that the researcher spell out the exact information requirement before undertaking a study.

DATA SOURCES

The next phase in the research process is identifying data sources. There are many data sources available for international research. Data source selection is governed by many factors. Some of the critical factors in data source selection are cost, time (how long it takes to obtain the information), and the appropriateness of the information to the current problem.

There are two main data sources for research—*secondary* and *primary*. Secondary data are those that were developed for a purpose other than helping to solve the problem at hand. Primary data are data that are collected to help solve a particular problem or take advantage of an opportunity on which a decision is pending. Figure 3.3 presents a classification of international research data sources.

Secondary Data

One of the cardinal rules in data collection is to exhaust all secondary data sources before conducting a primary study. Secondary research generally is less expensive and takes much less time than primary research. In some instances, secondary research can help resolve the problem at hand and avoid costly primary research. For example, an American farm-equipment manufacturer attempting to market its products in Asia commissioned a research supplier to analyze the potential for its products in a few select Asian countries. The research supplier searched for background information using secondary research and came across a study done by the U.S. Department of Commerce on market potential for small equipment including farm equipment in Asian countries. The cost of the report was $2.50. Being an ethical company, the research supplier submitted its report using the secondary data and shelved further primary research, saving thousands of dollars and time for the company.

Secondary data can be used at the initial phases of international research in defining research problem(s) and also during the latter phases of research. For example, secondary data can assist a researcher in developing questionnaires for primary research or in defining the population for sampling purposes. Because of its versatility and low cost, secondary data is very popular among international researchers. In fact, in some instances, difficulties encountered in gathering primary research often lead to the use of secondary data as the only feasible source of information.

Figure 3.3   **Classification of International Data**

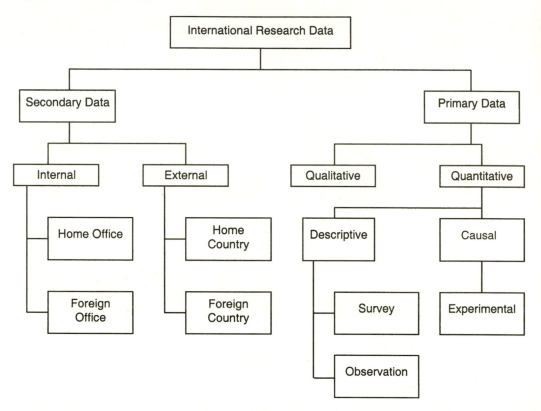

Secondary data can be classified as internal or external. Internal data consist of information generated within the company, such as sales records, financial statements, and budget reports. International companies use internal data to evaluate markets, compare cost-effectiveness of operations, and identify target customers. International companies have also used production reports from various countries to compare labor costs in manufacturing across countries in order to identify process efficiencies. Likewise, sales reports from various markets have been used to select target markets and to focus on specific consumer segments. Since internal data are specific to the firm and can be located easily, they are often used in defining problem areas and deciding on what actions to take in the near future.

External data are those that are generated by organizations other than the firm. External secondary data may be obtained from published materials, online services, or research suppliers that specialize in collecting data for a specific industry or industries (called syndicated services). External data are most often free, except in the case of syndicated services. Data collected from external sources generally provide both firm-specific as well as macro information. Firm-specific secondary information that is widely available includes market share by competitors, sales by distribution channel, characteristics of supply-chain strengths of leading competitors, advertising expenditures by company, media allocation by brand, consumer demographics, and product usage rate by segment.

Some of the macro information that is available from secondary sources includes economic trends, general information about competitors, political and legal conditions, census data, developments in technology, and sociocultural trends by country. Macro information is helpful in evaluating the present market, planning general strategies, and providing a direction for further research. A detailed description of secondary data sources and their uses is presented in detail in chapter 4.

Primary Data

Primary data collection is the heart and soul of any research. It involves many steps, is time-consuming, and tends to be expensive. Primary data are supposed to fill any void in the information needed for making business decisions after secondary sources have been exhausted.

In spite of the inherent difficulties and costs involved in collecting primary data, it is an important step in the research process. Because information collected through primary sources is specific and deals with the issues at hand, it is used in strategic as well as tactical decision-making situations. In addition, relevant and accurate primary data can often guarantee the success of a business plan. In some instances, data collected from primary sources have provided information that has helped a company avoid costly mistakes.

Primary research is classified into many categories. At the broadest level, primary data may be classified as qualitative or quantitative. Qualitative research (also called exploratory research) provides insights into and understanding of the issues at hand. It is concerned with discovering the general nature of the problem and the variables that relate to it. In specific situations, qualitative research is able to explore the feelings of respondents and why they react in certain ways. On the other hand, quantitative research seeks to find relationships and uses statistical means to explain the relationships.

In most instances, researchers conduct qualitative research before embarking on quantitative research. Qualitative research is helpful in providing input for developing questionnaires and also in the design of primary research studies. In some cases, qualitative research might answer key questions, thereby avoiding further studies.

Qualitative research generally uses small samples, and consequently the results are not projectable or used in forecasting situations. Focus groups, in-depth interviews, projective techniques, and thematic apperception tests (TATs) are the most commonly used qualitative research techniques in international research. In international research, qualitative techniques are particularly helpful in assessing unfamiliar market conditions. Qualitative techniques enable researchers in the international field to identify research constructs, to define products and services, to understand local variations in terminology and standards, and to identify attitudinal and behavioral aspects of the market. Because no prescribed conceptual model is imposed a priori on a sample, qualitative research avoids the imposition of cultural bias.

The most generally used quantitative technique in primary data collection is the *survey*. The survey is a technique for collecting information directly from respondents. Through the use of a questionnaire, surveys obtain information from a representative sample of the population. A questionnaire consists of a series of questions on a specific topic in which the researcher is interested. A questionnaire may contain both structured questions (which have a reasonably fixed number of responses and are unidimensional) and unstructured or open-ended questions (to which the respondents' answers may differ widely). Surveys can provide descriptive data such as attitudes, feelings, ownership, and personal characteristics. Because survey research employs large sample sizes, its results are projectable. Survey research is flexible and easy to execute and provides rich data, and therefore it is a very popular research technique and is the most common method of collecting primary data for business decisions.

In international research, surveys are often used to obtain business-related information. There are, however, inherent difficulties in designing and executing international surveys. International questionnaire preparation is difficult because of language and cultural differences. Sample selection is troublesome in some countries because of lack of demographic and other related data. Administrating questionnaires and supervising fieldwork are laborious due to lack of trained staff and inadequate infrastructure. Nonavailability of computers often creates problems in data analysis. Nonetheless, surveys are still a mainstay of international research for gathering critical and specific information.

A second data collection technique using the primary research format is the *experiment*. Experiments are also referred to as causal research designs, as they are able to specify the functional relationship between two or more variables. Experiments are used primarily in production, R & D, and marketing situations. For example, an international firm might want to determine the effect of worker-training programs on productivity levels. The best way to isolate the effects of the training program on worker productivity is to design an experiment with one group of workers undergoing training and a second group not undergoing training and then to compare the productivity levels of the two groups of workers. Experiments are generally difficult to design and, if not properly administered, may result in biased findings.

A third type of primary data collection is *observation*. This technique uses some form of observation of subjects, situations, events, objects, or some combination of these to gather information. Observation involves recording the behavioral or other actions of the subjects being observed. There is no direct contact between the researcher (the observer) and the subjects. Information is recorded as events take place or is culled from historical data. Observation may be used as the sole means of collecting data or it may be used in conjunction with other means.

Observation methods include personal observation, mechanical observation (audiovisual monitoring), audits (used in accounting and marketing functions), trace analysis, and content analysis. Trace analysis is the observation of physical traces. For example, in locations where electronic devices are not available or are too costly, the researcher notes the wear and tear of roads to determine vehicular traffic patterns. Content analysis is used in communication and cultural studies to identify interests and views on certain subjects of people in a community or country by observing the use of words, symbols, and characters in the public media.

The three primary data collection techniques are explained in detail in chapters 6, 7, and 8.

DATA ANALYSIS

Once data has been collected, the researcher must analyze them in order for them to be of use in decision making. Analysis of data is the process of transforming data into information. The way the raw data from a research study are prepared for analysis and the manner in which the summary and descriptive statistics are calculated can often make a substantial difference in the usefulness of the report.

Data analysis consists of two distinct steps: the data-preparation phase and the actual data-analysis stage. The data-preparation phase includes editing and coding. Editing ensures that the data are readable and accurate. Coding involves establishing categories and assigning codes to them. Coding transfers responses from written to alphanumeric format for entering the data into computers for analysis. In the actual data-analysis stage, responses are tabulated and inferences drawn through quantitative manipulations.

In international research, depending on the research expertise of local personnel, availability of computers, and complexity of the research, a researcher may tabulate and analyze the data manually. Manual data analysis has its limitations. Some of the more advanced statistical techniques for data analysis cannot be employed if high-powered computer systems are not available.

We can use simple tabulations as well as complex statistical techniques to interpret the data. Simple tabulations include frequency tables (tallies of responses by question), which provide basic information. The most commonly used statistics associated with frequency tables are mean, standard deviation, and skewness. Whereas frequency tables describe only one variable, cross-tabulation describes two or more variables simultaneously. Cross-tabulations show the nature of association between a pair of variables.

Some of the more sophisticated techniques in data analysis include chi-square analysis, hypothesis testing, analysis of variance, factor analysis, and regression analysis. Chi-square analysis is used to test the statistical significance of the observed association in a cross-tabulation. Hypothesis testing evaluates population values. Analysis of variance, also called ANOVA, examines differences among more than two means. Factor analysis is a procedure used primarily for data reduction and summarization. Regression analysis analyzes relationships of a dependent variable and one or more independent variables. These techniques generate useful information in addition to providing the statistical significance of the findings. The specific technique used to analyze a set of data will depend on the nature of the data, the country in which research is conducted, and the objectives of the research.

PRESENTATION OF RESEARCH FINDINGS

Once a research project is completed, it has to be presented to the appropriate decision makers. Effective communication between the research user and the researcher is extremely important to the research process. A formal presentation usually will play a key role in the communication effort. In the presentation of the research results, decisions associated with the research purpose are addressed, and the advisability of conducting further research is often considered. Since researchers are close to the project and know the results very well, they have a tendency to assume that the audience's level of knowledge matches their own, and consequently they skim over some of the important observations. The research user is not often as well informed as the researcher assumes. Therefore, researchers have to make sure that the results are presented completely and clearly both in a written format and orally.

The written report is a complete description of the research. It includes background information, statement of objectives, outline of the methodology, data presentation, analysis of data, recommendations, and necessary exhibits. A copy of any questionnaires used should be included as part of the exhibits. The findings and recommendations must be clearly spelled out and should identify the limitations of the study.

Oral presentations help management grasp the key findings and clarify issues and questions with the researchers. The object of an oral presentation is to provide a synopsis of the research and to draw the attention of decision makers to the key findings. Multimedia presentations, slide projections, and presentation of charts and graphs are all useful tools in communicating key findings. A good oral presentation should pique the interest of the executives and motivate them to read the full report.

INTEGRATION OF RECOMMENDATIONS INTO DECISION MAKING

To develop an international business plan, executives need a tremendous amount of information on the target country. Research findings are an excellent source of information for these executives. The key task here is to operationalize the findings into a few tactical steps for managers to implement.

Depending on the task at hand, an international executive has to review the results of the research and develop a feasible strategy. If, for example, a firm had sought information on the various funding options available to it, the results of a research study should enable the executives to choose a funding option that optimizes its resources. Similarly, a concept test for a new product idea should enable managers to decide whether to proceed with the product idea or consider alternatives.

STORAGE AND RETRIEVAL OF RESEARCH REPORTS

Since a completed primary study is an excellent source for future research, it should be stored for easy access. As international research costs more and takes a much longer time to complete, internal secondary sources such as past studies help the information collection process tremendously. For example, a study on plant location in Germany might prove useful when management is weighing a similar decision in France. If earlier studies are not totally adaptable to the new situation, at least portions of the research report might be of help in designing the research for the current problem.

International firms often use past research studies to build longitudinal data sets that are very useful in identifying issues, tracking trends, and pinpointing areas for future research. For example, a study done on the use of cellular phones in Japan in the late 1980s, if compared to a similar study done in the mid-1990s, might reveal interesting data to telecommunications companies regarding consumer concentration, brand preferences, usage patterns, and the like.

The three most critical considerations in data storage are *ease of data retrieval, confidentiality,* and *safety.* A principal goal of information storage is fast data retrieval. Research reports stored on computer disks or tapes are easy to access. But in countries where this method is not feasible, storing data on microfilm or microfiche or in files or folders may be the only available option.

Computer storage requires that a good directory (cross-referenced by project name, country, or date) be maintained to assist in the retrieval process. Computer storage requires the least amount of space, and, at the same time, it is the fastest method for retrieving data. However, computer systems are expensive and may not be available in many countries.

The second consideration in storing research data is confidentiality. Industrial espionage is rampant, and research reports provide valuable information to competitors. For example, if a competitor were able to acquire the plans for the introduction of a new product, it might introduce a version of the product earlier and negate the efforts of the company whose research was stolen. Therefore, safeguards in storage of research studies should be developed so that only a few key decision makers can access the information.

The third factor in the storage of research reports is safety. Safety refers to the possibility of loss of stored data through damage. Damage to file folders, films, or computer disks is a concern of researchers in storing data. Many firms have backup disks created to avoid problems of loss or damage. Storage of data is part of the research process and should not be treated lightly.

RESEARCH PROPOSAL

A research proposal is a written document that explains what has to be done, how it is done, who is going to do it, how long it will take, and how much it will cost. Essentially, the proposal is a contract between the researcher and the user of the research output. A proposal assists management in assessing the value of the research. It is a plan for conducting and controlling a research project. A proposal should be developed before a research project is begun. A proposal helps ensure that the decision maker and the researcher are in agreement on the basic management problem, the information required, and the overall research methodology. It also presents the researcher with an opportunity to sell the project to the final user.

As an agreement, a proposal eliminates many problems that might arise after the research has been conducted. Research proposals are required when dealing with research suppliers. They are equally useful when research is developed internally. A proposal assists subordinates in better organizing the research process and makes them aware of the difficulties in setting up mutually agreeable research objectives.

A typical research proposal consists of the following eight steps:

1. Introduction and background—includes the environmental context of the problem, discussion of present circumstances with an emphasis on the overall research problem, and identification of any information gaps.
2. Research objectives—defines the information to be obtained in terms of the research questions to be answered. This information must be related to the problem at hand. It includes explicit description of the scope of the proposed research, the specific informational needs, and the nature of the project (i.e., descriptive, evaluative, or predictive study). For example, a commercial bank may state its objectives as determining its customers' experiences and level of satisfaction with various banking services in order to decide what services are still needed.
3. Research hypotheses or specific questions to be answered—includes identification of research issues that need to be tested, determination of factors influencing research design, and development of a list of questions to be explored.
4. Research methodology—presents the important features of the research methods to be used, with justification of the strengths and limitations of the selected approach. It is a nontechnical description of the data-collection method, measurement instrument, sampling frame, and analytical techniques. The methodology section includes a list of information sources, a statement of preferences for secondary versus primary data collection, a rationale for using specific data-collection methods, pretesting of questionnaires and scales, a definition of the population under study, a sampling scheme, sample selection, standards for staff selection and training, an analytical design, and an interpretation of results. In the bank example above, the research methodology may include a survey of 500 present and future bank customers selected on the basis of a probability scheme. The sample may be contacted through personal interviews. The method of data analysis would be simple tabulations and cross-tabulations.
5. Presentation—specifies whether intermediate reports will be presented after each stage is completed and whether the presentations will involve both written and oral reports.
6. Time and cost estimates—explains the time and cost estimates for the planned methodology. This encompasses all negotiated aspects, including total fees, payments, special provisions, treatment of contingencies, and time schedule for completion of the project. It is sometimes useful to submit a PERT (program evaluation and review technique) chart to show the timeline.
7. Special conditions—includes the designation of responsibility for handling costs and status reports. Provisions for discontinuing the project should be explained in this section.
8. Appendixes—contain any statistical or other technical information that only a few of the potential readers may be interested in; they should be placed at the end of the proposal.

CHAPTER SUMMARY

This chapter outlined the research process. The research process identifies the various steps involved in undertaking international research. The steps in international research are as follows: preliminary phase, problem definition, management levels, secondary data collection, primary data collection, analysis of data, presentation of findings, integration of recommendations and decision making, and storage and retrieval. The research process in international business corresponds to the research process in domestic business, though the individual steps may be more involved in international research.

Some of the steps outlined in the research process are more critical than others. Problem definition is an important step, as it sets the direction for the remainder of the steps that follow. Data collection is another critical step. Similarly, the selection of the type of analysis to which the data is to be subjected is equally important.

Even though the research process is a series of sequential steps or stages, the stages are interrelated. Also, not all stages are completed in every research project. If the researcher obtains the necessary information through secondary sources, subsequent stages might be skipped. Similarly, after the research team has completed the exploratory research, management may feel that it has sufficient information to decide on a plan of action.

A research proposal describes the various activities to be completed in performing a research project. It serves as a control mechanism and helps avoid problems that arise from miscommunication. The research process and the accompanying proposal are necessary guides for the international researcher to proceed systematically. In addition, the process quite often serves as a planning tool.

CHAPTER REVIEW

1. Identify the steps in international research.
2. In your opinion, which are the three most important steps in international research? Justify your choice.
3. What are some of the key factors to be considered in defining a research problem?
4. What are the key informational sources in international research?
5. Describe the various techniques used in primary data collection.
6. What is a questionnaire?
7. What are the three main methods of collecting observational data?
8. What are some of the techniques used in analyzing research data?
9. What are some of the aids used in oral presentations?
10. Why is storage of research reports important? What are some of the methods used in storing research reports?
11. What is a research proposal, and what are its uses?
12. Enumerate the steps in a research proposal.

Notes

1. Paul Lewis, "Do Your Homework," *Successful Meetings* 46, no. 3 (1997), pp. 120–121.

2. Stewart A. Smith, "Research and Pseudo-Research in Marketing," *Harvard Business Review* (March–April 1974), pp. 73–76.

3. Elrick and Lavidge Inc., "Questions Marketing Research Planners Should Ask When Planning a Study," *Marketing Today* (1977), pp. 1–2.

Additional Reading

Books

Creswell, John W. *Research Design: Qualitative, Quantitative, and Mixed Method Approaches.* 2nd ed. Thousand Oaks, CA: Sage Publications, 2002.

Green, Paul E., Donald S. Tull, and Gerald Albaum. *Research for Marketing Decisions.* Upper Saddle River, NJ: Prentice-Hall, 1988.

Articles

Barabba, Vincent P. (1991) "Market Research Encyclopedia." *Harvard Business Review* (January–February), pp. 105–116.

Gandz, J., and T.W. Whipple (1977) "Making Marketing Research Accountable." *Journal of Marketing Research* (May), pp. 202–208.

Wilson, Dale R. (1996) "Research Design: Qualitative and Quantitative Approaches." *Journal of Marketing Research* 33 (2), pp. 252–255.

4 Secondary Data

All secondary data sources must be fully exhausted before other research procedures are undertaken.

LEARNING OBJECTIVES

This chapter explains the importance of secondary data, its sources, problems associated with it, and other issues involved in using secondary data to gather information. After reading this chapter, students should be able to

- Define the nature of secondary data
- Identify the international environment
- Pinpoint the advantages and disadvantages of secondary data
- Recognize the different types of secondary data
- Determine criteria for evaluating secondary data
- Identify the sources of international secondary data
- Recognize the uses and applications of secondary data
- Identify some of the unique problems in gathering international secondary data

The definition and general concepts related to secondary data are covered in chapter 2, and the present chapter details secondary data sources. Secondary data collection is an important step in the international research process, and students must understand the subject clearly.

Secondary data consist of information gathered for purposes other than the one at hand. The operational features of secondary data are that it already exists and is easily available. In international research, secondary data can be quite versatile and is used for many purposes. Because of the general problems associated with international research, especially when primary sources are too expensive or not feasible, secondary sources take on a much larger role. As explained in appendix 1.1 in chapter 1, assessing opportunities in foreign markets or identifying countries for international entry may be accomplished quite easily by using secondary sources. Also, when the size of a potential country is small, using secondary sources is more appropriate than undertaking expensive primary studies. Insufficient knowledge is the single biggest reason for failures in the international marketplace, especially for smaller companies. By using secondary sources intelligently, exporters can conduct cost-effective research of foreign markets.[1] The key to accomplishing low-cost research programs is to make effective use of secondary sources. Secondary data that are free or can be purchased for a modest price are also available from governments of many developed countries.[2]

ADVANTAGES OF SECONDARY DATA

Secondary data offer several advantages over primary data. Some of the advantages of using secondary data are as follows:

- *Accessibility.* Secondary data are much more easily available than most other data. Because the information is already collected, international managers need not set up elaborate organizations to collect it.
- *Cost.* Secondary data are relatively inexpensive. The costs associated with secondary data lie in compiling the information, which can be achieved with minimal costs.
- *Speed.* Since secondary data already exist and are readily available, much less time is needed to gather them. Time is a critical factor in a competitive international environment.
- *Availability.* Some data, such as census (population, labor, industries) or registration (birth, death, automobile registration) data, are available only through secondary sources. Due to the sensitive nature of these data and the cost involved in collecting them, no single firm or industry group can gather and maintain them.
- *Flexibility.* Data collected from secondary sources can be used for a variety of situations including identifying or defining problems, developing an approach to the problem, and answering preliminary research questions.

DISADVANTAGES OF SECONDARY DATA

Because secondary data have been collected for purposes other than the problem at hand, their usefulness to the current problem may be limited. Secondary data do not provide answers to specific questions. Before secondary data can be used as the only source of information to help solve a business problem, they must be *available*, *relevant, accurate*, *current*, and *sufficient*. If one or more of these criteria are not met, primary data have to be used.

- *Availability.* For some international problems, secondary data are not available. For many developing countries, information on proportion of expenditure by categories is not compiled and therefore not available. Similarly, some basic economic data for some countries are also not available.

- *Relevance.* Relevance refers to the extent to which the data fit the information needs of the research problem. Even when data that cover the same general topic as that required by the research problem are available, they might not fit the requirements of the particular problem. Two general issues reduce the relevance of data that would otherwise be useful. First, there is often a difference in the *units of measurement;* that is, the unit of measurement required by the problem does not match the unit of measurement used in the secondary data. For example, detailed information on the characteristics of the population is required for the evaluation of market size across countries. However, available demographic statistics may be organized by county in one country and by village in another. A second factor that can reduce the relevance of secondary data is the *definition of classes or categories.* Social class, age, income, and firm size and similar category-type breakdowns found in secondary data are not uniform across countries.

- *Accuracy.* Since the researcher did not conduct the original study, there may be problems in the study's design and methodology. The real problem is not so much obvious inaccuracy as it is the difficulty of determining how accurate or inaccurate the data are likely to be. When using secondary data, if possible, the original source should be used. Using the original source allows the data to be examined in context and may provide a better basis for assessing the quality of the data.

- *Currency.* A common problem associated with secondary data is the currency of the data. Research problems require current data. Most secondary data, on the other hand, have been in existence for some time. Some of these data may be many years old. For example, the United Nations' *Statistical Yearbook* is a major source of country information for international researchers, but the yearbook takes two to three years to compile, and data collected by individual countries may be even older; the 2003 yearbook might have data for the year 2000 or 2001.

- *Sufficiency.* Secondary data may be available, relevant, accurate, and current but still may not be sufficient to meet the data requirements for the problem being researched. In such cases, primary data must be obtained.

Since many factors affect the usefulness of secondary data, secondary research must be carefully evaluated before it is adopted.

CRITERIA FOR EVALUATING SECONDARY DATA

It is recommended that the secondary data projected for use in a research situation be systematically checked for its applicability. Following are some of the steps used to evaluate secondary sources:

- *Accuracy of data.* Errors in secondary data may be traced to poor research design. This may include the research process, including questionnaire design, data-collection techniques, sample design, and analytical techniques. The key factors in assessing the accuracy of secondary data is to determine the *who, why,* and *how* of data collection. The reputation or experience of the people (who) or the firm collecting the data quite often provides a clue to the accuracy of the data. An examination of the specific reasons why the data was collected also provides clues to the validity of the data. For example, in comparable studies of readership, one conducted by a magazine and one conducted by an independent research firm such as Simmons, the data from Simmons would tend to be considered more reliable. The magazine needs to sell advertising pages based on readership; consequently, it may overstate its numbers. Equally important in establishing the accuracy of secondary data is identifying the sources of information (how) used by the original researcher.

- *When the data were collected.* To gain the most effective input from secondary data, the researcher must find the latest possible secondary information. If there is a considerable time lag between data collection, its actual publication, and its use in research, the data will be less valid. If the data are old, the researcher may use estimation techniques to update them.

- *Content of the data.* Data should be examined for internal consistency, including consistency of key variables, units of measurement, and category breakdowns. Quite often the measurement variables do not fit the present research classification, negating their usefulness. A good example of a measurement problem is economic data from Eastern European countries. Gross national product (GNP) or gross domestic product (GDP) is the most commonly used measure for identifying the economic strength of a country. But in Eastern European countries, economic strength is measured by the net material product (NMP). NMP is the measure of a country's physical production and those services used in the physical production. Net material product does not include services such as banking, education, health, and the like. NMP is not equivalent to either GNP or GDP. These differences in secondary data create problems for international researchers.

- *Rigor of research design.* Do the research design and methodology follow acceptable standards (how scientific is the study)?

- *Other factors.* These include an evaluation of the quality of the publication in which the study appeared, the intended audience, the reputation of the person or group conducting the research, the purpose of the research, and the reputation of the sponsor of the research.

A good way to check for accuracy of secondary data is to obtain information from multiple sources and compare them. The fewer the deviations between the various sources, the greater is the likelihood that the research is accurate.

Most secondary sources provide valuable information on the external business environment. Evaluation of the external environment is probably the first step undertaken by international businesses to assess the market potential for a given product. To evaluate the external environment, researchers need to first identify these variables.

INTERNATIONAL BUSINESS ENVIRONMENT

All businesses, whether domestic or international, operate within a given environment that influences their decisions. Most of these external variables are beyond the control of the firm. Business executives need to understand these variables in order to develop effective strategies. An *external environment* is defined as a force surrounding and influencing the progress, development, and decision-making aspects of a firm. Domestic as well as international firms are affected by similar external variables. The key difference between the domestic and the international external variables is in the complexity of these variables. International external variables are more complex and dynamic. In addition, these variables are often unfamiliar to international executives. By definition, international companies operate in multiple countries. Consequently, they are affected by environmental variables that may be different in many aspects from each other.

The key international environmental variables are:

- *Competitive:* size and strength of competitors, types of competitors, and their location
- *Economic:* aggregate economic variables such as the GNP or the GDP, unemployment rate, national debt, balance of payments, personal consumption expenditures, and so forth, which all have a bearing on the operations of the firm
- *Financial:* interest rates, rate of inflation, exchange rates, tax rate, and so on
- *Political:* elements of a nation's political climate, political stability, form of government, nationalization policies, nationalism, and so on
- *Legal:* business regulations, ownership requirements, local laws, and the like
- *Infrastructural:* transportation systems, telecommunications networks, energy production, and distribution facilities
- *Technological:* technical skills and equipment that affect resource conversion, R&D expenditures, patent registrations, and the like
- *Demographic:* population size, characteristics, distribution by age, literacy rate, family and household sizes, and so forth
- *Sociocultural:* values, lifestyles, and cultural traits of a society including mores, attitudes, beliefs, and opinions
- *Geographic:* topography of the country, natural resources, climate, and so on

As mentioned previously, for international managers these external variables are quite often alien and difficult to assess and forecast. For example, host governments of developing countries may prefer that an international firm invest in low-technology industries to resolve high unemployment problems. This preference may be the opposite of the government policy adopted by the country in which the firm is incorporated. The international environment becomes even more unpredictable if the firm produces its product in one country but markets it in another country. Such operations complicate the attempt to understand the environments of many countries at the same time. For example, international companies operating in the Middle East are affected by political conflicts in that region. Therefore, a product produced in Israel cannot be marketed in Syria because these two countries are at war.

Following are the key difficulties faced by international executives in addressing external factors.

- *Unfamiliarity.* The domestic environment is a known entity for the international managers; the foreign environment is an unknown.
- *Assessment.* Environmental factors in foreign countries are difficult to evaluate. The historical origins and reasons for some of these factors are less obvious to foreign executives, and, therefore, they are that much harder to understand.
- *Interrelationships.* Environmental factors in many countries are interrelated to one another. Management practices and ownership rules are very much culture bound and vary from country to country. Because of this linkage, researchers have difficulty in forecasting the trends and directions of these external factors.
- *Influence.* International companies are less likely to influence the policies of the host governments than are domestic firms. This situation places the foreign firm at a competitive disadvantage.
- *Self-reference criterion.* Self-reference criterion, or SRC, is the unconscious reference to one's own cultural values when judging behavioral actions of others in a new or different environment. International executives will ascribe to others their own preferences and reactions (because of their familiarity with their own culture) and fail to use or consider local values and preferences (because of their unfamiliarity with these cultures). This lack of understanding or recognition of cultural differences has been identified as one of the major reasons for many international business failures.

In an effort to understand the significance of the environmental variables in international business and the need to gather relevant information on these factors for business decisions, the following discussion offers a detailed description of each environmental variable.

DESCRIPTION OF THE INTERNATIONAL BUSINESS ENVIRONMENT

COMPETITIVE ENVIRONMENT

The number, size, strength, and position of competitors in a particular country will affect a firm's ability to compete successfully in that country. Competitive analysis is a useful and necessary step in any business decision. Increased competition in the global marketplace has forced companies to be cautious in their approach to entering new markets. The level and complexity of international competition makes it harder to evaluate competitors.

In the international arena there are competitors from the local country, from other foreign countries, and also some from the home country. Each one of these competitors has different strengths. Some may have more knowledge of the local market, some may have more influence with the local government, and a few others may have the backing of their home governments. For example, General Motors in Japan has to compete with Toyota, Nissan, and Honda (local competitors). General Motors is at a disadvantage with respect to its influence with the Japanese government compared to the local manufacturers. In Japan, General Motors also competes with BMW, Fiat, Hyundai, Mercedes-Benz, and Volvo (foreign competitors). If the relationship between the government of Japan and the governments of the home countries of these foreign competitors is strong, GM may have less influence. In addition, GM competes in Japan with Ford and Chrysler (home competitors). In this case, GM's influence is on par with the other firms from its home country.

In some industries there are just a handful of international competitors who have a commanding share of the market and exert tremendous influence on the market. Examples of these industries include shaving equipment (Gillette), soft drinks (Coca-Cola and PepsiCo), detergents (Unilever and Procter & Gamble), electronics (Panasonic and Philips), and airplanes (Boeing and Airbus). On the other hand, in the automobile industry there is less global dominance by one or two firms. Firms such as General Motors, Ford, Toyota, Volkswagen, Fiat, and Nissan have much smaller shares of the total global market. The level of competition in the latter group is intense, and one firm's strategic actions are easily duplicated by the others. Thus, competitors in the second group try to maintain their market share and therefore adopt a defensive strategy. In industries with few world competitors, firms are interested in continuing their dominance, and as a result these firms tend to adopt an offensive global strategy.

Competitive analysis involves evaluating the strengths and weaknesses of the major players in the industry. An international firm is deemed to have strength in an area when it has a distinctive advantage over its competitors in that area. Similarly, weakness in a business function would be a disadvantage. For example, if a firm's plant is located very close to raw material sources, and it is the only manufacturing facility located there, then that firm has strength in that area. A company could also develop strengths in such areas as size (revenue, market share, number of employees, etc.), position (dominance), financial strength (availability of cash, capital structure, profitability, etc.), marketing (brand image, product quality, distribution coverage, etc.), and service quality (customer service).

To survive in the fierce international markets, a firm has to identify its competitors, evaluate their strengths and weaknesses, and anticipate their future strategies. Information is the key to conducting a thorough competitive analysis. As in other international situations, it is more difficult to obtain useful information for competitive analysis than it is in domestic situations. Some secondary sources such as the U.S. government, especially the Department of Commerce, can provide useful industry and competitor information. Similarly, the Findex directory contains a listing of the most readily available research reports for use in analyzing competitors. Government reports are quite often available without a fee; private sources, such as the Findex directory, are available at a cost. Also, competitive information is dependent on the level of economic development of a country. For example, it is much easier to obtain secondary competitor information in the United States, Canada, Western Europe, and Japan than in some Asian and African countries.

ECONOMIC ENVIRONMENT

The most significant external variable for international businesses is the economy. Total output of goods and services and the manner in which they are consumed are of critical importance to business executives. The utilization of a country's resources in the production and distribution of goods and services is part of the economic environment. Economic activities vary from country to country, and each has its own set of factors and levels of development. Lack of information in some instances makes analyzing the economic variable difficult.

The economic environment is made up of the GNP (or GDP), distribution of income, personal consumption expenditure, private investment, wages and salaries, and balance of payments. These factors vary greatly from one country to another. For example, Japan had a positive balance of payments in current accounts of US$75 billion at the end of 2003; India, on the other hand, had a negative balance of US$5 billion for the same time period.

Following is a simple explanation of the components that constitute the economic variables of a country.

Gross National Product

GNP is the market value of the final output of goods and services claimed by the residents of a country in a year. The World Bank and other international organizations such as the International Monetary Fund (IMF) and United Nations (UN) use estimates of GNP as the main yardstick of economic activity for a country. GNP at market prices may be calculated through a *production approach*, an *income approach*, or an *expenditure approach*. Using the production approach, GNP is calculated from the net output of agriculture, mining and manufacturing, construction, utilities, trade and transport, government services, and net factor income from abroad. Using the income approach, GNP is calculated by totaling wages and salaries, company profits, income from self-employment, rental and interest income, depreciation, net indirect taxes, and net factor income from abroad. Using the expenditure approach, GNP is computed by totaling private consumption, general government consumption, total investments, exports of goods and nonfactor services, and net factor income from abroad.

Since the output of a country is an indicator of its economic activity, the GNP is often used as a key factor in evaluating a country's economic strength. The five largest economies in the world based on their GNP are the United States, $7 trillion; Japan, $2.5 trillion; Germany, $1.1 trillion; France, $873 billion; and China, $393 billion.

Using the GNP as a basis, the countries of the world are classified into four categories. These categories are *highly industrialized countries*, *newly industrialized countries*, *developing countries*, and *less developed countries*. Appendix E presents the GNP for many countries of the world. This appendix also contains a few key country statistics.

The general characteristics of highly industrialized countries are high per capita incomes (over $10,000), a greater proportion of the workforce in the manufacturing or service sector, and significant export activity with a population that is concentrated in urban areas. Less developed countries, on the other hand, have very low per capita incomes (under $700); a majority of their workforce is in the agriculture sector; they are marginally involved in trade; and they have a population concentrated in rural areas.

Per capita GNP is the measure most often used to determine the well-being of the people of a country and its market potential. Though GNP per capita is very often used to compare countries, such measures create difficulties related to the purchasing power of local currencies and the existence of underground economies. For example, because of the high cost of living in Japan, its per capita income of $24,420 fell to an adjusted level of only $14,311 (using the purchasing power parity or PPP). On the other hand, China's per capita income of $670 rose to an adjusted level of $1,200 (once again, using the PPP) because of its low cost of living. In countries such as India, Mexico, and Russia, where a thriving underground (black market) economy exists, the true GNP per capita may be much higher. Comparisons of absolute GNP per capita do not provide the true economic strength of a country.

Gross Domestic Product

GDP measures the value of final goods and services produced by a country's domestic economy. GDP also can be estimated using production, income, or expenditure methods. The major difference between GNP and GDP is that in GNP the net factor income from abroad is added.

Balance of Payments

Balance of payments (BOP) is a financial statement that summarizes all economic transactions between a country and its trading partners for a given period of time. BOP is presented as a double-entry accounting statement in which total credits and debits are always equal. A country has a positive BOP when its receipts are greater than its disbursements. A deficit exists when a country pays out more than it receives in trade and related activities.

A country's BOP is a very important indicator for international business managers, as it reflects a country's propensity for consumption of foreign goods. BOP can also indicate the existing climate for foreign direct investment and other potential government actions toward foreign operations. If a country's BOP is in deficit, the local government may impose trade restrictions, devalue its currency to make imports more expensive in the short run, or impose currency controls to make it more difficult for locals to import goods.

BOP data are divided into *current account, capital account, official reserves account*, and *net statistical discrepancy*. The current account records the flow of goods, services, and transfers. The capital account shows public and private investment and lending activities. The official reserves account measures changes in holdings of gold and foreign currencies (reserve assets) by official institutions. The net statistical discrepancy reflects errors and omissions in collecting data on international transactions.

FINANCIAL ENVIRONMENT

National monetary policies, rate of inflation, and fluctuations in exchange rates greatly affect international operations.

Exchange Rates

Exchange rates represent the number of units of one currency needed to acquire one unit of another currency. Exchange rate operations assist international firms in transacting business across national boundaries. On the other hand, fluctuations in the world's currencies affect transfer of funds among international companies. International executives must understand how to protect against losses and optimize gains from currency fluctuations. Another problem encountered by international executives occurs when a government suspends or limits convertibility of its currency. In such situations, companies try to foresee and minimize losses resulting from large holdings in local currencies. Collecting historical data on currency rates and tracking the pattern of government intervention can help minimize the risks in currency transactions.

Inflation

Inflation is a condition in which the price level increases rapidly. Inflation affects international operations in many different ways. Through its influence on interest rates, exchange rates, and cost of living, inflation affects the general confidence in a country's economy. Inflation rates vary widely across countries. Industrialized countries generally try to control inflation. Therefore, countries such as Germany, Japan, and the United States have very low inflation rates (5% or lower). In contrast, some of the developing countries of Asia and Latin America experience hyperinflation. In the spring of 1985, Bolivia's inflation rate was running at 25,000 percent per year, the highest recorded rate in history. As recently as 1993, Brazil's inflation rate was over 1,000 percent. International companies doing business in these countries experience difficulty in planning for the future. Concerns regarding costs, cash flow, and inventory are some of the issues faced by firms in countries with hyperinflation.

Monetary and Fiscal Policies

A country's monetary and fiscal policies also affect the financial decisions of multinational companies. Governments introduce policies that may affect exchange rates, inflation, cost of living, and trade. Through the actions of wage and price controls, taxes, manipulation of the money supply, and decisions on government expenditures, governments effectively control consumption, production, and the way businesses operate.

POLITICAL ENVIRONMENT

A country's political system and philosophy influence the decisions made by an international firm. A friendly and stable government invites and encourages foreign investment. The business climate provided by these governments attracts foreign firms to establish operations in their countries. Other governments are hostile to foreign investments because of differences in political ideology (democracy versus communism, for example) or differences in economic philosophies (capitalism versus socialism, for example). Based on past experiences, a system of democratic government with a strong market economy is generally preferred by the international business community.

International companies prefer a political climate that is stable with very few upheavals. For international companies, political actions such as nationalization of businesses or government appropriation of property are prescriptions for disaster. A constant monitoring of political climate in foreign countries is an essential step in conducting business abroad.

LEGAL ENVIRONMENT

National laws affect how critical elements of the management process are performed. Some national laws that regulate local business activity influence both domestic and foreign companies, in the areas of employment practices and contractual obligations, for example. Laws also exist that affect only international companies, for example, investment of capital and repatriation of earnings.

Both democratic and totalitarian countries have legal systems, but the independence of the law from political control may differ from one to another. Generally, democratic countries have a more independent judicial system. Legal systems usually fall into three categories: common law, civil law, and theocratic law. Common law is based on tradition and precedent. The United Kingdom and the United States practice common law. Civil law is based on a very detailed set of laws that are organized into a code. Japan, Germany, and France follow the civil law system. Theocratic law is based on religious doctrine. Muslim countries that follow Islamic law fall under the theocratic legal system.

By nature, legal systems vary from country to country. Understanding the differences and operating in such diverse legal systems require a thorough knowledge of each country's laws.

INFRASTRUCTURE

The activities that facilitate education, transportation, communication, and distribution are collectively called infrastructure. Infrastructure is needed to ship raw materials and finished goods from source to user. Convenience of market reach under favorable costs is a key component of a firm's competitive position. International transportation is a major concern to the international firm because transportation determines how and when goods will be received. Infrastructure also helps companies to contact suppliers and customers, store goods, access foreign currencies, and transact business internationally through tele-transfers.

Extreme variations exist in the type of transportation systems available across countries. In some countries, for example, railroads may be an excellent transportation mode, as in many European countries. In others, trucking may be the preferred mode of transportation, as in the United States. In most industrialized countries, the infrastructure tends to be excellent. But in many countries of Africa, Asia, parts of Eastern Europe, the Middle East, and Latin America, the network of roads, railways, telecommunications, and storage systems is inadequate, and this may affect distribution of goods.

TECHNOLOGY

Technology is the usable knowledge that a society applies and directs toward attainment of economic and cultural objectives. It is significant in the efforts of developing countries to improve their standard of living. It is also a critical factor in the competitive strategies of international companies. By increasing the demand for new products and services, technology has an enormous impact on international business. Much of what we take for granted today, such as powerful desktop computers, is the result of technology that has been developed only in the last decade. Technology has contributed to improvements in the processing of raw materials, has improved quality of life, sped up the communication and transportation process, and offered time-saving conveniences in our day-to-day lives.

A country's technological environment is a combination of people skills, innovations, and advances in scientific and medical fields. Technology makes it possible for automobile manufacturers to use computers to design cars quicker, for doctors to study human anatomy using magnetic imaging techniques, and for businesses to communicate effectively across countries. Technology enables the application of science to production, marketing, finance, and management.

DEMOGRAPHIC ENVIRONMENT

Demography is the study of human populations in terms of size, density, location, age, gender, race, occupation, and other statistics. The world population is growing at an explosive rate. There were more than 6 billion people in the world at the beginning of the twenty-first century. There are vast differences in population sizes, from more than 1 billion inhabitants in China to less than 1 million in Luxembourg. Total population is the most general indicator of a potential market. The explosive population growth rate is a boon to international businesses for selling goods in untapped markets of the world. But most of the population explosion is taking place in developing countries that cannot afford the goods and services offered by international companies. Hence, a growing population does not necessarily mean a growing market. Nevertheless, demographics are an important variable in identifying potential markets.

SOCIOCULTURAL ENVIRONMENT

Social factors relate to family and societal influences. Cultural factors are those that influence a group or society. Because society is composed of people and their culture, it is not possible to speak of one without relating to the other. Therefore, anthropologists often use the terms interchangeably or combine them into one word, *sociocultural*. Businesspeople are interested in both social and cultural factors.

Culture affects a society's values, beliefs, attitudes, perceptions, codes of conduct, and communications. Both cultural and social factors affect how businesses are run. They affect employer-employee relations, buyer-seller interaction, business-to-business interchange, and government-to-business negotiations. Lack of understanding of these factors has resulted in many international business failures.

There are as many sociocultural patterns in the world as there are societies. When businesses operate in cultures that differ from their own, the problems they encounter in dealing with a single set of cultures are multiplied by the number of cultural sets they find in each of their foreign markets. Culture shock (being totally exasperated by customs and practices in a foreign country) is a phrase often used by international executives to describe their frustrations in dealing with foreign cultures.

It is easier to market products in foreign countries when the sociocultural factors are similar compared to when cultural patterns are diverse. In evaluating countries for potential entry, international companies study the sociocultural patterns to isolate factors that are similar and those that are dissimilar.

GEOGRAPHY

International business executives who know geography can better determine the location, quantity, quality, and availability of the world's resources. The uneven distribution of resources results in different products and services being produced in different parts of the world. For example, Middle Eastern countries have the world's richest oil deposits, but the same terrain that is conducive for oil deposits forces these countries to import most of their agricultural products. Similarly, countries such as Indonesia, Japan, and the Philippines are made up a series of islands, and they have vast coastlines that provide abundant seafood but make distribution of goods and services very expensive.

The probability of natural disasters such as earthquakes and hurricanes makes it riskier to invest in some parts of the world. Selection of countries for market entry is also influenced by geographic proximity. Geographic proximity makes it easier for international companies to control their foreign operations.

TYPES OF SECONDARY DATA

Secondary data sources are grouped into two categories, the distinction being whether the data are available within the company (*internal*) or must be obtained from outside sources (*external*). Most companies collect information in the everyday course of conducting business. The accounting department prepares financial statements and keeps detailed records of sales and costs. Manufacturing plants report on production schedules, shipments of finished products, and inventories. The sales department reports on sales by customer type and geographic territory. International managers can use information gathered from these sources to identify opportunities and evaluate performance. Multinational companies frequently use their international salespeople as sources of market-related information. Information gathered by the sales force can be valuable in overcoming cultural barriers, as the information provided by the salespeople may be based on firsthand experience.[3] Numerous sources external to the firm also may produce data relevant to the firm's requirements. The major sources of external secondary data are various government agencies, journals, databases, and the Internet.

Internal Secondary Sources

In collecting *internal* secondary data internationally, a researcher has to search for information both at the home office and at the local office. In addition, those companies that use a regional operating structure may have data available through their regional offices. Home office data are either collected by the home office or acquired by the home office from its foreign units. The key benefits of internal data are ready availability, reasonable accessibility, and relevance to the organization. Some internal reports are sufficiently detailed and can be used immediately. For example, production reports may provide useful information about total output by shifts, output per employee, or material usage per unit output.

Following is a list of internal data that are most commonly used in international business:

1. *Production.* Reports from foreign units may be used to monitor production runs, plan material requirements, and make workforce assignments. By reviewing historical records, management can improve the scheduling process. Similarly, inventory reports may be used to improve material requirements planning.

2. *Finance.* Financial reports such as balance sheets and income statements provide information to investors, creditors, and others who commit financial resources to a firm. In addition to the reports developed for external use, companies often prepare reports for planning purposes. Documents such as *cash flow statements* and *budget reports* provide useful information about company operations. Cash flow statements provide historical cash receipts and disbursements for a specific time period, and *budgets* provide a summary statement of plans expressed in financial (expenditure, cash, or capital) terms for a specific period of time.

3. *Marketing area.* Management gets information about the effectiveness of its marketing plan in several ways. The most important sources are the sales report, market share data, the distribution report, and the advertising media report. Sales reports consist of plans for future activities and write-ups of completed activities. The best example of a plan for future activities is the work plan that salespeople submit periodically. The work plan describes intended calls and routing. From this report, the sales manager can plan sales calls and schedule activities for each salesperson. This report also provides a basis for comparing plans across countries. Similarly, market share information from various countries can be used to compare marketing effectiveness. Sales by product line, by distribution channels, or by consumer segments are all very useful secondary data, especially in comparing results across countries.

4. *Human resources management.* Companies generate various reports that deal with employees. Reports such as man-hour efficiency and productivity are useful in evaluating results. Comparing such reports across countries provides management with a baseline for evaluating international operations. These reports are also useful in planning expansions.

In tracking internal secondary data, it is customary to develop databases. Through the use of computers, various internal data are categorized and stored for future use. For example, a firm might track customer segments and their purchase patterns in different countries. This information can be analyzed at the head office or regional office and disseminated to local offices for use in developing marketing programs. Similarly, production reports from various plant locations can be stored and analyzed for use in improving assembly-line setup. Figure 4.1 is a flow diagram outlining the sequence of steps necessary to systematically search for secondary sources.

A wide variety of external secondary sources are available internationally. Interestingly, there are far more avenues to collect external data internationally than there are in domestic situations. Besides the available information in the home country, useful information can be obtained from the region as well as the local country. In addition, information is available from many government and independent sources.

As mentioned in chapter 3, one source of external secondary data is from the home country's government agencies; the U.S. Department of Labor's *International Price Index* is one example. Similarly, foreign governments make available useful secondary data, for example, the Japan Development Bank's *Economic Data of Japan*. Commercial publishers offer compendia of data at home and in foreign countries, for example, *Euromoney*'s Country Risk Analysis. Other useful secondary sources include international organizations such as the IMF and the United Nations, which provide extensive country statistics, and service companies such as Price Waterhouse, which provide country-specific regulatory information. In addition, trade organizations such as the World Trade Club, universities (for example, the University of Chicago), nonprofit organizations such as the Netherlands Chamber of Commerce, professional research companies such as D&B Marketing Information Services, and electronic information retrieval services such as the Dow Jones Newswires provide valuable secondary information. Figure 4.2 identifies the major sources of external secondary data.

International firms have an advantage in that they can tap into many countries for acquiring secondary data through their subsidiaries. As in domestic situations, they can obtain information from the government, public sources, and private sources. In addition, some of the large international agencies such as the IMF, the United Nations, and the World Bank gather statistics that are useful to international companies.

The information available through these sources ranges from very general to specific data. Some of the information obtained through external secondary sources includes economic data, statistics on extractive industries, social and demographic data, legal and tax information, country statistics, ownership of automobiles and household appliances, industrial output, media usage by various segments of the population, and market data. Because of the vast number of sources, one of the challenges in international research is to sort out the relevant from the immaterial information.

EXTERNAL SECONDARY INFORMATION SOURCES

Secondary information sources can be classified either by data source or by type of data. Either approach is useful, but the following classification is based on data sources.

Figure 4.1   **Flow Diagram for the Systematic Search of Secondary Sources**

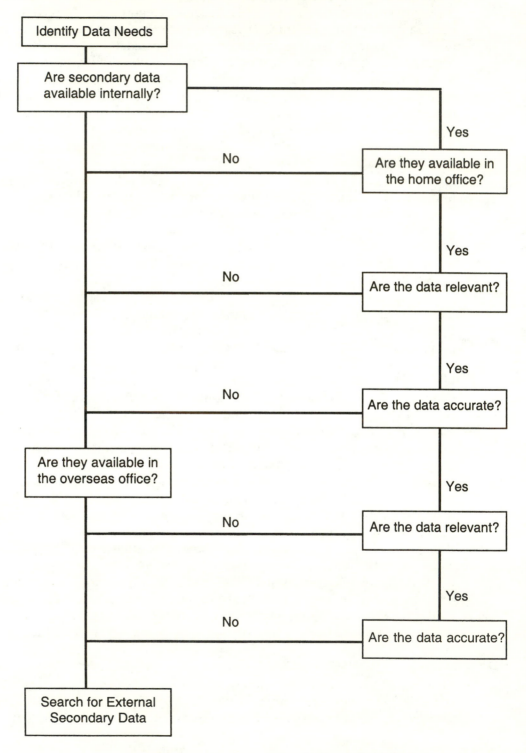

Figure 4.2 **Major External Secondary Sources**

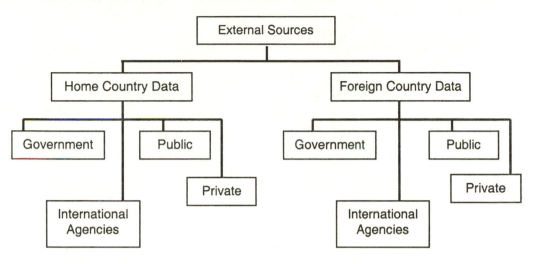

Since most governments collect an array of data to monitor economic and social shifts within their countries, government publications provide a practical starting point.

Government

Government agencies produce an abundant amount of data. Naturally, the more developed a country is, the greater the quality and diversity of information. Governments of countries such as the United States, Japan, the United Kingdom, Germany, and France have a wealth of useful information for international businesses. The U.S. Department of Commerce provides macro and micro information as well as other data services. Other federal departments such as the Department of Agriculture, the State Department, and the Department of the Treasury are equally useful sources of critical information. Most federal governments provide data on population trends, trade statistics, agriculture output, and other useful information.

Any government search should start with the home country sources. Proximity, knowledge of the sources, and specialized agencies or departments within the government assigned to help firms explore foreign markets make starting with the home country government sources a practical approach.

Besides the home country government sources, researchers should also consult secondary sources from foreign country governments. Most industrialized countries compile a variety of data to evaluate social and economic programs. Census and registration data gathered by government agencies are useful to researchers. Many countries actively seek foreign direct investment, and to encourage these flows, they assist foreign companies with incentives and by providing useful business-related information. Some examples of these publications are as follows:

1. *Yearbook Australia*—includes information on Australian history, government, physical geography, and climate, as well as statistics on population, employment, manufacturing, exports, and imports.
2. *China Statistical Yearbook*—presents a broad range of statistical material for the People's Republic of China, including natural resources, employment and wages, investments, public finance, and prices.
3. *Japan Statistical Yearbook*—presents statistics on population, transportation, commodity prices, and public finance.
4. *Korea Statistical Yearbook*—includes statistics on population, wages, foreign trade, national accounts, wholesale and retail trade, construction, mining, and manufacturing.
5. *Annual Abstract of Statistics*—provides statistical information for the United Kingdom, including education, trade, banking, transportation, energy, and agriculture.

The U.S. government is recognized as a leader in the collection and dissemination of business-related information; hence, any international search should begin with this source. The U.S. Census Bureau is the world's largest source of statistical data. The quality of census data is excellent, and they contain detailed information. The U.S. Census Bureau collects a wide variety of information, including population figures, consumer expenditure surveys, and American housing surveys. The bureau also provides international demographic and economic data through its Center for International Research.[4] Census data are available at a nominal fee, and some are even available on computer tape. The *Guide to the Economic Census* gives a complete list of all the census reports published by the U.S. Census Bureau.

The U.S. Department of Commerce operates the National Trade Data Bank (NTDB). The NTDB consists of 133 separate trade- and business-related programs. The NTDB provides information on export opportunities, population figures, socioeconomic conditions for several countries, and how-to market guides. Small and large companies can make use of this database to identify potential markets for their products.

In addition to the census data, the U.S. government collects and publishes a great deal of other statistical data. These publications include *Agricultural Statistics* (annual statistics on cost, consumption, prices, and production), *Business America* (domestic and international commercial news), *Economic Indicators* (monthly publication of general economic statistics), and *Statistical Abstract of the United States* (annual compilation of statistical tables covering demographic, economic, political, and social topics). U.S. businesses seeking a desirable location for expanding their operations overseas can make use of this published information. Details of selected U.S. government data sources are listed in Appendix B.

International Organizations

International organizations such as the United Nations, the World Bank, the IMF, the Organization for Economic Cooperation and Development (OECD), and others collect data at the international level. These collections are a useful source of secondary data.

The International Research Institute on Social Change (RISC) conducts worldwide research on social trends using surveys, in-depth interviews, and other qualitative techniques. Trends are measured every year from large samples in 30 countries. The insights gained can be applied to identify segments within a given population.[5] The main problem with secondary data collected by international agencies is that the information collected by these agencies is often quite dated. Because of the time needed to compile, sort, and publish worldwide data, there is a two- to three-year lag between the collection of data and its publication.

Following is a partial list of the major secondary sources provided by international organizations.

United Nations. The UN Statistical Yearbook is the official source of statistical data compiled by various organizations. This yearbook contains information for nearly 200 countries on such varied topics as agriculture, balance of payments, consumption, culture, education, energy, housing, industrial production, manufacturing, national accounts, population, transport, and wages and prices. Other publications of the United Nations include:

- *Industrial Statistics Yearbook*—contains basic data on industrial activity and detailed information on world production of industrial commodities
- *International Trade Statistics Yearbook*—provides import and export statistics for more than 150 countries covering five years
- *National Account Statistics*—presents detailed national accounts estimates for more than 160 countries
- *World Economic Survey*—includes statistics on population, foreign debt, per capita income, trade balances, and essays providing an overview of developments in international trade and policy

World Bank. The *World Atlas,* published by the World Bank, provides useful general data on GNP, GDP, growth trends, and population figures for most countries of the world. The other publications of the World Bank are:

- *World Development Report*—contains information about food production per capita, life expectancy, adult literacy, rate of inflation, and annual growth rates
- *World Tables*—contains current and historical data on gross national income, GDP, value of merchandise imports and exports, and private consumption
- *World Currency Yearbook*—includes information on the history of currency, transferability of currency, and recent developments in foreign exchange regulations
- *The World in Figures*—includes rates of exchange, growth rates, resources, production, and trade for most countries

International Monetary Fund. Some of the IMF publications that are helpful to international companies include:

- *The International Financial Statistics and IMF Annual Report*—contains information about national accounts, trade statistics, exchange rates, consumer prices, and money supply for the various countries of the world
- *Balance of Payment Statistics*—contains statistics on goods and services and long-term and short-term capital and reserves for more than 110 countries
- *Balance of Payment Statistics Yearbook*—contains eight-year balance-of-payment figures for more than 110 countries
- *Direction of Trade Statistics*—details central government revenues, expenditures, lending figures, financing options, and figures on a country's external debt

Organization for Economic Cooperation and Development. The OECD publishes many statistics and reports, including the following:

- *OECD Financial Market Trends*—contains information on financial markets for some industrialized countries
- *OECD Financial Statistics*—contains information on central government finances, new security issues, and interest rates for financial instruments
- *OECD Economic Surveys*—contains information on member countries including recent developments in demand, production, employment, prices, and wages
- *OECD Main Economic Indicators*—explains some of the most recent changes in the economy of OECD member countries

Service Organizations

Service organizations such as accounting firms, airlines, banks, and publishing houses provide a wide variety of secondary information. These organizations are able to supply information on such topics as business practices, regulatory requirements, and trade and financial data for many countries of the world. Notable publications by some of these service organizations include:

- *Moody's International Manual*—contains data on balance of payments and exports
- *Dun & Bradstreet's Exporters Encyclopedia*—provides information on tariffs and tax regulations
- *The Arthur Andersen European Community Sourcebook*—provides information on key strategic issues of the single European market and contains a brief background sketch with data for each member country
- *PricewaterhouseCoopers Doing Business in _____* (formerly *PriceWaterhouse Doing Business in _____*)—contains regulatory information for many countries of the world

Syndicated Services

Syndicated services collect information and make it available for subscribers. These companies use surveys, scanners, and audits to amass data that are of particular importance to many companies. Generally, these data are designed to serve information needs shared by a number of clients. Unlike service organizations, which may not have a particular client list and provide secondary information as part of their overall service, syndicated services sell their reports to specific clients. Syndicated services also differ from custom research firms, which collect data for a specific client and for a specific project.

A good example of a syndicated service for international firms is the macroeconomic country data collected by Business International. The Business International report contains a number of key variables including historical population of labor statistics, wages and prices, foreign trade, and production and consumption data. These data are computerized and regularly updated. By subscribing to this report, a client has access to information that may serve its international research needs. Business International also produces a country ranking report. This report ranks countries based on economic, political, financial, and other related factors. Other publications of Business International include:

1. *Market Key Index*—a cumulative, cross-referenced index to the entire Business International set of services.
2. *Updated Reference Services for Doing Business* contains information on investing, licensing, and trade conditions abroad. Regional reports provide detailed information on economic and political conditions in various regions of the world; *Business Latin America* is an example of such a report.

Euromonitor is another major syndicated service that collects and publishes data on a variety of subjects. Some of its publications include *European Food Databook*, *The World's Major Companies Directory*, and *The World Healthcare Marketing Directory*.

Euromonitor also publishes *Market Research International*, a journal for the research industry; *Market Reports,* which contain sales and consumption data for such products as beer, cosmetics, appliances, and food; and strategy reports, such as *The World Market for Meat and Poultry in Year 2000.*

ACNielsen, a division of D&B Marketing Information Services, is a large U.S.-based research company with operations in 90 countries. Nielsen provides a vast number of syndicated research reports. Its Scantrack measures retail consumer purchases through scanners in 3,000 supermarkets in all 50 U.S. states. Similarly, its 40,000-member in-house consumer panel provides customer profiles by brand and gauges customer loyalty. A useful syndicated service for bankers is the Investext reports. The Investext group provides bank executives approximately 1 million reports from 330 international investment banks, brokerage houses, consulting firms, and research companies. These reports contain competitive information including data on the total market as well as individual segments within the market.[6]

Trade Associations

Trade associations represent groups of individual firms. Every industry has its own association that collects information for the benefit of its members. Some of these trade associations are country based, such as the Association of Home Appliance Manufacturers in the United States, and others such as the international chambers of commerce are worldwide. These associations often collect a wide variety of data from their members, which are then published in an aggregate form. *The Beverage Annual*, published by the members of the beverage industry in the United States, is one such publication. The annual contains information on aggregate production, average costs, consumption rates, industry sales growth, and other related information. Most of these associations represent the viewpoints of their members and sometimes lobby host governments on their behalf.

Databases

Databases store a wide array of information. Some are managed internally by companies to develop a strategic advantage in securing real-time information. Others are maintained by government agencies, research suppliers, or private firms. For a fee, international companies can subscribe to online databases or information-retrieval companies. For example, the Eurobases and Euroscope databases provide a wealth of information on commercial, legal, and cultural aspects of European countries. In the United States, the Donnelly Demographics database provides demographic data from the U.S. census.

There are close to 5,000 databases available in the world, and a majority of them are produced in the United States. Computerized (electronic) databases tend to be current, are easier to access, and contain information on a wide variety of topics. Databases are classified as *bibliographic, empirical, text-based,* and *directory* databases. *Bibliographic* databases such as ABI/Inform include citations to articles. *Empirical* databases provide statistical information such as census data, economic data, and industry statistics. Compustat is an empirical database that lists major companies of the world along with financial and other related information for the reporting companies. *Text-based databases* contain complete texts of documents, usually newspapers. Financial Times Index is a good example of a text-based database. *Directory databases* provide information on individuals, organizations, and services. A good example of a directory database is the *European Communities Encyclopedia and Directory,* which contains the names, addresses, and telephone numbers of businesses and business contacts for European countries.

Most large companies devote a considerable amount of time on developing their own internal databases for their informational needs. This trend is expected to continue, and databases are expected to be the most important informational source for international researchers. Because of the growing importance of databases, chapter 5 discusses this source in greater detail.

Locating Secondary Research Reports

In the era of information explosion, it is difficult to locate the right source of secondary information. To assist in this task, some companies have developed guides that help researchers locate what they need in the vast amount of information that is out there. Following is a list of some useful guides for international business.

- *A Guide to European Financial Centers* contains information on 17 Western European countries
- *Directory of World Stock Exchanges* contains information on trading hours, volume of trade, and membership structure
- *Statistics Europe: Social, Economic, and Market Research* lists name, address, and telephone number of the central statistical office for each country
- *Using Government Information Sources: Print and Electronic* is a guide to U.S. government publications.

Internet Services

The Internet provides unlimited access to the world's information sources. Many international agencies such as the United Nations and the World Bank have Internet sites that can be used to obtain information.

The Internet provides instant access to information, with an extensive geographic reach, and can be used at a time most convenient to the researcher. There are hundreds of search engines available to Internet users. To scan or evaluate secondary data, the user simply types in one or more key words for documents worldwide. [7]

Two useful research Web sites are Euromonitor (http://www.euromonitor.com) and IMRMall (http://www.imrmall.com).

Some other useful World Wide Web index sites are

- Internet World (http://www.iw.com)
- One World Network (http://us.oneworld.net/)
- LYCOS, the Catalog of the Web (http://lycos.cs.cmu.edu/)
- Regional sites, Asia (http://www.asianbusinesswatch.com/)

Uses and Applications of Secondary Data

Secondary data are by far the most popular source of international business information. Secondary data are readily available and are often sufficient to answer the research question under study. In some instances, there is no other way to obtain information but through secondary sources. Governments, for example, can require businesses to divulge sales, expense, and profit information, which would not be revealed to anyone else.

Secondary data also may facilitate the research process by expanding the researcher's understanding of the problem. Other benefits of starting the research process by exploring secondary sources are as follows:

- Secondary data may help suggest a hypothesis.
- Secondary data may assist in setting up research design alternatives and indicating a preliminary basis for selecting alternative designs.

- Secondary research may help in planning the sample and provide a basis for validating the selected sample.

Decision makers in all areas of international business can employ secondary data to their advantage. When they are selecting plant sites, plant managers use secondary data to gather information on suppliers and manufacturing regulations. Finance managers use secondary data to assist in funds management by monitoring changes in the economic environment and plotting trends in the financial markets. The accounting staff uses secondary data to study new tax regulations. R & D personnel make use of secondary data to study the latest developments in technology. Human resources managers use secondary data to plan staff recruitment and training. Marketing managers use secondary data to assess market potential and to create preliminary demand analyses. More specifically, secondary data are used for the following purposes:

- Selecting countries for entry
- Developing entry strategies
- Selecting manufacturing plant sites
- Making financial decisions
- Making market-related decisions

SELECTING COUNTRIES FOR ENTRY

Country selection is one of the most important decisions an international company will make in its global expansion strategy. A wrong choice in selecting a country could set back a firm for many years. Even though vast improvements have come with the emergence of global databases, international online data services, and global research agencies, market-related data quality is still usually uneven, and comparing data across countries is very difficult. Long-term projections tend to be inaccurate when researchers are not familiar with the foreign market. U.S. businesses seeking a desirable location for a foreign venture have access to considerable background information and opinions on specific countries or foreign situations without ever leaving the United States. Organizations such as the Congressional Committee, the Carnegie Council, and the Business Council for International Understanding have a wealth of information on foreign countries.[8]

The process of evaluating foreign countries for market entry can be divided into three stages: country identification, screening, and selection. During each of these stages, secondary data can be of great help. The choice of countries in the first stage is based on easily available secondary data such as statistics on GNP, economic growth rates, population, and demographic breakdowns. During the screening stage, countries are rated using information such as political stability, economic development, and financial considerations (as shown in appendix 1.1 in chapter 1). In the final selection stage, information on target market, demand, competition, and forecasted costs and revenues is used to find the country with the best potential for achieving a company's goal. Available published data on market size, growth, and competition could help international companies to arrive at the final choice.

DECIDING ON AN ENTRY STRATEGY

International business may be conducted in various ways. For example, a company may produce at home or abroad. If producing abroad, the company may operate independently or it may join a local company. Essentially, there are four modes of entry into a foreign market: exporting, licensing, joint venture/strategic alliance, and wholly owned subsidiary. For most companies, immediate global expansion into all markets is usually not feasible. The mode of entry and the extent to which the expansion may take place depend on many factors. Financial and managerial factors, corporate objectives, resource constraints, and entry barriers dictate the selection of a particular type of foreign entry. Immaterial of the mode of entry, information in the form of secondary sources is invaluable in selecting a type of entry.

For companies with no experience in international business, the exporting option is often the most attractive mode of entry, especially if the market is small and the company is unsure of the endeavor's future potential. Exporting requires minimal effort and cost. If, however, the foreign market appears very attractive and there are indications that other companies are interested in the same market, an international company may decide to enter the market either through a joint venture or by setting up a wholly owned subsidiary. This strategy may also be the result of local laws that discourage imports and encourage foreign investment. Secondary information generated on market size, local laws, level of competition, and economic strength of the country are all useful in guiding decision makers in their choice of an entry strategy.

DECIDING ON PLANT LOCATION

The plant location decision is significant because of its effect on both production and distribution costs. Sometimes local governments provide incentives to locate manufacturing plants away from major cities. But these incentives may be offset by the increased expense of distribution to serve these major markets. Internationally, location decision for setting up a plant is an integral part of the strategic planning process.

Plant location decisions are long-term commitments by the international company, and incorrect decisions may have adverse effects on the company's expansion plans. In addition, a decision on plant location has an impact on the operations, investment requirements, operating costs, and revenues of the firm. Management must therefore ascertain that adequate labor, raw materials, and utilities such as water, power, and telephone lines are available before deciding on a location. Management's choice may be modified by market requirements such as the competitors' plant locations, employee preference (quality-of-life issues), and conditions imposed by the local government.

Secondary sources can provide substantial information to help executives make an informed location decision. Labor statistics, demographic data, geographic data, data on natural resources, and infrastructure information are available through many of the secondary sources identified earlier in this chapter.

MAKING FINANCIAL DECISIONS

The corporate finance function involves the acquisition and allocation of financial resources among the company's potential activities. International companies need to gain access to capital markets in different countries in order to finance expansion. International managers have to understand the nature of capital markets, cash management, and financial risk. Information is the basis for making financial decisions in the international area. Identifying sources of funds, transferring money and profits, dealing with transfer pricing, arranging for intercompany loans, and making royalty and dividend payments are all activities that require information. International funds management faces many obstacles and carries higher risks resulting from shifts in the economy, exchange rate fluctuations, and government actions, so an international firm collects information to reduce these risks.

As a result of technological advances in telecommunications and computers, the financial markets have become more efficient. This efficiency assumes a constant inflow of information. Data on interest rates, government intervention in currency markets, political upheavals, and fluctuations in economic activity need to be collected and disseminated on a real-time basis. Most of these data are available through secondary sources. By using Internet services and other scanning approaches, a funds manager is able to access information from any part of the world instantly.

MAKING MARKETING DECISIONS

Although the basic functions of domestic and international marketing are the same, the international markets served often differ widely because of great variations in external factors. The international marketing manager's task is complex. He or she must frequently plan and control a variety of marketing strategies in different countries. The manager must develop marketing strategies by assessing the firm's potential markets and analyzing the many alternative mixes. His or her aim is to select target markets that the firm can serve at a profit and to formulate combinations of strategies for product or service, price, promotion, and distribution that will best serve those markets.

Although some of the specific information necessary to identify target markets and develop marketing strategies is obtained from primary research, there is substantial information available through secondary sources that can assist international managers in their market planning. Information on general market data, demographic statistics, historical sales for the firm and industry, and competition are available through secondary sources. Similarly, forecasting sales and estimating demand rely on secondary sources. Data on sales, costs, and R & D expenditures from internal sources and more defined information from industry associations and syndicated services help to develop marketing strategies in the areas of product, package, price, distribution, and communication.

Secondary sources can be very useful for international businesses during the early phases of expansion into overseas markets. International research is more complex and expensive, but secondary sources provide an excellent option for gathering the necessary information.

CHAPTER SUMMARY

International research and domestic research follow similar processes and make use of the same techniques and tools. International research differs from domestic research in that the international environment from which information is gathered is more diverse. The international environment is much more dynamic and includes factors that ordinarily do not affect domestic businesses. Exchange rates, duties and tariffs, hyperinflation, and shifting government policies are factors more often found in international business. Therefore, assembling relevant and up-to-date information is critical in international business.

Conducting international research is made more difficult due to time constraints, varying costs, lack of expertise, and inefficient infrastructure. Given the difficulties and scarcity of resources, international firms have to find ways to obtain information creatively and inexpensively. Secondary sources appear to be a good solution for gathering information quickly and at minimal cost. Secondary data are those that have been collected already and are available for use.

Secondary data can be internal or external. Internal data are those that exist within the organization. Sales reports, accounting data, budgets, and past primary studies are all useful in evaluating markets, production decisions, and other functional decisions. A firm should first exhaust all its internal data before starting an external search.

External secondary data are available from various national governments, international organizations, syndicated services, service organizations, and publishing houses. With the globalization of markets, the availability of secondary data on markets in different countries has grown exponentially. In some instances only secondary sources may be available for international researchers. A case in point is census and registration data. Secondary data from overseas markets may suffer from problems of timeliness, reliability, and comparability, however.

Secondary data are very useful in the early stages of a research project. They are useful in defining problems, designing research, and answering simple research problems. By providing information on the external environment in areas such as economy, competition, demography, government regulations, culture, technology, and infrastructure, secondary data may aid decision making in a variety of international business situations. Secondary data are useful in evaluating countries, identifying locations for manufacturing plants, assessing financial markets, and developing marketing strategies.

A detailed list of secondary sources can be found in Appendix B.

CHAPTER REVIEW

1. What are the differences between primary and secondary data?
2. Why is it important to obtain secondary data before primary data?
3. What are the differences between internal and external secondary data? Give some examples of internal secondary data.
4. Identify the key external data sources in international secondary research.
5. What are the advantages and disadvantages of using secondary data?

6. What are some of the problems encountered in international secondary sources?
7. What are some of the criteria used for evaluating secondary data?
8. How is secondary data used in the early stages of an international marketing research project?
9. What are the strategic uses of secondary data?
10. If you were assigned to evaluate the Latin American market for a new medicated shampoo, how would you go about completing this project?

NOTES

1. Michel R. Czinkota and Ilkka A. Ronkainen, "Market Research for Your Export Operations," *International Trade Forum,* no. 3 (1994), pp. 22–23.
2. Michael R. Czinkota, "Take a Shortcut to Low-cost Global Research," *Marketing News* 29, no. 6 (1995), p. 3.
3. Lawrence B. Chonko, John F. Turner Jr., and Ellen Reid Smith, "Selling and Sales Management in Action: The Sales Force Role in International Marketing Research and MIS," *Journal of Personal Selling and Sales Management* 11, no. 1 (1991), pp. 69–79.
4. Diane Crispell, "How to Navigate the Census Bureau," *American Demographics* 11, no. 11 (1989), pp. 46–47, 66.
5. Larry Hasson, "Monitoring Social Change," *Journal of the Market Research Society* 37, no. 1 (1994), pp. 69–80.
6. Crispell, "How to Navigate the Census Bureau."
7. Nigel Bradley, "An Internet Tour for Market Research," *ESOMAR News Brief* (April 1998), pp. 12–13.
8. Benjamin Weiner, "Sources of Information (and Misinformation)," *Management Review* 81, no. 1 (1992), pp. 24–26.

ADDITIONAL READING

BOOKS

Dochartaigh, Niall O. *The Internet Research Handbook: A Practical Guide for Students and Researchers in the Social Sciences.* Thousand Oaks, CA: Sage Publications, 2002.
Nelson, T.A. *Measuring Markets: A Guide to the Use of Federal and State Statistical Data.* Washington, DC: U.S. Department of Commerce, 1979.
Stewart, David W., and Michael A. Kamins. *Secondary Research: Information Sources and Methods.* Thousand Oaks, CA: Sage Publications, 1993.

ARTICLES

Anonymous (1996) "Investext Offers Bird's-eye View of Business." *Bank Marketing* 28 (3), p. 53.
Castleberry, Stephen B. (2001) "Using Secondary Data in Marketing Research: A Project That Melds Web and Off-Web Sources." *Journal of Marketing Education* 23 (3), pp. 195–203.
Chisnall, Peter M. (2002) "Marketing Research: State of the Art Perspectives." *International Journal of Market Research* 44 (1), pp. 122–125.
Lemon, Katherine W., and Stephen M. Nowlis (2002) "Developing Synergies between Promotions and Brands in Different Price Quality Tiers." *Journal of Marketing Research* 39 (2), pp. 171–185.

Luk, Sherriff, T.K. (1999) "The Use of Secondary Information Published by the PRC Government." *Journal of the Market Research Society* (July), pp. 355–365.

Rabianski, Joseph S. (2003) "Primary and Secondary Data: Concepts, Concerns, Errors, and Issues." *Appraisal Journal* (January), pp. 43–56.

Vogelstein, Fred (2002) "Looking for a Dotcom Winner? Search no Further." *Fortune* (May 27), pp. 65–68.

5 Databases and Management Information Systems in International Research

Databases, collections of numeric data and textual information stored in computers, are secondary sources available in computer-readable form for electronic distribution. Management information systems (MIS) are a set of interrelated components that collect, process, store, and disseminate information to support decision making.

LEARNING OBJECTIVES

This chapter introduces the field of database management and its applications. After reading this chapter, students should be able to

- Define database management
- State its role in information management
- Describe the characteristics of a database system
- Understand the benefits of using database management
- Understand the problems associated with database management
- Know how to use databases
- Be able to explain the role of MIS

The purpose of MIS is to provide decision makers with a continuous flow of information. Specifically, information systems transform data into meaningful management information. Data are organized around files arranged so that duplication and redundancy are avoided. Information systems allow files to be accessed individually or across file boundaries. For example, a regional sales manager is able to capture sales organized by country and by name of the salesperson (individual access). A bank branch manager, for example, can access information on various accounts (savings account, checking account, and so on) for each customer (across files). Current management information systems use a variety of languages or data windows to obtain information. For example, senior executives may obtain information through voice recognition, line managers may use menu-driven systems to access information, and systems professionals may use programming language to interact with the system.

A company's MIS should be able to collect information about its external environment, including customers and competitors. Data is the key element that drives management information systems. Information systems provide the necessary inputs for executives to make decisions. Information is critical in planning and developing strategies. With the use of modern technology, managers can access a wealth of information instantaneously. Databases have emerged as the main component of an information system and the key resource for the collection and dissemination of information. Global information systems combine advanced computer hardware, integrative software, high-tech telecommunication systems, electronic data interchange (EDI), radio frequency identification (RFID), and interactive media technology.

Poor operating results can often be traced to insufficient data about internal operational variables as well as lack of information about external factors. Global companies such as Ford, Grand Metropolitan PLC, and Wal-Mart have invested in sophisticated EDI and RFID systems to improve intracompany information sharing. EDI and RFID systems assist companies in improving communication and improving management of their inventories. A starting point for management information systems is to first identify variables or factors about which information is desired. For example, for Unilever a large Dutch-UK-based packaged goods company, the variables identified in Table 5.1 may be critical in setting up its MIS.

WHAT IS A DATABASE?

Databases are defined as "a shared collection of logically related data, designed to meet the information needs of multiple users."[1] In a database, information concerning an ongoing or interesting activity is collected and arranged by category. Each subsystem (category) can be accessed individually or collectively from the same source.

Databases have become the major information tool for international businesses. They are accessible across countries in real time and contain a wealth of information. As newer databases are created on a daily basis, their utility for business decision making has also grown. As a secondary source, they are quickly accessible and relatively inexpensive. A major problem associated with most secondary sources is their currency, but a database often contains up-to-date information, giving it a clear advantage over other secondary sources. For example, Nestlé has successfully pilot tested a database system in Malaysia that it plans to use for a one-on-one communication program.[2]

Companies may generate databases for their own internal use, or independent suppliers may develop them for the purpose of providing useful information to other individuals or organizations. Technology has afforded businesses the luxury of targeting customers' suppliers and funding sources to maximize sales, marketing, and research efforts. Companies that deal with other companies (business-to-business marketing) can identify target customers by job function, title, industry, geography, firm size, and organizational structure. Some independent research suppliers have also set up databases for developing strategic business plans that can be purchased by other

Table 5.1   **Variable List in Developing an MIS for Unilever**

Variable	Description
Market potential	Demand estimates, consumer factors, market factors
Competitor information	Number of competitors, strengths, and weaknesses
Resource information	Availability of qualified personnel, financial resources
External factor information	Economic and political conditions, legal restrictions
Foreign exchange	Exchange rate fluctuations, restrictions on expatriation

companies. For example, a New York–based research company offers a database of executives at 900,000 organizations in 172 countries. The company owns the data, and it is constantly updated.[3] In contrast, Japan External Trade Organization (JETRO) a national government agency, provides information free of charge. Created to help small and medium-size Japanese companies to gain export markets, it also provides valuable information to foreign companies that are interested in the Japanese market. JETRO maintains a database that is available free to users and contains articles on trade issues and also publishes a statistical yearbook that contains critical demographic data useful for companies planning to invest in Japan.[4] In recent years, the availability of both internally developed databases and those provided by outside suppliers has grown exponentially. The availability and convenience provided by databases has given an impetus to the use of this data for a wide variety of business situations.

Databases are simply storage systems that contain data. Data can be numeric or textual. Numeric data may include production runs, inventories, stock prices, and customer order entries. A good example of a numeric database is the online database of the OECD, providing country statistics for its member countries. Textual information may include full text of a document, directories, and bibliographic information. Frost & Sullivan Research Reports Abstracts is a good example of a textual database. This database contains citations and abstracts from nearly 1,500 research reports providing analyses for a wide variety of industries. Abstract Business Information (ABI/Inform) is another good example of a textual database.

ADVANTAGES OF DATABASES

Many international firms set up their own internal databases to monitor the activities of their far-flung operations. An internal international database system consists of the basic information required by international companies to coordinate their various operations in different parts of the world. An international database may contain costs of raw materials in different countries, salaries of employees, sales revenues by country, customer orders, and transportation costs for shipping raw material and finished products to different parts of the world. Researchers use these internal data for generating cash-flow statements, forecasting, strategic planning, selecting plant sites, managing inventory control, media planning, and providing customer service. Database information is stored in computer memory banks. The wide acceptance of computers, with their flexibility and abundant storage space, has contributed tremendously to the growth in the number of databases.

For some time now, consumer packaged goods companies such as Procter & Gamble, General Mills, and Unilever have used databases successfully to track, attract, and sell their products to specific market segments. Recently, more and more financial institutions have recognized the usefulness of databases in marketing their services. For example, many of the major banks are using a variety of refined database-modeling techniques to gain a clearer perception of their customers' buying habits and financial needs.[5]

Most data transmission from databases to users is accomplished electronically. One of the key benefits of databases is the real-time nature of the data access. A user can connect to a database at any time and be able to obtain information instantaneously. Internally developed databases are centrally managed; therefore, access, control, and security of the information are made easier. Other main advantages of databases are as follows:

- *Many people can access the data at the same time.* Many users can access the database through terminals that are connected to a server in which the database is stored. The limiting factor here is the number of terminals connected to the server. In many externally supplied databases, thousands of users can simultaneously obtain information from a single database.
- *Data is always current.* Both internal and external databases are updated frequently, some even on a daily basis. External database compilers use computers and modern telecommunication technology to collect and store data. Some of the large databases are kept current by entering data and information from the latest reports. Some of these reports can be downloaded directly from the source's computers, speeding up the process.
- *A wide variety of data is available.* Database management has contributed tremendously to the collection of data from a wide variety of sources on a vast number of topics. The variety of topics covered through databases has made it possible for researchers to obtain comprehensive information on almost any topic.
- *Databases are easy to use.* Recognizing the need for user-friendly systems, many software developers have introduced menu-driven interface devices. The menu-driven interface systems have grown in popularity among novice database users. The simple logic of the interface makes it self-instructive. The search process is simplified by the fact that most external database providers use simple common search commands and protocols for accessing the data. The common language commands developed for accessing databases have made the task of retrieving data simple.
- *Electronic retrieval of data is very convenient.* Using databases, researchers can retrieve information from any location—home, the workplace, or anywhere the user has access to a computer, including while flying 33,000 feet above sea level. Development of computer networks and growth in the use of modems for computer connectivity have created an environment in which it is convenient to use databases. Databases are accessible any time of the day or night; such convenience is not available with other data-retrieval methods.

- *Database information is relatively inexpensive.* Developments in technology have reduced the cost of computer access. As a result, the cost of database development and management has gone down. Because of a large user base, the external vendors also offer their services at a reduced rate.

Databases can be classified as internal or external. Internal databases are all those generated by a company from inside and outside sources for the sole use of company personnel. Independent companies generate and manage external databases for use by any individual or company for a set fee. Internal data tend to be company specific. External databases are market driven, and therefore each supplier focuses on certain users or applications. In addition to the internal versus external factor, databases are classified according to the mode of access, that is, online or off-line.

In online information processing, transactions are entered directly into the computer. The user is able to work from a computer terminal and instantaneously access the data. Online systems provide convenience and flexibility. Telecommunication networks provide the access for an online system. In off-line information processing, the information is not accessed directly from the database. The user obtains the information from a floppy disk or CD-ROM. In off-line data retrieval, the user is not connected to a database. Some data is available only off-line. For example, the census of U.S. labor or census of U.S. industries is available only on CD-ROM, and the user is not able to connect directly to the database of the U.S. Census Bureau.

MANAGEMENT INFORMATION SYSTEMS

Databases form the core of a management information system. An MIS can be defined as a set of interrelated components that collect (or retrieve), process (analyze), store, and distribute information to support decision making and control in an organization. Management information systems provide managers and other decision makers with reports and other useful information through online access to the firm's current performance and historical records; databases play a key role in the retrieval and storage stages of the information system. There are four contemporary environmental factors affecting a global corporation's reliance on MIS: emergence of the global economy, transformation of industrial economies into knowledge-based economies, transformation of business enterprises, and technological development.

Industrialized countries depend heavily on trade. International trade has contributed to an increase in demand for both industrial and consumer goods. This demand is fueled by the emergence of newer economies, such as Brazil, China, India, Singapore, South Korea, and Taiwan, that have prospered in the last decade. Global corporations also have played a key role in the growth of the world economy. Through direct investments and transfer of technology, many global companies have changed the economic structure of some of the world's emerging countries. For example, in the last decade, China has become the leading manufacturer of parts and components for a variety of finished goods.

In the advanced economies of America, Asia, and Europe, knowledge and information are becoming the key ingredients in creating wealth, while manufacturing has moved to low-wage countries. The service sector accounts for more than 65 percent of the U.S. GNP. Many American workers are employed in such industries as telecommunications, computers and software, manufacturing design, health care, and financial services. In knowledge-based economies, MIS becomes a strategic asset for global corporations. MIS is used to optimize the flow of information and to maximize the firm's knowledge resources.

Large global corporations are undergoing a transformation that is reflected in their organizational structure. Through downsizing and flatter organizational structures, companies are entrusting decision making to lower-level employees. MIS has made it possible to disseminate information through the employee ranks quickly and efficiently. Computer networks and MIS have made possible location independence, teamwork, flexibility, and employee empowerment.

Much of what we take for granted today results from technology that was developed within the past two decades. Advances in transportation, telecommunications, computers, and biotechnology have all contributed to better products and an improved quality of life. By increasing the demand for new products and services, technology has had a tremendous impact on global business. As the demand for goods and services increases, so do the number of international business transactions. Improved communications, faster transportation systems, and more efficient MIS accelerate interactions and improve a managers' ability to control foreign operations.

DEVELOPMENT OF AN MIS

There are four stages in the development of a management information system.

- The first stage is the initiation, in which the developers define the project, perform a study of the environment and systems, and evaluate the information needs of the organization.
- The second stage is the technical development. Hardware, software, and telecommunications pose special challenges in an international setting. Ad hoc–based application proliferation and expansion result in incompatible networks that do not communicate among systems. The primary hardware challenge is finding a way to standardize a company's systems across countries. The major software challenge is finding applications that are user-friendly and that improve the productivity of international work teams. The major telecommunications challenge is making the data flow effortlessly across the global networks.
- The third stage is implementation. Implementation refers to the coordinated activities of a global organization that culminates in the adoption, management, and regular use of the MIS. This stage focuses on the integration of applications and the use of databases.
- The fourth stage of building a global information system is putting in place the operational and maintenance procedures. This stage involves evaluation of the system after it is in operation. Users and specialists will audit the MIS to see how well the system meets the needs of the organization.

Figure 5.1   **Model of a Management Information System**

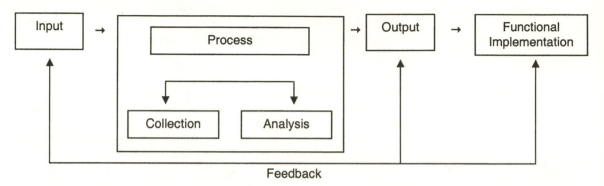

The basic elements of an MIS system are input, process, output, and functional implementation.

- *Inputs* are the source of information. They include information about customers, competitors, suppliers, governments, and other environmental forces.
- The *process* involves collection of data and analysis of data collected.
- *Output* creates the reports and recommendations for management use.
- *Functional implementation* allows managers to make use of the reports and recommendations.

Figure 5.1 is a schematic presentation of a basic MIS.

USES OF MIS

Corporate MIS can be used in a variety of situations, including strategic decision making, management control, knowledge-level decision making, and operational control. In the strategic area, companies use MIS to establish corporate goals and develop plans for productive use of their basic resources. In the management control area, MIS is used to monitor how efficiently a company uses its resources. In making knowledge-level decisions, MIS can be used for appraisal of new product ideas and establishment of internal communications networks. MIS is used in the operational control area by establishing the tactical components of business strategies. A critical output and use of databases is *data mining.*

In marketing, data mining enables firms to discover previously undetected facts about customers: their patterns of consumption, their choices, and other related information that is stored in various database management systems (DBMS). Increasingly, large amounts of critical business data are now stored electronically. Data-mining tools discover useful environmental and consumer-related facts that are often buried in the raw data. Data mining can be particularly effective for banks in retention campaigns. By evaluating patterns of transaction behavior and product purchase, banks can now predict those customers most susceptible to being wooed away by a competitor.[6]

Figure 5.2   **Decision Support System Architecture for Data Mining**

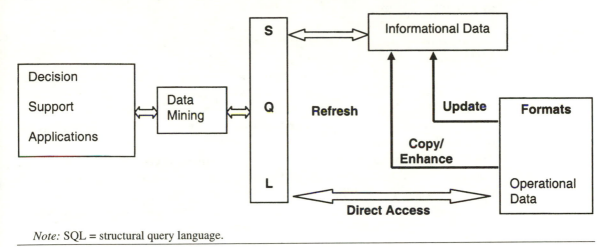

Note: SQL = structural query language.

More advanced decision support systems (DSS) facilitate data mining.[7] With the existing technology, it is now possible to link customer profiling expertly with each customer's real-time sales value.[8] A typical DSS used for data mining is shown in Figure 5.2.

Through data mining, large and small companies are able to track repeated interactions by customers, suppliers, and other institutions. By storing large-scale data warehouses fed from credit cards, help desks, and other sources, an international firm can form the foundation for understanding and reacting to each customer's or supplier's needs.[9]

MIS SUBSYSTEMS

Many factors promote efficiency, effectiveness, and success of an MIS. The efficiency of a system is the ability of the technology to help the company maximize the use of its resources. Effectiveness is the capacity of the system to assist the users in identifying and solving problems. Depending on the level of decision making, different types of MIS subsystems are developed. The most often utilized subsystems are

- *Executive support system* (ESS)—combines data from various internal and external sources. Executive support systems filter, compress, and track critical data, emphasizing the reduction of time and effort required in obtaining information useful to executives.[10] It helps managers to decide what business the firm should be in, how to track and evaluate competitors' actions, how to respond to cyclical patterns, and how to determine the earnings impact of various business decisions.[11]
- *Decision support system* (DSS)—used to assist managers in making decisions that are unique, rapidly changing, and not specified in advance. Decision support

systems have advanced capabilities that permit the user to employ sophisticated models to analyze information. For example, distribution networks may use a DSS to analyze transportation, inventory, and cost by evaluating the type of cargo, distances to be shipped, carrier to be used, timing of delivery, and so forth.

- *Knowledge work system* (KWS) and *office automation system* (OAS)—used to create, store, and communicate documents. These documents may be in the form of written reports, images, or data from any part of the organization. One good example of KWS is *digital image processing*—the conversion of documents and images into computerized form so that they can be stored and retrieved through computer networks.
- *Transaction-processing system* (TPS)—performs and records the daily transactions necessary in the conduct of the business. The master file in each of the systems is composed of discrete pieces of information called data elements. The elements on the master file are combined in different ways to create reports of interest to management. A payroll system is a good example of a TPS system.

Figure 5.3 explains these subsystems and their uses.

DEVELOPING A DATABASE

The first step in developing a database is to organize the information within the company. The type and extent of an internal database depends on many factors—the size of the firm, its involvement in international operations, and the number of subsidiaries it has worldwide. For a small firm exporting to a few countries, the database requirements may be very simple. The exporter may develop on a personal computer a sales database containing information on customers, sales volume, and location. In contrast, a large international firm with manufacturing operations in many countries may have to develop a more complex database. Such a firm may have databases at many locations with information on plant output, raw material requirements, supplier information, cash flows, unit costs, inventory levels, customer orders, and data on staffing needs.

There are two types of internal database structures (architectures): centralized and distributed. In a centralized database, all necessary data are located at a single location, usually the headquarters of the firm. Executives and other users of the database are connected through a network and can access the required data from any location. The centralized database architecture provides the greatest control for management in the collection and dissemination of data. Costs of developing and maintaining a centralized database are considerably lower than those for other architectures, as the centralized database reduces duplication of efforts by individual departments. In addition, a common database technology can be adopted in a centralized architecture. The critical disadvantage of a centralized database is its vulnerability to failure. Since all the data are located in one location, any technical or other problems render the database nonusable and ineffective.

In a distributive structure, a single logical database is spread physically across computers in many locations. Because distributed structures do not depend on the

Figure 5.3 **MIS Subsystems and Their Uses**

Types	Description				
	Strategic-Level Systems				
Executive Support System (ESS)	5-year sales trend forecasting	5-year operating plan	5-year budget forecasting	Profit planning	Manpower planning
	Management-Level Systems				
Management Information System (MIS)	Sales management	Inventory control	Annual budgeting	Capital investment analysis	Relocation analysis
	Sales analysis	Production scheduling	Cost analysis	Pricing analysis	Contract cost
	Knowledge-Level Systems				
Knowledge Work System (KWS)	Engineering workstations		Graphics workstations	Managerial workstations	
Office Automation System (OAS)	Word processing		Image storage	Electronic calendars	
	Operational-Level Systems				
Transaction-Processing System (TPS)	Marketing	Manufacturing	Finance	Accounting	Human Resources Management
	Order tracking	Machine control	Payroll	Auditing	Compensation
	Order processing	Plant scheduling	Accounts payable	Tax reporting	Training and development
		Material movement control	Accounts receivable	Cash management	Employee record keeping

Source: Kenneth C. Louden and Jane Price Louden, *Management Information Systems: Organization and Technology* (New York: Macmillan Publishing, 2001), p. 36.

availability of the resources at one central location, they are less likely to fail. The advances in computer technology and the innovations in communications and user interfaces have contributed to the growth in distributed database structures. In many firms, previously stand-alone personal computers are being linked together to benefit from multiple-location databases.

Distributed database structures are further categorized as homogeneous or heterogeneous. Homogeneous databases use common technology and share similar data. This type of structure simplifies data sharing by all users from different locations. To achieve a homogeneous system, international firms have to make sure that the computers used in all locations are the same (or compatible), the software and the management information system are the same, and the data terminology and definitions are also the same. Homogeneous databases are the ultimate goal of all international firms, but to achieve this goal, firms need to exert considerable control and plan ahead to develop a homogeneous structure.

Heterogeneous databases are the more common structures found among international firms. Databases in companies evolve over time depending on the needs of various departments and individuals. Database applications are developed on a one-by-one basis, creating problems in the integration of the data files. As each country or division acquires its own computer systems and develops its own databases, the overall system becomes a medley of structures with inherent problems. This type of system inhibits the use and application of databases.

In developing an internal database, a firm has to first make a comprehensive list of all its activities. The list may include the number of products it sells, manufacturing locations, raw materials used, work orders, inventory levels, customer invoices, vendor or supplier lists, customer orders, and a list of its present and potential customers. The next step is to identify the various decisions related to each of the areas listed above. Then the firm needs to determine the type of information needed to make these decisions and to identify the sources that can be directly linked to the database. After this step, the necessary data are collected and stored in the database.

The final step in setting up a database is to identify all the interactions among the various activities of the firm. For example, a computer manufacturer links suppliers of components to the manufacturing plant or assembly line. Similarly, the warehouse may be linked to the dealers for processing orders. This step is critical and provides management with valuable information about how the organization functions and the various relationships and interactions required for the smooth operation of its business.

The major components of an internal database are the following:

- The *database* is a collection of logically classified data that meet the informational needs of different users in a firm.
- The *database management system* includes the software and hardware to develop, maintain, and provide access to the database.
- The *repository* is the centralized knowledge base containing data definitions, report formats, and definitions of all related systems that protects and controls the resources.

- *Computer-aided software engineering* is tools to design databases and application programs.
- *Application programs* are the programs that help users obtain the data and information from a database.
- The *user interface* consists of languages and menus used for interaction among the systems.

System developers and system maintenance staff manage the various components of a database and also design new application programs. Data administrators are responsible for collecting and assembling the inputs for the database.

Databases are used by a variety of people within an organization. Top management uses databases to review strategies and develop future plans. Middle managers make use of databases to develop tactical plans based on the latest data. Information system managers, programmers, and system analysts use databases to evaluate and monitor data and their usage. The greatest value of databases lies in their use in strategic planning and control. Both top and middle management groups use databases when they need information. System analysts may use the databases for long periods of time to develop production programs and other applications. The views of management personnel and technical staff sometimes conflict on the use of databases. Line managers generally seek effectiveness in the use of databases, whereas systems personnel opt for efficiency.

USES OF EXTERNAL DATABASES

The growth in computer technology coupled with the need for fast and accurate information has encouraged many research suppliers and service companies to offer their clients and other interested firms shared databases for a fee. Each day, new suppliers are entering the business with specialized data. Database information is also available from the government. Commerce Department data on export sources and the State Department's daily updates of news from major embassies around the world are two useful government databases. Nowadays, one can find information on any topic through databases. Proliferation of external data suppliers has made the task of researchers and decision makers much easier. Databases can be found for all the functional areas of a business. Marketing managers may use ScanTrack, an ACNielsen database that provides data on sales and household purchases of a variety of product categories for many industries. Similarly, Profit Impact of Market Strategies (PIMS) is an ongoing Strategic Planning Institute database that analyzes strategic actions and performances of a few hundred companies.

In the finance area, databases such as Global Vantage, Datastream International, DRI/McGraw-Hill, Standard & Poor's database, International Finance Corporation (IFC) databases, the Bloomberg Terminal, Citibank database, the Chicago Research in Security Prices (CRSP) database, and the International Monetary Fund databases are all very useful in analyzing financial markets. Following is a brief description of some of these databases.

- The Global Vantage database provides extensive coverage of the world marketplace. It contains critical financial information on a wide range of industrial, insurance, banking, and other financial service companies. Financial information in Global Vantage includes income statements, balance sheets, and other data. It is useful in cross-border analyses of financial data. The database contains financial and market data from the year 1983 on for more than 11,000 companies from 70 countries.
- Datastream International provides financial information to the securities industry worldwide. With this information, a firm can evaluate investment opportunities and corporate performance, compare international financial markets, analyze fund holdings, and manage investment portfolios. The database contains historical data for more than 20 years. Some of the fundamental indicators contained include earnings, yields, balance sheet, and financial ratios. The Datastream database covers 140,000 securities and financial instruments from markets worldwide.
- The Bloomberg Terminal is a global distributor of information services, combining news, data, and analysis for all financial markets and businesses. It provides real-time historical pricing data on demand 24 hours a day. The database contains information on earnings, balance sheets, cash flow, debt/equity ratios, and exchange transactions. The information on transaction data includes volume, moving averages, money flows, volatility, and option sensitivity for all regions.
- The Chicago Research in Security Prices database is an extensive collection of stock prices and returns on the American and New York stock exchanges. The monthly prices and yields on stocks are available from 1926; the daily returns, from the year 1962 on.
- International Monetary Fund databases include international financial statistics, government financial statistics, balance of payments statistics, and direction of trade data for most countries of the world. These data are organized by country and contain information on interest rates, exchange rates, inflation rates, imports, exports, and balance of payments. Statistics are available on a monthly, quarterly, or annual basis. Annual statistics are available from 1948, and monthly data are available from 1957.

Like marketing and financial databases, production databases are used to develop plans and execute strategies. These databases help management to track raw material supplies, check inventory levels, monitor work orders, and assign staffing responsibilities.

PROBLEMS IN INTERNATIONAL DATABASES

International firms confront many challenges in the development of databases for managing international operations. Cultural differences, social expectations, legal constraints, and different hardware standards all make the creation of a database difficult. In developing an international database, the management and technical teams have to be cognizant of the various factors that affect the system. Following is a brief description of some of these factors.

- *Cultural differences*. Differences in cultural values affect the general business environment, including the political and legal framework of a country. Culture plays a role in how information is received and disseminated. Societies treat information selectively. For example, the French take pride in their cultural heritage and are reluctant to receive foreign television programs that might influence their culture. Culture has influenced or played a major role in laws governing transmission of information, privacy of citizens, and origins of software in information systems.
- *Regulations*. Regulations affect the transborder flow of data, that is, the transfer of information across countries. Many European countries have very strict laws concerning information flow to the citizens of their country from other countries. Some countries prohibit the processing of financial information outside their boundaries, effectively banning financial institutions' practice of performing back-office operations in offshore banking centers or low-wage countries. These regulations force international firms to develop a decentralized network of information systems in various countries, making the coordination of activities among the different units difficult.
- *Standards*. Different telecommunication systems and EDI (i.e., direct computer-to-computer exchange between organizations) create problems in setting up international database systems. In addition, data transfer speeds differ from country to country. Some, like the United States, have high-speed data transfers, but Asian, East European, and Latin American countries have slow data transfers.
- *Network reliability*. Telecommunication networks in many countries are not reliable and in some instances may be down for hours during peak times. In addition, the shortage of skilled technicians hampers network repair and maintenance.
- *Language*. Differences in language among countries have further complicated the development of global database systems. Though English is emerging as a common language among businesspersons, there are countries where English is not commonly used.

International firms face difficulties in planning a database system appropriate to the firm's global strategy and organizational structure. Whatever the organizational structure or the strategy employed by an international firm, powerful competitive challenges in the global market place force firms to develop an efficient and effective international database system.

CHAPTER SUMMARY

A database is a collection of data classified, stored, and arranged to facilitate retrieval and use for planning, operational control, and managerial control. A database includes all data, regardless of form, found within the organization. The database and computerized data processor combine to create value by converting data inputs into information. A database is part of an overall management information system. An MIS is an information system that facilitates management control by producing structured, summarized reports on a regular basis. In other words, an MIS is the design and use of effective information systems in business.

An integrated information system implies centralized, coordinated information planning and control activities through decentralized information-processing activities. Decentralization makes it possible for information to be processed through data collection, coding, and data conversion. Many users may be linked to a single database. Database design involves the definition, classification, selection, and coding of the data elements to be stored.

Databases can be internal or external. Internal databases are developed by companies to assist them in their information needs. Internal databases are company specific and therefore can be used for various activities within the firm. External databases, organized by research suppliers and governments, form a strong base of secondary sources. Some of these external databases, especially from the government and other international organizations, are available at no cost. In contrast, private research companies charge a fee for the use of their databases.

CHAPTER REVIEW

1. What is a database?
2. What is a management information system?
3. How is a database designed?
4. What are the types of databases?
5. How are databases used?
6. Identify and explain some of the frequently used databases.
7. How is an MIS developed?
8. What are the various parts of an MIS?
9. What are the uses of an MIS?
10. What are some of the problems associated with the development of international databases?

NOTES

1. Kenneth C. Laudon and Jane Price Laudon, *Management Information Systems: Organization and Technology,* 8th ed. New York: Palgrave Publishing Company, 2003.

2. Suzzane Bidkale, "Nestle Database in Asia," *Advertising Age* (January 12, 1998), p. 34.

3. Victoria Ocken, "Making the Most of Online Databases," *Marketing News* (September 30, 2002), p. 17.

4. Lee H. Murphy, "Japanese Keeping Fewer Secrets from U.S. Firms," *Marketing News* (June 21, 1999), p. 6.

5. Katherine Morrall, "Technology Updates Market Research Methods," *Bank Marketing* (April 1994), pp. 15–18.

6. Anonymous, "Beyond the Data Warehouse: Data Mining," *Bank Strategies* (November–December 1996), pp. 198–202.

7. Takeshi, Fukuda, Morimoto Yasuhiko, Morishita Shinichi, and Takeshi Tokuyama, "Data Mining with Two-dimensional Association Rules," *ACM Transactions on Database Systems* 26, no. 2 (2001), pp. 179–213.

8. N.R. Muranyi, "Database Marketing FMCGs: What Is the State of the Art?" *Journal of Database Marketing* 4, no. 1 (1997), p. 21.

9. Paul Buta, "Building Customer Relationships with Datamining," *Chain Store Age Executive* (November 1996), pp. 1–3.

10. Laudon and Laudon, *Management Information Systems: Organization and Technology*.

11. Peter Keen, "A Walk through Decision Support," *Computerworld* (January 14, 1985), p. 14.

ADDITIONAL READING

BOOKS

Drozdenko, Ronald G., and Perry D. Drake. *Optimal Database Marketing*. Thousand Oaks, CA: Sage Publications, 2002.

Laudon, Kenneth C., and Jane Price Laudon. *Management Information Systems: Organization and Technology*. 8th ed. New York: Palgrave Publishing Company, 2003.

Martin, James. *Information Engineering: Planning and Analysis*. Englewood Cliffs, NJ: Prentice Hall, 1990.

McFadden, Fred R., and Jeffrey A. Hoffer. *Modern Database Management*. Redwood City, CA: Benjamin/Cummings Publishing, 1994.

Miller, Thomas W. *Data and Text Mining: A Business Applications Approach*. Upper Saddle River, NJ: Pearson-Prentice Hall, 2005.

ARTICLES

Halliday, Jean (2000) "Carmakers Learn to Mine Databases." *Advertising Age* (April), pp. S6–S8.

Kotabe, Masaaki (2002) "Using Database in International Marketing Research." *Journal of the Academy of Marketing Science* 30 (2), p. 172.

Tenopir, Carol (2001) "Links and Bibliographic Databases." *Library Journal* 126 (94), pp. 34–35.

Wisner, Scott (1999) "Realities of Datamining." *Catalog Age* (January), pp. 1–2.

Yoffie, Amy J. (1998) "The Sampling Dilemma Is No Different On-line." *Marketing News* 32 (8), p. 16.

6 Primary Data Collection: Exploratory Research

Exploratory research that employs qualitative research techniques is useful in understanding a subject's thought processes and provides insights into attitudes and perceptions. Such research is helpful in defining issues and helps generate ideas for execution.

LEARNING OBJECTIVES

After reading this chapter, students should be able to

- Identify the role of research
- List the differences between qualitative and quantitative research
- Identify the major techniques in qualitative research
- Identify the critical conditions that are necessary for conducting international research
- Identify emerging technologies that can be applied in qualitative research

Exploratory research (also called qualitative research) is a primary data collection technique. Data is collected for a given research project for which relevant information does not already exist. The principal purpose of exploratory research is to shed light on the nature of a situation and to identify whether a researcher needs to conduct additional research. Exploratory research is a useful tool for hypotheses formulation and for understanding consumer vernacular. It is a very easy and cost-effective technique.[1]

Exploratory research techniques, though used mostly to understand consumers and markets, are equally applicable in other situations, including production and operations management, finance, and R & D. For example, in the production area, exploratory research would be useful for understanding workers' concerns about assembly-line problems. In finance, exploratory research may be used to determine traders' expectations of exchange rate fluctuations, and in R & D the same technique can be used to identify new product ideas.

Qualitative research is an unstructured research method based on small samples and intended to provide answers to underlying issues. This type of research also is useful in clarifying problem definitions. Exploratory research differs considerably from the more quantitative research techniques (also referred to as conclusive research). The key difference between the two research techniques is that exploratory research is used to gain insights and employs small samples, whereas conclusive research is used to test hypotheses and employs large samples. Qualitative research is not a competitor to quantitative research, but rather a complement to it. Each technique represents different methods and can be used to obtain specific information.[2] The exploratory research method is flexible and versatile. This type of research is more concerned with validity than with reliability. Conclusive research is covered in greater detail in chapter 7.

Exploratory research is a good platform on which to develop the more involved conclusive research techniques. It is an excellent intermediate step after completing secondary data collection. In some situations, the relevant subject group may be unwilling or unable to answer questions or provide accurate answers for conducting conclusive research (for example, questions on sensitive issues such as a person's medical history, outstanding loans, or social life). In these cases, an unstructured, disguised questionnaire design (a form of qualitative technique) may yield better results.

USES OF EXPLORATORY RESEARCH

Exploratory research may be the only choice a researcher has in situations where sufficient data are not available, information is hard to obtain, a quick turnaround in research is crucial, or funds are insufficient. In international research, because the researcher is not familiar with the foreign market, qualitative research is very useful in defining issues, developing the necessary research design, and generating relevant research hypotheses.

In the initial stages of international research, qualitative research, along with secondary sources, can guide the researcher to specific problem areas and can also help the researcher develop an approach for further research by generating relevant questions and hypotheses. Though qualitative research is very much part of many American companies' repertoire, it is gaining acceptance equally in other parts of the world. There are highly skilled qualitative research professionals in Asia, Europe, and South America.[3]

Specifically, exploratory research may be used for the following reasons:

- *To formulate a problem*. In research, the issue at hand often is not apparent, and it needs to be defined so that a researcher can design an approach to collect and analyze data. In some instances, a thorough search of secondary sources may provide direction and help identify critical issues, but it is never as useful as the qualitative technique. Because qualitative research is conducted with the relevant target groups, it is better able to clarify critical issues. For example, a plant manager wanting to understand the difficulties encountered by the assembly-line workers with a new processing technique can use one of the qualitative research techniques to define the problem.

- *To develop hypotheses.* In order to test a hypothesis, a researcher must first develop a few statements about the population of interest or the issues under consideration. To develop these statements, the researcher needs to have some ideas or know some facts about the subject at hand. Qualitative research techniques are ideal for developing the relevant hypothesis that needs to be tested. For example, a multinational firm considering investing in a foreign market is concerned about the direction of the local interest rates, which are critical to its decision. If the local interest rates remain under 9 percent, then it would be willing to invest; however, if the interest rates go very high, the firm may not consider investing in that country. By interviewing a small sample of experts in that country, the multinational firm can determine the range of interest rate possibilities and then set the criteria (hypotheses) for investing in the foreign market.

- *To isolate key variables.* In developing an international research design, the researcher often has many variables to consider. Some of these variables are very easy to identify; others are not so evident. By using qualitative research techniques with their much lower cost and relatively short time to complete, the researcher can identify the critical variables that ought to be studied. For example, an international product manager wishing to understand consumer behavior for a product is not sure whether some of the psychological variables critical to the customers in the home market are relevant in the foreign market. Before conducting a large sample study, he or she would be wise to conduct an exploratory study to isolate the key variables.

- *To assist the development of a questionnaire.* In addition to identifying key variables, qualitative techniques assist the researcher in identifying questions to be asked of subjects to obtain critical information. Qualitative research techniques are better able to isolate items of interest that need to be included in a questionnaire. For example, a qualitative study may help the manager of an international bank to list questions pertaining to unique saving patterns among local citizens.

- *Gaining insight for further research.* Qualitative research techniques often assist the researcher in identifying the next step in the research process. The information gathered through secondary sources consulted earlier and information gained from qualitative techniques would dictate whether the next step in the research process should be a survey, an experiment, or an observational design. For example, if the qualitative research conducted by the R & D department of a consumer package goods firm points to further research in the area of packaging rather than redesigning the product, a researcher may use controlled test marketing to identify the potential of the new package concept.

- *Answering research questions.* In some instances, qualitative research may provide answers to problems, negating the need for further research. For example, an international advertising manager wanting to find out the most salient theme to be used in an advertisement for a product may obtain this information by using a series of focus group sessions, an excellent qualitative research technique.

QUALITATIVE RESEARCH TECHNIQUES

Qualitative research involves collecting, analyzing, and interpreting data using unstructured questionnaires with small samples. Because of the sample size, these techniques do not permit a researcher to quantify and project the data to a larger group. Qualitative research techniques may be disguised or nondisguised. In *nondisguised,* or direct, approaches, the true purpose of the study is revealed to the respondents. The assumption is that there is nothing much to be gained from not identifying the purpose of the study or that the scope of the project is obvious to everyone. Focus groups and depth interviews are the two most commonly used techniques in nondisguised qualitative research.

In a *disguised* approach, the true nature or purpose of the study is not disclosed. The idea here is to obtain as much objective information as possible, and the assumption is that respondents may be biased once they know the purpose of the study. This approach is equally useful when respondents are not able to provide true information. Disguised or indirect approaches include projective techniques such as association techniques, completion techniques, Rorschach tests, and the thematic apperception test (TAT).

In international research, cultural attitudes influence which qualitative research techniques should be used and how they should be implemented. One may use focus groups in one country, but for the same study in another country, a projective technique may be more appropriate. Therefore, the task of the international researcher when designing qualitative research projects is compounded by variations in cultural differences among countries.

FOCUS GROUPS

Of all the techniques utilized in qualitative research, focus groups are probably the most widely used procedure by researchers. Focus groups remain the most popular tool for supporting many marketing decisions. They have been used for understanding the key issues to charting alternate pricing strategies. Focus group research is the most useful technique available as the first step in the research process.[4] Focus groups provide users with valuable qualitative data that are not readily obtained with any other data-collection techniques. Focus groups help business executives to gain information about marketing programs, personnel issues, service quality, and other areas that require fast and inexpensive information.[5] The focus group technique is versatile, flexible, and easy to execute. Used in most industrialized and some developed countries, focus groups are applied in a variety of situations. In the United States alone in 2002 there were more than 300 focus group facilities with trained moderators.[6] It is a $2 billion industry in U.S. companies such as VideoFocus Direct, which is a network of independent focus group facilities in 16 U.S. states and in more than 10 foreign countries. Firms such as VideoFocus Direct can arrange for multiple-site focus groups that can speed up the time to complete the research and at the same time be cost-efficient. In the international context, the importance and appreciation of cultural differences and the recognition of common versus specific cultural characteristics must be taken into consideration in developing focus group studies.[7]

Focus groups bring together qualified individuals (such as consumers) and recognized experts (such as financial analysts or manufacturing engineers) in an organized setting to develop, evaluate, and synthesize their individual points of view on a particular topic. *Focus groups* are defined as small group interviews conducted by a trained moderator through a non-structured discussion guide in an informal setting.

The role of focus groups is to

- *Help generate ideas for later execution.* For example, focus groups can aid in the exploration of consumer/subject behavior, attitudes, language, and so on.
- *Obtain early feedback.* Focus groups provide some basis for screening out ideas. In international research, this could be useful in avoiding costly and time-consuming research and/or market entry.
- *Aid in further research.* Focus groups provide sufficient insights into situations or issues, particularly when the client or firm does not have significant prior experience.
- *Help in generating hypotheses* for markets for which management does not have enough information (when entering a new country for the first time), in introducing new products, and in gaining insights into competitive activities.

Critical Factors in Focus Group Interviews

Focus groups are very useful in situations where respondents' feelings, attitudes, opinions, and thought processes need to be identified. To be effective, focus groups must be formulated with care. The success of focus groups depends on many factors, the most important of which are described below.

Group Composition. The effectiveness of a focus group depends on the characteristics of the participants. Members of a focus group should be homogeneous in key characteristics. For a focus group designed to identify key voter concerns, the characteristics of a focus group of potential voters such as demographic, lifestyle, socioeconomic status, geography, and psychographic status must be as homogeneous as possible. The intent of commonality in a group is to avoid confusion among numerous interacting respondent variables. To attain representation of the population, researchers conduct two or more focus group sessions. The collective characteristics and responses, therefore, should reflect those of the overall population. Thus, a focus group of British factory workers for an industrial study should separate the men from the women, the single from the married, and the college educated from the non–college educated. When a research study is broad and may benefit from a mix of respondents, the use of heterogeneous samples may be appropriate.

Using respondents who have some basic knowledge of the issues as part of the focus group is helpful. For example, in conducting a focus group for an analgesic product, the respondents should have used and be familiar with such a product. In selecting focus group members, care should be taken to avoid so-called professional respondents (people who have participated in many focus group sessions and are considered experts; they are not representative of the typical population). Friends and relatives should not be included in the same group because they may talk among themselves and negate group dynamics.

Group Size. A focus group is normally made up of 8 to 12 participants. This number has evolved from past practices and is universally accepted as the desired size. Because the group dynamic is supposed to generate freewheeling discussion and contribute to the information generated, a number less than 8 is deemed too small to generate the momentum. Likewise, a group with more than 12 may be too crowded, stifling discussion and discouraging the natural participation by all participants.

Moderator. The moderator plays an important role in the success of a focus group. The role of the moderator is to stimulate the flow of discussion among all the participants and at the same time ensure that the thrust of the discussion remains focused on the topic or issue under study. In addition, the moderator must know the issues, understand human dynamics, establish rapport with the members of the group, probe the group members to elicit insights, keep the discussion moving forward, avoid being drawn into the discussion, be sensitive, and be firm. This multifaceted assignment puts a tremendous burden on the moderator, and topics must be selected with care.

Generally, the moderator is also involved in analyzing and interpreting the information culled from the focus group session. Moderators must be able to go beyond what the participants say and make note of such nonverbal communication as tone of voice, emotional outbursts, facial expressions, and intensity. These nonverbal cues become more important in countries where the culture inhibits frank expression of opinions.

Physical Setting. Focus groups are generally held in relaxed and informal settings. In many countries there are designated centers with modern focus group facilities. These facilities provide a comfortable and friendly atmosphere, have unobtrusive electronic devices for recording and taping the sessions, have one-way mirrors that allow decision makers to observe the sessions, and are conveniently located. In countries where modern focus group facilities are not available, sessions have been held in small conference rooms, classrooms, and residents' living rooms.

Time Duration. Focus groups generally last one to two hours. Less than an hour does not permit the moderator to really get into the issues and may affect the full participation of all respondents. When sessions last longer than two hours, factors of fatigue or lethargy affect participants, and the sessions may prove to be counterproductive.

Recording. Focus group sessions are recorded on audiocassettes as well as on videocassettes, CDs or DVDs (whenever available) for subsequent replay. The recordings are transcribed and the discussion is analyzed. Decision makers use these transcripts to learn more about the issues and make a better assessment of the problem. Recording focus group sessions increases the cost of focus group sessions and may make respondents feel self-conscious and uncomfortable. The latter might affect the results of the study. As this discomfort may affect the results of the study, modern focus group facilities have the recording equipment concealed.

Concealment of recording equipment creates an interesting ethical dilemma. Should the respondents be informed of the recording devices and the secret observations by the decision makers, thus possibly inhibiting open discussion by the participants, or should they be kept in the dark to achieve a true, unhindered dialogue? Most researchers are of the opinion that the respondents must be informed about any recordings or observations that will take place during the session. Researchers may want to stress that there are no ulterior motives behind the recordings or observations, but that these recordings assist researchers in gaining truer insights. If the researchers are able to ease the participants' fears, they may respond positively or at least be neutral to the recordings.

Planning for Focus Group Research

Normally focus group sessions follow preliminary investigation by the researchers. Most often some form of secondary research has enabled the researcher to define the central issues to be studied. Using this problem definition, the researcher must state a specific objective for exploratory research. At this stage, the researcher has to determine whether focus groups are the best procedure for attaining the exploratory research objectives. Figure 6.1 describes the planning process for focus group interviews.

Key Steps in Focus Group Research

State Objectives. If focus groups are the desired exploratory research technique for the given problem, then a list of objectives for the focus group needs to be identified. These goals can be translated into a set of questions that the moderator will use as a discussion guide to ensure that all the key areas of interest are addressed in the discussion.

Screen Participants. Selecting suitable participants is an equally important task in focus groups. Researchers select the relevant group in accordance with the target audience that can provide the necessary information about the product, service or issue at hand. The group should be homogeneous in terms of demographic and socioeconomic characteristics. To select the appropriate group, researchers develop a screening questionnaire to query potential participants about their past experience with the focus group topic. The questionnaire is made up of just a few questions on the essential participant characteristics followed by questions on participants' knowledge about the issues. Questions designed to weed out professional respondents may be introduced at this point.

Create Discussion Guide. A detailed discussion guide is generally developed after consultation among the research team, the user of the research, and the moderator. For example, in developing advertising copy for a product in a foreign country, the

Figure 6.1   **Steps in Focus Group Research**

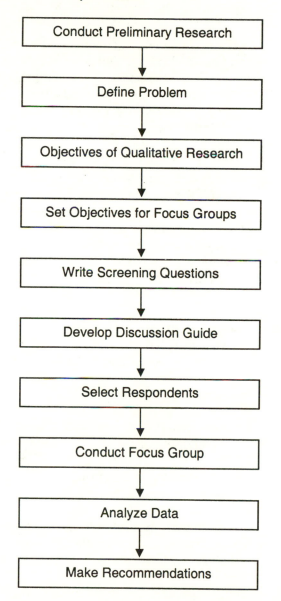

creative staff of an advertising agency may use one or two focus groups in that country to develop an understanding of the concerns of potential consumers. In this instance, the discussion guide may include a profile of the user as well as the key decision variables in the purchase of the product, usage behavior, and product knowledge.

When more than one moderator is used, the discussion guide serves to cover the same issues among the different focus group sessions. For international firms, the discussion guide ensures a consistent and uniform approach in focus group sessions across countries.

Conduct Focus Group Sessions. In conducting focus group sessions, the moderator makes the participants feel relaxed and comfortable by serving light refreshments at the start of the session and making them available throughout the session. A skilled moderator also creates an atmosphere conducive to open and frank discussion by approaching the participants in a warm and friendly manner. Probing participants and encouraging discussion among participants are other important tasks of the moderator.

Analyze Responses. In analyzing the focus group discussion, the moderator or analyst reviews the tapes and the notes made during the session. The object is to cull new ideas, identify participants' concerns, isolate relevant opinions, obtain general findings, and make note of specific comments and body language. Since the number of participants in each session is small, reliable findings are not practical. Neither should the researchers attempt quantitative analysis of the data. Conclusions are stated as "majority" opinions or "divided' opinions.

Identify Actions to Be Taken. Focus group research can generate important hypotheses for further exploration. Most often, the focus group or other qualitative research is followed by an extensive primary study. In some instances the focus group may provide basic answers to a few key issues and make further research unnecessary.

Benefits of Using Focus Group Research

Focus groups, if conducted properly, provide a wealth of information for researchers and decision makers. Following are some of the key advantages of focus groups.

Value of Information. Because of the group composition, focus groups may generate a wide range of information, insight, and ideas. The responses of participants tend to be more creative in a group setting. They are also less likely to feel inhibited in the company of others who are similar to them. Comments made by one participant in the focus group may evoke insights, thoughts, or ideas among other participants. These insights may not be forthcoming in a one-on-one interview.

Flexibility. Focus groups allow for coverage of a wide range of topics, and each topic can be covered in depth. The groups can provide insight into a great variety of problems in the area of finance, manufacturing, marketing, R & D (ideas for new products), and human resources issues. They are equally applicable in discussions of concepts, ideas, services, or products. Used in conjunction with other qualitative techniques such as projective techniques, focus groups can strengthen the information generated.

Study of a Variety of Participants. Focus groups may contain adults, children, senior citizens, professionals, or executives. Some of these special respondents are more likely to provide answers in group settings than in individual ones. In countries where speaking to strangers is taboo, focus groups are more likely to be acceptable. Professionals and executives may not be willing to participate in one-on-one interviews but may more likely be receptive to a group interview, which gives them an opportunity to be with their peers.

Usefulness. In focus groups, decision makers can be actively involved from the beginning of the research and may observe the sessions themselves. In this way they can learn about the issues, problems, and concerns firsthand. This contact increases the motivation of these executives, and they tend to demonstrate more interest in and enthusiasm for the results of these interviews than they do for the voluminous reports with all the empirical tables in other primary studies. Interesting remarks from participants are quite often more valuable to decision makers than descriptive analysis (mean, median, and mode).

Time Factor. One critical concern in conducting research is time. The faster the information is gathered, the more quickly the recommendations can be implemented. In focus groups, because a number of participants are interviewed at the same time, information is collected much faster than it is in other relevant research techniques. The fact that focus groups are conducted with small sample sizes also speeds up the process.

Problems with Focus Group Research

Active participation and unsolicited comments by respondents are important for a successful focus group. Internationally, due to cultural and other reasons, this success is not always possible. In addition, the willingness of people to interact freely and express their views openly differs from country to country. Under these conditions, the reliability and comparability of focus group findings across countries are questionable. The specific problems associated with focus groups are discussed below.

Results Cannot Be Generalized. By definition, focus group findings cannot be generalized and therefore are not conclusive. Information is not definitive, and since it is collected from small samples, the results cannot be projected to a larger population. The small sample sizes that provide some benefits also create problems in terms of representing the views of the general population. As they do not reflect the opinions of the population as a whole, focus group findings cannot be projected. Therefore, focus group findings should not be the only basis for decision making.

Interpretation Problems May Arise. The information generated from focus group interviews is only as good as the quality of the moderator. Since focus groups are informal, the information they provide is varied. Moderators and decision makers with preconceived notions about an issue may be able to find support for their positions by interpreting the information selectively. The moderator's interpretation of the sessions is just one opinion and should be recognized as such in formulating plans and strategies.

In international research, the moderator not only has to be trained in focus group methodology but should also be familiar with the language, culture, and social interactions prevailing in a given country. An Asian housewife's concept of being a homemaker may be different from that of a European housewife. Even within Europe, a housewife in France may have impressions regarding keeping the home clean that are different from those of a British housewife. Similarly, the views of factory workers on unionization may differ from country to country. In European countries where unions are strong and participate in board meetings, workers favor union membership; in China, membership in organized unions is nonexistent, and Chinese workers may view unions with apathy.

Furthermore, the interpretation problem is compounded by the fact that it is very difficult to find highly trained and experienced moderators in all countries. Since moderators have to be able to discern the minute differences in body language and other nonverbal cues to be able to garner the most information from these sessions, they must have full knowledge and understanding of different cultures. Such skilled observers may not always be available.

Potential Exists for Bias. Focus groups tend to suffer from both participant and moderator biases. Typically, respondents who agree to participate are different in many aspects from the concerned population. Professional respondents may bias focus group findings due to heavy participation. Professional respondents tend to participate in many focus group sessions to gain some financial benefits. These respondents may not represent the views of the population as a whole and may be more aggressive than others in their population segment.

Moderators may inject bias arising from their strong views about issues and countries. For example, focus group sessions among Japanese financial analysts conducted by a European moderator may be subjected to bias resulting from the strong opinions of the moderator about Japanese government policies on international trade.

Costs May Not Be Justified. The cost of a single focus group session is generally lower than that of a single primary study. Most often though, two or three focus group sessions may be conducted for a given situation, which can increase the total cost of the study. Furthermore, focus groups quite often are just a prelude to more conclusive studies. Hence, the total costs associated with information gathering for an issue may run into thousands of dollars. More important, due to other incidental costs such as participant-recruiting costs, incentive fees paid to participants, refreshments served, focus group facility charges, and moderator fees, cost per participant for focus group research may be higher than that for other research methods. Internationally, costs of conducting research vary from country to country. Generally speaking, a focus group study that might cost $3,000 to $5,000 in the United States can cost $7,000 to $10,000 in the United Kingdom and close to $20,000 in Japan.

For the above reasons, focus group sessions should be undertaken only after researchers have identified a specific need for such information. In Hungary, for example, focus groups are seldom used; most decisions are made on the basis of descriptive research.[8]

Hence, the use of focus group research varies from country to country. In spite of the inherent problems associated with focus group research, international executives do make constant use of focus group research as it can be executed quickly.

Applications of Focus Group Research

Focus group sessions can be used in any situation requiring understanding of and insights into a group. They are most often used in developing marketing strategies, determining attitudes and interests of consumers, unearthing human resources issues, identifying shifts in environmental concerns, discovering manufacturing process issues, revealing trends in financial markets, and preparing political campaign ideas.

In developing marketing strategies, focus group sessions could be used in product planning, generating ideas for new products, developing creative concepts and copy material for advertisements, studying responses to new package designs, obtaining feedback from consumers about new product introductions, and understanding consumers' perceptions and attitudes toward products and services.

In international marketing situations, focus groups have been used to explore the feasibility of transferring product ideas across countries, translating advertisements and questionnaires into other languages and cultures, and standardizing strategies in regional or global markets.

Variations in Focus Group Research

The previous section described in detail the basic focus group technique used in most instances. There are a few variations of the basic approach, and these include:

- *Dual-moderator group.* This type of focus group research has two moderators. One controls the flow of discussion, and the other controls the issues. Researchers use these groups mostly when technical topics are discussed.
- *Respondent-moderator group.* In this type of focus group research, the moderator selects a few respondents to play the role of the moderator temporarily to improve group dynamics.
- *Two-way focus groups.* In this method, the researcher uses two separate groups; one group listens in while the other is discussing. Researchers employ this procedure in professional situations where the two parties—for example, doctors and patients or lawyers and clients—are at either end of an exchange.
- *Telephone-based focus groups.* Focus group sessions are conducted using conference calls. While this method offers some convenience and flexibility, it suffers in group dynamics because participants feel the lack of face-to-face contact.
- *Group support systems.* In a group support system (GSS), participants input their responses through a computer terminal. The GSS approach is also a group interview run by a moderator or facilitator and a technical person who assists in setting up and managing the GSS system. GSS focus groups involve small groups of participants who interact through workstations that are connected by a local area network. Through the use of sophisticated software, the GSS allows

Table 6.1   **Key Elements of Focus Group Research**

Factor	Actions
Respondents	8 to 12 per group
Composition	Representative of the target population
Method	Discussion led by a trained moderator
Instrument	Discussion guide designed to meet specific areas of interest
Time	90 to 120 minutes
Setup	Takes about three to four weeks
Feedback	Immediate

participants to respond to requests for inputs on various subjects. In comparing the GSS with the traditional focus group sessions on general impressions, attitudes, feelings, and amount of information produced, researchers found that the GSS approach had substantial advantages over traditional focus groups.[9] In using GSS, the technical competency of the person administering the session is important, and in some countries this could pose a problem, as there may not be a sufficient number of fully qualified technicians available to manage the computer and software part of the focus group.

Table 6.1 summarizes the key elements of focus group research.

DEPTH INTERVIEWS

A *depth interview* is defined as a direct unstructured personal interview in which a single respondent is probed by an interviewer. Since it is a one-on-one interview, the interviewer can explore various ideas in depth with the respondent. Depth interviews generally use small sample sizes. Consequently, their results cannot be projected to the wider population.

Depth interviews are used in situations where the respondents have significant knowledge of a topic. Depth interviews are used when it is desirable to customize questions to respondents, companies, or both. Specifically, when a researcher is trying to collect information from professionals such as doctors, accountants, or engineers and in industrial marketing situations, this technique is particularly useful. Such respondents do not react favorably to the rigidity of a formal, structured interview. These respondents have a thorough understanding of their field and can add to the overall knowledge of the topic if given free rein. Professionals have limited time flexibility and blocking them into a time slot for a group interview like the focus groups is often difficult. Most of these respondents get an honorarium for their troubles, and these fees tend to be much higher than the allowances paid to focus group participants.

The main idea in depth interviews is to let respondents provide as much information as possible in an unrestricted fashion. After the interviewer has asked preliminary questions, the subsequent direction of the interview is determined by the respondent's replies. Depending on the response, the interviewer decides how much to explore (probing) one idea and when to move on to the next topic. This kind of flexibility and opportunity to cull information from the respondent make the depth interview a powerful technique in collecting information.

In conducting depth interviews, the interviewer prepares a checklist of relevant issues or topics as a guide but does not prepare a formal questionnaire. The early questions tend to be broad and purely exploratory. As the respondent warms up to the interview process, more substantive topics are discussed. The format, wording, and sequence of the questions are influenced by the responses. The goal is to make the interview flow smoothly and naturally.

Advantages of Depth Interviews

In depth interviews, the interviewer can probe an individual's feelings and thought processes and gain insights into his or her views and opinions. Depth interviews have been known to uncover more information than common focus group techniques can. Depth interviews also permit the researcher to customize the questions to a respondent's characteristics, such as background and personality.

Unlike focus group research, in which it is difficult to pinpoint a particular response to an individual, depth interview responses may be linked to a specific respondent. In addition, depth interviews result in a freer exchange of information than may be possible in other types of exploratory research techniques.

Disadvantages of Depth Interviews

The key to the success of the depth interview technique is the qualifications and skills of the interviewer. Internationally, the availability of such interviewers is often problematic, and there is a wide variability in the skills of those who are available, especially in the developing countries. Furthermore, the problem of dealing with multiple languages in the international arena makes the convertibility of the results difficult.

Because of the specialized skills required by the interviewers and the one-on-one format, depth interviews are expensive. Other disadvantages associated with depth interviews are as follows:

- The small size of the samples makes the drawing of inferences for the larger population inappropriate.
- The lack of structure in depth interviews makes the results of this technique vulnerable to the interviewer's influence (bias).
- As in the case of focus group research, because of the small sample size and the nature of the responses, the results are typically more difficult to analyze.
- Finally, depth interviews are very expensive due to the time required to complete the interviews, the high cost of the interviewers, and the honorarium paid to the respondents.

Applications of Depth Interview Research

As an exploratory research technique, depth interviews are valuable when a firm is seeking information from a specialized respondent group. Though not used as often as focus group techniques, depth interviews have their own niche in the international research area. For firms exploring markets and ideas abroad, depth interviews can provide precious information.

Some situations in which depth interviews could provide needed inputs are as follows:

- A pharmaceutical company seeking alternative ways to treat patients in foreign markets may conduct depth interviews with medical professionals in the target countries to understand the inherent problems with existing medications or therapies.
- Investment firms may gather information using depth interviews to identify the investment needs of some of their wealthy clients.
- Software companies could make use of depth interviews to develop the next generation of software by conducting depth interviews with programmers and hardware installers.
- Manufacturing engineers can use depth interviews to gain insights on supply networks and plant location sights in overseas markets by gathering information from their current suppliers.

Depth interviews can also be effectively employed in situations where the researcher is trying to gather sensitive information of either a personal or confidential nature and in cases where many firms in the same industry need to be contacted (competitive situation to predict industry trends). Depth interviews may also prove useful when respondents need to be probed, as in the case of insurance sales, when searching for complex behavior, as in medical or business decision making, and in situations where product consumption is based on emotional factors, for example, cosmetics.

INDIRECT OR DISGUISED EXPLORATORY TECHNIQUES

In disguised research techniques, the purpose of the study is not obvious and is not explained to the respondents. These techniques are used to solicit information without the respondent feeling inhibited. By making the respondents project their inner thoughts and feelings freely to an unrelated setting, researchers are able to learn about the respondents. Projective techniques generally involve offering study subjects an ambiguous stimulus and gauging from their reactions the inner self of these subjects. Specifically, respondents are asked to interpret the behavior of others rather than their own behavior. In interpreting the behavior of others, respondents will project their own thoughts to explain an issue or situation. A word association test is an excellent example of a projective technique.

Projective techniques are defined as an unstructured and indirect form of questioning that encourages respondents to project their underlying motivations, beliefs, attitudes, or feelings regarding the issue of concern. In most projective techniques, the stimuli are deliberately kept vague and ambiguous. The vagueness and ambiguity of the stimuli force the respondents to rely more on their own experiences to state their inner feelings.

Projective techniques are applicable in cross-cultural research and also when the researcher is interested in the "why" of an issue. In cross-cultural study, if the researcher is trying to determine the traits of a society, projective techniques might be more reliable than a structured direct questionnaire, in which people may not be able to state their cultural traits. Similarly, when marketing decision makers are interested in knowing why certain consumers buy a particular type of product, projective techniques are useful. For example, a wealthy person buying clothing from a discount store may not admit to this behavior on straightforward questioning lest he or she be labeled "cheap." A well-developed projective technique, though, might unearth this behavior and provide the marketing manager an alternative to sell clothing to such an individual.

Some of the commonly used projective techniques are word association, sentence completion, expressive techniques, thematic apperception test (TAT), and, to some extent, Rorschach tests.

Word Association

In most association tests, respondents react to stimuli and respond with the first thing that comes to mind. In word association techniques, the stimuli are a list of words. The basic tenet of this approach is that association allows respondents to show their true feelings for the issue at hand.

In developing and conducting word association tests, the researcher needs to observe the following procedures:

- Select a set of test words that have some relevance to the topic at hand.
- Intersperse some neutral words throughout the test words to disguise the study.
- Record the response to each word verbatim.
- Record the elapsed time between mentioning the test word and the response.

For example, in a study about automobile purchases, words such as "safety," "comfort," "style," and "performance" may be included as test words. In the same study, words such as "landscape," "comedy," and "art" may be used as neutral words.

In analyzing the word association tests, a researcher has to

- Count the frequency with which any word is given as a response to a test word.
- Note the amount of time taken by respondents to react to a test word. The elapsed time is a good indicator of the conviction of a respondent's answer to a test word. If respondents try to reason out or hesitate, the more time they take to respond (more than three seconds), the less sure they are about their choice of response.

• Record the number of respondents who do not respond at all. Respondents may not respond if they are unfamiliar with the test word or are so emotionally involved with the test subject that they block out their response.

For example, in the automobile study, 50 respondents out of a sample of 100 mention the word "airbags" for safety, and 35 mention "seat belts." Furthermore, 10 mention the word "Volvo," and 5 respond with the word "Mercedes-Benz." The researcher could conclude that respondents in this sample associate safety with airbags and seat belts and also that the two most recognized brands in this area are Volvo and Mercedes-Benz. If you are the executive from Volvo or Mercedes-Benz, you should feel very positive about the buyers' perceptions about your brand of automobiles.

The word association tests are classified as favorable, unfavorable, or neutral. Each respondent's pattern of responses reveals information about his or her attitudes and inner thoughts. The collective responses of the whole sample give the researcher an understanding of the general population. The researcher then develops a hypothesis, structures more conclusive studies, or draws some basic conclusions.

Word association tests have been used to segment markets, develop new products, identify copy themes for advertisements, and identify differences between the domestic and foreign markets. Some early research studies have shown that word association techniques in different cultures and countries tend to produce similar results. In countries where people are hesitant to discuss their feelings in a group setting or in depth interviews, projective techniques are used as an alternative.

Using word association techniques, American firms have found that the Japanese consumers have a positive association between fruit, the beach, and the sun and an equally strong association between clothing and skyscrapers. Therefore, for example, Washington apple producers should use the West Coast beaches in their commercials to sell apples, and Donna Karen should use Manhattan skyscrapers in her ads to sell her line of designer clothes to the Japanese.

SENTENCE COMPLETION

In sentence completion tests, respondents complete statements. They use the first word or phrase that comes to mind in completing the statements. For example, in determining the image that vacationers have toward a Caribbean country, the researcher may pose the following question: "When I think of a vacation, the country that comes to mind is . . ." By completing the question, respondents indicate their perceptions or images about the countries they would like to visit on their vacation. The same problem may also be stated as follows: "Caribbean islands are . . ."

Story completion techniques are sometimes used with the same objectives. Sentence completion or story completion techniques are more direct than word association tests, as the respondents may be able to determine the purpose of the study more easily. The fact that respondents can guess the purpose of the study can sometimes reduce the richness and accuracy of the information gathered from this technique. On the other hand, sentence completion techniques typically provide better and more descriptive information than some other projective techniques.

EXPRESSIVE TECHNIQUES

In expressive techniques, the researcher presents the respondent with a verbal or visual situation and then asks the respondent to relate the feelings and attitudes of other people to the situation. Because they feel they are expressing the views of others, respondents tend to be more open. The two most widely used expressive techniques are role-playing and the third-person technique.

In both role-playing and the third-person technique, the respondent is asked to assume the role of some other individual in responding to stimuli. The rationale behind this technique is that respondents initially may identify and express the view of the third person, but after some time they will revert back to their own experiences in responding to given stimuli. For example, the researcher could ask respondents how their neighbor might spend $1,000 and make note of the purchases indicated. The critical information emerges when the respondents shift from the third person to the first person. When this happens, the respondents are really thinking of their desires rather than their neighbors'.

In situations where respondents may be embarrassed in responding to some issues, the expressive techniques work very well. For example, in trying to understand why some people do not fly, researchers found that when asked, "Are you afraid to fly?" very few people said yes. However, when asked, "Do you think your neighbor is afraid to fly?" the respondent indicated that the neighbors would use alternative means of traveling, as they were afraid to fly. From this, researchers surmised that probably the respondents themselves were afraid to fly.

THEMATIC APPERCEPTION TEST

Thematic apperception tests, or picture response techniques, make use of pictures to gather information from respondents. The pictures portray social interaction or a consumer purchase situation. After viewing the pictures, respondents express their understanding of what is happening in the picture. In some cases, cartoons may be used instead of pictures. In other instances, the respondent fills in a blank space or balloon to express what the individual(s) in the picture may be saying or thinking.

Originally developed for measuring personalities, these tests have been used to gather information on consumers. These techniques may be administered to one respondent at a time or to a group. In a typical TAT, the test subjects are each shown a series of pictures for a short period of time (20 to 30 seconds) and asked to describe the story unfolding in the picture.

The characters or objects in the pictures are clear in some instances and vague in others. The respondents may be asked to describe such things as what is happening in the picture, why it is happening, and what the feelings of the characters might be. The respondents' interpretation of the pictures provides a clue to their behavior patterns.

TAT and other similar tests are useful in identifying consumers' personalities and their inner desires. Well-selected pictures can trigger people's hidden anxieties and cravings, which may not be revealed on direct questioning. These tests are also useful for developing images and art for advertisements, packaging, and perceptions of service offerings.

ADVANTAGES OF PROJECTIVE TECHNIQUES

Generally, projective techniques help researchers to get information from respondents that is not easily expressed under direct questioning. Lack of self-consciousness on the part of respondents may help to reveal their genuine reactions. The respondents' extreme reactions, either positive or negative, are definitely useful to researchers in formulating specific strategies. Actions by decision makers may be justified by quantitative interpretation of the test results.

Information regarding personal matters, sensitive issues, or strong social norms is more apt to be revealed under projective techniques than through focus group or depth interviews. Internationally, this issue is more apparent when researchers have to deal with traditional value systems.

DISADVANTAGES OF PROJECTIVE TECHNIQUES

Projective techniques are more difficult to execute than direct questioning. They also tend to be more laborious to analyze. An additional question that is often raised about projective techniques and other clinical studies is their applicability to practical business situations.

The other key drawbacks of projective techniques are that

- They tend be subjected to interpretation biases. The data analysis in projective techniques is subjective, as the analysis depends on one person's interpretation of the collected information.
- It is difficult to set up a common coding and analytical scheme across countries, which may further bias the results.
- The establishment of parity in verbal and nonverbal responses in different cultures with variations in language is next to impossible.
- The lack of highly trained interviewers in many of the developing countries makes these techniques ineffectual in these countries.
- Because of the technical capabilities required by the interviewer and interpreters, projective techniques may be expensive.
- Since projective techniques require respondents to engage in unusual behavior such as role playing, those who agree to these procedures may not represent the whole population or reflect the views and opinions of the population at large.

The use of indirect and unstructured research techniques in international research should be developed with extreme care. The sociocultural environments in which international business takes place are marked by divergence and tend to be dynamic. In such an environment, it is difficult to establish comparability and equivalence. As a general rule, researchers employ exploratory research techniques only in situations where there is a significant amount of human interaction involved.

New Directions in Exploratory Research

Researchers continually seek ways to better understand their customers or other subjects. Focus group techniques, depth interviews, and other exploratory methods, though useful, are still unable to give all the answers to research questions. There seem to be limitations to exploratory techniques. Even the conclusive research techniques go only so far in attaining the relevant answers. A recent development in the field of exploratory research is the technique of seeking true-life anecdotes that reveal some of the innermost feelings and desires of respondents. Used by a few researchers and companies in the United States, mostly in marketing studies, this method has allowed researchers and firms to find some success in understanding their customers better.

Many marketing companies are finding that they are really unable to fathom fully what motivates their customers. There is substantial evidence suggesting that respondents may not reveal all their feelings in focus group sessions. In fact, some respondents do not recall facts about a brand or product and may not admit to this in a group. Some respondents lie about their feelings if the rest of the group disagrees with them.

One way to deal with these issues is to approach the respondents from a different angle. A method that depends less on group dynamics and more on the day-to-day occurrences in the lives of these respondents may be more revealing. Researchers focus on respondent anecdotes and use more probing research techniques.

The technique of storytelling greatly depends on the ability to isolate subtle changes in human behavior. These changes cannot be captured within a focus group session or through the use of depth interviews. Since the changes take place over time and are not obvious, they need to be tracked and recorded. This tracking should unearth not only the emotion-laden events in a respondent's life but also some of the unspoken impulses.

True-life research may be conducted in a laboratory setting or at the homes of respondents. In both instances the idea is to have respondents deal with issues from a day-to-day perspective rather than an isolated event in their lives. Professor Zaltman of Harvard Business School has set up a laboratory that uses metaphors to cull the concerns of respondents. The technique requires respondents to define an issue, thought, or concern using other terms. Asking respondents to spend a few minutes thinking about how they would visually represent their experiences with a brand or a company draws out these metaphors. In one such session for the U.S.-based chemical company DuPont, which supplies raw materials for pantyhose, women brought pictures representing their concerns and thoughts about pantyhose.

One woman brought a picture of a spilled sundae, capturing her rage, she feels, when she spots a run in her stockings. Another brought a picture of a woman with baskets of fruit, suggesting that buying stockings should be as easy as picking fruit from an outdoor stand, and so on. The upshot of the research was that whereas women in focus group studies have always said that "they wear pantyhose because they have to, and they hate it," the metaphor study at Harvard revealed that women wear pantyhose to be sensual.

Similarly, Kimberly-Clark, a maker of disposable diapers called Huggies, sent a team of employees who themselves were bringing up toddlers to the homes of their customers to hear real-life stories. These sessions revealed a few concerns of mothers bringing up infants that did not surface in focus group sessions. For example, "the stress in toilet training came from the parent's feelings of failure," something that was never brought up in previous research. Kimberly-Clark's solution to this problem was to introduce Huggies Pull-Ups training pants. The product was a huge success.

The true-life approach is an alternate technique available to researchers to explore the inner psyche of consumers. The technique is in its developmental stages and should be used in situations where additional exploratory research may assist researchers in better understanding consumers. As the method becomes more popular and more researchers gain experience, the technique may spread to other countries. Similarly, other countries may have developed new methods for gaining insights into the reactions of consumers and respondents that have not yet been applied internationally.[10]

CHAPTER SUMMARY

Exploratory or qualitative research is characterized by unstructured and flexible data-collection techniques. The information is gathered from small samples. The samples are useful in generating information that cannot easily be surmised through structured and quantitative techniques. In international research situations, qualitative techniques become even more beneficial, because the researcher is often not familiar with the markets and the cultural mores in these countries. Qualitative research in these situations may provide some insights into research issues that otherwise might have been difficult to obtain.

Qualitative research is often used to identify aspects to be studied in subsequent phases of research. Specifically, qualitative research tends to provide direction in the initial stages of international research by helping formulate problem areas, generating relevant research questions, and assisting in the design of further research. Hence, qualitative research is generally conducted as a complement to conclusive research.

There are two main types of qualitative research: *nondisguised,* or direct, and *disguised,* or indirect. In nondisguised techniques, respondents most often understand the purpose of the study; in disguised techniques the research objectives are not known to the respondents. The direct methods most often employed by researchers are focus groups and depth interviews.

Focus groups are popular among researchers. They are versatile, relatively easy to conduct, flexible, and reveal salient information about the subjects. The three major determinants of effective focus groups are group composition, moderator effectiveness, and group dynamics. Focus groups commonly have 8 to 12 participants with some homogeneity among group members. Moderators of focus groups should effectively control the smooth flow of discussions, guide the discussion, and at the same time be able to establish rapport with the respondents.

Depth interviews are unstructured and nondisguised research techniques. These are one-on-one interviews with a loosely developed discussion guide. The wording and sequencing of the questions are predicated by the responses given by the study subjects. The idea is to let respondents provide as much information as possible in an open setting. Depth interviews are apropos when the respondents are professional or in industrial business exchanges.

The disguised or indirect techniques are collectively classified as projective techniques. In most projective techniques, the respondents are presented with fairly ambiguous stimuli, and the resulting reactions are noted to discern the inner feelings and thought processes of these respondents. Commonly used projective techniques are word association tests, sentence completion tests, expressive techniques, and TAT.

Projective techniques are flexible and can be tailor-made to fit many research situations. They are useful in identifying respondents' beliefs, attitudes, feelings, and motivations. Furthermore, they are ideal in cases where respondents are unable or unwilling to provide information through other research methods.

The key advantages of qualitative research are its flexibility, versatility, and efficiency (the short time it takes to complete them). Hence, they are well suited as exploratory research techniques. Collectively these techniques help international researchers to understand the key differences between domestic and international markets. The divergence in cultural patterns should be the deciding factor in selecting one type of technique over the other.

Some of the problems encountered in qualitative research are associated with the interpretation of data. Since individuals draw conclusions based on opinions and personal views, the findings are subjective and may suffer from biases. The nature of these research techniques requires special skills both in developing an appropriate procedure and also in interpreting the data. Finally, since most exploratory research is conducted with small samples, its results cannot be projected to the larger population.

As exploratory research continues to develop, we see newer methods being tried to explore the emotions and inner desires of respondents. One such technique is the true-life anecdote approach. This technique helps researchers to identify concerns normally not obtained through existing exploratory research. As more and more such new methods become available, they will assist researchers in understanding their subjects better.

CHAPTER REVIEW

1. What are the differences between conclusive research and exploratory research?
2. What are the primary differences between direct and indirect research?
3. What are the main characteristics of focus group research?
4. Describe the focus group research planning process.
5. Why is the moderator so critical to the success of a focus group?
6. What are some of the uses and benefits of focus group research?
7. What are some of the uses and benefits of depth interviews?
8. Identify the commonly used projective techniques.
9. List some of the test and neutral words you would use for a well-known detergent brand in identifying the consumer's interests, attitudes, and motivations for that brand.
10. Develop 10 statements or questions for developing advertising copy for a women's fragrance as a sentence-completion test.

NOTES

1. Alvin A. Achenbaum, "When Good Research Goes Bad," *Marketing Research* 13, no. 4 (2001), pp. 13–15.
2. Ellen Day, "Know Consumers through Qualitative Research," *Marketing News* (January 5, 1998), p. 14.
3. Patricia Sabena, "Ten Tips for the U.S. Client," *Marketing News* (February 28, 2000), pp. 18–19.
4. Kevin J. Clancy and Peter C. Krieg, "Surviving Death Wish Research," *Marketing Research* 13, no. 4 (2001), pp. 8–11.
5. Zane K. Quible, "A Focus on Focus Groups," *Business Communication Quarterly* (June 1998), pp. 28–38.
6. "2002 Directory of Focus Group Facilities and Moderators," advertising supplement to *Marketing News* (February 2002), pp. 22–45.
7. Jeffery S. Nevid and Nelly L. Sta Maria, "Multicultural Issues in Qualitative Research," *Psychology and Marketing* (July 1999), pp. 305–325.
8. David C. Bangert, "Hungary: Exploring New European Management Challenges," *International Studies of Management and Organization* 24, no. 1 (1994), pp. 209–230.
9. Jillian C. Sweeney, Geoffrey N. Soutar, Douglas R. Hausknecht, Raymond F. Dallin, and Lester W. Johnson, "Collecting Information from Groups: A Comparison of Two Methods," *Journal of Market Research Society* (April 1997), pp. 397–411.
10. Ronald B. Leiber, "Story Telling: A New Way to Get Close to Your Customer," *Fortune* (February 3, 1997), pp. 102–108.

ADDITIONAL READING

BOOKS

deVaus, David A. *Research Design in Social Research.* Thousand Oaks, CA: Sage Publications, 2002.
Edmonds, Holly. *The Focus Research Handbook.* Chicago: American Marketing Association, 1999.
Kassarjian, Harold H. "Projective Methods." In *Handbook of Marketing Research,* ed. Robert Ferber. New York: McGraw-Hill, 1974.
Kerlinger, Fred N. *Foundations of Behavioral Research.* 4th ed. New York: Holt, Rinehart and Winston, 1999.
Morgan, David L. *Planning Focus Groups.* Thousand Oaks, CA: Sage Publications, 1997.

ARTICLES

Bakken, David (1996) "State of the Art in Qualitative Research." *Marketing Research: A Magazine of Management and Applications* 8 (2), pp. 4–5.
Blackburn, Robert (2000) "Breaking Down the Barriers: Using Focus Groups to Research Small- and Medium-Sized Enterprises." *International Small Business Journal* 19 (1), pp. 44–67.
Dalbec, Bill (2001) "Stage an Intervention for the Focus Group." *Marketing News* (February 26), p. 46.
Greenbaum, Thomas L. (1996) "Understanding Focus Group Research Abroad." *Marketing News* 30 (12), pp. H14, H36.
Grunert, Klaus G., and Suzzanne C. Grunnert (1995) "Measuring Subjective Meaning Structures by Laddering Method: Theoretical Considerations and Methodological Problems." *International Journal of Research in Marketing* 12 (3), pp. 209–225.

Padilla, Belkist (1999) "Projective Techniques: Do They Work in the Hispanic Market?" *Quirk's Marketing Research Review,* no. 0483 (April).

Rentz, Kathryn C. (2002) "Reflexive Methodology: New Vistas for Qualitative Research." *The Journal of Business Communication* 39 (1), pp. 149–156.

Sweet, Casey (1999) "Anatomy of an Online Focus Group." *Quirk's Marketing Research Review,* no. 0548 (December), pp. 1–2.

Wade, Kenneth (2002) "Focus Groups' Research Role Is Shifting." *Marketing News* 36 (5), p. 47.

Wheeler, David R. (1988) "Content Analysis: An Analytical Technique for International Marketing Research." *International Marketing Review* 5 (4), pp. 34–40.

Wilk, Richard R. (2002) "The Impossibility and Necessity of Re-Inquiry: Finding Middle Ground in Social Science." *Journal of Consumer Research* 28 (2), pp. 308–312.

Zimmerman, Alan S., and Michael Szenberg (2000) "Implementing International Qualitative Research: Techniques and Obstacles." *Qualitative Market Research* 3 (3), pp. 158–164.

7 | Primary Data Collection: An Introduction to Conclusive Research

Conclusive research requires researchers to have clearly defined objectives, data requirements, and specific uses for the results obtained from the research.

LEARNING OBJECTIVES

After reading this chapter, students should be able to

- Understand the major issues in collecting primary data for international business
- Understand conclusive research designs
- Know the different techniques used to conduct conclusive research
- Know the differences between causal and descriptive research
- Understand different observational methods
- Know the advantages and disadvantages of observational methods
- Understand different experimental designs
- Know the advantages and disadvantages of experimental designs
- Understand the validity issues in experimental designs
- Provide an overview of survey methods

Secondary data provide broad-based information, and exploratory research provides more specific information using small samples; but to obtain detailed and very specific information, a researcher has to design conclusive research. Conclusive research provides the necessary information for executives to develop action plans. Exploratory research and conclusive research are both primary data-collection techniques. Because of its cost, primary research is used internationally far less than it should be. Primary data collection for international business is a complex undertaking because of unique problems faced by researchers. The following section summarizes some of these factors.

FACTORS INFLUENCING PRIMARY DATA COLLECTION

The three key factors to be considered in primary data collection in international research are the following.

COMPARABILITY OF DATA

Due to differences in measurements, variable definitions, and applicable range in responses, data collected across countries may not be comparable. The reason companies want to collect data in a multicountry context is to be able to develop uniform strategies. If environmental conditions permit, most multinational companies would like to standardize their operations and strategies. Using standardization, multinational firms are able to realize potential synergies from operating in several countries. Additionally, considerable cost savings may be achieved in areas such as R & D, accounting procedures, human resources, assembly-line operations, financial management, and marketing programs. Standardization is becoming increasingly important, as firms tend to view markets from a global perspective.

The standardization philosophy relies on the availability of information that can be compared across countries. As languages, cultural traits, business customs, and measurement systems vary from country to country, the information collected from various countries needs to be understood uniformly. It is important to know whether the data collected from several countries all have the same meaning.

The problem of data comparability implies that international research designs must be carefully developed and implemented. Diversity in international markets has to be recognized as given, and research methodology developed for one country cannot be transferred into another environment with a different language, a different level of literacy rate, and unique cultural patterns without modifications. These modifications have to take into account the problem of comparability of the information collected in these two different environments.

CULTURAL BIAS

Cultural bias exists in most international business situations. Researchers with different cultural backgrounds, language proficiency, and skills conducting research in one country may not draw similar conclusions when shown research reports from another country with a different set of cultural traits. Language and cultural differences among researchers are known to create problems when an international firm tries to merge two sets of research results. Whereas problems in comparability of data are rooted in the research process, cultural bias is a product of the people conducting the research.

The interaction between executives and researchers from different cultures is a common and natural consequence of conducting business on a global scale. Conducting international business research in various countries will result in researchers from different cultures being involved in a research study at the same time.

Besides the interactive cultural bias among researchers from different cultures, another area of bias is in the interaction between researchers and respondents from different cultures. When researchers translate questionnaire instruments from their language to that of the target group and translate responses from the language of the target group back to their own, both instruments and responses are subject to cultural bias. Bias caused by differences in culture between the respondents and the researchers is indirectly proportional to the level of knowledge and understanding the researcher has of the culture in which the study is conducted. That is, the more unfamiliar the researcher is with the foreign culture, the greater is the bias. From a business point of view, researchers assigned to conduct information gathering in foreign markets should be experienced in diverse cultures in order to reduce cultural bias.

EQUIVALENCE OF DATA

Of equal importance to comparability of data is the issue of equivalence in international research. Equivalence applies to the equality of the various constructs, scales, concepts, categories, calibrations, translations, and samples used in cross-cultural studies. Each one of these areas needs to be addressed separately in order to reduce the problems related to data equivalence.

Construct Equivalence

Constructs in research are characteristics that a researcher wishes to measure. Construct equivalence deals with the question of whether the constructs have the same meaning and significance in different countries. Constructs may differ from country to country, and researchers must account for these differences as they compile the results of a research study. For example, the leadership construct might have different degrees of significance and meanings in a traditional Asian society than it does in a European society.

Scale Equivalence

Scale or metric equivalence is the scoring equivalence of the measure used. Researchers have to be concerned with establishing equivalency to specific scoring procedures used to measure a construct and also with the response to a given measure in different countries. Aware of the problem with scale equivalence, researchers may want to consider different scales and response categories for different cultures.

A common problem observed in scale equivalence occurs when a researcher uses a Likert scale to predict purchase patterns. Do responses in the top two boxes (commonly used to predict likelihood of purchase) indicate a similar pattern of intention to purchase in different countries, or is it a reflection of cultural or other differences that make respondents select these response boxes?

Concept Equivalence

Concept equivalence refers to the interpretation of specific business ideas in different cultures. The focus here is on individual variation in attitudes and behavior, rather than on identifying cultural values or norms. Does the term "financial declaration" mean the same in all of the countries? In determining saving patterns or investment needs of respondents, the results from different countries and cultures differ vastly. In countries where true financial disclosures are required by law and unreported income is a small percentage of the total, the responses tend to be different from those of respondents from countries or cultures where traditionally all incomes are not fully reported.

Conceptual equivalence is also concerned with the interpretation of behavior or reactions of people in different societies to external stimuli. For example, in many Asian societies, being with friends and colleagues and having a party during the middle of the week is quite common. On the other hand, in some Western cultures, parties are set aside for the weekends except when entertaining business clients. Similarly, purchasing new and innovative products and telling friends and neighbors about these purchases is a common trait among Americans. In France, people have an equal propensity to purchase new and innovative products but seldom talk about these purchases.

Category Equivalence

Category equivalence refers to the differences in the ways countries and societies classify people, situations, and objects, including consumer products. For example, in the UK, office staff is categorized into many levels and treated accordingly, including having separate dining rooms for each level. In a Japanese office, the staff has fewer layers and very few individual offices, and all eat in one large cafeteria.

Job classifications and titles vary from country to country. In the accounting profession, accountants who have passed the board exams and are qualified to audit company reports in the United States and the Philippines are called certified public accountants (CPAs). In the United Kingdom and other Commonwealth countries, they are called chartered accountants (CAs). Additionally, the prestige attached to different jobs varies from country to country. For example, salespeople are highly respected in some Asian countries but are not so highly regarded in some European countries.

Regional and national differences are observed in product classifications as well. Beer is treated as an alcoholic drink in the United States and is sold only in designated retail outlets. In European countries, however, beer is treated more like a soft drink and is available in many types of retail stores.

Calibration Equivalence

Calibration equivalence refers to the variations found in the units of measurement and perceptual cues from country to country, for example, differences in monetary units (British pound, European euro, Indian rupee, Filipino peso, and American dollar), in distances (kilometer and mile), in volume (liter and gallon), and length (foot and meter).

Similarly, there are considerable variations in perceptual cues among countries. Color as a symbol of a society's values and norms is the most often mentioned categorization problem in international research. Different societies identify with different colors to signify an event or a situation. In China, red is the royal color and is used on festive occasions. In many Western societies, white is the symbol of purity and is also worn by brides; in China, Japan, and a few other Asian societies, white is the color of mourning. Green is the sacred color for Muslims around the world. In the United States, marketers use green in products and packaging to signify coolness (e.g., for mentholated products). Besides the symbolism of color, international researchers also have to realize that basic colors may be recognized the world over but, color variations may not be familiar in some countries. For example, the color fuchsia may be familiar to many American women, but in some parts of Middle East and southern Africa it is relatively unknown.

Conversion tables may be used to solve the problem of unit of measurement equivalence. The cost of raw materials in British pounds is easily translated into American dollars for a report submitted to an American company. It is much more difficult, however, to determine equivalents in perceptual cues. Researchers have to use caution and try to use multiple factors to compensate for nonverbal instrument calibration.

Translation Equivalence

Translation equivalence refers to the conversion of written and spoken language in questionnaire instruments. When researchers want to use the same instrument in different countries to develop a successful comparative study, they are faced with the problem of language equivalence. Researchers' concern here is that the translation is clear and has the same meaning to all respondents irrespective of country of origin or language.

Translation equivalence is critical in developing constructs. Constructs are the key measurement variables, and problems in their definition across countries may create validity concerns. Therefore, researchers must develop approaches to overcome the language equivalency problem. Two commonly used methods are back translation and parallel translation. Recognizing that a straightforward unidirectional translation may not capture the true meaning and intent of the question, researchers have successfully used the aforementioned translation techniques to develop questionnaires for different countries.

In back translation, the questionnaire is translated from its original (base) language to the target language by a bilingual speaker whose native language is the target language. This translated version is then retranslated into the original language by a bilingual speaker whose native language is the original, or base, language. This translation technique helps to identify translation errors that may be corrected to obtain an improved translated questionnaire.

In the parallel translation approach, a group of translators, each of whom is well versed in both languages, simultaneously translates the questionnaire and then compares their translations to make modifications agreeable to all the translators.

The previous techniques help to translate only the verbal component of the questionnaire and do not address the perceptual cues or other symbols in usage, which are much harder to translate. The same product may have different functional uses in different countries; for example, bicycles in the Netherlands are mainly used as a means of transportation, but in the United States they are mostly used for leisure. In some countries the product's function may be unfamiliar; for example, consumers in many Western countries use electric toothbrushes, a product virtually unknown throughout Latin America, where people use small manual toothbrushes.

Translation equivalency is a major concern for researchers. Not only must questionnaires possess linguistic equivalence, but they also must have perceptual and cultural equivalence.

Sampling Equivalence

Sampling equivalence concerns itself with the similarity of the samples drawn from more than one country. In drawing samples, researchers need to ensure that the sample drawn is representative of the population in each of the countries in which they are conducting the study and also that the respondents selected are able to express views for themselves and for a wider group.

Due to the differences in the availability of various demographic and census statistics, drawing representative samples is not always possible. Where there are abundant statistics available, drawing statistically randomized samples is much easier, and the possibility of their being a representative sample is much greater. In countries where data availability is a problem, drawing representative samples is very difficult. In many developing countries, data on total output and number of workers employed in an industry is unavailable, making the selection of a sample for a comparative manufacturing study difficult.

The other sampling concern is how to incorporate the responses of one individual speaking on behalf of a larger group. In many developing countries where the economy is largely agricultural, the village elders, who are respected in the community, are able to speak for the whole village, offering opinions, views, interests, and explanations of the needs of individual members. In some Middle Eastern cultures, the male head of the household is generally the spokesperson for all the family members. In contrast, in the United States, the views expressed by one member of the family may not be representative of the whole family. Since people in the United States tend to enjoy more individual freedom and independence, each member may have unique opinions and views and would not hesitate to express them.

To assure sampling equivalence, researchers have to consider whether a sample is representative of the wider population and also whether a single respondent should be used to represent a household or organization. Since there are considerable differences among countries, equivalence of samples when conducting studies from more than one country may pose methodological problems.

CONCLUSIVE RESEARCH

Conclusive research is designed to assist managers in selecting a course of action. All conclusive research techniques are considered *primary* data-collection techniques, that is, data collected specifically for a given research project for which no relevant information exists.

In our previous discussions of secondary and exploratory research, we concluded that these techniques are useful in defining problem areas, gaining insights into the business environment, providing directions for future research, and addressing general issues. In business decision making, the insights gained through secondary and exploratory research, though useful, are really not designed to arrive at a decision, answer very specific issues, or decide between two or more alternatives. To do the latter, we need to conduct some form of conclusive research.

Conclusive research is defined as research with a clear and well-defined objective, where variables of interest are pre-specified, a given level of reliability is sought, and a specific course of action can be suggested. To operationalize this definition to a research situation, we must be able to define the purpose of research, identify the data needs, use a structured format to collect information, employ a relatively large sample, apply quantitative analysis, and execute or implement some of the recommendations of the research study.

TYPES OF CONCLUSIVE RESEARCH

Conclusive research is broadly classified as *descriptive* or *causal*. Descriptive research helps researchers generate data that can explain the composition and characteristics of relevant groups. These groups could be customers, employees, organizations, or other service providers. Descriptive research can furnish precious understanding about the groups under inquiry and the interrelationships among variables. In contrast, causal research, also called experimental research, helps a researcher draw inferences about relationships among variables. Causality takes place when the occurrence of one variable increases the probability of the occurrence of a second variable. For example, interest rates have a causal influence on home buying. As interest rates rise, home buying decreases (cause-and-effect relationship). If we can systematically manage the levels of the cause variable, we can study the impact of the effect variable, keeping all other factors constant. Data collected through experimental research therefore tend to be more powerful than data collected through other research techniques.

Selection of appropriate research is crucial to the success of the research project. The main issues to be considered in selecting a technique are research objectives, cost-effectiveness, and comparability across different countries and cultures.

DESCRIPTIVE RESEARCH TECHNIQUES

Observations, surveys, and *longitudinal studies* are the three basic approaches for collecting descriptive research data. In observation research, information is gathered by observing people, objects, or events. By observing present behavior or the results of past behavior, researchers are able to collect useful information. Rather than invite potential consumers into artificial testing situations, such as focus groups, researchers observe and examine consumers at work, in stores, and in some cases even in their homes.[1] For example, using 200 field observations of parents and children, a retailer was able to ascertain the factors that influence the in-store purchasing decisions of parents shopping with children.[2] Observational techniques require the researcher to observe the behavior of subjects either as it is taking place or later if it has been mechanically or otherwise recorded.

Direct observational techniques have received a great deal of attention in new product development. Motorola, Gillette, and Xerox have used observational research to identify opportunities for new products. For example, direct observations led juice companies to offer juices in smaller convenient-to-carry bottles rather than the large and bulky containers that they were previously packaged in.[3] Hewlett-Packard (HP) is another company that uses observational research. In one case, HP researchers, by observing surgeons operating on patients, were able to develop a surgical helmet with goggles that cast images right in front of a surgeon's eyes. This was a tremendous improvement over the existing practice of using television monitors (which were often blocked by other surgical staff moving around) for observing their scalpel movements.

Observational techniques are particularly helpful in cross-border research, as the researcher may not be familiar with local conditions or societal patterns. These techniques are valuable in obtaining information on sensitive topics or when respondents are unable or unwilling to provide information. Observations are often used in actual situations without the subject's knowledge; consequently, the data is free of response biases.

SURVEYS

Survey research is the procedure most commonly used in international research. The general effectiveness of this method may not be uniform across countries. The data collected through survey research may be affected by many factors including cultural difficulties, sampling problems, and varying education levels. It does, however, act as a useful primary informational source. In surveys, respondents provide information through a structured questionnaire. The questionnaire consists of queries that deal with respondents' interests, intentions, likes, dislikes, knowledge, problems, behavioral patterns, life style, and demographics. The main difference between observation and surveys is the respondents' level of participation in the research. When researchers employ observation techniques, the role of the respondents is passive. In surveys, the respondents play an active role. In addition, survey research requires a level of communication and interaction between the respondent and the interviewer that rarely occurs when researchers use observation techniques. Primary research can be gathered in different ways. Some are specific to situations or industries. In the marketing of financial services, for example, surveys may not be the best technique to gather information in international markets due to the secrecy and confidentiality attached to these services.[4]

A major advantage of the survey technique is its versatility in terms of the types of data it is capable of generating. Respondents may answer a questionnaire verbally, in writing, or over the Internet. Many Japanese companies make use of surveys to gather primary data, but they try their instincts first. For example, research on the Walkman, Sony's lightweight portable cassette player, showed that consumers would not buy a tape recorder that did not record. The company's chairman, Akio Morita, decided to introduce the Walkman anyway, and the rest is history. Today, the Walkman is Sony's most successful product.[5] Survey research is used to gather information for many of the functional areas of business. Surveys, if done correctly, are quite reliable. A major portion of this book deals with survey procedures. A detailed discussion of surveys starts in chapter 9.

LONGITUDINAL STUDIES

Longitudinal studies involve collecting data from the same sample of individuals or households over time. These samples are often referred to as "panels." A panel is a fixed sample of elements. The elements could be individuals, stores, banks, dealers, or other entities. The panel remains relatively constant over time, although there are periodic additions to replace dropouts or to keep the panel representative. The sample members in a panel are measured repeatedly, as contrasted with the one-time measurement in a survey. Individuals who are selected as members of commercial panels are generally compensated with cash or other gifts for their cooperation. Some large companies maintain internal employee panels that provide information for quality control, product usage satisfaction, and new product development. R.J. Reynolds, the large tobacco company, has an internal panel of 350 employees who are called on to smoke, draw on unlit cigarettes, and smell new tobacco mixtures to provide useful information on new and existing brands. These studies assist the company in obtaining valuable confidential information.[6]

In the United States, the three major companies that conduct offline and online panels are National Family Opinion Inc., IPSOS-NPD, and Market Facts. All three companies maintain panels of more than 400, 000 households. Dunn & Bradstreet has an online panel of more than 1 million. According to Gerry Grise, senior vice president for global research services at Ipsos-Reid Corporation, panel studies are used a lot more in North America than anywhere else in the world, but they are quite common in Western Europe and are sometimes used in Japan and Australia. In Western Europe, average panel size is roughly 25,000, with some variance from market to market. It is extremely difficult to recruit, build, and maintain a panel that is representative of the entire population. In Japan, the panels are built from an exceptionally low response rate (single digit) and therefore costs are comparatively higher, sometimes twice those of a U.S. panel. It is not possible to conduct longitudinal studies in Africa, Asia (except Japan), Eastern Europe, and Latin America, as no panels exist in these regions.

In panel studies, members may be contacted by telephone, in person, or by a mail questionnaire. Panels rely on repeated measurements of the same variables. Typically, panel members record repetitive behavior of purchase, consumption, or use (or some combination of these factors) of products and services, which are then mailed back to the research organization.[7] ACNielsen, a large U.S.-based research company, maintains a panel of more than 40,000 households nationwide as a basis for its Scantrack service. The panel members use a handheld scanner to record all their purchases by passing the scanner across the Universal Product Codes (UPCs) on the packages of purchased items. On their return from shopping trips, they answer a programmed set of questions asking them where they purchased the product, how much they paid for it, and so on, by responding to a series of prompts from the scanner. Longitudinal studies enable the investigator to track repeat purchase behavior and changes in purchasing habits and to analyze the effects of specific marketing strategies such as price changes or special promotions.[8]

OBSERVATION TECHNIQUES

Observation techniques vary widely. They are classified on the basis of *how* the observations are made, *who* makes the observation, and *what* is observed. In all types of observational methods, the key element is recording situations and events as they happen. Observational techniques are generally best used as a complement to survey and other research methods and not as a stand-alone technique.

Observational techniques are classified by the way in which they are administered. Researchers use each of these techniques in different situations to provide the necessary information for decision makers. Some, such as personal and mechanical observation methods, are more popular than others.

Discussions of the major observational methods follow.

Personal Observation

In personal observation, a trained observer records events, subjects, situations, and behavior as they occur. Neither the respondent nor the observer influences or effects changes with the event or in the behavior. Personal observation techniques are flexible and applied in very many situations.

In personal observation, the observer studies behavior patterns by being present at the site or location of an event of interest to the researcher. These techniques are used to study behavior in specific communities; to gather anthropological or cultural information; to study interactions in marketing situations; to observe assembly-line workers in manufacturing plants; to study group dynamics in offices; and to evaluate sales-customer dyads in sales transactions.

When a researcher is attempting to understand other cultures, it is particularly important to obtain firsthand information. Observing people in their daily routines and natural habitat can be much more illustrative than just listening to peoples' responses.[9] When used to study cultures, observations may make note of expressive behavior including body language, voice intonations, and facial expressions. Such data are useful in better understanding the different cultural patterns of various societies and may be applied to business situations.

Many large companies make use of personal observation techniques to obtain relevant international information. Fast-food companies such as McDonald's and Pizza Hut use personal observations to understand traffic patterns in selecting store sites. They may also use this type of research to classify target customers in a particular area. In overseas markets, researchers use personal observation to study shopping behavior, including time spent on searching for products and time spent on selecting each product category. Researchers observe, among other things, the interaction between the buyer and store personnel, other buyers, or even family members. This type of observation is useful in providing insights into how people make purchasing decisions in different countries.

Commercial banks make use of personal observation to identify specific consumer needs at bank branches, and large manufacturing companies use personal observation to monitor the assembly-line system to understand delay patterns and to improve line efficiencies.

Large international firms have used personal observation techniques to gather information on customers, suppliers, and distributors in order to be more market responsive. In the 1980s, for example, Canon Camera Company of Japan used personal observation to study the customer service provided by their independent distributors. After observing a lack of efficient and competent service by the distributor, the company decided to use its own sales office to improve customer service.[10]

Retail establishments and large mall operators have used observational techniques to study traffic patterns and record automobile license plates to track the geographic spread of their customer base. They have used this information in organizing merchandise displays, selecting store locations, and designing a store's layout.

Personal observation methods offer significant benefits to researchers. They generally offer some degree of disguise, are not difficult to set up, are flexible, and offer an excellent opportunity to observe the subjects in natural settings. Since subjects respond and react under natural conditions, the researcher gains an understanding of the differences in behaviors in different countries and cultures.

A major criticism of personal observation techniques is that they are, to a large degree, subjective in their interpretation of the observed phenomena. Since setting prespecified guidelines on the events or behavior to be observed is different, no one is sure whether the observed behavior is the norm or the exception. For this reason, personal observation techniques are subject to both observer bias and analytical bias.

Mechanical Observation

Mechanical observation is a continuous monitoring and recording of events and subjects using some form of mechanical device. In mechanical observation, the observed individuals or objects do not interact with the researcher and are usually unaware of the observation. The resulting observations tend to be bias free.

Researchers commonly use video monitors and other mechanical devices to gather information. Merchants use on-site video cameras to plan floor displays, arrange aisles, and assess effects of specific marketing campaigns. City planners use traffic monitors to understand the flow of traffic and to improve traffic bottlenecks. Building managers and mass transportation systems use turnstiles to count the number of people entering a building or to count the number of users of a transit system.

Mechanical devices are useful for recording information for an extended time (for many hours). It is difficult to place observers at the same spot for 24 hours without being noticed. In addition, the costs of personal observation tend to be higher when observations need to be recorded for a number of days or months.

In international research, mechanical observation has been used in a variety of situations. In manufacturing, engineers have used mechanical devices to monitor flow of parts and components from warehouse to assembly line. Investment and financial service companies have used them to evaluate the effectiveness of brokers. Marketing companies have used this approach to study sales techniques employed by their sales personnel. Retailers have set up monitors to track theft by employees. Consumer packaged goods companies have used mechanical devices to study the effects of new package design on sales by observing consumer purchase patterns. And telemarketers have used observations to monitor staff sales pitches.

Use of optical scanners in conjunction with the Universal Product Codes (UPC) has helped generate single-source data for use by researchers. These data help track inventory, assist in better controlling inventory, monitoring sales by brand category and by store type, and understanding effects of price on sales volume. In addition, single-source data also track overall product category sales.

One of the early users of mechanical observation was ACNielsen, which used the audimeter (an electronic device attached to the television sets of a representative panel of households across the United States) to track the television viewing patterns of households in different parts of the country. Using this data, Nielsen is able to project the ratings (viewership by households of each segment of a given program) in television markets. This information aids advertisers in placing their commercials in their most desired programs.

Most mechanical observation techniques do not require the participation of the subjects of the study. A few, however, require the subject to be an active participant. Though these devices are more intrusive than those that don't require subject participation, they are still valuable in obtaining critical information. Some of these techniques are *eye cameras, pupilometers,* and *psycho-galvanometers.* The eye camera records the movements of the eye, tracking the respondent's eye contact with a stimulus or advertisement. The pupilometer measures the dilation of pupils. Chinese jade merchants have employed these devices to study the interest of customers in an object at different price levels. A respondent demonstrates greater pupil dilation when interested in a particular object or stimulus. Psycho-galvanometers measure changes in the electrical resistance of the skin. The theory behind these tools is that physiological changes (increased perspiration, for example) accompany emotional reaction. By judging the strength of the response, a researcher is able to draw inferences about the respondent's interest level and attitude toward specific stimuli. Another technique, voice-pitch analysis, measures emotional reactions by recording changes in the pitch of the respondent's voice. As a respondent gets excited or interested, the pitch of his or her voice rises, providing hidden clues to the researcher.

Mechanical observation techniques are relatively easy to use and are not subject to many of the problems associated with personal observation methods. They are relatively easy to set up and produce data with low observational and analytical biases. Problems associated with mechanical observation devices are that they tend to offer less opportunity to observe subjects in natural settings and in some cases may be intrusive.

Trace Analysis

Trace analysis uses physical and other evidence of objects or events to reveal behavior. These techniques differ from personal observation in that they report traces of behavior rather than actual behavior. Trace analysis techniques are useful in tracking incidences or frequencies of certain behaviors.

The evidence gathered through trace analysis may include wear and tear of roads, automobiles, magazines, and other objects people use more than once. If used creatively, trace analysis can provide information that may otherwise be impossible to discover. Analyzing consumers' trash, for example, may reveal valuable patterns of consumption. Trace analysis has been used in industrial espionage cases, though such use is generally deemed unethical. Trace analysis is relatively inexpensive and tends to have low observational bias since subjects are unaware of the observation.

In international settings where respondents may be reluctant to answer questions, trace analysis tends to offer an alternative in collecting data. By observing wear and tear of roads, researchers can estimate the flow of traffic to various markets and stores. Similarly, by observing the wear and tear of machine dials, engineers can estimate the speeds at which certain assembly-line machines are operated when there is less supervision.

Examining historical artifacts is another trace method of gaining information from subjects. The presence of physical facilities such as places of worship, schools, open markets, and community centers is a sign of heavy traffic and population density. Such information may be helpful in making decisions about setting up businesses or providing services.

Trace analysis is subject to interpretation bias. It is, after all, the opinion of one researcher viewing the traces. If another observer viewed the same trace evidence, he or she could interpret the data differently. Inferences drawn by linking an indicator to a behavioral pattern may not have any logical basis. There may be some other logical reason for such behavior, and the researcher may not identify this. Trace analysis relies on physical wear and tear to draw conclusions, but this wear and tear may not be caused by use but by time, in which case the interpretation may not be valid. Trace analysis is recommended only when other observational techniques are not feasible.

Content Analysis

Content analysis is the systematic, quantitative, and objective description of the content of media and other communication vehicles. Used mostly in cultural and communications research, this technique has been found to be extremely useful when subjects are unable to describe their own behavioral patterns. By studying words and pictures, researchers using content analysis are able to study beliefs, values, ideologies, role perceptions, norms, and other elements of a culture. The key to content analysis is the analytical part of the technique. The analysis has to be done carefully and by one who has at least a basic understanding of the technique.

The analysis of the observed media may include usage and frequency of different words, appearance of characters in the form of individuals or objects, coverage of various topics, length of the message, and general theme of the message. By classifying the total content of the media by the aforementioned units, researchers are able to draw inferences about the norms of a society, the overwhelming concerns of the society, and the topics of interest.[11]

In international research, content analysis is generally used in planning advertising and communication campaigns. By analyzing the contents of various media in different countries, researchers are able to determine whether there is any convergence of ideas and traits among various societies. If such convergence does exist, standardization of advertising and other promotional campaigns may be feasible across national boundaries.

If used correctly, content analysis provides the user with a high degree of disguise and a low analytical bias. Content analysis is quite difficult to set up, and it requires highly trained researchers painstakingly going over several media for a long period of time to draw inferences about a society. It is not very flexible, and its use is limited to cross-cultural studies and to developing communication programs.

Audits

Audit analysis is an inventory of items and other objects found in different places, for example, households, retail stores, or corporate offices. In audits, the researcher physically counts brand names, package sizes, and quantities of items in stock in a home or in retail stores. Since they are actual counts of items, audits provide a good inventory of usage by consumers.

In some industrialized countries, pantry audits (so called because they literally take inventory of pantries) are useful in establishing consumer purchase patterns. These observations provide a more realistic usage count and tend to be highly reliable.

Audits are generally difficult to implement, because the researcher needs to obtain the consumer's permission to conduct this type of study. It has also been found to be very expensive to conduct an audit. The strong points of audits are that they tend to have low observational and analytical biases and occur in natural surroundings. On the other hand, they are not disguised and are very difficult to implement.

Store audits are much more common in many countries. The owners of retail stores have an interest in knowing the exact physical count of the items on their shelves and in storage; they tend to conduct these audits periodically. There are many specialized suppliers who do store audits, and these audits are easy to conduct.

OTHER CLASSIFICATIONS OF OBSERVATION TECHNIQUES

Observational techniques may be further classified by degree of structure, level of disguise, and type of environment in which they are conducted.

- *Structured observation.* Structured observation is a technique researchers use when they are able to specify the behavior to be observed and are able to define the observational method to be applied. In this technique, the data gathered pertain to discrete, clearly defined events and are therefore recorded by merely making entries in categories on an appropriate observation form. Structured observations are used in conclusive research situations. They are generally reliable and reduce observer biases. A good example of a structured observation is a store audit.

- *Unstructured observation.* Unstructured observation is a technique in which the researcher observes all events and objects but does not specify the details of the observation beforehand. In the unstructured approach, there is no prior definition of behavior or method. Unstructured methods are flexible and are appropriate when the researcher is not sure of the problem. This type of observation suffers from observer bias and is used mostly as an exploratory research technique. Personal observation techniques such as observing shoppers in retail store settings fall under this category.

- *Disguised observation.* Disguised observation is a method in which the respondents or subjects are unaware of being observed. Disguised observation techniques provide data about respondents' natural behavior and are generally bias free. Most mechanical devices tend to be disguised approaches, and even some personal observations are disguised. As mentioned earlier, disguised observations may be ethically questionable.

- *Undisguised observation.* Undisguised observation is a method in which the subject or respondent is aware of the observation. This approach removes the ethical dilemma associated with disguised techniques, but it is subject to respondent or subject biases. Knowing that they are being observed, subjects may not behave naturally, and the resulting findings may not reflect a true behavioral pattern. Pantry audits are a good example of an undisguised observational technique.

- *Natural environment observation.* Subjects are observed in the natural environment in which an event normally takes place. For example, consumers purchasing products in stores provides a natural environment; consumers in mock stores do not.

- *Contrived or set-up environment observation.* Subjects are observed in an environment in which the event normally does not take place. Observing consumer choice processes and preferences in test kitchens is an example of observation in a contrived environment.

BENEFITS OF USING OBSERVATION METHODS

Observational techniques normally are disguised and provide a measurement of actual subjects' behaviors or events. Most other research techniques collect information on intended or expected behaviors. From a researcher's point of view, observational techniques are more revealing about actual behaviors than techniques that focus on expected behaviors.

When the subjects are unable to verbalize their responses or are unable to provide concrete information through surveys or other means, observational devices tend to fill the gap and provide the necessary information. Hence, observational techniques are useful in gathering information from countries where the literacy rates are low as well as when the respondents are small children who may not be able to communicate with the researchers. As observational devices basically record the events as they take place, they are relatively free of interviewer and reporting biases.

PROBLEMS ASSOCIATED WITH OBSERVATION METHODS

Observational techniques are often consuming and in some instances may be very expensive. Observational devices also suffer from interpretational biases caused by the selective perception of the observer. Observational devices are limited to particular activities and subjects and do not have the same flexibility as survey methods. Finally, the researcher may not come to know the reasons for the observed behavior and the underlying attitudes, beliefs, and motives of the subjects.

There is also a major debate among users of observational devices about the ethics of observing subjects without their knowledge. In some of the personal observation techniques and mechanical observation methods, subjects are not told that they are being observed, and this may violate their privacy.

CHAPTER SUMMARY

One of the more widely used primary data-collection techniques is conclusive research. Conclusive research is used to test specific hypotheses and examine relationships. Conclusive research generally uses large sample sizes. The research process is formal, information need is clearly defined, and data analysis is quantitative. The information gathered from conclusive research is used for decision making. Conclusive research designs may be classified as descriptive or causal.

There are major issues surrounding primary data-collection techniques for international operations. Since international research involves conducting data collection in more than one country, the issues of comparability, equivalence, and cultural biases are major problems when one tries to use the data collectively.

Comparability addresses the issue of whether data collected from different countries have the same meaning, accuracy, reliability, and precision of measurement. Equivalence refers to the similarity in the data at various levels among studies across countries. The equivalence issue looks at the construct, scales, concepts, categories, calibration, translation, and sample. The cultural bias issue addresses the problem of communication between researchers and respondents from different countries.

In descriptive research, the major objective is the description of business or market characteristics or functions. In causal research, the researcher is trying to find cause-and-effect relationships between variables; that is, Will the occurrence of one variable increase the probability of the occurrence of a second variable?

Descriptive research can be undertaken through observational techniques, surveys, or longitudinal studies. Worldwide, surveys are the most widely used research technique to gather information. In a survey, research information is gathered from a sample of respondents or elements by use of a questionnaire. Because it is the most widely used technique, many of the chapters that follow discuss this technique at length. Longitudinal studies are a survey of groups of respondents (panels) at different points in time, which allows researchers to analyze changes over time. Panels are very popular in the United States and also are used in Australia, Japan, and Western Europe.

The major observational techniques used are personal observation, mechanical observation, trace analysis, content analysis, and audits. Each of these methods can be applied in specific situations. Each also provides somewhat unbiased information. Observational techniques are relatively easy to set up, and they provide information in situations where information might otherwise not be obtainable.

Observational devices may be classified by the degree of structure, level of disguise, and type of environment in which the observation takes place. The more structured, disguised, and natural the environment, the better is the quality of the information gathered.

The benefits of observational methods are that they allow researchers to measure the subjects' actual behavior, reporting and interviewer bias is low, and some data can only be obtained from observational techniques. The problems associated with observational techniques are that variables such as attitudes, beliefs, and motives behind behavior are not clear in observational techniques. In addition, observational techniques are time-consuming and tend to be expensive. Some observer biases exist in this type of technique, and ethical issues arise when researchers observe subjects without their knowledge.

Observation devices are useful in some situations and, when applied with other research methods, can provide valuable information.

CHAPTER REVIEW

1. What is conclusive research?
2. What is the difference between descriptive and causal research?
3. What is a longitudinal study?
4. How and when are longitudinal studies undertaken?
5. Enumerate the major observational techniques.
6. How are observational techniques classified?
7. How is personal observation technique used in collecting information?
8. Where and why would one use content analysis?
9. What are the advantages of observational devices?
10. What are some of the problems in the use of observational devices?
11. Identify countries in which you feel observational techniques might work better for collecting information than survey techniques. State your reasons.
12. If you were a store owner, what type of information would you want to track using observational techniques?

NOTES

1. Robert Becker, "Take Direct Route When Data Gathering," *Marketing News* (September 27, 1999), p. 1.

2. Langbourne Rust, "Observations: Parents and Children Shopping Together: A New Approach to the Qualitative Analysis of Observation Data," *Journal of Advertising Research* (July–August 1993), pp. 65–70.

3. Bill Abrams, *The Observational Research Handbook.* Chicago: NTC Business Books, 2004, p. 14.

4. Craig C. Gordon, Denise D. Schoenbachler, Geoffrey L. Gordon, and Thomas M. Rogers, "Taking a 'Real-Time' Approach to International Marketing Research," *Journal of Professional Services Marketing* 11, no. 2 (1995), pp. 189–205.

5. Johny K. Johansson and Ikujiro Nonaka, "Market Research the Japanese Way," *Harvard Business Review* (May–June 1987), pp. 16–22.

6. Margaret Loeb, "Testers of Cigarettes Find On-Job Puffing Really Isn't a Drag," *Wall Street Journal,* August 22, 1984, pp. 1, 15.

7. S. Sudman, "On the Accuracy of Recording of Consumer Panels," *Journal of Marketing Research* (August 1964), pp. 69–83.

8. Venkatram Ramaswamy and Wayne S. DeSarbo, "SCULPTURE: A New Methodology for Deriving and Analyzing Hierarchical Product-Market Structures from Panel Data," *Journal of Marketing Research* (November 1990), pp. 418–427.

9. Felipe Korzenny and Ann Korzenny, "Trends in Hispanic Research," *Quirk's Marketing Research Review* (February 1998), p. 2.

10. Johansson and Nonaka, "Market Research the Japanese Way."

11. David R. Wheeler, "Content Analysis: An Analytical Technique for International Marketing Research," *International Marketing Review* 5, no. 4 (1988), pp. 34–40.

ADDITIONAL READING

BOOKS

Abrams, Bill. *The Observational Research Handbook.* Chicago: NTC Business Books, 2000.

Fowler, Floyd J., Jr., *Survey Research Methods.* 3rd ed. Thousand Oaks, CA: Sage Publications, 2001.

ARTICLES

Baumgartner, Hans, and Jan-Benedict E.M. Steekamp (2001) "Response Styles in Marketing Research: A Cross-National Investigation. *Journal of Marketing Research* (May), pp. 143–156.

Edris, Thabet A., and A. Meidan (1990) "On the Reliability of Psychographic Research." *European Journal of Marketing* 24 (3), pp. 23–41.

Han, Min C., Byoung-Woo Lee, and Kong-Kyun Ro (1994) "The Choice of a Survey Mode in Country Image Studies." *Journal of Business Research* 29 (2), pp. 151–162.

Kahle, Lynn R., Gregory Rose, and Aviv Shoham (1999) "Findings of LOV throughout the World, and Other Evidence of Cross-National Consumer Psychographics." *Journal of Euro Marketing* 8, pp. 1–13.

Netemeyer, Richard G., Srinivas Durvasula, and Donald R. Lichtenstein (1991) "A Cross-National Assessment of the Reliability and Validity of the CETSCALE." *Journal of Marketing Research* 28 (3), pp. 320–327.

8 Experimental Research

Experimentation is a type of conclusive research in which the objective is to understand cause-and-effect relationships between variables.

LEARNING OBJECTIVES

After reading this chapter, students should be able to

- Understand causal research
- Know what the conditions for causality are
- Understand validity in experimental designs
- Know the various experimental designs
- Understand the application of designs for various research objectives
- Be familiar with the use of experimental designs in test marketing
- Understand the general benefits of using experimental designs
- Know the problems associated with experimental designs

International executives need to understand why certain decisions they make have a greater impact on business results than some others. Will sales always rise when prices are lowered? Will factory workers always increase output when offered incentive bonuses? Causal research can help with these types of decisions. By scientifically isolating variables that have a greater impact on an outcome, managers can improve their decision-making skills. Experiments are widely used in product testing, trade-off analysis, and test marketing.[1]

Most causal research techniques are able to isolate those variables that have an effect on another variable. Furthermore, they help in determining the nature of the relationship between the cause variable and the effect variable, and they help predict the effect. Most causal research designs are structured and require careful planning. The major causal research technique used in business settings is experimentation. With the advent of computers and the ability to customize them easily, many researchers are using this technology. For example, researchers have found computer-generated experimental designs to be better than traditional designs for both "discrete choice" and "preference based" conjoint studies.[2]

KEY TERMS IN EXPERIMENTAL RESEARCH

Following are some of the key terms used in experimentation:

- In conducting experiments, the variable that causes the effect is referred to as the *independent variable* and the one that is affected is referred to as the *dependent variable*. Independent variables are the ones that the researcher generally changes or manipulates to measure the resulting effect. In business situations, independent variables could include price, package design, rebate offers, advertisements, new service offerings, improvements in working conditions, and employee bonuses. The corresponding dependent variables for these independent variables may be changes in sales, customer satisfaction, improvements in productivity, and employee satisfaction.
- The individual subjects or elements whose responses are sought using an independent variable are called *test units*. In experimentation, test units may be employees, service clients, customers, or organizations. For example, if a large telecommunications firm wants to study the effect of a new cable system it is installing on its business customers, it may use targeted businesses as test units.
- Besides the independent and dependent variables, there are other variables in the business environment that might have some effect on the dependent variable. These *extraneous variables* include all variables other than the independent variable that affect the outcome of the test units. Extraneous variables have to be accounted for in order to isolate the effects of the independent variable. In experiments, researchers commonly use control groups to isolate the effect of the independent variable. In marketing studies, researchers may want to determine the effect of a new campaign on sales, but at the same time they would like to be sure that the changes in revenues were not caused by another variable, including an extraneous variable.

EXTRANEOUS VARIABLES IN EXPERIMENTS

Following are the critical extraneous variables that affect the results of experiments:

- *History*. The specific events that are external to the experiment but that occur at the same time as the experiment may affect the final outcome. The longer the time interval between observations, the greater is the possibility that history will affect the outcome.
- *Maturation*. Maturation is a change observed in the test units caused by the passage of time. The test units may have gained experience, may be tired, or may

have matured over time, affecting the dependent variable. It is difficult to measure the effects of maturation.

- *Testing effects*. Testing effects occur when a prior observation affects a later observation or when a prior measurement affects the test unit's response to the independent variable. In the first case (called the main testing effect), posttreatment attitudes are influenced more by pretreatment attitudes than by the independent variable (treatment) itself. In the second case (called interactive testing effect), prior knowledge of the variable through prescreening or other factors affects the outcome.
- *Instrumentation*. Instrumentation effects result from changes in the measuring instrument. These changes may be the effect of the researcher's variations in observing the results. These can occur when both a pretest and a posttest are involved. Another source of the instrumentation effect is a change in the measurement of the outcomes of the post study.
- *Statistical regression*. Statistical regression occurs when test units shift their positions or results from the extreme to the middle during the course of the experiment. This shift creates problems for researchers, since the change in observed effect may be influenced by statistical regression and not by the independent variable.
- *Selection bias*. Selection bias occurs when the researcher subjectively or improperly assigns test units to treatment conditions.
- *Mortality*. Mortality occurs when test units are lost during the experiment. Mortality often happens when test units are unwilling to continue to be part of the experiment after the pretreatment period. Mortality affects the test results, since researchers are unsure of the way the lost test units would have responded.

To rectify (or control) the problems associated with extraneous variables, researchers often randomize test units or use specific designs that may be exposed to fewer extraneous variables.

EXPERIMENTAL DESIGNS

An *experimental design* is a set of procedures that outlines the format of an experiment. The design includes a definition of test units, an identification of the independent and dependent variables, and a description of how the extraneous variables are to be controlled.

In practice, researchers use a variety of designs in conducting experimental research. These designs range from very simple to very complex. Though the complexity does not necessarily provide better reliability, the more complex designs do tend to be less biased and offer a better account for the effects of extraneous variables.

Elements of experimental designs are symbolically presented as follows:

X = Sample or groups (test units) who are exposed to the independent variable
O = Measurement of the dependent variable on the sample or test units
R = Random assignment of test units to separate treatments

AFTER-ONLY DESIGN

In after-only experimental design, a single test unit is subjected to a variable or treatment, and then a single measurement on the dependent variable is taken. This is a simple and easy experiment to design and provides some basic answers.

Symbolically this experimental design may be represented as follows:

A single group of test units is exposed to a treatment (X), and then a single measurement on the dependent variable is taken (O_1).

A good example of an after-only experiment would be one in which a group of factory workers in a manufacturing plant are given one additional break during their shift; the additional break would be the independent, or treatment, variable X. If management measured the workers' output (dependent variable), and the group had produced 1,000 units in one shift (O_1), the output of 1,000 units would be the effect of the additional break given to the factory workers.

There are many problems associated with this design. The test units are not randomly assigned, and therefore the results may be biased. This design does not provide a basis for comparing level O_1 to a before (pretest) situation, and it does not control for extraneous variables. Hence, the findings of this experiment may be heavily influenced by extraneous variables and the researcher will not definitively conclude that the results were caused by the independent variable X.

ONE GROUP PRE-POST TEST DESIGN

In this design, a group of test units is measured twice, once before the independent variable is introduced and once after. First, a pretreatment measure is taken (O_1), and then the group is exposed to the independent variable or treatment (X). Then once again a measurement is taken, the posttreatment measurement (O_2). The effect of the independent variable is measured by subtracting the pretreatment measure from the posttreatment measure ($O_2 - O_1$).

Symbolically, this design can be represented as follows:

$$O_1 \quad X \quad O_2$$

Using the earlier factory-worker example, management would record one shift output of the study group (or take it from historical records), and find that 900 units were produced by the workers (pretreatment measurement, O_1). The independent variable would be the additional break (X), and the effect of the independent variable (posttreatment measurement, O_2) is 1,000 units. Management may conclude that the additional break produced an increase in output of 100 units ($O_2 - O_1$, or $1000 - 900 = 100$). This design produces much more useful information for management.

This is a definite improvement over the after-only design. The pre-post testing ensures the contribution of the independent variable to the final effect on the dependent variable. But, as there is no control group, the effect may have been contributed by extraneous variables. Also, pretreatment measurements may contribute to testing effects on the group and alter the group's natural responses. When respondents recognize that they are part of an experiment, that knowledge may have an impact on their responses. They may tailor their responses to those they feel the researcher desires or that may seem to offer them some benefit. In the example of the additional break, for instance, workers may improve production initially to gain the benefit of the extra break. Once the advantage is earned, production may slip back to previous levels.

AFTER-ONLY WITH CONTROL OR STATIC GROUP DESIGN

The after-only with control or static group design requires two groups. The first group is called the experimental group and is exposed to the independent variable. The second group is the control group and is not exposed to the independent variable. Measurements on both groups are made only after the treatment.

This design is symbolically presented as follows:

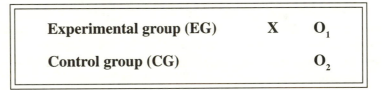

Experimental group (EG)   **X** O_1

Control group (CG) O_2

When this design is applied to the factory worker example, management would be selecting one test group as the control (CG); the original group of workers would be the experimental group (EG). Management would measure the effect of the additional break with the experimental group ($O_1 = 1,000$) and would also measure the output of the control group that has not been exposed to the independent variable. If the control group produced 950 units during the same shift period (O_2), then the effect of the independent variable is $1,000 - 950 = 50$ units ($O_2 - O_1$).

This design provides a slight improvement over the previous design, as it tries to account for extraneous effects by having a control group. But, as this design does not measure the values before exposing the groups to the independent variable, one is not sure of the total effect of the independent variable. In addition, the groups are not randomized, and some group differences that could affect the results may exist.

BEFORE-AFTER WITH CONTROL GROUP DESIGN (OR PRE-POST TEST WITH CONTROL GROUP DESIGN)

The before-after with control group design is truly a complete experimental design and is used quite often. In this design, two groups are randomly selected; one is assigned as the experimental group and the second is the control group. Symbolically this could be expressed as follows:

Experimental group	R	O_1	X	O_2
Control group	R	O_3		O_4

Measurements of both groups of the dependent variable are taken before introduction of the independent variable (O_1 and O_3). The experimental group (EG) is subjected to the independent variable, but the control group (CG) is not. Once again measurements are taken of both the groups (O_2 and O_4). The effect of the variable is measured as

$$(O_2 - O_1) - (O_4 - O_3)$$

The difference in measurement between the experimental group's pretreatment and its posttreatment ($O_2 - O_1$) gives the effect of the independent variable plus the effects of the extraneous variables. The difference in measurement between the posttreatment and pretreatment of the control group ($O_4 - O_3$) gives the effect of the extraneous variables only (as the control group has not been exposed to the independent variable). The difference between the first and the second isolates the effect of the extraneous variables, producing the effect of the independent variable.

In the factory worker example, management would randomly select two different groups of workers before measurements (output) were taken for both groups for a shift. Suppose the experimental group produces 900 units and the control group produces 910 units (technically, if both groups were identical, their outputs would be the same, but in practice it is impossible to achieve perfectly identical groups). The output of the experimental group is $O_1 = 900$ units and the output of the control group is $O_3 = 910$ units. Now, management would have the experimental group take one extra break (X), and measurements of output of both groups would be taken again. Suppose the experimental group produced 1,000 units (O_2) and the control group produced 925 units (O_4). The true effect of the independent variable would be $= (1000 - 900) - (925 - 910) = 100 - 15 = 85$. The effect of the additional break on worker productivity is 85 units.

This is a reliable design because it imposes controls for most of the extraneous variables. In addition, the difference between the experimental group and the control group is reduced considerably as a result of the random allocation of the test units into the two groups. One problem associated with this design is the effects of testing on the experimental and control groups.

AFTER-ONLY WITH CONTROL GROUP OR POSTTEST WITH CONTROL GROUP DESIGN

In the after-only with control group design, no measurements are taken before the test. Two groups are selected randomly. One of the groups, the experimental group, is exposed to the independent variable, but the second, the control group, is not. Measurements are taken of both the groups after the experimental group has been exposed to the independent variable. The effect of the independent variable is measured by subtracting the measurement of the experimental group from that of the control group.

Symbolically, this design can be expressed as follows:

Experimental group (EG)	**R**	**X**	$\mathbf{O_1}$
Control group (CG)	**R**		$\mathbf{O_2}$

The effect of the independent variable $= O_2 - O_1$.

In the factory worker example, management would randomly select two groups of workers, with one group receiving one additional break (EG). The production output of the experimental group would be measured after the introduction of the break. Suppose their output is 1,000 units (O_1). Now the output of the second group (CG), which was not given the additional break, would be measured, and this output equaled 935 units (O_2). The effect of the one additional break on the factory workers would equal:

$$1000 - 935 \text{ units} = 65 \text{ units.}$$

This design is easy to implement, and because no pretreatment measurements are taken, the researchers avoid effects that arise from the group's awareness that a test is under way. Next to the before-after with control group design, this is the most widely used technique in experimentation. In this design, though, one is not truly able to determine the effect of the independent variable, as the pretreatment measurements are not known.

TIME SERIES DESIGN

This experimental design involves periodic measurements on the dependent variable for a group of test units. Then the independent variable is either introduced by the researcher or occurs naturally. After the introduction of the independent variable, once again periodic measurements are undertaken to determine the effect of the treatment.

In effect, this is not a true experimental design, because the researcher sometimes has no control over the introduction of the independent variable or the measurements. Therefore, these procedures are considered quasi experiments. These techniques are popular with some researchers. These methods are useful when employment of regular experimental designs is not possible or when the researcher is under time and cost pressures.

Symbolically, time series designs are expressed as follows:

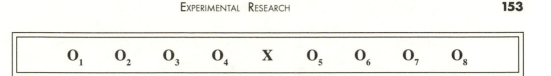

$$O_1 \quad O_2 \quad O_3 \quad O_4 \quad X \quad O_5 \quad O_6 \quad O_7 \quad O_8$$

In this design, there is no randomization of test units to the various treatments. Also, the researcher has no control over which test units receive the treatment or when the treatment is administered. The researcher has less control over the history of the measurements. In addition, the test results may be affected by the interactive testing in undertaking multiple measurements.

RANDOMIZED BLOCK DESIGN

The randomized block design is a statistical design in which test units are blocked on the basis of an external variable to ensure that the various experimental and control groups are closely matched on the given variable.

Though complicated, randomized block designs help researchers to account for those variables that may influence the dependent variable. For example, in our factory worker study, if the additional breaks given had time limits, say 10 minutes, 15 minutes, and 20 minutes, would the productivity of the workers be affected by the time interval of the break? Management strongly feels that the productivity is closely tied to the seniority of the workers (number of years with the company). The seniority is the blocking variable. The selected workers are assigned to three blocks: workers with less than five years' experience form the first block, workers with five to ten years' experience form the second block, and workers with more than ten years' experience form the third block. The workers with different levels of experience (blocks) are now randomly assigned to the three breaks (10 minutes, 15 minutes, and 20 minutes). The results will help management to verify the impact of experience with different time breaks on productivity.

A randomized block design may be set up as follows:

Block Group	Treatment Group		
5 years' experience	10-minute break	15-minute break	20-minute break
5 to 10 years' experience	10-minute break	15-minute break	20-minute break
More than 10 years' experience	10-minute break	15-minute break	20-minute break

In most business situations, many external variables influence the dependent variable. It is important to isolate the effect of these variables. The experimental designs mentioned earlier could not account for the external variable's influence on the dependent variable, including the completely random design. On the other hand, the randomized block design permits the researcher to isolate the influence of external variables.

Even though randomized block designs help control the influence of external variables, they can do so for only one external variable. If the situation requires more than one external variable, the researcher has to resort to another experimental design, such as the factorial design, described below.

Factorial Design

The factorial design is another statistical design used by researchers to measure the effects of two or more independent variables at various levels and to allow for interactions among variables. Unlike randomized block design and the Latin square design (a method to reduce the number of groups involved when interactions of variables between the groups are relatively unimportant), factorial design allows for interaction between variables.[3] Interaction of variables occurs when the simultaneous effect of two or more variables is different from the sum of their separate effects taken one at a time. For example, some consumers may prefer high-performance sports cars and low gas consumption, but it does not follow that these consumers would prefer sports cars that are low in gas consumption, as that combination may be contradictory to their assumptions about a sports car. The interactive nature of variables poses a problem for researchers, and the factorial design alleviates this problem.

Factorial designs have many practical uses that help companies resolve the effects of contradictory or conflicting variables on the consumption of products. Take, for example, the problem faced by Heineken, the Dutch beer marketer. Heineken wants to determine which combination of caloric content and taste levels it should use in its Amstel Light brand. To combine the two variables in a taste test, the company will have to fix the caloric content and experiment with the different taste levels or do the reverse. But this test would not take into account any interaction between the caloric content and the taste level. The best combination may lie somewhere between high-calorie beers, with the best taste, and low-calorie beers, with the worst taste. To determine the interactive effects of variables, researchers use factorial designs.

Table 8.1 presents a factorial design table for the Heineken problem. Each level of calorie content is represented in a row and each level of taste is represented in a column. In factorial designs, there must be a cell for every possible combination of treatment variables. That is, if there are three values for each variable, there must be nine cells, as shown in Table 8.1.

To determine the interactive nature of calorie content and taste, Heineken would have to conduct a taste test among beer drinkers on a rating scale (like versus dislike) and record the average rating for each combination. Then using some form of statistical analysis, such as analysis of variance, the company can determine the effect on preferences of calorie content and taste level, and the interaction between the two.

In most statistical designs, several experiments are conducted simultaneously, and at the same time researchers are able to conduct statistical analyses of external variables. Statistical designs allow the measurement of more than one independent variable, and some extraneous variables can be statistically controlled. Statistical designs are complex and difficult to execute. They also cost substantially more than other experimental designs.

Validity in Experimentation

The two key concerns of researchers in conducting experiments are *internal validity* and *external validity*.

Table 8.1   **Factorial Design**

Taste Level			
Calories	1	2	3
1			
2			
3			

- Internal validity is a measure of the accuracy of an experiment. It is a test of the effect of the independent variable on the dependent variable. Thus, internal validity allows researchers to conclude whether the observed effects on the test units were caused by the treatment variable or by other variables. Internal validity permits researchers to draw conclusions about the effects of the independent variables on the test group.
- External validity refers to the cause-and-effect relationships found in the experiment and whether they can be generalized to a broader group. Can the results be extended to a different test unit, different time frame, other independent and dependent variables, and other experimental situations?

PRECONDITIONS FOR CONDUCTING EXPERIMENTS

The three key conditions to be satisfied for assuming causality are *concomitant variation, time order of occurrence of variables,* and *elimination of other possible causal factors.*

CONCOMITANT VARIATION

Concomitant variation is concerned with the extent to which the independent variable (cause variable X) and the dependent variable (effect variable Y) occur together or diverge in the way they are predicted by the hypotheses. In the example of the factory workers, did the additional break produce a higher output, or did those workers with no additional break have lower output in relation to the ones with the break? In this case, there is the possibility of drawing cause-and-effect relationships between additional breaks and output. However, if the workers with additional breaks produced the same amount as the workers without additional breaks, we would find it difficult if not impossible to show a cause-and-effect relationship between the two variables.

TIME ORDER OF OCCURRENCE OF VARIABLES

Time order of occurrence of variables assumes that the independent variable (cause variable X) occurs before the effect or simultaneously with it but cannot occur after it. This is a simple and obvious requirement. By definition, an effect cannot be produced by a variable (cause) that happens after the effect has taken place.

Absence of Other Possible Causal Factors

Absence of other possible causal factors assumes that the independent variable under consideration is the only one that has the potential of effecting a change. Essentially, this assumes that all other possible variables besides the variable under consideration have been controlled and do not affect the outcome. This condition is one of the reasons we consider some of the experiments described here to be inferior, as they do not isolate other independent variables that may have an effect on the dependent variable.

Problems in Conducting Experiments

Experiments are no doubt the best technique to identify causality. International companies use the results of experiments in a variety of business situations. Identifying problem areas, improving the planning process, and developing strategic action plans are some of the common uses of causal research. But developing experimental designs and executing them are difficult in international markets. In many instances, test units are not willing to participate in experiments, qualified researchers are not available, and infrastructure and computers may be lacking; finally, problems of control are more problematic in international markets. Controlling test subjects, test sites, and test results are more difficult in some foreign markets.

At the micro level, the key problem areas are *time, cost,* and *execution.*

Time

Most experiments tend to be longitudinal; that is, they study test units over time. In international business decision making, time is of the essence. Executives need the results quickly and may not have the luxury to wait for test results. The conflict may lead researchers to take shortcuts or executives to make premature decisions. In either case, the results of the experiments may be compromised.

Cost

Experiments may involve large samples. For example, in a test market situation, a whole market may be subjected to the experimental variable. Sometimes the cost of an experiment is exorbitant and beyond justification. For example, in the case of the factory workers who received additional breaks, management may incur costs due to loss of production while the experiment is being conducted. In the factorial design examples, if Heineken wanted to study three variables instead of two, the number of cells would increase from 9 to 27, requiring a much larger sample.

Execution

Experiments involve large numbers of activities, beginning with the need for specially trained staff. Other activities that play a critical role in experiments include managing the treatment variable, measuring the results, and controlling the extraneous variable. All these tasks can make conducting an experiment administratively difficult.

CHAPTER SUMMARY

Causal research or experimentation helps decision makers to identify cause-and-effect relationships. Isolating those independent variables that have some effect on the outcome of another variable is a powerful finding and can improve strategic actions and help management avoid costly mistakes. Experiments are useful in all functional areas of a business.

In causality, one can draw inferences only about relationships but not about specific causes. In other words, if we find that the dependent variable has been affected by an independent variable, then we claim that the independent variable is one of the causes of the effect on the dependent variable. This does not conclusively prove that it is the only independent variable that is affecting the dependent variable.

In an experiment, the researcher may manipulate one or more independent variables to measure the effects on a single dependent variable, at the same time controlling for other external variables (called extraneous variables). There are many experimental designs available for researchers. From simple to highly sophisticated, each design progressively eliminates many of the common problems and reduces the effects of extraneous variables. But no experimental design totally eliminates the effect of extraneous variables.

Extraneous variables can be categorized by their history, maturation, testing effects, instrumentation, statistical regression, selection bias, and mortality. Each group affects the outcome differently. Researchers try to control the extraneous effects by randomizing testing units or by improving on the design of the experiment.

In designing an experiment, researchers must consider internal and external validity. Internal validity looks at how much of the effects on the dependent variable actually were due to the manipulation of the independent variable. External validity explains to what extent the results of the experiment may be generalized.

In many countries experiments cannot be conducted or may be influenced by many external forces that are not easy to control. Other limitations of experiments in the international area include time consideration, cost factors, and administrative issues.

CHAPTER REVIEW

1. What is causality?
2. Distinguish among independent variable, dependent variable, and extraneous variable.
3. Identify the types of extraneous variables.
4. How do researchers control for the effects of extraneous variables?
5. What is the difference between a post-only experiment and a pre-post design?
6. What are the advantages of using statistical designs over other experimental designs?

7. What is internal validity? How is it different from external validity?
8. What are some of the major problems associated with experiments?
9. What are some of the unique problems faced by international researchers?
10. Suppose you were asked to design an experiment to study the effects of shorter lines at bank branches. What are some of the steps you would undertake?

NOTES

1. Gordon A. Wyner, "Experimental Design," *Marketing Research: A Magazine of Management and Applications* 9, no. 3 (1997), pp. 39–41.

2. Warren F. Kuhfeld, Randall D. Tobia, and Mark Garratt, "Efficient Experimental Design with Marketing Research Applications," *Journal of Marketing Research* 31, no. 4 (1994), pp. 545–557.

3. Stephen J. Brown and L. Melamed, *Experimental Design and Analysis.* Newbury Park, CA: Sage Publications, 1990.

ADDITIONAL READING

BOOKS

Bausell, R. Barker. *Conducting Meaningful Experiments.* Newbury Park, CA: Sage Publications, 1994.

Berger, Paul, and Robert Maurer. *Experimental Design with Applications in Management, Engineering and the Sciences.* Boston: Boston University Press, 2002.

Gould, Grant F., and James L. Gould. *Biostats Basics: A Student Handbook.* New York: W.H. Freeman, 2001.

ARTICLES

Lynch, John G., Jr. (1982) "On the External Validity of Experiments in Consumer Research." *Journal of Consumer Research* (December), pp. 225–244.

Nevin, John R. (1974) "Laboratory Experiments for Estimating Consumer Demand: A Validation Study." *Journal of Marketing Research* (August), pp. 261–268.

Rosenbaum, Paul R. (2002) "Attributing Effects to Treatment in Matched Observational Studies." *Journal of the American Statistical Association* 97 (457), pp. 183–192.

Sengupta, Jaideep, and Gerald J. Gorn (2002) "Absence Makes the Mind Grow Sharper: Effects of Element Omission on Subsequent Recall." *Journal of Marketing Research* 39 (2), pp. 186–201.

Sobel, Michael (2000) "Causal Inference in the Social Sciences." *Journal of the American Statistical Association* 95 (450), pp. 647–651.

9 Questionnaire Design

Questionnaires are instruments used to obtain information from respondents. A well-developed questionnaire must not only elicit reliable and complete information but should also motivate respondents to complete the questionnaire.

LEARNING OBJECTIVES

After reading this chapter, students should be able to

- Recognize the importance of questionnaires in survey research
- Know the purpose of a questionnaire
- Learn the process of developing a questionnaire for international research
- Know the importance of developing questions that encourage responses in multiple-country settings
- Understand the unique problems faced by researchers in developing questionnaires internationally

Surveys are one of the most widely used research techniques. Questionnaires are generally associated with survey research. Surveys are used for generating information for a variety of functional areas, including marketing, finance, human resources, production, and R & D. Though the discussion and examples used in this chapter may be attuned to marketing, they can be applied equally to other functional areas. Surveys are also popular with not-for-profit organizations and government agencies. Government agencies collect information about the general population. For example, the ministry of health may undertake a survey to determine the food habits of the country's population.

A survey is only as good as the questions it asks. Questionnaires used for international research should be sensitive to the local cultural norms and values. Questionnaires used in surveys tend to be more structured than those used in exploratory research techniques. A questionnaire can be structured or unstructured. Structured questionnaires contain a specific set of questions in a predetermined sequence asked of all respondents. This form of data gathering also tends to be direct, as each respondent is contacted separately and individually. Surveys using structured questionnaires tend to be the most widely used technique for collecting detailed and specific information. In contrast, unstructured questionnaires contain open-ended questions that respondents answer in their own words, and the question sequence may depend on subjects' responses. Some questionnaires may contain both structured and unstructured questions. Questions in a questionnaire should be based on the information required by the objectives of the research.

A *questionnaire* is defined as a series of questions on a specific topic, based on specific information needs or research goals, that a respondent answers. Questionnaires are also referred to as instruments or interview forms. The role of a questionnaire is to translate the research objective(s) into specific questions that are asked of respondents. Questionnaires serve as permanent records of the research. Therefore, if more information needs to be extracted in the future, questionnaires may be reviewed or analyzed again.

BASIC REQUIREMENTS OF A QUESTIONNAIRE

In developing a questionnaire, researchers adhere to the following guidelines:

- *Be complete*. Respondents do not volunteer information; therefore, each questionnaire must be complete and include all relevant questions for which answers are sought. It is important that researchers develop questions on the basis of what they want to know. Researchers get only one chance with a given questionnaire to obtain information from a given sample. Therefore, the burden is on the researcher to make sure that all necessary and critical information is addressed in the questionnaire.
- *Motivate*. Questionnaires must motivate and encourage respondents to answer the questions. Given a choice, most respondents would rather not answer a questionnaire. Questionnaires should be developed with the respondents in mind. Through use of simpler language, better appearance, and smooth and logical flow, questionnaires may be developed to foster cooperation and keep respondents motivated throughout the interview. The critical nature of the study may also be used as a way to motivate respondents.
- *Reduce errors*. A goal of questionnaire development should be to reduce the response errors. A common problem with surveys is that they may lead to response errors, that is, errors due to wrong answers given by respondents or errors due to recording responses incorrectly. To assume that people will understand all the questions in a questionnaire is a common mistake by researchers. Respondents may not know what is being asked. They also may not be aware of the issue at hand, or the question may not mean the same thing to everyone interviewed. Developing easy-to-answer questions, asking simple questions, and recording information slowly and legibly may reduce some of these response errors.

Questionnaire Design

Designing a good questionnaire is not easy. Although much progress has been made, designing questionnaires is still considered an art. There are very few theories on the development of a questionnaire. Most of the suggestions or guidelines are derived from past experiences of other researchers. These suggestions are pieced together to form a set of procedures, which are followed by most researchers in developing a questionnaire. Experience and creativity are critical in the development of questionnaires. *Relevancy* and *accuracy* are the two basic criteria to be met in questionnaire design.

Questionnaire development is a process that starts with the research objectives and ends with a final set of questions. The guiding force in the design of a questionnaire is the original research objectives. It is in the translation of these objectives that we often fail to maintain relevancy and accuracy. Figure 9.1 presents a questionnaire development process that is commonly followed by many researchers. Experience indicates that it is rarely possible to develop a questionnaire in a step-by-step fashion. Researchers tend to work back and forth within the process to come up with an adequate questionnaire.

As shown in Figure 9.1, the questionnaire design process is made up of 10 steps. These steps help researchers to focus on the critical aspects in the design of a questionnaire. Questionnaires go through many drafts before they are tested. As questions are constructed, researchers quite often review alternate formats or wordings to design the most appropriate question. Language and cultural differences create difficulties for researchers in developing questionnaires for multicountry surveys. In an effort to maintain comparability among data collected from various countries, researchers pay close attention to the use of terms describing concepts and behavioral measures applicable to a particular country.

Descriptions of Questionnaire Design

Research Objectives and Problem Definition

Research objectives and problem definition were discussed in chapter 2. Questionnaires are developed to answer the questions raised in the problem statement or to meet the needs of research objectives outlined during the early stages of the research. Every research project is undertaken with an expectation of obtaining relevant information that can be used to make decisions. Research objectives provide the researcher with important clues of what management wants to get out of a research study. This in turn provides the necessary direction in developing a questionnaire.

Once the researcher is clear on the information needs, then it is possible to think in terms of questions that need to be asked of the respondents. For example, a commercial bank with a research goal to understand and quantify the demand for a new banking service could develop a set of questions to address the stated objective. In general, the research objectives or problem definition will indicate the specific information to be collected.

Figure 9.1 **Questionnaire Design Process**

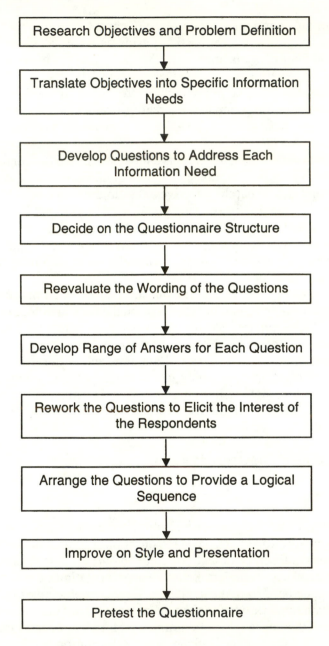

For international firms, the research goals established for multiple countries may have to be adapted to local needs. In essence, researchers will need to be able to tailor research questions, adapt research instruments, and modify questionnaire administration procedures to adjust to the differences among countries.[1] The adaptation of the research objectives to fit each country's requirements may be influenced by cultural, language, or other environmental factors. Therefore, in a country with very low literacy rates, some of the market or product-related objectives have to be adjusted to ensure that the questions reflect the respondents' literacy levels.

Translation of Objectives into Information Needs

Research objectives guide the researcher to the specific information that needs to be gathered from a given sample. Information obtained from the sample should help researchers address stated objectives, problems identified, or hypotheses outlined. The objectives of a research study should lead to a list of information items that need to be collected. The list may include a set of variables that need to be explored. For example, in a marketing study, the researcher may want to know: (a) *who* the customers or clients are, (b) *where* the customers shop for goods, (c) *how* often they shop, and (d) *what* their preferences are. The variable *who* requires the researcher to collect information about the consumer—information such as age, gender, occupation, and so on. Hence, information about a variable that a researcher is seeking may be converted into a set of questions. All the questions collectively become a questionnaire.

Internationally, problems exist in collecting some of the demographic data. For example, data on working women had different time periods—for Brazil it was 10 years, in Mexico it was 12, and in Italy it was 14.[2] Similarly, educational categories may not have equivalency from country to country. For example, in India and the Philippines, a high school diploma requires only 10 years of education; in the United States, students have to complete 12 years for a high school diploma, and in some European countries, the same takes 13 years. Therefore, to obtain accurate educational data, it is better to ask the number of years of schooling rather than requesting the highest degree attained. Generally, comparability in demographic characteristics is much easier to achieve than comparability in behavioral data. For example, motivational variables tend to have a cultural bias and may not have the same significance in two different societies. Individualism in the West is a positive trait, whereas in many Eastern societies that practice collectivism, it is viewed as negative.

In international research, if the researcher expects to use the questionnaire in more than one country, more attention has to be paid to the translation of the variables and the specific questions that will be put to a respondent. There is enough anecdotal evidence to indicate that international research sometimes has failed in part due to translation problems. Even regions that have many common characteristics and are considered uniform are not necessarily comparable in their interpretation of language and cultural artifacts. For example, there are basic differences in the Spanish language spoken among the various Latin American countries. For example, automobile tires are called "*gomas*" in Puerto Rico; "*llantas*" in Mexico, Peru, and a few other countries; and "*cauchos*" in Venezuela. Similarly, though Western Europe is often viewed as a single entity, there are differences in language, religion, habits, and preferences among Europeans. For example, in taking medicine pills the French prefer purple pills whereas the Dutch prefer white ones. In translating questions, sometimes the key words may be translated incorrectly. For example, in a survey of industrial seals, the Italian word used was "beeswax," a totally different term than originally intended.

DEVELOPING QUESTIONS

Information items identified previously form the basis for developing questions. Each and every question developed should have some informational value to the researcher. The effectiveness of a questionnaire is judged by the relevancy of the information obtained. All necessary questions should be included in the questionnaire. At the same time, researchers have to be sensitive to the length of the questionnaire and the time it takes to complete. Questions that have marginal value or those for which answers are available from secondary sources should be avoided. For example, sales revenues of all publicly traded companies are available through many business and trade publications; therefore, in questioning executives of these companies, there is no need to ask for sales figures. Unnecessary questions invariably extend the time of the interview, which may result in respondents losing interest in the study and not answering all the questions. This is especially true in countries where the population is not used to surveys or in those societies where people do not respond to strangers.

The number of questions that need to be asked for each item or variable differs from parameter to parameter. For some items, just one question may be enough to elicit the relevant information; for others, we may have to ask many questions to obtain the information required. For example, in a study of coffee consumption, if the researcher wished to find out whether the respondents drank coffee or not, the researcher has to ask just one question. On the other hand, if the researchers wished to find out *who* drinks coffee, they would need about six or seven questions to develop the profile of the user. Researchers therefore do not normally set a limit on the number of questions to ask, but allow the importance of the information to dictate the number of questions.

Developing a question's precise wording is often difficult. In designing a question, the ultimate goal is to devise a question that will elicit a factual response without injecting any bias (influence). A response bias is a systematic tendency on the part of an individual respondent to bias his or her responses to a questionnaire item(s) on something other than the specific item content. One of the most commonly observed biases in international research is related to social desirability, that is, "the need for social approval, or acceptance, and the belief that the approval or acceptance can be achieved through culturally acceptable and appropriate behaviors."[3] Product purchase patterns and people's behavioral reactions differ from society to society. If the wording of the phrase representing a particular behavior is not clearly stated, it may lead to incorrect or biased responses. Response bias is quite often the result of the phrasing of a question. In international questionnaire development, this problem is compounded. Based on collective experiences of international researchers, the following are some of the dos and don'ts in questionnaire development for international research projects:

Each question should focus on a single topic: respondents should not be confused by a question. Respondents' confusion can be greatly reduced by a focused question.

During the question development stage, it easy to lose sight of the specific topic under study. Use secondary sources to understand the respondent before developing a questionnaire. Do not assume that all respondents are well informed about a given issue or topic. Because of their experience and involvement with the project, researchers may be experts in the topic, but they can not assume that the respondents have a similar understanding of the topic that is being investigated. For example, the question "When you travel, do you fly first class or coach?" may be interpreted differently by different respondents, which may lead to response errors.

The problem with this question is that it does not clarify whether this travel is for business or vacation. Unless it is clearly explained, some respondents will assume this to be business travel and others, vacation travel. A better question in this instance would be "When traveling on business, do you fly first class or coach?" This question may be followed by a second question related to vacation travel.

Questions should be brief: respondents should be able to remember the questions in order to answer them correctly. Respondents may have difficulty comprehending the central idea of a question when the question is too long. Respondents may also lose interest in the survey when asked long questions that require them to concentrate. For example, in a questionnaire of bank customers, one of the questions asked was, "When selecting a bank for checking services, what are the factors that come to mind which will determine the selection of one bank over the other?" A better and more straightforward version of the question would be, "What are the critical factors in selecting a bank for checking services?"

Researchers should eliminate redundant words from questions. Answering questions is not among the top priorities for a respondent. Therefore, they exhibit short attention spans and have even shorter memories when it comes to responding to questionnaires.

Researchers should use simple words; they should assume respondents to be less technical and sophisticated than they are.

Researchers often use words familiar to them based on their experience and knowledge of the subject matter, but respondents may not easily understand these terms. The core vocabulary used in a questionnaire should reflect everyday language. In international studies, if the researcher is not too familiar with the language, he or she may use words that are found in mass media such as newspapers. Related problems in questionnaire wording are that if some but not all respondents understand a word or phrase, it may lead to response errors. Technical terms such as "derivatives," "CAD" (computer-assisted design), "cognitive dissonance," or even "Caucasian" are unfamiliar to many respondents. In a study conducted in France, the word "Caucasian" was interpreted as people from the Caucasus, a region in Northern Europe.

Given a choice between difficult versus simple words, questionnaire designers should use simpler terms. For example, the question "Is the offer of a premium an important consideration for you in selecting a brand?" assumes that all respondents understand the word "premium." A better question to ask would be, "Is the offer of a free gift an important consideration for you in selecting a brand?"

Other potential sources of bias in international research stem from social norms and cultural traits found in a given country. In many Eastern societies, it is not polite

to say no to requests; therefore, in research studies respondents may agree to asser-
tions, irrespective of their actual positions. Similarly, a cultural trait of humility may
dictate that respondents undervalue their incomes and assets, whereas in societies
where boasting is a common trait, respondents may overvalue their incomes and
worldly possessions.

THINGS TO AVOID IN QUESTIONNAIRE DEVELOPMENT

There are many don'ts in developing questions for a questionnaire. In fact, there are
more don'ts than there are dos in constructing a questionnaire. The following points,
which have been identified through years of experience, are generally accepted as
things to avoid in constructing a question.

Avoid Leading Questions

A leading question uses words that influence responses. Leading questions suggest
what the answer should be or indicate the researcher's own point of view. A leading
question assumes the respondent will agree with its basic premise. For example,
consider the following question[4]:

> **Do you feel that limiting taxes by law is an effective way to stop the govern-
> ment from picking your pocket every payday?**
>
> ____ **Yes**
> ____ **No**
> ____ **Undecided**

This questionnaire was sent to a large sample as part of a study sponsored by the
National Tax Limitation Committee of the United States. The results were to be made
available to members of Congress and state legislators. Use of the leading words
"picking your pocket" by the National Tax Limitation Committee, a group interested in limiting taxes, was intentional and may have distorted the results. Further,
it is unlikely that the questionnaire that was used was part of the final report to the
legislators. Similarly, a survey on airbags by an automobile company may contain
the following question:

> **Shouldn't anyone worried about driving a safe automobile expect an air bag
> to come as standard equipment?**
>
> ____ **Yes**
> ____ **No**

This question assumes that respondents concerned with safe driving must favor air
bags as standard equipment, and communicates such expectations. This is a leading
question.[5] The same question could be phrased as follows:

Should automobile manufacturers include air bags as standard equipment?

___ Yes
___ No

Leading questions are a major concern in international research. Because of language and cultural differences, many words or phrases in one language may have different meanings in another language or may be viewed differently in another culture. For example, in Italian and a few other languages, there is no word that is equivalent to the English word "households." The word used in these countries to indicate households is "family" (in Italian, the word is "*famiglia*"), which has a totally different meaning in the United States. Similarly, in Swahili (the language spoken in many East African countries), there is no word for "research"; the closest phrase is "look carefully in order to uncover new news"—not exactly what the researcher originally had in mind.[6]

Avoid Ambiguous Wording

Ambiguous wording results in each respondent using his or her own interpretation of the meaning of the words. The same is true for ambiguous questions. Words such as "often," "occasionally," "usually," "frequently," "good," and "fair" are too general and may have different meanings for different people. This is a major concern for researchers, as cultures differ in their interpretation of "good" and "bad," "small" and "large," "often" and "sometimes," and so forth. For example, for the question, "Do you go to the movies often?" one respondent may interpret "often" to mean once a week and another, once a month. In some societies minute variations are difficult to comprehend. For example, in some East African countries, given a five-point scale (1 = definitely will, 2 = probably will, 3 = might, 4 = probably will not, and 5 = definitely will not), respondents tend to dichotomize the scale and will select either a 1 or a 5. In some cultures it is not polite to comment negatively about people or objects. In these societies, a scalar question with a five-point scale where 1 is extreme like and 5 is extreme dislike, respondents will only select the positive choices, that is, check off one of the first three ratings.

Other cultural and social differences that may cause ambiguity are related to product usage patterns. People's product usage behavior may be influenced by their culture, social status, and economic background. For example, in some Asian countries, purchasing on credit is not a common practice, whereas in the United States, purchasing using credit cards is a commonly accepted behavior. In Europe, use of debit cards is much more common than in the United States. Therefore, in questioning consumers on their payment habits, researchers need to be careful not to provide a list of payment options that is not clear or is ambiguous to respondents from different countries.

If a question is ambiguous or an ambiguous word is used in a question, different respondents may interpret the question itself differently. For example, consider the following question:

Do you usually shop alone?

_____ **Yes**
_____ **No**

The above question is not context specific. Therefore, each respondent may interpret the question differently. Some would assume this to mean grocery shopping for the family or household and may answer yes; some other respondents may assume this to mean shopping for furniture or appliances and may answer no. In countries where shopping is done strictly by gender (shopping for household items is the domain of the female), this may lead to further confusion. This question would be less ambiguous, if it were worded as follows:

When you shop for groceries for the family, do you shop alone?

_____ **Yes**
_____ **No**

Avoid Double-Barreled Questions

A question covering more than one issue at once is referred to as double-barreled. These questions call for two or more responses, creating confusion for the respondents. For example, consider the following question: "What is your evaluation of the fairness and honesty of your supervisor?" This question asks the respondents to react to two separate qualities by which a supervisor could be described. If the supervisor happens to be honest but not fair, respondents may have difficulty in responding to this question. Similarly, consider a question such as:

Do you feel that international firms today are concerned about customers and the environment?

_____ **Yes**
_____ **No**
_____ **No opinion**

This question raises two separate issues but only provides one set of responses. A better question to ask would have been:

Do you feel international firms today are concerned about their customers?

_____ **Yes**
_____ **No**
_____ **No opinion**

A separate question should be asked to obtain respondents' views on the environment.

Avoid Making Assumptions

Questions are sometimes framed so that there is an implied assumption about what will happen as a consequence. Consider the following question:

Should the company continue its successful training program for employees?
____ Yes
____ No

This question contains the implicit assumption that the employees believe the training program was successful. By answering yes, employees imply that the training program is fine. By answering no, they imply that the company should discontinue the training program. Either answer may not be true. The responses from the employees may have been a direct consequence of the implicit assumption in the question. A better set of questions to consider would have been:

In your opinion, was the company's employee training program successful?
____ Yes
____ No

If the answer was yes to the previous question, a possible follow-up question could be:

Should the company continue the training program?
____ Yes
____ No

Avoid Burdensome Questions

Questions about past events or past purchases and questions that require respondents to recall events from the past might be difficult and taxing. In many instances, respondents may forget things and events. Therefore, asking questions about past behavior and events should be avoided at all cost. If the researcher suspects a problem in terms of respondents' memory, it may be worth adding aided-recall questions or providing specific reference points. For example, in a study of factory workers, the following question was asked about quality of incoming parts during assembly:

On an average, how many parts did you reject as you assembled a television set?
____ 1 to 5
____ 6 to 10
____ 11 to 20
____ 21 or more

The above question poses problems for the assembly workers. First of all, they may not remember the number of defective parts. Second, it is not clear whether the question addresses one particular part or all the parts assembled by the workers.

Similarly, in a study of advertising recall, after establishing respondents' favorite program, the following question was asked:

Do you recall any advertisements from your favorite television program?

___ Yes
___ No

If the answer to the previous question was yes, a follow up question was asked:

What brands were advertised?

The above two questions measure unaided recall, and many consumers may not remember any of the advertisements. To assist the respondents, these questions may be rewritten as follows:

Did you watch your favorite television program last week?

___ Yes
___ No

If the answer to the previous question was yes, the following question would be asked:

Do you recall whether there was a brand of shampoo advertised on that program?

___ Yes
___ No

If the answer is yes, the next question could be, "What shampoo brands were advertised on that program?"

Avoid Generalizations and Estimates

Questions should be asked in specific terms rather than generalities. Respondents should not be subjected to mental arithmetic in responding to questions. Questions should be easy enough for the respondent to answer, and if there are any further calculations to be done, they should be done by the researcher. For example, consider the following question asked of a group of stockbrokers:

How many clients did you contact last year? _____

To answer the question, the stockbroker would probably first estimate the number of clients called in a day or week and then multiply by the appropriate number of working days or weeks in a given year to arrive at the answer. A better question in this situation would have been:

How many clients do you contact on average in a given working day? _____

The researcher can do the math to arrive at the total number of clients contacted in a year.

In international research, estimates create many problems, as guesses in various countries may not have an equivalent base. Response estimates vary from country to country. A large sum in one society may not represent the equivalent amount in another country. Therefore, researchers have to be cautious in presenting generalized estimates. Wherever possible, numerical ranges must be provided.

QUESTION STRUCTURE

Three basic structures are used in developing questions: structured-direct (also called close-ended), unstructured (open-ended), and scaled-response questions. A questionnaire may contain just one format, or all three structures may be found in a single questionnaire. Structured-direct questions provide specific answers and are easy to tabulate. Unstructured questions provide the most information and may include details that help the researcher to understand the issues better. Scaled-response questions are useful in understanding respondents' opinions, feelings, attitudes, and the like.

Structured questions prespecify the set of response alternatives and the response format. A structured question may be dichotomous or multiple-choice. Most questions in a structured direct questionnaire are fixed-response questions; that is, there are a limited number of possible responses to each question. For example, a dichotomous question would be:

Did you work overtime last week?

____ **Yes**
____ **No**

A multiple-choice question might be:

How many hours does it take you to complete an industry analysis?

____ **10 hours or less**
____ **11 to 20 hours**
____ **21 hours or more**

A dichotomous question has only two response alternatives, such as "Yes" and "No." In some instances a researcher may supplement the dichotomous response with a neutral option such as "Do not know" or "No opinion." Dichotomous questions are very easy to tabulate and analyze.

When the underlying decision-making process reflects uncertainty or when the response is spread over a wide range of possibilities, it is better to use multiple-choice responses. In multiple-choice questions, the researcher provides a choice of answers, and respondents are asked to select one or more of the alternatives given. The response alternatives in a structured direct question should be collectively exhaustive and mutually exclusive. That is, response choices must include all possible choices (collectively exhaustive) and they should not overlap (mutually exclusive). It is useful to list all alternatives that are important and also to include an alternative: "Other—please specify." This enables the researcher to obtain information on choices that may be important to some respondents or those that are not widely known.

In the examples presented above, there is a finite number of possibilities for the two questions. A close-ended response assumes that a researcher can specify in advance all the possible answers to a particular question. This is difficult in international research, as the researcher may not understand a society's norms and values clearly enough to be able to identify all relevant response categories. In such instances, use of open-ended questions is a good option.

In an open-ended question, no response options are presented to the respondent. The respondent answers the questions in his or her own words. Since open-ended questions do not impose any structures, they may be used to avoid cultural biases. Therefore, questionnaires with open-ended questions may be more appropriate in international research. The response to an open-ended question depends on the topic and the makeup of the respondent. An open-ended question may have as many responses as the number of respondents. For example:

What is your opinion of the common European monetary unit?

or

What should industrialized countries do to eliminate world hunger?

The above questions may elicit many views and opinions from the respondents; if there are 100 respondents, there may be 100 different responses. One problem associated with open-ended questions in international research is the inability of these types of questions to elicit information from respondents who may be less educated or are illiterate. In addition, these open-ended questions assume some sophistication and general knowledge on the part of the respondents, and this may not be universally true.

In situations where literacy levels are suspect, especially in Africa and some Asian countries, use of nonverbal stimuli is a common practice. In nonverbal stimuli questioning, respondents react to pictures or other graphic stimuli. Interviewers first ask questions and then show respondents cards that depict a possible response option.

A third type of question used in a survey is the scaled-response question. A scaled-response question utilizes a scale to measure the attributes of some construct under study. The response options are identified on the questionnaire. For example, a bank interested in comparing its image to the images of its competitors may ask bank customers to answer a set of scaled questions as follows:

	Disagree	Neither Agree nor Disagree	Agree
Bank staff is helpful	☐	☐	☐
Bank offers courteous service	☐	☐	☐
Bank has convenient hours	☐	☐	☐
Bank has convenient locations	☐	☐	☐

In a scaled-response format, scales are identified with some descriptor. Commonly used descriptors in research include agree versus disagree, important versus not important, satisfied versus dissatisfied, and favorable versus unfavorable. By evaluating the degree of agreement and disagreement for each statement presented, researchers are able to ascertain the respondents' views on a given construct such as bank image or other variables under study.

REEVALUATING THE WORDING OF THE QUESTIONS

In developing questions for a questionnaire, the ultimate goal is to devise a way to obtain the respondents' true responses without influencing them. In any given research, the researcher gets only one chance to accomplish the objectives of the survey without any biases. Therefore, the wording of every question is critical.

Question wording is the transference of the desired question into words that respondents can clearly and easily understand. Deciding on question wording is perhaps the most critical and difficult task in developing a questionnaire. In the international context, this issue becomes even more critical. Because research is directed by the parent company and originates from the home country, most questionnaires require some translation. Not knowing or understanding the various nuances within languages and cultures can create difficulties in questionnaire translation. Evidence of errors exists because of poor questionnaire translations. Language is a chronic barrier for many foreign companies seeking information in Japan. For example, a simple "I agree with you" in Japan may actually mean that the respondent understands you, though he or she doesn't endorse your opinion.[7] Similarly, the word for children in Chile is "*guagua*" and in Venezuela it is "*niños*," and both countries have Spanish as their official language.

If a question is worded poorly, respondents may refuse to answer the question (nonresponse) or may answer it incorrectly (response error). Both the nonresponses and the response errors can make analysis of the results difficult. In developing the wording of a question, the researcher must ensure that both the researcher and the respondent will assign the same meaning to each and every question. Otherwise, the results of the study will be seriously biased.

In most research questionnaires, there is always the possibility of poorly worded questions. Take, for example, the following set of questions:

- "Do you think that items in Gucci's stores are very exorbitantly priced?" This question is biased as it overstates the condition of high price.
- "Isn't driving a Ferrari an ultimate driving experience?" This question leads respondents to say yes, or maybe it is beyond the respondent's experience.
- "Should the American government buy Hitachi super computers and hurt local computer industry?" This is a loaded question, as it implies that the purchase of foreign computers necessarily hurts the American industry.

In each question, there are critical terms that focus on the main issues under study. These words or phrases should be carefully developed to avoid previously mentioned problems. In constructing questions, it is suggested that each question be divided into key phrases for evaluation. For example, a commercial bank interested in learning the banking habits of its customers may develop the following questions:

- "In a typical month, how often do you visit your bank?"

The key terms in this question are "visit your bank," "how often," and "in a typical month." In reevaluating the wording of the questions in a questionnaire, a researcher should be totally convinced that each of these terms or phrases reflects exactly what the study objectives are. Are these terms very clear and easy to understand?

- "Do you think the service provided by our bank tellers is to your satisfaction?"

The key terms or phrases in this question are "service provided," "by our bank tellers," and "satisfaction." Here, too, the researcher needs to be totally convinced that each key term is easy to understand and not beyond the scope of the respondent's understanding.

TRANSLATION OF QUESTIONNAIRES INTO OTHER LANGUAGES

As mentioned previously, use of language, use of specific terms, and translation of questionnaires into foreign languages are critical in international business research. Words or terms used should mean the same to both the researcher and the respondent. In international research, the task of the researcher is further complicated by differences in language, cultural nuances, and lack of specific words to describe certain events or situations. In conducting cross-country research studies, researchers pay close attention to how a particular questionnaire is translated into other languages.

The most commonly used translation method in international research is back translation. In back translation, a bilingual individual who is a native speaker of the language into which the questionnaire is being translated, translates a questionnaire from the base language. Another bilingual person, whose native language is the base language, translates the newly translated version back into the original language.[8] For example, a questionnaire constructed in French that is to be translated into Japanese is translated by a French-speaking individual who is well versed in Japanese and back translated by a Japanese-speaking individual who is well versed in French. This enables the questionnaire developers to identify errors. The errors could be corrected by repeated back translations or by using a jury of three or four bilingual experts to correct the errors. Either approach takes time, but it is important that the approach be adopted to avoid costly mistakes. Ricks, Arpan, and Fu report many translation errors committed by multinational companies that have caused both problems and embarrassment for these companies. For example, "body by Fisher" in German was translated as "corpse by Fisher," and "full airplane" was translated as "pregnant airplane" in French.

In translating questionnaires, one has to be aware of the multiple meanings associated with words in some countries. For example, the word "*bola*" in Spanish, when translated in Latin American countries, could mean a ball, a revolution, or a lie (fabrication). Similarly, in German, the word "old-fashioned," used to convey tradition and, therefore, a positive attribute, translates as "outdated," just the opposite of what it is intended to imply. Likewise, the phrase "come alive" translates as "out of the grave" in German. In Arabic, words such as "dummy" and "load," commonly used computer terms, translate as "false pregnancy," creating confusion for respondents and embarrassment for questionnaire developers.[9]

DEVELOPING THE RANGE OF ANSWERS FOR EACH QUESTION

Whether questions are structured, unstructured, or scaled, they are all meant to elicit meaningful responses from a group of respondents. The responses may be a simple yes or no or a detailed description of events. Wherever possible, it is desirable to provide the respondents with choices that make the response process easier and more convenient. The actual response categories vary with the nature of the variable in question, the type of data desired, and the profile of the respondent. However, as a general rule if categories are preassigned, as mentioned earlier, the response choices must be collectively exhaustive and mutually exclusive. That is, all choices taken together should provide for every possible answer a respondent might have (collectively exhaustive), and the choices should not overlap (mutually exclusive). For example, to a question "Do you buy stocks from an independent broker?" the response choices are: "Yes," "No," or "Don't know." Together these choices cover all possible responses, and they are mutually exclusive responses.

For some questions, the range or categories of responses are quite obvious or easy to construct (for example, questions dealing with a respondent's age or consumption pattern). Therefore, one can easily construct response categories that are exhaustive and exclusive. In such instances, researchers first determine the total range of possible answers for the question and then divide the range into as many suitable categories as the data requirements dictate. Therefore, for age of respondents, the range may be from one day old to 125 years. This range may be broken down into six or seven categories. The division into categories is often based on accepted standards. In the case of age ranges, the category breakdown may reflect the demographic breakdown as reported by the local census bureau, or it may reflect some industry practices. That is, in some states in the United States the minimum drinking age is 21; therefore, the age breakdown may be constructed around this threshold. To determine the age of respondents, the question asked may be:

In which of the following categories does your age fall?

____ **Less than 11 years**
____ **11.1 to 18**
____ **18.1 to 30**
____ **30.1 to 45**
____ **45.1 to 65**
____ **Over 65**

The response categories in the above question fulfill both the collectively exhaustive and mutually exclusive rules. However, if the response categories include both the option 11 to 18 and the option 18 to 30, the question would have violated the mutually exclusive rule, as the choice of 18 years appears twice.

For a question on consumption of beer, the range of responses may range from zero to a case or two of beer per day. This range could again be divided into five or six categories. But there may be industry statistics showing the range of beer drinking by light, medium, and heavy drinkers that may be used to develop the ranges. Therefore, for the question on beer consumption, "On the average, how many 12-ounce cans of beer do you drink per week?" the response categories could be structured as follows:

On the average, how many 12-ounce cans of beer do you drink per week?

____ **Do not drink beer**
____ **1 to 3 cans/week**
____ **4 to 6 cans/week**
____ **7 to 12 cans/week**
____ **13 to 18 cans/week**
____ **More than 18 cans/week**

There are no specific rules to follow in determining the optimum number of categories. Past experience and judgment of the researcher is often used to develop categories. In the absence of experience, it is useful to examine past studies similar to the one being contemplated. Another alternative to response categorization is to make use of secondary data. Data on the general public's demographic characteristics are readily available through government sources. Therefore, a researcher could make use of the classification scheme developed in the census to obtain demographic data. For example, if the government classifies household size as 2 or less, 3 to 4, or more than 4 in a questionnaire dealing with household data, the same classification may be used in a questionnaire for business research. In international research, categorization is difficult, as different countries may use different classifications to record the same type of information. For example, in developing countries, data on households are not collected; therefore, government census reports do not contain this information. The U.S. Census Bureau does collect information on the size of the household.

Response categorization is also affected by how the questionnaire is administered (i.e., via mail, by telephone, or by personal contact). In questionnaires administered by mail, using many categories may increase the length of the questionnaire, resulting in higher mailing costs as well as discouraging respondents from filling out the questionnaire. In telephone or personal interviewing, a long list of categories may lead to response errors, as respondents may not recall all the categories after each question is asked. In addition, too many choices may lead to increased interview time and therefore increase the cost of research. The longer interview time may also, in all probability, irritate the respondent. In these situations, it is best to list the most likely responses (a shorter list) along with an "other" category. Another option to avoid the problems of long lists of response categories is to ask an open-ended question. For example, in determining age of respondents, the question could be

What is your age? _____

This will provide the exact age of the respondent and avoid categorization problems. After obtaining the specific information, the researcher then can categorize the data to fit into predetermined groups. A drawback of open-ended questioning is that it is much harder to computer code open-ended responses due to the wide diversity in responses. Also, responses to sensitive questions involving age of individuals, family income, and so on are better obtained through categorization, as respondents can conceal their true age and other demographics by responding to a range.

Developing response categories for questions dealing with respondents' views, opinions, motives, and beliefs is very difficult. For these variables, each respondent may have a unique response. This makes categorization of responses difficult. For such questions, researchers typically do not furnish specific response categories but provide sufficient space for the responses. For example,

What was your reaction to the president's State of the Union address?

This question may draw a simple one-sentence response from one respondent, such as, "I thought it was a great speech" or a lengthy one-page discourse about the merits of each of the major programs suggested by the president from another respondent.

While responses to open-ended questions are difficult to computer code for analysis, they provide rich and useful information on various topics and are very valuable to researchers. In international research, where prior information on categories may be difficult to obtain, open-ended questions may be more appropriate.

REWORKING THE QUESTIONS

After developing the right questions, it is now time to fine-tune them to generate high response rates. Response rate is directly proportional to the interest of the respondents in the topics and the fluidity of the questions asked. Therefore, it is critical that researchers rework the questions with response rates in mind.

Researchers should not assume that respondents are able to provide accurate or reasonable answers to all questions. It is the responsibility of the researcher to overcome a respondent's inability to answer. Certain factors limit the respondent's ability to provide the desired information. Respondents may feel embarrassed to answer some questions, may not be able to articulate certain types of responses, may not have any interest in some topics and therefore may not respond to questions on those topics, may not remember the specific answers to some questions, and finally may genuinely not be well informed enough to respond to some questions.

As mentioned earlier, answering questionnaires is not a top priority for most respondents. Therefore, many respondents are unwilling to devote much time and effort to providing information to strangers, to unknown companies, or on uninteresting issues. It is the responsibility of the researchers to use words and form questions to motivate respondents to answer questionnaires. For example, if a researcher is interested in identifying the supplier characteristics that are important to a purchasing manager, either the researcher could ask the respondent to list those characteristics or he or she could provide a list of key characteristics and ask the purchasing managers to check the applicable ones. The second option would generate a greater response rate, as it requires less effort from the generally busy purchasing managers.

Following are some of the most common areas that create difficulties for respondents in answering questions in survey research.

Embarrassing Questions

A common problem faced by researchers is how to encourage respondents to provide information that they are unwilling to give. Typically, sensitive topics are the hardest to obtain information on. Typical sensitive topics include company revenues, profits earned by small and medium-sized companies, especially if they are privately owned, R & D budgets, taxes paid, marketing expenses, career goals of company employees, and future investment plans.

Because these items are considered sensitive information, company executives may be unwilling to provide answers to such questions about them. Similarly, members of the general public may have difficulty providing information on household income, their age, their weight, and their medical history.

Respondents may be encouraged to provide information on sensitive questions by using some of the following techniques:

- Preface the question with a statement that the information or behavior of interest is common for that group. A question could be prefaced with "Recent studies show that," "Government reports suggest," or "According to your neighbors."
- Provide response categories rather than asking for specific figures. Do not ask, "What is your personal annual income?" Instead, ask the respondent to check one of the income categories provided in the question.
- Place sensitive questions or topics at the end of the questionnaire. If the sensitive questions are placed toward the end of the questionnaire, by then respondents' initial mistrust has been overcome and better rapport may have been built. This may induce respondents to be freer with their responses.

Articulation Problems

In some instances, respondents may be unable to articulate their responses. Asking about ethical practices of employees or asking bank patrons to describe the atmosphere of their branch may pose problems for respondents. If respondents are unable to articulate their responses to a question, they are likely to ignore that question and refuse to respond to the rest of the questionnaire. In such situations, it is useful to assist the respondents in phrasing their responses without leading them. In addressing abstract topics or difficult issues, respondents may be provided with alternative descriptions. Internationally, design of instruments that employ visual as well as verbal stimuli and occur in a familiar and realistic setting rather than requiring abstract cognitive skills will be more effective.[10] These are very practical in international research, as respondents in many developing countries may not have the same level of general or technical knowledge that is found among respondents in more developed countries.

Respondents' Memory Problems

It is not uncommon for people to forget things. The inability of respondents to remember leads to errors of *omission, telescoping,* and *creation.* Omission is the inability to recall events. Telescoping is remembering an event as occurring more recently than it actually occurred. Creation is recalling an event that did not actually occur. All three conditions lead to response errors.

People tend to remember events that are important, that occur frequently, or that are unusual. Factory workers will recall the specifications of items they assemble, bank managers will recall interest rates of the previous week or month, and individuals will remember their birthdays. Other events that are less important may not be recalled that easily. Once again, providing aids or cues is one way to minimize respondents' memory problems. For example, if respondents are asked to recall the advertisements they may have seen for an automobile brand during the past week, many might not recall the specific name of the automobile at all. However, if the question is reworded as "Which of the following brands of automobiles were advertised last week?" respondents may recall some of the automobile advertisements. The aided-recall approach attempts to stimulate the respondents' memory by providing cues related to the issues of interest to the researcher.

Context and Legitimacy Issues

Respondents may view some questions in a questionnaire as inappropriate, or they may doubt the real purpose of the questions and therefore refuse to answer them. For example, questions about the following topics may create doubts in the minds of respondents, which may lead to their refusal to answer questions:

- Number of employees in a company
- Fringe benefits offered to employees
- Markets served by a company

Questions about the above topics may be appropriate when asked by a government agency such as the U.S. Department of Commerce but not in a study sponsored by a competitor or other individuals. Similarly, respondents may be unwilling to provide information if they are not sure of the purpose of the research. For example, if a research study asks questions about personal hygiene or tax-related topics and the study sponsor is not revealed, respondents may be suspicious of the purpose of the study and not respond to such questions. Even in legitimate studies such as one on consumer preferences of cosmetic items, respondents may question why the firm wants to know their age, income, and occupation.

To avoid the above-mentioned problems, it is always good to explain up front why the information is needed to assure the respondents of the legitimacy of the study. The purpose of the study should be conveyed early on so as not to plant doubts in the minds of respondents about the legitimacy of the study.

ARRANGING THE QUESTIONS

The order or sequence of questions provides a logical flow that may result in improved response rates. Questionnaires must be organized to move the respondent smoothly from one question to the next. Simple questions should be placed early in the questionnaire, and complicated or difficult-to-answer questions should be placed deep in the body of the questionnaire. Demographic and classification questions are normally placed at the end of the questionnaire. Following is a general outline of a questionnaire.

Lead Questions

Also called the opening questions, lead questions should be simple, interesting, easy to answer, and nonthreatening. Asking easy-to-answer questions allows respondents to build confidence and helps them slowly get involved in the questionnaire process. If respondents' curiosity is not aroused at the beginning, they can lose interest in the research and refuse to answer further questions. Quite often, a broad question is asked in the beginning that captures a vast respondent pool. For example, for a study of beer consumption patterns, the following lead question may be asked to gather in as many respondents as possible into the survey:

> **Which of the following beverages have you consumed in the previous month?**
>
> ____ **Sodas**
> ____ **Coffee**
> ____ **Tea**
> ____ **Juices**
> ____ **Beer**
> ____ **Others (please specify)**

In some instances, the first few questions could be screening questions that will determine whether or not the potential respondent qualifies to participate in the study based on certain selection criteria that the researcher has deemed essential. For example, in a study of stock purchases by consumers, a good lead question would be, "Have you purchased any stock in the past month?" If they have not purchased any stock, the interviewer may be instructed to terminate the interview or obtain just the demographic information.

Questions that ask respondents for their opinions can also be good lead questions. Most people like to express their opinions and views. For example, asking consumers, "What do you think of the recent rise in the Dow Jones Industrial Average?" could make the respondents feel very important and arouse their interest in the study.

Warm-up Questions

Lead questions may be followed by warm-up questions. Warm-up questions are general in content and easy to answer. These questions help to elevate the interest of the respondents. For example, in the earlier stock purchase question, the researcher could ask, "How often do you read up on news about stocks?" This serves as an excellent warm-up question.

Transition Questions

Transition questions address some of the peripheral or secondary objectives of the study. They seek definite content or information and serve to move the respondent into the main body of the questionnaire. These questions are more detailed and can be used to develop the "skip patterns" (i.e., questions that try to capture all possible scenarios). For example,

"Did you speak to your stock broker this week?"

____ **Yes (If yes, go to next question.)**
____ **No (If no, skip to question #___.)**

Main Body of the Questionnaire

The body of the questionnaire contains the most critical questions; it also normally contains the bulk of the questions. These questions address the main objectives of the study. They tend to be very detailed, complicated, and often difficult to answer. Researchers constantly have to go back to the original objectives of the study to ensure that all the important issues are translated into questions in the main body of the questionnaire. Scaled-response questions and other multiple-response questions are quite often found in this section. Questions that seek respondents' opinions and preferences, "what if" questions, and similar types of questions are found in the body of the questionnaire. An example of this type of question is, "Rate each of the following criteria in selecting a stock broker on a five-point scale, where 1 = very important and 5 = least important."

The main questions are placed in the body of the questionnaire for two important reasons. First, by this time the respondent is in a decisively answering mode (i.e., into the heart of the questionnaire and caught up with the topic), and second, it conveys to the respondent that the interview is in its last stages.

Classification Questions

It is common practice for most questionnaires to end with classification or demographic questions. Because demographic questions and company classification data tend to be sensitive, they are placed at the end to keep respondents from breaking off the survey.

Questions dealing with educational levels or personal incomes may be embarrassing to some. Respondents may be ashamed to tell strangers that they did not finish high school or that they earn the minimum wage, and therefore they would refuse to answer these questions, but the refusal comes at the very end of the questionnaire process. If it had occurred at the beginning of the questionnaire, the respondent might refuse to answer the rest of the questionnaire.

The sequence described here is referred to as the funnel approach, or inverted cone approach. That is, the questionnaire starts off with the most general questions leading to very specific ones.

An outcome of the sequencing of questions is called *order bias*. Order bias is caused by the influence of earlier questions in a questionnaire or by the position of a choice in a set of choices, for example, the respondents' selection of the first choice in an array of choices. Quite often, a specific question may influence a more general question. If a question about the use of a specific beer brand is asked prior to the questions concerning the criteria for selecting the beer brand, respondents may not provide a consistent response. For example, consider the following questions:

What is your favorite brand of beer? _____

From the following attributes of beer, select the most important attribute of your favorite brand of beer (check as many attributes as apply).

____   **Taste**
____   **Flavor**
____   **Price**
____   **Color**
____   **Calories**

What are the most important attributes you look for in the beer you buy?
_____

In this case, the first two questions are very specific (related to a brand), and the last question is general (product related). It is possible that respondents who state that they drink a beer that is low in calories may also state that calories are not as important an attribute as they really believe it is, to avoid being inconsistent.

STYLE AND PRESENTATION

The layout and the physical attractiveness of the questionnaire are of crucial importance in most survey research. Similarly, the format, spacing, and positioning of questions can have a significant effect on the results. Whether the questionnaire is self-administered, completed by telephone, or conducted through personal interview, the style and presentation make a difference in terms of response rates. A better laid-out questionnaire tends to improve response rates. If the survey is conducted by mail, the layout may reflect high professionalism and encourage greater response. In the case of telephone or personal interviews, a well-organized questionnaire may reduce interviewer errors.

Following are important considerations in the layout of a questionnaire:

- The questionnaire should not be overcrowded.
- Divide the questionnaire into several parts.
- Label each part to help respondents in understanding the type of the questions that follow.
- Adequate margins improve the appearance of the questionnaire.
- The questionnaire should be numbered sequentially.
- Questions in each part should be sequentially numbered.
- Colors should be used to separate items of importance or questions from responses.
- Avoid confusing matrices.

Questionnaires should be designed to appear as brief and small as possible. Questionnaire length can affect survey rates significantly, particularly when the importance of the research is great and the questionnaire is too long.[11] If the questionnaire is long, it is advisable to use a booklet form rather than a large number of pages stapled together. It is possible to develop simple matrices to accommodate multiple questions. For example, in a survey of office personnel regarding preferences for morning and afternoon breaks, the following question was asked:

Given the choice, would you rather have two 15-minute breaks, one 30-minute break, or no break but leave early by 30 minutes at the end of the workday?

	Yes	No	Not Sure
Two 15-minute breaks?	____	____	____
One 30-minute break?	____	____	____
No break at all, but leave 30 minutes early?	____	____	____

Researchers have also found that inserting appropriate titles to emphasize the importance of the research induces a higher response rate. For example, adding "A Worldwide Study of Financial Analysts" or "Survey of Top Business School Deans" is a useful technique to underline the importance of the research. Equally useful labels are "Confidential," "Highly Technical Study," and "Only for Statistical Purposes" (when requesting demographic data).

Layout is especially important when questionnaires are long or require the respondent to fill in a large amount of information. Questionnaires should be presented in an eye-pleasing manner to which respondents can reply easily and with minimal confusion.

PRETESTING THE QUESTIONNAIRE

Very rarely can a researcher fulfill all the requirements of a questionnaire in just one attempt. It is assumed that many initial drafts will be produced and modified based on the researcher's judgment. Even after a researcher's self-evaluation of the questionnaire, it may have some problems or errors. A pretest allows the researcher to try out the questionnaire with an external group to isolate problem areas. Pretests involve administering a questionnaire to a limited number of potential respondents to identify inherent problems and point out design flaws. Pretests, if conducted scientifically, should identify ambiguity in questions, problems of redundancy, question-sequencing issues, use of incorrect or difficult words, unanswerable questions, problems in skip patterns, and an estimate of the time it takes to complete a questionnaire. In international research, where the chances of making errors are greater, pretesting is of utmost importance.

Pretests are sometimes improperly conducted or misused. Pretests are not a substitute for the careful thought and attention given to the preparation and design of a questionnaire. If pretests are used in lieu of careful preparation, there could be serious flaws in the questionnaire, as respondents alone may not be able to point out all the problems. It is incorrect to assume that respondents will be able to uncover all the potential limitations of a questionnaire. Pretests must be viewed as a tool for shedding light on specific features or issues in a questionnaire that the researcher is particularly concerned about. For example, a pretest may identify problems in response choices (Are the response choices mutually exclusive? Is the sequencing of questions logical? Are there words that may be misconstrued or have more than one meaning in different countries?).

Even though pretests are conducted with a smaller sample, they should be tabulated and analyzed. Tabulating the results of a pretest helps determine whether the questionnaire addresses the key issues of the research. Results from the pretest may confirm the direction of the research or point out insufficiencies in the questions selected.

CHAPTER SUMMARY

A questionnaire is a collection of questions that draw out the desired information from a sample. Good questionnaire design is a key to obtaining the right information. In designing a questionnaire, a researcher has to make sure that it is easy to administer, clear, and easily understood by a majority of the population. Questionnaire design is a complex undertaking requiring the researcher to follow some basic rules. Accuracy and relevancy are the two basic criteria to be met in developing a questionnaire. Question wording is the most critical determinant of data accuracy. Researchers normally follow a 10-step procedure in designing a questionnaire. The process starts with the objectives of the research, followed by identification of information needs, question content, question structure, phrasing of the questions, developing response categories, question sequencing, layout of the questionnaire, style and presentation of the questionnaire, and pretest.

Questions can be open-ended, soliciting a broad set of responses from the respondents. These are difficult to tabulate. Standardized response questions are easier for respondents to answer and easier for the researcher to code. Fixed-alternative questions are easier to administer as well as to answer.

In designing questions, a researcher should follow some basic guidelines, such as using simple language in anticipation of a wide variation in the education levels of respondents, avoiding ambiguity in questions, avoiding long questions, avoiding double-barreled questions, and avoiding leading questions.

In international research, it is important that question wording be precise and translated correctly. There is a higher likelihood of response bias in international research than in domestic or single-country research. Low levels of literacy, unique cultural traits (e.g., tendency to be polite in some cultures), lack of technical knowledge or sophistication, and a general mistrust of strangers all lead to low response rates or response biases in cross-cultural research. In some cases, use of nonverbal stimuli can aid researchers in obtaining information in international research.

CHAPTER REVIEW

1. What is a questionnaire?
2. What are some of the requirements of a questionnaire?
3. Enumerate the questionnaire design process.
4. Which of the steps in the questionnaire design are the most critical?
5. What is a questionnaire structure? Distinguish between structured versus open-ended questions.
6. Identify some of the inherent biases in questionnaire design.
7. Why is it important to pretest a questionnaire?
8. What is a leading question? How would a researcher avoid leading questions?
9. What is a nonverbal stimulus or cue? Why do researchers use nonverbal stimuli?
10. What are some of the difficulties in developing international questionnaires?
11. Explain the procedure followed to reduce translation errors.
12. Evaluate and comment on the following questions:
    a. Should the company continue its generous life insurance program?

        ____ Yes
        ____ No

b. After the disastrous currency problems faced by many of the Asian countries, would the stock market in these countries rebound during the next year?

____   Yes

____   No

____   Do not know

c. Do you use a credit card or a debit card?

____   Credit card

____   Debit card

d. What is your age?   ____

e. What is your educational level?

____   High school

____   College

13. Translate the following questions into a language other than English.

a. When was the last time you cleaned your oven?

____   Within the last month

____   More than one month to two months ago

____   More than two months to three months ago

____   More than three months to six months ago

____   Seven months ago or more

b. Which phrase listed below describes the condition of your oven at the present time?

____   Not at all dirty

____   Slightly dirty

____   Moderately dirty

____   Very dirty

14. Cross-translate the questions listed in question 13 back to English and compare them to the original questions. Are you satisfied with the original translation?

____   Yes

____   No

If not, try to correct the questions to make the translated questions as accurate as possible.

APPENDIX 9.1. SAMPLE QUESTIONNAIRE   1-3

Detergent Questionnaire

Hello, my name is _____ from the Institute of Research Inc., an independent market research firm. We are conducting a survey of household cleansing products in your area and would like to include your views. This survey will take about 15 minutes.

PART 1

1. Are you the one who decides on the brand of detergents to be purchased in your home?

    ____ Yes   **5-1**
    ____ No   **5-2**

(If no, ask to speak to the person most responsible for making decisions on household items. If no one is available, thank the respondent and terminate the interview.)

2. Who does the washing of clothes in your home?

    ____ Self   **6-1**
    ____ Spouse   **6-2**
    ____ Others—Children (specify):   **6-3**
                                                          6-4

3. How often do you wash clothes in your home?

    ____ Every day   **7-1**
    ____ Two to three times a week   **7-2**
    ____ Once a week   **7-3**
    ____ Once in two weeks   **7-4**
    ____ Other (specify):   **7-5**

4a. Do you own a washing machine?

    ____ Yes   **8-1**
    ____ No   **8-2**

4b. If you do not own a washing machine, how do you do your laundry?

    ____ Laundromat   **9-1**
    ____ Laundry services   **9-2**
    ____ Washboard   **9-3**
    ____ Other (specify):   **9-4**

5. Do you use detergents to wash your clothes?

    ____ Yes   **10-1**
    ____ No (Go to Question 10)   **10-2**

6. What brand of detergent do you most often buy?

    ____ Ariel   **11-1**
    ____ Persil   **11-2**
    ____ Omo   **11-3**
    ____ Dash/Duz   **11-4**
    ____ Other (specify):   **11-5**

7a. Besides the brand mentioned above, do you buy any other brands?

    ___ Yes   **12-1**
    ___ No   **12-2**

7b. If yes, what are the names of the other brands you use?

    ___ Ariel   **13-1**
    ___ Persil   **13-2**
    ___ Omo   **13-3**
    ___ Dash/Duz   **13-4**
    ___ Skip   **13-5**

8. What is the size (in weight) of the detergent box/container you usually buy?

    ___ 500 g   **14-1**
    ___ 750 g   **14-2**
    ___ 1 kg   **14-3**
    ___ 2 kg   **14-4**

9. Besides using a detergent, do you also use any other cleaning agents to wash your clothes?

    ___ Bleach   **15-1**
    ___ Fabric softeners   **15-2**
    ___ Other (specify):   **15-3**
    _____   **15-4**

10. If you do not use detergents, what other product(s) do you use to wash clothes?

    ___ Soap   **16-1**
    ___ Home products   **16-2**

Part 2

Following are some statements that pertain to washing clothes. For each statement indicate whether you fully agree with the statement or fully disagree with the statement.

	Statements	Fully Agree	Agree	Neutral	Disagree	Fully Disagree	
1	Existing detergents/products that are available for washing clothes are reasonably good.	1	2	3	4	5	**17-1,2,3,4,5**
2	The brand of detergent I buy should have a bleaching agent in it.	1	2	3	4	5	**18-1,2,3,4,5**
3	Most detergents in the market are environmentally unsafe.	1	2	3	4	5	**19-1,2,3,4,5**

Statements	Fully Agree	Agree	Neutral	Disagree	Fully Disagree	
4 Existing brands of detergents come in convenient packages.	1	2	3	4	5	20-1,2,3,4,5
5 I wish the detergents in the market were not caustic.	1	2	3	4	5	21-1,2,3,4,5
6 I would like to see a more concentrated brand of detergent in the market.	1	2	3	4	5	22-1,2,3,4,5
7 Current detergent brands in the market are undistinguishable.	1	2	3	4	5	23-1,2,3,4,5
8 Price is critical in my selection of a detergent brand.	1	2	3	4	5	24-1,2,3,4,5
9 I rely on information provided by friends and relatives in selecting a detergent brand.	1	2	3	4	5	25-1,2,3,4,5
10 It is really messy to measure and get the required amount of detergent for each load from the existing packages.	1	2	3	4	5	26-1,2,3,4,5

PART 3

Scientists of a detergent company have developed a highly concentrated detergent powder that has the following benefits when compared to existing brands of detergents:

a. It requires only 1 tablespoon of detergent per normal wash load.
b. It is less caustic.
c. The package has a dispenser that automatically dispenses the necessary amount of detergent.
d. The package size for a normal 40-load wash weighs only 1 kilogram.

12. If a brand such as the one described above were now available, would you be interested in buying such a product?

　___ Yes 　　　　　　　　　　　　　　　　　　　　　　27-1
　___ No 　　　　　　　　　　　　　　　　　　　　　　27-2
　___ Do not know 　　　　　　　　　　　　　　　　　　27-3

(If the answer to Question 12 is "No" or "Do not know," go to Question 19.)

13. Setting aside the question of price for the moment, which of the following statements best describes how interested you would be in this new product? Would you:

　___ Definitely be interested in it 　　　　　　　　　　28-1
　___ Probably be interested in it 　　　　　　　　　　28-2
　___ Possibly be interested in it 　　　　　　　　　　28-3

14. Assuming that you will buy the new detergent and that the volume you buy will give you the same number of loads as your current brand, would you buy it if it were priced at 8.00 euros?

    ___ Yes   **29-1**
    ___ No   **29-2**
    ___ Do not know   **29-3**

15. Supposing the new detergent was priced at 7.00 euros, would you buy it?

    ___ Yes   **30-1**
    ___ No   **30-2**
    ___ Do not know   **30-3**

16. Supposing the new detergent was priced at 9.00 euros, would you buy it?

    ___ Yes   **31-1**
    ___ No   **31-2**
    ___ Do not know   **31-3**

17. Now supposing the new detergent was priced at 12.00 euros, would you buy it?

    ___ Yes   **32-1**
    ___ No   **32-2**
    ___ Do not know   **32-3**

18. Supposing the new detergent product was available in stores today, please tell me which statement best describes how soon you would most likely buy the product. Would you buy it

    ___ Within the next few days   **33-1**
    ___ Within the next few weeks   **33-2**
    ___ Within the next few months   **33-3**
    ___ Not in the foreseeable future   **33-4**

PART 4

Finally, I would like to ask a few questions that are used for classification purposes only. No one will see your individual responses.

19. What is your marital status?
    ___ Married   **34-1**
    ___ Single   **34-2**

20. Including you, how many people live in your house?
    ___ 2   **35-1**
    ___ 3–4   **35-2**
    ___ 5 or more   **35-3**

21. What is your occupation?

   ____ Homemaker   **36-1**
   ____ Office worker   **36-2**
   ____ Factory worker   **36-3**
   ____ Professional   **36-4**

22. Please tell me which category best describes your age.

   ____ 21–35   **37-1**
   ____ 36–50   **37-2**
   ____ 51–65   **37-3**
   ____ 66 or older   **37-4**

23. How many years of formal schooling do you have?

   ____ Less than 13 years   **38-1**
   ____ 13 years   **38-2**
   ____ More than 13 years   **38-3**

24. Finally, which of the following groups best describes your total family income?

   ____ Under 20,000 euros   **39-1**
   ____ 20,001–35,000   **39-2**
   ____ 35,001–50,000 euros   **39-3**
   ____ 50,001–75,000 euros   **39-4**
   ____ Over 75,001 euros   **39-5**

Thank you very much for your time.

NOTES

1. Susan Douglas and C. Samuel Craig, "The Changing Dynamic of Consumer Behavior: Implications for Cross-Cultural Research," *International Journal of Research in Marketing* 14 (1997), pp. 391–395.

2. Rena Bartos, "International Demographics Data? Incomparable!" *Marketing Research Today* (November 1989), pp. 205–211.

3. Bruce Keillor, Deborah Owens, and Charles Pettijohn, "A Cross-Cultural/Cross-National Study of Influencing Factors and Socially Desirable Biases," *International Journal of Market Research* 43, no. 1 (2002), pp. 63–84.

4. Gilbert A. Churchill Jr., *Marketing Research Methodological Foundation.* New York: Dryden Press, 1995, p. 425.

5. Alvin C. Burns and Ronald F. Bush, *Marketing Research.* Upper Saddle River, NJ: Prentice-Hall, 1995, p. 300.

6. Gerald E. Fryxell, "Inside Story: Inside East Africa, Outside the Research Culture," *Organizational Studies* 13, no. 1 (1992), pp. 111–117.

7. Lee H. Murphy, "Japanese Keeping Fewer Secrets From U.S. Firms," *Marketing News* (June 21, 1999), p. 6.

8. Richard Brislin, "Back-Translation for Cross-cultural Research," *Journal of Cross-Cultural Psychology* 1 (1970), pp. 185–216.

9. David Ricks, J.S. Arpan, and M.Y.C. Fu, *International Business Blunders.* Columbus, OH: Grid, 1974.

10. Susan Douglas and C. Samuel Craig, "Implications for International Marketing Research in the Twenty-first Century," *International Marketing Review* 18, no. 1 (2001), pp. 80–90.

11. Andrew G. Bean and Michael J. Roszkowski, "The Long and Short of It: When Does Questionnaire Length Affect Response Rate," *Marketing Research: A Magazine of Management & Applications* 7, no. 1 (1995), pp. 20–26.

10 | Scale Measurements

Scale measurements provide quantitative responses to respondents' characteristics or items of interest to a researcher.

LEARNING OBJECTIVES

After reading this chapter, students should be able to

- Understand the concept of measurement
- Understand scale characteristics
- Understand the primary scales of measurement
- Classify and discuss scaling techniques
- Develop scaled-response questions
- Measure behavioral intentions
- Understand the unique characteristics of scale measurements in international research
- Understand reliability measures in scales
- Understand the issues involved in the decision to select a scale

Measurement of variables is an important aspect of international research. Researchers are interested in measuring people's attitudes, the importance they place on certain attributes of products, their behavior patterns, and their views on various issues.

Measurement is defined as "assignment of numbers to observations according to some set of rules."[1] It determines how much of a particular characteristic is possessed by an individual. By quantifying characteristics, researchers can summarize responses more efficiently. In addition, quantified responses permit researchers to analyze the data using a variety of quantitative techniques. Data analyzed through quantitative techniques provide the researcher with useful insights on issues of interest that otherwise may go undetected.

Respondents have objective and subjective characteristics. Objective variables include age of respondent, volume of output of a manufacturing plant, and interest rate charged by a bank. Objective characteristics are physically verifiable and easy to measure. In contrast, subjective characteristics such as respondents' attitudes, behavior patterns, or feelings cannot be easily observed or quantified. Hence, subjective characteristics are difficult to measure. A researcher has to measure both objective and subjective characteristics.

For subjective characteristics, researchers ask respondents to convert their views, feelings, opinions, and other subjective properties onto a continuum of intensity otherwise called a *scale*. Developing a scale is a complex undertaking. It requires the researcher to design questions with possible responses that measure the amount of intensity of the characteristic under study. Typically researchers develop a number of statements reflecting the issue under study, and then have these statements rated on a predetermined scale.

CHARACTERISTICS OF SCALES

There are many varieties of scales. Each scale has its own characteristics. The four main characteristics of a scale are

1. Description
2. Order
3. Distance
4. Origin

Description refers to the label assigned to each response or designation in a scale. The descriptor could be a simple "yes" or "no" or a specific item such as a company's sales revenue. A descriptor could also be more complex, for instance, the level of agreement versus disagreement on a continuum.

Order reflects the relative size of the descriptor. The size of the descriptor may be identified with such terms as "major customer" versus "minor customer," "more important" versus "less important," or "large company" versus "small company." Here the defining term is "relative," as no one can be sure of the fine distinctions between one descriptor size and another. That is, when one identifies a large company in terms of sales revenue, it may be twice the sales of the small company or it may be ten times the sales of the small company.

When differences between descriptors are known and can be expressed in units, the difference is termed the *distance*. Therefore a company with sales of 10,000 units per month has twice (distance) the sales of another company with sales of 5,000 units per month. Distance characteristics also inform us about the order of the scale. That is, the company with sales of 10,000 units is bigger than the company with 5,000 units of sales.

When a scale has a unique beginning such as a zero, it is said to have the characteristic of an *origin*. Therefore, in the previous example of monthly sales, it is very clear that the starting point (or origin) is zero. It is not always possible to establish the origin in scales. In cases where true origin is not established, researchers have arbitrary starting points. For example, for a response of "Neutral" to a question that asks "Do you agree or disagree with the current International Monetary Fund policy on stabilizing troubled Asian economies?" there is no true starting point.

TYPES OF SCALES

The number system we use has certain properties that we normally take for granted. But these properties have great significance when setting up measurement scales. Following are some of the properties of the number system:

- The number system has a unique starting point (i.e., zero).
- The number system follows a rank order (i.e., 2 is greater than 1; or 4 is less than 8).
- The *intervals* between pairs of numbers can be compared (i.e., the interval between 4 and 2 is the same as that between 8 and 6).
- We can divide one number by another and interpret the resulting ratios (i.e., 4 is twice as large as 2, or 4 is half of 8).

In surveys, quantifying responses as if they were numbers is sometimes inappropriate. That is why researchers measure responses to determine under which categories these responses fall. There are four categories of quantified responses: nominal, ordinal, interval, and ratio scales.

NOMINAL SCALE

Nominal scales serve as labels and are used mainly to identify and categorize respondents or responses. Each number is assigned to only one person or response. In many countries, people are given identification numbers at birth that are then used in all official correspondence and transactions. The social security number, used in the United States, is one example of a nominal scale. Student identification numbers assigned to students taking national exams in some countries are another example. When a nominal scale is used for identification, there is a one-to-one correspondence between the number and the person.

Nominal scales may also be used to identify responses. For example:

What is your favorite brand of beer?

1. **Heineken**
2. **San Miguel**
3. **Kirin**
4. **Corona**
5. **Budweiser**
6. **Other (specify):** _____

In this case the numbers accompanying the response categories identify that particular brand. In the above responses, the number 3 refers to the Kirin brand. Note that the nominal scale used in this context has none of the properties of a number system mentioned earlier. In other words, we could have used any set of numbers to identify the beer brands (25 for Heineken, 35 for San Miguel, and so on).

The numbers in a nominal scale do not reflect any rank order or the amount of a characteristic possessed by a person or an object. In the previous example, a high number (5, Budweiser beer) does not imply that this brand is in some way superior to a lower number (1, Heineken beer). Nominal scales are useful in tabulating results. They can be used to count the number of responses per category and also to perform simple statistical analysis such as percentages, modes, chi-squares, and binomial tests.

ORDINAL SCALE

An ordinal scale is a more powerful scale than a nominal scale. More information can be derived from this scale. The numbers assigned in an ordinal scale indicate the relative extent to which the objects possess a specific characteristic. It shows whether one object has more or less of a characteristic than another object. However, an ordinal scale is not able to show how much more or less of a characteristic one object has. Consider the following example:

How many hours of overtime do you work in an average week?

(Suggested value)

____	**One hour or less**	1
____	**One to two hours**	2
____	**Two to three hours**	3
____	**Three to four hours**	4
____	**More than four hours**	5

The values 1, 2, 3, 4, and 5 assigned to the response categories serve first as a nominal scale, and, second, they serve as an indication of the number of hours of overtime an employee works in an average week. Therefore, a worker checking choice 3 puts in more overtime per week than a worker selecting choice 2. But, if a third worker also checks choice 2, we are not able to distinguish whether the second or the third worker is the one putting in more overtime. Since the exact overtime cannot be discerned from the values, intervals between them cannot be interpreted. Thus, an ordinal scale indicates relative position, but not the magnitude of the difference between the two values.

In an ordinal scale, equivalent objects receive the same rank. Therefore, we can assign any values in an ascending order to form an ordinal scale. As long as the values preserve the order relationship between objects, any values may be assigned. For the above example, a researcher could have easily assigned the numbers 2, 5, 7, 9, and 10 instead of the numbers 1, 2, 3, 4, and 5. In addition to the counting operation performed in a nominal scale, the ordinal scale can measure the mode, median, percentile, and quartile of the responses as well as perform other statistical analyses such as rank-order correlation.

INTERVAL SCALE

An interval scale contains all the properties of an ordinal scale, and, in addition, allows the researcher to compare the differences between objects. The values in an interval scale tell us how far apart the objects are with respect to a specific characteristic. The difference between the scale values 1 and 2 is the same as the difference between the scale values 2 and 3. Furthermore, the difference between the scale values 2 and 4 is twice the difference of that between the scale values 1 and 2.

In interval scales the subjective judgments of respondents are translated into quantitative information. By designing an interval, a researcher is able to achieve a higher level of measurement than with nominal and ordinal scales. Sometimes, the researcher is forced to impose equal intervals between descriptors. The researcher would assume that the difference between one descriptor and the next on a scale using "very strongly agree," "strongly agree," "agree," "neutral," "disagree," "strongly disagree," or "very strongly disagree" was one unit. The values assigned to this set of responses run from 1 through 7. Respondents will treat the differences between adjacent response categories as equal.

In an interval scale, the location of the starting point (zero) is not fixed. Both the zero and the units of measurement are arbitrary. For example, temperature measurement for a day in a city ranged between 20°Fahrenheit (F) and 40°F. From these values, can we conclude that the high temperature of 40°F was two times as hot as the low temperature of 20°F? The answer is no. This can easily be proven by converting the temperature from Fahrenheit to centigrade (C). The low temperature of 20°F is equal to –7°C, and the high temperature of 40°F is equal to 4°C (this is because the starting point for the Fahrenheit scale is 32 degrees and for the Centigrade scale is 0 degrees). The high temperature of 4°C is not twice as hot as the low temperature of –7°C. The ratio of high temperature to low temperature in degrees Centigrade is much different from the one indicated by the Fahrenheit scale. In interval scales, we are able to preserve any positive linear transformation of the form $y = a + bx$. In other words, two interval scales that rate two objects as 1 and 2 or 13 and 16 are equivalent (obtained by assigning $a = 10$ and $b = 3$). As in an ordinal scale, it is not useful to take ratios of the scale value in the interval scale, as the starting point is arbitrary. The ratio 1:2 is not the same as the ratio 13:16.

The permissible statistical analysis for interval scales includes all those applicable in a nominal scale and ordinal scale, and, in addition, we can calculate the mean, standard deviation, and correlation analysis.

RATIO SCALE

In ratio scales a true zero exists. Therefore, the researcher can construct ratios. Workers' salaries, company sales volume, ages of respondents, and number of cans of soda consumed can all be used to construct ratios. Analytically, ratio scales are very pow-

Table 10.1   **Properties of Scales**

Scale	Characteristics	Examples	Statistics Applied	
			Descriptive	Inferential
Nominal	Identification, classification	Player's jersey number, age, gender	Percentages, mode	Chi-square, binomial test
Ordinal	Relative position, rank order, not magnitude of differences	Quality rankings, preference rankings	Percentile, median	ANOVA
Interval	Can compare differences, arbitrary 0	Temperature, attitudes	Mean, standard deviation	T-tests, ANOVA, regression, factor analysis
Ratio	Fixed 0; ratios can be computed	Length, sales, income, costs	Geometric mean, harmonic mean	Coefficient of variation

Source: Adapted from Naresh K. Malhotra, *Marketing Research: An Applied Orientation*, 4th ed. (Upper Saddle River, NJ: Prentice-Hall, 2004), p. 256.

erful. They possess all the properties of the nominal, ordinal, and interval scales. For example, a worker earning $400 per week earns twice as much as a worker earning $200 per week, and a worker earning $600 per week earns three times the wages of the worker earning $200 per week.

Ratio scales allow only the proportionate transformation of the scale values and not the addition of an arbitrary constant as done in interval scales. A proportionate transformation function takes the form $y = bx$, where x represents the original values, y represents the transformed values, and b is a positive constant. For example, in converting feet to inches, all the relationships among the objects are preserved. Here $b = 12$; therefore, in the example of the lengths of two pieces of cloth, one of 1 foot in length and the other 3 feet, the ratio is 1:3. When converted to inches, the ratio is 12:36 = 1:3.

Ratio scales allow researchers to undertake many varieties of statistical analysis including coefficient of variation, geometric mean, and harmonic mean. Table 10.1 summarizes the properties of all four scales.[2]

SCALE QUESTION FORMS

Researchers are often interested in the subjective properties of respondents or objects. Most of these properties are concerned with the psychology of respondents. The psychological properties of interest to researchers are intentions, perceptions, attitudes, opinions, views, beliefs, and evaluations. These constructs are not observable and tend to be very subjective. Therefore, they are difficult to measure. It is the responsibility of the researcher to develop instruments to measure the direction and intensity of these impressions. One way of obtaining responses for subjective properties is through scaled-response questions.

Most psychological properties exist on a continuum, ranging from very low to very high. Because the respondents make use of this continuum to respond to subjective properties, researchers construct scaled-response questions in an assumed interval scale format. The intensity continuum may be set up to start from either an extreme positive or an extreme negative through a neutral to the other extreme. Following are some examples of a continuum:

1	2	3	4	5
Extremely important	Important	Neither important nor unimportant	Unimportant	Extremely unimportant

1	2	3	4	5
Extremely dissatisfied	Somewhat dissatisfied	No opinion	Somewhat satisfied	Extremely satisfied

In international research, scale calibrations are complex and more difficult to develop than those in domestic research. Because the cultural, societal, and environmental contexts differ from country to country, the response formats and corresponding scales have to be adjusted accordingly. For example, Latin Americans tend to use the high end of the scale; therefore, a weak response may still be rated as "7" or "8." The British tend to be more critical in their evaluations and may rate the same factor a "5" or "6." Asian respondents tend to prefer the middle of the scale, even if their view is very negative.[3] Some of the difficulties arise out of the interpretation of the starting and ending point of the scale. In some cultures "1" implies very good, and in others "1" is a low number and therefore implies "not so good" compared to a higher number. Because of lower literacy levels in some countries, the scales may not be clearly understood by respondents. Language differences may further compound the process of determining equivalent or similar verbal descriptions from country to country.[4]

If an international researcher does adapt the scales to fit local differences, then he or she faces additional challenges in the form of comparability. How would you compare data from various countries if the scales were not uniform? One solution is to transfer responses back to a common scale. That is, if in one country the high end of the scale is "1" and in another country it is "5," convert one of the scales to the most commonly used numerical value for comparison purposes.

Researchers use many scales to obtain behavioral and attitudinal measures. Some of the most commonly used scaled-response formats are the Likert scale, the equal-appearing interval scale, and the semantic differential scale. These scales have been developed and tested over many years; therefore, it is not necessary for researchers to customize scales.

LIKERT SCALE

In a Likert scale, respondents are asked to indicate their agreement or disagreement on a symmetric scale for a series of statements. The researcher develops a large number of statements that reflect qualities of objects or attributes of a service. These statements could be generated on the basis of the researcher's prior experience with the topic, through discussion with experts in the area, or through secondary sources. The statements developed have to reflect all attributes of the object that may lead to an opinion or views. These statements are then edited to remove ambiguous, irrelevant, and awkward statements. The remaining statements are then presented to a panel of judges or a small representative sample to sort statements by their degree of preference.

In assigning scale values, each judge would be instructed to group the statements into 9 or 11 piles based on their degree of agreement or disagreement. Only statements with a consensus view among the judges are selected, and the ones with wide disagreement are dropped from the questionnaire. A scale value is determined for each statement by the frequency with which the statement is placed in each of the piles. The statements are then screened on the basis of two criteria: the dispersion in judgments exhibited by the selected judges and the scale values.

International researchers have observed that verbal rating scales are easily understood and grasped by people in many parts of the world. Because these scales are easy to administer and seem to be acceptable to a vast group of respondents, they are often used to discern behavioral aspects in international research.

Likert scales generally reflect the "agree/disagree" response options. A Likert scale captures the intensity of the respondent's feelings. For example, in evaluating the services of an investment bank, a researcher may develop the following scaled statements:

Statement	Strongly agree	Somewhat agree	Neutral	Somewhat disagree	Strongly disagree
The investment bank offers many funds.	1	2	3	4	5
The investment bank offers courteous service.	1	2	3	4	5
The performance of the funds has been consistently good.	1	2	3	4	5
The brokers of the bank are knowledgeable.	1	2	3	4	5
The research reports of the investment bank are not very good.	1	2	3	4	5

SEMANTIC DIFFERENTIAL SCALE

The semantic differential scale consists of bipolar adjectives that are used to cull the reactions of respondents to issues or objects. Researchers have sometimes used phrases instead of adjectives at each end of the scale. By using the semantic differential scales, researchers have been able to develop profiles of employees, products, companies, and other organizations.

Semantic differential scales have been tested extensively in the international research field with a high rate of consistently similar results. The semantic differential scale is considered a truly pan-cultural scale and is widely used by international research managers. Osgood, May, and Miron have extended this type of study to many countries covering a wide range of different adjectives.[5] In their studies, three common factors emerged as the most dominant: the *evaluative, potency,* and *activity* factors. The evaluative factor is based on a good/bad dimension, the potency factor is based on a strong/weak dimension, and the activity factor is based on a fast/slow dimension. This technique is useful in capturing "affective" meaning and discerning notable dimensions on which to measure values. The semantic differential scale can be used for various situations in international research.

The construction of a semantic differential scale begins with the determination of a person, an object, a company, a concept, or an idea to be rated. Next, the researcher generates a large list of bipolar adjectives or phrases to be used to describe a subject's salient properties. Depending on the subject, phrases or adjectives such as "convenient/inconvenient," "friendly/unfriendly," or "useful/not useful" may be used in obtaining the necessary information. The opposites are positioned at the end-points of a continuum of intensity. The intensity continuum is usually separated by an odd-numbered scale. By tradition, most scales are either a five-point or a seven-point scale. The respondents then indicate their evaluation of the subject by checking the appropriate level in the scale. The extreme points on the scale reflect the higher intensity of a respondent's evaluation of the subject. The general thrust in using the semantic differential scale is to be able to select the appropriate sample of adjective pairs or phrases from which a score could be generated for a subject's dimensions and then used to compare it to other subjects.

For example, in the earlier example of an investment bank study, the following bipolar phrases may be used to evaluate the services of the bank:

The bank offers many funds.	___	___	___	___	___	The bank offers very few funds.
The bank offers very high yields.	___	___	___	___	___	The bank offers very low yields.
The bank's personnel are courteous.	___	___	___	___	___	The bank's personnel are discourteous.

The scale would then be administered to a sample of respondents. Each respondent would be asked to read each set of bipolar phrases to check the cell that best described his or her feelings toward the bank. The individual items may be scored 1, 2, 3, 4, and 5 if a five-point scale is used (or +1, +2, 0, −1, and −2) or 1, 2, 3, 4, 5, 6, and 7 if a seven-point scale is used.

A major advantage of the semantic differential scale is that it provides the researcher with the data needed to compute averages and to plot a profile of the salient features of the subject. After the scale is administered to a sample, the average score for each pair of bipolar phrases is computed. In the investment bank example, the average score for a sample of 100 respondents for the first pair of bipolar phrases was 4.1. The respondents seem to suggest that the investment bank offers very few funds or that the bank has failed to communicate effectively the number of funds it does offer.

Even with the frequent use of the semantic differential scale and its applicability to international research, the researcher must exercise caution in using this method.

Given cultural differences in terms of color preferences, functionality of products and services, variability in value judgments, and differing experience levels in the use of products, setting up appropriate rating scales suitable for all countries and cultures may be difficult. If the object is comparative analysis, these cultural differences compound the difficulties.

Issues in the Use of Scales

In using scale formats, a researcher has to address two issues. First, should a middle or neutral response option be included? If a neutral option is included, those respondents who do not have an opinion should have an opportunity to respond. However, many respondents may use the neutral option to hide their opinions. If a neutral position is not available, respondents may be forced to indicate their true opinions. The second issue concerns the need to have a symmetrical scale. Quite often researchers have only a positive side to a scale. It is critical before settling on one format that both symmetrical and one-sided scales be tested to see whether or not the respondents will use the negative side of the scale.

In international research, avoiding inherent problems in scaled responses requires the researcher to develop an alternative approach. Assuming that culture-free uniform scales across countries are difficult if not impossible to develop, researchers have tried developing questionnaire formats that use a self-defined cultural norm. One such approach is Cantril's self-anchoring scale.[6] This technique requires respondents to indicate their own anchor point in relation to a culture-specific stimulus set. Researchers have successfully used this approach to study attitudes toward female roles, social activities, and communication.

Scaled-Response Question Formats

Scaled-question formats can take many forms. The most commonly used formats are

- Graphic rating scale
- Itemized rating scale
- Percentage scale
- Staple scale

Graphic Rating Scale

Because of low literacy rates in many countries, international researchers use graphic rating scales. Graphic rating scales use pictorial representation to indicate intensity of response. The "smiley" scale is a commonly used graphic rating scale. The smiley scale represents sad-to-happy faces on a continuum to indicate intensity. A very happy face denotes agreement and a very sad face indicates disagreement.

Even when using graphic scales in international research, researchers have to be careful to adapt the pictures to local happy-face depiction. For example, the typical

Figure 10.1   **Example of Graphic Scale: Sad-to-Happy-Face Scales—United States and Africa**

Source: C.K. Corder, "Problems and Pitfalls in Conducting Marketing Research in Africa," in *Marketing Expansion in a Shrinking World,* ed. Betsy Gelb. Chicago: American Marketing Association, 1978.

happy face in the United States has a round face with two circles for eyes and an inverted (concave) arc representing a smiling mouth. The round face remains the same throughout the continuum, but the mouth changes from happy (concave arc) to sad (convex arc). In African countries, the shape of the face changes from a circle to an oval as the scale moves from happy to sad. In addition, the eyes and mouth take on different shapes as the scale moves from happy to sad (see Figure 10.1).[7]

ITEMIZED RATING SCALE

Itemized rating scales use numbers to indicate the intensity of the response and are very popular. For example:

How would you rate your local phone service?

Poor	Fair	Good	Very Good	Excellent
1	2	3	4	5
——	——	——	——	——

PERCENTAGE SCALE

Percentage scales use percentages to indicate the intensity of response. For example:

How satisfied are you with your local telephone service?

Very Satisfied	Satisfied	Neither	Dissatisfied	Very Dissatisfied
100%	75%	50%	25%	0%
——	——	——	——	——

STAPLE SCALE

Staple scales use positive and negative numbers to indicate the intensity of response. For example:

How would you rate your local telephone service?

Excellent	Very Good	Fair	Poor	Very Poor
+2	+1	0	–1	–2
——	——	——	——	——

Because these standard formats have been in use for quite some time, they have undergone many tests for reliability and validity. Therefore, a researcher can forgo tests to validate the scaled-response formats. Additionally, using standard formats saves time in the preparation of a questionnaire.

In designing scaled-response formats for international research, researchers need to develop scales that a wide variety of respondents from different countries and cultures can easily understand. The two key issues in this type of research tend to be convertibility and comparability of findings across national boundaries.

RELIABILITY MEASUREMENTS IN SCALED RESPONSES

Reliability measures are critical in scaled-response formats. Reliability measures a respondent's consistency of response to a question. If the questions are constructed and administered correctly, there should not be any variability in the answers provided by a respondent to two identical questions. Researchers can have confidence in their questionnaire if two identical questions elicit similar answers. There are many degrees of reliability measures. Some will exhibit perfectly consistent responses and some perfectly opposite responses. Researchers face problems when the reliability measures indicate wild swings in responses.

One easy way to measure reliability is to conduct a test-retest. In this type of test, after a questionnaire has been administered, a follow-up set of questions is asked of the same group of respondents after an interval. For example, in the earlier telephone study, a respondent may have checked –1 (poor) on the service question, indicating displeasure with the service. To measure the reliability, the researcher may conduct a follow-up study two weeks later with the same sample. After the respondent's participation in the earlier survey is verified, he or she is asked to rate the quality of the operator service on a five-point scale, with 1 being excellent service and 5 being poor service. If a respondent selects 5, then the respondent has been consistent. Therefore, the scale used in the questionnaire is deemed highly reliable.

In a test-retest situation, if the responses to identical or similar questions are identical or close, we conclude that the scale is reliable. The follow-up question does not have to be the original or identical question, as long as it conveys the same meaning or concept. In a retest of scaled responses, all questions are not repeated; only a few critical questions are selected. Even the scale need not be the same. A researcher can use a Likert scale in the original questionnaire and a semantic differential in the retest. The reliability test isolates the consistency from randomness.

Besides the test-retest method, researchers can also use a split half test to measure reliability. In this approach, the respondent sample is divided into two equal groups, and the scaled responses of the two subsamples are compared. If the two groups are assumed to be identical, the average responses of the two samples should be similar. If the responses are not similar, then one may deduce that the scale used in the questionnaire is not reliable. Usually, the researcher conducts statistical tests to determine the degree of similarity. A major drawback of the split half test is the difficulty in isolating subgroup similarities and differences. For example, using a five-point scale with 1 being "very important" and 5 "not at all important," the average responses for one subsample was 3. This average score was a result of one-half of this sub-sample selecting 1 and the other half selecting 5. In contrast, the second subsample's average of 3 was a result of all the respondents in this subsample selecting 3.

Once the reliability measures have been completed, a researcher can use the tests to weed out questions that are not reliable. In some instances, the researcher may also reduce the scale values by combining some of the scales. For example, a seven-point Likert scale as shown below:

Extremely Favorable 1	Very Favorable 2	Somewhat Favorable 3	Neutral 4	Somewhat Unfavorable 5	Very Unfavorable 6	Extremely Unfavorable 7
—	—	—	—	—	—	—

If it appears that the scale is unreliable, the researcher can reduce the seven-point scale to a five-point scale by combining choices 1 and 2 and choices 6 and 7 or even reduce it to a three-point scale, with choice 1 as "favorable," 2 as "neutral," and 3 as "unfavorable."

VALIDITY OF MEASUREMENTS IN SCALED RESPONSES

Validity is the ability of a scale or measuring instrument to measure what was intended to be measured. It is an assessment of the accuracy of the measurement. It is possible to have a scale that is totally reliable but does not measure what it is supposed to measure. Verification of responses is not always easy. Respondents' answers to scaled questions may not always reflect their actual behavior, and quite often researchers may incorrectly interpret the true meaning of a response. For example, in questions relating to a respondent's personal achievements, there is a tendency to overstate one's accomplishments. Achievements such as educational levels, income, number of foreign trips taken, and the value of stock portfolios are all subject to overstatement. Respondents may answer in the same manner in repeated retests. The consistency of the responses fulfills the reliability criteria, but the response is not accurate and therefore is invalid. Similarly, in a scaled questionnaire of factory workers, the responses may show a high level of absenteeism, but the researcher cannot measure the morale of the workers using the absenteeism factor because there may not be a correlation between absenteeism and morale. Therefore, the result, though accurate, may not be valid.

Researchers can test for validity in a variety of ways. The most commonly used tests are

- Content validity
- Predictive validity
- Construct validity
- Discriminant validity

Content or *face validity* is defined as the agreement among professionals that a scale appears to be accurately measuring what it is intended to measure. Content validity asks the question, "Does it look like" it measures what the test is supposed to measure? If the measure appears to a group of experts to have adequate coverage, a measure has content validity. The assessment is purely a judgment call, and each question or statement is developed and tested in a similar fashion. Because of the subjectivity of this approach, content validity is the least accurate of the measures.

Predictive validity is defined as a classification of criterion validity whereby a new measure predicts a future event or correlates with a criterion measure administered at a later time. Predictive validity seeks to establish the extent to which a particular measure predicts or relates to other measures. Advertising agencies tend to use predictive validity by comparing recall scores of rough commercials with finished commercials. Similarly, buyers' positive attitudes toward products from certain countries, such as electronic products from Japan, would be supported by a high incidence of purchase of Japanese brands of electronics among the same group of consumers.

Construct validity is defined as the ability of a measure to concur with a group of related hypotheses from other concepts that have a theoretical basis. Construct validity tries to establish a high correlation between empirical evidence and conceptual logic. Statistical analysis is used to understand the findings, which are then compared to theoretical models. If the measure behaves as it is conceptualized, then we conclude that there is a high degree of construct validity to the question.

Discriminant validity is defined as the ability of some measures to have a low correlation with measures of dissimilar concepts. It asks the question, "Do measures of different constructs differ as you expect them to?" For example, in a study of factory workers, you expect the workers to rate the question, "Is safety important to you?" very highly. On a five-point scale with 1 being very important, the average score should be close to 1. In contrast, one expects the workers to rate a question such as "Is wearing a suit at work important to you?" low or at best indifferent with an average score close to 5.

Generally researchers should be concerned about the concepts of reliability and validity. Some, such as face validity, are standard procedures and are followed in every instance. If a measure is unreliable or not valid, the whole research study may be inappropriate or inaccurate.

INTERNATIONAL CONSIDERATIONS IN SCALE DEVELOPMENT

Increased globalization has generated considerable interest in testing theories and constructs in other countries that were developed in the United States or in Europe. Are the scales developed in Western societies appropriate to measure constructs in other regions of the world? A requirement for any cross-cultural or cross-national research should be that scales and measurements of constructs can be applied across countries. The question also is whether all the items used in the scale can be applied to all the sample subjects. Recent studies have shown that it is possible to apply Western-based scales to test theories and constructs across countries. Using the generalizable theory (G theory) in conjunction with a confirmatory factor analysis can provide supplementary evidence of measurement invariance across countries.[8] It is also possible to use multiple-item scales in international research situations. Some studies have shown that, in international research, multiple-item scales for measuring constructs can be developed. These scales have been found not only to measure the constructs, but also to meet precise measurement criteria.[9]

A second consideration in international research is the effect of ethnocentrism on international transactions. Ethnocentrism is the belief that one's own culture is superior to others. The effect of ethnocentrism is to disregard the environmental differences that may exist between the home country and the foreign country. Research suggests that one construct and associated measure that may have great potential for international consumer research are consumer ethnocentrism and its measurement using the CETSCALE[10] (consumer ethnocentric scale). Shimp and Sharma developed an instrument to measure consumer ethnocentric behavior related to purchasing of foreign- versus American-made products. The authors found that ethnocentric behavior is more of a tendency than an attitude. Research suggests that consumer ethnocentrism and the related CETSCALE used to measure it may be useful for applications in measuring constructs in international research. Using samples from the United States, Japan, France, and Germany, researchers found strong support for the CETSCALE's factor structure and reliability across the four countries.[11]

CHAPTER SUMMARY

In international research, there is a need to measure behavioral and other subjective properties of people, objects, and issues. These research problems require the use of an appropriate measurement system. Scales should assist researchers in obtaining the desired information. In using scaled questions across countries, researchers must formulate the questions in exactly the same manner in all situations. In designing scales for use in international research, the key issue is the development of a scale that is easy to understand and easy to administer in different cultural contexts. The concepts to be measured must have an operational definition that specifies how they will be measured. Measurement systems use numbers to quantify variables. Measurements can employ nominal, ordinal, interval, or ratio scales.

Nominal scales are used for identification purposes. Ordinal scales arrange items according to their magnitude in an ordered relationship. Interval scales measure distance, and ratio scales are absolute scales with a zero as the starting point. As the researcher moves from the nominal to the ratio scale, more information is gained. Internationally, some scales are more useful than others. For example, semantic differential scales and graphic scales have some benefits over other types of scales.

As constructed, these scales try to measure respondents' behavioral patterns and their feelings about certain objects. In measuring complex variables such as attitudes, researchers use composite measures of these variables. The use of several questions to identify and understand one concept is a common practice among researchers.

Scaled instruments are evaluated for reliability and validity. Reliability reflects the degree to which the measurement provides consistent results. Validity refers to an instrument's ability to measure the concept the researcher wants to measure. Researchers measure reliability using either the test-retest or the split half test method. Researchers use four approaches to establish validity: face validity, predictive validity, construct validity, and discriminant validity.

CHAPTER REVIEW

1. What is scale measurement?
2. Identify and distinguish among the four basic scales.
3. What are the permissible statistics for each of the four scales?
4. What is a continuum along which subjective properties can be measured?
5. Is the use of an odd-numbered scale better in measurements than an even-numbered scale? Explain.
6. What is a Likert scale? Construct a Likert scale to measure students' interest in the study of international business.
7. What is a semantic differential scale? Construct a semantic differential scale to measure students' interest in watching movies on television.
8. Why is the semantic differential scale popular among international researchers?
9. What is a common graphic representation scale? How is it used in international research?

10. What is reliability in scaled-response questions? How does one test for reliability?
11. What is validity in scaled-response questions?
12. Distinguish among face validity, predictive validity, construct validity, and discriminant validity.

Notes

1. Gene F. Summers, ed., *Attitude Measurement.* Chicago: Rand McNally, 1970, p. 1.

2. Naresh K. Malhotra, *Marketing Research: An Applied Orientation,* 4th ed. Upper Saddle River, NJ: Prentice-Hall, 2004, p. 256.

3. Jennifer Mitchell, "Reaching across Borders," *Marketing News* (May 10, 1999), p. 19.

4. Reinhard Angelmar and Bernard Pras, "Verbal Rating Scales for Multinational Research," *European Research* 6 (1978), pp. 62–67.

5. Charles E. Osgood, William H. May, and Murray S. Miron, *Cross-Cultural Universals of Affective Meaning.* Urbana: University of Illinois Press, 1975.

6. A. Cantril, *The Pattern of Human Concerns.* New Brunswick, NJ: Rutgers University Press, 1965.

7. C.K. Order, "Problems and Pitfalls in Conducting Marketing Research in Africa," in *Marketing Expansion in a Shrinking World,* ed. Betsy Gelb. Chicago: American Marketing Association, 1978, pp. 86–90.

8. Subash Sharma and Danny Weathers, "Assessing Generalizability of Scales Used in Cross-National Research," *International Journal of Research in Marketing* 20, no. 3 (2003), pp. 287–295.

9. Ingrid M. Martin and Sevgin Eroglu, "Measuring a Multi-Dimensional Construct: Country Image," *Journal of Business Research* 28 (1993), pp. 191–210.

10. T. Shimp and Subash Sharma, "Consumer Ethnocentrism: Construction and Validation of CETSCALE," *Journal of Marketing Research* 24 (1987), pp. 280–289.

11. Richard G. Netemeyer, Srinivas Durvasula, and Donald R. Lichtenstein, "A Cross-National Assessment of the Reliability and Validity of the CETSCALE," *Journal of Marketing Research* 28, no. 3 (1999), pp. 320–327.

Questionnaire Administration

Questionnaire administration is the means through which respondents are contacted to obtain the necessary information.

LEARNING OBJECTIVES

After reading this chapter, students should be able to

- Know the various data-collection methods
- Become knowledgeable about the details of different types of survey data-collection methods
- Understand when personal interviews, telephone interviews, mail interviews, self-administered surveys, and the Internet should be used
- Know the advantages and disadvantages of each method of questionnaire administration
- Understand the emerging techniques of data-collection methods

Researchers trying to collect data from primary sources need to have a mechanism to reach the identified sample respondents. Primary data may be collected by questioning respondents via mail, over the telephone, in person, or through self-administered questionnaires. A mail questionnaire involves mailing the questions to a predetermined sample of respondents with an accompanying cover letter. The respondents complete the questionnaire and mail their replies back to the researcher. A researcher conducts a telephone interview by questioning respondents over the phone. In a personal interview, a one-on-one interaction between the interviewer and a respondent is used to cull the information. The self-administered survey is one in which respondents complete the survey on their own without a medium involved. The researcher mails the self-administered questionnaires or delivers them in person to the respondents. Self-administered surveys are generally treated as a type of mail survey. In international surveys, cultural differences can affect administration of questionnaires. Based on the experiences of research suppliers such as SRG International, the following generalizations can be made for Asia and Latin America. Asian respondents are more noncommittal than respondents of other nationalities and will answer questions to please the interviewer, that is, they will respond with the answer the respondent believes the interviewer wants to hear rather than with what they really think. In Latin America, however, personal interviews are the best survey choice, as Latinos are more forthcoming in person than in other survey scenarios. Latin American respondents also like to overstate their responses to some types of personal questions.

Internationally, conducting interviews can be difficult. In some countries the mail system is poor; in others telephone penetration among households is less than 10 percent; and in other countries there may not be sufficient qualified interviewers to conduct the interviews. According to Gerry Grise, senior vice president of global research services at Ipsos-Reid Corporation, in Asia and Latin America respondents are most commonly contacted through personal interviews, with interviewers going door-to-door, since telephone penetration is still low in many markets and postal services are not always reliable. These difficulties are not limited to just developing countries. Even in some highly industrialized countries conducting interviews has its own problems. For example, in Japan, the postal rates are high, with a one-ounce letter costing 75 cents to mail (compared to 41 cents in the United States and 30 cents in Germany). Nippon Telegraph and Telephone, the state-owned monopoly, charges dearly for toll-free numbers and is reluctant to share its database of regular phone numbers.[1]

MAIL INTERVIEWS

Before undertaking a mail interview, the researcher must evaluate the country's existing mail service for speed of delivery and quality of service. Mail services vary in efficiency from country to country. Some developing countries and a few industrialized countries are notorious for their poor mail service. In these countries, a large percentage of mail does not reach the addressee. Inadequate infrastructure, lack of dwelling-unit identification, incorrect or inappropriate zoning systems, and manual sorting of mail are some of the problems that contribute to poor mail service. In addition, mailing lists, which are easily available in some industrialized countries, are nonexistent in many other countries, making the task of identifying potential respondents difficult. If the mail system in a country is found to be adequate and useful mailing lists are available, mail surveys may be used for reaching preselected respondents.

ADVANTAGES OF MAIL INTERVIEWS

- In mail surveys, respondents control at what time they respond to a questionnaire and they can also control the pace at which they complete the questionnaire. Being more relaxed and not under any pressure, respondents may provide more complete and thorough responses to questions.
- Mail surveys allow for a high degree of anonymity, as the respondent does not interact with an interviewer. This is critical for many sensitive-issue studies. Mail surveys provide a higher response rate than other methods in these instances.

- Mail surveys are very useful when the respondents are geographically wide-spread. If the respondents are located away from city centers, are geographically dispersed, and have a low level of telephone usage, mail surveys may be the only option available because using personal interviewers may be prohibitively costly. In special cases, such as in reaching busy executives or professionals, mail surveys may be more appropriate than personal or telephone interviews.
- Mail surveys are attractive to researchers because they are self-administered. Self-administration of the questionnaires saves researchers time and money in training interviewers. By eliminating the need for an interviewer or interviewing devices such as telephone lines and computers, researchers can realize significant cost savings. In addition, interviewer bias, which tends to be a problem with telephone and personal interviews, can be avoided.

Because of their low cost, mail interviews are used heavily in many developed countries. For example, in Canada, 6.2 percent of all interviews are conducted through mail.[2]

DISADVANTAGES OF MAIL INTERVIEWS

Mail surveys are plagued by the following problems:

- In mail surveys, control of the survey is in the hands of the respondent. Therefore, mail surveys have one of the poorest response rates among all the available survey methods. Typically, mail surveys achieve less than 20 percent response rates, and in some situations the rate can go as low as 2 to 3 percent.
- Mail surveys are one of the least flexible contact methods. Flexibility refers to the convenience of making appointments with respondents at a time when it is most suitable for them to answer questions, the availability of respondents to explain and clarify difficult questions, and the freedom to probe respondents in unstructured questions. Because there is no interaction between the respondent and the interviewer in mail surveys, they have low flexibility.
- Mail surveys suffer from response biases due to self-selection. Self-selection means that respondents who respond to the questionnaire have certain characteristics that are totally different from the rest of the sample. Therefore, the researcher has the least amount of sample control in mail surveys.
- Compared to other methods, mail surveys take the longest time to complete. Unlike personal or telephone interviews, a researcher cannot add more interviewers to speed up the process. In mail surveys, the researcher is at the mercy of the respondent.
- Mail surveys are ineffective in developing countries. Because of low literacy rates, population diffusion in many villages or rural areas, and the fact that the mail services in these countries are inadequate, surveys using the postal services are difficult if not impossible.
- In mail surveys, there is greater possibility than in other types of surveys that respondents will not complete the questionnaire. A lack of supervision and en-

couragement from outside sources may lead to partial completion of the questionnaire, late returns, or refusals.

- There is a greater burden on the researcher in mail surveys than in other types of surveys to make the self-administration of the questionnaire work. Therefore, the questionnaire has to be very clear, follow-up instructions must be well spelled out, and the questionnaire should contain constant reminders of important items.

Recognizing the problem of low response rate in mail surveys, researchers have developed a number of techniques to increase response rates. These include sending follow-up letters, making follow-up phone calls, designing attractive questionnaires, writing stimulating cover letters, personalizing cover letters, and composing easy-to-answer questions. In some countries even these additional details may not generate the necessary response rates. For example, using preliminary notification and detailed project explanation in Denmark did not have the desired response rates for a mail survey.[3]

A growing trend in mail surveys is to include a gift with the questionnaire. These gifts include money, coupons, gift certificates to select stores, and other items such as key chains and pocket diaries. In many countries the addition of a gift seems to increase the response rates. Results from a study across five countries—Canada, France, Germany, the United Kingdom, and the United States—suggest that an inexpensive and symbolic incentive such as a commemorative stamp can significantly increase response rates, especially for business executives.[4] Similarly, monetary incentives accompanying questionnaires and follow-up letters appear to be the most consistently effective techniques to increase response rates among consumers, especially in Japan, the United States, and the United Kingdom, but produce opposite results in Hong Kong.[5] In Hong Kong monetary rewards in mail surveys are viewed negatively and hence should not be used to increase response rates. In international research, researchers must be careful in the selection of the gifts they include with the surveys. In some Asian countries coupons are not viewed favorably by the public, who link coupons with poorer-quality merchandise that the seller is trying to get rid off.

Mail surveys are a feasible research tool in Japan and in other cultures where intended respondents are literate and can be contacted through a dependable postal system.[6] In some other countries, however, cultural differences may cause respondents to ignore mail questionnaires because they view questions from strangers and unknown persons as inappropriate. Also, in countries with totalitarian governments, the public mistrusts the mail system and fears that government agents may read their correspondence. In these situations, researchers have tried hand delivering mail or using private letter carriers.[7]

STEPS IN CONDUCTING MAIL INTERVIEWS

The first step in conducting mail interviews is to develop the mailing package. A typical package contains a cover letter, the questionnaire, a stamped return envelope, and an incentive of some sort. The cover letter is an important element to the success rate of a mail survey. The letter should draw the attention of the respondents to the questionnaire and motivate them to respond. A cover letter typically plays on the importance of the issues contained in the questionnaire and of the contribution of the respondents. Incentives such as token payments or coupons to redeem products are commonly used by researchers.

Mail surveys are by design short, as it is difficult to maintain the attention of respondents for a long time without prodding from interviewers. Mail surveys are quite often used to collect sensitive information concerning sexual preferences or health issues. With no interviewer present or listening to their answers, respondents feel freer to reveal information that otherwise might not be provided.

Before mailing questionnaires, a researcher first has to identify the respondents. Obtaining a valid mailing list in countries where such lists are available speeds up this process. For example, in the United States, researchers can obtain a wide variety of mailing lists, including lists broken down by zip code, profession of respondents (doctors, lawyers, accountants, etc.), and age group. In many industrialized countries, such as the United Kingdom, it is possible not only to buy mailing lists but also to obtain labels or labeled envelopes. Equally attractive to researchers are the service companies who for a fee stuff the envelopes with the questionnaires and mail them.

If mailing lists are not available, a researcher has to undertake the additional task of creating them. This procedure adds to the cost and time of completing a mail survey. Magazine subscription lists may be used in developing mailing lists in some countries. These lists are fairly accurate and current. The main problem with this type of list is that the sample may be skewed toward better-educated and urban segments of the population and fail to represent a wider population. In business surveys, mailing lists can be compiled from customer rosters or trade-association memberships. Mailing lists can also be compiled from telephone directories. Mailing lists should be carefully checked to make sure that the right population is represented and that the addresses in the lists are accurate and current.

Telephone Interviews

Telephone interviews are becoming one of the primary methods of contacting respondents in international business research. As the familiarity of respondents with the telephone survey grows, they are more willing to provide detailed and reliable information on a variety of topics over the phone. As telephone technology improves, with faster and better service, this method is becoming very popular among researchers. In addition to the improvements in technology, penetration of telephones into households is rapidly increasing in many countries of the world. Countries such as Argentina, Hong Kong, Malaysia, Singapore, South Korea, Turkey, and Uruguay have at least 10 percent of households with telephones compared to less than 5 percent just a few years ago.

Telephone interviews involve phoning a sample of respondents to obtain information. In traditional telephone surveys, the interviewer records the responses directly onto the questionnaire. In many instances, the interviewers are in one central location. This arrangement helps reduce cost and enables the researcher to better monitor the interviewers. Wherever available, Wide-Area Telecommunications Service (WATS) is purchased from local telephone companies to assist in conducting telephone interviews. WATS lines offer fixed rates for calls within a wide geographic area, reducing the cost of calls. Telephone interviews are also known to produce high-quality samples. By using random dialing procedures and proper callback measures, telephone interviewing can supply a very good representative sample in countries with a high usage rate of telephones.

In many industrialized countries, traditional telephone interviewing is replaced by computer-assisted telephone interviews. In computer-assisted telephone interviews, the questionnaire is not printed out for interviewers but available on a computer monitor (screen). Specific software programs help researchers to perform a variety of tasks through the computers. One software program aids in telephone number selection and automatic dialing. A second one helps in selecting samples randomly. Upon command, the computer dials the telephone number. After establishing contact with the selected respondent, the interviewer reads questions from the screen and records the answers directly into the computer. Yet another software program can supply daily status reports on the number of completed interviews.

Computer-assisted telephone interviewing has greatly improved the quality and accuracy of telephone interviewing. In a computer-assisted interview, the system leads the interviewer through the questionnaire one question at a time. The computer checks the responses for appropriateness and consistency. Skip patterns within the questionnaire are controlled by the system. The variability between interviewers is kept to a minimum in a computer-assisted telephone interview.

ADVANTAGES OF TELEPHONE INTERVIEWS

Telephone interviewing has the following advantages:

- Telephone interviewing has a cost advantage over personal interviews, its chief rival in terms of flexibility and usage. In some instances, telephone interviewing costs are half those of personal interviews, especially for a geographically diffused sample of respondents.
- Telephone interviewing is relatively faster than personal interviews. Because telephone interviews can be accomplished from one location and many phone lines can be tapped at the same time, this form of interviewing has advantages over other methods. Commercial establishments wishing to survey employees or customers can easily reach them over the phone, and all the interviews can be completed within a day or two. Internationally, interviewing can be initiated from any country, as long as the interviewers are fluent in the language of the target country. This method also significantly reduces the time required to organize interviewing of respondents in many countries. Researchers can institute better quality-control checks when interviewing is done from one location.
- Since respondents do not see the interviewer, they are more willing to answer confidential or embarrassing questions. Questions that relate to individuals' health, their income, and their sexual orientation may be personally threatening to some respondents. Questions addressing these issues have high refusal rates in all methods, but to a lesser degree in mail and telephone interviewing.

- Telephone interviewing reaches respondents who may be geographically isolated. People in some neighborhoods are reluctant to allow strangers to come into their houses for security reasons. Some apartment complexes or gated communities may prohibit strangers from entering their premises. In some countries people regard privacy very highly and are reluctant to talk to strangers. People at work may not like to respond to interviews. All these groups may be easily reached by telephone.
- Callbacks to respondents who may not have been home or were otherwise engaged are easier via telephone.
- By using random-digit dialing (using a random numbers table to generate telephone numbers), a fairly representative sample may be obtained. Even when a large percentage of the phone numbers in an area are unlisted, this method of dialing overrides this problem.

DISADVANTAGES OF TELEPHONE INTERVIEWS

Telephone interviewing has the following disadvantages:

- Low telephone usage in many countries of the world makes obtaining representative samples for telephone interviewing more difficult. In countries such as Bangladesh, India, Indonesia, Mali, Nigeria, Pakistan, Paraguay, Peru, Philippines, Sri Lanka, Uganda, and Zimbabwe, where per capita telephone usage is less than 10 percent, only a small group of wealthy and upper-middle-income groups own telephones, and obtaining a large representative sample may not be possible.
- A limitation of telephone interviewing is the absence of face-to-face contact. The facial reactions and other body-language signals of respondents are a valuable source of hidden information for the researcher. A grimace, creasing of the brow, or smile on the face of a respondent all can mean something to an observer with knowledge in this area. The inability of the interviewer to see the respondent is a major disadvantage of telephone interviewing. Also, the interviewer is not able to make various judgments and evaluations of the respondents' surroundings. For example, researchers cannot make judgments regarding a respondents' wealth based on the home in which they live and other outward signs of economic status. In addition, the interviewer is not able to see whether the respondent has completed answering the previous question and may continue talking, resulting in a garbled response.
- Lack of face-to-face contact also limits the flexibility of using visual aids in telephone interviewing. Interviewers cannot show respondents anything. Telephone interviewing does not allow the researcher to obtain reactions to samples or pictures. For the same reason, scaled-response formats needing graphic scales cannot be used in telephone interviewing. This severely limits a researcher's flexibility in questioning respondents with limited education.
- Another disadvantage of the telephone interview is that the length of the interview is limited. Respondents who feel that the interview has taken too much time may simply refuse further questioning and hang up.

- Low levels of technology utilized in some countries result in static and other interference that may cause problems in understanding questions and responses.
- Finally, the growing use of answering machines, caller ID, and other recognition devices in many industrialized countries is making telephone surveys much harder to complete.

Internationally, traditions, social interactions, and cultural differences make telephone interviewing more complex. Language difficulties and telephone usage behavior in some countries restrict the use of telephones (in some countries the telephone is viewed as an emergency contact device and not one for social interaction). Telephone costs are often high in many countries, and this factor adds to the cost of the research. Also, flat-rate arrangements available in industrialized countries may not be available in some nonindustrialized countries. For these reasons, in international research telephone interviewing may be more appropriate for business-to-business research.

PERSONAL INTERVIEWS

In personal interviews, researchers interview respondents face-to-face. These interviews may be conducted at the respondents' homes, in offices, at factory sites, or in large shopping areas. When conducted in large shopping areas, the interviews are also called mall-intercept interviews since the respondents are intercepted while they are shopping. The advantage of mall-intercept interviews is that the interviewers may contact a large number of respondents very quickly and efficiently. In addition, in these situations the respondents meet the interviewer rather than the other way around, saving cost and time in contacting respondents.

Personal interviews are the oldest form of contacting respondents. Egyptians and Romans used to conduct personal interviews to gather census and other population-related information. In the fifteenth century, European business enterprises used surveys and other information sources from various parts of the world to gain an advantage over their competitors.

The interviewer's task in personal interviews is to contact the respondents, ask questions, and record the responses. As personal interviews require two-way communication, they tend to be more reliable than other interviewing methods. Two-way communication provides an opportunity for instant feedback. Personal interviews are also the most flexible and versatile of the interviewing approaches. Researchers can select interviewers to reflect the demographic and other social factors of their respondents. For example, in conducting surveys among heavily concentrated Italian communities in Argentina, a researcher can pick interviewers with an Italian background in an effort to make respondents feel more comfortable.

ADVANTAGES OF PERSONAL INTERVIEWS

Personal interviews have many advantages. Following is a list of these advantages:

- Personal interviews are ideally suited for lengthy questionnaires that take time and effort. Both mail and telephone interviews are restrictive and tend to be designed for speedy completion. Telephone interviews are shorter because it is hard to maintain respondents' attention for long periods of time. Mail interviews do not provide opportunities for coaxing respondents to answer lengthy questionnaires. A personal interview, however, is tantamount to chitchat and has a social interaction component to it. In larger cities, where establishing social contacts may be difficult, personal interviewers are welcomed by respondents as a way to spend time in the company of people. In addition, interviewers can encourage respondents to take the necessary time to complete a questionnaire.

- Personal interviews can be used to obtain insightful information based on respondents' reactions to questions. Their facial expressions and body language can be noted down on the questionnaire to further analyze the respondents' state of mind in answering the questions. Personal observations also may be used to identify sensitive demographic factors such as age and income.
- An important aspect of personal interviews is the opportunity to probe. If a respondent's answer appears to be incomplete or unclear, the interviewer can ask questions and encourage the respondent to be more explicit or add to the answer. In all methods of interviewing, the interviewer is trained to remain within the script of the questionnaire to maintain uniformity in questioning. Probing is allowed when it seems that the respondent has not responded fully to a question. Personal interviews are definitely appropriate when the questionnaire has unstructured questions that require a certain amount of probing to obtain complete responses.
- Personal interviews allow the researcher to use visual aids and other props when needed. Researchers can easily incorporate graphic scales, plant layouts, package designs, or prototype products in personal interview questionnaires.
- Personal interviews provide a more representative sample of the population than other methods of interviewing. In some Latin American countries, respondents may be unwilling to respond to mail or telephone interviews but may not object to a personal interview.
- Personal interviews appear to increase the number of subjects willing to respond to a questionnaire. The fact that the interview is often conducted in a friendly environment such as the respondent's home or workplace relaxes the respondent. People are generally sociable, and personal interviews offer the opportunity to share information and insights. Interviewers are trained to be friendly and sympathetic to respondents to reflect the social nature of interviews.
- Internationally, personal interviews serve researchers in situations where telephone and mail interviews are not feasible due to low telephone usage and poor mail service. In addition, in countries with low literacy rates, the interviewer may employ graphic scales and verbal translation to complete the questionnaires.

DISADVANTAGES OF PERSONAL INTERVIEWS

The main disadvantages of personal interviews are as follows:

- In personal interviews, the respondent sees the interviewer, and therefore the survey loses its anonymity. In most questionnaires there are a considerable number of questions that ask the respondent to reveal sensitive information. A respondent may be reluctant to answer these sensitive questions when the interviewer is present.

- Personal interviews are generally more expensive than other forms of interviews, because they require more man-hours than other interviewing methods. Other factors that contribute to the increase in costs are travel time to the respondents' premises, the high percentage of nonrespondents associated with personal interviews, the length of a typical personal interview questionnaire, additional costs incurred with personal interview callbacks, and the complexity of the questionnaires.
- The demographic characteristics of interviewers are more likely to influence and have an impact on the results in personal interviews than in other methods. Studies have shown that male interviewers produce larger variance in answers than female interviewers for surveys with female samples.[8]
- Personal interviews are also prone to more biases. A respondent may take cues from the interviewer, altering the true nature of the answers. The intonation of words, voice modulation, and facial expressions of the interviewers may influence the responses.
- Personal interviews are more difficult to control with regard to the quality of the interviewing process. Unlike in telephone interviewing, where the interviewer can be monitored, in personal interviews monitoring of the actual interview is virtually impossible. Therefore, in countries that have fewer trained interviewers, cheating is possible. The interviewers could complete part of the questionnaire or fill in the entire questionnaire by themselves.
- In personal interviews a researcher has to go through an additional step of entering the data into a computer for analysis. This not only takes time but also may lead to errors in entry. In a computer-assisted telephone interviewing process, this factor is greatly reduced.

In international research, personal interviewing methods are the most popular.[9] Lower cost for interview staff and lack of other useful methods to reach respondents make personal interviewing a popular technique in contacting respondents in international research. The biggest concern of international researchers is the wide variance in the willingness of respondents to answer questions in personal interviews. In many countries, union activity, business practices, political affiliations, personal hygiene, and other personal care products are never addressed in public, and questions relating to these topics would be totally rejected by respondents in personal interviews. Similarly, in a few countries female respondents are unwilling to participate in surveys, even if the interviewers are females. In such situations, a third party known to the respondent may be used to complete the questionnaire.

TECHNOLOGY-DRIVEN APPROACHES TO INTERVIEWING

Recent advances in computer graphics and three-dimensional modeling have made it possible for marketers to re-create an actual store on a computer screen, providing opportunities for a unique way to contact customers and make surveys as realistic as possible. Virtual-shopping simulations are easy and inexpensive to create using readily available data. Researchers can change the assortment of brands on display in a store setting or the features of any given brand within minutes. By combining computer techniques with traditional low-tech tools of market research, product developers can quickly assess new ideas and concepts for business-to-business global markets.[10] Many companies have already used this approach with success. For example, the Goodyear Tire & Rubber Company had traditionally sold its tires through its own retail stores but was planning to expand distribution to general merchandise outlets. To evaluate consumers' preferences to the change in distribution, the company conducted a study of nearly 1,000 people who were planning to buy Goodyear tires. Each respondent took a trip through a number of different virtual tire stores stocked with a variety of brands and models. Across respondents and shopping trips, the computer varied the prices and warranty levels of the competing brands of tires. Goodyear managers judged a tire to have strong brand equity if it could command a higher price than the competitors' offerings, draw sales away from competitors when its price was reduced, and retain sales in the face of competitors' price cuts. The study proved to be very effective for the company, results they could not have achieved without the new research tool.[11] Similarly, many Realtors in the United States and other countries have started virtual-reality home tours that assist buyers to view homes from a distance. By scanning up and down as well as side to side, the viewer can zoom in and out to get a really good picture of a house. This helps buyers to narrow their choices and save time.

As the computer and other communications technology grow in popularity around the world, there appears to be a movement toward using the link among telephones, cable systems, and computers to harness the power of these newfound communication tools for research purposes. A good example of this trend is the growing use of the Internet to contact potential respondents. Internet-based research is becoming increasingly popular as international companies regularly conduct online studies more quickly. According George Gallup Jr., the renowned pollster, the day is not far off that technology will enable researchers to complete worldwide surveys in a matter of hours.[12]

Use of the Internet for international research in some industrialized countries is very high, and could be tapped to reach a wide segment of respondents. In Singapore, 90 percent of the households are connected to the Internet; in Finland the percentage is 75; and in the United States it is more than 50 percent. The Internet is becoming a favorite in the market researcher's collection of tools because it is cheaper, faster, easier than surveys, and can be used in a variety of settings. Researchers can conduct wide-open, anybody-can-answer polls; opt-in, invitation-only surveys; password-protected research sites and forums; and Internet-based panels. To the extent that Web sites are increasingly likely to be accessed by users worldwide, information on an international sample can be gathered. In addition, this technology allows researchers to track behavior at the site, revealing interest relating to the products and services.[13]

Many studies have shown that the Internet and online data collection can significantly improve data collection.[14] The Internet has also been found to be very cost-effective (average savings of more than 40 percent over other data-collection methods) and efficient. In a study comparing time taken in preparing and sending surveys and the associated costs of using mail, fax, and the Internet to 100 respondents, researchers found that it took eight hours and cost $371 to prepare and send a survey through the mail, two hours and $169 to send it by fax, and two hours and only $59 to send it by e-mail.[15] For example, King Brown & Partners of San Francisco was able to conduct an online study of the Discovery Channel, a cable channel in the United States that airs interesting historical and scientific stories. The cable operators were interested in measuring the usage, perceptions, and demographic characteristics of the Discovery Channel's recently installed Web site. Using a Java-based intercept link on various pages of the Web site, King & Brown researchers were able to survey a relatively nonbiased audience in a fraction of the time a survey would normally take and at a relatively low cost.[16]

While researchers are finding ways to translate their scientific methods for online use, there are concerns about the validity and inherent biases in such methods. But some companies find the results of surveys done through the Internet comparable to traditional methods in data correlation. For example, Avon Products Inc., a cosmetic and beauty products firm based in New York, has used the Internet for data collection and finds the results highly reliable. For years, the company dispatched interviewers to survey Avon representatives in meetings at local malls. But in 1997, the company decided to conduct side-by-side product research studies—one via the Internet and the other through traditional methods. The result of the Internet surveys proved to be comparable to the result of the traditional methods, with high data correlation.[17] The research industry and its clients are becoming more comfortable with online research's results, and the use of the Internet to conduct surveys is expected to grow in the years to come.

Given the infancy of the Internet's infrastructure, researchers are currently unable to take full advantage of its potential. But, like the high penetration of telephones and the resulting use of the phone for contacting large samples, it is expected that in due course, the Internet will also be a valuable tool in conducting surveys.

Contacting respondents through the Internet has some obvious benefits. It is relatively inexpensive and has a much faster turnaround time. Contact via the Internet can be targeted to specific respondents, and there is very little paperwork involved. Internet-based surveys also reduce interviewer biases, and the system is quite flexible in terms of the length of the questionnaire and type of questions asked. In addition, it may be useful for extracting answers to sensitive questions.[18]

Generally speaking, data collection on the Internet falls into the same category as data collection via the mail. Like the mail data-collection method, the Internet is cost-efficient (about 50 percent less expensive than telephone data collection), it can be used for graphical illustrations, and sampling frames can be easily obtained.[19] In addition, the Internet is much faster, so the normal data-collection window is reduced dramatically. Where a study would have taken four to six weeks to field with a mail survey and two to three weeks using the telephone, it may require only two to three days to collect data using the Internet.

Though the Internet has some very attractive benefits as a data-collection medium over other commonly used techniques, it is not used widely due to some major limitations.

On the negative side, there is not much academic research on the validity and reliability of data collected through the Internet. Access to the Internet is still limited to certain segments of the population, making it difficult to gather data that represent the general population. This may lead to sample biases. Worldwide, only a small percentage of the population is hooked up to the Internet; consequently, large-scale, cross-country studies are not practical. In addition, holding the attention of respondents for lengthy questionnaires may be difficult in an Internet setting. Some of the other drawbacks of the Internet are the following:[20]

- *Limited instrument capabilities.* Internet users are used to navigating through volumes of information and are very adept at skipping sections of information content that they are not interested in with the click of a mouse. When confronted with a lengthy questionnaire, they can easily move around these questionnaires, responding to only some portions, which results in partially completed surveys. Therefore, existing Internet infrastructure allows researchers to ask only simple questions.
- *Unobserved data collection.* Like in mail surveys, respondents are neither observed nor prompted while responding to a survey. This limits the researchers' ability to probe for answers as well as note physical cues for additional information.
- *Interface difficulties.* The variations in respondents' browser setup and compatibility to run applications make the process of uniformly administering questionnaires difficult.

Even with the difficulties of using the Internet to obtain data, some international researchers have started tapping into this medium to obtain information from selective clients, suppliers, and service organizations. Especially in business-to-business transactions, the type and amount of data that could be collected is unimaginable.[21] The Internet has also been found to be very useful in internal employee surveys; e-mail is still a novelty, and it arouses the curiosity of its users, drawing the attention of respondents.

SELECTING AN INTERVIEWING APPROACH

Selection of an interview method depends on several factors:

- The type of information required
- Time constraints
- Budgetary limitations
- Respondent characteristics
- Target-country characteristics
- Geographical breadth of the study

All of the above factors affect the choice of interviewing method. The best data-collection methods vary even in countries that are located in the same geographic region. For example, in a study conducted in Europe, researchers found that in Swit-

Table 11.1 **Factors Affecting the Use of a Particular Interviewing Method**

Factors	Mail	Telephone	Personal	Internet
Can be used in many countries	Moderate	Low	High	Low
Speed	Low	High	High	High
Cost	Low	Moderate	High	Low
Interviewer bias	None	Moderate	High	None
Flexibility	Low	Moderate	High	Moderate
Use of visual aids	Moderate	No	High	High
Length of questionnaire	Moderate	Moderate	High	Moderate
Diversity of questions	Moderate	Low	High	Moderate
Sample control	Low	High	High	Low
Anonymity	High	Moderate	Low	High
Response rate	Low	Moderate	Moderate	Low
Wide geographic coverage	High	Moderate	High	Low

zerland and the United Kingdom personal in-home interviews were the most common, whereas in France, street interviews were used most often, and in Sweden, telephone interviews were the norm.[22] The German public also prefers telephone interviews: almost 38 percent of all interviews conducted in Germany are telephone interviews.[23] In some circumstances all three methods may be simultaneously employed. If the mail system in a country is poor, and the people lack telephone access, a personal interview may be the only method available to a researcher. Table 11.1 presents some of the factors that may influence a particular approach.

Most international researchers prefer personal interviews over other techniques in conducting international surveys.

CHAPTER SUMMARY

To conduct a survey, researchers must contact potential respondents directly using a questionnaire. The questionnaire may be administered through the mail, by telephone, or in person. Of these methods, personal interviewing is the most widely used in international research.

Mail questionnaires are less expensive than other methods. Respondents can answer them at leisure. Mail surveys are quite useful in obtaining information for sensitive questions. Mail questionnaires need to be clear, and all necessary instructions must be spelled out. Typically, mail surveys have low returns, but response rates can be improved by providing incentives, creating imaginative cover letters, and stressing the importance of the respondent's contributions on important issues.

Mail surveys are constrained by the mail delivery system. In many countries, mail services are poor, making it very difficult to conduct mail surveys. The probability of nonresponse biases is much higher with mail surveys than with other techniques.

Telephone interviews are fast and quite inexpensive. The researcher is able to monitor the interviewers in telephone surveys. By using computer-assisted telephone interviews, researchers can speed up the data-collection and analysis process. However, not all households have telephones. In many countries telephone penetration rates are less than 10 percent. This situation causes problems in obtaining a representative sample when using telephones for international research.

Personal interviews are flexible, have a wide geographic reach, and are useful when visual aids are needed. Personal interviews have high response rates and are useful in culling nonverbal information. In international research, they are probably the most convenient method for collecting data. Personal interviews can cause interviewer bias, though, and are very expensive. Selecting and training qualified interviewers can be a problem in cross-country research.

In international research, comparability of data and quality of data collection are two key factors that need to be controlled. Reaching a selected sample of respondents efficiently in various countries must be a top priority of international researchers. It may be necessary to employ more than one technique in some countries to complete a survey. Cultural, language, and social differences among countries may require researchers to take some unique approaches in contacting respondents.

Electronic questionnaire distribution is becoming popular in countries where the technology exists. Surveys are conducted through the Internet. As the technology becomes available to more individuals, this form of contacting respondents may grow at a quicker rate.

CHAPTER REVIEW

1. What is questionnaire administration?
2. What are some of the major benefits of using mail questionnaires?
3. In what circumstances would you not use the mail to contact respondents?
4. What are some of the advantages of telephone interviewing over other methods?
5. Is telephone interviewing a good method for conducting international research?
6. What are the strong points of computer-assisted telephone surveys over traditional methods?
7. Why and when would a researcher use personal interviews?
8. What is interviewer bias?
9. If you had to conduct a survey of employees in a large corporation, which approach would you use and why?
10. Should a researcher use only one approach to contact respondents in international research situations?

NOTES

1. Lee H. Murphy, "Japanese Keeping Fewer Secrets from U.S. Firms," *Marketing News* (June 21, 1999), p. 6.

2. D. Monk, "Marketing Research in Canada," *European Research* (November 1987), pp. 271–74.

3. Gerald Albaum and Jesper Strandskov, "Participation in a Mail Survey of International Marketers: Effects of Pre-contact and Detailed Project Explanation," *Journal of Global Marketing* 2, no. 4 (1989), pp. 7–23.

4. Scott Dawson and Dave Dickinson, "Conducting International Mail Surveys: The Effect of Incentives on Response Rates with Industry Population," *Journal of International Business Studies* (Fall 1988), pp. 491–496.

5. L. Kanuk and Conrad Berenson, "Mail Surveys and Response Rates: A Literature Review," *Journal of Marketing Research* (November 1975), pp. 440–453.

6. Raymond A. Jussaume Jr. and Yoshiharu Yamada, "A Comparison of the Viability of Mail Surveys in Japan and the United States," *Public Opinion Quarterly* 54, no. 2 (1990), pp. 219–228.

7. Lewis C. Winters, "International Psychographics," *Marketing Research: A Magazine of Management and Application* (September 1992), p. 48.

8. John Frieman and Edgar Butler, "Some Sources of Interviewer Variance in Surveys," *Public Opinion Quarterly* (Spring 1976), pp. 79–81.

9. Philip Barnard, "Conducting and Coordinating Multicountry Qualitative Studies Across Europe," *Journal of the Market Research Society,* no. 24 (1982), pp. 46–64.

10. John B. Elmer, "Travel the High-Speed Road to Global Market Research," *Marketing News* (September 23, 1996), p. 44.

11. Raymond R. Burke, "Virtual Shopping: Breakthrough in Marketing Research," *Harvard Business Review* (March–April 1996), pp. 120–129.

12. George Gallup Jr., "Survey Research: Current Problems and Future Opportunities," *Journal of Consumer Marketing* 5, no. 1 (1988), pp. 27–30.

13. F. Frost, "Electronic Surveys: New Methods of Primary Data Collection," in *Proceedings of the 27th European Marketing Academy Conference, Marketing Research,* ed. P. Anderson. Stockholm: EMAC, 1998, pp. 213–232.

14. Steve Baron, Nigel M. Healey, and Janet Illieva, "On-line Surveys in Marketing Research," *International Journal of Marketing Research* (July 2002), p. 362.

15. Rick Weible and John Wallace, "Cyber Research: The Impact of the Internet on Data Collection," *Marketing Research* (Fall 1998), pp. 19–24.

16. Jeff Rosenblum and Chris Grecco, "The Future of On-line Research," *Quirks Marketing Research Review* (July 1998), pp. 1–5, http://www.quirks.com. Accessed April 2005.

17. Dana James, "Precision Decision," *Marketing News* (September 27, 1999), p. 23.

18. Bill MacElroy and Bill Geissler, "Interactive Surveys Can Be More Fun than Traditional," *Marketing News* (October 24, 1994), pp. 4–5; Aileen Crowley, "E-mail Surveys Elicit Fast Response, Cut Costs," *PC Week,* (January 30, 1995), p. 11.

19. Tregg Farmer, "Using the Internet for Primary Research Data Collection," Info Tek Research Group, 2000, pp. 1–6, http://researchinfo.com.

20. Ibid.

21. Duane Bachmann, John Elfrink, and Gary Vazzana, "Tracking the Progress of E-mail vs. Snail-mail," *Marketing Research* (Summer 1996), pp. 30–36.

22. Naresh K. Malhotra, "Administration of Questionnaires for Collecting Quantitative Data in International Marketing Research," *Journal of Global Marketing* 4, no. 2 (1991), pp. 63–92.

23. Ian P. Murray, "Surveying a Decade of Surveys in Germany," *Marketing News* (September 23, 1996), p. 33.

ADDITIONAL READING

ARTICLES

Becker, Bob (1999) "Taking Direct Route When Data-Gathering." *Marketing News* 33 (1), p. 29.

Cobanoglu, Cihan, Bill Warde, and Patrick J. Moreo (2001) "A Comparison of Mail, Fax, and Web-Based Survey Methods." *International Journal of Market Research* 43 (4), pp. 441–452.

Cooper, Hester R., Ann Holway, and Michelle Arsan (1998) "Cross-Cultural Research—Should Stimuli Be Psychologically Pure or Culturally Relevant?" *Marketing and Research Today* (February), pp. 67–72.

Dodd, Jonathan (1998) "Market Research on the Internet—Threat or Opportunity." *Marketing and Research Today* (February), pp. 60–66.

Feid, Nimr (1997) "Market Research with Women in the Arab Gulf Countries." *Marketing Research Today* (May), pp. 52–57.

Jobber, David, and John Saunders (1988) "An Experimental Investigation into Cross-National Mail Survey Response Rates." *Journal of International Business Studies* (Fall), pp. 483–489.

Keown, Charles F. (1985) "Foreign Mail Surveys: Response Rates Using Monetary Incentives." *Journal of International Business Studies* (Fall), pp. 151–153.

Siu, Wai-Sum, and Lewis Long-Fing Chau (1998) "Teaching Marketing Research with the Internet." *Journal of Education for Business* 74 (1), pp. 44–49.

Sweeney, Jillian C. (1997) "Collecting Information from Groups: A Comparison of Two Methods." *Journal of the Marketing Research Society* 39 (2), pp. 397–411.

12 Sampling

Sampling makes it possible to draw conclusions about a large population based on observations of only a select portion of the population.

LEARNING OBJECTIVES

After reading this chapter, students should be able to

- Understand the terms "sample," "population," "sampling frame," "element," and "census"
- Learn about the reasons for selecting a sample
- Understand issues concerning the identification of the target population and the selection of a sampling frame
- Understand the differences between probability and nonprobability sampling methods
- Understand sampling errors
- Understand how to choose an appropriate sample design
- Be able to develop a sample plan

A sample is a subset of the units of a population. Most primary studies in international research involve surveying a sample of respondents from a population. In order to understand how information can be gathered from surveys or other primary research techniques, we must distinguish between a sample and a population. A *sample* may be defined as the portion of the population that has been selected for analysis. A population, or universe, in contrast, is any set of individuals (or objects) having some common observable characteristics. Therefore, a *population* is the totality of items or objects under consideration. A sample is a subset or some part of the population. Sampling enables researchers to estimate some unknown characteristic (also called a parameter) of the population.

In many industrialized countries, the general population reads about opinion polls during election time. News groups, research companies, and the government periodically issue reports describing national public opinion on a wide range of current issues. Most of these polls are conducted by selectively questioning a small group from the overall population. In some countries, even the national population data (census) is gathered by surveying a small sample from the population. Sampling makes it possible to draw conclusions about a large population by studying a selected portion of the total population. The use of samples to study large populations is an accepted approach around the world. Sampling saves money and time while providing useful and accurate information. In developing countries, identifying the population and determining the sample elements is difficult. But in a study conducted in Saudi Arabia, researchers found that using students as surrogates for the population worked well. In fact, this approach also helped cut down the cost of sampling and reduced data-gathering problems associated with research in developing countries.[1]

An option other than sampling for collecting data is to contact everyone in the population. When each and every member of the population is contacted for information, it is called a *census*. Therefore, a census is the measurement of each element in the population of interest. By definition, census data are more accurate and reliable than sample data and also reflect the true sentiment of the population. Samples, on the other hand are approximations of a given population's views. Every 10 years, the United States conducts a census of its population to accurately determine the number of people residing in the country. Censuses are prohibitively expensive, time-consuming, and difficult to conduct. Therefore, censuses are conducted when the population size is relatively small. For example, surveys of industrial consumers are frequently in the form of censuses, as there are few of them in each product category.

In business research, the unit or entity upon which a measurement is made is called an *element*. An element could be individual consumers, employees, businesses, organizations, or other subjects. A *sampling unit* is a collection of elements. For example, a household or a firm is a sampling unit. The *sampling frame* is a physical listing of all the units in a population that is used to select the listing units, the sampling units, or both. A list of all households or a directory of businesses is a good example of a sampling frame. A sample is a collection of sampling units selected from a sampling frame. A number of households or a number of business firms is a sample that can be used to infer information about the respective populations.

Advances in communication technology are creating sampling problems for researchers. The use of cell phones, pagers, faxes, the Internet, call-forwarding features, and other convenient services offered to phone subscribers complicates random-digit dialing techniques.[2]

As stated earlier, dealing with an entire population is usually costly, cumbersome, and time-consuming. Therefore, population characteristics or other variables are estimated using samples. For example, the Social Security Administration, which is responsible for social welfare in the United States, wishes to estimate the percentage of the population that needs government assistance. It will have to interview thousands of people to obtain this information. Instead, the agency questions a sample of the population to get the same information. Based on the outcome of the sample, conclusions may be drawn

Figure 12.1 **Sampling Techniques**

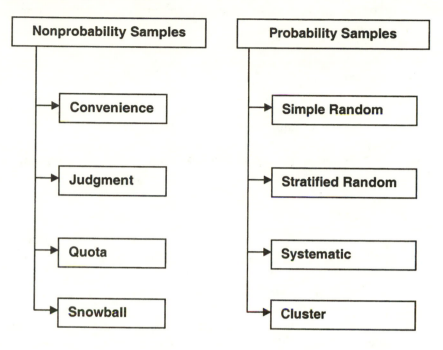

concerning the need for government assistance. Similarly, the production manager of an appliance company will not test the thousands of toaster-ovens it produces to study the quality of the finished product. Instead, only a sample of the toaster-ovens will be selected, and based on the results, conclusions will be drawn concerning the quality of the entire batch of ovens produced. How much of the sample represents the overall population is the key to inferring information about the population.

TYPES OF SAMPLES

Samples can be selected using statistical procedures called *probability* samples, or they can be selected on the basis of nonstatistical approaches, called *nonprobability* samples. Nonprobability samples do not use probability theories in the selection of sample units. In nonprobability samples, the relative probability that any given unit will be included in the sample is not known. Therefore, the researcher has no prior knowledge of the probability that any particular member of the population will be chosen or not. The various sampling techniques used in research are presented in Figure 12.1.

The selection of sampling units in nonprobability sampling is quite arbitrary. Therefore, there is no probabilistic way of interpreting how representative of the overall population the particular sample is. Nonprobability samples are usually much simpler and cheaper to obtain than probability samples. International researchers rely on nonprobability samples because of their ease and convenience. Procedures such as convenience samples, judgment samples, quota samples, and snowball samples are some of the most commonly used nonprobability sampling approaches.

Nonprobability Sampling Procedures

Convenience Sampling

Convenience samples are selected at the convenience of the researcher. They could be a collection of subjects easily grouped, such as members of a particular class, churchgoers, factory workers, persons responding to a promotion, or individuals who visit a shopping center. As the selection of the sample units is done with very little thought to composition of the population, it is very difficult to obtain a truly representative sample through this approach.

Judgment Sampling

Judgment samples are selected on the basis of the expert opinion either of the researcher or an outside specialist. The researcher is assumed to have a thorough knowledge of the population, and the selection is left entirely to the discretion of the researcher or interviewer. Once again, this is an efficient and economical way of selecting a sample. Like the convenience sample, the single greatest drawback of the judgment sample is that there is no probabilistic way of estimating how representative such selected samples are.

Quota Sampling

Quota samples are selected on the basis of the distribution of the defined population across control characteristics. In selecting a quota sample, the only requirement is that the elements selected fit the control characteristics. Once the quotas have been assigned, there is considerable freedom in selecting the elements to be included in the sample.[3] In quota sampling, selection of sample units is constrained by preestablished characteristics, such as age, education, income, number of years of experience, or managerial level, which try to simulate known population characteristics. Quota samples also suffer from the representation issue; therefore, it is not appropriate to use such samples to make inferences of the entire population.

Snowball Samples

Snowball samples are selected on the basis of referrals. In snowball sampling, an initial group of respondents is selected using probability methods. After being interviewed, these respondents are asked to identify others who belong to the target population of interest. Subsequent respondents are then obtained from information provided by the first group of respondents. By obtaining referrals from referrals, this process may be carried out in waves, thus leading to a snowball effect. As the referrals will have respondent characteristics more similar to the person referring them than will respondents selected by chance, snowball sampling is considered a nonprobability sampling design.

The major advantage of snowball sampling is that it substantially increases the likelihood of locating the desired characteristic in the population. This is a low-cost sampling approach and is used in industrial (business-to-business) research or to locate members of rare populations. Snowball sampling is ideal in situations where the government wants to study a segment of the population that may have contracted some illness, such as AIDS, or a scattered minority population. Snowball sampling suffers from sampling biases due to the selection process, which may produce similar respondents representing only a small group within the population. For example, a researcher studying the suppliers of manufactured components for the textile industry in a foreign market may know only a few suppliers. To obtain a larger sample of this group, the researcher may use one or two of the known suppliers to identify the rest of the sample. The most economical way to survey 10 suppliers is to find the first 2 and ask them for the names of other suppliers.

In nonprobability sampling techniques, the researcher can purposely avoid certain locations or groups for safety or accessibility reasons. Results obtained from such samples are biased since entire groups are omitted from the selection process. The appropriate way for researchers to make sure that the sample is representative of the population is to use probability sampling techniques in selecting samples.

PROBABILITY SAMPLES

In probability sampling, the relative probability that any given unit in the population will be included in the sample is left entirely to chance. In addition, in probability sampling each element of the population has a known chance of being selected. Probability sampling techniques allow researchers to draw statistical inferences about a population parameter based on a sample that is quite small in relation to the population. In critical situations, where the results of a research study have far-reaching implications, it is important that the estimate determined through samples be as accurate as possible to the population estimate. Careful sampling procedures are especially important when the population is diverse. By minimizing the subjective selection of the sample, probability techniques are able to select samples that are representative of the overall population. In probability sampling procedures, sampling frames can be designed to come very close to the population by using random-digit telephone samples that may represent all telephone exchanges and households. Similarly, company lists of customers, when used as sampling frames, may also provide excellent representation of the population.[4]

Probability sampling techniques are based on the *central limit theorem*. The central limit theorem states, "If a random sample of 'n' observations is selected from a population, then, when 'n' is sufficiently large, the sampling distribution of the means of the sample ($\bar{x}$) will be approximately a normal distribution." The significance of this theorem is that the population mean is equal to the expected value of all sample means, and the standard error of the mean is the standard deviation of the theoretical distribution of sample means. The central limit theorem assures us that the sample means can be treated as if they were distributed normally, and we can calculate confidence intervals about the sample means. For example, the 95 percent interval will be

$$\bar{x} \pm 1.96 S\bar{x}$$

where $\bar{x}$ is the sample mean and $S\bar{x}$ (standard error of the mean) $= s/\sqrt{n}$. The four most commonly used probability sampling techniques are simple random sample, systematic sample, stratified sample, and cluster sample.

Simple Random Sample

Simple random sample is defined as a sample in which each unit of a given population has a known and equal chance of being included in the sample. Using simple random samples, a researcher is able to calculate the mean and standard deviation for a population. One way to conduct a simple random sample is to assign a number to each element of the population, write these numbers on individual slips of paper, toss them into a hat, and draw the required number of slips from the hat. This approach is possible only if the population is small. For larger populations, random drawing is done through the use of computer-generated random-number tables.

In many instances, the elements of the population are already numbered with, for example, worker identification numbers, household telephone numbers, driver's license numbers, or social security numbers. Once each element of the chosen population has been assigned a unique number, samples can be selected at random. Some research suppliers, such as Survey Sampling Inc., can provide random-digit samples for the United States and about 18 countries in Europe.[5]

Stratified Random Sample

A stratified random sample is obtained by separating the population into mutually exclusive sets, or strata, and then drawing simple random samples from each stratum. Any stratification must be done so that the strata are mutually exclusive. This means that each member of the population must be assigned to only one stratum. Stratifying assures the researcher that all the different subsets within the population are represented in the sample. One advantage of this sampling procedure is that if the strata are relatively homogeneous, the variability within each stratum and the overall variability are reduced. A second advantage of a stratified random sample is that the researcher can draw inferences about each stratum individually.

For example, suppose a researcher wants to estimate the average education level of people living in a city. The researcher could draw a simple random sample of 500 people from the city and estimate the education level of the population. In this case, it is possible that a high proportion of females or older people may be selected even though the population of the city includes an equal number of males and females and the segment of the older people in the city's population is only 25 percent. Instead of a simple random sample, the researcher could stratify the population by age and gender and draw random samples from each stratum to improve the estimate.

Cluster Sampling

Cluster sampling is a simple random sample of groups or clusters of elements. When the clusters are geographic, this technique is called area sampling. In cluster sampling, each stage of sampling involves selecting clusters of sampling units, then listing the units within each selected cluster and sampling again from the resulting lists. Cluster sampling is useful when it is difficult or costly to develop a complete list of the population members. It is also useful whenever the population elements are widely dispersed.

For example, suppose a researcher wants to estimate the average annual household income for Milan, Italy. Using a simple random sample would require a complete list of households in Milan. To use stratified random sampling, the researcher would need a list of households and would also need to have each household categorized by age and education of the head of the household in order to develop the strata. Instead, the researcher could let each block within Milan represent a cluster. Suppose there are 10,000 city blocks in Milan. Further, if there are 50 households on average in each block, to obtain a sample of 500, the researcher could select 50 blocks at random from the 10,000 blocks and from each block could select 10 households at random to arrive at the desired sample of 500 (50×10) households. By reducing the distances between respondents, the costs of interviews could be reduced.

Systematic Sampling

In systematic sampling, a researcher selects every kth element after a random start from the first k elements. The sampling interval k equals N/n, where N = population size and n = sample size. Systematic sampling is usually more efficient than simple random sampling and in some instances is more accurate. One problem that can arise using this procedure is a cyclical pattern that would yield biased results.

For example, in the average household income study for Milan, if the number of households in Milan is 500,000 and the researcher wants a sample of 500 households, using systematic sampling the researcher would obtain the interval (k) by dividing 500,000 by 500 = 1,000 (k). Next, the researcher would pick at random 1 household from the first 1,000 households. Then the researcher would select every thousandth household as part of the sample.

SAMPLING PROCESS

In practical terms, selecting a sample involves accomplishing a series of steps. The sequence of steps, called the sample plan, is what a researcher goes through in order to select a sample for a research study. The sample plan involves the following steps:

- Define the target population
- Obtain an accurate list of the population
- Determine an appropriate sampling method
- Plan the procedure for selecting sampling units

- Determine the sample size
- Draw the sample

DEFINE THE TARGET POPULATION

The target population is the total number of elements of a specific population relevant to the research project. This is most often influenced by the objectives of the research study. In some studies, the target population is very well defined and is easy to identify. For example, a human resources management (HRM) director is trying to determine the training needs of a company. For the HRM director, all the employees in the company are the target population. The target population has to be defined very clearly. This requires the researcher to describe the population through some characteristics. Demographic descriptions such as age, income, educational level, and marital status are often used in population definitions. If the population is business firms, characteristics used may include sales volume, number of employees, type of industry, and geographic location.

In some instances, defining the target population may be more complex. For example, in a beer-consumption study, should the researcher include all males and females above the drinking age or only those who presently are beer drinkers? Should the researcher include occasional drinkers in the population? Similarly, in a study of telecommunication needs of business customers, should the population include just purchasing managers or should it also include the telecommunications specialist? Fundamentally, the question for the telecommunications study is, Is the population the company or its managers?

In either case it is very important that the population be defined correctly. If the population includes subjects who are not part of the intended group, then questioning a few of them may skew the results and make the study invalid. Similarly, not including the right units of the population may hurt the sample as it may result in not questioning some that ought to have been included in the study. For example, if a political scientist wishes to estimate the percentage of votes that a candidate will receive in a presidential election, he or she will interview a sample of the population. The political scientist defines the population as all adults above the age of 21 (21 years of age is the voting age in the country). Selecting a sample of 1,000 from the population, the scientist proceeds to establish their voting preference. Suppose in this country there is a large worker population of aliens who are over 21 years old but are not eligible to vote, as they are noncitizens. The results are not going to reflect the true sentiments of the population, as the population defined here includes invalid units. The outcome of the poll will not bear out in the actual elections. A better definition of the population for the political scientist would have been "all registered voters."

In international research, defining the population is not easy. The relevant respondents may differ from country to country. In the male-dominated societies of the world, women may not play any role in the purchase of some durable goods, or the role of children in the selection and consumption of food products may be different in different countries. These differences need to be recognized in defining a population for sampling. In developing countries, where the numbering of dwelling units is haphazard or nonexistent, defining a population for area sampling becomes impossible.

Obtain an Accurate List of the Population

After defining the population, the researcher needs to look for a suitable list of the population, called the sampling frame. A sampling frame is the list of all elements from which the sample may be drawn, for example, a list of all stockbrokers at the London Stock Exchange or a list of all doctors in an area may be used as a sampling frame.

In business-to-business research when the population is other business organizations, the task of identifying the sampling frame is more complex. Technological innovations and competitive pressures are redefining industries and businesses. How do you define the sampling frame in these times of virtual business, in-home business, never-ending mergers and acquisitions, and flat organizational decision-making teams?[6] A way out of this problem appears to be to define business entities by revenues and number of employees and thus simplify the process of identifying sampling frames.

In some countries, directories with names and addresses are easily available, including such lists as homes with phone connections, lists of automobile owners, and lists of the general population (through identification numbers such as social security or food ration programs). In other instances, a list of a specific population group is available through research suppliers for a fee. These companies provide mailing lists broken down by specific characteristics, such as zip codes, profession, or telephone exchange. Mailing lists contain the names, addresses, and telephone numbers of specific populations. Mailing lists are sometimes compiled from magazine subscriptions or credit card ownership. In countries where the government has enacted strict privacy laws, mailing lists are difficult to obtain.

The quality and availability of sampling frames across countries vary dramatically. In most industrialized countries it is easy to obtain sampling frames. In some of the newly industrialized countries of Asia, reliable sampling frames are easily available. These tend to be updated often, as the governments of these countries spend considerable time and money compiling statistics of their populations.[7] In developing countries, lists are not available or are inaccurate. Governments in these countries do not conduct censuses of their populations, and accurate maps of cities and towns are not available. These conditions lead to sampling frame errors in most developing countries. In such instances, researchers have to create their own lists at tremendous cost and expenditure of time.

It is rarely possible to have a complete list that includes all the members of a population. When a list does not contain all the members of a population, it suffers from sampling frame errors. A sampling frame error occurs when certain sample elements are excluded or when an entire population is not accurately represented in the sampling frame. Most lists suffer from sampling frame errors. The key to assessing sampling frame errors is to judge how different the people listed in the sampling frame are from the population so as to estimate what kinds of subjects in the population

Table 12.1 **Comparison of Sampling Techniques**

Type of Sample	Usage	Strengths	Weakness	Costs
Convenience	High	Simple; no need for lists	May not be representative; cannot measure variability; cannot project data	Low
Judgment	Moderate	More representative; can meet some specific objectives	Judgment bias; cannot project data	Moderate
Quota	High	Use of stratification; no need for lists	Errors from population cannot be estimated; cannot project data	Moderate
Simple random	Low	Simple to use; easy to analyze data	Requires sampling frame; some segments may not be represented	High
Stratified random	Moderate	Representative segments within population can be analyzed	Requires a good list sample	High
Cluster	High	No need for lists; good yield	Potential for error; possible duplication or omission of elements	Low
Systematic	Moderate	Simple and easy to use	High variability	Moderate

are not listed in the sampling frame. If a complete list of population elements is not available, geographic sampling frames may be substituted instead.

Determine an Appropriate Sampling Method

There are several ways of taking a sample. As discussed earlier in this chapter, a researcher can use either a nonprobability sampling approach or a probability sampling design. Table 12.1 provides a summary comparison of the various sampling techniques. The choice depends on many factors including the implications of the study, accuracy desired, cost of research, and time considerations.

Accuracy

Researchers have to make sure that the sample selected is representative of the target population. But the tolerance for sampling and nonsampling errors may vary from project to project. Depending on how critical the study's outcome is, budget considerations may influence the degree of accuracy desired. If the research study is going to be used for investing large sums of money and if the sample result must be an accurate representation of the target population, then the researcher will select a sample with a very high level of accuracy.

Cost of Research

More sophisticated sample designs cost considerably more than simple designs. If a researcher has unlimited funds and a large support staff, he or she may be willing to spend a substantial amount of money in selecting a sample that is representative of the target population and has a very high level of accuracy. Researchers concerned with the cost of the research versus the value of information may select a nonprobability sampling design to cut down on the total cost of the research.

Time Consideration

Researchers who need to complete a project quickly, as is often the case in the international arena, will likely opt for a nonprobability sampling design to save time. A convenience sample may be selected and contacted within one or two days, whereas a stratified random sample may take a few weeks.

A researcher designing a sample for a specific project will identify a number of sampling criteria and evaluate the relative importance of each criterion before selecting a sample design. Regardless of the size of the sample, the specific sampling design must be clearly articulated by the researcher. The sample design varies according to the objectives of the research study.

PLAN THE PROCEDURE FOR SELECTING SAMPLING UNITS

Planning the procedure for selecting sampling units includes all necessary steps to draw the sample. In selecting sampling units, all events should be considered carefully and all potential problem areas should be anticipated. This helps the researcher to develop contingency plans. In international situations, problems occur very frequently and the more prepared the researcher is, the greater the probability that the study can be completed on time. For example, if a stratified random sample is going to be used, the researcher should identify the various strata, obtain information on each stratum, and be prepared to substitute the strata if one is not easily identifiable or cannot be reached. In some countries, information on population and demographic breakdowns may not be available; therefore, planning a stratified random sample in these countries is not feasible. Hence, the researcher will have to plan some other equally reliable sampling design.

DETERMINE THE SAMPLE SIZE

Sample size refers to the number of elements to be included in the study. One of the most common questions asked in research studies is, How large should the sample be? There is no simple answer to this question. Some of the factors that should be considered in determining the sample size include the importance of the decision, the type of research (exploratory versus conclusive), the number of parameters, the type of analysis desired, the yield (number of useful responses obtained from the total contacts made), and the resource constraints.

Research that provides information for making critical decisions, for example, in the case of approval of a new drug or regarding large outlays of funds, generally calls for large and precise samples. The size of the sample naturally affects the cost of the research. Therefore, if there are budgetary constraints, a researcher may not be able to afford large samples, even though the large sample may add to the accuracy of the research.

The type of research also has an impact on the sample size. By definition, exploratory research is conducted with smaller samples. Research methods such as focus groups or depth interviews are meant to draw insights and are not used for predictions about the total population. In contrast, for research methods such as surveys, sample sizes need to be large, as they are used for forecasting.

If the research is conducted to collect information on a large number of variables, larger samples are required. The cumulative effects of sampling error across variables are reduced in a larger sample. Similarly, if more complex analytical techniques are desired, the sample size should be large. Some of the techniques, such as multivariate analysis, can be performed only with large sample sizes. Also, if the data need to be analyzed for subsamples, the sample size should be large.

Finally, the sample size decision is guided by the availability of the resources. If funds are not available, time is critical, or the skills of the researchers are limited, then sample sizes tend to be small. This situation is more prevalent in international research. In international research, quite often the circumstances and local conditions dictate the size of the sample. Even though this type of sample size determination may not be ideal from a statistical point of view, researchers are forced to adapt to this method due to difficulties of determining sample sizes in these countries. If the conditions permit and the researcher has sufficient time and funds, a statistically derived sample size is recommended.

If the sample size is determined using judgment, experience, convenience, or a combination of these, the sample size may not be appropriate. In addition, the researcher is in no position to estimate the confidence interval of the information obtained from the sample. If statistical techniques are employed, the sample size depends on three factors:

- The parameter to be estimated
- The desired confidence level of the interval estimator
- The maximum error of estimation

Determining sample size is discussed in detail in chapter 13.

DRAW THE SAMPLE

Drawing the sample is a two-step process. First, the sample unit must be selected. Second, information must be obtained from the selected units. The problem arises when the selected person or element is unwilling to provide the necessary information. Internationally, due to cultural and other societal norms, the rate of rejection is often very high. Researchers have to devise creative measures to obtain responses in such societies. In one example, researchers used the influence and offices of village elders in African tribal communities to have the members of the village respond to a questionnaire.

Typically, all identified members of a sample may not complete the questionnaire. This leads to substitutions. Substitutions occur whenever an individual who was qualified to be in the sample is unsuitable, unavailable, or unwilling to respond. Substitutions must be handled carefully so as not to inject any sampling bias. There are three different substitution methods available: drop-downs, oversampling, and resampling.

The drop-down substitution is often used with systematic sampling. In this form of substitution, if the identified caller is unavailable or unwilling, the researcher goes to the next person on the list and tries to complete the questionnaire. After that, the researcher resumes the originally established skip interval. For example, the head of the public works department of a city wants to get inputs from the department's approximately 10,000 staff members to find out ways to improve the processing of bids from contractors on public projects. The department head uses a systematic sampling design and decides on a sample of 100. The skip interval (k) in this case is 10,000 ÷ 100 = 100. Using the alphabetical list of his staff as the sampling frame and in accordance with the systematic sampling procedure, the department head selects the first person at random from the first 100 staff members in the list. After the department head identifies the first respondent from the list, every hundredth name from the list is selected for contact. If one of the selected respondents is not available, the interviewer is instructed to contact the next staff member on the list. After that, the skip interval is resumed. There is no limit to the number of drop-downs to be followed for obtaining a qualified respondent.

Oversampling assumes some prior knowledge of the population or experience with similar studies or both. The researcher has firsthand knowledge of incidence rates and nonresponse rates and uses this knowledge to add more elements to the sample. For example, if the researcher knows from experience that in a certain country the response rate for a mail survey is approximately 10 percent, then the researcher would mail out 2,000 questionnaires to obtain a final sample of 200 respondents.

Resampling is yet another option available to researchers to make up for the loss of original members of the sampling frame. In this procedure, the sampling frame is tapped for additional names after the initial sample is drawn. Care should be taken to ensure that the prospective respondents appearing in the original sample are not included in the resample.

Sampling techniques and procedures vary in accuracy, reliability, and cost from country to country. If the same sampling procedures are used in each country, the results may not be comparable.[8] To achieve comparability in sample composition and representation, it is recommended that researchers use different sampling techniques in different countries when the sampling frames are not identical.

Because of the lack of sampling frames, the inaccessibility of certain respondents (such as children, women, and other groups in some cultures), and the lack of research infrastructure, probability sampling techniques are rarely used in some of the developing and less developed countries. In many of these countries, quota and snowball sampling have been used quite effectively.

CHAPTER SUMMARY

Sampling is a procedure that uses a small number of elements of a given population as a basis for drawing conclusions about the whole population. Because of cost and time constraints in conducting a survey of the total population (a census), sampling is often the only efficient method available to obtain information from the population. Samples taken with care and accuracy can provide useful information for decision makers.

Sampling design starts with population definition. Population definition identifies and describes the elements of the population. Incorrect definition of the population is likely to produce biased results. After defining the population, a researcher has to determine the sampling frame. A sampling frame is a representation of the elements of the target population. It consists of a list of elements or individual members of the overall population from which a sample is drawn. A sampling unit is a single element subject to selection in the sample. In international research, the lack of information, differences in cultures, and unfamiliarity with the culture all compound defining the target population.

The next step in the sampling process involves selecting a sampling technique and determining the sample size. In addition to quantitative analysis, several qualitative considerations should be taken into account in determining the sample size. Sampling techniques may be classified as nonprobability and probability. The most commonly used nonprobability sampling techniques are convenience sampling, judgment sampling, quota sampling, and snowball sampling. Nonprobability sampling techniques are relatively inexpensive and easy to use. They do not, however, permit an objective evaluation of the sample results. Also, the results obtained through nonprobability sampling techniques are not statistically projectable to the population.

The probability sampling techniques that are more frequently used are simple random sampling, stratified random sampling, systematic sampling, and cluster sampling. In probability sampling techniques, sampling units are selected by chance. Each sampling unit has a known and nonzero probability of being selected. Probability sampling allows researchers to obtain a more precise sample. Through probability techniques a researcher can prespecify the probability of selecting each sample, determine the precision of the sample estimates, and make reliable projections to the target population.

The choice between nonprobability and probability sampling should be based on the type of research, degree of accuracy desired, relative magnitude of errors, variability in the population, and operational considerations. There are two sources of errors in estimating parameters using samples. One type of error is random sampling error arising from the chance variations of the sample from the population. Nonsampling errors are the result of sample bias.

The key steps in developing a sample are defining the target population, obtaining an accurate list of the population, selecting a sampling frame, determining appropriate sampling methods, developing a procedure for selecting sampling units, determining the sample size, and drawing the sample. When conducting international research, it might be necessary to use different sampling techniques in different countries to achieve comparability in sample compositions across countries.

CHAPTER REVIEW

1. Define "population," "sample," "sampling frame," and "sample element."
2. Why do researchers use samples to estimate population parameters?
3. Describe the difference between a nonprobability sample and a probability sample.
4. Describe briefly each of the nonprobability sampling methods.
5. Describe briefly each of the probability sampling methods.
6. Describe each of the three methods of substitution for individuals who refuse to participate in a survey.
7. Identify some of the unique problems associated with sampling in international research.

NOTES

1. Ugur Yavas, "Research Note: Students as Subjects in Advertising and Marketing Research," *International Marketing Review* 11, no. 4 (1994), pp. 35–43.

2. Ibid.

3. Gordon A. Wyner, "Representation, Randomization, and Realism," *Marketing Research* (Fall 2001), pp. 4–5.

4. Ibid.

5. "Business Sampling Options Grow," *The Frame* (April 1999), p. 1.

6. "Shifts in Technology Impact Sample Design," *The Frame* (January 2000), p. 1.

7. Wyner, "Representation, Randomization, and Realism."

8. Lucy Webster, "Comparability in Multi-Country Surveys," *Journal of Advertising Research* (December 1966), pp. 14–18.

ADDITIONAL READING

BOOKS

Levy, Paul S., and Stanley Lemeshaw. *Sampling of Populations: Methods and Applications.* 3rd ed. New York: John Wiley & Sons, 1999.

Seymour, Sudman. *Applied Sampling.* San Francisco: American Press, 1976.

Thompson, Steven K. *Sampling.* New York: John Wiley & Sons, 2002.

ARTICLES

Assael, Henry, and John Keon (1982) "Nonsampling vs. Sampling Errors in Sampling Research." *Journal of Marketing* (Spring), pp. 114–123.

Brock, Sabra E. (1989) "Marketing Research in Asia: Problems, Opportunities, and Lessons." *Marketing Research* (September 1989), p. 47.

Gillett, Raphael (1989) "Confidence Interval Construction by Stein's Method: A Practical and Economical Approach to Sample Size Determination." *Journal of Marketing Research* (May), pp. 237–240.

Kjell, Gunnar (2000) "The Level-Based Stratified Sampling Plan." *Journal of the American Statistical Association* 95 (452), pp. 1185–1191.

Laird, London E., Jr., and Sharon K. Banks (1977) "Relative Efficiency and Bias of Plus-One Telephone Sampling." *Journal of Marketing Research* 14 (3), pp. 294–299.

MacFarlane, Phyllis (2002) "Structuring and Measuring the Size of Business Markets." *International Journal of Market Research* 44 (1), pp. 7–30.

Reiter, Jerome P. (2002) "Topics in Survey Sampling/Finite Population Sampling and Inference: A Prediction Approach." *Journal of the American Statistical Association* (March), pp. 357–358.

Walker, J. (2002) "A Sequential Discovery Sampling Procedure." *Journal of the Operational Research Society* 53 (1), p. 1.

13 | Sample Size Determination Using Statistics

Statistical inference allows a researcher to draw conclusions about a population parameter based on samples.

LEARNING OBJECTIVES

After reading this chapter, students should be able to

- Understand the concepts of descriptive and inferential statistics
- Understand frequency distributions
- Understand the concepts of standard deviation and the characteristics of a normal distribution
- Distinguish among population distribution, sample distribution, and sampling distribution
- Be able to compute confidence interval estimates
- Understand sample size determination for means and proportions
- Understand the nonstatistical factors that influence sample size
- Understand nonresponse issues in sampling

The first part of the chapter discusses the statistical applications that are useful in understanding determining sample sizes.

Statistical procedures are used in determining sample sizes. In practice, in some international settings, a researcher may use his or her experience or judgment to determine sample sizes. Though not the best way to determine sample sizes, this approach is necessary in some situations where the researcher may be forced to bypass statistical techniques due to time constraints or the inability to use statistical designs.

Before discussing sample size selection, it may be useful to present some of the key statistical concepts that are used in deriving sample sizes. Statistics are divided into two categories: descriptive and inferential. Descriptive statistics deal with methods of organizing, summarizing, and presenting numerical data in a convenient form. Tables presented in the *United Nations Statistical Yearbook,* which provides national data about population, gross national product, and economic growth, are good examples of descriptive statistics.

Inferential statistics allow decision makers to draw conclusions or inferences about characteristics of a population based on information available in a sample taken from the population. For example, a large multinational company is planning to introduce one of its successful products that did very well in Europe to the Asian market. After financial analysis, the company has determined that the proposed new product must capture at least 10 percent of the Asian market in order to attain break-even levels. To obtain additional information before arriving at a decision on whether to introduce the new product or not, the company decides to conduct a survey of 400 potential consumers in the Asian market. On the basis of a sample product, each consumer is asked whether he or she would buy the new product if offered at a prespecified price. If 80 out of the 400 respondents (20 percent) in the sample indicate intent to buy the new product, the company may decide to introduce the product in the Asian market because of the positive response.

The decision made by the multinational company is based on inferential statistics. The company is drawing a conclusion about the entire target market on the basis of information provided by the sample. Statistical inference is the process of making an estimate about a population based on sample information.

FREQUENCY DISTRIBUTION

A very simple way to present descriptive data is through frequency distribution. In frequency distribution, data are grouped into intervals called classes, and the number of observations in each class is recorded. For example, a commercial bank has data on the weekly deposits for each of its customers. Table 13.1 summarizes the deposit rates for 20 of the bank customers.

Using the data for 20 customers, the bank manager can draw some conclusions about the deposit rates. One way to analyze the bank deposit data would be to determine the proportions of all deposits that lie within various intervals between the lowest and highest deposit amounts. The bank manager may want to find out what percentage of deposits fall above $150. This information can be obtained by forming a frequency distribution of the deposits into six intervals: 40–60, 61–80, 81–100, 101–120, 121–140, and 141–160. The resulting distribution is presented in Table 13.2.

The data presented in Table 13.2 are a frequency distribution. Frequency distribution provides more useful information to the researcher than other tabulations. From the table, the bank manager can conclude that 65 percent of bank deposits based on the sample of 20 bank customers are between 81 and 140.

Before constructing a frequency distribution, researchers must decide on the appropriate number, size, and limits of classes to use. The objective of the research project, the variables to be studied, and a researcher's experience are all factors that assist in setting up class limits. Some researchers use a trial-and-error method to determine the most useful class intervals. Class intervals are set up such that the intervals are nonoverlapping, the intervals contain all observations, the intervals are limited to just

Table 13.1 **Deposits by Customers**

Customer Number	Deposit ($)	Customer Number	Deposit ($)
1	115	11	75
2	50	12	105
3	65	13	160
4	100	14	110
5	85	15	125
6	90	16	70
7	120	17	95
8	175	18	120
9	110	19	135
10	45	20	140

Table 13.2 **Frequency Distribution of Bank Deposits**

Intervals	Frequency	Percentage of Deposits in Each Interval
40–60	2	10
61–80	3	15
81–100	4	20
101–120	7	35
121–140	2	10
141–160	2	10
Total	20	100

a few (usually between 5 and 20), the width of the interval is predetermined, and the width remains constant for a set of data.

The nonoverlapping condition implies that each observation falls into exactly one interval. For example, in setting up a frequency distribution of grades for an English class, the instructor sets the following intervals:

Interval	Grade
1	1 to 2
2	2 to 3
3	3 to 4

The intervals for the English class grades in the above example are overlapping. A student who earns a grade of 2 may be placed in interval 1 or in interval 2. The correct intervals for the English class grade distribution would be as follows:

Interval	Grade
1	1 to 2
2	2.1 to 3
3	3.1 to 4

In frequency distributions, the number of intervals used is normally relatively small (ranges between 5 and 20). If the number of intervals used is too large, deducing the major clusters becomes difficult. Once the number of intervals has been decided, the approximate size or width of each interval is determined by:

Size of interval = (Largest value − Smallest value) ÷ Number of intervals

In the example of bank deposits, the largest deposit is 160 and the smallest is 40. The range values for bank data are 160 − 40 = 120. If the bank manager uses 6 intervals, the width of each interval will be 120 ÷ 6 = 20.

Researchers also keep the width of the interval the same for a given set of data to facilitate interpretation of the frequency distribution. Therefore, for the bank deposit example, the width of each interval for bank deposits would be kept at 20. Finally, simple (integral) values should be chosen as the intervals.

The absolute frequency shown in Table 13.2 can be shown as proportion or percentage of measurements falling into the various intervals. When presented as percentages, the distribution is called relative frequency.

Relative frequency = Interval frequency ÷ Total number of measurements

The resulting relative frequency distribution for the bank deposit data is presented in Table 13.3.

CENTRAL TENDENCY

Frequency distributions enable the researcher to summarize large sets of data and draw useful conclusions. The researcher is able to see how the data are distributed between two extreme values. Summarized data may be further improved by computing numerical descriptive measures. These measures provide precise values that are easy to manipulate, interpret, and compare with one another. These measures are collectively called "central tendencies" or "measures of central location." The measures of central location provide more powerful analysis of the data than do frequency distributions. Central location measures are most useful when the data represent a sample from which inferences will be drawn about the entire population. The three most widely used measures of central location are the mean, the median, and the mode.

THE ARITHMETIC MEAN

The arithmetic mean is commonly referred to as the average. The mean is easy to compute, interpret, and mathematically manipulate. For researchers, it is the best measure of central location. The one main drawback of the measurement of mean is that it is inordinately influenced by extreme observations. For example, the mean value of 1, 2, and 3 is 2 and that of 1, 2, 3, and 18 is 6. The mean of a set numbers is

Mean = Sum of measurements ÷ Number of measurements

Table 13.3 **Relative Frequency Distribution for Bank Deposits**

Interval	Relative Frequency
40–60	2/20 = 0.10
61–80	3/20 = 0.15
81–100	4/20 = 0.20
101–120	7/20 = 0.35
121–140	2/20 = 0.10
141–160	2/20 = 0.10
Total	20/20 = 1.00

Many symbols are used in dealing with samples. These are:

N = Population size
n = Sample size
μ = Mean of the population
$\bar{x}$ = Mean
Σ = Summation

Using the symbols, the sample mean of n measurements $x_1, x_2, x_3, \ldots x_n$ can be expressed as

$$\bar{x} = \frac{\sum_{i=1}^{n} x_i}{n}$$

Therefore, the mean of bank deposits from the sample, 115, 95, 120, 135, and 145 is

$$\bar{x} = \frac{115 + 95 + 120 + 135 + 145}{5} = 122$$

Similarly, the population means of N measurements $x_1, x_2, x_3, \ldots x_N$ can be expressed as

$$\mu = \frac{\sum_{i=1}^{N} x_i}{N}$$

MEDIAN

The median of a set of measurements is the value that falls in the middle when the measurements are arranged in order of magnitude. When an even number of measurements is involved, any number between the two middle values may be used as the median. For example, to compute the median deposit value for nine bank customers from Table 13.1, the data first have to be arranged in order of magnitude as 70, 75, 95, 105, 110, 115, 120, 135, and 160. The median value is then obtained by selecting the fifth value (for nine data points the midpoint is the fifth value). The middle value of this series is the fifth value—115. Therefore, the median value of this series is 115. That is, half the bank deposits fall below 115 and half fall above 115.

The median value is often preferred by researchers, especially if there are extreme observations. The median is the most appropriate measure of central location to use when the data under consideration have an ordinal scale. If the data collected are from a scale that measures "preferences" or "degree of difficulty," then the use of the median is more fitting.

MODE

The mode of a set of measurements is the value that occurs most frequently. For the bank deposit example, the branch manager observes the following deposit pattern for a typical week—100, 150, 125, 150, 175, 200, 150, 225, and 175. Of the nine different deposits, 150 appears three times, more than any other deposit amount. The mode of the deposits for that given week is 150. The mode is useful when demand for an item or occurrence of an event is of interest.

MEASURES OF DISPERSION

The mean, median, and mode summarize the central tendency of frequency distributions. But these measures do not convey the complete picture. For example, the mean defective rate for a company at its plant in Osaka, Japan, was 8 per employee per week; at its Kuala Lumpur, Malaysia, plant, it was 7.5 per employee per week. From the data presented, it appears that the Kuala Lumpur plant produces better-quality product than the one in Osaka. On further investigation, it was found that the defective rate per employee in the Osaka plant ranged between 5 to 10 defects per employee per week. In contrast, the defective rate ranged between 2 and 15 defects per employee per week in Kuala Lumpur. From this additional information, it appears that though the Osaka plant has a higher rate of defects per employee per week, it has a much lower variability in the defective rate. Therefore, the arithmetic mean alone may not be sufficient to draw inferences about a given population. It is equally important to consider the variability in the results to be more precise about the population characteristic under study.

Once the arithmetic mean of a set of measurements is computed, the next important measure to determine should be how typical the average value is. Therefore, it is important to know how far the values depart from the central location, in other words, how spread out the measurements are from the mean. The concept of variability is critical to understanding statistical inferences. There are two measures of variability—the *range* and the *percentiles*. The range measures the numerical difference between the largest and smallest measurements. For percentiles, the *p*th percentile of a set of measurements is the value for which at most *p* percent of the measurements are less than that value and at most $(100 - p)$ percent of the measurements are greater than that value. In other words, the 95th percentile of a distribution $p_1, p_2, \ldots$, and p_{95} is such that 5 percent of the data fall below p_{95}.

In the bank deposit example in Table 13.1, the lowest bank deposit for the week was 45 and the highest was 175, so the range would be $175 - 45 = 130$. The range is a useful measure to know, but it does not provide information about the dispersion of the values falling between the smallest and the largest measurements. Information concerning the dispersion can be observed through percentiles.

The pth percentile is exactly like the median—the value for which 50 percent of the measurements are smaller, and, at most, 50 percent of the measurements are greater. Therefore the median is the 50th percentile. But the median is just one percentile measure. The other commonly used percentile measures are quartiles and deciles.

In quartile measurements, the data is divided into quarters, as shown below:

> First (lower) quartile = Q_1 = 25th percentile
> Second (middle) quartile = Q_2 = 50th percentile (also called median)
> Third (upper) quartile = Q_3 = 75th percentile

In deciles, the data is divided into tenths, as shown below:

> First (lower) decile = 10th percentile
> Ninth (upper) decile = 90th percentile

Using the bank deposit data in Table 13.1, it can be demonstrated how the computation of quartiles and deciles could be done. To find the quartiles for the bank deposits—115, 50, 65, 100, 85, 90, 120, 175, 110, 45, 75, 105, 160, 110, 125, 70, 95, 120, 135, and 140, we must first arrange the measurements in ascending order:

45, 50, 65, 70, 75, 85, 90, 95, 100, 105, 110, 110, 115, 120, 120, 125, 135, 140, 160, 175

      ↑   ↑   ↑

  lower quartile   median   upper quartile

The lower quartile is the value for which, at most, $0.25 \times n$ of the measurements are smaller and, at most, $0.75 \times n$ of the measurements are larger. That is, for the bank deposit data, $0.25 \times 20 = 5$ of the measurements are smaller and $0.75 \times 20 = 15$ of the measurements are larger. The only measurement satisfying these criteria is 75. Therefore, 75 is the first or lower quartile. Similarly, we can establish that the median is 107.5 (when the percentile falls between two of the measurements, you select the midpoint between the two measurements, i.e., $105 + 110 \div 2 = 107.50$) and the third quartile is 125.

Percentiles are widely used as measures of relative position or performance. For example, the price/earnings ratio of a company's stock could be evaluated whether it is in the upper quartile, middle quartile, or lower quartile. Similarly, students' grades on an SAT could be easily evaluated from a quartile point of view.

VARIABILITY IN DATA

The two most widely accepted measures of variability are *variance* and *standard deviation*. Variance and standard deviation take all the data into account and are fundamental to statistical inferences. The standard deviation can be used to describe differences among all measurements. The standard deviation describes a certain distance. The measure described by each unit of standard deviation depends on the distribution of measurements. The size of a standard deviation unit is fixed for any set of measurements.

The variance of a population of N measurements $x_1, x_2, x_3, \ldots x_N$ having a mean μ is given by

$$\sigma^2 = \frac{\sum_{i=1}^{N}(x_i - \mu)^2}{N}$$

The variance of a sample of n measurements $x_1, x_2, x_3, \ldots x_n$ having a mean $\bar{x}$ is given by

$$s^2 = \frac{\sum_{i=1}^{n}(x_1 - \bar{x})^2}{n-1} \qquad s^2 = \frac{1}{n-1}\left[\sum_{i=1}^{n}x_i^2 - \frac{\left(\sum_{i=1}^{n}x_i\right)^2}{n}\right]$$

The variance of a sample is computed as follows:

- Calculate the arithmetic mean of a set of measurements ($\bar{x}$).
- Calculate the deviations by subtracting the mean from each measurement individually ($x_i - \bar{x}$), where x_i is the individual measurements.
- Square each difference.
- Total (sum) all the squared differences.
- Divide this total for a sample by the number of measurements minus 1, ($n - 1$). The result obtained is the sample variance, s^2, where n is the total number of measurements.

STANDARD DEVIATION

The standard deviation of a set of measurements is the positive square root of the variance of the measurements. While variance is a useful measure of the relative variability of two sets of measurements, it is useful to determine variability that is expressed in the same unit as the original measurements, just as the mean is. Therefore, the standard deviation of a sample with a variance of s^2 is

$$s = \sqrt{s^2}$$

For example, the following table gives the weekly sales for a department store:

Sales (000)	Mean ($\bar{x}$)	$(x_i - \bar{x})$	$(x_i - \bar{x})^2$
$x_1 = 90$	100	−10	100
$x_2 = 100$	100	0	0
$x_3 = 110$	100	10	100
$x_4 = 105$	100	5	25
$x_5 = 95$	100	−5	25
Total = 500	500 ÷ 5 = 100	0	250

Therefore, the variance and standard deviation for the department store sales are:

$$s^2 = \frac{1}{n-1}\left[\sum_{i=1}^{n}x_i^2 - \frac{\left(\sum_{i=1}^{n}x_i\right)^2}{n}\right]$$

$$s^2 = \frac{250}{n-1} = \frac{250}{4} = 62.5$$

$$s = \sqrt{62.5} = 7.91$$

Variances help to assess the true value of the mean. The mean by itself may distort the significance of the central tendency. In analyzing sales, profits, or return on investment, a larger variance corresponds to a higher level of risk. For example, a multinational company has two wholly owned subsidiaries in two different countries. The average annual return on investment (ROI) over the past 10 years for these two subsidiaries (X and Y) is as follows:

Subsidiary	1	2	3	4	5	6	7	8	9	10
ROI (%) X	11.0	8.5	7.5	6.0	9.0	10.0	12.0	10.0	7.0	9.0
ROI (%) Y	12.5	8.5	5.0	9.5	15.5	20.5	15.0	8.5	4.0	11.0

The mean ROI for subsidiary X is

$$\bar{x} = \frac{11.0+8.5+7.5+6.0+9.0+10.0+12.0+10.0+7.0+9.0}{10} = \frac{90}{10} = 9$$

The mean ROI for subsidiary Y is

$$\bar{x}_Y = \frac{12.5+8.5+5.0+9.5+15.5+20.5+15.0+8.5+4.0+11.0}{10} = \frac{110}{10} = 11$$

For each subsidiary, the variance of the ROI needs to be calculated. For subsidiary X,

$$\sum_{i=1}^{10} x_i = 90$$

$$\sum_{i=1}^{10} x_i^2 = (11)^2 + (8.5)^2 + (7.5)^2 + (6)^2 + (9)^2 + (10)^2 + (12)^2 + (10)^2 + (7)^2 + (9)^2$$

$$= 840.5$$

$$S_X^2 = \frac{1}{n-1}\left[\sum_{i=1}^{10} x_i^2 - \frac{\left(\sum_{i=1}^{10} x_i\right)^2}{n}\right] = \frac{1}{9}\left[840.5 - \frac{(90)^2}{10}\right] = 3.39$$

For subsidiary Y,

$$\sum_{i=1}^{10} x_i = 110$$

$$\sum_{i=1}^{10} x_i^2 = (12.5)^2 + (8.5)^2 + (5)^2 + (9.5)^2 + (15.5)^2 + (20.5)^2 + (15)^2 + (8.5)^2 + (4)^2 + (11)^2$$

$$= 1438.5$$

$$s_Y^2 = \frac{1}{n-1}\left[\sum_{i=1}^{10} x_i^2 - \frac{\left(\sum_{i=1}^{10} x_i\right)^2}{n}\right] = \frac{1}{9}\left[1438.5 - \frac{(110)^2}{10}\right] = 25.39$$

The mean ROI is higher for subsidiary Y, but its variance is much higher compared to subsidiary X. The standard deviations for the two ROIs are:

$$s_Y = \sqrt{s_Y^2} = \sqrt{25.39} = 5.04$$

$$s_X = \sqrt{s_X^2} = \sqrt{3.39} = 1.84$$

Therefore, in the long run, subsidiary X is a more stable investment.

COEFFICIENT OF VARIATION

Another useful statistic or measure to know is the coefficient of variation. The coefficient of variation (CV) of a set of data is the standard deviation of the data divided by its mean. For a population, $CV = \sigma \div \mu$, and for a sample, $CV = s \div x$.

In many cases, comparing standard deviation and coefficient of variation leads to the same conclusion. Therefore, for our example of comparing ROI for the two foreign subsidiaries, the CV for subsidiary X is 2.43/9.0 = 0.27, and for subsidiary Y, 5.03/11.0 = 0.46.

DISTRIBUTIONS

There are three types of distributions that need to be clarified in determining sample sizes. These are population distribution, sample distribution, and sampling distribution. A frequency distribution of the population elements is called a population distribution. The mean of the population distribution is represented by μ, and its standard deviation by σ. A frequency distribution of a sample is called a sample distribution. The sample mean is represented by $\bar{x}$ and the sample standard deviation, by S. The sampling distribution is the distribution of the sample means. It is the distribution of the values of a sample statistic computed for each possible sample that could be drawn from the target population. The sampling distribution is a theoretical probability distribution that is hardly ever calculated. The sampling distribution's mean is called the expected value of the statistic. The expected value of the mean of the sampling distribution is equal to μ. The standard deviation of the sampling distribution is called the standard error of the mean.

The earlier bank deposit statistic of a sample of 20 bank customers (Table 13.1) is an example of a sample distribution. The relative frequency distribution of the values of the mean of these 20 different samples would specify the sampling distribution of the mean (Table 13.3).

Sampling distribution of the mean and the corresponding proportion have unique properties that are useful in calculating sample sizes. For large samples (defined as samples of 30 or more) the important properties are as follows.

The sampling distribution of the mean is a normal distribution. Normal distribution is a continuous distribution that describes the distributions of numerous random variables. Revenues of companies, heights of people, and grades of students tend to fall under a normal curve. The normal distribution provides a useful approximation to many other distributions, including the discrete binomial distribution. In addition, the normal distribution provides the basis for statistical inferences representing the distribution of the possible estimates of a population parameter arising from different samples. The normal curve is a symmetrical bell shaped curve, shown in Figure 13.1.

The sampling distribution of a proportion is generally a binomial, but for large samples, it can be approximated to the normal distribution.

The sampling distribution of the mean ($\bar{x}$) or of the proportion (p) tends to be equal to the corresponding population parameter value, that is, the population mean (μ) or population proportion (π).

Standard error is the standard deviation of the sampling distribution of the mean or the proportion. It can be calculated by using the following formulas:

Figure 13.1 **Sampling Distribution of the Mean**

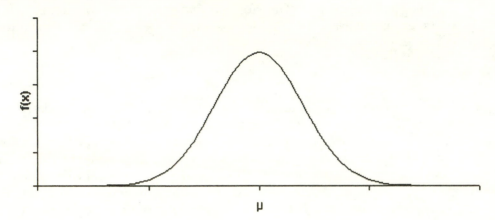

Mean

$$\sigma_{\bar{x}} = \frac{\sigma}{\sqrt{n}}$$

Proportion

$$\sigma_p = \sqrt{\frac{\pi(1-\pi)}{n}}$$

In many cases, the *standard deviation of the population* (σ) is unknown. In such instances, the population standard deviation can be estimated as follows:

$$s = \sqrt{\frac{\sum_{i=1}^{n}(X_i - \bar{X})^2}{n-1}}$$

or

$$s = \sqrt{\frac{\sum_{i=1}^{n} X_i^2 - \frac{\left[\sum_{i=1}^{n} X_i\right]^2}{n}}{n-1}}$$

When σ is estimated by s, the standard error of the mean $\sigma_{\bar{x}}$ is

$$\sigma_{\bar{x}} = \frac{s}{\sqrt{n}}$$

Similarly, the *standard error of the proportion* can be estimated using the sample proportion p as an estimator of the population proportion π:

$$s_p = \sqrt{\frac{p(1-p)}{n}}$$

The area under a normal curve between any two points can be calculated in terms of z *values*. The z value for a point under a normal curve is the number of standard errors a point is away from the mean. The z is calculated as

$$z = \frac{\bar{X} - \mu}{\sigma_{\bar{x}}}$$

The area under one side of the normal curve between the mean and points that have z values of 3 is 0.4986, and for 1 it is 0.3413. A complete set of z tables is provided in appendix C. The computation of z values for the proportion is the same as that for the mean.

SAMPLE SIZE TO ESTIMATE THE MEAN (μ)

One of the most common questions asked of researchers is how large the sample for a study should be. The answer to this question depends on several factors:

- The parameter to be estimated
- The desired confidence level of the interval estimator
- The maximum error or precision (e) of estimation ($\bar{x} - \mu$)
- The importance of the decision
- The nature of the analysis
- The incidence rates
- The resource constraints (costs, staff, infrastructure, etc.)

Depending on the incidence rates (the number of respondents willing to answer a survey) and completion rates, the final sample size may have to be increased. The statistical approach in determining the sample size is based on the construction of confidence intervals around sample means or proportions using the standard error formula.

Suppose the quality control manager of an automobile parts company is interested in finding the mean (μ) defect rate of automobile parts produced at one of the company's factories. The confidence interval estimator, assuming a normal distribution with a known standard deviation (σ), is

$$\bar{x} \pm z_{\alpha/2} \frac{\sigma}{\sqrt{n}}$$

If the quality control manager wishes to estimate μ to within a specified error (e), the manager would want the confidence interval estimator to be

$$\bar{x} \pm e$$

Therefore, e could be rewritten as

$$e = z_{\alpha/2} \frac{\sigma}{\sqrt{n}}$$

Solving for n will obtain the mean defective rate. A formula for the size of a sample can be derived from the above equation. It is

$$n = \left(\frac{z_{\alpha/2}\sigma}{e} \right)^2$$

Suppose the quality control manager wants to estimate the defects with 95.5 percent confidence interval and within 10 defects of the actual population mean, $e = 5$ and $z_{\alpha/2} = 2$ (from the z tables in appendix C), and based on past experience, the manager estimates the standard deviation (σ) to be 25; the required sample to estimate the auto parts defect rate at the factory is

$$n = (2 \times 25 \div 5)^2, n = (50/5)^2$$

$$n = (10)^2, n = 100.$$

In this study, the sample size would have been different if the standard deviation of the population was different. If we assume that the standard deviation of the population is 50 instead of 25, the new sample size would be

$$n = (2)^2(50)^2 \div (5)^2 = 400$$

Whereas, if the standard deviation was only 10, the required sample size would be

$$n = (2)^2(10)^2 \div (5)^2 = 16$$

In other words, when the population variance of the parameter to be estimated is small, a researcher needs only a small sample; when the population variance is large, the sample size required to estimate is also large. Intuitively, this is easy to explain. If the sample size variation was 0, in other words, if all the elements of the population had the same value, we need to consider only one element of the population as the sample to estimate the mean, and the estimated parameter would be exactly equal to the population parameter. However, if the variance is α, the researcher has to consider every element of the population to determine the exact value of the parameter.

Besides the variance, the other two variables that affect the sample size are confidence interval and error. If, in the example of the auto parts, the quality control manager wished to reduce the error rate to, say, within 2 from 10, then the sample size would be

$$n = (2 \times 25 \div 2)^2 = 625.$$

In this case, the new sample size with an error of 2 is more than six times the original sample size with an error of 5. As the accuracy rate is increased, the sample size also increases.

Similarly, if the researcher raises the confidence interval from 95.5 percent to 99.7 percent, the resulting sample size will increase to

$$n = (3 \times 25 \div 5)^2 = 225 \text{ from 100 at 95.5 percent.}$$

Unknown Population Standard Deviation

In practice, the standard deviation of a population may not be known. In such instances, a rough estimate of the standard deviation may be used. Two popular methods of approximating the standard deviations follow.

Through past experience or industry studies, it may be able to determine the average lowest and highest consumption or the value of a parameter. Using this range, researchers are able to approximate the value of the population standard deviation by finding the difference between the highest and the lowest values and dividing it by 6. The assumption is that the standard deviation under a normal curve is divided into +3 and −3 standard deviations. This method is quite effective, since 3 standard deviations on either side of the mean create an interval that contains about 99.7 percent of the population. For example, a beverage manufacturer knows from experience that the heavy drinkers of its product consume on an average about 146 twelve-ounce bottles per month and the light drinkers about 26 bottles. In this case, the population standard deviation can be approximated by

$$\sigma = 146 - 26 \div 6 = 20.$$

The second approximation for determining the population standard deviation calls for conducting a small pilot study and using the study results to estimate the population standard deviation.

SAMPLE SIZE TO ESTIMATE THE PROPORTION

Similar to determining the sample size for the mean, the size of the sample to determine proportion (p) depends on the desired confidence level ($z_{\alpha/2}$) and the error factor (e). The confidence interval estimator of p is

$$\hat{p} \pm z_{\alpha/2}\sqrt{\frac{\hat{p}\hat{q}}{n}}$$

where p is sample proportion and q is $1 - p$. As in the case of the sample for calculating means, we can determine the required sample size as

$$n = \left[\frac{z_{\alpha/2}\sqrt{pq}}{e}\right]^2$$

This formula assumes that the researcher has information on the values of p and q, which may not be the case. In situations when the population proportions are unknown, the researcher can use $p = 0.5$ and $q = 0.5$. The rational for this approach is that under values of 0.5 for p and q, the sample size obtained would be the highest and provides the largest possible sample size, because any other combination of values for p and q will be lower than the value at 0.5 ($0.5 \times 0.5 = 0.25$). The second method to determine sample size without knowing the value of p is to use some prior knowledge or experience to estimate the values of p and q.

For example, suppose a bank manager is interested in finding the number of mistakes made by data-entry clerks in the branch and wishes to check a sample of data entries. What should the sample size be at a 95.5 percent confidence interval and a proportion of estimate of wrong entries (e) within 0.03? To solve for n we need to know p and q. But these values are unknown at the present time. Based on the previous discussion, the values of p and q are assumed to be 0.5. Therefore, for the data-entry problem the sample size would be

$$n = \left[\frac{2\sqrt{(.5)(.5)}}{.03}\right]^2 = 1111.11 = 1112$$

In calculating sample size, decimals are always rounded up.

The bank manager could also use historic information for determining the values of p and q instead of assuming the values to be 0.5. For example, the bank manager may be able to review the historical records of data entries and determine that the error rate in entries is 0.3. This information, along with the estimate of error (e), can be used to determine the new sample size. Suppose the branch manager once again wants to estimate the proportion of errors in entries to within 0.03. Sample size can be determined as

$$n = \left(\frac{2\sqrt{(.3)(.7)}}{.03} \right)^2 = 933.33 = 934$$

Summary of Steps in Determining Sample Size for Means and Proportions

- Specify the desired level of confidence—68.26 percent, 95 percent, 95.5 percent, or 99.74 percent.
- Determine the corresponding z value associated with the confidence level from appendix C—1.0, 1.96, 2.0, or 3.0.
- Designate the level of the acceptable error estimate or precision.
- Ascertain the population standard deviation or the value of the population proportion from secondary sources, pilot studies, or other methods.
- Determine the sample size using the following formula:

For means:

$$n = \left(\frac{z_{\alpha/2}\sigma}{e} \right)^2$$

For proportions:

$$n = \left(\frac{z_{\alpha/2}\sqrt{pq}}{e} \right)^2$$

From the above examples, it is clear that whether the sample size is determined through probability techniques or nonprobability techniques, the final size of the sample (n) is not affected by the size of the population (N). It is possible to obtain relevant information from a large population with a sample of only 100 elements.

Sample Size Estimation for Measuring Multiple Parameters

Often, research studies are conducted to measure more than one variable. For example, in the quality control study, the manager may not want to know only the mean defect rate but also the average number of hours spent by checkers on the assembly line. There are now two means to be determined. Suppose both means are estimated with a 95.5 percent confidence interval and the desired error factor is within 10 defects and within 10 minutes of the hours spent on checking for defects, respectively. Furthermore, the standard deviation of the population for defects is 25 and for time spent by checkers is 60 minutes. The resulting sample sizes would be as follows:

$n = (2)^2(25)^2 \div (5)^2 = 100$ for defects

$n = (2)^2(60)^2 \div (5)^2 = 576$ for average number of hours spent by checkers

The study to determine two parameters produces two different sample sizes. Should the sample size be 100 or 576? Some researchers would suggest a sample of 576, as it would ensure meeting the precision levels of both studies. This sample size would drive up the research cost, however. In addition, if the average hours spent by quality checkers is less critical than the defective rate, the 576 samples would be a waste. For this reason, researchers prefer first to establish the importance of the multiple parameters to be studied and then to focus on the most important parameter in estimating sample size. For the quality control example, the final sample size selected would be 100 to satisfy the requirement of the defective rate.

ADJUSTMENTS TO SAMPLE SIZE

Sample sizes determined through probability techniques assume that the number of respondents selected would be available or willing to provide the necessary information. In practice, this level of compliance may be difficult to achieve. In many instances, sample elements (people) may not be willing to answer questions; employees of companies may be traveling or reluctant to be respondents; and government officials may be prohibited from responding to questions. The two factors that affect the final response rates are *incidence rate* and *completion rate.*[1]

Incidence rate is the percentage of people in a specific population that fits the qualifications of those people that the researcher desires to have interviewed. For example, a brokerage house wanting to start a Web site–based stock-trading network plans to conduct a survey among customers to determine the potential for this type of service. Suppose only 50 percent of households in that country have Internet connectivity and of those who have Internet service only 50 percent buy and sell stocks; then only 25 percent (0.5 × 0.5) of all households fall into the qualified category. This incidence rate means that only one out of every four households contacted at random would qualify for questioning on Internet stock trading. One approach to adjust for the loss of respondents is to increase the sample size to offset for the low incidence rate. For the above example, the researcher may decide to increase the final sample size by a factor of 4 (1.0 ÷ .25 = 4).

Another potential problem faced by researchers is high refusal rates from selected respondents. This problem affects the completion rate too. The completion rate is the percentage of qualified respondents who complete an interview. As mentioned in earlier chapters, in some countries cultural and other societal factors interfere with respondents' willingness to participate in a survey. Because of either general suspicion of strangers or the desire for privacy, respondents in many countries refuse to participate in research studies. Some respondents are also turned off by the topic of study and are therefore unwilling to participate in the survey. Researchers have to be prepared for low completion rates and must adjust their sample size accordingly. For example, if a researcher expects only a 75 percent completion rate of eligible respondents, the number of contacts should be increased by a factor of 1.34 (100 × [25 ÷ 75]). Before sample sizes are adjusted, researchers may want to try proven methods such as the use of incentives, group dynamics, or soliciting influential leaders to endorse research studies to increase the completion rates.

The incidence rate and the completion rate problems should be built into the sample size as adjustments. The initial sample size should be larger than originally computed to adjust for a lower incidence rate, a lower completion rate, or both. In general, when response rates are expected to be lower, the final sample size can be adjusted as follows:

Final sample size = (Initial sample size) × (Incidence rate × Completion rate).

For example, the initial sample size for a study was determined to be 200. From our previous examples we have the incidence rate and completion rate as 4 and 1.34, respectively. For this example the final sample size will be:

Final sample size = 200 × 4 × 1.34 = 1072.

RESPONSE PROBLEMS IN SAMPLING

Response bias is a major problem in studies involving surveys. Response biases occur due to nonresponses by selected sample elements. Nonresponse or low responses occur due to either refusals or not-at-homes (or not available). Nonrespondents may differ from respondents in some critical characteristics, such as demographic or other variables. If this happens, the completed study would be biased, as the responses do not reflect the sentiments of the true population. Increasing response rates to reduce response bias is often the goal of researchers.

Recognizing the existence of the sampling biases, researchers often undertake steps to increase response rates. As mentioned earlier, incentives are often used to increase response rates. Notifying respondents in advance of a forthcoming survey may also help. Motivating respondents by stressing the importance of the study or the prestige of the organization that is conducting it is also useful. Other techniques that could improve response rates are designing an easy-to-follow questionnaire, improving the presentation of the questionnaire by having it developed professionally, using field-workers who have characteristics in common with the respondents (female field-workers to ask questions of female respondents) to administer the questionnaire, and finally, conducting follow-up calls.

Response biases may be addressed by actually reporting the percentage of non-responses so that the effects of the bias may be estimated. To estimate the effects of nonresponses, link the nonresponse rate to estimated differences between respondents and nonrespondents. If no estimates can be computed, a researcher could adopt the following approaches to adjust for nonresponse errors:

- *Use subsamples*. By contacting subsamples of the nonrespondents, researchers are able to prorate the information to the nonrespondent group.

- *Substitute*. Other elements from the sampling frame are substituted for the nonrespondents. The sampling frame may be stratified into subgroups that are homogeneous in terms of respondent characteristics. These subgroups are then used to identify substitutes who are similar to nonrespondents but differ from the group that has already responded. This assures a wider variety of respondents in the sample.
- *Replacement*. If both the above approaches do not result in an improved response rate, nonrespondents in the study are replaced. Replacements may be obtained from a group of subjects from earlier similar studies who did not respond to the original survey. Again, the idea is to obtain a good representation of the total population—those who normally respond and those who do not.

CHAPTER SUMMARY

Accurate sample size determination requires knowledge of statistics. Descriptive and inferential statistics are used in estimating sample sizes. Descriptive statistics are concerned with methods of summarizing and presenting the basic information contained in either a population or a sample. Grouping the measurements through a frequency distribution can summarize quantitative data. The frequency distribution shows how frequently each response or classification occurs. A proportion shows the percentage of a group having a particular characteristic.

Numerical measures can be used to describe some of the central characteristics and dispersion of the data. The three most often measured central characteristics are the mean, the median, and the mode. The mean is the arithmetic average, the median is the halfway value, and the mode is the most frequently observed value. The range, percentiles, variance, and standard deviation measure the information regarding the dispersion (variability) of the data. The range is the difference between the largest and smallest values observed. The variance and standard deviation are the most useful measures of dispersion.

The normal probability distribution is the most useful and important continuous distribution. The normal distribution is symmetrical about its mean, with equal mean, median, and mode. The area under the normal curve is 1 (100 percent) and lies within ±3 standard deviations of the mean.

The process of drawing conclusions about the properties of a population based on information obtained from a sample is called statistical inference. Statistical inference draws on the relationships among the population distribution, the sample distribution, and the sampling distribution. The cornerstone of statistical inference is the central-limit theorem. According to the central-limit theorem, if relatively large samples of size of n are drawn from any population, the sampling distribution of $\bar{x}$ is approximately normal and the value of the sample mean tends to be equal to the population mean (μ).

The selection of a sample size depends on many factors, including the parameter to be estimated, the desired confidence level of the interval estimator, the maximum error of estimation, the importance of the decision, the nature of the analysis, the incidence rates, and the resource constraints.

Formulas for calculating the sample for means and proportions, respectively, are as follows:

$$n = \left(\frac{z_{\alpha/2}\sigma}{e} \right)^2 \qquad n = \left(\frac{z_{\alpha/2}\sqrt{pq}}{e} \right)^2$$

Sample sizes determined through probability techniques assume that the number of respondents in the original sample will be available and that all will respond to the questionnaire. Often, respondents are not available, and some are not willing to complete a questionnaire. In such instances, researchers have to be ready to make adjustments to the sample size and must also be prepared to incur response biases, which must be resolved.

CHAPTER REVIEW

1. Distinguish between descriptive statistics and inferential statistics.
2. What is a frequency distribution and what are its characteristics?
3. Explain central tendencies and explain how researchers use these measures.
4. Students in an introductory international business class obtain the following marks on the final exam: 60, 85, 82, 73, 55, 66, 65, 74, 83, 67, 86, 74, 89, 90, 71, 78, 82, 71, 69, and 60. Determine the mean, range, median, mode, and standard deviation for the final exam marks.
5. In determining a sample size, what are some of the key factors that a researcher needs to consider?
6. What is the confidence level of the interval estimator?
7. What is the error or precision in calculating sample size?
8. If the population standard deviation is unknown, how would you determine the sample size to determine the average salaries of bank tellers in Japan?
9. The health ministry of South Korea is planning to determine the average annual family medical expenses of its urban population. The ministry wishes to be 95 percent confident that the sample average is correct within ±50.00 won of the true average family medical expense. Historically, the standard deviation for medical expenses has remained at about 400 won. How large a sample size should the health ministry consider? If the health ministry wishes to obtain the sample average expenditure within ±25.00 won, what would the new sample size be?
10. A factory manager plans to sample his workers to determine the annual average absentee rate at the factory. He wishes to have a 90 percent confidence level and an error factor of not more than 5 days. The national rate of absenteeism for factory workers in the country is 6 days. What would the required sample size be?
11. Philips, a Netherlands-based company, is planning the introduction of a new high-resolution television set. In planning the introduction of the new TV, the marketing department wants to estimate the acceptance rate of this new TV

so as to develop an effective promotion program. A survey of the households in five European countries is planned to estimate the potential demand. Management wishes to be 95 percent confident with an error rate of not more than ±25 households. Based on past experience, the marketing group estimates the standard deviation for such consumer studies as 400 households. How large a sample should the company consider? If in the past only about 80 percent of the respondents contacted completed the survey, what should the new sample size be?

12. The management of a large investment banking firm in Japan wants to determine the average savings rate of its present customers. At a confidence level of 99 percent and an error estimate of not more than ¥100, what should the sample size be if in the past the variance (σ) in savings has been around ¥1000?

13. In a country's parliamentary elections, the ruling party would like to estimate the proportion of voters who will vote for the party. The party chief would like to be 95.5 percent confident that his prediction is correct within ±5 percent of the true proportion. What sample size is required? If the party chief wishes to attain a 90 percent confidence interval and an error estimate of ±10 percent, what should the new sample size be?

14. The *Daily Mirror* of London would like to estimate the proportions of its readers who would pay an additional charge for home delivery service of its newspaper. The newspaper group would like to have 95 percent confidence that its estimates are correct within ±5 percent of the true proportion. Newspapers in other countries have a 30 percent home delivery rate. What is the required sample size?

15. A multinational bank operating in the United Kingdom wants to estimate the proportion of its bank customers that would sign up for the bank's credit card. It estimates that about 25 percent of its present customers do so. In order to get an accurate estimate it plans to conduct a survey of its customers. What should the sample size be if the bank wants to be 95.5 percent confident and wants the results to be within 5 percent of the true proportion?

NOTE

1. Louis G. Pol and Sukgoo Pak, "The Use of Two-Stage Survey Design in Collecting Data from Those Who Have Attended Periodic or Special Events," *Journal of Marketing Research* 36 (October 1994), pp. 315–326.

ADDITIONAL READING

BOOKS

Churchill, Gilbert A., Jr., and Tom J. Brown. *Basic Marketing Research.* 5th ed. Cincinnati, OH: South Western Publishing, 2004, pp. 397–464.

Lind, Douglas A., William G. Marchal, and Samuel A. Wathen. *Statistical Techniques in Business and Economics.* 12th ed. New York: McGraw-Hill Irwin, 2005, pp. 250–281.

Malhotra, Naresh K. *Marketing Research: An Applied Orientation.* 4th ed. Upper Saddle River, NJ: Prentice-Hall, 2004, pp. 312–383.

Zikmund, William G. *Exploring Marketing Research.* 8th ed. Cincinnati, OH: South Western Publishing, 2003, pp. 415–471.

ARTICLE

"RDD Sampling in 15 Countries." *The Frame* (November 1998), p. 1.

14 Data Analysis: Fundamentals

Data analysis is the process that converts raw data into meaningful information.

LEARNING OBJECTIVES

After reading this chapter, students should be able to

- Understand data editing and coding
- Understand computerized data entry
- Understand cross-tabulations
- Understand hypothesis testing
- Understand tests of independence using chi-square analysis

Analyzing data is a very important step in the research process. Analysis generates meaning from data and leads to insights that can be used to make business decisions. A thorough understanding of data-analysis techniques can assist a researcher in formulating better research objectives and designing a comprehensive research plan.

However good the data analysis is, it cannot make up for a poorly conceived research study. If the objectives of the research are not clearly stated, if the questionnaire design is flawed, or if the study hypotheses are not practical, then no amount of sophisticated analysis can salvage the research study. Similarly, poor or weak data analysis has the potential to undermine a well-designed study. In analyzing data, a researcher has to first categorize the data, edit and clean the data, and finally set up a coding system that converts the data into a machine-readable format.

ESTABLISHING CATEGORIES

Analysis of data requires that the data be grouped into categories. Categorical variables have a limited number of distinct values. For example, the variable gender may only be categorized as "male" or "female," or in the case of a category scale that has a particular evaluative dimension, as "excellent," "fair," or "poor." By establishing categories, a researcher is able to consider alternative responses in more detail. Categorization also helps in designing a better-organized questionnaire.

EDITING

Editing is a quality control step for cleaning the raw data. When editing is done while administering the questionnaire (field editing) it helps control the field staff and also helps identify glaring omissions. Editing helps in isolating problems of *completeness, legibility, compressibility, consistency,* and *uniformity.* The role of editing is to clean the research data, that is, to ensure that the data is readable and accurate. Most often, completed questionnaires have incorrect or missing data. In international research this happens quite frequently, as the research capabilities in some countries are subpar. Therefore, before subjecting the data to analysis, a researcher has to make sure that all the inconsistencies have been clarified. Editing of raw data should be done immediately after the completion of the fieldwork, as the interviewers may not accurately recall parts of the interview if this step is delayed. Interviewers and their supervisors should be questioned to correct any glaring omissions. Editing is normally centralized so as to ensure consistency and uniformity in treatment of the data. Specifically, editing helps researchers identify problems such as omissions, ambiguities, ineligible respondents, interviewer errors, and inconsistent responses.

- *Omissions.* Respondents sometimes fail to answer one or more questions either inadvertently or deliberately. If the questionnaires are long or very complex, respondents might purposely omit some questions, resulting in incomplete questionnaires.
- *Ambiguity.* A response might not be legible, or the response category may not be clear. For example, in answers to multiple-choice question, it could be unclear which of the two boxes is checked.
- *Ineligible respondent.* The person responding to a questionnaire may not be the right respondent. For example, in a study of middle-level managers, a few of the entry-level managers might have also been questioned, or in a study of the head of the household, children may have been included.
- *Interviewer errors.* Interviewers may be giving incorrect instructions to respondents or they may be explaining the questions when they are not supposed to. Internationally, due to literacy problems, the interviewer often ends up explaining the questions to the respondents. If interviewers are not careful, their explanations may lead to biased results or they may not be explaining the question uniformly, leading to inconsistent responses.
- *Inconsistencies.* Sometimes two responses from a single respondent can be logically inconsistent. For example, a respondent who checks his or her income as over $50,000 might have selected that they work only part-time. Similarly, a respondent may indicate that he or she is not aware of a particular brand, but then selects that brand as one that he or she frequently uses.

There are many ways to deal with editing problems. If there are many problems with a few completed questionnaires, it is best to contact the respondents again to resolve the identified problems. A second approach is to either throw out the whole questionnaire or disregard just the problematic responses. Sometimes this course of action leads to response or sampling biases. A third approach is to code illegible or missing answers into a different category such as "Don't know." Still another alternative is to use the information by applying judgment or extrapolation techniques. It is sometimes possible to infer what the response should be from other data on the same questionnaire, responses from all the other questionnaires, or external data sources. Some questionnaires contain more missing data than others do. A researcher must decide how much and what type of missing data constitutes grounds for discarding or deleting a questionnaire.

If the researcher decides to reconstruct the information using extrapolation methods, he or she can accomplish this by applying an average value for the variable obtained from all the responses. For example, in a survey of 100 purchasing managers, 3 did not respond to the question about education level. If the mean number of years of education for the remaining 97 is 16 years, the researcher could assign 16 years of schooling to each of the 3 respondents who did not answer that question.

In some instances, a researcher could also use available secondary data to plug in missing values. For example, in a survey of detergent usage in Berlin, Germany, the question on family income is left blank by a few respondents; the researcher can obtain government information on family incomes for Berlin and use this information to complete the missing data. Before changing or discarding seemingly ambiguous or logically inconsistent information, the researcher should consider the possibility that there may be a significant underlying cause for the ambiguity. If there is such a problem, the researcher should investigate further to pinpoint the causes of ambiguity. A researcher should also be alert to individual questions that frequently are left unanswered or produce ambiguous responses. Such questions can be altered to improve response quality during the interview.

One of the problem areas in international research is the unit of measurement. As explained earlier, units of measurements across countries vary, and data comparison may show inconsistent results. If the units of measurement are not comparable, such as in the case of weights, classifications of target groups, or currencies (American dollar, British pound, European euro, Japanese yen, etc.), normalization of the data may be necessary.

CODING

Coding is a process of categorizing raw data and transforming them into symbols. In other words, coding is the means by which responses are converted into machine-readable (computer) formats by using alpha-numeric codes. Assigning numerical symbols allows the transfer of data from survey responses that can be read by computers for faster data analysis. As is demonstrated later in this book (see appendix D), entering verbal responses into computers for data analysis is cumbersome and impractical. But, with newer software programs, coding even open-ended responses is made easier. This software program merges similar responses with the help of keyword search techniques and automatically generates coded data.[1] Coding can also be done on questionnaires before the data are collected; this is called precoding. The assignment of codes after the data are collected is called postcoding. Precoding is done to categories on structured or close-ended questions. Postcoding is done with unstructured or open-ended forms. For example, the following three structured questions may be precoded as follows:

Question 1. Do you use automatic teller machines (ATMs) to transact your banking needs?

___	Yes	1	
___	No	2	(10)

Question 2. How often do you use an ATM machine?

___	At least once a day	1	
___	Two to three times a week	2	
___	Once a week	3	
___	Two to three times a month	4	
___	Once a month	5	
___	Other (please specify)	6	(11)

Question 3. For what purpose do you most often use an ATM? Choose as many as apply.

___	For money withdrawals	1	
___	For deposits	2	
___	For transferring funds	3	
___	For investment banking purposes	4	
___	Other (please specify)	5	(12)

In the above example, numbers 10, 11, and 12 are categories (i.e., 10 = use ATM or not; 11 = how often use ATMs; and 12 = for what purpose ATMs are used) and would be entered in respective columns to indicate categories. The responses for question 1 are coded as 1 and 2, that is, code 1 = yes and code 2 = no. The responses for question 2 are coded from 1 through 6, and for question 3, they are coded from 1 through 5.

There are two basic rules to be followed in constructing a coding scheme. First, the coding categories should be exhaustive. That is, coding categories should be provided for all responses. Second, the coding categories should be mutually exclusive and independent. That is, there should be no overlap between the categories—a response can be placed in only one category. As a general rule, coding schemes should not be too elaborate, but easy to use and less complicated.

The first step in setting up a coding scheme is to develop a data matrix. A data matrix is a spreadsheet arrangement of data into rows and columns. Each row in the matrix represents a subject that is the fundamental unit of analysis, for example, "a respondent." Each column represents a particular field. The second step in coding

Table 14.1 **Example of a Codebook for the Detergent Questionnaire**

Variable Number	Column Number	Variable	Question Number	Instruction
1	1–3	Respondent ID		001 to 101
2	4–5	Project code		Same for all respondents
3	6–7	Interview code		As coded on questionnaire
4	8–13	Date code		6 digits—month-day-year
5	14–19	Time code		6 digits—hours-minutes-a.m./p.m.
—	20–21	Blank		To separate responses
6	22	Decision maker	1	Yes = 1
				No = 2
7	23	Who buys	2	Self = 1
				Spouse = 2
				Others (a) = 3
				Others (b) = 4
8	24	How often	3	Every day = 1
				2–3 times/week = 2
				Once a week = 3
				Once in 2 weeks = 4
				Other = 5
9	25	Own washing machine	4	Yes = 1
				No = 2

is to develop a codebook. A codebook identifies each variable in the study and its location in the data matrix. The book is used to identify a variable's description, code name, and field.

The first variable in a codebook is usually the respondent identification. Depending on the sample size, the first two, three, or four columns could be assigned for identifying respondents. The column numbers correspond to the number of digits of the sample. That is, if the sample is fewer than 99 subjects, the number of columns required for respondent identification is two; if the sample size is between 100 and 999, the number of columns needed is three, and so on. The second variable is the project code. This is for internal control, especially if there is more than one study being undertaken. The third variable is the interviewer code, which identifies the interviewer. This helps the project director to monitor the performance of an interviewer. Variable number four is the date code. The fifth variable is the time code. Variable number six and those that follow it deal with the responses of individual respondents. The responses for each question of the questionnaire are entered in these columns. Table 14.1 presents an example of a codebook for the detergent questionnaire presented in appendix A.1.

For missing data, sometimes no value is assigned, leaving a blank. Another common approach to dealing with missing data is the use of the number 9. A third approach is to assign the missing data category a value that is one number larger than the largest response value. Thus, for our ATM question, for missing data to question 1, a value of 3 would be assigned, for question 2 a value of 7 would be assigned, and for question 3 a value of 6 would be assigned.

Coding for open-ended questions is time-consuming and difficult. Usually, a researcher might wait for all the questionnaires to be returned and then decide on categories to be selected based on the responses to the open-ended questions, or he or she could develop a lengthy list of possible responses (based on prior knowledge) and then place responses into one of the list items. In international research, because of the diversity of the respondents and lack of prior knowledge of the country factors, it is recommended that categorization be done after all the questionnaires are returned.

For an open-ended question such as "What is the future of the euro?" there could be as many answers as there are respondents. Therefore, open-ended questions are hardly ever precoded, but instead, the researcher waits for the responses to come back to categorize them into uniform response categories. In the case of the euro question, after all the responses are reviewed, the researcher may categorize them into four groups:

- Category 1: The euro will succeed in the long term
- Category 2: The United Kingdom and Denmark will join the European Monetary Union
- Category 3: The euro will be used by only some of the European members
- Category 4: The euro will fail and the group will not pursue a common monetary unit

Categorization of open-ended responses is a judgment decision and depends on the experience and knowledge of the researcher. In some international research situations, an editor-coder may be assigned to actually do the editing and coding work. In regional research activities (Asia, Europe, Latin America), the regional office may assign a person in each country to do the editing and coding function to assure consistency.

COMPUTERIZED DATA ENTRY

With improvements in hardware and software technology, more and more of the actual analysis of data in international research is done through the use of computers. To start the analysis process, researchers need to convert the questionnaire output into computer-readable format. Powerful desktop computers can undertake sophisticated analytical procedures and do so more efficiently than humans can. Through the use of network- or personal-computer-based statistical packages such as SAS® (Statistical Analysis System) or SPSS® (Statistical Package for the Social Sciences), researchers can undertake complex analyses including factor analysis, discriminant analysis, multiple regression, and analysis of variance (ANOVA). In addition, large sample sizes pose little problem for computer-driven analysis. In developing countries where the use of computers is limited, most analysis is done manually. This limits the researcher's ability to subject the data to statistical analysis that may show significance levels and improve data interpretation. Furthermore, manual analysis places constraints on the sample size.

Advances in technology have made the process of data entry simple and fast. Data can be entered as the survey is being conducted, as in the case of computer-assisted telephone interviewing. If data are not directly entered into the computer, data from the completed questionnaires need to be entered into the computer using a keyboard. Often entry errors are made while the data are input into the computer. Since data-entry errors cause incorrect analysis, researchers most often have a second keyboard operator checking the accuracy of the data entered into the computer to reduce the data-entry errors.

To facilitate data entry, researchers often convert information from the questionnaires into a coding sheet. A coding sheet is a multicolumn matrix that is an exact replica of the data matrix. Appendix D explains data entry for statistical packages such as SAS and SPSS.

DATA ANALYSIS

The purpose of data analysis is to produce information that will address the issue(s) at hand. Therefore, the selection of data-analysis strategy should be derived from the research objective(s) and research design. For example, if the research design is an experiment, the data analysis may involve ANOVA.

In selecting a particular statistical technique, the researcher should be aware of the properties of the technique and its underlying assumptions. The use of a specific technique depends on the kind of analysis a researcher wishes to do. Statistical techniques are used for a variety of situations. They can be used to forecast outcome of variables, for examining the differences between variables, and for determining the intensity of relationships among the variables. It is always useful to use a range of techniques to obtain the maximum possible information from a set of data.

CLASSIFICATION OF DATA-ANALYSIS TECHNIQUES

The two basic types of data analysis are univariate and multivariate. When there is a single or several measurements of each element or object, a univariate analysis is more appropriate. When there are two or more measurements on each element and the variables are analyzed simultaneously, multivariate analysis is applicable.

The focus of univariate analysis is on means and variances. Multivariate analysis, on the other hand, focuses on simultaneous relationships among variables and the degree of such relationships. Correlation and covariance are measures determined through multivariate analysis.

SIMPLE DATA ANALYSIS

The easiest and the quickest data analysis can be accomplished through frequency distribution (also called simple tabulation) and cross-tabulation.

Frequency Distribution

Frequency distribution is usually the first step in data analysis. It involves tabulating each question in a questionnaire by itself. The most common way to present this type of data is through a frequency table. Frequency distribution of a set of observations is an arrangement that shows the frequency (number of observations) of occurrence of the values of the variable in ordered classes. A frequency distribution reports the number of responses that each question received. Tabulating this information is completed by counting the number of responses in each data category. This type of analysis provides the researcher with a quick overview of the research study.

For example, in a study of milk consumption by households, the following three questions were part of a broader questionnaire:

Question 1. Do you or a member of your household buy milk?

____ Yes
____ No (If no, go to Question ___.)

Question 2. How often do you or a member of your household buy milk?

____ Once every day
____ Twice a week
____ Once a week
____ Other (specify)

Question 3. What is the amount of milk purchased each time by you or a member of your household?

____ One quart
____ Two quarts
____ Three quarts
____ A gallon or more

Suppose the survey was conducted among a sample of 200 consumers; a frequency distribution (simple tabulation) for the first question may be presented as shown in Table 14.2. A frequency distribution for the three questions may be presented as shown in Table 14.3.

In Table 14.3, we have the responses not only in absolute terms but also in percentages and in a bar graph. Percentages are easy to use when comparing data. The frequency distribution is able to provide more information than the single-variable tabulation shown in Table 14.2. Frequency distributions may be used to measure the central tendencies of a set of data. These and other measures such as variability were discussed earlier in conjunction with the discussion on sampling.

Cross-Tabulation

Cross-tabulation involves the simultaneous counting of the number of observations that occur in each of the data categories of two or more variables. When data have discrete components, especially qualitative data such as socioeconomic data, cross-tabulations are a useful means of analyzing the data.[2] Cross-tabulations show how respondents

Table 14.2 **Simple Tabulation**

Buy Milk	Number of Respondents
Yes	175
No	25
Total	200

with a given value on one variable responded to one or more other variables. A cross-tabulation is one of the more commonly used techniques in analyzing data.

The steps in a two-way cross-tabulation are as follows:

- On the horizontal axis, list the name for each category of the first variable.
- On the vertical axis, list the name for each category of the second variable.
- For the total sample, count the number of responses for each category of the two variables.

In cross-tabulation, the percentages can be calculated either by columns or by rows. The general rule is to calculate the percentages in the *direction* of the independent variable (for example, demographic variables) and *across* the dependent variable (for example, purchase behavior). Table 14.4 presents an example of a two-way tabulation.

Using the number of respondents as base, researchers can calculate percentages for each cell in a cross-tabulation. This helps the researcher understand the relationship between variables through relative comparison. For example, from Table 14.4, we can surmise that 25 out of 200, or 12.5 percent, of the sample buy milk every day and buy one quart of milk each time, compared to 10 out of 200, or 5 percent, of the respondents who buy one quart of milk once a week. If a researcher is interested in the relationship between two variables, he or she can choose one of the variables or questions as a base. In the above example, the amount of milk purchased is the base variable.

With modern computers, tabulations can be done very easily and quickly. Any spreadsheet program can easily do tabulations. For more sophisticated tabulations and analysis with statistical inferences, one can use a standard statistical package such as SAS, BMDP (Biomedical Computer Programs), or SPSS. These programs have simplified data analysis by eliminating the tedious task of writing a computer program every time a researcher wants to analyze data.

In a given questionnaire, the possibilities for cross-tabulation of two or more variables become enormous. Unless the sample size is large, it is likely that some of the values in the cross-tabulation cell may be very small and will not provide useful information. For this reason, key variables for cross-tabulations should be very carefully selected. The selection of variables for cross-tabulation should be based on strategic reasons. Usually, one of the variables selected for cross-tabulation is the respondent profile or demographic variable.

Table 14.3 **Frequency Distribution**

Do you buy milk?

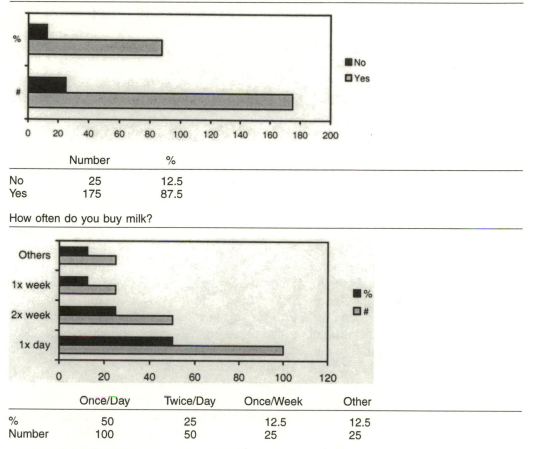

	Number	%
No	25	12.5
Yes	175	87.5

How often do you buy milk?

	Once/Day	Twice/Day	Once/Week	Other
%	50	25	12.5	12.5
Number	100	50	25	25

What was the amount of milk purchased?

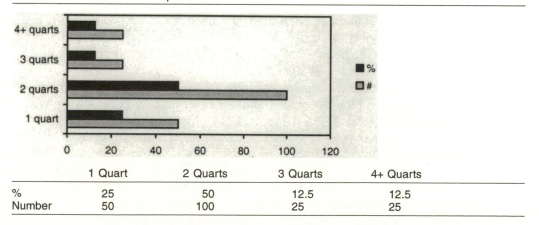

	1 Quart	2 Quarts	3 Quarts	4+ Quarts
%	25	50	12.5	12.5
Number	50	100	25	25

Table 14.4 **Cross-Tabulation: Amount of Milk Purchased by Number of Times Milk Purchased**

Amount of Milk Purchased	Number of Times Milk Purchased				
	Once/Day	Twice/Day	Once/Week	Other	Total
1 quart	25	15	10	0	50
2 quarts	60	30	5	5	100
3 quarts	10	5	5	5	25
1 gallon or more	5	0	5	15	25
Total	100	50	25	25	200

HYPOTHESIS TESTING

Global managers receive data and information every day from different parts of the world about various aspects of their businesses. Some of this information may simply reflect random fluctuations in daily operations. At the same time, managers may receive information that signals critical shifts in the operations of the company. Managers have to distinguish between random and significant shifts in their operations. Hypothesis testing is a technique that assists managers to isolate random events from significant changes. Hypothesis testing is used to draw statistical inferences. The objective of hypothesis testing is to determine whether or not data from a sample support a proposition about the population. Because they test the value of a population parameter, hypothesis tests are also called *parametric tests*. Parametric tests also assume that the variables are measured on an interval scale.

The hypothesis is an unproven proposition that tentatively explains some facts about a population. Hypotheses are developed to provide a plausible explanation to address management's concern. A hypothesis thus guides research intended to test an explanation or a proposition linked to a theory. Hypothesis testing is different from estimation. The major difference between the two techniques depends on the predetermined idea or notion of the state of the population being sampled. If some information about the population is suspected, hypothesis testing is the right technique to apply. However, if nothing is known or suspected about the population, estimation is used to provide point or interval estimates about population variables. For example, an R & D manager may hypothesize that the research productivity of the scientists in the department is highly correlated to the number of scientific projects they are involved with. The greater the number of projects worked on by the scientists, the poorer the results.

Hypothesis testing is a measure of the differences observed between the sample and the population parameter. Hypothesis tests are used to make statistical inferences about population parameters and population distributions. Concepts such as sampling distribution, standard errors, and confidence intervals are all useful to know in understanding hypothesis testing. Hypothesis tests could be undertaken in many different ways. When using parametric tests with metric data (interval scale), the statistical procedures presented in Figure 14.1A are possible. When using nonparametric tests

Figure 14.1A **Parametric Tests**

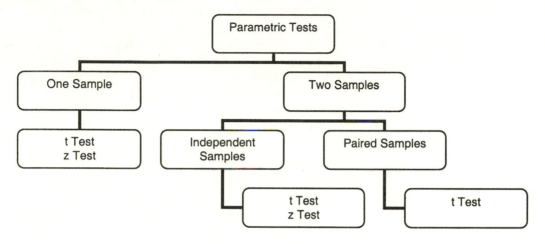

Figure 14.1B **Nonparametric Tests**

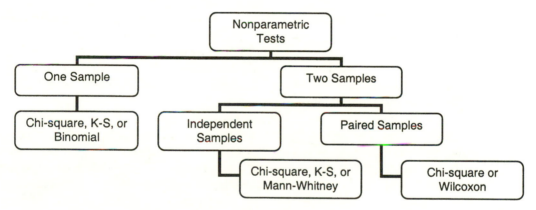

Source: Naresh K. Malhotra, *Marketing Research: An Applied Orientation,* 4th ed. Upper Saddle River, NJ: Pearson-Prentice Hall, 2004.

with nonmetric data (nominal or ordinal scale), the statistical procedures presented in Figure 14.1B are applied.

Elements of Hypothesis Testing

The four key elements of hypothesis testing are

- Null hypothesis
- Alternative hypothesis
- Test statistic
- Rejection region

Null Hypothesis. Testing of a hypothesis should be approached very cautiously, as researchers can be bold in conjectures but have to be exact in testing. For this reason, a hypothesis is stated in a null form (H_0). A null hypothesis is a conservative statement that communicates the opinion that any change from what has been thought to be true or observed in the past will be due to entirely random error. Hence, the null hypothesis is a statement about status quo. The purpose of setting up the null hypothesis is to be able to nullify it after the tests are complete. The null hypothesis, H_0, must specify that the parameter is equal to a single value. For example, a financial analyst might want to examine the association between financial risk and a firm's value. One approach to this problem is to compare values for firms with high and low financial risk. Suppose firms with higher financial risk exhibit higher values than firms with lower financial risk. This could be stated as:

$$H_0: F_{lr} = F_{hr}$$
$$H_A: F_{hr} > F_{lr}$$

where F_{lr} are firms with low risk and F_{hr} are firms with high risk.

Alternative Hypothesis. The alternative hypothesis is a statement about the population that must be true if the null hypothesis is false. The alternative hypothesis (or H_A) is the opposite of the null hypothesis. The alternative hypothesis, H_A, answers the question by specifying that the parameter is greater than the value shown in the null hypothesis, less than the value shown in the null hypothesis, or different from the value shown in the null hypothesis.

Test Statistic. The test statistic is the criterion upon which the researcher bases the decision. For parametric tests of hypotheses, the test statistic is the point estimator of the parameter being tested. For example, in tests of hypotheses of population mean (μ), the sample mean ($\bar{x}$) will be used as the test statistic.

Rejection Region. The rejection region is a range of values such that if the test statistic falls into that range, the researcher decides to reject the null hypothesis. To determine the rejection region, the researcher must determine when the value of the test statistic is sufficiently different from the hypothesized value of the parameter to enable us to reject the null hypothesis. For example, suppose we would like to test $H_0 = 200$. If the sample means (test statistic) is very different from 200, we conclude that $\bar{x}$ falls into the rejection region and reject the null hypothesis. However, if $\bar{x}$ is close to 200, we cannot reject the null hypothesis. In hypothesis testing, the term "not reject" is used as opposed to "accept."

The objective of a hypothesis test is to use sample values to select between the null and alternative hypotheses about a pertinent value of a given population. The key question in hypothesis testing is, Has the sample mean deviated from the mean of hypothesized sampling distribution by a large enough value to conclude that this large deviation would be somewhat rare if the statistical hypothesis were true?

Table 14.5 **Type I and Type II Errors**

State of Null Hypothesis	Decision	
	Accept Null (H_o)	Reject Null (H_o)
Null (H_o) is true	No error	Type I error
Null (H_o) is false	Type II error	No error

Errors in Hypothesis Testing

Hypothesis testing is based on the probability theory. Hence, it is not possible to make any statement about samples with certainty. Therefore, there is always a chance that an error can be made. There are two possible types of errors that a researcher could make in testing a hypothesis—type I and type II.

A type I error is made when the null hypothesis is rejected when it is true. A type II error is made when the null hypothesis is *not* rejected when the alternative hypothesis is in fact true. A type I error has the probability of alpha (α), the level of statistical significance that the researcher has set up. The probability of making a type II error is called beta (β). There are no errors made (1) if the null hypothesis is true and the decision is made to accept it and (2) if the null hypothesis is false and the decision is made to reject it. Table 14.5 summarizes the two types of errors.

Because of the inverse relationship between type I and type II errors, researchers cannot simultaneously reduce both types of errors. If the researcher reduces the probability of a type II error, then the probability of a type I error is increased. In business situations, researchers tend to focus more on type I errors than on type II errors. Type I errors are more problematic and are of greater concern; hence, researchers concentrate on determining significance level more with α than with β.

Steps in Hypothesis Testing

Following are the critical steps to follow in hypothesis testing:

- State the null and alternative hypotheses
- Assume the null hypothesis is true
- Specify a confidence level ($1 - \alpha$)
- Take a random sample from the population under investigation
- Compute the test statistic
- Evaluate the likelihood of selecting the test static from the assumed sampling distribution (see appendix C2)

Hypothesis testing can be conducted for one population mean, one population proportion, two population means, two population proportions, paired observations, one population variance, or two population variances.

Example 1. The Indian managers of a large European multinational company operating in India feel that they are underpaid in comparison to managers in other Asian countries. The average salary for midlevel managers in India is US$10,000. To prove to the Indian managers that they are not underpaid, the senior management of the multinational company obtains the mean salaries of 100 managers from the region. The mean salary for the midlevel managers in the sample is US$10,500. Based on company data, the standard deviation of the midlevel managers' salary is US$2,500. Is the average salary obtained by the management (US$10,500) close enough to claim that the differences between the Indian managers and the rest of the managers in the Asian region are not significant? To show the Indian managers that they are not underpaid, the management of the multinational company decides to conduct a hypothesis test at a confidence interval of 95 percent ($\alpha = .05$).

The hypothesis to be tested is as follows:

H_0: $\mu = 10,000$
H_A: $\mu \neq 10,000$

where μ is the average annual salary of Indian managers.

The management cannot reject H_0 if the value US$10,500 is too small or too large. For this example,

$n = 100$
$\mu = 10,000$
$\sigma = 2500$
$z_{\alpha/2} = 1.96$ (from the z tables in appendix C2, at $\alpha = .05$)

$$\pm z_{\alpha/2} = \frac{\bar{x} - \mu}{\sigma/\sqrt{n}} = \frac{\bar{x} - 10,000}{2500/\sqrt{100}} = \pm 1.96$$

$$\bar{x} - 10,000 = \pm 1.96 \left(2500/\sqrt{100} \right)$$

$\bar{x} = -1.96(2500/10) + 10,000$
$\bar{x} = +1.96(2500/10) + 10,000$
$\quad = -490 + 10,000 = 9510$ or
$\quad = +490 + 10,000 = 10,490$

Therefore, the rejection region is

$\bar{x} < 9510$ or $\bar{x} > 10490$

Since the mean salary of the sample is US$10,500, outside the rejection region of $10,490, the conclusion of the management should be to reject H_0. There is sufficient evidence to conclude that H_A is true, that is, $\mu \neq 10,000$. The Indian managers are right in assuming that their salaries are less than those of the rest of the managers in the Asian region.

The critical region may be constructed with the point estimator, as demonstrated in the above example, or through the z value, as demonstrated below.

Example 2. A human resources (HR) director is concerned about the effectiveness of the company's employee training program. In an effort to determine employee perceptions about the program, the HR director conducts a confidential survey among a sample of the employees. One of the questions asked in the survey is "On a five-point scale, where 1 indicates a highly *ineffective* training program and 5 indicates a highly *effective* program, overall how would you rate the effectiveness of the company's training program?" The HR director expects that the employees will be neutral to the effectiveness question. Therefore, the HR director formulates the null hypothesis that the mean score is equal to 3.0 (midpoint of the scale), and the alternative hypothesis is that the mean does not equal 3.0:

$$H_0: \mu = 3.0$$

$$H_A: \mu \neq 3.0$$

Assuming the distribution of perceptions to be normal (at least approximately), the HR director wishes to test this hypothesis at the 95 percent confidence level (0.05 α). That is, if the sample mean lies within the region of acceptance, the HR director would conclude that the null hypothesis is true. The range of acceptance identifies those acceptable values with a difference between hypothesized mean in the null hypothesis and also shows a difference in this range to be so small that we would conclude that the difference was due to a random sampling error rather than a false null hypothesis.

Suppose the HR director sampled 196 employees and obtained a mean score ($\bar{x}$) of 3.65 for the question on training effectiveness. Suppose the sample standard deviation (s) was estimated to be 3.92. The HR director now has sufficient information to test the hypothesis.

The 0.05 level of significance suggests that in the long run, the probability of making an incorrect decision when H_0 is true is less than 5 times in 100. From the standardized normal distribution in appendix C2, the z score for a 0.05 confidence level is 1.96 standard error from the population mean (μ). That is, 1.96 represents a probability of 0.025 that a sample mean lies above 1.96. It also implies a probability of 0.025 that a sample mean will lie below 1.96 standard error from population mean (μ). The values that lie exactly on +1.96 and −1.96 are called the critical values. Critical values lie on the boundary of the region of rejection. See Figure 14.2 (next page).

Figure 14.2

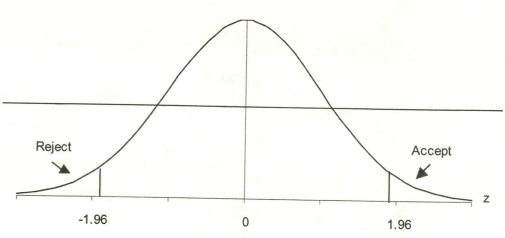

Critical value: upper limit $= \mu + z s_{\bar{x}}$ or $\mu + z \dfrac{s}{n}$

$$= 3.0 + 1.96 \left(\frac{3.92}{\sqrt{196}} \right)$$

$$= 3.0 + 1.96 (0.2)$$

$$= 3.0 + .392 = 3.392$$

Critical value: lower limit $= \mu + z s_{\bar{x}}$ or $\mu - z \dfrac{s}{n}$

$$= 3.0 - 1.96 \frac{3.92}{\sqrt{196}}$$

$$= 3.0 - 1.96 (0.2)$$

$$= 3.0 - .392 = 2.608$$

The rejection region for the test of this hypothesis is shown in Figure 14.3.

The employee survey resulted in a mean score of 3.65 for the effectiveness of training. Since the sample mean is greater than the critical value, 3.392, the HR director concludes that the sample result is statistically significant at the 0.05 level. The result indicates that the employees feel the training to be effective.

Hypothesis testing could also be accomplished in terms of the z statistic. In this case the decision rule is established in terms of z values. Knowing the sample mean $\bar{x}$, the researcher can calculate the observed z statistic and then have it compared to the theoretical z value based on accepted confidence intervals.

Figure 14.3

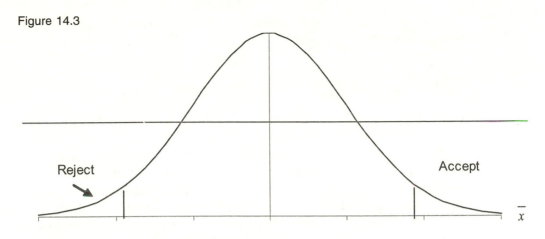

The observed z statistic for a given $\bar{x}$ is:

$$z_{obs} = \frac{\bar{x} - \mu}{s_{\bar{x}}}$$

In the case of the employee training effectiveness study,

$$z_{obs} = \frac{3.65 - \mu}{s_{\bar{x}}}$$

$$z_{obs} = 3.65 - 3.0 \div 0.2$$

$$= .65 \div 0.2 = 3.25$$

As the observed z value is greater than the theoretical z value of $+1.96$ at the 0.05 level, the HR director can come to the same conclusion as in the previous calculation. That is, the employees feel that the training program is effective.

One-Tailed versus Two-Tailed Tests

In the previous example of the employee training effectiveness study, the mean scale value tested was either equal to μ or not equal to μ. What if a researcher is interested in finding out whether the retirement age of employees in private businesses is going up (employees are retiring at a later age)? In this example, the test is not either equal or not equal, but more a case of μ being greater than, say, 60 years of age. In this case, the test of a hypothesis is similarly computed, but the null and the alternative hypotheses are stated differently. When the researcher is interested in only one alternative, the test is referred to as a *one-tailed* test. Therefore, a one-tailed test is one in which the alternative hypothesis indicates a direction—either greater or less than. For example,

$$H_0: \mu = 1,000$$
$$H_A: \mu > 1,000$$

A *two-tailed* test is one in which the alternative hypothesis does not specify direction. For example,

H_0: $\mu = 1,000$
H_A: $\mu \neq 1,000$

Example 3. A multinational company with thousands of employees wants to estimate the average age at which its employees retire. The company's official retirement age is 65. In the 1980s management did observe that most employees retired at the mandatory retirement age. But lately, the company senses that its employees are retiring at an earlier age due to improved economic conditions and alternative lifestyles. Since the question involves a downward change only, a one-tailed test should be used. Following the steps in testing hypotheses, the company management establishes the following null and alternative hypotheses:

H_0: $\mu \geq 65$
H_1: $\mu < 65$

A random sample of 225 employees is drawn from the company's list of retirees during the 1990s and their retirement age is noted. The mean age for recent retirees is observed to be 62. The standard deviation of ages in the population of retirees is estimated to be 15 years. Management establishes a 95.5 percent confidence level to test the above hypothesis.

$$z_{obs} = \frac{\bar{x} - \mu}{\sigma_{\bar{x}}}$$

where $\bar{x}$ = Sample mean
μ = Hypothesized population mean
$s_{\bar{x}}$ = Standard error of mean

$$\text{Standard error of the mean} = \frac{\sigma}{\sqrt{n}} = \frac{15}{\sqrt{225}} = 1.0$$

$z_{obs} = 62 - 65 \div 1.0 = -3.0.$

See Figure 14.4.
The z observed value from appendix C2 (–3.0) is below the critical z value (2.005) from the standard table for 47.75 percent (95.5 ÷ 2). The decision rule calls for rejection of the null hypothesis. That is, such a low sample mean is quite unlikely to have come from a sampling distribution with a mean of 65. Employees are retiring at a much earlier age.

The Probability Value (p Value) of a Hypothesis Test

Up to this point, the statistical test procedures explained testing of hypotheses through preset criteria. That is, based on a reject region (α) selected prior to conducting a test,

Figure 14.4

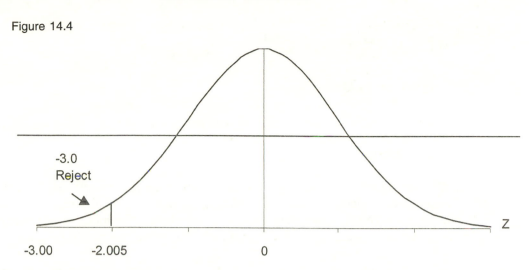

-3.0
Reject

-3.00   -2.005   0   Z

the conclusion is stated in terms of rejecting or not rejecting the null hypothesis. A different method of presenting the results of a statistical test would be to see to what extent the test statistic disagrees with the null hypothesis. That is, what percentage of the sampling distribution lies beyond the sample statistic curve? This percentage value is reported in terms of a p value, where p value is explained as the smallest value of α that would lead to rejection of the null hypothesis. In other words, the p value is the probability of observing a sample value as extreme as, or more extreme than, the value actually observed, given that H_0 is true. The following example should clarify the concept of the p value of a hypothesis test.

Example 4. The top management of a French department store is planning to introduce a new billing system for its credit card customers. Based on a financial analysis, it is determined that to be cost-effective, the average monthly account per customer cannot be less than €350. To test the effectiveness of the new program, management wants to determine the monthly expenditure per customer. From a random sample of 200 monthly accounts, the mean expenditure is obtained as €330. Using a confidence level of 95 percent, management wants to know whether there is sufficient evidence to conclude that the new system would be cost effective. Historically, the population standard deviation for credit card customers has been around €150.

In this case, the hypothesis can be stated as

$$H_0: \quad \mu = 350$$
$$H_A: \quad \mu < 350$$

The test statistic is:

$$z_{obs} = \frac{\bar{x} - \mu}{\sigma \sqrt{n}}$$

$$z_{obs} = \frac{330 - 350}{150/\sqrt{200}} = \frac{-20}{10.6} = -1.89$$

The rejection region is:

$$z < -z_\alpha$$
$$< -z_{.05}$$
$$< -1.645$$

As the calculated z value (-1.89) is less than the critical value (-1.645), the null hypothesis is rejected. There is sufficient evidence from the sample to allow the management of the department store to conclude that the mean monthly expense for the credit card customers is less than €350. Therefore, the new billing system would not be cost-effective.

Management is also concerned with issues other than cost-effectiveness. For example, would the new billing system improve customer service? If it does, will it, in the long run, increase customer spending? Moreover, based on the hypothesis test, the management of the department store did not prove that the system would be costly, just that the statistical evidence existed to that effect. What the department store management really should consider is a measure of how much evidence exists so it can be weighed in relation to other key business variables. In this instance, the p value of the hypothesis test comes into play.

For the department store management, the value of the test statistic was $z = -1.89$ and the rejection region ($\alpha = .05$) was $z < -1.645$. Because $z_{calculated}$ was less than $z_{critical}$, management rejected the null hypothesis. But management could have come to a different conclusion with a change in the confidence interval. At a confidence level of 98 percent ($z = -2.05$) or 97.5 percent ($z = -1.96$), management could not have rejected the null hypothesis. Table 14.6 summarizes the critical values of z that affect the rejection or nonrejection regions for the department store managers.

From Table 14.6, it appears that the smallest value of α that would lead to the rejection of the null hypothesis lies between .029 and .030. This particular value is called the p value. That is, the p value is the probability that $z < -1.89$. From Table C5 in the appendix that provides the area under the normal curve,

$$p \text{ value} = P(z < -1.89) = 0.0294 \ (0.5000 - 0.4706)$$

The calculation of the p value depends to some extent on the alternative hypothesis. The following example will demonstrate this concept.

Example 5. A manager at an investment banking company wants to know whether the average fee charged by the company's brokers is equal to 100 or greater. To test this hypothesis, the manager takes a random sample of 225 records and obtains 102.5 as the average fee charged by the company. In the past, the variations in fees have been around 25.

Table 14.6 **Rejection Region for a Variety of Confidence Intervals**

Confidence Interval (%)	Rejection Region	Decision with $z = -1.89$
99.00 ($\alpha = 0.010$)	$z < -2.33$	Do not reject H_0
98.00 ($\alpha = 0.020$)	$z < -2.05$	Do not reject H_0
97.50 ($\alpha = 0.025$)	$z < -1.96$	Do not reject H_0
96.20 ($\alpha = 0.029$)	$z < -1.90$	Do not reject H_0
96.00 ($\alpha = 0.030$)	$z < -1.88$	Reject H_0

The manager sets the null and alternative hypotheses as follows:

H_0: $\mu = 100$
H_A: $\mu > 100$

$$z_{obs} = \frac{\bar{x} - \mu}{\sigma / \sqrt{n}} = \frac{102.5 - 100}{25 / \sqrt{225}} = \frac{2.5}{5/3} = 1.5$$

Because the rejection region is $z > z_\alpha$, the p value is the probability that z is greater than 1.50. In this case the p value is

p value $= P(z > 1.50) = 0.0668$ (area under the normal curve)

Based on the test, the manager will conclude that the $100 fee charged by the company underestimates the true total fee charged by the company. The outcome is based on the fact that the alternative hypothesis was set as greater than instead of not equal to.

p Value for a Two-Tailed Test

For a two-tailed test, the procedure is the same, except that the z value is doubled to reflect the two sides of the curve. The following example demonstrates the two-tailed test.

Example 6. A battery manufacturer claims that the company's new batteries last for 1,000 hours. An independent laboratory is hired to test this claim. The lab tests 100 batteries and finds the average life of the batteries to be 1002.5 hours. Historically, the standard deviation for the life of batteries has been 20. The lab sets the following null and alternative hypotheses:

H_0: $\mu = 1000$
H_A: $\mu \neq 1000$

$$z_{obs} = \frac{\bar{x} - \mu}{\sigma / \sqrt{n}} = \frac{1002.5 - 100}{20 / \sqrt{100}} = \frac{2.5}{2} = 1.25$$

Because this is a two-tailed test, the rejection region is $|z| > z_{\alpha/2}$. The probability that z is greater than 1.25 must be doubled in order to determine the p value.

p value $= 2P(z > 1.25)$

From the tables in appendix C2, a z of $1.25 = 0.1056(0.5000 - 0.3944)$. Therefore, the p value is $2(0.1056) = 0.2112$.

Interpreting the p *Value*

The p value measures the amount of statistical evidence that supports the alternative hypothesis. The p values can be interpreted as follows: When the p value is small, there is sufficient evidence to support the alternative hypothesis. However, when the p value is large, there is little evidence to support the alternative hypothesis.

Example 7. The management of an appliance company wants to provide its customers with the exact time of the washing cycle for its newest washing machine. The company's goal is to have the machine take only 30 minutes to complete the wash. To determine the time of the wash, the company takes a sample 36 of the new machines and finds that the time it takes the machines to complete a wash is 35.5 minutes. In the past, the variation in washing cycles has been around 12 minutes. The management sets the following hypothesis:

H_0: $\mu = 30$
H_A: $\mu \neq 30$

$$z_{obs} = \frac{\bar{x} - \mu}{\sigma/\sqrt{n}} = \frac{35.5 - 30}{20/\sqrt{36}} = \frac{5.5}{2} = 2.75$$

Because this a two-tailed test, we need to double the p value.

p value $= 2P(z > 2.75)$
$= 2(0.0030)$
$= 0.0060$

The large value of $\bar{x}$ provides more evidence to support the alternative hypothesis that the washing machine cycle is not equal to 30 minutes. The large sample mean has also produced a very small p value.

In the previous example, suppose the time to complete the wash cycle was 31 minutes instead of 35.5. The z value for this scenario is

$$z = \frac{31-30}{12/\sqrt{36}} = \frac{1}{2} = 0.50$$

$$p \text{ value} = 2P(z > 0.50) = 2(0.3085)$$
$$= 0.6170$$

The average cycle of 31 minutes for completing a wash provides very little evidence to indicate that the alternative hypothesis is true. In this case the p value is very high.

Calculating p Value under Three Different Alternative Hypotheses

1. If $H_A: \mu > \mu_0$, where μ_0 is the value of the mean specified under the null hypothesis:
   p value $= P(z > z_a)$, where z_a is the actual value of the test statistic.
2. If $H_A: \mu < \mu_0$:
   p value $= P(z < z_a)$
3. If $H_A: \mu \neq \mu_0$
   p value $= 2P(z > z_a)$ if $z_a > 0$, or
   $\qquad = 2P(z < z_a)$ if $z_a < 0$

HYPOTHESIS TESTING WITH UNKNOWN STANDARD DEVIATION (σ^2) USING STUDENT T DISTRIBUTION

The previous section discussed the confidence level estimator based on knowing the standard deviation and the knowledge that the test statistic

$$\frac{\bar{x} - \mu}{\sigma/\sqrt{n}}$$

is normally distributed. More often than not, the researcher has no idea of the standard deviation. Therefore, the test statistic is not

$$\frac{\bar{x} - \mu}{\sigma/\sqrt{n}}$$

and cannot be the basis for the confidence interval estimator.

Because the standard deviation is unknown, it is substituted with the sample standard deviation(s). However, the test statistic

$$\frac{\bar{x} - \mu}{s/\sqrt{n}}$$

is not normally distributed, but the distribution is a student t distribution (appendix C3) if the population distribution is normal. The

$$\frac{\bar{x} - \mu}{s/\sqrt{n}}$$

is called the t statistic.

The t distribution has the following characteristics:

- It is symmetrical about zero
- It is more widely dispersed than the standard normal distribution; therefore, it is shaped like a mound.
- Its actual shape depends on the sample size n. The t statistic has $(n - 1)$ degrees of freedom.

Following is a problem involving unknown population standard deviation.

Example 8. A computer company in Taiwan assembles motherboards for American PC manufacturers. The company can assemble 1,000 motherboards per day. In an effort to improve the memory power of the motherboard as well as increase production, the PC manufacturer has come up with a new design that it plans to implement immediately. During an experimental run of one week, the plant workers were able to assemble the newly designed motherboards at the rate of 1008, 1009, 1010, 1011, 1010, and 1012 per day. Did the new design increase the production rate at the plant? Use a confidence level of 95 percent.

The sample mean = 1,010 and the sample standard deviation = 1.58. The parameter to be tested is μ, with an unknown population standard deviation. Therefore, the test statistic is $t = (\bar{x} - \mu)/(s/\sqrt{n})$.

The null and alternative hypotheses for this problem are:

$$H_0: \mu = 1000$$
$$H_A: \mu > 1000$$

$$t_{obs} = \frac{1010 - 1000}{1.414/\sqrt{6}} = \frac{10}{.566} = 17.67$$

Rejection region:

$t > t_{\alpha, n-1}$
$t > t_{.05}, 5$
$t > 2.015$ (from the t tables in appendix C3).

See Figure 14.5.

Figure 14.5

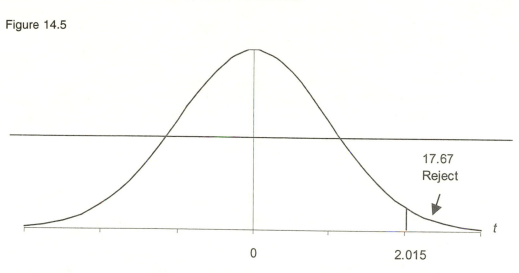

Since the calculated t is greater than the critical t, we reject the null hypothesis. There is enough evidence to show that the average daily output has increased due to the design changes.

Hypothesis testing could also be used when a researcher has to compare results from two populations that are related to each other. Paired observation hypothesis testing is useful in experiments where observations are made on the same subjects before and after treatment. The sample mean can be expressed as μ_1 and μ_2 for the two populations, and the difference between the two means is denoted by μ_d, where $\mu_d = \mu_1 - \mu_2$. For a one-tailed test, the null and alternative hypotheses are written as

$$H_0: \mu_d = 0$$
$$H_A: \mu_d < 0 \text{ or}$$
$$H_A: \mu_d > 0 \text{ (when } \mu_2 \text{ is less than } \mu_1.)$$

When conducting a two-tailed paired comparison test, the null and alternative hypotheses can be written as:

$$H_0: \mu_d = 0$$
$$H_A: \mu_d \neq 0$$

The test statistic for the paired observations is given by

$$t_{(n-1)} = \frac{\bar{d}}{S_d / \sqrt{n}}$$

where $t_{(n-1)}$ is the student t statistic with $(n-1)$ degrees of freedom;

$$\bar{d} = \frac{\sum d_i}{n}$$

where $\bar{d}$ is the observed mean of the paired differences, $d_i = X_{1,i} - X_{2,i}$ is the ith paired difference, and $X_{1,i}$ and $X_{2,i}$ are the respective ith observations on population 1 and population 2; and

$$S_d = \sqrt{\frac{n\sum d_i^2 - (\sum d_i)^2}{n(n-1)}}$$

where S_d is the standard deviation of the paired differences and n = number of pairs.

Example 9. The marketing manager of a beverage company wants to test the strength of its new vitamin-fortified sport drink. The objective of the test is to determine whether the sport drink increases the stamina level of athletes measured by time. The results of 10 randomly selected respondents, which form a sample of 100, are given in Table 14.7. The marketing manager wants to test the results at a significance level of 0.01 ($\alpha = 0.01$).

$$\bar{d} = \frac{\sum d_i}{n} = -24/10 = -2.4$$

$$S_d = \sqrt{\frac{n\sum d_i^2 - (\sum d_i)^2}{n(n-1)}} = \sqrt{\frac{10(66) - (-24)^2}{10(9)}} = 0.93$$

The null hypothesis, H_0, is $\mu_d = 0$; that is, the vitamin-fortified sport drink does not increase an athlete's stamina.

The alternative hypothesis, H_A, is $\mu_d < 0$; that is, the vitamin-fortified sport drink increases an athlete's stamina.

The test statistic is

$$t_9 = \frac{\bar{d}}{S_d/\sqrt{10}}$$

at 9 degrees of freedom ($10 - 1$). Therefore, based on Table 14.7,

$$t_9 = \frac{-2.4}{.93/\sqrt{10}} = -8.28$$

Table 14.7 **Stamina Levels of Athletes**

Subject Number	Stamina before Sport Drink = X_{1i}	Stamina after Sport Drink = X_{2i}	Paired Difference = d_i	d_i^2
1	27	28	−1	1
2	27	29	−2	4
3	31	34	−3	9
4	30	32	−2	4
5	26	27	−1	1
6	33	35	−2	4
7	30	34	−4	16
8	32	35	−3	9
9	29	32	−3	9
10	27	30	−3	9
Total			−24	66

From appendix C3, the t statistic at the significance level of 0.01 and 9 degrees of freedom, $t_9 = -2.821$. Therefore, the rejection region is $t_9 < -2.821$.

Since the calculated t statistic, −8.28, is less than −2.281, it falls in the rejection region. Therefore, we must reject the null hypothesis. In other words, at a .01 level of significance, the marketing manager can conclude that the vitamin-fortified sport drink is effective. That is, the drink increases the stamina level of athletes.

CHI-SQUARE DISTRIBUTION

The previous section dealt with inferences about central location of the population, such as the mean. Since the data obtained are interval scaled and they assume the underlying population to be normally distributed, these tests are classified as parametric tests. A wide variety of data may not be interval scaled or may not come from a normally distributed population. In such cases, researchers apply other techniques that are less restrictive. One such technique is called chi-square. Chi-square tests can be applied when the data is nominal or ordinal scaled.

The chi-square technique can be used for the independence of nominal scale on two categorical variables. That is, it can be used to determine whether a relationship exists between the two variables. This technique could also be used for goodness of fit of a sample of frequency distribution to an actual or theoretical distribution.

In many business situations, executives are sometimes interested in the measure of variability, that is, the population variance (σ^2). For example, a company planning to invest its excess funds in financial instruments will evaluate the variance of the returns as a measurement of risk inherent in the instrument.

As the sample mean was the unbiased estimator of the population mean, so also the sample variance (s^2) is an unbiased estimator of the population variance (σ^2). The sample variance is distributed differently than the population means distribution. The particular distribution associated with the sample variance is called chi-square (χ^2) distribution. The *chi-square distribution* is defined as follows: In repeated sampling from a normal population whose variance is σ^2, the variable $(n-1)s^2/\sigma^2$ is chi-square

Figure 14.6

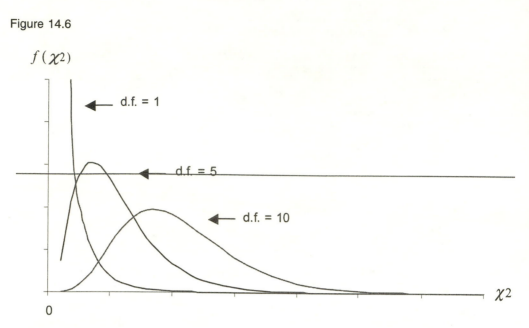

distributed with $(n - 1)$ degrees of freedom. The variable $(n - 1)s^2/\sigma^2$ is called the chi-square statistic. Chi-square distribution can take values between 0 and ∞. See Figure 14.6.

The chi-square variable assumes only positive values, and therefore is noted differently from the z or t values, which take on both negative and positive values. The value of chi-square to its right under the curve is equal to α and is noted as χ^2_{α}. Therefore, $\chi^2_{1-\alpha}$ is the point for which the area to its right is $1 - \alpha$ and the area to its left is α. See Figure 14.7.

Confidence Level Estimator of Variance

For a chi-square distribution,

$$\text{Lower limit} = \frac{(n-1)s^2}{\chi^2_{\alpha/2}}$$

$$\text{Upper limit} = \frac{(n-1)s^2}{\chi^2_{1-\alpha/2}}$$

The above figures are obtained from $P(\chi^2_{1-\alpha/2} < \chi^2 < \chi^2_{\alpha/2}) = 1 - \alpha$ and by substituting for χ^2 with $(n-1)s^2/\sigma^2$. Following is an example that uses the chi-square distribution for setting up confidence intervals.

Example 10. An investor looking for potential investments tracks different financial instruments over a period of time and observes the following returns:

Figure 14.7

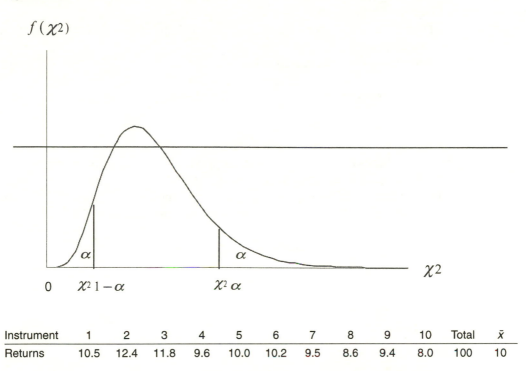

Instrument	1	2	3	4	5	6	7	8	9	10	Total	$\bar{x}$
Returns	10.5	12.4	11.8	9.6	10.0	10.2	9.5	8.6	9.4	8.0	100	10

The investor would like to explain the variance (σ^2) of the returns.

The returns are a single population and they are in an interval scale. To determine the risk associated with these financial instruments, the investor assumes a 90 percent confidence interval for the population variance (σ^2). The sample mean of the population ($\bar{x}$) = 10.00.

For the chi-square distribution, the lower limit = $(n-1)s^2/\chi^2_{\alpha/2}$ and the upper limit = $(n-1)s^2/\chi^2_{1-\alpha/2}$

$$\Sigma(x_1 - \bar{x})^2 = (n-1)s^2 \quad \left(\text{sample variance } s^2 = \frac{\sum\limits_{i=1}^{n}(x_i - \bar{x})^2}{n-1} \right)$$

From the data of the returns,

$$\sum_{i=1}^{n}(x_1 - \bar{x})^2 = (10.5-10.0)^2 + (12.4-10.0)^2 + (11.8-10.0)^2 + (9.6-10.0)^2$$

$$+ (10.0-10.0)^2 + (10.2-10.0)^2 + (9.5-10.0)^2 + (8.6-10.0)^2$$

$$+ (9.4-10.0)^2 + (8.0-10.0)^2 = 19.00$$

For a confidence level of 90 percent, $1 - \alpha = .90$, therefore $\alpha/2 = .05$ and degrees of freedom $= 9(10 - 1)$.

Therefore, $\chi^2_{.05, 9}$ from the chi-square tables in appendix C4 $= 16.919$ and $\chi^2_{.95, 9} = 3.32511$.

Therefore, the lower limit $= (n - 1)s^2/\chi^2_{\alpha/2} = 19 \div 16.919 = 0.006$, and the upper limit $= (n - 1)s^2/\chi^2_{1-\alpha/2} = 19.00 \div 3.32511 = 5.71$.

The 90 percent confidence interval estimate of variance for the returns is 0.006, 5.71.

Example 11. A soft drink bottler claims that the standard deviation of the cans filled by its machines is less than 1 cubic centimeter (cc). In a random sample of 10 fills, the sample standard deviation was 0.90 cc. At a 95 percent confidence level, determine whether there is sufficient evidence to verify the claim of the soft drink bottler.

The null and alternative hypotheses in this case are as follows:

H_0: $\sigma^2 = 1$ ($\sigma = 1$ and therefore, σ^2 is also $= 1$)
H_A: $\sigma^2 < 1$

Test statistic:

$$\chi^2 = \frac{(n-1)s^2}{\sigma^2}$$

$$\chi^2 = \frac{(n-1)s^2}{\sigma^2} = \frac{9(0.90)^2}{1} = 7.29$$

Rejection region:

$$\chi^2 < \chi^2_{1-\alpha, n-1}$$
$$\chi^2 < \chi^2_{.95, 9}$$
< 3.32511 (from the chi-square tables in appendix C4)

Since the chi-square calculated is greater than critical, we reject the alternative hypothesis. There is not enough evidence to support the bottler's claim.

CHI-SQUARE DISTRIBUTION AND CONTINGENCY TABLES

In many business situations the data collected is often nominal or ordinal data. These types of data could be subjected to a test that determines whether two categorical variables are related. Governments may be interested to know whether the labor force is shifting from an agricultural to industrial or service sector. To determine if one categorical variable is related to another, researchers use a contingency table or data matrix. A contingency table test is referred to as a *test of independence* since the null hypothesis being tested states that the two categorical variables are independent.

Table 14.8 **Contingency Table—Car Buyer Survey**

Technical Knowledge	Male	Female	Total
Has knowledge	40	20	60
Has no knowledge	70	70	140
Total	110	90	200

The data necessary for the contingency table test consist of sample measurements on two categorical variables. The data is arranged in a tabular or matrix form (also called cross-tabulation table).

Example 12. The marketing vice president of a large automobile manufacturer wants to know if the technical knowledge possessed by female car buyers is the same as those of male car buyers. To test this hypothesis, the marketing executive randomly surveyed 200 potential car buyers. The survey results are presented in Table 14.8 arranged as a matrix or contingency table.

Contingency table tests are used to contrast a demographic variable such as age, income, or size with a usage, attitude, or opinion variable. Therefore, for the above example on car buyers' technical knowledge, the marketing executive is interested in knowing whether the first variable knowledge is independent of the second variable buyer's gender.

The null and alternative hypotheses that the researcher must choose between is

H_0: The row and column variables (knowledge and gender) are independent
H_A: The row and column variables (knowledge and gender) are not independent

In Table 14.8, the probability that a person has technical knowledge is calculated by dividing 60 by 200, or = 0.30. If gender and technical knowledge are independent, the marketing executive would expect 30 percent of the 110 males (33) and 30 percent of the 90 females (27) to be technically knowledgeable about cars (note that the expected frequencies for the knowledgeable individuals must total 60, the observed frequencies). Using this approach, the marketing executive can now show the expected frequencies for each cell of the contingency table.

Technical knowledge	Male		Female		Total
Has knowledge		40		27	
	33		20		60
Has no knowledge		77		63	
	70		70		140
Total	110		90		200

The upper right-hand corner of each cell shows the expected frequencies, and the lower left-hand corner values of each cell show the observed frequencies. If the observed frequencies are close to the expected frequencies, the test statistic should indicate that the marketing executive could not reject the null hypothesis, that is, that gender and technical knowledge are independent. If the observed and expected frequencies are different, the test statistic should lead to the rejection of the null hypothesis, that is, that gender and technical knowledge are not independent.

The chi-square (χ^2) statistic is computed as

$$\chi^2 = \Sum \frac{(f_o - f_e)^2}{f_e}$$

where f_o = observed frequency, and f_e = expected frequency.

$$\chi^2 = \frac{(40-33)^2}{33} + \frac{(20-27)^2}{27} + \frac{(70-77)^2}{77} + \frac{(70-63)^2}{63} = 4.71$$

The critical chi-square value from the table in appendix C4 for 1 degree of freedom [df = $(column - 1)(row - 1) = (2-1)(2-1) = 1$] and a confidence level of 95.00 percent is 3.841. The decision rule is, if the calculated chi-square value is larger than 3.841, we will reject the null hypothesis. Since the calculated chi-square, 4.71, is greater than the critical value, 3.841, the null hypothesis is rejected. Gender and technical knowledge are not independent.

Example 13. The secretary of labor of the Philippine government would like to determine whether the sick days associated with factory workers are related to age. In a random review of 450 sick-leave statistics compiled by the department, the following pattern is observed.

Sick leave per annum (days)	Age (years)			Total
	≤30	30.1–50	≥50.1	
0–5	90	50	10	150
6–10	50	60	40	150
11 or more	10	40	100	150
Total	150	150	150	450

The labor secretary sets a significance level of 0.05 to determine whether sick leave is age related.

    H_0: Age and sick leave are independent
    H_A: Age and sick leave are not independent

Frequency table:

Sick leave per annum	Age (years)			Total
	≤ 30	30.1–50	≥50.1	
0–5	50	50	50	150
	90	50	10	
6–10	50	50	50	150
	50	60	40	
11 or more	50	50	50	150
	10	40	100	
Total	150	150	150	450

$$\chi^2 = \frac{(90-50)^2}{50} + \frac{(50-50)^2}{50} + \frac{(10-50)^2}{50} + \frac{(50-50)^2}{50} + \frac{(60-50)^2}{50}$$

$$+ \frac{(40-50)^2}{50} + \frac{(10-50)^2}{50} + \frac{(40-50)^2}{50} + \frac{(100-50)^2}{50} = 147.00$$

In the chi-square tables in appendix C4, the chi-square value for a 95 percent confidence interval and 4 degrees of freedom [df = (3 – 1)(3 – 1)] = 9.488.

The chi-square observed (147.00) is greater than chi-square critical (9.488). Therefore, the null hypothesis is rejected. The sick leave absences of factory workers are not independent of age.

INTERPRETING CHI-SQUARE RESULTS

Chi-square analysis is a method to determine whether a nonmonotonic association exists between two variables. It is able to indicate the strength of the association by its size, but not the nature of the association. It is a good prerequisite for looking more closely at the variables to understand the nature of the association between them. If the chi-square analysis results in a relationship between variables, a researcher needs to investigate this relationship very closely. When the computed chi-square value is small, then the null hypothesis or the hypothesis of independence between variables is assumed to be true. The chi-square analysis tells the researcher the probability of finding evidence in support of the null hypothesis

Table 14.9 summarizes some of the previously discussed procedures for analyzing research data.

CHAPTER SUMMARY

Data analysis is the process of transforming data into information. Data analysis starts with editing. Editing consists of reviewing responses to identify incomplete, illegible, ambiguous, and inconsistent responses. Requestioning the sampled respondents, returning to the field for clarification, assigning missing values, or disregarding the responses may correct the problems identified during the editing phase of data analysis. Data cleaning requires treatment of missing responses. Options available to correct missing responses include substitution of a neutral value, such as the mean,

Table 14.9 **Statistical Analytical Approaches**

Statistical Question	Type of Scale	Test of Significance
Differences between sample and population mean	Interval scale	z test for large samples t test for small samples
Categorization of variables	Ordinal scale	Chi-square test
Independence of variables	Nominal scale	Chi-square test
Proportion of categories		t test of proportions
Determine associations		Cross-tabulation or correlation
Statistical forecasting		Regression

or case-by-case deletion. Researchers can also make use of weighting to adjust for the missing responses.

Coding is the next step in the process. In some situations, a researcher may precode the questionnaires. Coding involves assigning numeric or alphanumeric codes to represent a specific response. Coding helps researchers to enter data into computers for analysis. When conducting cross-country studies, researchers have to make sure that the units of measurement are comparable across countries.

Frequency distribution is used to obtain counts for each variable in the questionnaire. Frequency distribution is also used to obtain percentages and cumulative percentages for all the values associated with a given variable. The mean, median, and mode are measures of central tendency. The range, standard deviation, coefficient of variation, and quartile range describe the variability of the distribution. Cross-tabulations provide the joint distribution of two or more variables. Percentages and sample means of subgroups may be calculated through cross-tabulations.

Univariate statistical analysis allows the researcher to assess the statistical significance of various hypotheses about a single variable. Hypothesis testing is a univariate statistical procedure. In hypothesis testing, a researcher states a null hypothesis about a population mean. The null hypothesis is usually a statement about the status quo. The alternative hypothesis is a statement indicating the opposite of the null hypothesis. The z test (or the t test in the case of an unknown standard deviation) defines a region of rejection based on a significance level on the standardized normal distribution (or the t distribution) beyond which it is unlikely that the null hypothesis is true. If a sample mean is contained in the region of the rejection, the null hypothesis is rejected. The estimate of the variance (σ^2) is based on the chi-square distribution. Chi-square and t distributions both require that the populations from which the samples are taken be normally distributed. There are two possible types of error in statistical tests. A type I error occurs when a null hypothesis that is true is rejected. A type II error occurs when a false null hypothesis is accepted.

Bivariate or multivariate analysis is used when two or more variables are to be analyzed. Nonparametric statistical tests are used on nominal or ordinal data. Parametric tests are used for interval or ratio scales. The contingency table test is designed to examine the relationship between two or more categorical variables. One of the variables is arranged in the rows of the table, and the other along the columns. A chi-square test is used to see whether the variables are independent by measuring the degree of conformity between the observed frequencies and the expected frequencies for each cell in the contingency table.

* * *

NOTE: A data set containing responses from the detergent questionaire (chapter 9, appendix 9.1, page 186) is available on the publisher's Web site: www.mesharpe. com. Search for it by author name (Neelankavil) and there will be a link to the data set. This data set can be used by students to practice data analysis (chapters 14 through 16).

CHAPTER REVIEW

1. What are some of the key preliminary steps undertaken in analyzing data?
2. What is editing? Why is it important?
3. How are inconsistencies found in the editing process resolved?
4. What is coding? Why is it important?
5. What is computerized data entry?
6. How can we classify data?
7. What is a frequency distribution?
8. What is a cross-tabulation?
9. What is hypothesis testing?
10. How is hypothesis testing used?
11. What are the two errors found in hypothesis testing?
12. What are the null and alternative hypotheses?
13. Describe the steps in hypothesis testing.
14. What is the difference between a one-tailed and two-tailed hypothesis test?
15. What are the differences among the z, t, and chi-square distributions? What are the conditions that must exist for using each one of these distributions?
16. In a survey of bank customers on bank employees' efficiency in transacting business, a sample of 225 customers rated the efficiency of the bank employees 3.75 on a five-point scale, with 1 being very inefficient and 5 extremely efficient. The sample standard deviation = 1.5. At a 95 percent significance level, can the management of the bank claim that its employees are efficient?
17. A mutual fund manager claims that the fund she manages has historically maintained at least 15 percent returns. In order to test this claim, a financial analyst tracks the quarterly returns for the fund over a 25-year period and obtains a mean return of 15.5 percent with a sample variation of 2.5 percent. Is the claim of the mutual fund manager justified based on the sample mean?
18. The Ford Motor Company is planning to buy 1 million tires for an off-road vehicle that it plans to introduce in the near future. It wants the tires on the vehicles to last for at least 100,000 miles. The Goodyear Tire and Rubber Company has developed a new set of tires that it claims can meet Ford's tire specifications. To prove to Ford that its tires meet the standards, Goodyear

tests 25 tires on a testing machine and finds that the mean life of the tires is 97,000 miles with a standard deviation of 15 miles. At a significance level of 95 percent, is Goodyear's claim correct?

19. A pharmaceutical company has developed a new diet supplement that may help patients reduce their weight by at least 25 pounds over the course of six months. The company wants to initially test its experimental product on about 10 volunteers under close monitoring by a physician. After the trial period, the physician provides the following patient-weight-loss data to the company: 24, 28, 26, 23, 27, 22, 25, 27, 23, and 25 pounds. At a 99 percent significance level, determine whether the new diet supplement is effective.

20. A Japanese camera manufacturer is interested in determining the variability in dealer prices for its cameras in the European market. In 10 randomly selected retail stores, the following prices were observed (all in euros): 350, 400, 390, 370, 360, 410, 380, 375, 385, and 380. Estimate with a 95.5 confidence level the variance in price for the Japanese camera.

21. The CFO of a multinational company wants to determine the percentage of accounts receivable that are past due. Over the years, the companywide percentage has remained at about 5 percent. The regional manager for Asia suspects that the accounts receivable from Indonesian distributors are much higher than the company average. To test this, the CFO asks the regional manager to review the previous year's accounts receivable for Indonesia. Of the 500 invoices issued in a typical month, about 40 were past due. At a 95 percent significance level, is the accounts receivable rate in Indonesia higher than that in the company as a whole?

22. The German government wants to know whether its population is fully aware of the hospice program that it has recently introduced for elderly patients. It appears that more male patients are enrolling in the program than female. In a survey of 400 elderly persons (200 male and 200 female), the response rate for awareness of hospice is male 150/200 and female 100/200. At a 95 percent confidence level, are there any significant differences between male and female patients?

23. A plant manager wants to know whether employees' work experience results in higher productivity at his plant. He groups his workers into three categories—15 years' or more experience, 5 to 14.9 years' experience, and less than 5 years' experience. In reviewing 225 production runs, the plant manager obtains the following results:

Experience (years)	Productivity		
	High	Medium	Low
≥15	50	20	5
5–14.9	20	50	5
<5	5	20	50

At a 95 percent significance level, is the productivity level dependent on experience?

NOTES

1. Serge Luyens, "Coding Verbatim by Computer," *Marketing Research: A Magazine of Management and Applications* 7, no. 2 (1995), pp. 21–25.

2. William R. Dillon and Mathew Goldstein, *Multivariate Analysis: Methods and Applications.* New York, John Wiley & Sons, 1984, pp. 303–335.

ADDITIONAL READING

BOOKS

Churchill, Gilbert A., Jr., and Tom J. Brown. *Basic Marketing Research.* 5th ed. Cincinnati, OH: South Western Publishing, 2004, pp. 514–563.

Malhotra, Naresh K. *Marketing Research: An Applied Orientation,* 4th ed. Upper Saddle River, NJ: Prentice Hall, 2004, pp. 424–463.

Zikmund, William G. *Exploring Marketing Research.* 8th ed. Cincinatti, OH: South Western Publishing, 2003, pp. 499–544.

ARTICLE

Malhotra, Naresh K., Jane Agarwal, and Mark Peterson (1996) "Methodological Issues in Cross-Cultural Marketing Research," *International Marketing Review* 13, no. 5, pp. 7–43.

15 Data Analysis: Tests of Differences

Tests of differences let researchers conclude whether a given research result is statistically significant and confirm that it was not the result of chance.

LEARNING OBJECTIVES

After reading this chapter, students should be able to

- Understand tests of statistical significance
- Discuss reasons for conducting tests of differences
- Understand the various available tests and know when to apply them
- Understand the χ^2 (chi-square) goodness-of-fit test
- Understand the application of chi-square tests to contingency tables
- Understand the analysis of variance (ANOVA)
- Understand one-way analysis of variance and its effects

Researchers strive to obtain information that is actual, true, and representative of the values of the population. But often, research is conducted with samples. Samples are frequently biased; therefore, the results obtained or the findings culled from the sample may not reflect the underlying conditions in the population. Hence, researchers make use of various tests to determine the significance of the results obtained from the sample. These tests are commonly referred to as tests of statistical significance. In this chapter, two useful tests for examining the statistical significance of differences are presented. The differences examined might be between the sample result and an expected population value, or they might be between two or more sample results. The two tests discussed here are the χ^2 (chi-square) goodness-of-fit tests and the analysis of variance (ANOVA).

GOODNESS-OF-FIT TESTS

The chi-square distribution was used in chapter 14 as a way to test a hypothesis concerning the population variance (σ^2). The purpose was to describe a single population for which the interval scale data was used. In a test for statistical significance, the data in question has a nominal scale. Chi-square tests discussed in this chapter—the goodness-of-fit test—can be used to help determine whether it is reasonable to assume that the sample is from a normal distribution.

The sequence of steps for goodness-of-fit tests is similar to the hypothesis testing procedure discussed in chapter 14.

GOODNESS-OF-FIT TESTS: STEPS

- Set null and alternative hypotheses
- Select a significance level for rejection of the null hypothesis
- Draw a random sample of observations from a population
- Derive a set of expected (theoretical) frequencies under the assumption that the null hypothesis is true (assume that a particular probability distribution is applicable to the population under consideration).
- Determine the degrees of freedom (df) as number of cases (k) – 1.
- Compare the observed frequencies to the expected frequencies.
- Reject the null hypothesis if the discrepancy between the observed and expected frequencies is too great to be attributed to chance fluctuations.

The goodness-of-fit test can be illustrated by an example using a sample from a population with a uniform probability distribution. If equal probabilities are assigned to a discrete random variable, the distribution of the variable is said to be uniform.

Example 1. A food company selling packaged ice cream through food stores wants to find out whether consumers have specific preferences based on taste alone between its brand and three other competing brands. A comparison taste test was conducted among a randomly selected sample of 400 customers. The research team used an experiment to determine the taste preferences among the four brands. The experiment involved giving each consumer a scoop of vanilla ice cream from four containers labeled 1, 2, 3, and 4. Each brand of ice cream was presented to each consumer in a random order. Results of the experiment are presented in Table 15.1.

If there were no difference in preferences among the brands, 100 (25%) consumers from the sample would prefer one particular brand. Hence, the null and alternative hypotheses could be set as

H_0: $P_1 = P_2 = P_3 = P_4$ (the probability distribution is uniform)
H_A: $P_1 \neq P_2 \neq P_3 \neq P_4$ (the probability distribution is not uniform)

Table 15.1 **Consumers' Taste Preferences for Four Ice Cream Brands**

Brand Identity	Brand Preferences
1	95
2	110
3	115
4	80
Total	400

Applying the chi-square equation

$$\chi^2 = \sum_{i=1}^{n} \frac{\left(f_o - f_t\right)^2}{f_t}$$

where f_o is the observed frequency and f_t is the theoretical or expected frequency results in the calculation of chi-squares as presented in Table 15.2.

To complete the analysis, the computed chi-square must be compared to a critical value that is determined from the chi-square tables in appendix C4. To obtain the critical chi-square value, one needs to know the level of confidence and degrees of freedom (df). The df for the ice cream problem is the number of cases (k; in this case, four brands), minus 1, or $4 - 1 = 3$. Let us assume that the null hypothesis is tested at a 0.05 level of confidence ($\alpha = 0.05$). From the chi-square tables (appendix C4), the critical value for the 0.05 significance level and 3 df is 7.815. Therefore, the decision rule for the ice cream problem is as follows:

If $\chi^2 > 7.815$, reject H_0 (the null hypothesis)
If $\chi^2 \leq 7.815$, accept H_0 (the null hypothesis)

Since the computed chi-square value (7.50) is less than the critical value (7.815), the null hypothesis cannot be rejected. Therefore, it can be concluded that real differences do not exist in consumer preference among the brands of ice cream. In terms of goodness of fit, we reject the null hypothesis that the probability distribution is uniform (i.e., the uniform distribution is not a good fit to the sample data).

The goodness-of-fit test allows researchers to determine whether the research results are statistically significant. It basically answers the question, "Could the result have occurred by chance due to the sample, or does it indicate an underlying condition that exists within the population?" Goodness-of-fit tests are applied mostly to nominal data.

The following problem will further clarify the goodness-of-fit test.

Example 2. A regional bank is planning to introduce automatic bill payment services to its customers. It has three possible approaches to introduce this service. It could introduce the service through a personalized letter, it could ask its branch managers

Table 15.2 **Chi-square Statistic**

Brand	Observed f_o	Theoretical f_t	$(f_o - f_t)$	$(f_o - f_t)^2$	$(f_o - f_t)^2/f_t$
1	95	100	−5	25	0.25
2	110	100	+10	100	1.00
3	115	100	+15	225	2.25
4	80	100	−20	400	4.00
Total	400	400	0	0	7.50

$$\chi^2 = \sum_{i=1}^{n} \frac{(f_o - f_t)^2}{f_t} = 7.50$$

to personally introduce the service to customers when they visit the bank, or it could have bank representatives call its customers by telephone to introduce the new service. In the past the bank has had the best results in introducing new services when its branch managers spoke directly to bank customers. The telephone calls were next in obtaining favorable results, and the mail contact was the least successful. In fact, the personal approach brought in three times as many customers as mail, and telephone contact brought in twice as many as mail. Mail contacts are the cheapest and personal contacts are the most expensive. The bank wishes to test whether this pattern will prevail for the automatic payment services and conducts a study among a small sample of its customers. In a test of 120 of its customers, the bank obtained the following results:

Number of Customers Signing Up for the New Service

Personal Contact	Telephone Contact	Mail Contact	Total
75	30	15	120

Does the preliminary result indicate that the bank can expect a change in customer acceptance of the new service compared to previous customer contacts?

The null hypothesis is H_0: $P = 3{:}2{:}1$ ($P_1 = 3/6$; $P_2 = 2/6$; $P_3 = 1/6$)
The alternative hypothesis is H_A: $P \neq 3{:}2{:}1$

Therefore, the expected number of service acceptances for the sample is: personal contact $= (3/6)(120) = 60$; telephone contact $= (2/6)(120) = 40$; and mail contact $= (1/6)(120) = 20$.

Chi-square Statistic

Contact	Observed f_o	Theoretical f_t	$(f_o - f_t)$	$(f_o - f_t)^2$	$(f_o - f_t)^2/f_t$
Personal	75	60	15	225	3.75
Telephone	30	40	−10	100	2.50
Mail	15	20	−5	25	1.25
Total	120	120	0	0	7.50

If the bank has chosen a significance level of $\alpha = 0.05$, using the level of significance and the df, the chi-square critical can be obtained from appendix C4. For this test, the df is $(k - 1) = 3 - 1 = 2$. The chi-square critical value for a 0.05 significance level and a df of 2 is 5.991.

Since the computed chi-square value (7.50) is greater than the critical (5.991), the null hypothesis is rejected. That is, the acceptance rate of the automatic bill payment system will follow a different pattern, not 3:2:1, for personal, telephone, and mail contact, respectively.

Analysis of Variance (ANOVA)

The previously discussed chi-square test enabled us to test for the significance of the differences among sample *proportions*. The technique to test for the significance of the difference among sample *means* is the analysis of variance (ANOVA). Technically speaking, ANOVA is a test of variances, but in testing for variances, it also provides a test for the significance of the differences among means. The null hypothesis is that all means are equal. This technique is applied in many business situations including manufacturing, finance, human resources, and marketing.

Analysis of variance examines the differences in the mean value of a dependent variable (metric, meaning measured in an interval or ratio scale) with the effect of an independent variable (which is nonmetric, also called categorical data). When only one independent variable is involved, the test is called *one-way analysis of variance*. If two or more independent variables are involved, the test is called *n-way ANOVA*. If the independent variables are made up of both interval and categorical scales, the technique used to test the differences of means is called analysis of covariance (ANCOVA), and if the independent variables are made up of an interval scale, then regression analysis is used (see chapter 16).

The one-way analysis of variance uses a single variable measured on the sample items to test the null hypothesis that the population means are equal. That is, the null hypothesis under test is that all the populations being studied have the same mean value for the variable (dependent variable) under study. The variable can be interval or ratio scaled. The actual calculation of the ANOVA is typically handled by a computer program such as SAS or SPSS.

In ANOVA, it is assumed that all the populations being studied have the same variance regardless of whether their means are equal; that is, whether the populations have equal or unequal means, the variability of items around their respective means is the same. If this assumption is true, the null hypothesis of equal population means can be tested using the F distribution.

Basic Steps in ANOVA

The basic steps in ANOVA are as follows.

- A specific variable is measured from each of the populations under study.
- ANOVA can be done in two ways:

1. The first method, known as "within" (also called "between-row"), produces a valid estimate of the unknown common variance of the population regardless of whether the populations have equal means.

2. The second method (also called "between-column") produces a valid estimate of the variance of the populations only if the null hypothesis of the population means being equal is true.

- Under the null hypothesis, where the population means are equal, the between-column variation and the between-row variation would be expected not to differ significantly from each other (both reflect the same type of chance sampling errors). (The term "variation" in this context refers to a sum of squared deviations. When the measure of variation is divided by an appropriate number of degrees of freedom, it is referred to as "variance.") If the null hypothesis is false, and the population means are different, then the between-column variation should significantly exceed the between-row variation. The reason for the large difference in between-column and between-row variation is that the between-column variation would be produced by the differences among the column means as well as by the chance sampling error. The between-row variation is due only to chance sampling error.

- A comparison of between-column variation and between-row variation provides information about the differences among the column means.

- The formula for between-column variation is

$$\sum_j r\left(\bar{x}_j - \bar{\bar{x}}\right)^2$$

where r = number of rows
$\bar{x}$ = the mean of jth column
$\bar{\bar{x}}$ = the grand mean
$\sum_j$ = summation taken over all columns

- The between-row sum of squares is a summary measure of the random errors of the individual observations around their column means. The formula for the between-row sum of squares is

$$\text{Between-row} = \sum_j \sum_i \left(x_{ij} - \bar{x}_j\right)^2$$

where x_{ij} = the value of the observation in the ith row and jth column
$\bar{x}$ = the mean of the jth column
$\sum_j \sum_i$ = squared deviations first summed over all sample observations within a given column, then summed over all columns

- The test of the null hypothesis in ANOVA involves a comparison of the between-column variance and the between-row variance. The next step is to determine the degrees of freedom (df) associated with each of the measures of variation. For the between-column sum of squares, the degree of freedom is $(c - 1)$, where c = the number of treatments represented by the number of columns. The df associated with the between-row sum of squares is $rc - c = c(r-1)$, where c = number of treatments or columns and r = number of elements in each group or number of rows.

- The test of the null hypothesis that the population column means are equal is carried out by comparing the mean square of columns with the mean square of rows. The comparison of these two mean squares is made by calculating their ratio—called the F ratio (in the F ratio, between-column variance is always placed in the numerator). Under the null hypothesis that the population column means are equal, the F ratio would tend to be equal to 1 (F = Sampling error + Variance due to differences ÷ Sampling error). If the population column means differ, the F ratio will be greater than 1.
- The F ratio is given as

$$F(df_1, df_2) = MS_c/MS_r$$

where MS_c = between-column sum of squares $(SS_c) \div (c-1)$
MS_r = between-row sum of squares $(SS_r) \div c(r-1)$

- To complete the ANOVA, we must find out how large the test statistic F must be in order to reject the null hypothesis. This is given by the F random variable distribution. Appendixes C5 and C6 provide the values of the F ratio for frequently used significance levels and degrees of freedom.
- The underlying assumption for the above is that the two random samples are drawn from normally distributed populations with equal variances σ_1^2 and σ_2^2.

The following example illustrates the application of ANOVA.

Example 3. The human resources (HR) department of a multinational company wants to know of the three methods available for training new recruits, which is the most effective based on feedback from executives that employed these trainees. In the first method, the HR department used internal staffers to conduct the standard training course; in the second method, outside consultants were brought in to conduct the same program; and, in the third method, the standard program was conducted by both internal staffers and outside consultants. To conduct the study, the HR department used 24 new recruits that were recently hired. The new recruits were assigned randomly to the three training groups. After completion of their program, the executive in charge of the international division was asked to evaluate their performance on a 10-point scale, where 1 = poor and 10 = excellent. Table 15.3 presents the scores given by the executive for the 24 recruits.

The "between" method of ANOVA translates for the above example as "between-column" variation and the "within" method is basically "between–row" variation. That is, "between-column" variation refers to variation of the sample means $\bar{x}_1$, $\bar{x}_2$, and $\bar{x}_3$ around the grand-mean $\bar{\bar{x}}$. "Within" (also called "between-row") variation refers to the differences of the individual observations within each column from their respective means $\bar{x}_1$, $\bar{x}_2$, and $\bar{x}_3$.

The mean rating for each group of recruits is

$$\bar{x}_1 = 6.37; \ \bar{x}_2 = 7.0; \ \bar{x}_3 = 7.88$$

Table 15.3 **Evaluation Scores of 24 New Recruits**

Sample Number	Method 1	Method 2	Method 3
1	7	8	9
2	6	7	8
3	5	8	8
4	7	7	8
5	8	7	8
6	5	6	7
7	7	6	8
8	6	7	7
Total	51	56	63
Mean	6.37	7.0	7.88

The grand mean for the total sample is

$$\bar{\bar{x}} = \frac{6.37 + 7.0 + 7.88}{3} = 7.1$$

The research question is, "Can the three sample groups represented by the three means be considered as having been drawn from populations having the same mean?" That is, if μ_1, μ_2, and μ_3 represent the population means corresponding to the three sample means, respectively, the null hypothesis can be stated as

$$H_0: \mu_1 = \mu_2 = \mu_3$$

and the alternative hypothesis is

$$H_A: \mu_1 \neq \mu_2 \neq \mu_3$$

In essence, the researcher wants to determine whether the differences among the sample means are too great to attribute to the chance errors of drawing samples from populations having the same means. If the sample means differ significantly, it implies that the three training methods produce different results. In reality, the tests are actually done to determine whether the three samples are drawn from populations having the same means and variances.

BETWEEN-COLUMN VARIATION

The formula for between-column variation is

$$\sum_j r\left(\bar{x}_j - \bar{\bar{x}}\right)^2$$

For the training problem, the calculations for between-column variation are presented below:

$$\left(\bar{x}_1 - \bar{\bar{x}}\right)^2 = \left(6.4 - 7.1\right)^2 = 0.49$$

$$\left(\bar{x}_2 - \bar{\bar{x}}\right)^2 = \left(7.0 - 7.1\right)^2 = 0.01$$

$$\left(\bar{x}_3 - \bar{\bar{x}}\right)^2 = \left(7.9 - 7.1\right)^2 = 0.64$$

$$\sum_j r\left(\bar{x}_j - \bar{\bar{x}}\right)^2 = 24\left(0.49\right) + 24\left(0.01\right) + 24\left(0.64\right) = 27.36$$

Therefore, the between-column variation = 27.36.

BETWEEN-ROW VARIATION

The formula for the between-row sum of squares is

$$\sum_j \sum_i \left(x_{ij} - \bar{x}_j\right)^2$$

For the training problem, the between-row calculations are presented in Table 15.4. Therefore,

Total Variation = Between-Column Variation + Between-Row Variation

That is, for the training problem,

Total Variation = 27.36 + 17.2 = 44.56.

NUMBER OF DEGREES OF FREEDOM (DF)

For the training problem, $c = 3$. Therefore the df for the between-column = $3 - 1 = 2$ and for the between-row: $c = 3$ and $r = 8$. Therefore the df for between-row variation = $3(8 - 1) = 21$.

Now we are ready to complete the ANOVA analysis. The ANOVA table for the training problem is presented below.

Source of Variation	Sum of Squares	Degrees of Freedom	Mean Square (Col.2/Col. 3)
Between-column	27.36	2	13.7
Between-row	17.20	21	0.8
Total	44.56	23	

$F(2, 21) = 13.7 \div 0.8 = 17.125$

Table 15.4 **Between-Row Calculations**

Sample Number	$(x_{i1} - \bar{x}_1)$	$(x_{i1} - \bar{x}_1)^2$	$(x_{i2} - \bar{x}_2)$	$(x_{i2} - \bar{x}_2)^2$	$(x_{i3} - \bar{x}_3)$	$(x_{i3} - \bar{x}_3)^2$
1	7.0 – 6.4 = 0.6	0.36	8.0 – 7.0 = 1.0	1.0	9.0 – 7.9 = 1.1	1.21
2	6.0 – 6.4 = (0.4)	0.16	7.0 – 7.0 = 0	0.0	8.0 – 7.9 = 0.1	0.01
3	5.0 – 6.4 = (1.4)	1.96	8.0 – 7.0 = 1.0	1.0	8.0 – 7.9 = 0.1	0.01
4	7.0 – 6.4 = 0.6	0.36	7.0 – 7.0 = 0	0.0	8.0 – 7.9 = 0.1	0.01
5	8.0 – 6.4 = 1.6	2.56	7.0 – 7.0 = 0	1.0	8.0 – 7.9 = 0.1	0.01
6	5.0 – 6.4 = (1.4)	1.96	6.0 – 7.0 = (1.0)	1.0	7.0 – 7.9 = (0.9)	0.81
7	7.0 – 6.4 = 0.6	0.36	6.0 – 7.0 = (1.0)	1.0	8.0 – 7.9 = 0.1	0.01
8	6.0 – 6.4 = (0.4)	1.60	7.0 – 7.0 = 0	0.0	7.0 – 7.9 = (0.9)	0.81
Total		9.32		5.0		2.88

$$\sum_j \sum_i \left(x_{ij} - \bar{x}_j\right)^2 = 9.32 + 5.0 + 2.88 = 17.2$$

Suppose the HR department wishes to test the null hypothesis at an $\alpha = 0.05$ level of significance. From the F distribution (see appendixes C5 and C6), for $df_1 = 2$ and $df_2 = 21$ [$F_{.05}(2, 21)$] an F value of 3.47 would be exceeded 5 percent of the time if the null hypothesis were true.

Compare critical F (from the F distribution) $F_{.05}$ (2, 21) to calculated F (2, 21).

Since 17.125 > 3.47, reject the null hypothesis. The conclusion is that the sample mean of the training effectiveness in classes taught by the internal trainer, the external trainer, and a combination of the two differ significantly. That is, the inference about the corresponding population means is that they are not all the same. In fact, in comparing the three approaches in Table 15.3, we see that the training method using the internal and external trainers produces the highest ratings (7.9 versus 7.0 and 7.9 versus 6.4).

SUMS OF SQUARES

The above method of calculating ANOVA is time-consuming and cumbersome. A shortcut method to determine ANOVA is to apply the calculations of sums of squares. To apply the sums of squares approach, the following equations need to be clarified:

Sum of squares total (also called total sum of squares) = SST = $\sum\limits_{i=1}^{k} \sum\limits_{j=1}^{n} X_{ij}^2 - \dfrac{1}{kn} * T^2$

Sum of squares among = SSA = $\dfrac{1}{n} * \sum\limits_{i=1}^{k} T_i^2 - \dfrac{1}{kn} * T^2$

Sum of squares within = SSW = SST – SSA

where k = number of factors (in example 3, k is the three methods)

n = number of observations per factor (in example 3, n is 8)

X_i = individual observations

T = sum all observations

To obtain SST, first compute the sum of each individual value, i.e.,

$$\sum_{i=1}^{k}\sum_{j=1}^{n} X_{ij^2}$$

Step 1: $\sum (7^2 + 8^2 + \ldots\ldots 7^2) = 1228$

Next add all the values in the matrix, that is, T

Step 2: $(7 + 8 + \ldots 7) = 170$

Step 3: $1/kn \times T^2 = 1/24 \times 28900 = 1204$

Step 4:   Compute the value of SST = $1228 - 1204 = 24$

Step 5: $\dfrac{1}{n} * \sum_{i=1}^{k} T_i^2 = 1/8(51^2 + 56^2 + 63^2) = 1213$

Step 6: $\dfrac{1}{kn} * T^2 = 1204$

Step 7:   compute the value of SSA = $1213 - 1204 = 9$

Step 8:   compute the value of SSW = SST − SSA = $24 - 9 = 15$

The ANOVA table is

Source of Variation	Degrees of Freedom	Sum of Squares	Mean Square	F
Among	$k - 1$	SSA	MSA = SSA/k − 1	MSA/MSW
Within	$k(n - 1)$	SSW	MSW = SSW/$k(n - 1)$	
Total	$nk - 1$	SST		

For example 3, the ANOVA table is

Source of Variation	Degrees of Freedom	Sum of Squares	Mean Square	F
Among	2	9	4.5	4.5/0.7 = 6.4
Within	21	15	0.7	
Total	23	24		

As shown in appendixes C5 and C6, the value of F for (2, 21) at the 0.05 level is 3.47. Since 6.4 is greater than 3.47, reject the null hypothesis. We arrive at the same conclusion using both methods.

Table 15.5 **Tests of Suppliers' Components**

Sample Number	Supplier 1	Supplier 2	Supplier 3
1	10	8	9
2	11	8	8
3	9	3	6
4	6	10	12
5	15	1	11
6	3	2	14
7	2	6	9
8	11	5	13
9	10	2	5
10	6	10	10
Total	83	55	98

Example 4. Three different suppliers provide an electronic component to a mobile phone manufacturer (three competing suppliers are used to maintain quality and guarantee a continuous supply of the component). The quality of the electronic system determines the overall performance of the mobile phone. To measure the quality of each supplier, the mobile phone manufacturer randomly selects 10 samples of the component from each supplier and tests the component's performance on an internally developed measurement scale. The results are presented in Table 15.5.

Null hypothesis: H_0: $\mu_1 = \mu_2 = \mu_3$
Alternative hypothesis: H_A: $\mu_1 \neq \mu_2 \neq \mu_3$

To proceed with the analysis, the following calculations have to be made: total sum of squares (SST), sum of squares among (SSA), and sum of squares within (SSE). In Table 15.6, all the necessary calculations are made.

$$SST = \sum_{i=1}^{k} \sum_{j=1}^{n} X_{ij^2} - \frac{1}{kn} * T^2 = (833 + 407 + 1017) - \left(1/20 * [83 + 55 + 98]^2\right)$$

$$= 2257 - 1/20 * 55{,}696$$

$$= 2257 - 2785 = -528$$

$$SSA = \frac{1}{n} * \sum_{i=1}^{k} T_i^2 - \frac{1}{kn} * T^2 = 1/10\left(83^2 + 55^2 + 98^2\right)$$

$$= 1/10\left(6889 + 3025 + 9604\right)$$

$$= 1952$$

$$SSW = SST - SSA$$

$$= (-528) - (1952) = 1424$$

Table 15.6 **Calculations for ANOVA**

Sample Number	Supplier 1	( )2	Supplier 2	( )2	Supplier 3	( )2
1	10	100	8	64	9	81
2	11	121	8	64	8	64
3	9	81	3	9	6	36
4	6	36	10	100	12	144
5	15	225	1	1	11	121
6	3	9	2	4	14	196
7	2	4	6	36	9	81
8	11	121	5	25	13	169
9	10	100	2	4	5	25
10	6	36	10	100	10	100
Total	83	833	55	407	98	1,017
Mean	8.3		5.5		9.8	

The ANOVA table for example 4 is

Source of Variation	Degrees of Freedom	Sum of Squares	Mean Square	F
Among	2	1,952	976	976/53 = 18.4
Within	27	1,424	53	
Total	29	−528		

As shown in appendixes C5 and C6, the value of F for (2, 27) at the 0.05 level is 3.35. Since 18.4 is greater than 3.35, reject the null hypothesis. That is, the quality of the three suppliers is not equal.

TWO-WAY ANALYSIS OF VARIANCE (ANOVA)

In the two examples used for demonstrating ANOVA, only one variable was considered. In example 3 the variable was the method of instruction, and in example 4 the variable was the supplier. However, sometimes the results may be affected by a second variable, for example, in example 3, the style of instructor in addition to the method of instruction. In such instances, a two-way ANOVA is appropriate.

The procedure for the two-way ANOVA is similar in many ways to that for the one-way method. The differences are that the effects of the second variable should be accounted for, the number of degrees of freedom will change, and two sets of hypotheses (one for each variable) must be tested. The impact of the second variable basically affects the sum of squares within (SSW).

In spite of the small sample used, the ANOVA analysis is quite complex and time-consuming. In practice, the ANOVA is handled through computer programs that are developed to handle this type of analysis. An ANOVA problem solved using SAS is discussed at the end of this chapter (appendix 15.1).

CHAPTER SUMMARY

In most statistical analysis there is an assumption that the probability distribution of the population is known. We also assume that the theory of probability and mathematical models can be duplicated using samples. For example, in a binomial distribution, we assume that (1) the probability of a success (P) remains constant from trial to trial and (2) the trials are independent. In practice, these assumptions do not always hold true.

This chapter describes two statistical tests for examining differences. The differences to be studied might be between a sample result and an expected population value or between two sample results, such as means. The first is a goodness-of-fit test, which is based on samples taken from a single population of nominal data. The second, analysis of variance (ANOVA), lets us test for differences among populations when the data scale is interval.

The goodness-of-fit test is used to determine the validity of a hypothesis concerning the *multinomial distribution* of a single population of nominal data. The goodness-of-fit test may be used to determine whether a sample was drawn from a normal distribution. In other words, are the samples drawn from the same population? The test statistic used has an approximate chi-square distribution. In order for this approximation to be adequate, the sample unit must be large enough so that the cell frequency is greater than five.

In research studies, it is necessary to make a statement about the parent population mean (μ) in relation to the sample mean $\bar{x}$. ANOVA is an extension to testing the equality of means of more than two populations. ANOVA is applicable when there are more than two means to be compared. ANOVA enables us to test for the significance of the difference among means. It is an excellent procedure for use in experimental studies.

CHAPTER EXERCISES

1. A fast-food restaurant manager is concerned about staffing the appropriate number of waiters and busboys at his eatery. To determine the number of staff needed at various times of the day, he asks his assistant manager to record the number of patrons eating at the three busiest time periods: breakfast, lunch, and dinner. He wants to test the hypothesis at an 0.05 significance level that the three time periods handle equal numbers of patrons. The average number of patrons eating at the restaurant for a month is given below.

	Time Period 1	Time Period 2	Time Period 3
Number of Customers	96	120	84

2. The plant manager at a factory producing precision instruments believes that depending on the day of the week the number of defects in his plant fluctuates. To test his theory, he records the average number of defects over a six-month

period. Based on the results presented below, is the plant manager right at the 0.05 significance level? Will the test results change if the plant manager uses an 0.01 significance level?

Day of the Week	Number of Defects
Monday	44
Tuesday	65
Wednesday	42
Thursday	60
Friday	46
Saturday	43
Total	300

3. A multinational company has introduced its most popular brand of cereal in six Latin American markets. Based on its popularity and the uniqueness of the cereal, the company expects to have at least a 50 percent share of the market in each country after the third year of the introduction of the brand of cereal. In an effort to test its prediction, the company conducts a small market test and obtains the following data. Based on the results of its test, do you feel that the company has achieved its goal of 50 percent share of the market?

Country	Market Share
1	44
2	65
3	41
4	58
5	47
6	45

4. A detergent company is planning to introduce a new liquid detergent in an Asian market. To determine the price point for an average package, the company test markets three pricing treatments in four geographic regions. The results of the tests are presented below. Use a significance level of 0.05.

Market	Test Price 1	Test Price 2	Test Price 3
A	130	145	152
B	115	142	130
C	89	121	97
D	85	131	98

5. An investment banker in Hong Kong wants to find out whether the three independent brokers she employs execute the same average number of trades per hour. A random sample of six hourly trades is recorded for the three brokers, as shown below. The investment banker would like to see that all three of her brokers have the same number of trades per hour. Use a 0.05 significance level.

Number	Trades, Broker 1	Trades, Broker 2	Trades, Broker 3
1	12	15	11
2	23	18	9
3	16	19	12
4	24	22	10
5	19	15	14
6	20	21	11

6. The planning department of a large multinational company does the sales forecasts for all its divisions. The department uses three different methods of forecasting. The vice president in charge of the department would like to know which forecasting method is the most accurate. In an effort to determine the accuracy of the three methods, he selects 24 forecasts over a 10-year period and assigns them randomly to three forecasting approaches. The three approaches used by the company are a sales force composite, an exponential smoothing technique, and a multiple regression model. The recorded accuracies of the techniques are given below. Use a 0.05 level of significance to determine which forecasting method is the most accurate.

Number	Sales Force Composite	Exponential Smoothing	Multiple Regression
1	44	40	51
2	39	37	47
3	33	28	37
4	56	53	52
5	43	38	42
6	56	51	63
7	47	45	46
8	58	60	62
Total	376	352	400

7. An international bank with branches in Bonn, New Delhi, and Tokyo is interested in finding out which of its financing plans is attracting the highest amount of loans. Each branch has developed its own unique financing plans. The results of these plans for a typical 10-working-day period are given below (deposits are in US$000). At a 0.05 significance level, determine whether there are differences in deposits among the three branches.

Day	Bonn	Delhi	Tokyo
1	85	88	92
2	76	77	87
3	82	87	65
4	90	85	77
5	75	82	85
6	80	85	74
7	87	73	79
8	77	69	83
9	88	78	85
10	84	76	77

APPENDIX 15.1. SOLVED ANOVA PROBLEM USING SAS

The plant manager of a large European auto parts manufacturer with manufacturing facilities in China wants to determine which of the four training programs that the company has devised to train factory workers should be used to improve productivity at his plant. Each program is administered to 10 recently hired factory workers with similar backgrounds and experience. After the factory workers have completed the two-week training program, the following outputs per week by each sample group are observed. Are the four training programs equally effective?

Number	Program 1	Program 2	Program 3	Program 4
1	45	41	36	41
2	42	38	34	48
3	49	39	38	42
4	37	49	33	41
5	45	40	40	40
6	50	50	47	38
7	42	38	39	41
8	43	41	39	36
9	40	39	38	37
10	41	37	38	38

```
            Effectiveness of the Four Training Programs
      In Improving the Productivity of Recently Hired Factory Workers


                          The ANOVA Procedure

Dependent Variable: PerWeekOutput   Output Per Week


                          Sum of        Mean
Source              DF    Squares       Square      F Value   Pr > F
Model               3     162.0909091   54.0303030   3.58     0.0231
Error               36    543.4090909   15.0946970
Corrected Total     39    705.5000000


           R-Square      Coeff Var     Root MSE     PerWeekOutput Mean
           0.229753      9.534207      3.885189        40.75000


                                         Mean
Source              DF    Anova SS       Square      F Value   Pr > F
TrainingPgm         3     162.0909091   54.0303030   3.58     0.0231
```

Therefore, training programs do make a significant difference in the output of workers. Also there is significant difference among the four training programs at a 97.7 level.

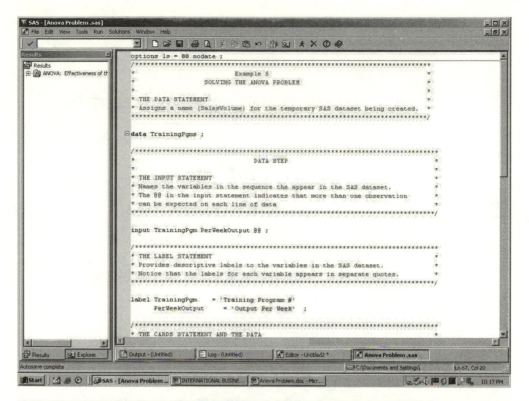

```
options ls = 80 nodate ;
/*******************************************************************************
*                              Example 5                                       *
*                     SOLVING THE ANOVA PROBLEM                                 *
*                                                                              *
* THE DATA STATEMENT                                                           *
* Assigns a name (SalesVolume) for the temporary SAS dataset being created.    *
*******************************************************************************/

data TrainingPgms ;

/*******************************************************************************
*                              DATA STEP                                       *
*                                                                              *
* THE INPUT STATEMENT                                                          *
* Names the variables in the sequence the appear in the SAS dataset.           *
* The 88 in the input statement indicates that more than one observation       *
* can be expected on each line of data                                         *
*******************************************************************************/

input TrainingPgm PerWeekOutput 88 ;

/*******************************************************************************
* THE LABEL STATEMENT                                                          *
* Provides descriptive labels to the variables in the SAS dataset.             *
* Notice that the labels for each variable appears in separate quotes.         *
*******************************************************************************/

label TrainingPgm    = 'Training Program #'
      PerWeekOutput  = 'Output Per Week'  ;

/*******************************************************************************
* THE CARDS STATEMENT AND THE DATA                                             *
```

```
/*******************************************************************************
* THE CARDS STATEMENT AND THE DATA                                            *
* Reads variable values in the sequence given in the INPUT statement above.    *
* Separate line for each observation follow immediately below the              *
*          CARDS Statement.                                                    *
* The Variable values for each observation are separated by atleast one space. *
* End the data section with a ';' on a separate line immediately following the *
*          last observation.                                                   *
*******************************************************************************/

cards ;
1 45 2 41 3 36 4 41
1 42 2 38 3 34 4 48
1 49 2 39 3 98 4 42
1 37 2 49 3 33 4 41
1 45 2 40 3 40 4 40
1 50 2 50 3 47 4 38
1 42 2 39 3 98 4 41
1 43 2 41 3 39 3 36
1 40 2 39 3 38 4 37
1 41 2 37 3 30 4 30
;

run ;

/*******************************************************************************
*                              PROC STEP                                       *
*                                                                              *
* proc Anova invokes the Anova Procedure and processes the identified data.     *
* The class statement identifies the independent variables (factors) for the   *
* experiment. The factors can be either quantitative or qualitative variables. *
* The model statement defines the model to be fit.                             *
```

Note to Appendix 15.1

The screen shots and code were generated using SAS software, version 8.2 of the SAS System for Microsoft Windows. Copyright © 2002–2007 SAS Institute Inc., Cary, NC, USA. All Rights Reserved. Reproduced with permission of SAS Institute Inc., Cary, NC.

SAS and all other SAS Institute Inc. product or service names are registered trademarks or trademarks of SAS Institute Inc., Cary, NC.

Additional Reading

Books

Churchill, Gilbert A., Jr., and Tom J. Brown. *Basic Marketing Research.* 5th ed. Cincinnati, OH: South Western Publishing, 2004, pp. 574–595.

Lind, Douglas A., William G. Marchal, and Samuel A. Wathen. *Statistical Techniques in Business and Economics.* 12th ed. New York: McGraw-Hill Irwin, 2005, pp. 386–413.

Malhotra, Naresh K. *Marketing Research: An Applied Orientation,* 4th ed. Upper Saddle River, NJ: Prentice Hall, 2004, pp. 466–492.

Zikmund, William G. *Exploring Marketing Research.* 8th ed. Cincinatti, OH: South Western Publishing, 2003, pp. 574–589.

16 Regression Analysis

Researchers use regression analysis to determine whether there is an association between two or more variables and also to find out the strength and functional form of this relationship.

LEARNING OBJECTIVES

After reading this chapter, students should be able to

- Understand the concept of correlation
- Understand simple regression models and how they are applied
- Understand the coefficient of correlation and coefficient of determination and how to compute them
- Understand multiple regression analysis

In regression analysis, researchers are interested in descriptive relations between two or more variables. For example, the chief finance officer (CFO) of an international company may be interested in determining the economic exposure and effects of a risk on transaction costs. By isolating the variables that may impact the subsidiaries' transaction costs, and using regression, the CFO is able to measure the vulnerability of the company to exchange rate risks in overseas transactions.[1] Or a factory manager may want to predict worker productivity based on the average number of years of experience that the plant workers have. In regression analysis, researchers are able to describe one unknown variable (exchange rate risks or worker productivity) through the knowledge of its relationship to another variable (economic variables and number of years of work experience).

Regression and correlation analysis are techniques that assist researchers in studying relationships between variables. Regression analysis is a technique that links the variables. Correlation analysis is a technique that measures the strength of the relationship between the variables.

Linear relations or approximated linear relations are commonly found in business situations. The term "linear" implies that the relationship between two variables can be functionally described in the form of an equation. In simple regression, the variable whose values we wish to estimate is referred to as the dependent/criterion variable, denoted by Y, and the variable from which the forecast (predictions) are made is called the independent/predictor variable, denoted by X.

SIMPLE LINEAR REGRESSION

The linear equation used in regression is in the form of $Y = a + bX$, where a and b are constants (these constants will be explained later) that describe the average relationship between the two variables. This implies that for a given value of X, one can establish the value of Y. For example, consider the linear model $Y = 2 + 3X$. If the value of $X = 10$, then the value of $Y = 2 + 3(10)$, that is, 32.

Example 1. Simple regression is best explained through an example. The vice president of operations for a large manufacturing company is attempting to forecast factory workers' average output per day in one of his plants. The average output for 10 randomly selected workers is presented below.

Average Factory Output

Average Working Hours (X)	7.1	7.4	6.1	8.4	8.9	7.8	9.3	6.0	8.6	6.0
Output/Worker/Day (Y)	72	76	80	83	87	87	95	65	81	65

The values of average working hours (X) and worker output (Y) are plotted on a graph as shown in Figure 16.1, called a scatter diagram.

The pattern of the plot appears to be linear. No straight line will pass through all 10 points; however, a single line seems to pass reasonably close to all 10 points.

SLOPE AND THE INTERCEPT

Referring back to the linear equation $Y = a + bX$, the two constants a and b can now be explained. The first constant, a, is the intercept, and the second, b, is the slope. The intercept, a, is defined as the value of Y when the value of X is 0 (the starting point of the straight line that intersects the y-axis). The slope, b, is the rate of change of Y for a unit change in the value of X, which provides the angle of the straight line. Given the starting point and the angle of the straight line, the linear function can be used to predict the values of the dependent variable (Y) for a given value of the independent variable (X).

To solve the linear equation, we need to calculate the two constants a and b. One method to estimate these values is the least squares estimation procedure. The closeness to the plotted actual data of the linear line drawn in Figure 16.1 is characterized by the vertical distances from the sample points to the linear (regression) line. The least squares procedure guarantees that these distances (errors) will be as small as possible. The minimization equations that result in determining the values of a and b are as follows:

Figure 16.1   **Working Hours and Worker Output**

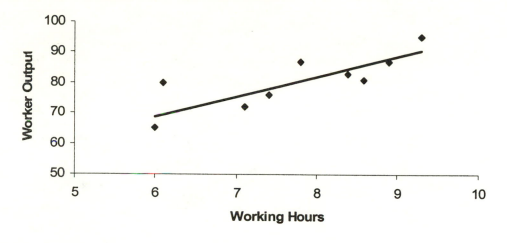

$$a = \bar{Y} - b_1\bar{X} \qquad\qquad (1)$$

$$b = \frac{n\sum(XY) - \sum X * \sum Y}{n\sum X^2 - (\sum X)^2} \qquad\qquad (2)$$

The numerator, $n\sum(XY) - \sum X * \sum Y$, is also referred to as SS_{xy}, and the denominator, $n\sum X^2 - (\sum X)^2$, is referred to as SS_{xx}. Therefore $b = SS_{xy} \div SS_{xx}$.

Since the intercept (a) value can be determined only after obtaining the value of the slope (b), b must be computed first. To compute the values of a and b, it is best to construct a table that calculates the desired data. Table 16.1 provides all the necessary data ($\bar{X}$, $\bar{Y}$, $\sum XY$, $\sum X^2$, $\sum Y^2$) to compute the slope and the intercept for example 1.

Applying the data from Table 16.1 and substituting the figures in equations 1 and 2,

$$b = n\sum(XY) - \sum X * \sum Y$$

$$b = (10)(6071.8) - (75.6)(791)/(10)(585.4) - (75.6)^2$$

$$= 1018.4/138.64$$

$$= 6.6$$

$$a = \bar{Y} - b_1\bar{X}$$

$$a = 79.1 - (6.6)(7.56)$$

$$= 79.1 - 55.188$$

$$= 29.2$$

Table 16.1   **Variables Necessary for Calculating the Intercept and the Slope**

Working Hours (X)	Worker Output (Y)	XY	X^2	Y^2
7.1	72	511.2	50.41	5184
7.4	76	562.4	54.76	5776
6.1	80	488.0	37.21	6400
8.4	83	697.2	70.56	6889
8.9	87	774.3	79.21	7569
7.8	87	678.6	60.84	7569
9.3	95	883.5	86.49	9025
6.0	65	390.0	36.00	4225
8.6	81	696.6	73.96	6561
6.0	65	390.0	36.00	4225
Totals = 75.6	791	6,071.8	585.44	63,423
Mean = 7.56	Mean = 79.1	$\Sigma(XY)$	$\Sigma(X^2)$	$\Sigma(Y^2)$

Therefore, the estimated regression equation for working hours and worker output is: $Y = 29.2 + 6.6X$. If the vice president of operations wants to find the output for, say, 10 working hours, the output could be estimated through the equation $Y = 29.2 + 6.6 \times 10 = 95.2$ units.

The coefficient b is equal to 7.3, which means that for each additional 1 hour of work put in by the workers, the output will increase by an average of 7.3 units. The intercept a is equal to 23.9, which means that when $X = 0$, the value of Y will be equal to 23.9. One might be tempted to interpret this to mean that when no work is done by the workers, the number of units produced will be equal to 23.9, which is not true. As a general rule, we cannot determine the value of Y for a value of X that is far outside the observed range of the value of X.

Example 2. A large multinational company selling cosmetics wants to know whether there is a correlation between consumers' trust in its products and the amount that a customer is willing to spend on the company's brand of cosmetics. A consumer study of 500 respondents was conducted in four major European cities. Among other questions, each respondent was asked to indicate on a 10-point scale (where 10 = complete trust and 1 = no trust at all) trust in the company's products and the amount they were willing to spend to buy its brand of cosmetics. Table 16.2 presents the partial results of the survey for 10 customers. The values necessary to calculate the intercept and the slope are presented in Table 16.3.

The intercept and the slope for the cosmetic example can be shown as follows.

$$\text{Slope } b = \frac{n\Sigma(XY) - \Sigma(X) * \Sigma(Y)}{n\Sigma(X^2) - (\Sigma X)^2}$$

$$= (10)(6,104.6) - (76.1)(790) \div (10)(592.01) - (76.1)^2$$

$$= (61,046 - 60,119) \div (5,920.1 - 5,791.21) = 927 \div 128.89 = 7.2$$

Table 16.2 **Consumer Trust and Their Spending on Cosmetics**

Trust in the Company	7.2	8.9	6.0	7.8	8.6	8.5	6.3	7.3	6.2	9.3
Amount Spent (€)	74	87	64	87	81	84	78	74	66	95

Table 16.3 **Variables Necessary for Calculating the Intercept and Slope**

Trust in the Company (X)	Amount (€) Spent on Cosmetics (Y)	XY	X²	Y²
7.2	74	532.8	51.84	5,476
8.9	87	774.3	79.21	7,569
6.0	64	384.0	36.00	4,096
7.8	87	678.6	60.84	7,569
8.6	81	696.6	73.96	6,561
8.5	84	714.0	72.25	7,056
6.3	78	491.4	39.69	6,084
7.3	74	540.2	53.29	5,476
6.2	66	409.2	38.44	4,356
9.3	95	883.5	86.49	9,025
Total = 76.1	790	6,104.6	592.01	63,268
Means $\bar{X}$ = 7.61	$\bar{Y}$ = 79.0	$\Sigma(XY)$	$\Sigma(X^2)$	$\Sigma(Y^2)$

Intercept $a = \bar{Y} - (b)(\bar{X})$

$$= 79.0 - (7.2)(7.61) = 79.0 - 54.792$$

$$= 24.2$$

The regression equation for the cosmetics example is as follows:

$Y = 24.2 + (7.2)X$. That is, a consumer who trusts the company at level 10 would spend
$Y = 24.2 + (7.2)(10)$
   $= €96.2$

STANDARD ERROR OF THE ESTIMATE

The least squares method of fitting the regression line from sample data is only an approximation of the actual regression line. As can be seen in Figure 16.1, the regression line drawn for working hours and worker output fits the data with a minimum amount of variation. Therefore, the regression line provides only an approximate predictor of a Y value for a given value of X. Hence, a statistic that measures variability of the actual Y values from the predicted must be developed (similar to a measure of variability of each observation around its arithmetic mean). The measure of variability around the line of regression is called the *standard error of the estimate* and can be calculated with the following formula:

$$S_{Y,X} = \sqrt{\frac{\sum_{i=1}^{n}\left(Y_i - \bar{Y}_i\right)^2}{n-2}}$$

where Y_i = actual value of Y for a given X_i

$\bar{Y}_i$ = predicted value of Y for a given X_i

The above equation could be simplified as:

$$S_{Y,X} = \sqrt{\frac{\sum_{i=1}^{n}Y_i^2 - a\sum_{i=1}^{n}Y_i - b\sum_{i=1}^{n}X_iY_i}{n-2}}$$

or

$$S_{Y,X} = \sqrt{\frac{\left[\sum(Y)^2 - n\bar{Y}^2\right] - b\left[\sum(XY) - n\overline{XY}\right]}{n-2}}$$

Either equation can be used to calculate the standard error of the regression estimate.

Using Computer Programs to Determine Linear Regression

Nowadays, simple regression coefficients are calculated not manually but through the use of scientific calculators or computers. The following example illustrates the use of computer programs to solve for regression coefficients.

Example 3. A large appliance manufacturer seeks to improve its sales forecast to assist the plant manager in scheduling the weekly production runs. The marketing department feels that the average family income is probably the most accurate single variable that can be used to predict appliance sales. From past sales records, appliance sales for 10 randomly selected families are obtained and presented in Table 16.4. The scatter diagram for the values in Table 16.4 is presented in Figure 16.2.

The computer program SAS® to solve the above problem is presented at the end of the chapter as appendix 16.1. The SAS readout for example 3 is shown below. Typically, most computer programs also print out different statistics as part of the regression analysis.

Table 16.4 **Annual Appliance Purchase and Annual Net Income for 10 Randomly Selected Families**

Family	Annual Net Family Income ($)	Annual Expenditure for Appliances ($)
1	20,000	4,600
2	4,000	1,400
3	8,000	3,000
4	12,000	3,400
5	16,000	4,600
6	14,000	4,400
7	8,000	2,000
8	12,000	2,800
9	14,000	4,000
10	12,000	3,600

```
          Annual Appliance Purchase and Annual Net Income
              Data from 10 Randomly Selected Families
               For Predicting Annual Appliance Sales $s

                      The REG Procedure
                      Model: MODEL1
Dependent Variable: ApplExpenditure Annual Family Expenditure on Appli-
ances (00)

                      Analysis of Variance

                      Sum of         Mean
Source            DF    Squares       Square     F Value    Pr > F

Model              1   904.69565    904.69565     42.35     0.0002
Error              8   170.90435     21.36304
Corrected Total    9  1075.60000

          Root MSE           4.62202   R-Square   0.8411
          Dependent Mean    33.80000   Adj R-Sq   0.8212
          Coeff Var         13.67461

                      Parameter Estimates

                                             Parameter   Standard
Variable      Label                     DF    Estimate    Error

Intercept     Intercept                  1    7.19130    4.34226
FamilyIncome  Annual Family Net Income (000)  1  2.21739    0.34074

                      Parameter Estimates

Variable      Label                     DF   t Value   Pr > |t|

Intercept     Intercept                  1    1.66     0.1363
FamilyIncome  Annual Family Net Income (000)  1   6.51     0.0002
```

This code was generated using SAS software, version 8.2 of the SAS System for Microsoft Windows. Copyright © SAS Institute Inc. SAS and all other SAS Institute Inc. product or service names are registered trademarks or trademarks of SAS Institute Inc., Cary, NC, USA.

Figure 16.2   **Expenditure on Appliances and Net Family Income**

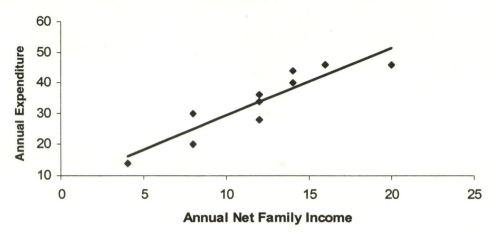

INTERPRETING THE SAS PRINTOUT

The f statistic of the model suggests that FamilyIncome is significant (at the 0.0002 level) in predicting the annual appliance expenditure of a family. The R-square value of 0.8411 implies that there is a high correlation between FamilyIncome and expenditures for appliances (that is, most of the variation is explained by the one variable, FamilyIncome). According to the output, the regression equation is

$$Y = 7.2 + 2.2X$$

EVALUATING THE REGRESSION MODEL

The least squares method produces the best straight line for a given set of independent and dependent variables. Producing a straight line fitting all the points on a graph does not necessarily mean that a linear relationship exists between the two variables. It is possible that no relationship exists between X and Y. If this is the case, a linear model may not produce useful results. To evaluate the model and its applicability, researchers may subject the model to further analysis. Following are some of the techniques used to assess the linear equation model.

ANALYZING THE SLOPE (b)

If the values of a and b for the total population were known and the resulting equation produces a straight line with slope > 0 (Figure 16.3), this would indicate that a linear relationship exists and that the linear model could be applied (as opposed to the slope being equal to 0, in which case the straight line would be parallel to the x-axis).

In most instances, the population parameter b, the slope, is unknown, and hence the above method of evaluating the linear function is not available. When the sample parameter b is known, the model can be evaluated by estimating the confidence interval

Figure 16.3   **Relationship Between *X* and *Y***

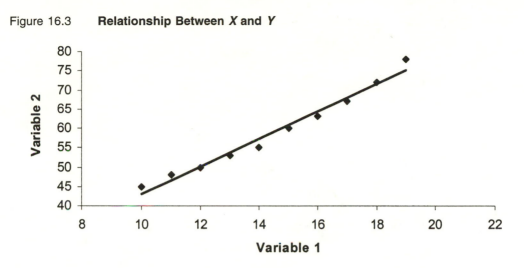

of the slope *b*. To evaluate a regression equation, a test of its slope will provide the necessary results. That is, if the data points fall close to a linear pattern, the slope is assumed to be nonzero and therefore a good linear fit. If the data points are widely dispersed about the regression line, the fit is poor and the slope near 0 (Figure 16.4).

For each value of *X*, the distribution of the points about the regression (mean of *a* + *bX*) is normal with mean 0 and a constant variance of σ^2 (as shown in Figure 16.4). The approximate regression equation for the sample is represented by

$Y_i = a_1 + b_1 X$ (the regression equation for the total population would be $Y = a + bX$)

To determine whether the slope is significantly different from 0, a *t* test could be applied. The following formulas are applied to test the regression equation (the derivation of the formula is complicated and not necessary for understanding the use of the formula).

$$t_{n-2} = \frac{b - b_1}{S_{Y.X}^2 / \sqrt{\sum\left(X^2\right) - n\bar{X}^2}}$$

where $S_{Y.X}^2$ = the variance of regression (the standard deviation is the square root of this). This can be computed by

$$\frac{\left[\sum\left(Y^2\right) - n\bar{Y}^2\right] - b\left[\sum\left(XY\right) - n\overline{XY}\right]}{n - 2}$$

The degree of freedom is *n* − 2 because the two parameters *b* (actual slope) and b_1 (assumed slope) are approximated in order to compute $S_{Y.X}$.

Figure 16.4

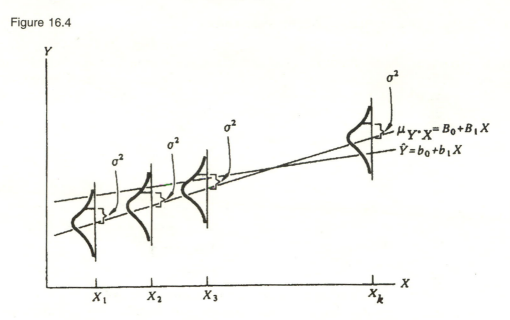

As discussed in chapter 14, to estimate the confidence interval, a test of hypotheses is carried out. Using example 2 (trust in the cosmetics company), we can demonstrate the confidence interval for the regression using hypothesis testing. Let us assume a 2.5 percent level of significance that the trust in the company is linearly related to the amount spent on its brand of cosmetics. The following hypothesis would be tested:

H_0: $b = 0$ A linear regression is not meaningful
H_A: $b \neq 0$ A linear regression is meaningful for $\alpha = 0.025$

The cosmetics company should reject H_0 if calculated t is greater than 2.306 (obtained from the t distribution table (appendix C3) for eight degrees of freedom [$n - 2$] and significance level of 0.025).

$$\text{Calculated } t = \frac{(b-0)}{S_{Y.X} / \sqrt{\sum(X^2) - n\bar{X}^2}} = \frac{(7.2-0)}{\sqrt{24.6/\sqrt{(10)(57.9)}}}$$

$t = 7.2/.21 = 34.2$

(See Table 16.3.)

The calculated t is greater than the t from the distribution table (2.306), so the cosmetics company should reject the null hypothesis. The trust in the cosmetics company and the amount of cosmetics purchased by its customers can be forecasted using linear regression.

Example 4. A stockbroker in London makes cold calls every day to potential buyers. Typically, he makes between 12 and 24 calls daily. Ten randomly selected days representing the number of calls made and the amount of sales closed by the broker (he felt that the face value of the stocks was a better reflector of his efforts than the number of buyers who bought shares from him) are presented in Table 16.5.

The SAS program output for example 4 is as follows.

```
            Value of Shares Sold in British Pounds (00)
                Data from 10 Randomly Selected Calls
                   For Predicting Value of Shares

                      The REG Procedure
                        Model: MODEL1
Dependent Variable: ValueOfShares Value of Shares Sold in British Pounds
(00)

                  Number of Observations Read     10
                  Number of Observations Used     10

                      Analysis of Variance

                         Sum of        Mean
Source              DF    Squares      Square      F Value    Pr > F

Model                1   371.92918    371.92918     5.60      0.0455
Error                8   531.51582     66.43948
Corrected Total      9   903.44500

           Root MSE             8.15104    R-Square    0.4117
           Dependent Mean      75.95000    Adj R-Sq    0.3381
           Coeff Var           10.73212

                      Parameter Estimates

                                            Parameter    Standard
Variable      Label                    DF    Estimate     Error

Intercept     Intercept                 1    41.24077    14.89466
NumCallsMade  Number of Calls Made      1     2.07840     0.87844

                      Parameter Estimates

  Variable      Label                    DF   t Value   Pr > |t|

  Intercept     Intercept                 1    2.77      0.0243
  NumCallsMade  Number of Calls Made      1    2.37      0.0455
```

This code was generated using SAS software, version 8.2 of the SAS System for Microsoft Windows. Copyright © SAS Institute Inc. SAS and all other SAS Institute Inc. product or service names are registered trademarks or trademarks of SAS Institute Inc., Cary, NC, USA.

Table 16.5 **Shares Sold through Cold Calls**

Sample Number	Calls Made	Value of Shares (£00)
1	20	85.5
2	12	54.9
3	18	63.6
4	14	82.0
5	22	87.5
6	16	78.5
7	19	81.5
8	14	73.5
9	15	75.0
10	17	77.5

INTERPRETING THE SAS PRINTOUT

The f statistic of the model suggests that the NumCallsMade is significant (at the 0.0455 level) in predicting the ValueOfShares. The R-square value of 0.4114 implies that 41 percent of variation in the ValueOfShares is explained by the NumCallsMade. This implies that there are other variables that affect purchase of shares. According to the output, the regression equation is

$$Y = 41.2 + 2.1X$$

COEFFICIENT OF CORRELATION IN REGRESSION ANALYSIS

The Pearson coefficient of correlation, also known as the Pearson product-moment correlation coefficient r, for a sample, is a measure of the strength of the linear relationship between two variables, X and Y. That is, it measures how much of the change in the dependent variable is explained by the independent variable. Hence, the coefficient of correlation measures the similarity of the changes in the values of X and Y. The coefficient of correlation ranges between -1 and $+1$. A value of 1 indicates a perfect relationship—that is, almost all the changes in the dependent variable can be explained by the independent variable. When the correlation is positive, the value of Y increases when X increases (direct relationship). When the correlation is negative, the value of Y decreases when X increases (inverse relationship). If the dependent variable is unaffected by the independent variable, then the coefficient of correlation is 0 or there is no linear relationship between X and Y. The coefficient of correlation for a population is denoted by the Greek letter rho (ρ).

Other values of the coefficient of correlation are explained with reference to the values of -1 and $+1$. Hence, if the value of $\rho = +0.85$, we conclude that there is a strong positive (direct) linear relationship between the variables. Similarly, if the value of $\rho = -0.80$, we can conclude that there is a strong negative (inverse) relationship between the independent and dependent variables. However, a value of $\rho = +0.30$ indicates that a weak positive relationship exists between the variables.

The correlation of coefficient ρ as explained above is a population parameter. Researchers most often deal with sample data. The sample coefficient of correlation is denoted by r and is calculated by the following formula:

$$r = \frac{n\Sigma(XY) - \Sigma X.\Sigma Y}{\sqrt{\left[n\Sigma(X^2) - (\Sigma X)^2\right]\left[n\Sigma(Y)^2 - (\Sigma Y)\right]^2}}$$

For the cosmetics example, all the necessary values have been calculated in Table 16.3. When we substitute the values from the table, the value of the correlation coefficient (r) for the trust in the cosmetics company and the amount of purchase by its customers is

$$r = \frac{(10)(6104.6) - (76.1)(790)}{\sqrt{\left[(10)(592.01) - (75.5)^2\right]\left[(10)(63,268) - (790)\right]^2}}$$

$$r = \frac{61046 - 60119}{\sqrt{\left[(10)(592.01) - (5791)\right]\left[(10)(63268) - (624100)\right]}}$$

$$r = \frac{61046 - 60119}{\sqrt{\left[(10)(592.01) - (5791)\right]\left[(10)(63268) - (624100)\right]}}$$

$r = 927/1052 = +0.88$

Based on the value of r, it appears that there exists a strong positive correlation between the trust in the cosmetics company and the amount of purchases by their customers.

COEFFICIENT OF DETERMINATION

The coefficient of determination is the square of the coefficient of correlation (r^2). It signifies the proportion of the total sample variability around the mean value of the independent variable $(\bar{Y})$ that is explained by the linear relationship between Y and X. In other words, the coefficient of determination, r^2, is equal to the variance explained by the regression equation over the total variance. When regression problems are solved with computers, the computer output will provide the value of the coefficient of determination.

MULTIPLE REGRESSION

At times, simple regression seems inadequate for analyzing research problems, especially if a single variable cannot fully explain the effects on the dependent variable. This is evident when the standard error of estimate, r^2, is low (say, $r^2 = 0.60$). There is still a large variation that is not explained. To reduce the proportion of unexplained variation and thereby increase the value of the standard error of estimate, it might be necessary to consider other independent variables that may impact a particular dependent variable. If and when the researcher ascertains that the dependent variable may be affected by more than one independent variable, multiple regression is the technique that is most applicable. Multiple regression is a logical extension of the simple linear regression. The multiple linear regression technique is similar to the simple linear regression and the fundamental concepts remain the same. The multiple regression model is represented as follows:

$$Y = a + b_1 X_1 + b_2 X_2$$

where Y is the dependent variable

X_1 and X_2 are two independent variables

a, b_1, and b_2 are constants—a is again the intercept, but it is interpreted as the value of Y when both X_1 and X_2 are equal to 0

The constant b_1 measures the change in Y per unit change in X_1 when X_2 is held fixed, and b_2 measures the change in Y per unit change in X_2 when X_1 is held fixed. In multiple regression, the b values are referred to as "net regression coefficients."

Example 5. The CFO of a U.S.-based multinational firm wants to hedge against currency fluctuations that the company faces in importing components from its overseas suppliers. The exchange rate fluctuations affect the company's cash flow. To determine the firm's economic exposure, the CFO reviews many of the exchange rate risk models that are in use and identifies two critical variables that have the most effect on a country's exchange rates—nominal interest rate and expected inflation rate. The CFO randomly selects 10 international transactions and their effect on cash flows over a 12-month period and notes the corresponding nominal exchange rate and the prevailing rate of inflation. The information the CFO obtained is presented in Table 16.6.

The CFO's cash flow problem can be represented as follows:

$$Y \text{ (the changes in cash flow)} = a + bX_1 + b_1 X_2$$

where X_1 = average nominal exchange rate for a particular time period

X_2 = average inflation rate for a particular time period

The least squares method could also be applied to multiple regression to obtain the best-fitting linear regression. Since multiple regression problems involve more than one variable, they cannot be represented on a two-dimensional scale. In a regression

Table 16.6 **Transactions Costs, Exchange Rates, and Inflation Rates**

Sample Number	Changes in Cash Flow ($ million)	Exchange Rate ($1 =)	Rate of Inflation (%)
1	19	7	4
2	10	4	2
3	22	8	6
4	20	7	6
5	14	4	3
6	17	6	4
7	23	8	6
8	15	5	4
9	14	4	3
10	23	7	6

problem involving three variables, the points are plotted on a three-dimensional plane (as in a cube, which has length, breadth, and height). Because there are three variables involved, three equations are solved to determine the values of a, b, and b_1.

The procedure to compute the constants and the variables in multiple regression is similar to the one used in simple regression. The calculations of the constants are first handled manually and then shown through the SAS program. Table 16.7 presents the necessary calculations to determine the values of the constants.

The formula for calculating the constants is presented below. (The actual derivation of the formula is not shown here, as most of the problem solving for a multiple regression problem would be done using a software package.)

$$\sum Y = na + b\sum X_1 + b_1 \sum X_2 \tag{3}$$

$$\sum X_1 Y = a\sum X_1 + b\sum X_1^2 + b_1 \sum X_1 X_2 \tag{4}$$

$$\sum X_2 Y = a\sum X_2 + b\sum X_1 X_2 + b_1 \sum X_2^2 \tag{5}$$

All the necessary figures to solve equations 3, 4, and 5 are found in Table 16.6

(Eq. 3) $170 = 10a + 60b + 40b_1$

(Eq. 4) $1095 = 60a + 384b + 267b_1$

(Eq. 5) $776 = 40a + 267b + 196b_1$

Solving these three equations simultaneously, we obtain the following values for the constants:

$a = 3.8; b = 0.8; b_1 = 2.1$

Therefore, the multiple regression equation for predicting the cash flow effects is

Table 16.7 **Calculations for Multiple Regression**

Sample Number	Cash Flow ($ million) Y	Exchange Rate X_1	Interest Rate X_2	X_1Y	X_2Y	X_1X_2	Y_2	X_1^2	X_2^2
1	19	7	4	133	76	28	361	49	16
2	10	4	1	40	10	4	100	16	1
3	22	8	6	176	132	48	484	64	36
4	20	7	6	140	120	42	400	49	36
5	14	4	3	56	42	12	196	16	9
6	17	6	4	102	68	24	289	36	16
7	23	8	6	184	138	48	529	64	36
8	15	5	3	75	45	15	225	25	9
9	7	4	1	28	7	4	49	16	1
10	23	7	6	161	138	42	529	49	36
Σ	170	60	40	1,095	776	267	3,162	384	196
Mean	17	6	4						

$$Y = 3.8 + 0.8X_1 + 2.1X_2$$

That is, if the nominal rate (X_1) shifts by one unit (say from 5 to 6 percent) and the inflation rate (X_2) stays the same; the resulting effect would be a decrease in the company's cash flow by $800.00 (0.8 × 1,000). Similarly, if the inflation rate went up by one unit (say from 4 to 5 percent) and the nominal rate remained the same, then the cash flows for the company would decrease by $2,100.00 (2.1 × 1,000).

If in a given year the change in the nominal rate was 7 percent and the rate of inflation was 6 percent, the resulting change in cash flows would be

$$Y = 3.8 + (0.8)(7) + (2.1)(6)$$

$$Y = 3.8 + 5.6 + 12.6 = 22.0$$

So the exposure is $22,000 ($Y$ is expressed in thousands dollars).

Example 6. In recent years, the stock price of a large multinational company has hit an all-time low, and investor confidence in the stock is very low too. To resolve the problem, the CEO of the company has asked the CFO to isolate the key reasons for the lack of investor confidence. In reviewing the stock prices and related data, the CFO was able to separate two variables that may be driving the company stock down—net profits and debt-to-equity ratio. To further verify her hunch, the CFO gathers data for 10 consecutive quarters. These figures are presented in Table 16.8.

To test for the effects of net profits and debt-to-equity ratio on quarterly stock prices, the CFO conducts a multiple regression that is expressed as

$$Y = a + bX_1 + X_2$$

where Y = company's quarterly stock prices
X_1 = quarterly net profit
X_2 = company's debt-to-equity ratio

Table 16.8 **Quarterly Stock Prices, Net Profit, and Debt Ratio**

Quarter	Stock Price	Net Profit ($ million)	Debt/Equity Ratio
1	32	31.1	0.2
2	24	20.5	0.3
3	38	42.3	0.2
4	19	18.9	0.5
5	25	26.5	0.4
6	30	29.8	0.3
7	26	24.3	0.3
8	32	38.1	0.3
9	39	52.0	0.2
10	17	16.0	0.5

The calculations necessary for obtaining the necessary variables are presented in Table 16.9.

$$\sum Y = na + b\sum X_1 + b_1 \sum X_2$$

$$\sum X_1 Y = a\sum X_1 + b\sum X_1^2 + b_1 \sum X_1 X_2$$

$$\sum X_2 Y = a\sum X_2 + b\sum X_1 X_2 + b_1 \sum X_2^2$$

$282 = (10)a + b(300) + b_1(3.2)$

$9159 = a(300) + b(10124) + b_1(87)$

$83 = a(3.2) + b(87) + b_1(1.14)$

Solving the above three equations (simultaneous equations), the following values for the constants are obtained:

$a = 29.8$

$b = 0.33$

$b_1 = -36$

Therefore, the company's stock prices can be estimated from the following multiple regression equation: $Y = 29.8 + 0.33X_1 + (-36)(X_2)$. If in a given quarter the company's net profits were $50 million and if it was able to maintain a debt-to-equity ratio of 0.1, its stock price based on the multiple regression equation would be:

$Y = 29.8 + (0.33)(50) + (-36)(0.1)$

$= 42.7$

Table 16.9 **Regression Value Calculations**

Quarter	Y	X_1	X_2	X_1Y	X_2Y	X_1X_2	Y_2	X_1^2	X_2^2
1	32	31.1	0.2	995	6.4	6.2	1,024	967	0.04
2	24	20.5	0.3	492	7.2	6.2	576	420	0.09
3	38	42.3	0.2	1,607	7.6	8.5	1,444	1,789	0.04
4	19	18.9	0.5	359	9.5	9.5	361	357	0.25
5	25	26.5	0.4	662	10.0	10.6	625	702	0.16
6	30	29.8	0.3	894	9.0	8.9	900	888	0.09
7	26	24.3	0.3	631	7.8	7.3	676	590	0.09
8	32	38.1	0.3	1,219	9.6	11.4	1,024	1,451	0.09
9	39	52.0	0.2	2,028	7.8	10.4	1,521	2,704	0.04
10	17	16.0	0.5	272	8.5	8.0	289	256	0.25
Σ	282	299.5	3.2	9,159	83.4	87.0	8,440	10,124	1.14
Mean	28.2	30	0.3						

Table 16.10 **Average Sales, Number of Calls Made, Years of Experience, and Territorial Experience**

Sample Number	Monthly Sales ($)	Number of Calls	Number of Years with the Company	Territory Experience
1	57,000	13	5	4
2	67,000	18	6	4
3	81,000	14	7	6
4	126,000	27	12	12
5	79,000	16	7	6
6	120,000	24	11	9
7	88,000	20	8	7
8	113,000	22	12	9
9	121,000	19	11	10
10	78,000	12	9	7

Example 7. The vice president of sales of a medium-size international company wants to test the theory that the sales volume produced by a salesperson is dependent on three variables, the number of potential customers contacted per month, the number of years of selling experience, and the number of years of territorial experience (i.e., the number of years a salesperson has been selling in a particular territory). Information for 10 randomly selected salespeople is presented in Table 16.10.

The multiple regression equation for the above example is $Y = a + bX_1 + b_1X_2 + b_2X_3$

where Y = average monthly sales
X_1 = number of sales call made per month
X_2 = number of years with the company
X_3 = number of years in the territory

Manual calculations are next to impossible with three independent variables, so it is best to solve this regression through the use of a computer program. Screen shots from the SAS program, used to solve the above problem, are presented as appendix 16.2 at the end of the chapter. The SAS output for the problem is presented below.[2]

```
          Annual Sales Volume Produced by a Salesperson
        Data from 10 Salespersons Over a Period of One Year
               For Predicting Annual Sales Volume $s

                       The REG Procedure
                         Model: MODEL1
          Dependent Variable: MonthlySales Monthly Sales ($000)

                       Analysis of Variance

                       Sum of         Mean
Source            DF   Squares        Square      F Value    Pr > F

Model             3    5308.19949     1769.39983    41.50    0.0002
Error             6     255.80051       42.63342
Corrected Total   9    5564.00000

          Root MSE              6.52943    R-Square    0.9540
          Dependent Mean      93.00000    Adj R-Sq    0.9310
          Coeff Var            7.02089

                       Parameter Estimates

                                          Parameter   Standard
Variable      Label                  DF    Estimate     Error    t Value

Intercept     Intercept               1     9.73603    9.52149    1.02
NumContacts   # of Contacts           1     1.04371    0.68669    1.52
YrsWithCo     # of Years with the Company 1 3.84751   2.63655    1.46
TerritoryExp  Territory Experience    1     4.06720    2.71667    1.50

                       Parameter Estimates

Variable        Label                             DF    Pr > |t|

Intercept       Intercept                          1     0.3460
NumContacts     # of Contacts                      1     0.1793
YrsWithCo       # of Years with the Company        1     0.1948
TerritoryExp    Territory Experience               1     0.1850
```

INTERPRETING THE SAS PRINTOUT

The f statistic of the model suggests that the NumContacts, YrsWithCo and Territory-Exp are significant (at the 0.0002 level) in predicting the MonthlySales. The R-square value of 0.9540 implies that 95 percent of variation in the MonthlySales is explained by the three independent variables. However, based on the t statistic of the individual variables, it appears that they are not significant at the 0.05 or 0.1 levels. Therefore, the researchers will have to do further diagnostics. It appears, based on logic, that all three independent variables appear to be correlated to one another, and hence the t statistic may be low. The multiple regression equation is as follows.

$$Y = 9.74 + 1.044X_1 + 3.85X_2 + 4.07X_3$$

CHAPTER SUMMARY

Regression analysis and correlation analysis analyze relationships between two or more variables. In regression analysis, an independent variable is used to make predictions about a dependent variable. Regression analysis can also be used to estimate the change in one variable, given a specific amount of change in another variable. Correlation analysis is used to measure the extent of the linear relationship between the independent and dependent variables. The correlation coefficient, r, indicates the strength and direction of the association of the two variables. The coefficient of determination, r^2, measures the amount of total variance in the dependent variable explained by the independent variable. Simple regression models are often used in forecasting.

Multiple regression is an extension of the simple regression model. In the simple regression model, only one independent variable is considered. In contrast, multiple regression analyzes many independent variables that may influence the dependent variable.

CHAPTER REVIEW AND EXERCISES

1. What is regression analysis?
2. Discuss the rules that must be followed before using regression analysis.
3. Distinguish between dependent and independent variables.
4. Explain the intercept and slope of the regression equation.
5. Explain the Pearson correlation coefficient.
6. What is the coefficient of determination?
7. When and how would you use multiple regression?
8. How do you test the regression model?
9. The country manager for a cosmetics company in Europe is requesting additional funds from the parent company to launch a new fragrance. The fragrance was successfully introduced in many other markets but has failed to reach the first-quarter sales targets during the first quarter of its introduction in the European country. To make his case, the country manager plans to use the success of a new product introduction that had encountered similar problem but was turned around after an advertising blitz. Though he cannot prove a direct relationship between advertising and sales, the country manager plans to show a relationship between advertising expenditures and change in attitude of consumers toward the new introduction. Based on the information provided below, is there sufficient evidence to show that the request for additional advertising expenditure is justified? Is there a high correlation between advertising expenditure and changes in consumer attitudes?

Month	Advertising Expenditure (€000)	Change in Attitude (1 = low; 5 = high)
1	30	1
2	30	1
3	30	2
4	40	2
5	45	2
6	50	3
7	60	3
8	75	4
9	75	4
10	75	5

10. The human resources director for a multinational company wants to see whether there is a relationship between an aptitude test administered to new employees and their work performance. The data for a random sample of 10 employees are presented below. Project the performance level of an employee who scores 100 in the aptitude test. Is the aptitude test able to explain all the variances in the performance of new hires?

Number	Aptitude Test Score (/100)	Performance Score (/10)
1	75	7
2	65	6
3	70	6
4	80	7
5	90	9
6	85	8
7	60	5
8	95	9
9	75	6
10	80	7

11. A pharmaceutical company that has developed a new type of drug to fight a new strain of bacterial infection is interested in investigating the relationship between the dosage level and the cure rate of the new drug. The scientist who developed the new drug wants to test the potency of the drug among lab animals before trying it out on humans. Accordingly, she selects 10 animals of equal weight and other characteristics, administers the new drug, and notes the animals' recovery rate. The data are shown in the table below. Based on the test, what should the recommended dosage level be? How confident can the scientist be of the results?

Number	Dosage Level (mg)	Recovery Rate (%)
1	0.100	50
2	0.150	50
3	0.200	55
4	0.225	60
5	0.250	60
6	0.275	75
7	0.300	80
8	0.325	80
9	0.350	80
10	0.375	80

12. An international charter airline servicing some of the Caribbean islands would like to attain a higher occupancy rate on its flights and, hence, achieve greater profitability for its routes originating from some of the major European cities. In the past the local (in Europe) weather and temperature seem to have provided some clues for the low occupancy rates, but management is not certain that this is the reason in this case. To make sure that the weather plays a role in Europeans' travel plans, the project-planning department of the company has compiled the following data. Are the weather and temperature major influences on travel plans for European leisure travelers? Can this be established with some certainty?

Month	Temperature (°C)	Occupancy rate (%)
January	0	95
February	5	100
March	5	85
April	10	80
May	15	80
June	25	65
July	30	65
August	30	70
September	20	65
October	15	70
November	10	65
December	5	60

13. The CFO of a medium-size company with subsidiaries in the Far East has been having difficulty remitting profits from these units due to volatile exchange rate fluctuations. To better predict the timing of these remittances, the CFO has been following the factors that seem to have a bearing on the rate shifts. The CFO has compiled the following quarterly changes in exchange rates and other economic variables for the previous five years. Do you agree with the CFO about the influence of the factors he selected? Is there a high correlation between the exchange rate and the selected variables?

Quarter	Change in Rate (%)	Variable 1: GDP/Capita	Variable 2: External Debt ($ million)	Variable 3: Trade Deficit ($ million)
1	10	875	100	2,000
2	15	875	1,000	3,500
3	16	875	1,000	3,000
4	15	875	1,500	2,500
5	5	950	500	1,000
6	5	950	350	1,000
7	6	950	400	1,200
8	6	950	400	1,000
9	8	1,000	1,000	3,000
10	9	1,000	2,000	3,500
11	15	1,000	3,500	5,000
12	15	950	3,500	5,500
13	16	950	3,500	5,500
14	20	975	5,000	6,000
15	20	975	5,000	4,000
16	16	1,000	4,000	4,000
17	12	1,100	3,000	2,500
18	10	1,100	2,500	2,000
19	8	1,100	500	1,000
20	5	1,100	300	500

14. The comptroller for a large global company has noticed that the cost associated with one of its subsidiaries is much higher than that associated with other similar-size operations. The local managers seem to have no solution to the problem. To get to the root of the cost problem, the comptroller assigns the task to one of her assistants. The assistant attempts to isolate the factors that cause costs to be incurred and their composite effects. The assistant uses weekly production as a proxy for the costs. The data collected by the assistant (partial) are shown below. Assuming that a multiple regression model can be used to explain the cost increases, address the following points.

a. Find the multiple regression equation.
b. Test the usefulness of the model using an $\alpha = 0.01$ (hint: use an F test).
c. Find r^2 and interpret your results.
d. In your opinion, did the assistant correctly identify the reasons for the cost variations at the subsidiary?

Week	Output (thousands of units)	Labor hours	Local Materials Used (kg)	Imported Materials (kg)
1	90	510	900	80.0
2	87	500	875	77.5
3	92	510	910	81.0
4	85	480	860	76.0
5	80	450	820	72.0
6	77	400	800	70.0
7	75	400	780	68.0
8	78	425	780	68.0
9	80	450	825	82.5
10	90	515	900	80.0
11	95	540	940	84.0
12	98	545	950	85.0
13	96	545	952	85.2
14	95	542	940	84.0
15	90	518	900	80.0
16	92	520	910	81.0
17	100	550	955	85.5
18	105	555	960	86.0
19	108	560	962	86.2
20	110	560	965	86.5
21	105	556	960	86.0
22	106	556	960	86.0
23	100	548	955	85.5
24	98	545	954	85.4
25	95	545	940	84.0

15. A financial analyst for an American investment banking firm based in São Paolo has had some difficulty in predicting the changes in share prices for the companies operating in the automotive industry. The volatile nature of the economy, coupled with inefficiencies within the industry, has caused the stock prices of automotive firms to rise and fall unevenly. In an attempt to understand the wide swings in stock prices, the analyst has compiled the following quarterly data for the industry. Do the variables identified by the

analyst explain the reasons for the stock price swings among the firms in the automotive industry?

Quarter	Average Stock Price ($)	Profits ($ million)	Investments ($ million)	Exports (000)
1	32.0	50.4	98.7	10.0
2	30.5	48.6	85.5	8.2
3	27.3	35.8	66.7	7.4
4	24.1	28.0	51.4	6.0
5	29.0	37.6	59.1	6.3
6	28.0	36.2	54.9	5.4
7	27.0	34.8	57.8	5.7
8	22.5	21.7	41.6	5.1
9	20.8	16.4	33.1	3.8
10	17.5	11.9	23.4	2.1

16. The regional brand manager for an aromatic liquid soap has collected the following data for one of his European markets. Using the data from the table, address the following points.

   a. Determine the value of the regression coefficients.
   b. What is the coefficient of determination (r^2)?
   c. What would you conclude based on the value of r^2?
   d. Are the regression coefficients (slope) statistically significant?

Month	Sales (€ million)	Company's Marketing Expenditure (€ thousand)	Competitor's Advertising Expenditures (€ million)
1	1.10	115	2.0
2	1.20	125	2.1
3	1.25	135	2.0
4	1.20	130	1.9
5	1.00	110	2.5
6	1.15	130	2.3
7	1.25	135	2.4
8	1.45	140	2.0
9	1.60	155	1.8
10	1.75	185	1.5
11	1.60	162	1.8
12	1.50	156	1.8

APPENDIX 16.1. SAS PROGRAM TO SOLVE SIMPLE REGRESSION PROBLEMS

These screen shots from SAS depict the income and appliance purchase problem discussed in example 3.

Figure 16.5   **SAS Program to Solve Simple Regression Problems, Window 1**

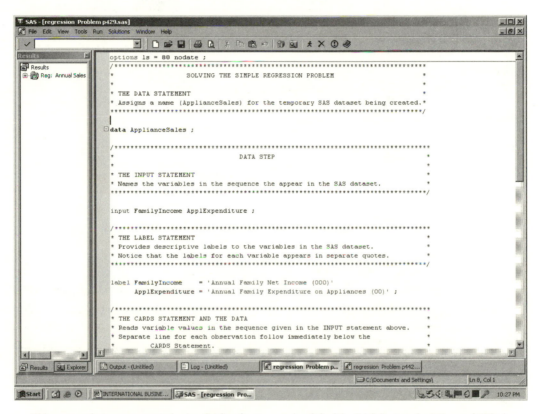

This screen shot was generated using SAS software, version 8.2 of the SAS System for Microsoft Windows. Copyright © SAS Institute Inc. SAS and all other SAS Institute Inc. product or service names are registered trademarks or trademarks of SAS Institute Inc., Cary, NC, USA.

Figure 16.6   **SAS Program to Solve Simple Regression Problems, Window 2**

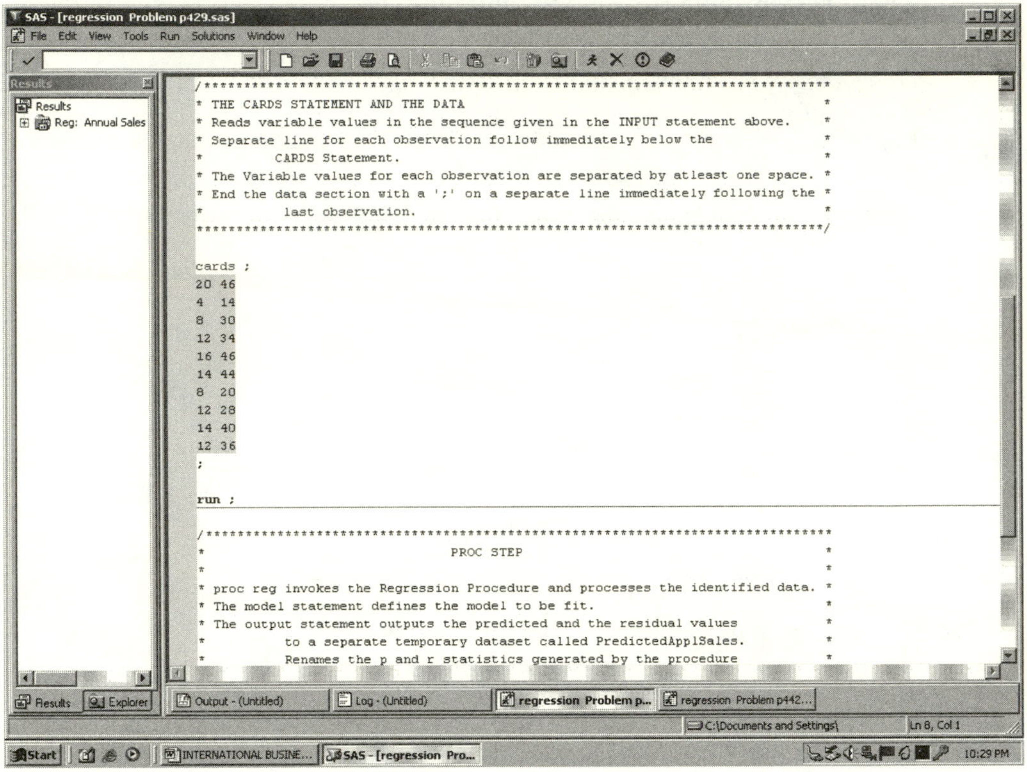

```
/*********************************************************************
* THE CARDS STATEMENT AND THE DATA                                   *
* Reads variable values in the sequence given in the INPUT statement above.  *
* Separate line for each observation follow immediately below the    *
*          CARDS Statement.                                          *
* The Variable values for each observation are separated by atleast one space. *
* End the data section with a ';' on a separate line immediately following the *
*          last observation.                                         *
*********************************************************************/

cards ;
20 46
4  14
8  30
12 34
16 46
14 44
8  20
12 28
14 40
12 36
;

run ;

/*********************************************************************
*                         PROC STEP                                  *
*                                                                    *
* proc reg invokes the Regression Procedure and processes the identified data. *
* The model statement defines the model to be fit.                   *
* The output statement outputs the predicted and the residual values *
*          to a separate temporary dataset called PredictedApplSales. *
*          Renames the p and r statistics generated by the procedure *
```

This screen shot was generated using SAS software, version 8.2 of the SAS System for Microsoft Windows. Copyright © SAS Institute Inc. SAS and all other SAS Institute Inc. product or service names are registered trademarks or trademarks of SAS Institute Inc., Cary, NC, USA.

Figure 16.7   **SAS Program to Solve Simple Regression Problems, Window 3**

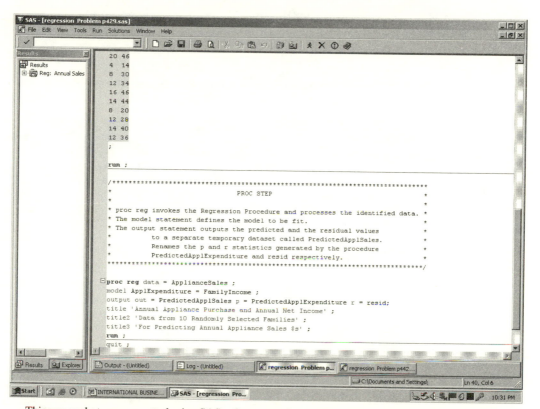

APPENDIX 16.2. SAS PROGRAM TO SOLVE MULTIPLE REGRESSION PROBLEMS

These screen shots from SAS depict the monthly sales, number of contacts made, years with the company, and territorial experience problem discussed in example 7.

Figure 16.8   **SAS Program to Solve Multiple Regression Problems, Window 1**

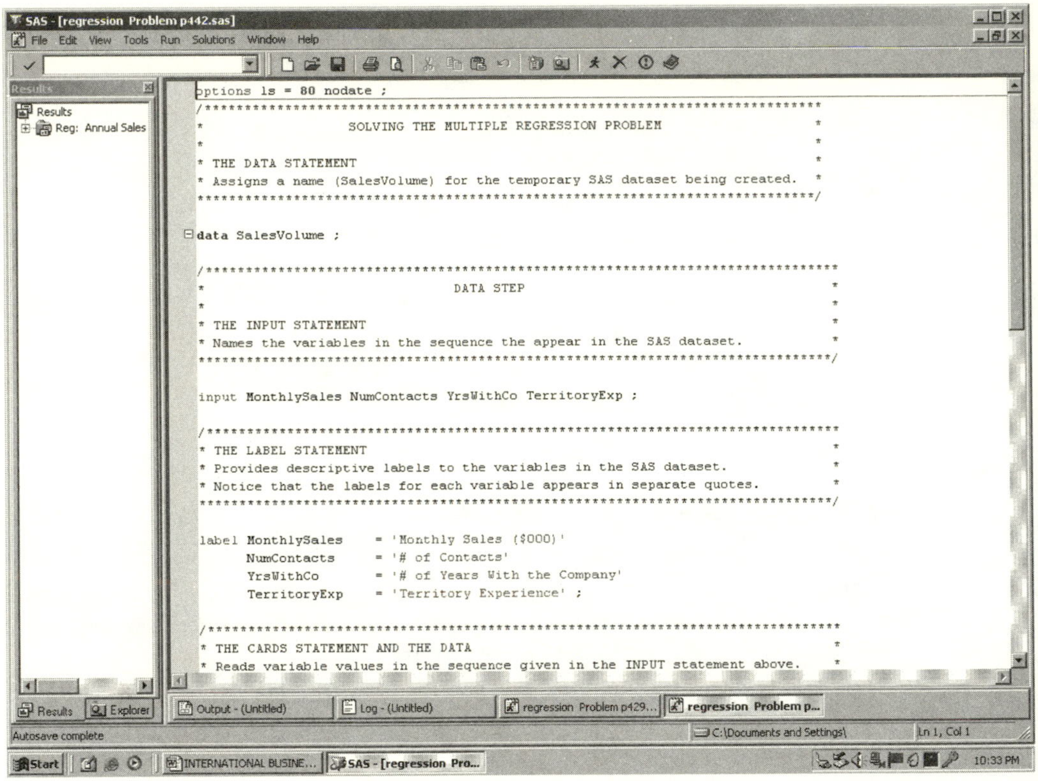

This screen shot was generated using SAS software, version 8.2 of the SAS System for Microsoft Windows. Copyright © SAS Institute Inc. SAS and all other SAS Institute Inc. product or service names are registered trademarks or trademarks of SAS Institute Inc., Cary, NC, USA.

Figure 16.9 **SAS Program to Solve Multiple Regression Problems, Window 2**

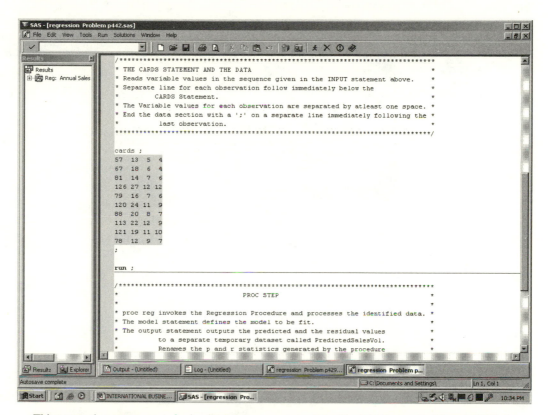

```
/**************************************************************
* THE CARDS STATEMENT AND THE DATA                            *
* Reads variable values in the sequence given in the INPUT statement above. *
* Separate line for each observation follow immediately below the *
*       CARDS Statement.                                      *
* The Variable values for each observation are separated by atleast one space. *
* End the data section with a ';' on a separate line immediately following the *
*       last observation.                                     *
**************************************************************/

cards ;
57  13   5   4
67  18   6   4
81  14   7   6
126 27  12  12
79  16   7   6
120 24  11   9
88  20   8   7
113 22  12   9
121 19  11  10
78  12   9   7
;


run ;


/**************************************************************
*                    PROC STEP                                *
*                                                             *
* proc reg invokes the Regression Procedure and processes the identified data. *
* The model statement defines the model to be fit.            *
* The output statement outputs the predicted and the residual values *
*       to a separate temporary dataset called PredictedSalesVol. *
*       Renames the p and r statistics generated by the procedure *
```

This screen shot was generated using SAS software, version 8.2 of the SAS System for Microsoft Windows. Copyright © SAS Institute Inc. SAS and all other SAS Institute Inc. product or service names are registered trademarks or trademarks of SAS Institute Inc., Cary, NC, USA.

Figure 16.10   **SAS Program to Solve Multiple Regression Problems, Window 3**

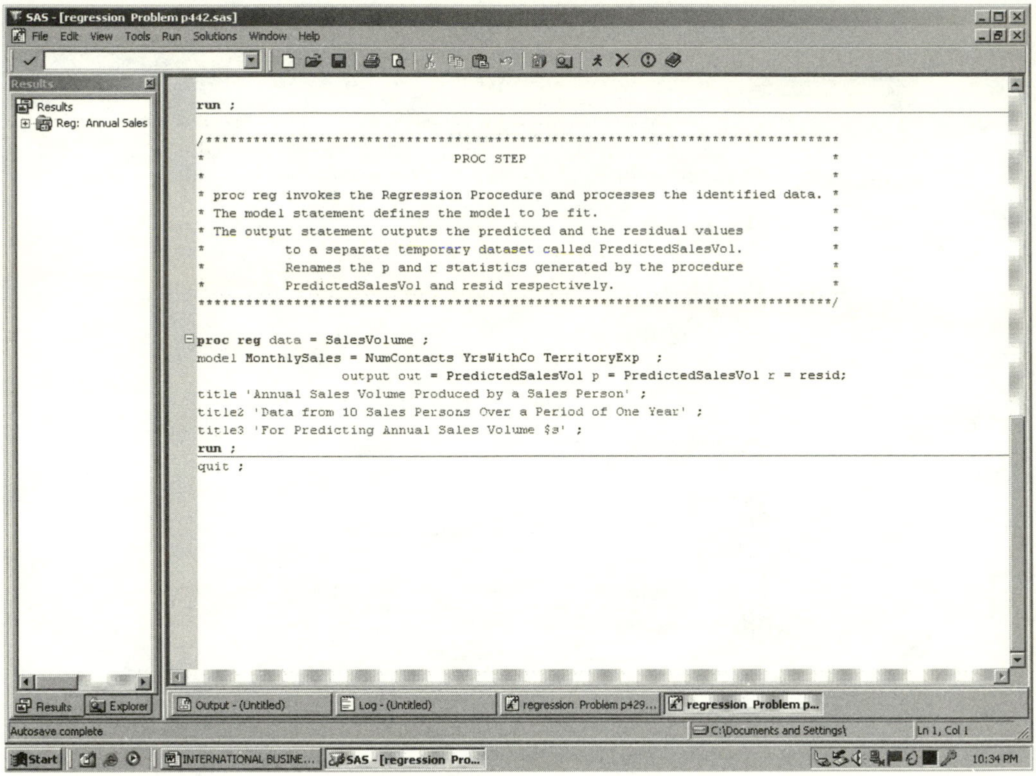

This screen shot was generated using SAS software, version 8.2 of the SAS System for Microsoft Windows. Copyright © SAS Institute Inc. SAS and all other SAS Institute Inc. product or service names are registered trademarks or trademarks of SAS Institute Inc., Cary, NC, USA.

NOTE

1. Kent C. Garner and Alan C. Shapiro, "A Practical Method of Assessing Foreign Exchange Risk," *Midland Corporate Finance Journal* (Fall 1984), pp. 6–17.

2. Created with SAS software. Copyright © 2002–2007 SAS Institute Inc., Cary, NC, USA. All Rights Reserved. Reproduced with permission of SAS Institute Inc., Cary, NC.

ADDITIONAL READING

BOOKS

Chen, Peter Y., and Paula M. Popovich. *Correlation: Parametric and Non-Parametric Measure.* Thousand Oaks, CA: Sage Publications, 2002.

Mendenhall, William, and Terry Sincich. *A Second Course in Statistics: Regression Analysis.* Upper Saddle River, NJ: Pearson-Prentice-Hall, 2003.

Wittink, D. *The Application of Regression Analysis.* Boston: Allyn and Bacon, 1988.

ARTICLES

Binder, John J. (1985) "The Multivariate Regression Model in Event Studies." *Journal of Accounting Research* 23 (1), pp. 370–383.

Darlinton, R.B. (1968) "Multiple Regression in Psychological Research and Practice." *Psychological Bulletin* 69, pp. 161–182.

Irwin, Julie R., and Gary H. McClelland (2001) "Misleading Heuristics and Moderated Multiple Regression Models." *Journal of Marketing Research* 38 (1), pp. 100–109.

Martin, W.S. (1978) "Effects of Scaling on the Correlation Coefficient: Additional Considerations." *Journal of Marketing Research* (May), pp. 304–308.

Schmitt, Neal (1999) "Estimates for Cross-Validity for Stepwise Regression and with Predictor Selection." *Journal of Applied Psychology* 84 (1), p. 50.

Zellner, Arnold (2001) "Further Results on Baysian Method of Moments Analysis of the Multiple Regression Model." *International Economic Review* 42 (1), pp. 121–140.

17 Multivariate Analysis

Researchers use multivariate techniques to analyze the effects of more than one variable considered one at a time.

LEARNING OBJECTIVES

After reading this chapter, students should be able to

- Distinguish between univariate and multivariate analysis
- Understand and apply factor analysis
- Understand cluster analysis
- Understand discriminant analysis
- Understand multidimensional scaling
- Identify and understand the differences among the various multivariate techniques

Univariate analysis lets the researcher analyze one variable at a time. Bivariate analysis involves two variables. When a problem involves three or more variables, researchers use multivariate techniques. For example, a potential investor in stocks would not only have to monitor the prevailing interest rates but also be concerned with corporate profits, inventory turnover, and consumer confidence level. Similarly, consumption of heating oil may depend on price of crude oil, use of gas heat, and severity of the weather. These business issues are ideally suited for conducting multivariate analysis.

The four techniques described in this chapter are classified as analysis of interdependence. In interdependence techniques it is not necessary to designate the dependent and independent variables. Interdependence techniques treat all variables equally. Basically, the technique explores for underlying patterns within a data set. In other words, analysis of interdependence attempts to give meaning to a set of variables or to find common features to group things together. An investment banking firm trying to group its various clients by size, financial ratios, and profits to identify differences in patterns of investment is a good example of the use of analysis of interdependence. In analysis of dependence techniques, an attempt is made to explain the dependent variable on the basis of one or more independent variables. Techniques such as regression analysis and discriminant analysis are dependence approaches. Chapter 16 discusses one of these techniques—regression analysis—in detail.

The four interdependence methods that are classified as multivariate analysis are factor analysis, cluster analysis, discriminant analysis, and multidimensional scaling. Only factor analysis is discussed in detail in this chapter. In using multivariate techniques, researchers have to be concerned about sample sizes. Smaller sample sizes may result in the tests identifying the significance of the results, or the results may fit very well but in reality may not be generalized for a larger population. Also, in many situations the data collected do not lend themselves to interval measurement. Most survey instruments use fixed-response questions that yield nonmetric response data such as ordinal or nominal data. Consequently, many of the traditional multivariate techniques are not suited to such data; therefore, it may be necessary to try other analytical techniques.[1]

FACTOR ANALYSIS

In factor analysis, interdependent relationships among variables critical to a research study are examined. This and other interdependent techniques allow a researcher to further understand the structure of a set of variables. This procedure is used primarily for data reduction and summarization. Factor analysis generates a small number of variables (*factors*) from a large number of variables. The factors are formed by taking advantage of the interrelationships among the original variables. Factor analysis is based primarily on a linear relationship. It assumes that the data are interval scaled. It is difficult if not impossible to undertake factor analysis manually. Most factor analysis is accomplished through computers using standard statistical software such as SPSS or SAS.

CONSIDERATIONS IN FACTOR ANALYSIS

- Does the research problem lend itself to *exploratory* or *confirmatory* factor analysis?
- If exploratory factor analysis is the chosen technique, is the grouping of *variables* (R-factor analysis) or *cases* (Q-factor analysis)? Summarizing many characteristics of a sample would use a correlation matrix of variables, whereas factor analysis of the individual respondents based on their characteristics would use cases. When individual respondents (Q factor analysis) are chosen, the statistical technique used is *cluster analysis*.
- What is the research design? That is, is the sample size adequate (greater than 100) for factor analysis, what variables are included (R type or Q type), and how are the variables measured (must be metric measurement)?

- Have the statistical considerations of normality and linearity been met, and is the sample homogenous?
- In selecting the factors, is the total variance or only the common variance analyzed?
- Should the factors be correlated (oblique) or uncorrelated (orthogonal)?

Factor analysis can be used either as an exploratory technique or as a confirmatory technique. When applied as an exploratory technique, it useful in data reduction or in searching for structure in a set of variables. When a researcher has an a priori hypothesis, factor analysis may be used to test the hypothesis. In this case, factor analysis is used as a confirmatory technique.

USES OF FACTOR ANALYSIS

- To examine the strength of the overall association among variables
- To describe data but not to draw statistical inferences
- To identify a new, smaller set of noncorrelated variables to replace the original set of correlated variables identified in other multivariate techniques such as regression
- To identify the underlying factors that explain the correlation among a set of variables
- To identify a smaller set of key variables from a larger set for use in subsequent multivariate analysis

In international business research, a large number of correlated variables may have to be reduced to a manageable level. The government of a developing country may be interested in determining the foreign investors' perception about the country's business climate. This factor may be measured by asking potential foreign investors to evaluate the country on a multitude of factors, such as economic risk, political risk, regulatory risk, exchange risk, and so on, through statements on a Likert scale. These statements explaining each of the factors evaluated may then be analyzed to determine the factors underlying the investment climate of the country.

The main purpose of factor analysis is to identify and test dimensions that may explain variables. Quite often, respondents are not able to state their intentions clearly. Therefore, researchers try to identify the underlying reasons for certain factors. In the study to determine a country's business climate, the researcher's interest is to see whether investors have a positive or negative view of the business climate. This may not be an observable variable, but, rather, it may be inferred from correlated measures that are observable such as the economic risk, political risk, and so on.

In the managerial study documented in chapter 16 (the questionnaire used for the managerial study is presented as appendix A2), prior to testing the main prediction of the study and to justify the pooling of data from the four countries, factor analyses were conducted to determine whether data from the four countries share similar data structure. Items that had dual loadings (the correlation of a variable with a factor) or very low loadings were dropped from the analysis to purify the data. This process

Figure 17.1   **Factor Analysis Example—Managerial Study**

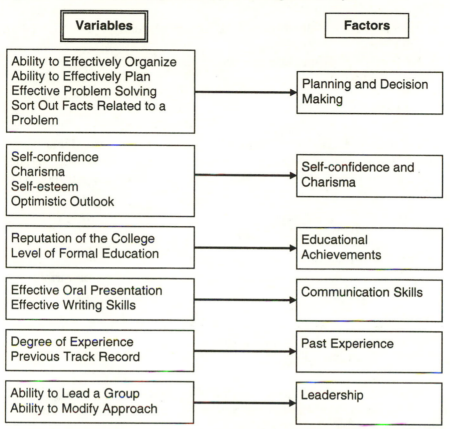

resulted in the retention of 18 of the original 42 items. Subsequent factor analysis produced five factors for three countries and six factors for the fourth country. This reduction in data is presented in Figure 17.1.

TERMS USED IN FACTOR ANALYSIS

- *Common variance.* Variance that is shared with other variables in the factor analysis
- *Communality.* Amount of variance an original variable shares with all other variables included in the analysis
- *Correlation matrix.* Table showing the intercorrelation among all variables
- *Factor.* Linear combination of the original variables representing the underlying dimensions, also called constructs, that summarize the original set of observed variables
- *Factor loadings.* Correlation between the original variables and the factors and the critical component that explains a particular factor. When squared, factor loadings indicate how much the factor explains the percentage of variance in the original variable

- *Factor matrix.* A table that presents the factor loadings of all variables on each factor
- *Factor rotation.* Adjustment of the factor axes to achieve more meaningful factor solutions
- *Factor score.* Composite measure created for each observation on each factor obtained from the factor analysis

FACTOR ANALYSIS MODEL

The variables in factor analysis are expressed as a linear combination of underlying factors. The amount of variance one variable shares with all other variables included in the analysis is referred to as communality. The factor analysis model is represented as

$$X_i = A_{i1}F_1 + A_{i2}F_2 + A_{i3}F_3 + \ldots A_{im}F_m + V_iU_i$$

where X_i = ith standardized variable

A_{ij} = standardized multiple regression coefficient of variable i on common factor j

F = common factor

V_i = standardized regression coefficient of variable i on unique factor i

U_i = unique factor for variable i

m = number of common factors

The unique factors are not correlated with each other or with the common factors. The common factors themselves can be expressed as a linear combination of the observed variables, as shown below.

$$F_i = W_{i1} X_1 + W_{i2}X_2 + W_{i3}X_3 + \ldots W_{ik}X_k$$

where F_i = estimate of the ith factor

W_i = weight of the score coefficient

k = number of variables

For example, a researcher tests for different brands of tires for

Total life of the tire (miles)	1
Strength of tire (resistance to foreign objects)	2
Skid resistance	3

To obtain the necessary feedback from tire users, the researcher conducts a survey of tire buyers. Each respondent is asked to evaluate seven statements that reflect the three dimensions that the company is interested in (life = 1, strength = 2, and skidding = 3) on a five-point scale. These statements are presented in Table 17.1.

There appear to be some common themes emerging from the statements listed in Table 17.1. Statements 1, 2, and 5 should lead to similar responses, as they all deal

Table 17.1   **Statements Used in the Study**

Statements	Strongly Agree	Agree	Neutral	Disagree	Strongly Disagree
1. Tires that I buy last very long.					
2. Most tires in the market have a long life.					
3. Tires are much safer now.					
4. Modern tires can handle icy conditions.					
5. Almost all tires last over 80,000 miles.					
6. Modern tires are puncture resistant.					
7. Tires I buy do not skid.					
8. Tire companies use very strong materials for treads.					

with *life of tires*. Statements 6 and 8 are concerned with *strength and puncture resistance*. Statements 3, 4, and 7 deal with *skid issues*.

Table 17.2 presents the three variables expressed as a standardized variate that has a mean of 0 and standard deviation of 1.

The purpose of working with standardized data is to reduce the influence of the original measurement units, which were probably chosen without much thought to their relevance.

FACTOR SCORES

As defined earlier, a factor is a linear combination of the original score. By assigning weights, a researcher can write the factor associated with a particular variable. For example, in the above tire problem, weights could be assigned to each variable—variable 1 (life of tire) = 0.4, variable 2 (strength) = 0.2, and variable 3 (skid resistance) = 0.1. Using these weights, a factor F_1 is presented as follows:

$$F_1 = 0.4X_1 + 0.2X_2 + 0.1X_3$$

The question is, How did the researcher choose these weights? Since the purpose of the factor analysis procedures is to select these weights according to certain criteria, there is no specific rule in selecting the weights. The various methods of factor analysis are differentiated in terms of the bases upon which the weights are selected. Each item has a factor score, where the weights are common for each object. For example, the factor score for the first tire brand (from Table 17.2) is

$$0.4(-0.28) + 0.2(-0.36) + 0.1(0.52)$$

Similarly, the factor scores for the other four brands of tires can be computed using the same weights. The new factor scores will be different, as the original scores were different across each of the tire brands.

Table 17.2   **Standardized Data Matrix**

Variable Description	Characteristic Number		
	1	2	3
Brand 1	−0.28	−0.36	−0.52
Brand 2	3.51	3.61	−0.55
Brand 3	−0.39	−0.34	−0.55
Brand 4	−0.06	−0.28	−0.55
Brand 5	0.38	−0.27	−0.46

In practice, the actual analysis is conducted through statistical software packages.

CLUSTER ANALYSIS

Cluster analysis is used to group elements such that the characteristics or traits of the grouped elements (clusters) are homogeneous. Cluster analysis can be used to segment markets, group employees for specific tasks, and group different suppliers according to location. Through database management and advances in technology, businesses (especially marketers) often have a vast set of data on costs, sales, vendors, and so on. Cluster analysis is able to reduce this vast data into meaningful groupings or classifications. Cluster analysis could be used to identify new market opportunities and new product opportunities, and to select test-market sites.

Cluster analysis can be divided into two categories: hierarchical and nonhierarchical. In hierarchical clustering, the outcome is characterized as a treelike structure (hierarchical), whereas in nonhierarchical clustering, the outcome is characterized by a sequential threshold, parallel threshold, and optimizing portioning.

Since many algorithms are available for conducting cluster analysis, it can be used with any type of data: nominal, ordinal, interval, or ratio. The basic principle underlying cluster analysis involves measuring similarity among objects on the basis of their values on various characteristics. The similarity measure among objects is determined through "distance measures," which are computed by complex computer programs. Determining how many distinct clusters there are and to which cluster each data point belongs is accomplished through trial and error; hence, the use of computers makes this process much easier.

DISCRIMINANT ANALYSIS

Discriminant analysis and cluster analysis are concerned with classification. Whereas cluster analysis requires no prior information about the cluster membership, discriminant analysis assumes prior knowledge of the cluster. Suppose a researcher is faced with a dependent variable that is nominal, such as domestic/foreign, buyer/nonbuyer, and cash purchase/credit card purchase. It is not possible to use multiple regression in this case. The multiple regression technique is applicable only when the dependent variable is interval scaled. In instances such as this one, discriminant analysis is a more appropriate analytical technique.

The purpose of discriminant analysis is to classify objects into two or more categories using a set of interval-scaled independent variables. In discriminant analysis, when the dependent variable has two categories, the technique is known as *two-group discriminant analysis*. In the case of two-group analysis, it is possible to derive only one discriminant function. When there are three or more categories of the dependent variable, the technique is called *multiple discriminant analysis*. In this case, more than one discriminant function may be calculated.

The discriminant analysis technique identifies the differentiating characteristics of subclasses of units that are maximally separated on a dependent variable. The model developed to run a discriminant analysis will effectively classify a large proportion of the cases. Hence, the mathematical principle of discriminant analysis is similar to multiple regression.

For example, a commercial bank wants to discover the distinguishing characteristics of homeowners who may be taking out a home-equity loan based on their age (X_1) and household income (X_2). Assuming that these are the most critical independent variables in determining whether a homeowner takes out a home-equity loan or not, the bank would like to predict the likelihood of homeowners with different ages and household incomes taking out home equity loans. If the bank has a set of data on the two variables for a sample of home-equity borrowers and a second set for nonborrowers, it could plot the samples on a graph, as shown in Figure 17.2.

The circled area shown in Figure 17.2 contains homeowners who have taken out a home equity loan and others who have not. As observed in Figure 17.2, there are wide sections that are distinct from each other, implying that there is a difference based on the two variables—income and age—between homeowners that take out home equity loans and those who do not. That is, income and age are good discriminators between homeowners who take out home equity loans and those who do not.

Using discriminant analysis, the bank can now use the data from the two samples to quantify the relative importance of X_1 and X_2. This analysis could also be used to develop a criterion for classifying prospective homeowners as potential customers for home-equity loans. The discriminant function could be set up as a linear function, represented by

$$Y_n = w_1 X_1 + w_2 X_2$$

where Y_n = homeowner's discriminant score for homeowner b
X_1 and X_2 = the two variables—age and household income
w_1 and w_2 = discriminant coefficients (constant)

The discriminant analysis selects the two coefficients in such a way that the variation in the discriminant scores (Y) between the two groups of homeowners is made as large as possible. That is, the coefficients selected maximize the ratio of between to within sums of squares of corresponding to the discriminant scores. Discriminant

Figure 17.2   **Equity Loan**

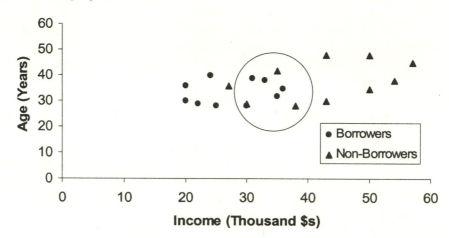

analysis is usually performed using statistical software programs such as SAS and SPSS. These software programs provide the discriminant coefficients and also the statistical significance of the functions.

MULTIDIMENSIONAL SCALING

Multidimensional scaling (MDS) is a procedure that shows relationships between variables through graphics rather than numbers alone. Multidimensional scaling techniques transform one-dimensional relationships into multidimensional relationships, providing an easy-to-understand visual analysis. Multidimensional scaling is used to infer underlying characteristics or dimensions from a series of similarity preference judgments provided by elements within a given set. While cluster analysis groups objects according to similarities inferred from data on prescribed dimensions, multidimensional scaling infers underlying evaluative dimensions from similarities or preferences or both. Multidimensional scaling can be applied to a wide range of marketing problems, in particular to perceptual mapping. The introduction of methods based on the "maximum likelihood principle" is one of the most important developments.[2] For example, a company wishing to determine its competitive position on two attributes that are critical to the purchase of the product may develop a spatial map that it can use to develop innovative strategies (see Figure 17.3).

In multidimensional scaling, respondents' preferences and perceptions are represented in multidimensional space, providing a visual display of the relationships among various stimuli. Perceptual differences between objects are measured as relative distances between objects. The MDS technique uses proximity or preference data as its input. The preference is explained as a number that indicates how similar or how different two objects are perceived to be (hence the name "perceptual maps"). Multidimensional scaling has been used to segment markets, to study the effects of advertising, to develop new services, and to develop scales. Both metric and non-metric data can be analyzed using multidimensional scaling. Like cluster analysis,

Figure 17.3   **Spatial Location of Competing Brands**

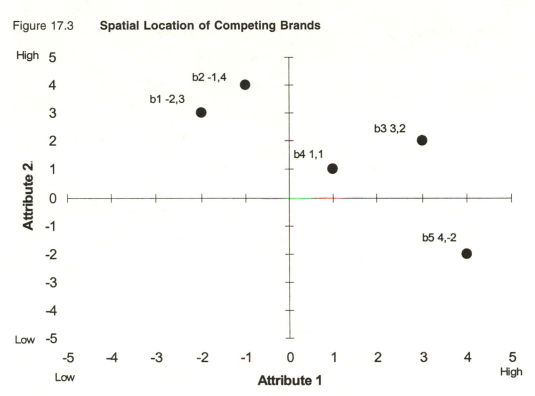

multidimensional scaling is a complex and time-consuming trial-and-error process. Many computer software programs can be used to analyze multidimensional scaling problems.

CHAPTER SUMMARY

Multivariate analysis is useful when three or more variables are involved. Multivariate techniques use two or more dependent variables to predict a dependent variable. Advances in computer technology and availability of user-friendly statistical packages have made multivariate analysis more popular. The various multivariate analytical techniques include multiple regression (chapter 16), factor analysis, cluster analysis, discriminant analysis, and multidimensional scaling.

Factor analysis is a powerful tool for effectively summarizing information from databases. It is essentially a multivariate statistical technique that can be used to define the underlying structure in a data matrix. Factor analysis addresses the problem of analyzing the structure of the correlations among a large number of variables by defining a set of common underlying dimensions called factors. By using factor analysis, a researcher is able to identify the separate dimensions of the structure and then determine the extent to which each variable is explained by each dimension. The primary uses of factor analysis are summarization and data reduction. Improved

Table 17.3 **Summary of Selected Statistical Methods for Analyzing Variables**

Statistical Technique	Scale Used	Number of Individual Variables	When Used
Cross-tabulation	Nominal	One	Number of users versus nonusers of items by a variable (age)
Chi-square			Usage of items by different levels of variables (different ages)
Analysis of variance	Interval/ratio	More than one	
Multiple regression	Interval/ratio	More than one	Usage by two or more variables
Factor analysis	Interval	More than one	To reduce number of factors from a large number of variables
Cluster analysis	Interval	More than one	To classify individuals into a small number of mutually exclusive and exhaustive groups
Discriminant analysis	Interval	More than one	To examine differences across groups
Multidimensional scaling	Depends		To measure objects in multidimensional space on the basis of judgments of respondents

and advanced computer technology has made factor analysis a widely used analytical research technique.

Cluster analysis classifies elements into a small number of homogeneous groups. The clusters are suggested by the data, not a priori. Useful in segmentation studies, cluster analysis provides a basis for determining how objects or elements should be assigned to groups to make sure that there will be as many likenesses as well as differences within groups. Clustering procedures may be hierarchical or nonhierarchical.

Discriminant analysis is used when the dependent variable is categorical and the independent variable is interval. This technique is useful in defining segments, identifying critical characteristics that could be used to distinguish between segments, and classifying prospective clients or customers. In finance, discriminant analysis can be used to identify characteristics that may predict bankruptcies among companies.

Multidimensional scaling explains perceived relationships by observing the attitude components making up the judgments. It measures objects in multidimensional space. That is, relationships (perceived or psychological) are represented as geometric relationships among points in space. This technique is useful in analyzing the perceptions and preferences of elements, especially consumers. Table 17.3 presents selected statistical methods for analyzing association and interdependence of variables.

CHAPTER REVIEW

1. Define factor analysis.
2. How and when can you make use of factor analysis?
3. Enumerate the steps in factor analysis.
4. Identify and discuss one or two problem situations for which factor analysis may be an appropriate statistical technique.

5. How would you apply the factor-loading matrix to interpret the underlying meaning of the factors?
6. Differentiate between cluster analysis and discriminant analysis.
7. When do researchers use discriminant analysis?
8. What are discriminant coefficients?

NOTES

1. William R. Dillon and Mark Goldstein, *Multivariate Analysis: Methods and Applications.* New York: John Wiley & Sons, 1984, pp. 303–335.

2. Tammo H.A. Bijmolt and Michel Wedel, "A Comparison of Multidimensional Scaling Methods for Perceptual Mapping," *Journal of Marketing Research* 36, no. 2 (1999), pp. 277–285.

ADDITIONAL READING

BOOKS

Bartholomew, David J., and Martin Knott. *Latent Variable Models and Factor Analysis.* London: Edward Arnold Publishers, 1999.

Green, Paul E., and Yoram Wind. *Multivariate Analysis.* Englewood Cliffs, NJ: Prentice-Hall, 1976.

Hair, Joseph F., Rolph E. Anderson, Ronald L. Tatham, and William C. Black. *Multivariate Data Analysis: With Readings.* 5th ed. Englewood Cliffs, NJ: Prentice-Hall, 1998.

Kemsley, E.K. *Discriminant Analysis and Class Modeling of Spectroscopic Data.* New York: John Wiley & Sons, 1998.

Malhotra, Naresh K. *Marketing Research: An Applied Orientation.* 4th ed. Upper Saddle River, NJ: Pearson, 2003, pp. 553–558.

ARTICLES

Dansky, Kathryn H., and Dianne Branon (1996) "Discriminant Analysis: A Technique for Adding Value to Patient Satisfaction Surveys." *Hospitals and Health Services Administration* 41 (4), pp. 503–513.

DeSarbo, Wayne S., and Martin R. Young (1997) "A Parametric Multidimensional Unfolding Procedure for Incomplete Nonmetric Preference Choice Set Data in Marketing Research." *Journal of Marketing Research* 34 (4), pp. 499–516.

Ding, Adam A. (1999) "Prediction Intervals, Factor Analysis Models, and High-Dimensional Empirical Linear Prediction." *Journal of American Statistical Association* (June), pp. 446–455.

Douglas, Carroll J., and Paul E. Green (1997) "Psychometric Methods in Marketing Research: Part II, Multidimensional Scaling." *Journal of Marketing Research* 34 (2), pp. 193–204.

Fenwick, Ian (1978) "A User's Guide to Conjoint Measurement in Marketing." *European Journal of Marketing* 12 (2), pp. 203–211.

Frank, Ronald A., and Paul E. Green (1968) "Numerical Taxonomy in Marketing Analysis: A Review Article." *Journal of Marketing Research* (February), pp. 83–98.

Franses, Philip Hans (2000) "A Test for the Hit Rate in Binary Response Models." *International Journal of Marketing Research* 42 (2), pp. 239–245.

Glen, J.J. (2001) "Classification Accuracy in Discriminant Analysis: A Mixed Integer Programming Approach." *Journal of the Operational Research Society* 52 (3), p. 328.

Kamakura, Wagner A., and Michel Widel (2000) "Factor Analysis and Missing Data." *Journal of Marketing Research* 37 (4), pp. 490–498.

Klastorin, T.D. (1983) "Assessing Cluster Analysis Results." *Journal of Marketing Research* (February), pp. 93–98.

Rummel, R.J. (1967) "Understanding Factor Analysis." *Journal of Conflict Resolution* 11 (4), pp. 444–480.

Wind, Yoram, Paul E. Green, and Arun. K. Jain (1973) "Higher Order Factor Analysis in the Classification of Psychographic Variables." *Journal of the Market Research Society* 15, pp. 224–232.

Wiseman, Frederick (1991) "Identifying Most Influential Observations in Factor Analysis." *Marketing Science* (Spring), pp. 145–160.

18 Research Reports

The successful implementation of research findings depends on how effectively the results have been communicated to decision makers.

LEARNING OBJECTIVES

After reading this chapter, students should be able to

- Understand the basic requirements in report presentation
- Understand the importance of written and oral reports
- Understand the process in making a successful oral report
- Learn how to incorporate the client's perspective in written and oral reports

Research reports may be presented in written or oral format, or both. Though the written report is an essential requirement of any research project, in most instances the client requests an oral report as well. To prepare a research report that is useful to the client or user, it is critical that the presenter put the focus on the needs of the client or user. A research project is undertaken to generate information that will help decision makers. The goal of the research report is to convey the research findings clearly and precisely.

WRITTEN REPORT

Most decision makers are involved with many facets of a business and have very little time on their hands. Business executives tend to be less interested in the technical details of a research project and more concerned with the results. In addition, it is conceivable that more than one decision maker will read the research report, and these decision makers are likely to differ in terms of interests, training, and reasons for reading the report. Finally, a report that is interesting, has useful information, and is easy to read will draw the attention of decision makers more than a report that is cumbersome to read and filled with unnecessary details. In the preparation of a written report, it is useful to develop an outline that reflects the tasks that are spelled out in the research proposal. The outline is then filled with relevant text material that forms the first draft of the final written report. The outline or format of a typical research report is presented below.

OUTLINE OF A WRITTEN REPORT

- Title page—contains the project title; the client's name and address; the researcher's name, address, and affiliation; and the date of the report
- Table of contents—contains a list of topics and subtopics arranged in order of their appearance and the corresponding page numbers on which these topics and subtopics appear. The table of contents should also list all the tables, charts, graphs, exhibits, and appendixes with their corresponding page numbers.
- Executive summary—is a summarized version of the full report that emphasizes the critical findings. It captures the essence of the report and in a nutshell is able to provide busy executives with what they should learn from the research.
- Introduction—is a brief description of the background of the study, industry characteristics, and the environmental context of the study. The introduction should set the stage for the study.
- Problem definition—specifies the issues and the basic questions that need to be addressed. The problem definition should clearly and concisely state the research problem that led to the commission of the present research. Discuss the types of information that management needs.
- Research methodology—details the specifics of how the research was conducted; discusses in detail all the research methods used, including secondary data analysis, qualitative research techniques, and primary sources. If primary research was conducted, the research methodology discusses the questionnaire development, scaling techniques, sampling frame and sample selection, field work, and analytical techniques used to interpret the data.
- Data analysis—is the most critical section in a research report and is a major portion of the overall report. This section should describe the data analysis framework and the types of techniques that are applied to obtain the results. Data analysis can be organized around the objectives of the study or in terms of the importance of the key findings. The analysis section should be carefully structured to make sure that the description of the findings or results is clearly presented. Some of the important analytical tables can also be presented in the text. But the detailed tables should be placed in the appendixes. This will help the readers of the report to concentrate on the important findings and not get bogged down in details.
- Limitations—are any weaknesses of the study and need to be discussed here. Without corrupting the overall quality of the report, limitations present those problems that may assist management to review the results within a realistic context.
- Conclusions and recommendations—are drawn using the objective as a guide. They could help management better understand the results of the study. After

drawing pertinent conclusions, a researcher could also recommend strategic actions that may assist managers to address the issues or problems that led to the research study in the first place.

- Bibliography—contains a list of any outside sources that have been used.
- Tables/charts/graphs—present the data and the detailed analysis that was applied. Tables included in the main text can be just the highlights, whereas in this section the detailed tables are included. Tables should have labels, and the conclusions drawn from these tables must be included in the main body of the text.
- Appendixes—include items that have limited interest. Items such as the questionnaire used, industry studies that were used as secondary sources, the fieldwork reports, detailed sampling frame, and any other information that may have some bearing on the study could be included here.

GUIDELINES FOR WRITING A COMPREHENSIVE REPORT

- *Focus*. The main focus of the research report should be on the objective of the study. The research may have been commissioned to arrive at a decision or solve a problem. The final report should be built around that decision or problem. Therefore, the report should show the relevancy of the information to the main objective of the study. The researcher should make sure that all key facts are included and are presented in detail.
- *Technical aspects of the report*. Most researchers are strong in methodology and analytical techniques. They also have a tendency to showcase their expertise. This often leads to detailed discussion of the sampling frame, discussion of statistical techniques, and the level of confidence achieved. Though these factors are critical to the richness of the study, they are of little importance to the user of the research. The user of the research is more interested in the findings and the usefulness of the findings to the decision or problem at hand.
- *Language*. The purpose of the report is to inform research findings and not demonstrate the writer's research skills. The language used must be simple and must include clarification or explanations of technical terms. For example, an expression such as "skewed response distribution" (a one-way table in which a large proportion of responses are piled toward one end of the range of data obtained) or "split-half reliability" (an indicator of the degree of consistency across ratings produced by items within a multiple-item scale) might have to be explained for those decision makers that do not understand these terms. It is also important to proofread the report to correct errors in spelling, grammar, and sentence construction. Misspelled words can confuse the reader and reflect poorly on the researcher. Nowadays, with advanced word processors, mistakes can be greatly reduced.
- *Writing style*. The writing style should be such that the report should be easy to read and the reader should have little difficulty in understanding the results of the research. The report should be interesting and well organized and should have a natural flow. Avoid unnecessary complexity and long-winded sentences.

- *Organization*. Organize the report with proper breaks, and avoid long paragraphs. Provide subtitles to help the reader identify relevant topics.
- *Tables, charts, and graphs*. Important figures and analytical findings are more useful when presented in easily readable tables. Placing numbers in sentences detracts from the significance of these numbers. For example, a section of the report that provides market share figures for various segments in relation to the industry average may read,

> The company's share of the total market for the year grew by 5 percent compared to the previous two years, whereas the total sales for the industry grew by 9 percent for the same period. More alarmingly for the company, its sales in some of its key market segments were much lower than industry growth rates. In three of its market segments, the sales growth was 6 percent, 4 percent, and 4 percent, respectively, whereas the industry growth rates for the same segments were 11 percent, 7 percent, and 6 percent, respectively.

> Though the findings represented are correct, it is impossible to discern what the results imply. These figures could have been presented in a table format, as shown in Table 18.1, with greater clarity.

Besides using tables to present data, the report could also employ pie charts or bar charts, with similar results. A pie chart is just a circle divided into sections, and each section represents the percentage of the total area of the circle associated with one variable. A section may often represent a row in a table. For the data discussed above, the researcher could have used a pie chart as shown in Figure 18.1.

The same information could have been presented as a bar chart instead of a pie chart. A bar chart is constructed by placing rectangles (bars) over each value of the variable. Each bar often represents a row in a table or a section in a pie chart. Figure 18.2 is the same information that was presented previously in a table format (Table 18.1) and a pie chart (Figure 18.1) ("A Series of Pie Charts," 1992).

Data can also be presented in other formats besides the pie and bar charts, including a three-dimensional bar chart, as shown in Figure 18.3.

ORAL REPORT

At the end of most research projects, the client or user of the research expects an oral presentation. The oral presentation is an opportunity for the researcher to clarify issues and focus the attention of the client on the key findings of the research. It also provides an opportunity for the client to ask questions and understand the results. In some cases, a client may simply recall the important findings based on the oral presentation. To make an oral presentation effective, the researcher has to customize it to suit the audience.

The oral presentation should demonstrate to the audience that the presenter has total grasp of the research project and is qualified and knowledgeable. Effective presentation implies that all the ideas that the presenter wants to convey have been strongly conveyed. The three critical elements of an oral presentation are:

- Drawing the *attention* and interest of each member of the audience without losing sight of the value of the results.
- Making the presentation *meaningful* to the audience.
- Giving a presentation that enables the audience to *recall* the key findings.

Figure 18.1 **Company vs. Industry Growth: Pie Chart**

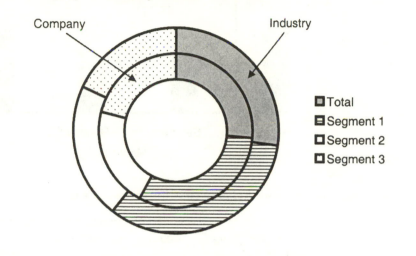

☐Total
⊟Segment 1
☐Segment 2
☐Segment 3

Table 18.1 **Sales Growth Comparisons: Company vs. Industry, 2003**

By Market	Company (%)	Industry (%)
Total	5	9
Segment 1	6	11
Segment 2	4	7
Segment 3	4	6

GUIDELINES FOR A SUCCESSFUL ORAL PRESENTATION

- *Focus the presentation on the needs of the audience.* The presentation should enumerate the objectives of the study and explain how the research results help in addressing the project objectives.
- *Make an outline of the presentation.* In preparing an oral presentation, develop an outline that helps the flow of the presentation. The most commonly used outline for an oral presentation includes an introduction, a description of the methodology used, an explanation of the basic analytical techniques used, a comprehensive discussion of the results, and finally general recommendations that are based on the results of the study.
- *Rehearse the presentation.* In most cases, oral presentations are limited to a predetermined time factor (60 to 90 minutes). It is important that the presenter not run out of time, and is able to present the key findings. Therefore, it always

Figure 18.2 **Company vs. Industry Growth: Bar Graph**

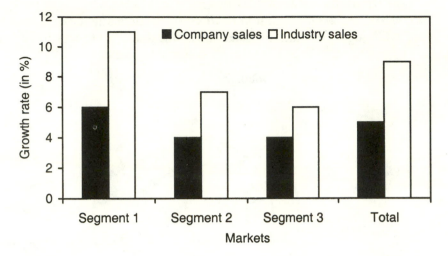

Figure 18.3 **Company vs. Industry Growth: Three-Dimensional Bar Graph**

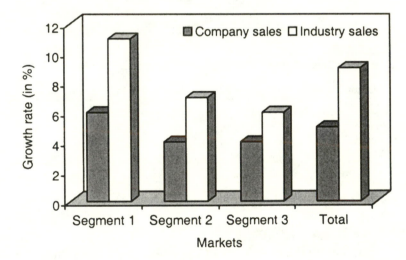

good to rehearse the script to ensure that the key findings are presented slowly and clearly.

• *Keep the audience's attention and interest.* It is important to maintain the audience's attention. Some suggestions to achieve this include making eye contact with the audience, speaking clearly so that everyone in the audience can follow the presentation, modulating the voice to make the presentation less monotonous, emphasizing key points, repeating findings that the client or user should recall, and always being ready to answer questions, even during the presentation.

- *Use audiovisuals.* Modern-day computer technology allows researchers to prepare very elaborate presentations. Audiovisual presentations increase the chances of maintaining the audience's attention. In addition, audiovisual presentations increase the audience's rate of recall of the key findings and other aspects of the research report. Audiovisual aids include charts, graphs, transparencies, slides, videos, and PowerPoint presentations. The primary purpose of an audiovisual aid is to complement and enhance a presentation. It is not a substitute for the presenter or for the presentation itself.

Audiovisuals are used to clarify and highlight the data or the findings of the study. As previously mentioned, these aids help the audience recall the key findings. The essential goals of the audiovisual presentations are to

- Create an interest in the results
- Focus the audience's attention
- Involve the audience
- Inject enthusiasm and
- Make the presentation flow smoothly

To achieve the above goals, audiovisual presentations should be creative, colorful, and demonstrative. It is critical that the presenter select key points that will benefit from audiovisual presentation (show important tables, charts, and graphs to make a point). By integrating the audiovisual presentation with the oral presentation, the presenter will achieve the complementary benefit of the technique and have room for explanations and clarifications. Modern technology provides presenters with an opportunity to make an oral presentation effective, efficient, and interesting. Use of PowerPoint and other presentation techniques can enhance the overall effectiveness of the presentation. In PowerPoint presentation, use of animation improves the presentation. Choose colors with sufficient contrast so that the text can be read easily. At the same time, the technical sophistication (too many bells and whistles) should not be distracting. The focus should always be the results and not the technical complexity of the presentation. Stay away from fussy backgrounds, distracting slide transitions, flying words, and funny noises. Other visual aids such as posters, charts, samples, displays, and handouts can be helpful. These aids also help relieve the potential monotony of the oral presentation.

- *Wrap up.* Gradually wind down the presentation. The transition from the key points to the end of the presentation should be smooth. As you conclude, briefly review the major findings that are of interest to your audience. Finish the presentation; don't just stop.
- *Questions and answers* (Q & A). It is important that time be made for questions from the audience. This is an excellent way to clarify points, draw the attention of the audience to key findings, and test the audience's understanding of the research findings. If there are no questions from the audience, it is likely that the presenter has not been able to convey the key points and hence may have lost

the audience's attention. (It should not be construed that the presentation was so good that all understood the key elements of the presentation.) The overall purpose of the oral presentation is to persuade or impress upon the user that the research study was able to uncover a few salient issues that were not previously known.

STORAGE AND RETRIEVAL OF RESEARCH REPORTS

Since a completed primary study is an excellent source of information for future research, it should be stored for easy access. As costs of conducting international research keep rising and as this research takes much longer time to complete, internal secondary sources such as past studies help the researcher in his or her efforts to collect information. For example, a study on plant location in Germany might prove useful when weighing a similar decision in France. If the earlier studies are not totally adaptable to the new situation, at least portions might be of help in designing the research for the current problem.

International firms often use past research studies to build longitudinal data sets that are very useful in identifying issues, tracking trends, and pinpointing areas for future research. For example, a study done on the use of cellular phones in Japan in the late 1980s, if compared to a similar study done in the mid-1990s, might reveal interesting data to telecommunications companies regarding consumer concentration, brand preferences, usage patterns, and the like.

The three most critical considerations in data storage are *ease of data retrieval, confidentiality,* and *safety.* A principal goal of information storage is fast data retrieval. Research reports stored on computer disks or tapes are easy to access. In countries where this option is not feasible, storing data on microfilm or microfiche or in files may be the only option available.

Computer storage requires that a good directory (cross-referenced by project name, country, or date) be maintained to speed (*ease*) the retrieval process. Computer storage requires the least amount of space and at the same time is the fastest for retrieving data. Computer systems are expensive, though, and may not be available in many countries.

The second consideration in storing research data is *confidentiality.* Industrial espionage is rampant, and research reports provide valuable information to competitors. For example, if a competitor was able to acquire the plans for the introduction of a new product, it may introduce a version of the product earlier and negate the efforts of the company whose research was stolen. Therefore, safeguards in storage of previous research studies should be developed so that only a few key decision makers can access the information.

The third factor in storage is *safety.* Safety refers to the possibility of loss of stored data through damage. Damage to file folders, films, or computer disks are all concerns of researchers in storing data. Many firms have backup disks created to avoid problems of loss or damage. Storage of data is part of the research process and should not be treated lightly.

CHAPTER SUMMARY

Reports are the culmination of a research project, and it is important that the results be presented to the decision makers in an easily readable manner. Most research findings are presented in both an oral form as well as a written format. The oral report helps the researchers to communicate the most critical findings to an audience and allows the decision makers to clarify issues. In an oral presentation, it is important that the presenter maintain the interest of the audience and draw their attention to the critical findings. Audiovisual aids help oral presentations in highlighting the basic findings.

The written report provides the details and becomes a permanent record that may be used in the future. The written report should be customized to meet the recipient's needs. Most research reports follow a specific format that includes an executive summary, introduction and background, description of methodology, results and findings, conclusion and recommendations, and limitations of the study.

The executive summary should be carefully developed and should include most of the key findings. In many instances, a busy executive may have the time to read only the executive summary and use it to understand the most relevant aspects of the study.

Tables, charts, and graphs should be used to present numerical data. These graphic aids are able to present a large amount of data in a concise manner. In addition, tables and charts are able to show relationships between variables.

CHAPTER REVIEW

1. Why is oral presentation important?
2. What are some of the key factors in oral presentations?
3. What are some of the techniques that are useful in presenting tables and charts?
4. Enumerate some of the techniques to maintain audience attention.
5. How can technology be incorporated into an oral presentation?
6. Discuss the outline of a written report.
7. Explain some of the key components of a written report.
8. Elaborate on some of the techniques used to make a written report readable.
9. How should tables, charts, and graphs be presented in a written report?
10. What are the three critical aspects in storing research studies?

ADDITIONAL READING

BOOKS

Arredinido, Lani. *The McGraw-Hill 36-Hour Course: Business Presentations.* New York: McGraw-Hill Publishers, 1993.

Leech, Thomas. *How to Prepare, Stage, and Deliver Winning Presentations.* 3rd ed. New York: American Management Association, 2004.

Lewis, Philip V., and William H. Baker. *Business Report Writing.* Columbus, OH: Grid, 1978.

ARTICLES

"A Series of Pie Charts" (1992) *Advertising Age International* (April 27), pp. 1–26.

Jaffe, Greg (2000) "What Is Your Point, Lieutenant? Please, Just Cut to the Pie Charts." *Wall Street Journal,* April 26, p. 1.

Low, George, S. and Jakki J.Mohr (2001) "Factors Affecting the Use of Information in the Evaluation of Marketing Communications Productivity." *Academy of Marketing Science Journal* 29 (1), pp. 70–88.

Leach, John (1993) "Seven Steps to Better Writing." *Planning* 59 (6), pp. 26–27.

Moody, Janet (2002) "Showing the Skilled Business Graduate: Expanding the Tool Kit." *Business Communication Quarterly* 65 (1), pp. 21–36.

Appendix A. Questionnaires

Note: The data set for A1. Detergent Questionnaire can be found at www.mesharpe.com. Search by author name (Neelankavil) and there will be a link to the data set.

A1. DETERGENT QUESTIONNAIRE

Hello, my name is _____ from the Institute of Research Inc., an independent market research firm. We are conducting a survey of household cleansing products in your area and would like to include your views. This survey will take about 15 minutes.

PART 1

1. Are you the one who decides on the brand of detergents to be purchased in your home?

___	Yes	5-1
___	No	5-2

   (If no, ask to speak to the person most responsible for making decisions on household items. If no one is available, thank the respondent and terminate the interview.)

2. Who does the washing of clothes in your home?

___	Self	6-1
___	Spouse	6-2
___	Other—Children (specify):	6-3
	_____	6-4

3. How often do you wash clothes in your home?

___	Every day	7-1
___	Two to three times a week	7-2
___	Once a week	7-3
___	Once in two weeks	7-4
___	Other (specify):	7-5
	_____	

4a. Do you own a washing machine?

    ___ Yes   8-1

    ___ No   8-2

4b. If you do not own a washing machine, how do you do your laundry?

    ___ Laundromat   9-1

    ___ Laundry services   9-2

    ___ Washboard   9-3

    ___ Other (specify):   9-4

_____

5. Do you use detergents to wash your clothes?

    ___ Yes   10-1

    ___ No (Go to Question 10)   10-2

6. What brand of detergent do you most often buy?

    ___ Ariel   11-1

    ___ Persil   11-2

    ___ Omo   11-3

    ___ Dash/Duz   11-4

    ___ Other (specify):   11-5

_____

7a. Besides the brand mentioned above, do you buy any other brands?

    ___ Yes   12-1

    ___ No   12-2

7b. If yes, what are the names of the other brands you use?

    ___ Ariel   13-1

    ___ Persil   13-2

    ___ Omo   13-3

    ___ Dash/Duz   13-4

    ___ Skip   13-5

8. What is the size (in weight) of the detergent box/container you usually buy?

    ___ 500 g   14-1

    ___ 750 g   14-2

    ___ 1 kg   14-3

    ___ 2 kg   14-4

9. Besides using a detergent, do you also use any other cleaning agents to wash your clothes?

    ___ Bleach   15-1

    ___ Fabric softeners   15-2

    ___ Other (specify):   15-3

_____ 15-4

10. If you do not use detergents, what other product(s) do you use to wash clothes?

___ Soap 16-1
___ Home products 16-2

PART 2

Following are some statements that pertain to washing clothes. For each statement, indicate whether you fully agree with the statement or fully disagree with the statement.

	Statements	Fully Agree	Agree	Neutral	Disagree	Fully Disagree
1	Existing detergents/products that are available for washing clothes are reasonably good.	1	2	3	4	5 17-1,2,3,4,5
2	The brand of detergent I buy should have a bleaching agent in it.	1	2	3	4	5 18-1,2,3,4,5
3	Most detergents in the market are environmentally unsafe.	1	2	3	4	5 19-1,2,3,4,5
4	Existing brands of detergents come in convenient packages.	1	2	3	4	5 20-1,2,3,4,5
5	I wish the detergents in the market were not caustic.	1	2	3	4	5 21-1,2,3,4,5
6	I would like to see a more concentrated brand of detergent in the market.	1	2	3	4	5 22-1,2,3,4,5
7	Current detergent brands in the market are undistinguishable.	1	2	3	4	5 23-1,2,3,4,5
8	Price is critical in my selection of a detergent brand.	1	2	3	4	5 24-1,2,3,4,5
9	I rely on information provided by friends and relatives in selecting a detergent brand.	1	2	3	4	5 25-1,2,3,4,5
10	It is really messy to measure and get the required amount of detergent for each load from the existing packages.	1	2	3	4	5 26-1,2,3,4,5

PART 3

Scientists of a detergent company have developed a highly concentrated detergent powder that has the following benefits when compared to existing brands of detergents:

a. It requires only 1 tablespoon of detergent per normal wash load.
b. It is less caustic.
c. The package has a dispenser that automatically dispenses the necessary amount of detergent.
d. The package size for a normal 40-load wash weighs only 1 kilogram.

12. If a brand such as the one described above were now available, would you be interested in buying such a product?

___	Yes	27-1
___	No	27-2
___	Do not know	27-3

(If the answer to Question 12 is "No" or "Do not know," go to Question 19.)

13. Setting aside the question of price for the moment, which of the following statements best describes how interested you would be in this new product? Would you:

___	Definitely be interested in it	28-1
___	Probably be interested in it	28-2
___	Possibly be interested in it	28-3

14. Assuming that you will buy the new detergent and that the volume you buy will give you the same number of loads as your current brand, would you buy it if it were priced at 8.00 euros?

___	Yes	29-1
___	No	29-2
___	Do not know	29-3

15. Supposing the new detergent was priced at 7.00 euros, would you buy it?

___	Yes	30-1
___	No	30-2
___	Do not know	30-3

16. Supposing the new detergent was priced at 9.00 euros, would you buy it?

___	Yes	31-1
___	No	31-2
___	Do not know	31-3

17. Now supposing the new detergent was priced at 12.00 euros, would you buy it?

___	Yes	32-1
___	No	32-2
___	Do not know	32-3

18. Supposing the new detergent product was available in stores today, please tell me which statement best describes how soon you would most likely buy the product. Would you buy it

____	Within the next few days	33-1
____	Within the next few weeks	33-2
____	Within the next few months	33-3
____	Not in the foreseeable future	33-4

PART 4

Finally, I would like to ask a few questions that are used for classification purposes only. No one will see your individual responses.

19. What is your marital status?

____	Married	34-1
____	Single	34-2

20. Including you, how many people live in your house?

____	2	35-1
____	3–4	35-2
____	5 or more	35-3

21. What is your occupation?

____	Homemaker	36-1
____	Office worker	36-2
____	Factory worker	36-3
____	Professional	36-4

22. Please tell me which category best describes your age.

____	21–35	37-1
____	36–50	37-2
____	51–65	37-3
____	66 or older	37-4

23. How many years of formal schooling do you have?

____	Less than 13 years	38-1
____	13 years	38-2
____	More than 13 years	38-3

24. Finally, which of the following groups best describes your total family income?

____	Under 20,000 euros	39-1
____	20,001–35,000 euros	39-2
____	35,001–50,000 euros	39-3
____	50,001–75,000 euros	39-4
____	Over 75,001 euros	39-5

Thank you very much for your time.

A2. Managerial Questionnaire (in English)

You have been selected to be a participant in a large-scale global study of the managerial decision-making process. Specifically, this research attempts to gather information critical in managing a modern-day business.

The attached questionnaire has two (2) parts: Part 1, Managerial Profile; and Part 2, Performance Factors. Please read the instructions that precede each section carefully. The survey should take approximately 15 minutes. Your responses will be held in complete confidence. The personal data requested is for statistical purposes only.

Thank you very much for your cooperation.

Part 1. Managerial Profile

Select the answer that most accurately describes your current personal situation. Please answer all questions. If an exact response is not possible, please use your best estimate.

Personal Data

1. Are you: ___ Male
   ___ Female
2. Are you: ___ Single
   ___ Married
   ___ Widowed/Divorced
3. What is your age? ___

Present Job Data

4. Present job title: _____
5. Present Functional Responsibility (check one)

   ___ Data Processing/Computer Science
   ___ Engineering/Technology
   ___ Finance/Accounting
   ___ Marketing/Sales
   ___ Personnel/Human Relations
   ___ Production
   ___ Research
   ___ Maintenance
   ___ Other (Specify): _____

6. Average number of hours per week spent on job: ____
7. Number of direct subordinates you supervise: ____
8. The title of executive you report to (direct supervisor): _____
9. Time on present job: ____ years   ____ months
10. Time with present company: ____ years   ____ months
11. General rating of current job satisfaction level (check one)

    ___ Very satisfied
    ___ Satisfied

___ Neither satisfied nor dissatisfied
___ Somewhat dissatisfied
___ Very dissatisfied

12. General rating of job pressure (check one)

___ Very high pressure
___ High pressure
___ Medium pressure
___ Low pressure
___ No pressure

Education

13. Number of years of formal schooling (including elementary and high school):
_____

14. Major course of study in college (e.g., accounting, engineering): _____
____

Firm

15. Name of your firm: _____
16. Major business of your firm (e.g., banking, computers, manufacturing of machinery): _____
17. Location of your office (e.g., Town: London, Country: UK):
Town: _____ Country: _____

PART 2. PERFORMANCE FACTORS

In this section you will find a list of brief statements that describe either ability, an approach to the job, or a personal characteristic. Using a five-point rating scale, where 1 = low, or far below average, and 5 = high, or far above average, evaluate these statements in terms of *level of importance*.

Scale: 1 = not at all important
2 = not very important
3 = somewhat important
4 = very important
5 = extremely important

Statement of ability/approach/characteristic:	Level of Importance				
	Not at all important				Extremely important
1. The ability to lead a group to accomplish a task without arousing hostility	1	2	3	4	5
2. The ability to modify your approach or behavior tendencies in order to reach a goal	1	2	3	4	5

3. Getting the endorsement of your boss before implementing your ideas	1	2	3	4	5
4. Getting the endorsement of your peers and subordinates before implementing your ideas	1	2	3	4	5
5. Recognizing your own strengths and weaknesses	1	2	3	4	5
6. Always keeping in mind that it is more important to please superiors than subordinates	1	2	3	4	5
7. Dealing with others with complete honesty and integrity	1	2	3	4	5
8. Doing high-quality work even when a lesser quality would be acceptable	1	2	3	4	5
9. The ability to effectively present an oral report to a conference group	1	2	3	4	5
10. The ability to effectively express your ideas in writing	1	2	3	4	5
11. Making an impact on others upon first encounter	1	2	3	4	5
12. Perceiving subtle cues in the behavior of others toward you	1	2	3	4	5
13. Maintaining a continuously high level of work activity	1	2	3	4	5
14. Maintaining performance stability under pressure or stressful situations	1	2	3	4	5
15. The ability to learn new things	1	2	3	4	5
16. The ability to effectively organize the work effort	1	2	3	4	5
17. The ability to effectively plan and follow through on those plans	1	2	3	4	5
18. Consistently making decisions in a timely manner	1	2	3	4	5
19. The ability to sort out all the relevant facts related to a problem or situation	1	2	3	4	5
20. The ability to solve problems effectively	1	2	3	4	5
21. The reputation of the college or university where degree was obtained	1	2	3	4	5
22. Level of formal educational achievement in terms of degrees and grades	1	2	3	4	5
23. Degree of experience, either on-the-job or in related jobs or fields	1	2	3	4	5
24. A track record of favorable results on previous assignments	1	2	3	4	5
25. The ability to get along with others	1	2	3	4	5
26. Maintaining a positive attitude toward the job	1	2	3	4	5
27. Having an optimistic outlook on life	1	2	3	4	5
28. Quality and amount of specific job-related training other than formal education	1	2	3	4	5
29. Having an attractive personal appearance	1	2	3	4	5
30. The ability to work independently to produce an output	1	2	3	4	5
31. The tendency to initiate action without prompting from others	1	2	3	4	5
32. Compassion for others	1	2	3	4	5
33. Corporate political know-how	1	2	3	4	5
34. Intimate knowledge of company operations	1	2	3	4	5

35. Always maintaining a bottom-line orientation	1	2	3	4	5
36. Degree of self-confidence	1	2	3	4	5
37. Attracting loyalty from people in higher-level management positions	1	2	3	4	5
38. Level of charisma	1	2	3	4	5
39. Level of self-esteem	1	2	3	4	5
40. Level of self-confidence	1	2	3	4	5

A3. MANAGERIAL QUESTIONNAIRE (IN GERMAN)

Si wurdenausgewählt um an einer umfassenden globalan studie über Enstscheidungsprozesse auf Führungsebenen teilzunehmen. Insbesonder versucht diese untersuchung, Informationen über Brennpunkte in der Führung eines mordenes unternehmens zusammenzutragen.

Der anhängende Fragebogen enhält zwei (2) Abschmitte: Teil 1, Persönlichkeitsprofil; Teil 2, Leistungsfaktoren. Bitte lessen Sie die vorangentallten Erläuterungen zu den einzelnen Sektionen. Die umfrage nimmt etwa 30 minuten in anspruch. Ihre Antworten warden absolute vertraultich behandelt. Die vielen dank für statistische Zwecke Verwendet.

Vielen Dank für Ihre Zussammenarbeit.

TEIL 1. PERSÖNLICHKEITSPROFIL

Wählen sie die Antwort, die Ihre gegenwärtige Situation am deutlichsten beschribt. Bitte beantworten Sie alle Fragen. Wenn eine exakte Antworrt nicht möglich ist, geben Sie das naheliegende an.

Persönchliche Daten

1. Sie sind: ___ Mann
   ___ Frau
2. Sie sind: ___ ledig
   ___ verheiratet
   ___ Verwitwet/geschieden
3. Wie alt sind Sie? ___

Aktuelle berufliche Daten

4. Gegenwärtige Berufsbezeichnung: _____
5. Derzerige function (nur ein kreuz)

   ___ Datenverarbeitung/ Informatik
   ___ Ingenieurwesen/ Technik
   ___ Fiananzen/Buchhaltung
   ___ Marketing/Verkauf
   ___ Personal/ Personalwesen
   ___ Produktion
   ___ Forshung
   ___ Insandhaltung
   ___ Andere (bitte angeben): _____

6. Durchschnittliche Wochenarbeitszeit: ____
7. Anzahl der direkten Untergebnen: ____
8. Berufsbezeichnung Ihres direkten vorgestzten: _____
9. Wie lange üben Sie Ihre derzeitige funktion aus? ____ Jahre ____ Monate
10. Wie lange sind sie ihrer jetzigen Firma Beschäftigt? ____ Jahre ____ Monate
11. Allgemeine Einschäzung bezüglich des Zufriedenheitsgrades in der derzeitigen Tätigkeit (ein Kreuz)

    ____ Sehr befreidgend
    ____ befreidgend
    ____ weder befreidgend noch unbefreidgend
    ____ etwas unbefreidgend
    ____ Sehr unbefreidgend

12. Allgemeine Einschätzung der Arbeitsbelastung (ein Kreuz)

    ____ Sehr hohe Belastung
    ____ hohe Belastung
    ____ mittlere Belastung
    ____ niedrige Belastung
    ____ keine Belastung

Ausbildung

13. Anzahl der Jahre in allgemeinbildendem Schulwesen (einscheileßlich Grundschule): _____
14. Hausptstudiengang an eiiner Hochshule (z.B. Wirtschaftslehre, Ingenieurwesen): _____

Betrieb

15. Name der Firma: _____
16. Hauptaufgabe Ihrer Firma (z.B. Bank, Computer, Maschinenbau):

    _____

17. Standort Ires Büros (z.B. Stadt: London, Land: UK):
    Stadt: _____ Land: _____

TEIL II. LEISTUNGSFAKTOREN

In diesem abschnitt finden Sie eine Auflistung kurzer Aussagen, die entweder eine Fähigkeit, ein Heran gehen an dir Tätigkeit oder eine persönliche Charakteristik beschreiben Stufen Sie diese Aussagen unter Anwendung einer fünfustufigen Wertungsskala ein, wobei Stufe 1 = niedrig oder sehr niedrig und 5 = hoch oder weit ü berdurchshnittlich bedeutet.

Skala: 1 = unwichtig
        2 = nicht sehr wichtig
        3 = etwas wichtig
        4 = sehr wichtig
        5 = außerordentlich wichtig

Wertungsskala

Aussage zu Fähigkeit/Angehensweise/Charakteristik:	Absolut extrem				Unwichtig unwichtig
1. Die Fähigkeit eine Gruppe so zu leiten, daß bei Erledigung einer Aufgabe Keine Feindseligkeiten enstehen	1	2	3	4	5
2. Die Fähigkeit Ihre Vorgehensweise oder Ihre Verhaltensweisen zuänderm, um ein Zeil zu erreichen	1	2	3	4	5
3. Die Zustimmung von Vorgesetzten einholen, bevor Sie eigene Ideen durchführen.	1	2	3	4	5
4. Die Zustimmung von kollegen and Unterrgebenen eicholen, Sie eigene ideen durchführen	1	2	3	4	5
5. Eigene Stärken und schwächen anerkennen	1	2	3	4	5
6. Immer daran denken, daß es wichtiger ist, dem Vorgestzten zu gefallen, als den Untergebenen.	1	2	3	4	5
7. Aufrichtigkeit und integritäit beim Umgang mit anderen	1	2	3	4	5
8. Qualitativ hochwertige Arbeit leisten, Wenn geringere Qualität ausreichend Wäre	1	2	3	4	5
9. Einer Konferenz effectiv einen mündlichen Bericht geben.	1	2	3	4	5
10. Die Fähigkeit, Ihre Ideen effectiv in schriftlicher Form ausudrücken.	1	2	3	4	5
11. Auf Anheib bei anderen einen starken Eindruck hinterlasssen	1	2	3	4	5
12. In dem Verhalten anderer Ihnen gegenüber subtile Fingerzeige wahrnehmen	1	2	3	4	5
13. Einen durchängig hohen Grad der Arbeitsintensität aufrechterhalten	1	2	3	4	5
14. Leistungsstabilität unter Druck und in Streßsituationen aufrechterhalten	1	2	3	4	5
15. Die Fähigkeit, neue Dinge zu Lernen	1	2	3	4	5
16. Die Fähigkeit, Arbeitsabläufe effectiv zu organisieren.	1	2	3	4	5
17. Die Fähigkeit jene Arbeitsabläufe effectiv zu planen und durchzuführen	1	2	3	4	5
18. Folgerichtige Entscheidungen agemessener Zeit zu treffen	1	2	3	4	5
19. Die Fähigkeit alle relevanten Faktoren, die ein problem oder eine Situation betreffen, herauszufilterm.	1	2	3	4	5
20. Die Fähigkeit Probleme effectiv zu loosen	1	2	3	4	5
21. Die Reputation einer Hochschule oder Universität von der der Titel erhalten wurde.	1	2	3	4	5
22. Höhe der in der formellen schulischen Bildung erzielten Titel und Grade	1	2	3	4	5
23. Grad der Erahrungen, entweder am derzeitigen Arbeitsplatz oder in verwandten Bereichen.	1	2	3	4	5
24. Ein schriftlicher Erfolgsnachweis vorteilhafter Leistungen bei vorangegangenen Anstellungen	1	2	3	4	5
25. Die Fähigkeit mit anderen gut auszukommen	1	2	3	4	5
26. Eine positive Eintellung zum Arbeitsplatz beibehalten.	1	2	3	4	5
27. Eine optimistsche Lebenseinstellung haben	1	2	3	4	5

28. Qualität Und Umfang Der speziellen Beruflichen Ausbildung, im Gegensatz Zu formellen Ausbildung	1	2	3	4	5
29. Ein attraktives persönliches Erscheinen zu haben	1	2	3	4	5
30. Die Fähigkeit, selbständig zu arbeiten und ein Ergebnis zu erzielen	1	2	3	4	5
31. Die Tendenz Prozesse zu initiieren, ohne von andered dazu angeregt worden zu sein	1	2	3	4	5
32. Mitleid für andere	1	2	3	4	5
33. Kenntnisse über interne Firmenpolitik	1	2	3	4	5
34. Vertrauliche Kenntnisse über Firmentätigkeiten besitzen	1	2	3	4	5
35. Immer eine profitorientierung beibehalten	1	2	3	4	5
36. Grad des selbstvertrauens	1	2	3	4	5
37. Die Loyalität von Leuten in höheren Managementpositionen auf sich lenken	1	2	3	4	5
38. Niveau des Charismas	1	2	3	4	5
39. Niveau des Selbstachtung	1	2	3	4	5
40. Niveau des Selbstvertrauens	1	2	3	4	5

Appendix B
Selected Secondary Sources

Most of the reports listed here are updated periodically by the publishers.

DATA FOR ASIAN-PACIFIC COUNTRIES

Asia-Pacific. Database covering the business, economics, and new industries of the Pacific Rim nations. (Aristarchus Knowledge Industries/Dialog Information Services, Inc., 1989)

Asian Data Disk. Comprehensive library of published demographic and economic data on 14 Asian countries from 1970 to 1994. (Asia Studies Ltd.)

Asian Wall Street Journal. Periodical covering subjects specific to Asian countries and international affairs. (*Wall Street Journal*)

Business Asia. Periodical covering subjects specific to Asian countries and international affairs. (NA)

China Statistical Yearbook. Annual that presents a broad range of statistical material for the People's Republic of China. (International Centre for the Advancement of Science and Technology China Statistical Information and Consultancy Service Centre, Hong Kong, 1988)

Consumer Asia. Regional handbook containing data including country-by-country statistical analysis of Asian countries. (Chicago, IL: Euromonitor International Inc., 1995)

Consumer China. Regional handbook that provides comprehensive statistical coverage of China's consumer markets with background data on business, economic, and social conditions. (Chicago, IL: Euromonitor International Inc., 1994)

Consumer Japan. Regional handbook that provides information including expert analysis of key trends and developments needed to compete effectively in Japan. (Chicago, IL: Euromonitor International Inc., 1993)

Economic and Social Survey of Asia and the Pacific. Publication presenting an overview of recent economic and social developments of concern to developing countries in the Asia/Pacific region. (Bangkok: Economic and Social Commission for Asia and the Pacific, 1974)

Far Eastern Economic Review. Periodical covering economic topics pertaining to countries in the Far East. (Hong Kong: E.E. Halpern)

International Historical Statistics: Africa and Asia. Information on climate, population, labor force, agriculture, education, trade, and boundary and currency changes. (New York: New York University Press, 1982)

Japan Economic Journal. Periodical covering economic topics specific to Japan and international affairs. (Tokyo: Japan Economic Journal)

Japan Statistical Yearbook. Annual that presents statistics specific to Japan, including population, climate, transportation, health, prices, and public finance. (Sorifu, Tokeikyoku, Tokoyo)

Japan Technology. Database containing abstracts of articles from the leading Japanese business, technical, and scientific journals. (SCAN C2C/Dialog Information Services, Inc., 1991)

Korea Statistical Yearbook. Annual that presents statistics specific to Korea, including population, wages, climate, health, foreign trade, retail trade, and manufacturing. (Seoul: Ky ongje Kihoegw on, 1961)

Retailing in China. Report on China's retailing structure and markets covering all aspects of this sector, including information on consumers, retail outlets, retail sales trends, and Chinese households. (Chicago, IL: Euromonitor International Inc.)

Retailing in South East Asia. Publication that provides expert market analysis and statistical data, focusing on relevant marketing parameters. (Chicago, IL: Euromonitor International Inc.)

The China Investment Guide. Publication that provides a general survey of the People's Republic of China as well as regional and industrial sector profiles. (New York: Longman, 1984)

Tokyo Business Today. Periodical covering general relevant business topics pertaining to Tokyo. (Tokyo, Japan: Toko Keizai Shinposha)

Travel and Tourism in South East Asia. Publication focusing on the region's markets and industry for the travel and tourism sector. (Chicago, IL: Euromonitor International Inc.)

Who Owns Whom: Australia and Far East. Section 1 lists parent companies alphabetically, section 2 lists parent companies registered outside with subsidiaries or associates in that area, and section 3 lists alphabetically parent companies, affiliates, and subsidiaries. (Skokie, IL: National Register Publication Co.)

DATA FOR DEVELOPING COUNTRIES

Economic and Social Survey of Asia and the Pacific. Publication that presents an overview of recent economic and social developments of concern to developing countries in the Asia/Pacific region. (Bangkok: Economic and Social Commission for Asia and the Pacific, 1974)

World Development Report. A World Bank publication that contains a discussion of key trends in the world economy and provides selected social and economic indicators for more than 100 countries. (New York: Oxford University Press)

DATA FOR EUROPEAN COUNTRIES

The Arthur Anderson European Community Sourcebook. Publication that provides information about the Signal Market Program of 1992 and its effect on business. (NA)

Business Europe. Periodical covering topics relevant to business in Europe and its international affairs. (NA)

Commission of the European Communities. Lists all magazines, parliamentary reports, and information bulletins the EC library has received from international organizations. (NA)

Consumer Europe. Publication that contains statistical information on consumer trends in Western Europe (Chicago, IL: Euromonitor International Inc., 1994)

Euromoney. Publication that focuses on the European money market, with statistics on eurodollar rates, interest rates, and exchange rates. (London: Euromoney Publications Ltd.)

Europa Yearbook. Annual that contains information on international organizations such as the UN, the OECD, and OPEC, with an alphabetical survey of countries. (London: Europa Publications)

European Business and Industry. Publication that contains biographies of top managers in international trade, business, and industry, and a survey of European business and industry and company profiles. (Hersching: Who's Who Edition, 1985)

The European Communities Encyclopedia and Directory. Guide to the European Communities that includes a chronology of the EC and a summary of treaties. (London: Europa Publications)

The European Development Directory. Guide to the maze of financial aid and business grants available in 27 European countries. (Chicago, IL: Euromonitor International Inc.)

European Directory of Medium Sized Companies. Book that provides detailed profiles of the 4,000 next largest companies across Eastern and Western Europe, including details such as company activity, ownership, subsidiaries, main products and brands, profit, sales, and recent company developments. (Chicago, IL: Euromonitor International Inc.)

European Historical Statistics (1750–1975). Historical statistics of various countries taken from official publications including population, labor force, external trade, and prices. (New York: Facts on File, 1981)

The European Legislation Handbook. Handbook guide to EC and national European business legislation emphasizing international business law. (NA)

European Marketing Data and Statistics. Reference book containing an updated edition of Euromonitor's statistical yearbook. (London: Euromonitor Publications, 1962)

European Marketing Information Database. Database containing more than 100,000 pieces of market data organized into clear, segmented sections. (Chicago, IL: Euromonitor International Inc.)

A Guide to European Financial Centres. Publication that provides information on 17 Western European countries with significant financial centers, with each country study containing information on laws, regulations, recent history, and financial markets (Chicago: St. James Press, 1990)

Market Research Europe. User receives six reports each month covering European food markets, European nonfood markets, secondary markets, and special market reports for France, Germany, Italy, Spain, Scandinavia, and Benelux. (Chicago, IL: Euromonitor International Inc.)

Statistics Europe: Sources for Social, Economic and Market Research. Arranged alphabetically by country, publication that includes name, address, and telephone number of each country's central statistical office and bibliography of statistical publications including production, external trade, and finance. (Detroit, MI: Gale Research)

Western Europe: A Political and Economic Survey. Publication that provides information on all countries in the European Communities and the European Free Trade Association as well as Cyprus, Malta, and Turkey, including information on macroeconomy, industry, agriculture, socioeconomic trends, tourism, transport, politics, and media. (NA)

Who Owns Whom: Continental Europe. Publication that lists parent companies by company name and those registered outside continental Europe with subsidiaries or associates in that area. (Skokie, IL: National Register Publishing Co.)

DATA FOR LATIN AMERICAN COUNTRIES

Business Latin America. Periodical covering topics relevant to business in or with Latin American countries. (NA)

Consumer Latin America. (1993) Euromonitor's guide to consumer markets, providing statistical and analytical information on Latin American countries, bringing together relevant information required for accessing growth areas and developing business potential. (Chicago, IL: Euromonitor International Inc.)

Dun's Latin America's Top 25,000. Publication that contains information on enterprises in 35 countries, including company sales, number of employees, location, and standard industrial classification (SIC). (Bethlehem, PA: Dun & Bradstreet Information Services, 1995)

Economic Survey of Latin America and the Caribbean. Publication that presents a discussion, supplemented with graphs and statistics, on a variety of topics including foreign trade, debt, inflation, investments, employment, and wages. (Santiago, Chile: United Nations, 1984)

Latin America: A Directory and Sourcebook. Publication that provides extensive details on more than 1,000 of Latin America's major companies, country-by-country listings of vital marketing information sources, and expert analysis of all the major trends and developments shaping the market. (Chicago, IL: Euromonitor International Inc.)

Retailing in Latin America. Publication containing a regional overview, with each country containing major economic indicators, retail sales developments, leading retail companies, and future outlook. (Chicago, IL: Euromonitor International Inc.)

Statistical Abstract of Latin America. Reference publication that gives socioeconomic and political characteristics of 24 independent nations in Latin America. (Los Angeles: University of California, Los Angeles)

Travel and Tourism in Latin America. Guide that provides an introduction to the travel and tourism industry and that contains information on major economic indicators, tourism infrastructure, domestic tourism, and the future. (Chicago, IL: Euromonitor International Inc.)

INTERNATIONAL DATA (GENERAL)

America's Corporate Families and International Affiliates. Resource that provides information on U.S. family members of foreign ultimate parent companies and foreign subsidiaries of U.S. ultimate parent companies. (Duns Marketing Services, 1983)

Background Notes. Resource that contains a political geography. (Washington, DC: Superintendent of Documents)

Business Information Sources. Reference source that provides information sources. (Berkeley: University of California Press)

Cities of the World. Compilation of U.S. government reports and original research on the social, cultural, political, and industrial aspects of more than 450 major cities in 140 countries. (Detroit, MI: Gale Research, 1983)

Computer-Readable Databases: A Directory and Data Sourcebook. Reference that describes specific databases that may be accessed. (White Plains, NY: American Society for Information Sciences)

Consumer International. Resource that provides information on a wide range of consumer markets all over the world; it allows for international comparisons. Topics include population trends, GDP, and consumer expenditure. (Chicago, IL: Euromonitor International Inc.)

Countries of the World and Their Leaders Yearbook. Annual publication that contains information on issues facing different countries, chiefs of state, cabinet members by country, U.S. embassies, consulates, and foreign service posts. (Detroit, MI: Gale Research, 1980)

Country Outlooks. Publication that provides annual projections of business conditions on a country-by-country basis. (San Francisco, CA: Bank of America World Information Services)

Cumulative Index. Reference source that provides access to the publications of the Conference Board by broad subject categories. (New York: Conference Board)

Directory of Directors. Listing of 58,000 directors of principal public and private firms in the United Kingdom along with the name of the company with which each is associated and its board members. (Haywards Heath, UK: Thomas Skinner Directories)

Directory of Multinationals. Profiles of more than 400 of the world's largest industrial corporations with significant international operations, including information on corporate structure, products, principal affiliates, and subsidiaries. (New York: Stockton Press, 1991)

Directory of United Nations Databases and Information. Comprehensive summary of data available through the United Nations. (New York: United Nations Publications)

Encyclopedia of Business Information Sources. Listings of various types of information sources including statistical publications, directories, and periodicals on 1,086 business topics. (Detroit, MI: Gale Research, 1991–1992)

Encyclopedia of Geographic Information Sources. Listings of various types of information sources by name of country, including statistical publications, directories, periodicals, and guides for doing business. (Detroit, MI: Gale Research)

F&S International. Publication that provides access to articles in business publications by industry, country, and company name. (Cleveland, OH: Predicasts, Inc.)

Global Guide to International Business. A comprehensive guide to information under 23 major headings. (New York: Facts on File, 1983)

Guide to International Business Information Databases. A comprehensive description of online computer sources and databases on international business. (College Park: University of Maryland, 1992)

Handbook of International Business and Management. Listing of definitions and key terms and concepts in the fields of international business and management. (Oxford: Blackwell, 1990)

Hoover's Handbook of World Business. Descriptions of global economic trends, foreign investment, rankings of companies, and profiles of economic regions and nations. (Austin, TX: Reference Press, 1991)

International Bibliography, Information Documentation. Index of books and periodicals issued by the United Nations and other intergovernmental organizations that are outside the United Nations. (New York: Bowker & Unipub, Inc.)

International Dictionary of the Securities Industry. A listing of world stock exchange indexes. (Homewood, IL: Dow Jones-Irwin, 1989)

International Business Series. Publication organized by country that includes characteristics of business entities, digest of principal taxes, and a national profile. (New York: Ernst and Whinney)

International Executive. Periodical, each issue containing abstracts of books, articles, and papers as well as a list of reference sources in international management. (Glendale, AZ: American Graduate School of International Management)

Management Administration and Productivity: International Directory of Institutions and Countries. Lists of more than 2,300 institutions and more than 1,000 key information sources in 140 countries. (Washington, DC: International Labor Office, 1981)

Master Key Index. A cumulative, cross-referenced index to the entire Business International set of services, which consist of sections on country, company, and management technique. (New York: Business International Corporation)

Moody's International Manual. Financial and business information on almost 4,700 major corporations in 108 countries, including profile, map, and financial statistics summary. (New York: The Service, 1981)

The Multilingual Commercial Directory. A listing of the most commonly used terms in international business in six languages. (New York: Facts on File, 1980)

Multinational Enterprise: An Encyclopedia Dictionary of Concepts and Terms. Detailed definitions including a list of bibliographies on multinational enterprises, an index, and references for further reading. (New York: Nicholas Publications, 1987)

National Trade Data Bank. Online computerized service updated continuously that gives latest information by country. (Washington)

Overseas Business Reports. Collection of reports on more than 100 countries that provides a brief introduction to economic and business trends. (NA)

Principal International Business. Publication containing information on 50,000 companies in 140 countries, listed geographically, alphabetically, and by SIC code. (New York: Dun & Bradstreet)

PTS Annual Reports Abstracts. Reports providing in-depth information on publicly held U.S. and selected international companies; a source in identifying companies according to product lines or service areas. (Cleveland, OH: Predicasts Inc.)

PTS International Forecasts. Abstracts of published forecasts for all countries of the world, including market and industry data for virtually all manufacturing and service industries, as well as economic and government indicators and demographics. (Cleveland, OH: Predicasts Inc.)

Survey of Research on Transnational Corporations. Publication that includes reports on 810 studies completed or under way in 1976. (New York: United Nations Centre on Transnational Corporations)

Travel and Tourism: The International Market. Publication providing market overview, market background, key trends and developments, market sectors, and outlook for each country included (Chicago, IL: Euromonitor International Inc.)

Ulrichs International Periodicals Directory. Index of internationally published periodicals covering business, literature, and science. (New York: R.R. Bowker Co.)

User's Guide to the Information System on Transnational Corporations. Guide on how to obtain and use information the United Nations has compiled on transnational corporations, including individual companies. (New York: United Nations)

Walden Country Report. Reports on current situations and outlooks on specific countries at irregular intervals. (London: Walden Publishing)

Washington's Best Kept Secrets: A U.S. Government Guide to International Business. List of services provided by eight different U.S. government agencies. (New York: John Wiley & Sons, 1983)

Who Owns Whom: UK and Republic of Ireland. Listing of subsidiaries and associates of parent companies registered in the United Kingdom and the Republic of Ireland. (Skokie, IL: National Register Publishing Co.)

World Business Cycles. Historical statistics for the period of 1950–1980, which contain information on world business cycles including gross domestic product, consumer expenditures, and government. (London: Economist Newspaper Ltd., 1982; Detroit, MI: Gale Research)

The World Directory of Business Information Libraries. Selective directory detailing more than 2,500 of the major libraries across the globe that provide public access business information. (Chicago, IL: Euromonitor International Inc.)

The World Directory of Exhibitions and Trade Fairs. Handbook that details more than 4,000 trade fairs and exhibitions in 50 countries across the world. (Chicago, IL: Euromonitor International Inc.)

World Class Business: A Guide to the 100 Most Powerful Global Corporations. Guide that provides information on each company's history, main areas of operation, present competitive position, and labor and environmental records. (New York: Holt, 1992)

The World's Major Companies Directory. Listing of both multinational and national companies arranged by country, which includes financial data, turnover, and major company rankings. (Chicago, IL: Euromonitor International Inc.)

World Factbook. Detailed reports on countries, possessions, and regions that presents information on geography, population, government, economics, communications, and defense forces. (Washington, DC: U.S. Central Intelligence Agency)

Year Book Australia. Annual publication that includes information on Australian history, government, physical geography, and climate, as well as statistics on population, employment, manufacturing, exports, and imports. (Canberra: Australian Bureau of Statistics)

NATIONAL DATA (GENERAL)

America's Corporate Families. Publication that provides company information, including subsidiary information. (Dun's Marketing Service)

Brands and Their Companies. Alphabetical listing of consumer products, including manufacturer's name and address. (Detroit, MI: Gale Research, 1990)

Business International. Periodical that includes topics relevant to international business. (New York: Business International Corporation)

Checklist of U.S. Public Documents 1789–1970. Listing that provides information from the U.S. Historical Documents Institute. (U.S. Historical Documents Institute)

Directory of American Firms Operating in Foreign Countries. Alphabetical listing of American firms that have overseas operations. (New York: Simon & Schuster, 1980)

Directory of Corporate Affiliations. Listing that provides company information including information on companies' subsidiaries. (Skokie, IL: National Register Publication Co., 1973)

Directory of Foreign Firms Operating in the United States. Listing of firms by parent company's country, including address, number of employees, and product or service. (New York: Simon & Schuster, 1969)

Directory of Foreign Manufacturers in the United States. Listing with entries that include manufacturer's name in the United States, name of parent company, products, and SIC code. (Atlanta: Georgia State University Business Press, 1993)

Dun's Business Identification Service. Publication that provides company information, which includes a listing of private companies both domestic and international. (Parsippany, NJ: Dun & Bradstreet, 1981)

Dun's Business Rankings. Listing of public and private companies by two- or three-digit SIC code; also ranked by sales and number of employees. (Parsippany, NJ: Dun's Marketing Services, 1982)

Dun's Census of American Business. Publication that counts the number of establishments in each SIC industry category by sales volume and number of employees, with data provided on the national, state, and county levels. (New York: Dun & Bradstreet)

Guide to U.S. Government Publications. Publication that provides information on available current and historical government publications. (Ithaca, NY: Cornell University Libraries, 1980)

Guide to U.S. Government Scientific and Technical Resources. Publication that provides information relevant to all branches of the U.S. government. (Littleton, CO: Libraries Unlimited, 1983)

Hoover's Handbook of American Business: Profiles of 500 Major U.S. Companies. Publication that provides information relating to specific public and private companies, including address, telephone number, officer's names, primary SIC codes, and products and services. (Austin, TX: Reference Press Inc., 1991)

Insider's Guide to Demographic Know-How. Directory of federal agencies, state and local sources, private companies, and nonprofit organizations that provide demographic information. (Ithaca, NY: American Demographics Press, 1990)

Million Dollar Directory. Listing that provides brief information regarding public and private companies. (Parsippany, NJ: Dun's Marketing Services)

Moody's Complete Corporate Index. Listing that allows the user to determine the manual in which his or her company of interest is located. (New York: Moody's Investors Service)

Moody's Industrial Manual. Reference providing an overview that includes a brief company history, company description, names of officers and directors, selected balance sheets, and more. (New York: Moody's Investors Service)

Moody's OTC Industrial Manual. Reference source that provides company overviews. (New York: Moody's Investors Service)

Moody's OTC Unlisted Manual. Reference that provides company overviews. (New York: Moody's Investors Service)

Moody's Public Utilities Manual. Publication providing overviews of public utility companies. (New York: Moody's Investors Service)

Moody's Transportation Manual. Reference providing overviews of transportation companies. (New York: Moody's Investors Service)

MRA Blue Book Research Services Directory. Publication that describes the services and facilities of data-collection companies, research companies, and suppliers of related services. It also includes topics such as central telephone facilities, focus group facilities, and interviewing specialties. (New York: Marketing Research Association)

New York Times Index. Periodical covering a wide array of up-to-date information. (New York: R.R. Bowker Co.)

Sourcebook of Demographics and Buying Buyer for Every Zip Code in the U.S.A. Listing of all zip codes, arranged by state, and associated demographic information including population size, population profile, income and employment statistics, and housing profile. Also included is the purchasing potential index, which is a statistic measuring of the likelihood that the residents of a zip code will purchase various categories of goods and services. (Fairfax, VA: CACI, Inc.)

Standard & Poor's Corporation Records. Publication that contains brief company history, description of business, and balance sheet statistics. (New York: Standard & Poor's Corporation)

Standard & Poor's Register of Corporations. Listing that provides brief information on companies, such as address, telephone number, officers' names, primary SIC codes, and description of products and services offered. (New York: Standard & Poor's Corporation)

Standard Industrial Classification Manual. Reference source that provides the SIC codes, which classify establishments by type of activity. (Washington, DC: U.S. Government Printing Office, 1967)

Thomas' Register of American Manufacturers. Listing that provides information on both public and private companies. (New York: Thomas Publishing Company, 1905)

Tracing the Multinationals. Publication that records the growth and spread of individual U.S. enterprises. (Cambridge, MA: Ballinger Publishing Company, 1977)

The USA and Canada. Comprehensive guide to the political, economic, and social structures of the United States and Canada. It also provides historical, geographical, and demographic data as well as essays on social issues and international relations. (London: Europa Publications)

U.S. Industrial Outlook. Publication that provides recent trends and forecasts for more than 250 industries. It also discusses developments in domestic and foreign markets. (Washington, DC: U.S. Department of Commerce)

Wall Street Journal Index. Periodical covering up-to-date business information. (New York: Dow Jones & Co.)

Ward's Business Directory of U.S. Private and Public Companies. Listing that provides information relating to both public and private companies. (Detroit, MI: Gale Research)

Who Owns Whom: North America. Listing of parent companies, head-of-office address, and main business activity. (Skokie, IL: National Register Publication Company)

Economic Data

Analyst's Handbook. Publication that provides financial data, both current and historical, such as earnings per share, price/earnings ratio, and dividend yields. (New York: Standard & Poor's Corporation)

Balance of Payments Yearbook. Publication that includes reports on goods, services, and unrequired transfers; capital (excluding reserves); allocations of special drawing rights; and reserves. (Washington, DC: International Monetary Fund)

Country Report Analysis of Economic and Political Trends. Quarterly reports on specific countries that include updates on current situations as well as outlooks. (London: Economist Intelligence Unit)

Direction of Trade. Publication on trade, by country, for 167 countries, including summaries of each country and 11 areas of comparison. (Washington, DC: International Monetary Fund)

Direction of Trade Statistics. Reference source that provides detailed statistical tables on central government revenue, expenditure, lending, financing, and debt. (Washington, DC: International Monetary Fund, 1981)

Economic and Social Survey of Asia and the Pacific. Publication that presents an overview of recent economic and social developments as well as an in-depth discussion of a topic of concern to developing counties in the Asia-Pacific region. (Bangkok: Economic and Social Commission for Asia and the Pacific, 1974)

Economic Indicators. Monthly publication of general economic statistics useful for measuring trends in business conditions. (Washington, DC: Council of Economic Advisors, Government Printing Office)

Economic Report of the President: Transmitted to Congress. Report that contains current and historical information on bond yields and interest rates and common stock prices and yields. (Washington, DC: U.S. Government Printing Office)

Economic Survey of Latin America and the Caribbean. Report that presents a discussion, supplemented with graphs and statistics, on a variety of topics including foreign trade, debt, inflation, investments, and employment and wages. (Santiago, Chile: United Nations, 1984)

The Economist. Periodical covering subjects relevant to economic topics. (London: Economist Newspaper Ltd.)

Euromoney. Periodical that focuses on the European money market, with statistics on Eurodollar rates, interest rates, and exchange rates. (London: Euromoney Publications Ltd.)

Europa Yearbook: A World Survey. Annual publication containing detailed information on the political, economic, commercial, and social institutions of the world. (London: Europa Publications)

Far Eastern Economic Review. Periodical covering topics relevant to the Far East and its markets. (Hong Kong: E.E. Halpern)

Foreign Economic Trends and Their Implications for the U.S. Periodical, each issue of which is dedicated to a country and contains information on key economic indicators, current economic situations, and trends and implications for the United States. (Washington, DC: U.S. Department of Commerce)

Foreign Trade and Economic Abstracts. Publication that offers worldwide economic information concerning market trends, economic developments, international trade, particular economic climates, management problems, and economic science. (Dialog Information Services, Inc., 1988)

Gallatin Business Intelligence. Publication that provides a review of economic, political, and social conditions, including legal restrictions and investment climate. (Gallatin Publications)

The Gallatin Letter. Weekly report of major economic, political, or social occurrences, with analysis of their impact on business. (New York: Gallatin International Business Service)

Guide to World Commodity Markets. Publication that includes an explanation of the role and functions of commodity markets in international trade, as well as a good description of methods of training. (New York: Nichols Publishing Co., 1985)

Highlights of U.S. Export and Import Trade. Publication that provides monthly tables from the Bureau of Customs that give the unadjusted and seasonally adjusted data on U.S. international trade, listed by commodity group, nation, product use, U.S. customs region, and method of shipment. (Bureau of Customs)

Index to International Business Publications. An index to the individual issues of *Foreign Economic Trends, Overseas Business Reports,* and several other Department of Commerce publications arranged by name of country. (Washington, DC: U.S. Department of Commerce)

Industry Norms and Key Business Ratios. Publication that provides financial ratios and balance sheet items for more than 800 lines of businesses, arranged by SIC code. (New York: Dun & Bradstreet Credit Services, 1983)

International Bibliography of Economics. Publication that provides a means to obtain global information about the previous year's publications in the field of economics. (London: Tavistock Publications)

International Economic Indicators and Competitive Trends. Publication that contains information on the United States and seven major competitor nations from *Overseas Business Reports*, including economic prospects and recent trends, changes in key indicators, basic data for indicators, and notes and sources. (Washington, DC: U.S. Department of Commerce)

International Monetary Fund. Publication that contains information about exchange rates, exchange controls, and so forth on currencies of all countries that are members of the IMF. (Washington, DC: International Monetary Fund)

International Trade Handbook. Publication that contains sections on basic principals of foreign trade, documentation and finance, legal aspects, selection and training of executives, case histories, operation of an overseas trade organization, and practical problems. (Chicago, IL: Dartnell Corp.)

International Trade Reporter: Export Shipping Manual. Listing of country-by-country shipping information including mail, telephone, time differentials, holidays, ports, tariffs, controls, documents required, and consulates in the United States. (Washington, DC: Bureau of National Affairs, Inc.)

International Trade Statistics Yearbook. Annual publication that provides import and export statistics for more than 150 countries. (New York: United Nations, 1985)

M.P.A. Market Profile Analysis: Consumer and Business Demographic Reports. Publication that includes four volumes on retail market factors, business market factors, new construction information, and competitive factors. (Santa Clara, CA: Strategic Mapping)

The Market Guide. Publication that surveys more than 1,500 daily and weekly newspaper markets in the United States, Canada, and selected foreign markets. Includes population, trade areas, principal industries, and maps. (Glen Head, NY: Market Guide Inc., 1990)

New Book of World Rankings. Publication that includes a comparison and ranking of more than 190 nations on the basis of their performance in 300 key areas, including national income, exports, balance of trade, commodities produced, and per capita consumption. (New York: Facts on File, 1991)

OECD Economic Surveys. An analysis of economic development and policies in one of the OECD member countries. Information provided in each survey includes recent development in demand, production, employment, prices and wages, conditions in the money and capital markets, and developments in the balance of payments. (Paris: OECD)

OECD Main Economic Indicators. Publication that provides, using tabular and graphic presentations, a picture of the most recent changes in the economy of OECD member countries. (OECD)

The Official Guide to the American Marketplace. Publication that includes information organized by factors that influence consumer markets such as population, income, spending, labor force, education, health, general attitudes, and household characteristics. (Ithaca, NY: New Strategist Publications, 1995)

One Hundred Years of Economic Statistics. Publication that includes statistical tables from Australia, Canada, France, Germany, Italy, Japan, Sweden, the United Kingdom, and the United States, including balance of payments, rates of productivity growth, share prices and interest rates, distribution of employment, and industrial production. (New York: Facts on File, 1989)

The Outlook. Periodical that provides weekly information on stocks and mutual funds. (New York: Standard and Poor's Corp.)

Pick's Currency Yearbook. Annual publication that provides a monetary glossary. (New York: Pick Publishing Corporation)

Predicast's Forecasts. Quarterly publication giving shortened long-term forecasts for economic indicators, industries, and products and basic statistical information on companies and industries. (Cleveland, OH: Predicasts, Inc.)

SRDS Newspaper Circulation Analysis. Publication that provides market data analysis, metropolitan area analysis, rankings by type of paper, and total circulation. (Nilmette, IL: SRDS Report)

Standard & Poor's Industry Surveys. Publication that provides basic data on more than 30 industries including financial comparisons of the leading companies in each industry. (New York: Standard & Poor's Corp.)

Stateman's Yearbook. Annual publication that includes statistical tables for selected commodities, and a listing of international organizations arranged by country including demographics, industry statistics, imports, and exports. (New York: St. Martin's Press)

Statistical Abstract of the United States. Publication that includes information on transportation, population, health, and education, maps, charts, and tables. (Washington, DC: U.S. Department of Commerce)

Survey of Buying Power. Publication that presents statistical data on buying power as well as demographic and retail sales information including sales, marketing, and advertising figures. (New York: Sales and Marketing Management)

Trade and Securities Statistics. Publication that provides current and historical information on investment statistics. (New York: Standard & Poor's Corp.)

U.S. Exports: Schedule B, Commodity by Country. Report that gives quantity and value of exports from the United States to each foreign country. Data are classified according to the *Standard International Trade (SIT) Classification Manual.* (Washington, DC: U.S. Census Bureau, U.S. Government Printing Office)

U.S. General Imports: Schedule A, Commodity by Country. Report that gives quantity and value of imports to the United States from each foreign country. Data are classified by SIT code. (Washington, DC: U.S. Census Bureau, U.S. Government Printing Office)

United Nations Statistical Yearbook. Annual publication of statistics on economics, manufacturing, agriculture, and social indicators for UN member nations. (New York: United Nations)

Western Europe: A Political and Economic Survey. Publication that provides information on all countries in the European Communities and the European Free Trade Association as well as Cyprus, Malta, and Turkey. (NA)

World Currency Yearbook. Annual publication in which entries are arranged alphabetically by country and include information on currency history, transferability, and recent developments. (Brooklyn, NY: International Currency Analysis, Inc.)

World Development Report. Annual report that includes an in-depth analysis of a major development issue such as poverty or financial markets. (New York: Oxford University Press)

World Economic Factbook (1994/95) Publication that presents reference information on 206 countries including information on growth markets, inflation, political risk, and more. (Chicago, IL: Euromonitor International Inc.)

World Economic Survey. Essays that provide an overview of developments in international trade and trade policy. Statistical tables include historical and current information on population, foreign debt, per capita income, and trade balances. (New York: United Nations)

The World in Figures. Publication that provides detailed statistics for every country including exchange rates, growth rates, resources, population, and trade. (New York: John Wiley & Sons, 1973)

World Tables. Publication that provides current and historical data on gross national income, gross domestic product, value of merchandise imports and exports, and private consumption. (Baltimore, MD: Johns Hopkins University Press)

World Trade Resources Guide. Publication that presents information on 80 of the largest and most significant trading nations of the world. Entries include information on currencies, economic and trade statistics, and principal commodities traded. (Detroit, MI: Gale Research)

Yearbook of National Accounting Statistics. Annual publication that gives the individual country's external trade performance in terms of the overall trends in current values, volume, and prices. It also shows the importance of trading partners and the significance of individual commodities. It includes annual data for 147 countries, arranged by SIT code. (New York: United Nations Statistical Office)

FINANCIAL AND INVESTMENT DATA

Almanac of Business and Industrial Financial Ratios. Publication that provides financial and operating ratios for more than 150 industries profiled in charts and graphs. (Englewood Cliffs, NJ: Prentice-Hall)

Amex Fact Book. Publication that provides data on equities, options, and government and corporate bonds. (New York: The Exchange, 1985)

Analyst's Handbook. Resource that provides both current and historic quarterly data, including earnings per share, price/earnings ratio, and dividend yields. (New York: Standard & Poor's Corp., 1993)

Annual Dividend Record. Report containing dividend payments on publicly owned American and Canadian preferred and common shares. (New York: Standard & Poor's Corp.)

Bond Guide. Monthly resource that provides information on both corporate and government bonds. (New York: Standard & Poor's Corp.)

Business International Money Report. Publication that provides information on finance and banking areas. (Geneva: Business International)

Daily Stock Price Record: American Stock. Report that includes daily volume, high, low, and close figures, as well as information on earnings and dividends. (New York: Standard & Poor's Corp.)

Daily Stock Price Record: New York Stock. Report that includes daily volume, high, low, and close figures, and information on earnings and dividends. (New York: Standard & Poor's Corp.)

Daily Stock Price Record: Over the Counter. Report that includes daily volume, high, low, and close figures, and information on earnings and dividends. (New York: Standard & Poor's Corp.)

A Dictionary of International Finance. Volume of definitions, some of which include references for further reading; also contains a bibliography of specialized dictionaries. (Westport, CT: Greenwood Press, 1979)

Directory of Obsolete Securities. Publication that profiles banks and companies whose original identities have been lost as a result of merger, name change, reorganization, or bankruptcy. (Jersey City, NJ: Financial Information, Inc.)

Directory of World Stock Exchanges. Publication that includes information on trading hours, trading volume, instruments traded and settlement procedures, exchange history, and membership structure. (Baltimore, MD: Johns Hopkins University Press, 1988)

Doing Business In . . . Series of guides that examine business conditions in various countries, including information on population, social patterns, living standards, cultural and social life, and an overview of foreign investment opportunities. (New York: PriceWaterhouse and PricewaterhouseCoopers)

Exporter's Encyclopedia. Entries include a country profile, trade regulations, marketing data, and information on documentation, communications, transportation, and business travel. (Dun & Bradstreet International)

Financial Times International Yearbook. Annual publication that presents information on 700 of the world's top companies, including state-owned enterprises. (London: Financial Times)

Guide to Mutual Funds. Arranged by type of fund, volume includes description of fund and assets under management and information on initial and subsequent investment requirements. (Washington, DC: Investment Co. Institute, 1987)

Hints to Business Men. Pamphlets arranged by country, giving travel, communication, economic, regulatory, business, government, and general information of interest to businesspeople. (London: British Overseas Trade Board)

Importers Manual USA: The Single Source Reference Encyclopedia for Importing to the U.S. Comprehensive source that includes information on international legal issues, international banking and letters of credit, U.S. customs entry and clearance, as well as packing, shipping, and insurance. (San Rafael, CA: World Trade Press, 1992)

International Dictionary of the Securities Industry. Volume that includes a listing of World Stock Exchanges indexes. (Homewood, IL: Dow Jones-Irwin, 1989)

International Directory of Marketing Research Houses and Sources. Publication that includes an alphabetical listing of research organizations including a description of services offered. (The Green Book)

Investment Companies. Publication that contains general information about investment company operations, glossary of terms, and current and historical information for individual funds. (New York: Practising Law Institute, 1983)

Investment Statistics Locator. Publication that includes statistics on stock and bond prices, mutual fund sale and assets, earnings, foreign trade exchange rates, and interest rates. (Phoenix, AZ: Oryx Press, 1995)

Investors Guide and Mutual Fund Directory. Resource that provides current information for funds listed by investment objective and management company. (New York: No-Load Mutual Fund Association, 1987)

IRM Directory of Statistics of International Investment and Production. Reference source that provides data on the international direct investment position of 80 countries, including a description of the main features of the international investment of the country, policies regarding inward and outward capital flows, and main sources of statistical data. (New York: New York University Press, 1987)

Journal of Banking and Finance. Academic journal that covers topics relating to the industry of banking and finance. (Amsterdam: North Holland Publishing Co.)

Moody's Bank and Finance Manual. Resource that provides an overview, including brief company history, description of the business, names of officers and directors, and selected balance sheet statistics. (New York: Moody's Investors Service)

Moody's Bond Record. Publication that provides current information on bonds, commercial paper, and preferred stock ratings. (New York: Moody's Investors Service)

Moody's Bond Survey. Publication that provides current information on bonds and prospective offerings. (New York: Moody's Investors Service)

Moody's Dividend Record. Resource that covers more than 20,000 issues, including 9,000 common and preferred paying stocks, 2,000 nonpaying issues, and payments on approximately 9,000 bond funds. (New York: Moody's Investors Service)

Moody's Handbook of Common Stocks. Reference source that provides current and historical data on common stocks. (New York: Moody's Investors Service)

Moody's Handbook of NASDAQ Stocks. Reference source that provides current and historical data on NASDAQ stocks. (New York: Moody's Investors Service)

Moody's Handbook of OTC Stocks. Reference source that provides current and historical data on over-the-counter stocks. (New York: Moody's Investors Service)

Moody's International Manual. Reference source that provides current and historical data. (New York: The Service, 1981)

Moody's Investors Fact Sheets: Industry Review. Ranked listing of leading companies in more than 140 industries, including financial, operating, and investment statistics. (NA)

Mutual Fund Directory. Reference source that includes current information on name changes, mergers, and dissolutions. (New York: IDD, Inc.)

Mutual Fund Fact Book. Reference source that contains information on assets, sales, redemptions, and net sales, including some historical information. (Washington, DC: Investment Co. Institute)

NASDAQ Fact Book. Reference source that contains listings of securities and share and dollar volume. (Washington: NASD)

The New Palgrave Dictionary of Money and Finance. Reference source that contains more than 1,000 essays arranged in alphabetical order. (New York: Stockton Press, 1992)

OECD Financial Market Trends. Publication that contains data on financial markets in 16 European countries, the United States, Canada, and Japan. (Paris: OECD)

The Outlook. Publication that provides current information on stocks and mutual funds. (New York: Standard & Poor's Corp.)

RMA Annual Statement Studies. Publication that contains financial and operating ratios for almost 300 lines of business, including balance sheet and income statement composites. (Philadelphia: Robert Morris Associates)

SEC Filing Companies. Resource that identifies public companies that have filed with the SEC. (Washington: Disclosure, Inc.)

Security Owner's Stock Guide. Reference source that provides information useful to investors. (New York: Standard & Poor's Corp.)

Standard & Poor's Stock Reports: American Stock Exchange. Reports that provide current and historical information relating to the American Stock Exchange. (New York: Standard & Poor's Corp.)

Standard & Poor's Stock Reports: New York Stock Exchange. Reports that provide current and historical information relating to the New York Stock Exchange. (New York: Standard & Poor's Corp.)

Standard & Poor's Stock Reports: Over the Counter. Provides current and historical information relating to the Over the Counter Exchange. (New York: Standard & Poor's Corp.)

Standard & Poor's/Lipper Mutual Fund Profiles. Resource that covers more than 750 funds and provides current pricing and asset information, investment policy, and performance evaluation. (New York: Standard & Poor's Corp.)

The Dow Jones Averages, 1885–1980. Resource that provides daily high, low, close, and sales figures. (Homewood, IL: Dow Jones-Irwin, 1982)

The Dow Jones Investor's Handbook. Resource that includes both current and historical information on Dow Jones averages, mutual funds, foreign stock market indexes, and foreign bonds. (Princeton, NJ: Dow Jones Books)

The Dow Jones-Irwin Business and Investment Almanac. Reference source that contains information on U.S. and foreign stock markets, options, futures, and commodities. (Homewood, IL: Dow Jones-Irwin)

The Dow Jones-Irwin Guide to International Securities, Futures and Options Markets. Resource that includes general information on investment strategies and presents a review of the economy, banking system, and primary financial markets in 15 countries. (Homewood, IL: Dow Jones-Irwin)

Trade and Securities Statistics. Reference source that provides current and historical information for selected industries. (New York: Standard & Poor's Corp.)

Trade Opportunities. Publication that contains live purchase requests by the international market for U.S. goods and services. (Washington, DC: U.S. Department of Commerce)

Value Line Investment Survey. Publication that provides an analysis of 1,700 companies in approximately 95 different industries. (New York: A. Bernhard)

MARKETING DATA

AD $ Summary. Index of brands with year-to-date total advertising expenditures. (New York: Leading National Advertisers, Inc.)

Advertising Ratios & Budgets. Publication that contains an analysis of advertising budgets for companies and industries, arranged by SIC code. (Evantson, IL: Schanfold & Associates, Inc.)

Adweek's Marketer's Guide to Media Markets. Publication that contains current rate and audience estimates for the major media. (NA)

Almanac of Consumer Markets. Reference source that provides demographic information needed to examine consumer markets, organized according to age, with cross-references to sex, income, education, and household structure. (Ithaca, NY: American Demographic Press)

American Marketing Association Bibliography Series. Detailed annotated bibliography of topics of interest to the American Marketing Association. (Chicago, IL: American Marketing Association)

The Bibliography of Marketing Research Methods. Reference source that contains more than 14,000 citations for materials in popular marketing and marketing research periodicals, handbooks, and conference proceedings. (Lexington, MA: Lexington Books, 1990)

Bradford's Directory of Marketing Research Agencies and Management Consultants in the U.S. and the World. Reference source that contains more than 900 agencies and consultants arranged alphabetically by state or country. (Middleburg, VA: Bradford's Directory of Marketing Research Agencies)

Census of Retail Trade. Publication that provides statistics by state, SMSA, and areas outside SMSA for more than 100 different retail enterprises. (Washington, DC: U.S. Department of Commerce, U.S. Census Bureau)

Census of Service Industries. Resource that provides data on approximately 130 service industries, with statistics on the number of establishments, payroll, and employment. (Washington, DC: U.S. Department of Commerce, U.S. Census Bureau)

Census of Wholesale Trade. Reference source that provides statistics for more than 100 kinds of wholesale businesses, with figures on number of establishments, sales, inventories, and kind of business detail. (Washington, DC: U.S. Department of Commerce, U.S. Census Bureau)

Circulation. Comprehensive print analysis showing circulation and penetration. (Northfield, IL: American Newspaper Markets, Inc.)

Commercial Atlas and Marketing Guide. Resource that presents useful marketing information in map format, such as demographic and economic data, manufacturing activity, and population change. (Chicago, IL: Rand McNally & Co.)

Consumer Power: How Americans Spend their Money. Publication that focuses on consumer spending patterns with an emphasis on national-level spending data. (Ithaca, NY: New Strategist Publications)

Dartnell Marketing Manager's Handbook. Information resource that covers marketing functions, developing the marketing plan, promotion, and international marketing. (Chicago, IL: Dartnell Corporation, 1994)

Dictionary of Advertising and Direct Mail Terms. Reference source that provides definitions to commonly used terms in the advertising and marketing field. (New York: Barron's, 1987)

Dictionary of Marketing. Reference source that includes information relevant to the marketing field. (New York: Fairchild Publications, 1988)

Dictionary of Marketing Research. Reference that includes a checklist for marketing researchers and the AMA marketing research code of ethics. (Chicago, IL: St. James Press, 1987)

Dictionary of Retailing. Reference resource that includes brief biographies of historical figures that have had an impact on retailing. (New York: Fairchild)

Direct Marketing Market Place. Resource that includes entries arranged alphabetically by product and service, with information on advertising and expenditures. (Hewlett Harbor, NY: Hilary House Publishers)

European Marketing Data and Statistics. Publication that contains the latest available data on key economic and marketing parameters in 32 European countries. (London: Euromonitor Publications)

European Marketing Information Database. Resource that contains more than 100,000 market data figures organized into segmented sections. (Chicago, IL: Euromonitor International Inc.)

Geographical Index to the Standard Directory of Advertisers. Listing of companies arranged by state and city, including parent company name. (Skokie, IL: National Register Publishing Co.)

Green Book: International Directory of Marketing Research Houses and Services. Alphabetical listing of services offered by major U.S. and international marketing firms. (New York: Marketing Association)

International Directory of Marketing Research Houses and Sources. Publication that contains an alphabetical listing of research organizations including a description of services offered. (The Green Book)

International Marketing Data and Statistics. Resource that includes data on business and marketing parameters, including literacy and education, consumer expenditure, and demographic trends and forecasts. (London: Euromonitor Publications Ltd.)

International Marketing Handbook. Reference source that contains marketing profiles for more than 140 countries, including customs information, import data, area guides, and a directory of assistance agencies. (Detroit, MI: Gale Research, 1988)

Macmillan Dictionary of Marketing and Advertising. Reference that provides information relevant to the marketing and advertising industry. (New York: Nichols Publishing Co., 1984)

Market Research Europe. Monthly reports broken down into sections on the European food and nonfood markets, secondary markets, and special market reports. (Chicago, IL: Euromonitor International Inc.)

Market Research International. Monthly reports broken down into sections on an international market review, global market trends and developments, U.S. market report, Japan market report, emerging market report, and market focus. (Chicago, IL: Euromonitor International Inc.)

Marketfull. Collection of full-text market research reports, with information on products, industries, markets, market share, pricing, consumer attitudes, consumption, and more. (Palo Alto, CA: Dialog Information Services, Inc.)

Marketing and Sales Management: An Information Sourcebook. Reference source that focuses on management techniques and the practical aspects of marketing and sales. (Phoenix, AZ: Oryx Press, 1988)

Marketing Information Guide. Publication that contains a monthly listing of current reports and statistics on marketing and distribution practices. (Washington, DC: U.S. Department of Commerce)

Marketing News International Directory of the American Marketing Association and the Marketing Yellow Pages. Listings of marketing consultants, marketing research services, marketing software producers, and names, addresses, and telephone numbers of more than 26,000 AMA members. (Chicago, IL: American Marketing Association, 1993)

Sales Manager's Budget Planner. Resource that presents information on 100 metropolitan market profiles, including vital statistics, meal and lodging costs, information on hotels, conference centers, and restaurant and travel costs. (Sales and Marketing Management)

Simmons Study of Media and Markets. Publication based on a survey of 19,000 households that measures usage of products and services by brand name, characteristics of the respondents, and their exposure to different media. (Simmons Market Research)

SRDS Newspaper Circulation Analysis. Publication that includes market data analysis, metropolitan area analysis, rankings by type of paper, and total circulation. (NA)

SRDS Report. Newsletter that focuses on media trends including graphs, charts, and statistics. (Wilmette, IL: SRDS Report)

Standard Directory of Advertisers. Listing of more than 25,000 advertiser companies, with entries including products advertised and media used. (Skokie, IL: National Register Publishing Co.)

Standard Directory of Advertising Agencies. Listing of approximately 5,000 agencies, with entries including information on approximate annual billing. (Skokie, IL: National Register Publishing Co.)

Standard Directory of Worldwide Marketing. Listings of advertisers and agencies, trade name index, and listing of foreign trade commissions/chambers of commerce. (NA)

Survey of Media Markets. Publication that presents population, income, and retail sales data for media markets, current sales statistics, and market projections. (New York: Bill Communications)

POLITICAL DATA AND GOVERNMENT INFORMATION

Area Handbook Series. Annual reports on countries, with specific coverage of variables useful for analysis of political risk. (Washington, DC: Library of Congress Federal Research Division)

Business Serials of the U.S. Government. Reports that contain information relevant to the U.S. government. (Chicago, IL: AIA, 1988)

Business Services and Information: The Guide to the Federal Government. Guide for identifying U.S. government publications, including an annotated list of publications and agency phone numbers and addresses. (New York: Management Information Exchange)

Census Catalog and Guide. Annual catalog of all information available from the Census Bureau since 1980, with Census Bureau phone numbers included. (Washington, DC: U.S. Department of Commerce, U.S. Census Bureau, 1985)

Census of Government. Publication that provides statistics on state and local government pertaining to local employment, size of payroll, operating budgets, and amount of indebtedness. (Washington, DC: U.S. Census Bureau, U.S. Government Printing Office)

Complete Guide to Citing Government Information. Resource that provides information relevant to finding resources available on the government. (Bethesda, MD: Congressional Information Services)

Consumers', Researchers' and Students' Guide to Government Publications. Resource that provides a listing of available government publications. (NA)

Country Report Analysis of Economic and Political Trends. Quarterly reports, each of which contains information on specific countries including updates on current situations as well as outlooks. (London: Economist Intelligence Unit)

Cumulative Subject Index to the Monthly Catalog of U.S. Government Publications. Publication that provides a listing of available government publications. (Washington, DC: Carrollton Press)

Directory of Government Document Collections and Librarians. Resource that provides a listing of libraries with significant collections of documents of particular agencies or in given subjects. (Bethesda, MD: Congressional Information Service, 1991)

Document Catalog. A listing of sources offering government information. (New York: Johnson Reprint Corp.; Kraus Reprint Corp.)

Europa Yearbook: A World Survey. Volume that provides detailed information on the political, economic, commercial, and social institutions of the countries of the world. (London: Europa Publications)

Federal Regulatory Directory, 5th ed. Publication that supplies information on independent regulatory commissions. (Congressional Quarterly Inc.)

Gallatin Business Intelligence. Resource that provides a review of economic, political, and social conditions, including legal restrictions and investment climate. (Gallatin Publications)

The Gallatin Letter. Weekly report of major economic, political, or social occurrences, with analysis of their impact on business. (New York: Gallatin International Business Service; Coply International)

Government Agencies. A guide to government agencies. (Westport, CT: Greenwood Press, 1983)

Government Documents Collections. Resource that identifies libraries that have significant collections of government documents. (Bellport, NY: The Council, 1992)

Government Publications and Their Use. A listing of government publications. (Washington, DC: Brookings Institution)

Government Reference Books. A listing of available books. (Littleton, CO: Libraries Unlimited)

Government Reference Serials. A listing of available serials. (Englewood, CO: Libraries Unlimited, 1988)

Government Reports Announcements and Index. A biweekly issue that publishes announcements. (Springfield, VA: U.S. Department of Commerce; National Technical Information Service)

Guide to U.S. Government Directories. A listing of available directories. (Phoenix, AZ: Oryx Press, 1981)

Guide to U.S. Government Publications. A listing of available publications. (Ithaca NY: Cornell University Libraries)

Guide to U.S. Government Scientific and Technical Resources. A listing of resources. (Littleton, CO: Libraries Unlimited, 1983)

Handbook on the Use of Government Statistics. Pamphlet designed to aid in understanding government statistics. (Charlottesville, VA: Taylor Murphy Institute)

International Tax Agreements. Lists of comprehensive information on the status of all agreements for the avoidance of double taxation and the prevention of tax evasion. (New York: United Nations Department of Economic and Social Affaires)

International Trade Handbook. Guide that contains sections on basic principals of foreign trade, documentation and finance, legal aspects, selection and training of executives, case histories, operation of overseas trade organizations, and practical problems. (Chicago, IL: Dartnell Corp.)

Introduction to United States Government Information Sources. A listing of government sources. (Englewood, CO: Libraries Unlimited, 1992)

Law and Policy in International Business. Journal that features articles on the political economy and legal aspects of international business. (Washington, DC)

Moody's Municipal and Government Manual. An overview that includes a brief company history, description of the business, names of officers and directors, selected balance sheet statistics, and more. (New York: Moody's Investors Service)

Political Data Handbook OECD Countries. A statistical guide to the government and politics of the 24 OECD countries. (New York: Oxford University Press, 1991)

Political Risk in Thirty-Five Countries. Publication that provides information on the special situations of 35 countries. (London: Euromoney)

Public Affairs Information Service Bulletin. (New York: Public Affairs Information Service)

Statistical Abstract of Latin America. Reference source that includes information on transportation, population, health, education, working conditions, and housing for 20 countries. (Los Angeles: University of California)

Statistical Abstract of the United States. Reference source that includes information on transportation, population, and more. (Washington, DC: U.S. Department of Commerce)

Subject Guide to Major United States Government Publications. A listing of publications. (Chicago, IL: American Library Association)

Subject Guide to U.S. Government Reference Sources. A listing of sources. (Littleton, CO: Libraries Unlimited, 1985)

Tapping the Government Grapevine: The User-Friendly Guide to U.S. Government Information Sources. A listing to information sources. (Phoenix, AR: Oryx Press, 1988)

U.S. Government Publications Relating to the Social Sciences: A Selected Annotated Guide. A listing of publications. (Beverly Hills, CA: Sage Publications)

U.S. Government Scientific and Technical Periodicals. A listing of available periodicals. (Metuchen, NJ: Scarecrow Press)

U.S. Industrial Outlook. Resource that contains recent trends and forecasts for more than 250 industries. (Washington, DC: U.S. Department of Commerce)

United States Government Manual. Publication that provides information on the U.S. government. (Washington, DC: Office of the Federal Register)

United States Government Publications Catalogs. A listing of publications. (Washington, DC: Special Libraries Association, 1988)

Using Government Information Sources: Print and Electronic. A listing of sources. (Phoenix, AZ: Oryx Press, 1994)

Western Europe: A Political and Economic Survey. Publication that contains a series of introductory essays on the European macroeconomy, industry, agriculture, tourism, recent history, and politics. (NA)

STATISTICAL INFORMATION SOURCES

American Statistics Index. (Washington, DC: Congressional Information Services)

Annual Abstract of Statistics. Yearly publication that gives statistical information for the United Kingdom, including vital statistics, social services, public health, education, trade, banking, transportation, energy, and agriculture. (London)

Asia Data Disk. Library of demographic and economic data on 14 Asian countries. (Hong Kong: Asia Studies Ltd.)

Balance of Payment Statistics. Publication that provides statistics on goods and services, long-term and short-term capital, and reserves for more than 110 countries. (NA)

Business Statistics. Publication that provides historical data on an annual, quarterly, or monthly basis. (Washington, DC: U.S. Department of Commerce, Bureau of Economic Analysis)

Catalogue of Publications, OECD. Publications that specialize in comparative statistical information on the OECD's member countries. (Paris: OECD)

Census of Retail Trade. Publication that provides statistics by state, SMSA, and areas outside SMSA for more than 100 different retail enterprises. (Washington, DC: U.S. Department of Commerce, U.S. Census Bureau)

Census of Service Industries. Publication that provides data on approximately 130 service industries. (Washington, DC: U.S. Department of Commerce, U.S. Census Bureau)

Census of Wholesale Trade. Publication that provides statistics for more than 100 kinds of wholesale businesses, with data on number of establishments, sales, inventories, and kind of business. (Washington, DC: U.S. Department of Commerce, U.S. Census Bureau)

China Statistical Yearbook. Annual that presents a broad range of statistical material for the People's Republic of China, including climate, natural resources, employment and wages, investments, public finances, and prices. (Hong Kong: International Centre for the Advancement of Science and Technology; China Statistical Information and Consultancy Service Centre, 1988)

Comparative World Data: A Statistical Handbook for Social Science. Reference source that includes information on military expenditures, gross domestic product, share in world exports, per capita income, strikes, and membership in international organizations. (Baltimore, MD: Johns Hopkins University Press, 1988)

Consumer Europe. Reference that contains the latest statistical information on consumer trends in Western Europe. (Chicago, IL: Euromonitor International Inc.)

Demographic Yearbook. A world summary is followed by groups of chapters dealing with detailed economic statistics, summary economic statistics, and social phenomena. (New York: United Nations Statistical Office)

Direction of Trade Statistics. Source that contains detailed statistical tables on central government revenue, expenditure, lending, financing, and debt. (Washington, DC: International Monetary Fund 1981)

Economic Indicators. Monthly publication of general economic statistics useful for measuring trends in business conditions. (Washington, DC: Council of Economic Advisers, U.S. Government Printing Office)

Encyclopedia of Business Information Sources. Lists of various types of information sources, including statistical publications, directories, and periodicals on 1,086 business topics. (Detroit, MI: Gale Research)

Energy Statistics of OECD Countries 1980–1989. Detailed statistics on production, trade, and consumption based on information obtained in annual OECD questionnaires on oil, natural gas, solid fuels, and manufactured gases. (NA)

Europa Yearbook. Annual that contains detailed information on the political, economic, commercial, and social institutions of the countries of the world. (London: Europa Publications)

European Historical Statistics: 1750–1975. Publication that provides historical statistics of various countries taken from official publications, including population and vital statistics, labor force, industry, external trade, prices, and national accounts. (New York: Facts on File)

European Marketing Data & Statistics. Reference that contains the latest available data on key economic and marketing parameters in 32 European countries. (London: Euromonitor Publications Ltd.)

Handbook on the Use of Government Statistics. Pamphlet designed to aid in understanding government statistics. (Charlottesville, VA: Taylor Murphy Institute)

Industrial Statistics Yearbook. Annual that contains basic data on industrial activity and structure as well as index numbers of industrial production and employment. (New York: Department of Economic and Social Affairs, Statistical Office of the UN, 1982)

International Financial Statistics. Reference source that includes exchange rates, money and banking statistics, interest rates, and government finance. (Washington, DC: International Monetary Fund)

International Historical Statistics: Africa and Asia. Reference source that contains information on climate, population, labor force, agriculture, industrial production, trade, and education. (New York: New York University Press, 1982)

International Historical Statistics: The Americas and Australia. Volume that presents statistics on population, climate, labor force, industrial production, agriculture, education, and trade. (Detroit, MI: Gale Research, 1983)

International Marketing Data and Statistics. Publication that provides data on business and marketing parameters, including literacy and education, consumer expenditure, and demographic trends and forecasts. (London: Euromonitor Publications Ltd.)

International Trade Statistics Yearbook. Annual containing import and export statistics for more than 150 countries. (New York: United Nations, 1985)

Investment Statistics Locator. Volume that includes statistics on stock and bond prices, mutual fund sales and assets, earnings, foreign exchange rates, and interest rates. (Phoenix, AZ: Oryx Press, 1995)

IRM Directory of Statistics of International Investment and Production. Reference that contains data on the international investment position of 80 countries, with a description of the main features of the international investment, policies regarding inward and outward capital flows, and main sources of statistical data. (New York: New York University Press, 1987)

Japan Statistical Yearbook. Annual containing statistics including climate, population, transportation, health and sanitation, disasters and accidents, prices, and public finance. (Sorifu, Tokeikyoku, Tokoyo)

Korea Statistical Yearbook. Annual that includes statistics on population, wages, climate, health and social security, foreign trade, national accounts, wholesale and retail trade, construction, and mining and manufacturing. (Seoul: Ky ongje Kihoegw on)

Marketing Information Guide. Monthly listing of current reports and statistics on marketing and distribution practices. (Washington, DC: U.S. Department of Commerce)

Monthly Bulletin of Statistics. Periodical containing comprehensive statistical data for more than 200 countries, including information on population, trade, manufacturing, and national accounts. (New York: United Nations Statistical Office)

National Accounts Statistics: Main Aggregates and Detailed Tables. Reference source that presents detailed national accounts estimates for more than 160 countries and areas. (New York: United Nations)

One Hundred Years of Economic Statistics. Volume that contains statistics for balance of payments, rates of growth of productivity, share prices and interest rates, distribution of employment, and industrial production. (New York: Facts on File, 1989)

Predicast's Basebook. Publication that provides economic forecasting statistics. (Cleveland, OH: Predicasts Inc.)

Rand McNally Commercial Atlas and Market Guide. Reference source that provides demographic data and statistical indicators of market potential for U.S. cities, counties, and regions. (NA)

SRDS Report. Newsletter that focuses on media trends, with graphs, charts, and statistics. (Wilmette, IL: SRDS Report)

Standard & Poor's Statistical Service. Resource that provides historical statistical data on a variety of industrial topics, including finance, production and labor, and income and trade. (New York: Standard & Poor's Corp.)

Stateman's Yearbook. Annual that includes comprehensive statistical tables for selected commodities, a list of international organizations, and data on demographics, industry statistics, imports, and exports. (New York: St. Martin's Press)

Statistical Abstract of Latin America. Volume that includes information on transportation, population, health, education, working conditions, and housing for 20 countries. (Los Angeles: University of California)

Statistical Abstract of the United States. Source that includes information on transportation, population, and more. (Washington, DC: U.S. Department of Commerce)

Statistical Yearbook. Digest of statistics for more than 270 UN member countries and territories, with information on manufacturing, finance, transportation, import/export trade, balance of payments, wages, and prices. (New York: United Nations)

Statistics Europe: Sources for Social, Economic and Market Research. Lists of name, address, and telephone number of central statistical office for each country, and principal libraries where statistical sources may be consulted. (Beckenham, UK: CBD Research, 1981)

Statistics Sources. Subject guide to information on business, industrial, social, educational, and financial information. (Detroit, MI: Gale Research)

Trade and Securities Statistics. Publication that provides current and historical information. (New York: Standard & Poor's Corp.)

United Nations Statistical Yearbook. Annual publication of statistics on economics, manufacturing, agriculture, and social indicators for UN member nations. (New York: United Nations)

USSR Facts and Figures Annual. Yearly publication that includes information on construction, industrial development, GNP, labor force, population, energy, agriculture, and transportation. (Gulf Breeze, FL: Academic International Press)

The World in Figures. Publication that provides detailed statistics for every country, including exchange rates, growth rates, resources, production, and trade. (New York: John Wiley & Sons)

World Trade. Summary as well as detailed trade statistics by commodity and trading partner. (New York: United Nations Statistical Office)

Yearbook of International Trade Statistics. Annual that gives the individual country's external trade performance in terms of the overall trends in current values, volume, and prices. (New York: United Nations Statistical Office)

Yearbook of National Accounting Statistics. Annual publication that gives GNP, national income, gross domestic product consumption, and more. (New York: United Nations Statistical Office)

Appendix C
Statistical Tables

Table C1.   **Random Numbers**

02711	08182	75997	79866	58095	83319	80295	79741	74599	84379
94873	90935	31684	63952	09865	14491	99518	93394	34691	14985
54921	78680	06635	98689	17306	25170	65928	87709	30533	89736
77640	97636	37397	93379	56454	59818	45827	74164	71666	46977
61545	00835	93251	87203	36759	49197	85967	01704	19634	21898
17147	19519	22497	16857	42426	84822	92598	49186	88247	39967
13748	04742	92460	85801	53444	65626	58710	55406	17173	69776
87455	14813	50373	28037	91182	32786	65261	11173	34376	36408
08999	57409	91185	10200	61411	23392	47797	56377	71635	08601
78804	81333	53809	32471	46034	36306	22498	19239	85428	55721
82173	26921	28472	98958	07960	66124	89731	95069	18625	92405
97594	25168	89178	68190	05043	17407	48201	83917	11413	72920
73881	67176	93504	42636	38233	16154	96451	57925	29667	30859
46071	22912	90326	42453	88108	72064	58601	32357	90610	32921
44492	19686	12495	93135	95185	77799	52441	88272	22024	80631
31864	72170	37722	55794	14636	05148	54505	50113	21119	25228
51574	90692	43339	65689	76539	27909	05467	21727	51141	72949
35350	76132	92925	92124	92634	35681	43690	89136	35599	84138
46943	36502	01172	46045	46991	33804	80006	35542	61056	75666
22665	87226	33304	57975	03985	21566	65796	72915	81466	89205
39437	97957	11838	10433	21564	51570	73558	27495	34533	57808
77082	47784	40098	97962	89845	28392	78187	06112	08169	11261
24544	25649	43370	28007	06779	72402	62632	53956	24709	06978
27503	15558	37738	24849	70722	71859	83736	06016	94397	12529
24590	24545	06435	52758	45685	90151	46516	49644	92686	84870
48155	86226	40359	28723	15364	69125	12609	49644	86857	31702
20226	53752	90648	24362	83314	00014	19207	57171	97016	86290
70178	73444	38790	53626	93780	18629	68766	69413	74639	30782
10169	41465	51935	05711	09799	79077	88159	24371	68519	03040
81084	03701	28598	70013	63794	53169	97054	33437	23259	96196
69202	20777	21727	81511	51887	16175	53746	60303	70339	62727
80561	95787	89426	93325	86412	57479	54194	46516	19197	81877
08199	26703	95128	48599	09333	12584	24374	52153	61782	44032
98883	28220	39358	53720	80161	83371	15181	31232	12219	55920
84568	69286	76054	21615	80883	36797	82845	11131	90900	18172

(continued)

04269	35173	95745	53893	86022	77722	52498	39139	22448	22571
10538	13124	36099	13140	37706	44562	57179	84193	67877	01549
77843	24955	25900	63843	95029	93859	93634	44693	66294	41218
12034	94636	49455	76362	83532	31062	69903	20205	65768	55949
10524	72829	47641	93315	80875	28090	97728	91186	34937	79548
68935	76632	46984	61772	92786	22651	07086	52560	44143	97687
89450	65665	29190	43709	11172	34481	95977	89754	25658	73898
90696	20451	24211	97310	60446	73530	62865	47535	13829	72226
49006	32047	93086	00112	20470	17136	28255	96574	07293	38809
74591	87025	52368	59416	34417	70557	86746	86328	53628	12000
06315	17012	77103	00968	07235	10728	42189	55809	51487	64443
62386	09184	62092	46617	99419	64230	95034	33292	07857	42510
86848	82122	04028	36959	87827	12813	08627	85481	13345	51695
65643	69480	46598	04501	40403	91408	32343	80699	49303	90689
11084	46534	78957	77353	39578	77868	22970	48130	09184	70603

Table C2.　**Area under Normal Distribution**

Example:
If z = 1.96, then
P(0 to z) = 0.4750

z	0.00	0.01	0.02	0.03	0.04	0.05	0.06	0.07	0.08	0.09
0.0	0.0000	0.0040	0.0080	0.0120	0.0160	0.0199	0.0239	0.0279	0.0319	0.0359
0.1	0.0398	0.0438	0.0478	0.0517	0.0557	0.0596	0.0636	0.0675	0.0714	0.0753
0.2	0.0793	0.0832	0.0871	0.0910	0.0948	0.0987	0.1026	0.1064	0.1103	0.1141
0.3	0.1179	0.1217	0.1255	0.1293	0.1331	0.1368	0.1406	0.1443	0.1480	0.1517
0.4	0.1554	0.1591	0.1628	0.1664	0.1700	0.1736	0.1772	0.1808	0.1844	0.1879
0.5	0.1915	0.1950	0.1985	0.2019	0.2054	0.2088	0.2123	0.2157	0.2190	0.2224
0.6	0.2257	0.2291	0.2324	0.2357	0.2389	0.2422	0.2454	0.2486	0.2517	0.2549
0.7	0.2580	0.2611	0.2642	0.2673	0.2704	0.2734	0.2764	0.2794	0.2823	0.2852
0.8	0.2881	0.2910	0.2939	0.2967	0.2995	0.3023	0.3051	0.3078	0.3106	0.3133
0.9	0.3159	0.3186	0.3212	0.3238	0.3264	0.3289	0.3315	0.3340	0.3365	0.3389
1.0	0.3413	0.3438	0.3461	0.3485	0.3508	0.3531	0.3554	0.3577	0.3599	0.3621
1.1	0.3643	0.3665	0.3686	0.3708	0.3729	0.3749	0.3770	0.3790	0.3810	0.3830
1.2	0.3849	0.3869	0.3888	0.3907	0.3925	0.3944	0.3962	0.3980	0.3997	0.4015
1.3	0.4032	0.4049	0.4066	0.4082	0.4099	0.4115	0.4131	0.4147	0.4162	0.4177
1.4	0.4192	0.4207	0.4222	0.4236	0.4251	0.4265	0.4279	0.4292	0.4306	0.4319
1.5	0.4332	0.4345	0.4357	0.4370	0.4382	0.4394	0.4406	0.4418	0.4429	0.4441
1.6	0.4452	0.4463	0.4474	0.4484	0.4495	0.4505	0.4515	0.4525	0.4535	0.4545
1.7	0.4554	0.4564	0.4573	0.4582	0.4591	0.4599	0.4608	0.4616	0.4625	0.4633
1.8	0.4641	0.4649	0.4656	0.4664	0.4671	0.4678	0.4686	0.4693	0.4699	0.4706
1.9	0.4713	0.4719	0.4726	0.4732	0.4738	0.4744	0.4750	0.4756	0.4761	0.4767
2.0	0.4772	0.4778	0.4783	0.4788	0.4793	0.4798	0.4803	0.4808	0.4812	0.4817
2.1	0.4821	0.4826	0.4830	0.4834	0.4838	0.4842	0.4846	0.4850	0.4854	0.4857
2.2	0.4861	0.4864	0.4868	0.4871	0.4875	0.4878	0.4881	0.4884	0.4887	0.4890
2.3	0.4893	0.4896	0.4898	0.4901	0.4904	0.4906	0.4909	0.4911	0.4913	0.4916
2.4	0.4918	0.4920	0.4922	0.4925	0.4927	0.4929	0.4931	0.4932	0.4934	0.4936
2.5	0.4938	0.4940	0.4941	0.4943	0.4945	0.4946	0.4948	0.4949	0.4951	0.4952
2.6	0.4953	0.4955	0.4956	0.4957	0.4959	0.4960	0.4961	0.4962	0.4963	0.4964
2.7	0.4965	0.4966	0.4967	0.4968	0.4969	0.4970	0.4971	0.4972	0.4973	0.4974
2.8	0.4974	0.4975	0.4976	0.4977	0.4977	0.4978	0.4979	0.4979	0.4980	0.4981
2.9	0.4981	0.4982	0.4982	0.4983	0.4984	0.4984	0.4985	0.4985	0.4986	0.4986
3.0	0.4987	0.4987	0.4987	0.4988	0.4988	0.4989	0.4989	0.4989	0.4990	0.4990

Table C3.   **t Distribution**

.10

Example: With
df = 9 and .10 area
in the upper tail,
t = 1.383

	Confidence Limits					
	80%	90%	95%	98%	99%	99.9%
	Level of Significance					
	0.100	0.050	0.025	0.010	0.005	0.0005
Degrees of Freedom (df)	Level of Significance for Two-Tailed Test					
	0.20	0.10	0.05	0.02	0.01	0.001
1	3.078	6.314	12.706	31.821	63.657	636.619
2	1.886	2.920	4.303	6.965	9.925	31.599
3	1.638	2.353	3,182	4.541	5.841	12.924
4	1.533	2.132	2.776	3.747	4.604	8.610
5	1.476	2.015	2.571	3.365	4.032	6.869
6	1.440	1.943	2.447	3.143	3.707	5.959
7	1.415	1.895	2.365	2.998	3.499	5.408
8	1.397	1.860	2.306	2.896	3.355	5.041
9	1.383	1.833	2.262	2.821	3.250	4.781
10	1.372	1.812	2.228	2.764	3.169	4.587
11	1.363	1.796	2.201	2.718	3.106	4.437
12	1.356	1.782	2.179	2.681	3.055	4.318
13	1.350	1.771	2.160	2.650	3.012	4.221
14	1.345	1.761	2.145	2.624	2.977	4.140
15	1.341	1.753	2.131	2.602	2.947	4.073
16	1.337	1.746	2.120	2.583	2.921	4.015
17	1.333	1.740	2.110	2.567	2.898	3.965
18	1.330	1.734	2.101	2.552	2.878	3.922
19	1.328	1.729	2.093	2.539	2.861	3.883
20	1.325	1.725	2.086	2.528	2.845	3.850
21	1.323	1.721	2.080	2.518	2.831	3.819
22	1.321	1.717	2.074	2.508	2.819	3.792
23	1.319	1.714	2.069	2.500	2.807	3.768
24	1.318	1.711	2.064	2.492	2.797	3.745
25	1.316	1.708	2.060	2.485	2.787	3.725
26	1.315	1.706	2.056	2.479	2.779	3.707
27	1.314	1.703	2.052	2.473	2.771	3.690
28	1.313	1.701	2.048	2.467	2.763	3.674
29	1.311	1.699	2.045	2.462	2.756	3.659
30	1.310	1.697	2.042	2.457	2.750	3.646
40	1.303	1.684	2.021	2.423	2.704	3.551
60	1.296	1.671	2.000	2.390	2.660	3.460
120	1.289	1.658	1.980	2.358	2.617	3.373
∞	1.282	1.645	1.960	2.326	2.576	3.291

Table C4.   **Chi-square Test**

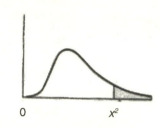

.Example: With 17
df and a .02 area in
the upper tail, $x^2 = 30.995$

0   x^2

Degrees of Freedom (df)	Right-Tail Area			
	0.10	0.05	0.02	0.01
1	2.706	3.841	5.412	6.635
2	4605	5.991	7.824	9.210
3	6.251	7.815	9.837	11.345
4	7.779	9.488	11.668	13.277
5	9.236	11.070	13.388	15.086
6	10.645	12.592	15.033	16.812
7	12.017	14.067	16.622	18.475
8	13.362	15.507	18.168	20.090
9	14.684	16.919	19.679	21.666
10	15.987	18.307	21.161	23.209
11	17.275	19.675	22.618	24.725
12	18.549	21.026	24.054	26.217
13	19.812	22.362	25.472	27.688
14	21.064	23.685	26.873	29.141
15	22.307	24.996	28.259	30.578
16	23.542	26.296	29.633	32.000
17	24.769	27.587	30.995	33.409
18	25.989	28,869	32.346	34.805
19	27.204	30.144	33.687	36.191
20	28.412	31.410	35.020	37.566
21	29.615	32.671	36.343	38.932
22	30.813	33.924	37.659	40.289
23	32.007	35.172	38.968	41.638
24	33.196	36.415	40.270	42.980
25	34.382	37.652	41.566	44.314
26	35.563	38.885	42.856	45.642
27	36.741	40.113	44.140	46.963
28	37.916	41.337	45.419	48.278
29	39.087	42.557	46.693	49.588
30	40.256	43.773	47.962	50.892

Table C5. F Distribution, $\alpha = 0.05$

.05

Degrees of Freedom for the Numerator

Degrees of Freedom for the Denominator	1	2	3	4	5	6	7	8	9	10	12	15	20	24	30	40
1	161	200	216	225	230	234	237	239	241	242	244	246	248	249	250	251
2	18.5	19.0	19.2	19.2	19.3	19.3	19.4	19.4	19.4	19.4	19.4	19.4	19.4	19.5	19.5	19.5
3	10.1	9.55	9.28	9.12	9.01	8.94	8.89	8.85	8.81	8.79	8.74	8.70	8.66	8.64	8.62	8.59
4	7.71	6.94	6.59	6.39	6.26	6.16	6.09	6.04	6.00	5.96	5.91	5.86	5.80	5.77	5.75	5.72
5	6.61	5.79	5.41	5.19	5.05	4.95	4.88	4.82	4.77	4.74	4.68	4.62	4.56	4.53	4.50	4.46
6	5.99	5.14	4.76	4.53	4.39	4.28	4.21	4.15	4.10	4.06	4.00	3.94	3.87	3.84	3.81	3.77
7	5.59	4.74	4.35	4.12	3.97	3.87	3.79	3.73	3.68	3.64	3.57	3.51	3.44	3.41	3.38	3.34
8	5.32	4.46	4.07	3.84	3.69	3.58	3.50	3.44	3.39	3.35	3.28	3.22	3.15	3.12	3.08	3.04
9	5.12	4.26	3.86	3.63	3.48	3.37	3.29	3.23	3.18	3.14	3.07	3.01	2.94	2.90	2.86	2.83
10	4.96	4.10	3.71	3.48	3.33	3.22	3.14	3.07	3.02	2.98	2.91	2.85	2.77	2.74	2.70	2.66
11	4.84	3.98	3.59	3.36	3.20	3.09	3.01	2.95	2.90	2.85	2.79	2.72	2.65	2.61	2.57	2.53
12	4.75	3.89	3.49	3.26	3.11	3.00	2.91	2.85	2.80	2.75	2.69	2.62	2.54	2.51	2.47	2.43
13	4.67	3.81	3.41	3.18	3.03	2.92	2.83	2.77	2.71	2.67	2.60	2.53	2.46	2.42	2.38	2.34
14	4.60	3.74	3.34	3.11	2.96	2.85	2.76	2.70	2.65	2.60	2.53	2.46	2.39	2.35	2.31	2.27
15	4.54	3.68	3.29	3.06	2.90	2.79	2.71	2.64	2.59	2.54	2.48	2.40	2.33	2.29	2.25	2.20
16	4.49	3.63	3.24	3.01	2.85	2.74	2.66	2.59	2.54	2.49	2.42	2.35	2.28	2.24	2.19	2.15
17	4.45	3.59	3.20	2.96	2.81	2.70	2.61	2.55	2.49	2.45	2.38	2.31	2.23	2.19	2.15	2.10
18	4.41	3.55	3.16	2.93	2.77	2.66	2.58	2.51	2.46	2.41	2.34	2.27	2.19	2.15	2.11	2.06
19	4.38	3.52	3.13	2.90	2.74	2.63	2.54	2.48	2.42	2.38	2.31	2.23	2.16	2.11	2.07	2.03
20	4.35	3.49	3.10	2.87	2.71	2.60	2.51	2.45	2.39	2.35	2.28	2.20	2.12	2.08	2.04	1.99
21	4.32	3.47	3.07	2.84	2.68	2.57	2.49	2.42	2.37	2.32	2.25	2.18	2.10	2.05	2.01	1.96
22	4.30	3.44	3.05	2.82	2.66	2.55	2.46	2.40	2.34	2.30	2.23	2.15	2.07	2.03	1.98	1.94
23	4.28	3.42	3.03	2.80	2.64	2.53	2.44	2.37	2.32	2.27	2.20	2.13	2.05	2.01	1.96	1.91
24	4.26	3.40	3.01	2.78	2.62	2.51	2.42	2.36	2.30	2.25	2.18	2.11	2.03	1.98	1.94	1.89
25	4.24	3.39	2.99	2.76	2.60	2.49	2.40	2.34	2.28	2.24	2.16	2.09	2.01	1.96	1.92	1.87
30	4.17	3.32	2.92	2.69	2.53	2.42	2.33	2.27	2.21	2.16	2.09	2.01	1.93	1.89	1.84	1.79
40	4.08	3.23	2.84	2.61	2.45	2.34	2.25	2.18	2.12	2.08	2.00	1.92	1.84	1.79	1.74	1.69
60	4.00	3.15	2.76	2.53	2.37	2.25	2.17	2.10	2.04	1.99	1.92	1.84	1.75	1.70	1.65	1.59
120	3.92	3.07	2.68	2.45	2.29	2.18	2.09	2.02	1.96	1.91	1.83	1.75	1.66	1.61	1.55	1.50
∞	3.84	3.00	2.60	2.37	2.21	2.10	2.01	1.94	1.88	1.83	1.75	1.67	1.57	1.52	1.46	1.39

Table C6. F Distribution, $\alpha = 0.01$

	Degrees of Freedom for the Numerator															
	1	2	3	4	5	6	7	8	9	10	12	15	20	24	30	40
1	4052	5000	5403	5625	5764	5859	5928	5981	6022	6056	6106	6157	6209	6235	6261	6287
2	98.5	99.0	99.2	99.2	99.3	99.3	99.4	99.4	99.4	99.4	99.4	99.4	99.4	99.5	99.5	99.5
3	34.1	30.8	29.5	28.7	28.2	27.9	27.7	27.5	27.3	27.2	27.1	26.9	26.7	26.6	26.5	26.4
4	21.2	18.0	16.7	16.0	15.5	15.2	15.0	14.8	14.7	14.5	14.4	14.2	14.0	13.9	13.8	13.7
5	16.3	13.3	12.1	11.4	11.0	10.7	10.5	10.3	10.2	10.1	9.89	9.72	9.55	9.47	9.38	9.29
6	13.7	10.9	9.78	9.15	8.75	8.47	8.26	8.10	7.98	7.87	7.72	7.56	7.40	7.31	7.23	7.14
7	12.2	9.55	8.45	7.85	7.46	7.19	6.99	6.84	6.72	6.62	6.47	6.31	6.16	6.07	5.99	5.91
8	11.3	8.65	7.59	7.01	6.63	6.37	6.18	6.03	5.91	5.81	5.67	5.52	5.36	5.28	5.20	5.12
9	10.6	8.02	6.99	6.42	6.06	5.80	5.61	5.47	5.35	5.26	5.11	4.96	4.81	4.73	4.65	4.57
10	10.0	7.56	6.55	5.99	5.64	5.39	5.20	5.06	4.94	4.85	4.71	4.56	4.41	4.33	4.25	4.17
11	9.65	7.21	6.22	5.67	5.32	5.07	4.89	4.74	4.63	4.54	4.40	4.25	4.10	4.02	3.94	3.86
12	9.33	6.93	5.95	5.41	5.06	4.82	4.64	4.50	4.39	4.30	4.16	4.01	3.86	3.78	3.70	3.62
13	9.07	6.70	5.74	5.21	4.86	4.62	4.44	4.30	4.19	4.10	3.96	3.82	3.66	3.59	3.51	3.43
14	8.86	6.51	5.56	5.04	4.69	4.46	4.28	4.14	4.03	3.94	3.80	3.66	3.51	3.43	3.35	3.27
15	8.68	6.36	5.42	4.89	4.56	4.32	4.14	4.00	3.89	3.80	3.67	3.52	3.37	3.29	3.21	3.13
16	8.53	6.23	5.29	4.77	4.44	4.20	4.03	3.89	3.78	3.69	3.55	3.41	3.26	3.18	3.10	3.02
17	8.40	6.11	5.18	4.67	4.34	4.10	3.93	3.79	3.68	3.59	3.46	3.31	3.16	3.08	3.00	2.92
18	8.29	6.01	5.09	4.58	4.25	4.01	3.84	3.71	3.60	3.51	3.37	3.23	3.08	3.00	2.92	2.84
19	8.18	5.93	5.01	4.50	4.17	3.94	3.77	3.63	3.52	3.43	3.30	3.15	3.00	2.92	2.84	2.76
20	8.10	5.85	4.94	4.43	4.10	3.87	3.70	3.56	3.46	3.37	3.23	3.09	2.94	2.86	2.78	2.69
21	8.02	5.78	4.87	4.37	4.04	3.81	3.64	3.51	3.40	3.31	3.17	3.03	2.88	2.80	2.72	2.64
22	7.95	5.72	4.82	4.31	3.99	3.76	3.59	3.45	3.35	3.26	3.12	2.98	2.83	2.75	2.67	2.58
23	7.88	5.66	4.76	4.26	3.94	3.71	3.54	3.41	3.30	3.21	3.07	2.93	2.78	2.70	2.62	2.54
24	7.82	5.61	4.72	4.22	3.90	3.67	3.50	3.36	3.26	3.17	3.03	2.89	2.74	2.66	2.58	2.49
25	7.77	5.57	4.68	4.18	3.85	3.63	3.46	3.32	3.22	3.13	2.99	2.85	2.70	2.62	2.54	2.45
30	7.56	5.39	4.51	4.02	3.70	3.47	3.30	3.17	3.07	2.98	2.84	2.70	2.55	2.47	2.39	2.30
40	7.31	5.18	4.31	3.83	3.51	3.29	3.12	2.99	2.89	2.80	2.66	2.52	2.37	2.29	2.20	2.11
60	7.08	4.98	4.13	3.65	3.34	3.12	2.95	2.82	2.72	2.63	2.50	2.35	2.20	2.12	2.03	1.94
120	6.85	4.79	3.95	3.48	3.17	2.96	2.79	2.66	2.56	2.47	2.34	2.19	2.03	1.95	1.86	1.76
∞	6.63	4.61	3.78	3.32	3.02	2.80	2.64	2.51	2.41	2.32	2.18	2.04	1.88	1.79	1.70	1.59

Degrees of Freedom for the Denominator

Appendix D
Statistical Software Packages

D1. AN INTRODUCTION TO SPSS

HELPFUL HINTS FOR SPSS

1. This handout will give a brief introduction to SPSS.[1] SPSS is a statistical program that can be used to perform data analysis in marketing research. We will use this program to do real data analysis this semester. I will demonstrate its use and discuss various analytical techniques in class, and you will use it to perform data analysis for your project. It is a very simple and user-friendly program. But it is important that you get started early and become familiar with the program so that you are ready to understand analytical techniques when we discuss them in class and to use it to perform analysis for your project in the latter part of the semester.

2. We start with the assumption that you are familiar with Windows XP operating systems and that you have visited the computer lab at least once. PCs in the Hammer lab are now equipped to run Windows XP applications. We will use the Windows XP version of SPSS for all analytical work this semester. Although you are free to use any version of Windows, class discussions, handouts, and class demonstrations will focus on the Windows XP version of SPSS.

3. To get started, you will need a 3.5" disk (high-density formatted) or a Zip disk. You will use this disk to save your data and output files. Step-by-step directions to get started are given below.

4. In the lab, start the PC and log on to the network. Instructions for logging on are posted in the lab.

5. From the Windows Program Manager, first select Database/statistical group and then select SPSS 11.5 or the available version of SPSS by clicking on the appropriate icons.

6. Selecting SPSS and choosing the Type Data option will open the SPSS application window, as shown in Figure D.1. In the main SPSS application window, you will see the menu bar at the top (consisting of File, Edit, Data, etc.). Under this you will see the toolbar (consisting of buttons for Open file, Save, Print, etc.). Some of the tools in the toolbar are core tools and others are window-specific tools. In the main SPSS

Figure D.1

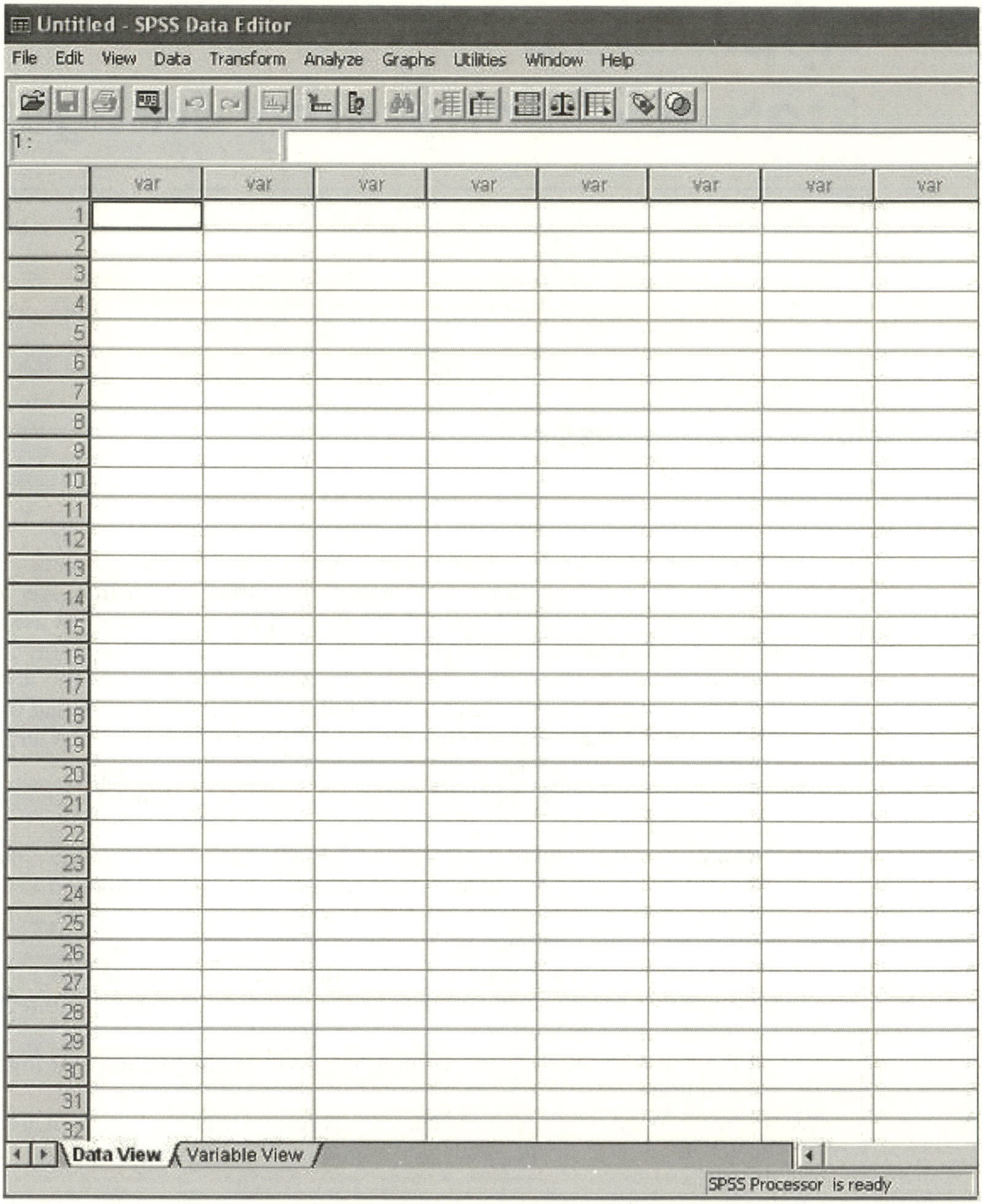

application window, you will see two cascading windows (Output and Newdata). At the bottom, under the main area, you will see the status line showing "SPSS processor is ready." The same status line will also show the description of specific tools as you point the cursor at the button for that specific tool.

7. Move your pointer across the toolbar and notice how the description in the status line changes. As you point to each button, the status bar will tell you what the function of that button is. For example, the first button is File Open.

8. The Newdata window (the Data Editor) looks like a spreadsheet, with "var" as the heading for each column and 1,2,3, and so on as row headings. You can enter your data into this spreadsheet or read your data from external files stored on your disk. SPSS supports many different formats for external data files. In any case, you will be able to see your data anytime during your SPSS session in this spreadsheet format. (More about this window later.)

9. The Output window will eventually show your program output. As you do some analysis, the output will go to this window. You can see the output as you go along, print it, save it, or edit it, if desired.

10. You can open many other windows as the need arises. For example, you can open a help window, syntax window, chart window, command structure window, or multiple data, output, and syntax windows. Also, these windows can be enlarged to occupy the whole area or reduced to a small size. Generally, you will maximize the window you are working with and minimize other windows.

11. You can exit SPSS as you exit any Windows program, by clicking on the top left-hand corner box and selecting Close. If on the first day you want to stop at this point, it is okay. If you are more daring, you can go on to the next step.

RUNNING A SAMPLE SPSS PROGRAM

12. For your first program, maximize the Newdata window and enter the following data in the spreadsheet. Each line represents a separate record (respondent), and the three columns represent three variables (age, income, sex). Notice that the sex variable is coded as 1 or 2. Here 1 represents "female" and 2 represents "male." Each variable will occupy a separate column. After you have entered all the data, your spreadsheet (data editor) will look like Figure D.2.

25	25000	1
24	26000	1
30	45000	1
35	42000	2
25	23000	2
22	18000	2
30	25000	2

13. If you like, you can give names to your variables. Go to the lower left corner of the screen and locate the Variable View button. Click it and you will see the screen shown in Figure D.3. To change the name of variable "var00001," highlight "var00001" (see Figure D.4) and type in the desired name, say, "age." You may do the same for the other two variables, changing them to "income," and "sex." See Figure D.5 for the result of this process. If you want, you can use the same dialog box to go to other dialog boxes to change settings for type of variable, variable label, value labels, missing values, and column formats (more about this in a little while). Finally, you may want to save the file you have just created under a name of your choice, say, "SPSS example1."

Figure D.2

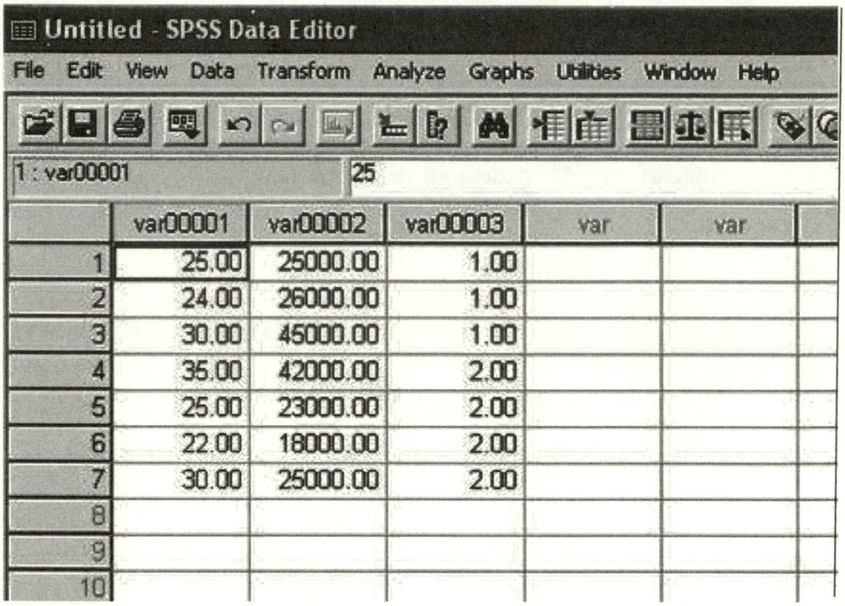

14. Since you know that for the variable "sex," 1 stands for "female" and 2 stands for "male," you can tell SPSS about this. To do this, go the same Variable View window and find the Values button for this variable, "sex." Currently, this button displays None to indicate that no values have been defined. Double-click on the Value (None) button for "sex" and you will see the pop-up window Value Labels, as shown in Figure D.6. In the space marked Value, type "1," and in the space marked Value Label, type its associated label "female." Click the Add button. As you do this, you will notice that '1.00="FEMALE" appears in the box next to the buttons. Similarly, type "2" in the space for Value and "Male" in the space for Value Label, and click the Add button. As you do this, '2.00="MALE" will appear in the box next to the buttons. Finally, click on Continue and OK to complete the task.

15. Now your data file has three variables: age, annual income, and sex (1 = Female, 2 = Male). Also, you have seven observations in the data file. These data are from a survey of individuals about their incomes (Figure D.7).

16. To perform any analysis, you can use the menu and dialog boxes. For simplicity, we will use menu and dialog boxes for almost all the analyses we perform this semester. Click on Analyze in the menu bar and select Descriptive Statistics and Frequencies from the submenus (Figures D.8 and D.9). This will open the Frequencies main dialog box (Figure D.10). In this dialog box, you will see that all the variables in your active data file are listed in the left-hand box. From this list you can select any number of variables for running frequencies. Select all three variables from the list and click on the right arrow. All three variables will appear in the Variable(s) box, indicating that you have selected these variables for the analysis. Click OK to run the Frequencies command.

Figure D.3

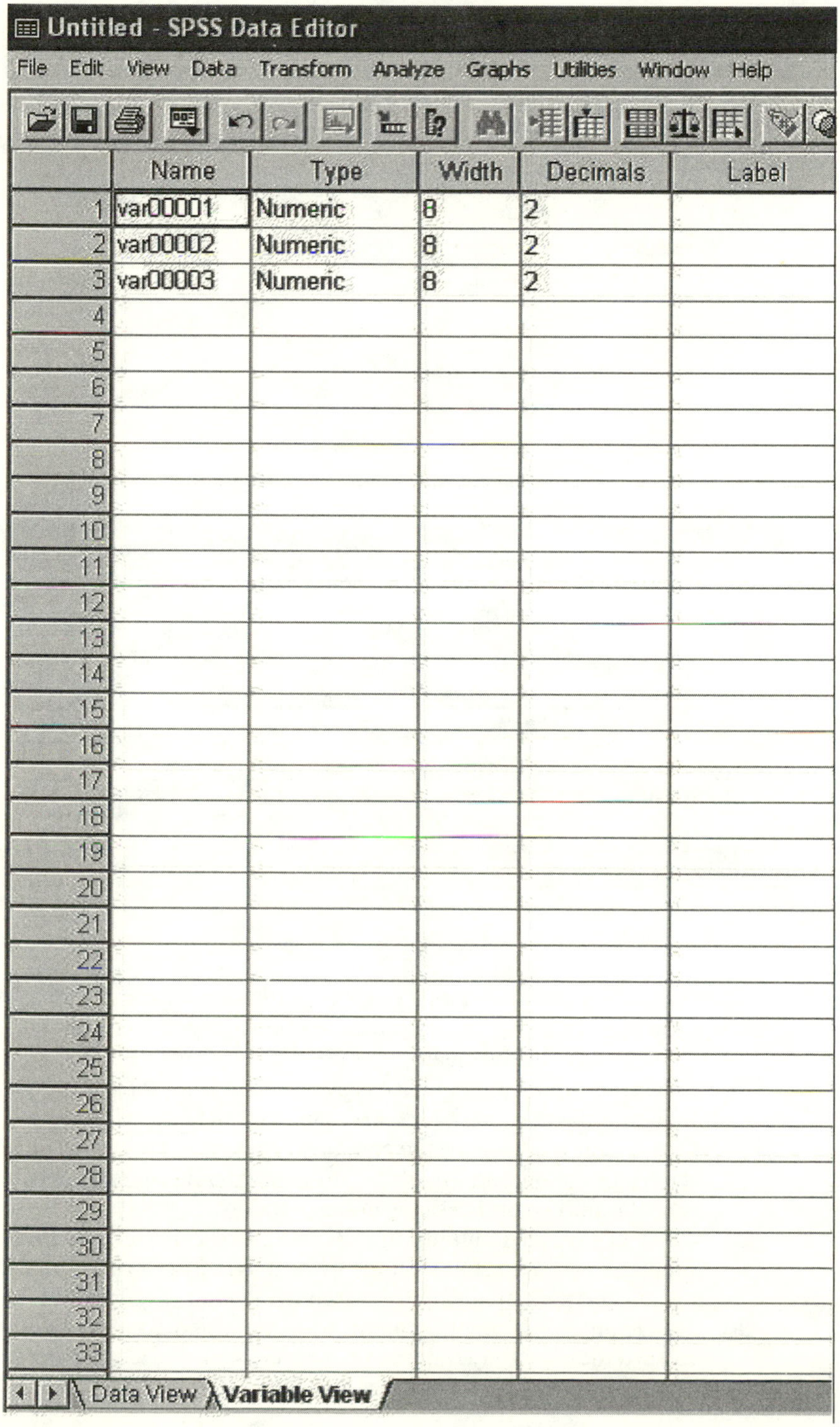

		Name	Type	Width	Decimals	Label
	1	var00001	Numeric	8	2	
	2	var00002	Numeric	8	2	
	3	var00003	Numeric	8	2	
	4					
	5					
	6					
	7					
	8					
	9					
	10					
	11					
	12					
	13					
	14					
	15					
	16					
	17					
	18					
	19					
	20					
	21					
	22					
	23					
	24					
	25					
	26					
	27					
	28					
	29					
	30					
	31					
	32					
	33					

Data View \ Variable View

Figure D.4

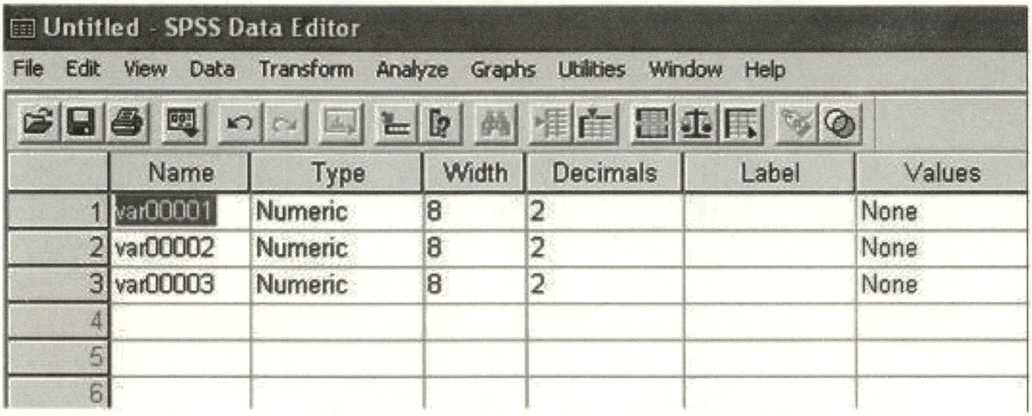

	Name	Type	Width	Decimals	Label	Values
1	var00001	Numeric	8	2		None
2	var00002	Numeric	8	2		None
3	var00003	Numeric	8	2		None
4						
5						
6						

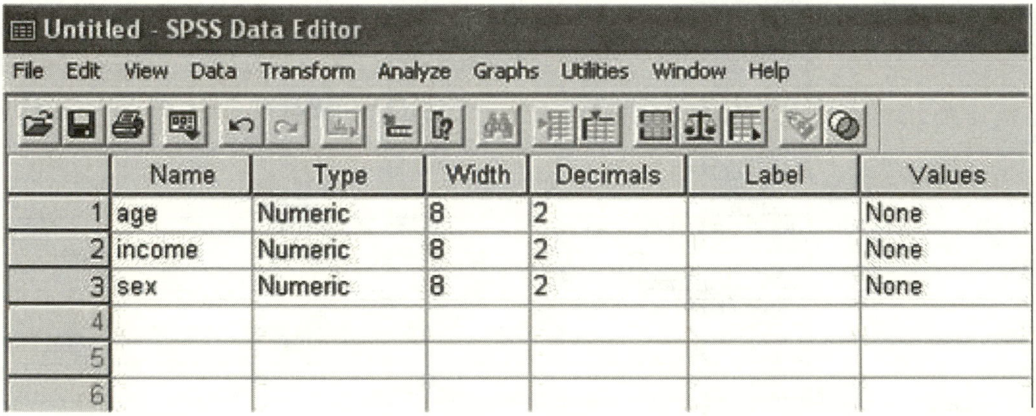

Untitled - SPSS Data Editor
File   Edit   View   Data   Transform   Analyze   Graphs   Utilities   Window   Help

Figure D.5

	Name	Type	Width	Decimals	Label	Values
1	age	Numeric	8	2		None
2	income	Numeric	8	2		None
3	sex	Numeric	8	2		None
4						
5						
6						

Untitled - SPSS Data Editor
File   Edit   View   Data   Transform   Analyze   Graphs   Utilities   Window   Help

17. As your command is being run, you will notice that the status line changes to "Running . . . ," and when the command sequence is complete, the status line shows "SPSS Processor Is Ready" again.

18. When the command sequence is over, you will see the output window with frequency tables for the three variables. You can maximize this window and scroll through your output. You will also see the command syntax that was used to generate this output at the top of the output. Finally, if your command sequence encountered any problem, you will find error messages in this window.

19. You can save this output, print it, or edit it. Click on the Print button to print this output. It will be printed on the default Windows printer attached to your PC. You can go and pick up this output from the printer (Figure D.11).

20. By default, your output, command syntax, and data files are not saved. You have to save them if you so desire. However, you will be prompted to save before you exit.

Figure D.6

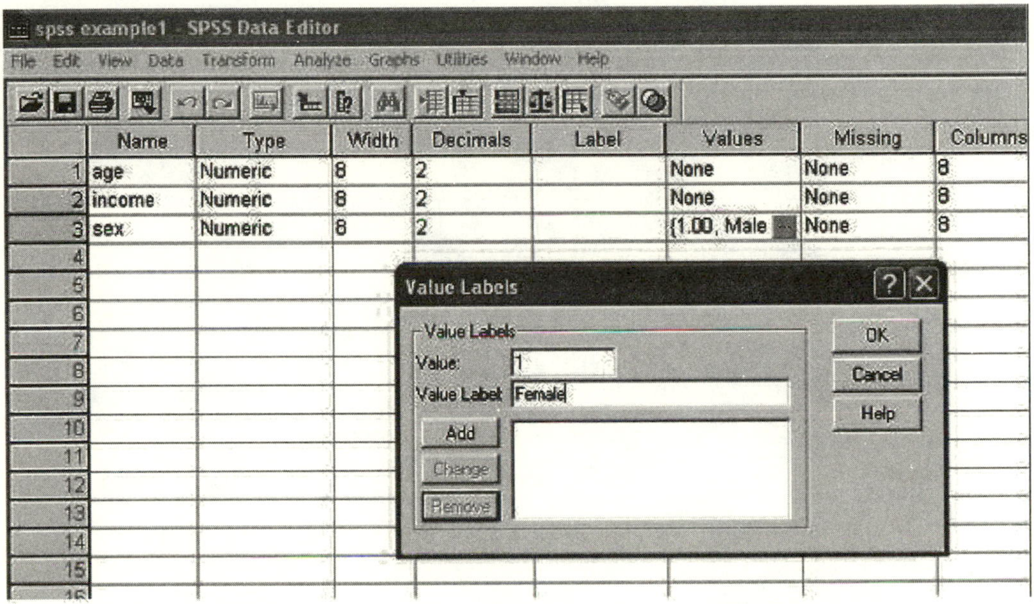

21. Before you exit the program, you may want to save your output file. To do this, go to the output screen and click on the Save button on the toolbar. At the prompt, provide an appropriate file name. Remember to choose the appropriate drive (drive A:) to which your file should be saved. Also, make sure your formatted diskette is in the drive. By default, SPSS uses ".lst" as the file extension for output files.

22. To save your data, go to the data editor and again click on the Save button on the toolbar. Provide a file name for the data file. SPSS uses the extension ".say" for data files. When you click Save, your file will be saved as an SPSS Windows system file. This system file contains all the data, variable names, value labels, and other information (we will discuss more of this later).

23. Now exit SPSS as you would exit any Windows program (by clicking on the top left-hand corner box and selecting Close).

24. If you have been able to get this far and get a printed output, you have accomplished a lot. If not, make a note of the problems you encountered and we will resolve them next time.

25. Good luck!

D2. A Brief Introduction to the SAS System

The SAS system is an integrated application system that gives you strategic control over your data-processing needs. The SAS system enables you to access, manage, analyze, and present data. In the Windows environment, the SAS Display Manager is one of the interfaces offered by SAS that enables you to access and work on the system. In this research, the SAS system will be used for data analyses.[2]

Figure D.7

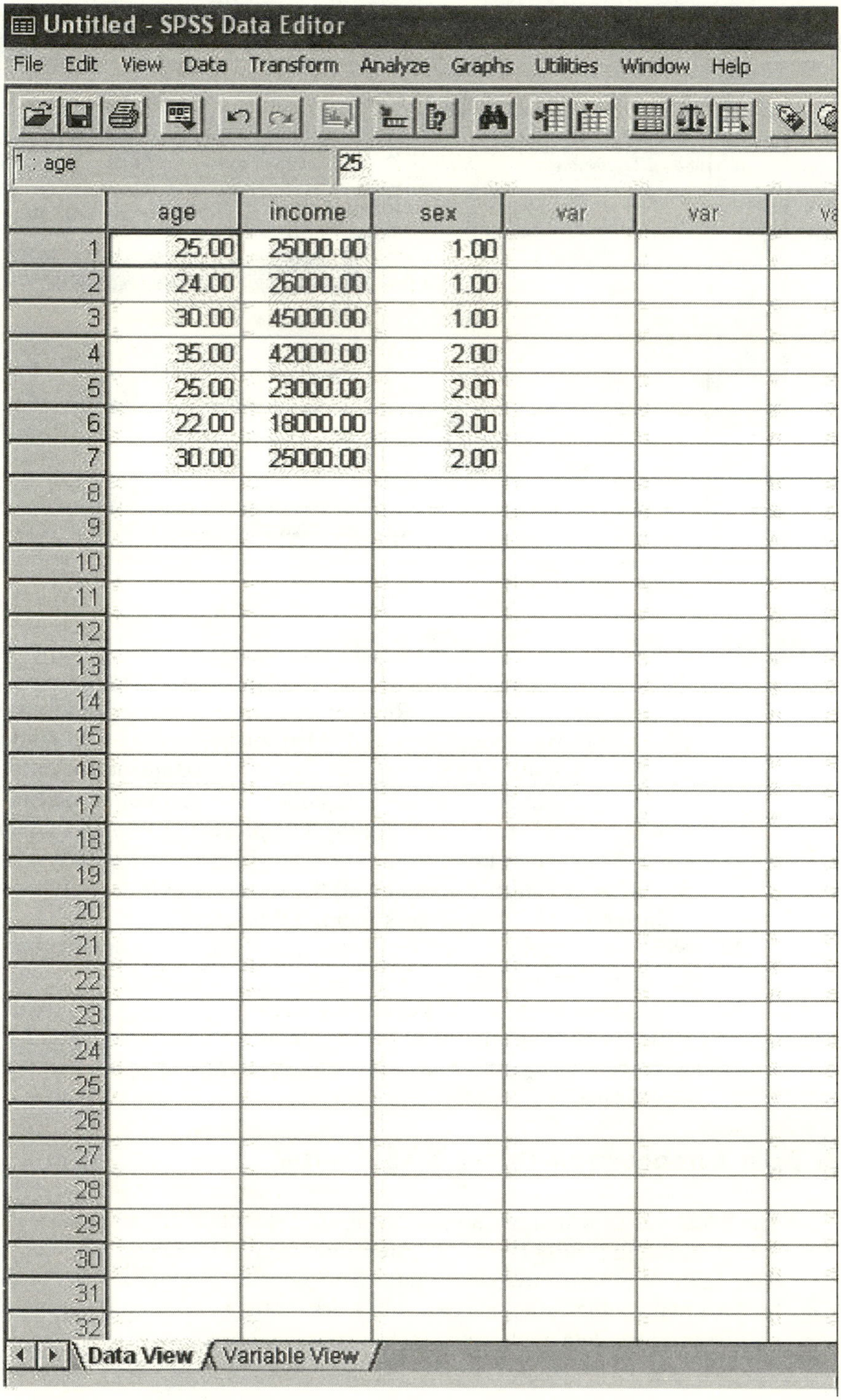

Untitled - SPSS Data Editor

File Edit View Data Transform Analyze Graphs Utilities Window Help

1 : age   25

	age	income	sex	var	var	va
1	25.00	25000.00	1.00			
2	24.00	26000.00	1.00			
3	30.00	45000.00	1.00			
4	35.00	42000.00	2.00			
5	25.00	23000.00	2.00			
6	22.00	18000.00	2.00			
7	30.00	25000.00	2.00			
8						
9						
10						
11						
12						
13						
14						
15						
16						
17						
18						
19						
20						
21						
22						
23						
24						
25						
26						
27						
28						
29						
30						
31						
32						

◄ ► \Data View ⋀ Variable View /

Figure D.8

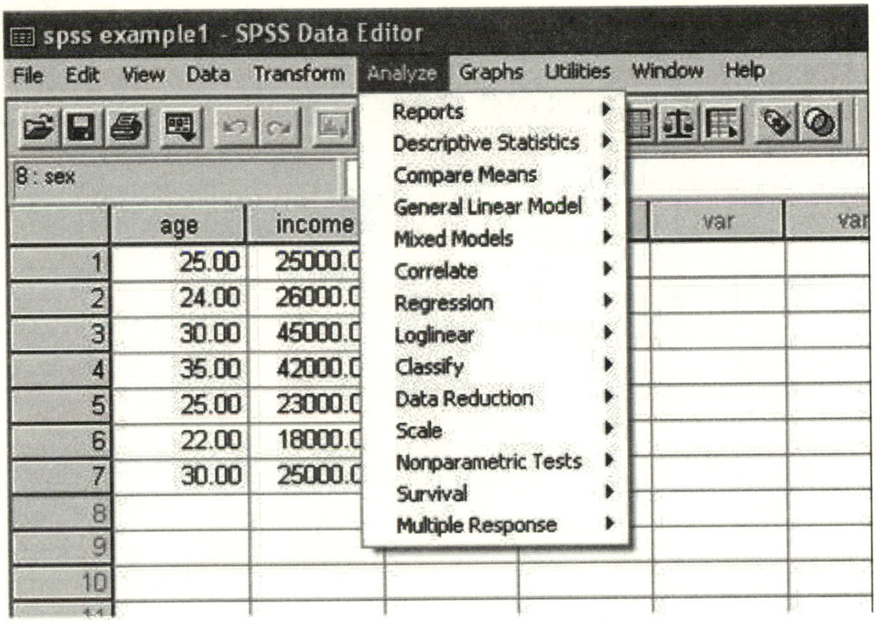

Figure D.9

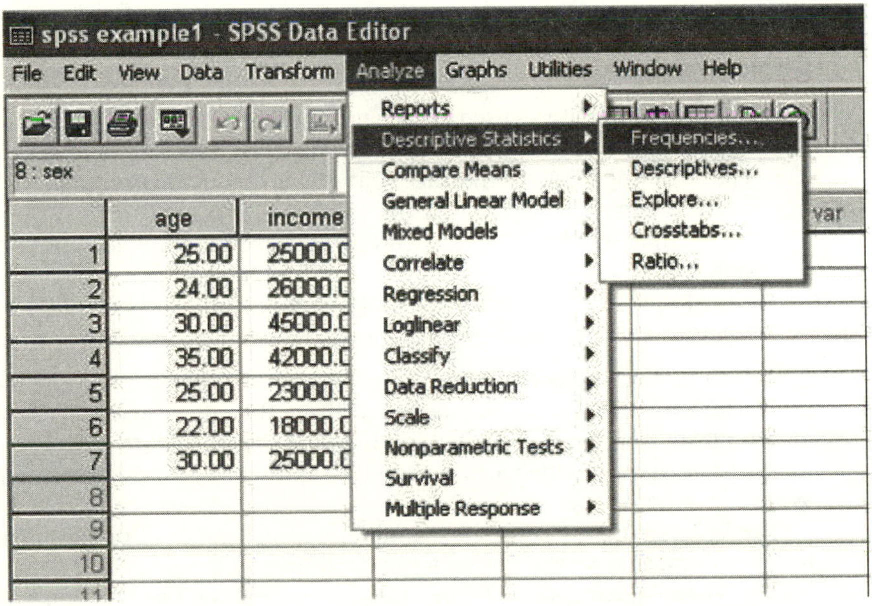

Figure D.10

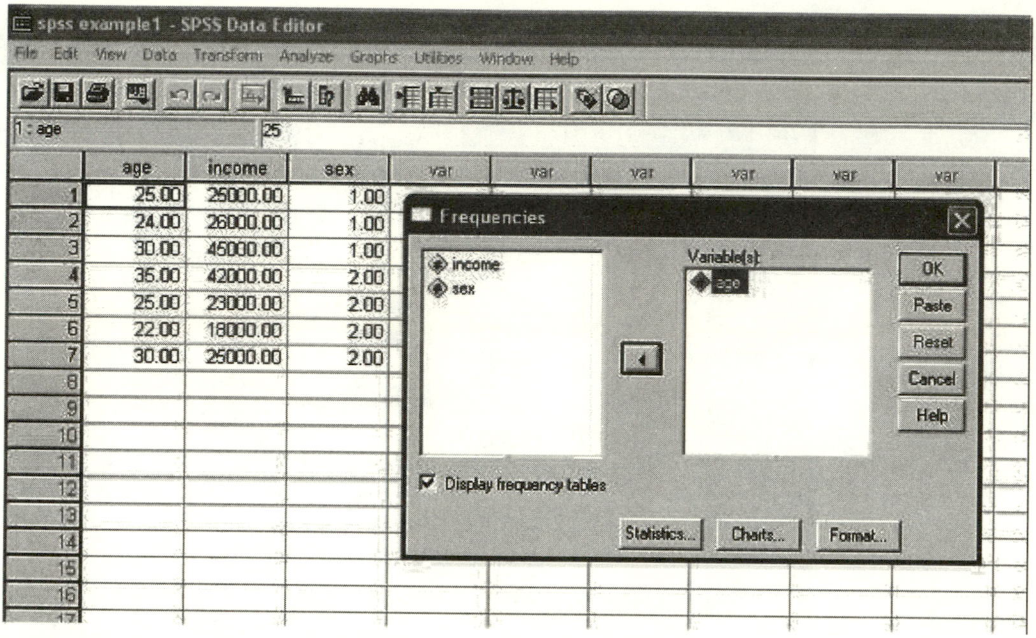

THE SAS DISPLAY MANAGER

SAS Display Manager is an interactive windows environment. Four windows constitute the Display Manager, and each window has particular capabilities.

- The Program Editor is used to open previously saved SAS programs, write new programs, edit programs, and submit SAS programs.
- The SAS Log displays messages and any errors in the programs you submit during the SAS session.
- The Output window is used to browse procedure outputs from your current SAS session.
- The Output Manager helps you navigate to specific portions of the results in the Output window and to the SAS work and user-defined libraries.

Although you see several windows at once on the screen, only one window is active at a time. The active window is where you will see the cursor and where you issue commands or enter text. To activate a displayed window, click the mouse button while pointing within the window. The windows can be scrolled and resized in the same manner used in other Windows applications.

The Program Editor is where you initially enter your SAS program. To submit a program for execution, activate the Program Editor containing the SAS program and click the Submit button. An hourglass appears while a program is running. The Log window displays messages about the program you are now executing (see Figure D.12). Watch out for error messages. You may need to activate this window to browse the messages. The Output window automatically opens after the execution is complete without any error in the program. The Output window

Figure D.11

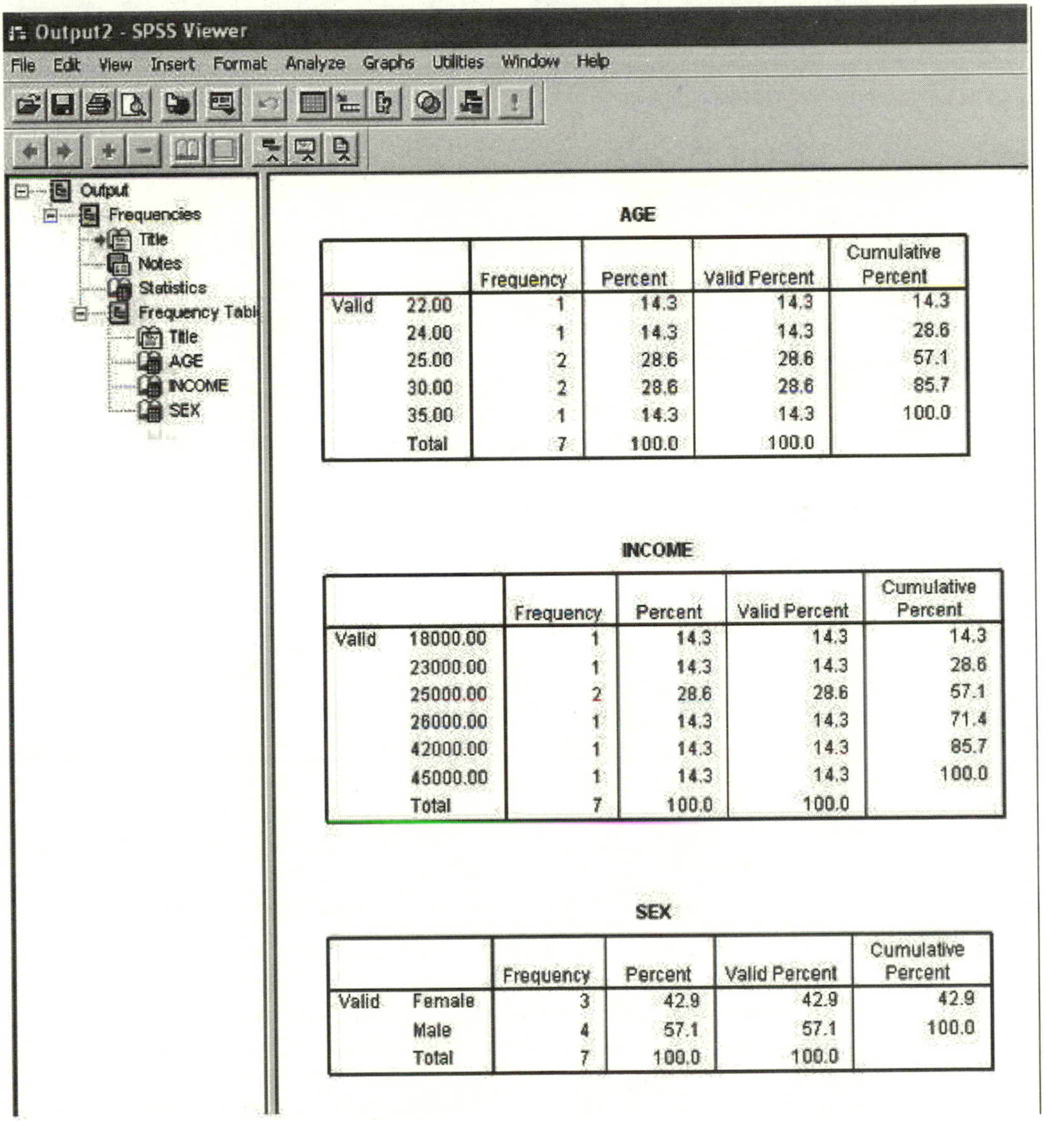

Output2 – SPSS Viewer

File Edit View Insert Format Analyze Graphs Utilities Window Help

- Output
  - Frequencies
    - Title
    - Notes
    - Statistics
    - Frequency Table
      - Title
      - AGE
      - INCOME
      - SEX

AGE

		Frequency	Percent	Valid Percent	Cumulative Percent
Valid	22.00	1	14.3	14.3	14.3
	24.00	1	14.3	14.3	28.6
	25.00	2	28.6	28.6	57.1
	30.00	2	28.6	28.6	85.7
	35.00	1	14.3	14.3	100.0
	Total	7	100.0	100.0	

INCOME

		Frequency	Percent	Valid Percent	Cumulative Percent
Valid	18000.00	1	14.3	14.3	14.3
	23000.00	1	14.3	14.3	28.6
	25000.00	2	28.6	28.6	57.1
	26000.00	1	14.3	14.3	71.4
	42000.00	1	14.3	14.3	85.7
	45000.00	1	14.3	14.3	100.0
	Total	7	100.0	100.0	

SEX

		Frequency	Percent	Valid Percent	Cumulative Percent
Valid	Female	3	42.9	42.9	42.9
	Male	4	57.1	57.1	100.0
	Total	7	100.0	100.0	

does not get populated if there are errors in the program. It is a good idea to clear the Log and Output windows periodically so that you do not confuse previous messages for new. To clear a window, activate the window and choose Clear All under the Edit menu.

- To see a list of the Output window's contents, you can activate the Results tab on the Output Manager window. From this window, you can browse, edit, delete, store, and print output.
- To close a window of the Display Manager, activate the window and choose Close from within the File menu.

Figure D.12

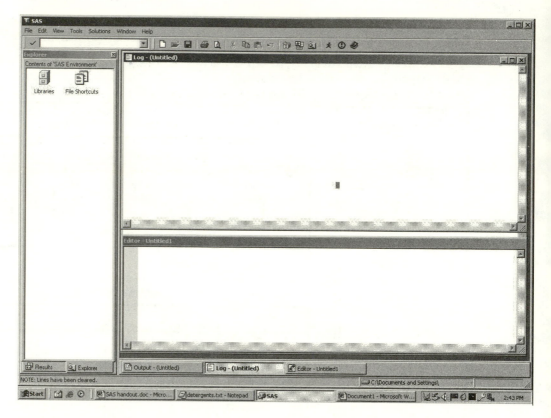

- You can clear text in a window by selecting Edit and then Clear or Clear All.
- You can save your file by selecting File and then Save.
- You can exit from the SAS system by selecting File and then Exit.

As you start writing and submitting programs, you'll notice that some of the errors (displayed in the Log window) may be due to misspelled keywords, forgotten semicolons, or invalid options. When SAS detects a syntax error, it prints the word "Error," identifies the possible location of the error, and prints an explanation of the error. Syntax error generally causes the SAS system to stop processing the step where the error is encountered. Errors are displayed in red. You may also notice warning messages in the Log window. Warning messages draw attention to minor discrepancies in the program. These messages are displayed in green. It is a good idea to check the warning messages thoroughly, as they might actually be due to an underlying problem with the code or the variables in question.

When you save an SAS program, it typically uses the file extension ".sas." The output files use the extension ".lst," and the log file uses the ".log" extension. The SAS data set of SAS version 8.2 uses the ".sas7bdat" extension.

Do not hesitate to access the SAS help system for information about individual procedures as well as general and host-specific help. Look for Syntax under the submenus.

SAS BASICS

At the outset, we must mention that SAS is a powerful and rich tool for analyzing data. The process is described below in the simplest terms. Once you gain understanding of this process, it will be easy to utilize the tool offerings to your best advantage. For more information, please refer to www.sas.com or the SAS manuals.

An SAS program consists of two steps: the data step and the procedure ("proc" for short) step. These two steps, alone or in combination, form all SAS programs. The data step typically creates SAS data sets but also can be used to produce custom-designed reports. The proc step typically analyzes and processes data in the form of SAS data sets. An SAS program is a group of step-by-step instructions called statements. Each statement has two important characteristics. It begins with an SAS keyword and ends with a semicolon. SAS is not case sensitive.

The data step is identified by its keyword, "data" and the procedure step by its keyword, "proc." The statements can begin and end in any column and can continue over several lines. Several statements can be on one line. It is a good idea to begin data and proc steps in column 1 and indent statements within a step.

SAS procedures, or proc steps, are programs that can process and analyze an SAS data set. A proc step always begins with a proc statement. The proc statement begins with the keyword "proc," gives the name of the procedure to be run, and ends with a semicolon.

In a proc step, you indicate:

- Which SAS data set is to be processed
- Which variables in the data set are to be processed
- Which options are to be invoked with the procedure

You can invoke any number of procedures to process data in a given SAS data set. If you do not use "data =" in the statement, SAS uses the most recently created SAS data set for the procedure. The title statement defines the text to be printed at the top of the output pages. You can specify up to 10 title lines. A title statement is in effect for all subsequent procedures unless it is redefined or canceled.

The general form of a title statement is

*title*n 'title';

where "n" immediately follows the keyword "title" to indicate the number of the title line.

STATEMENTS APPEARING BEFORE THE DATA OR THE PROC STEP

Before we examine the data step, let us take a look at three statements that precede the data and proc steps in our analyses. These statements provide some basic settings for the SAS system.

There are several *options* settings. We'll use the options statement to set the line size for the outputs to 80 characters.

The *libname* statement defines the library where we choose to save SAS data sets as permanent data sets. You need to define the path and give the library a name (we'll call the library "studying" our programs). The library definition needs to be given only once at the beginning of the SAS session. If the library statement is not used, the SAS system will create only temporary data sets stored in a library called "work." The work library is lost at the end of an SAS session. You can view the contents of the SAS library of the current session on the Explore tab of the Output Manager window.

An SAS data set has a two-level name. When the first-level name is not specified, the default name "work" is used. The name "work" indicates that the SAS data set is temporary. To store an SAS data set permanently, you must specify the two-level name. The first level of the name points SAS to the data library. The second level of the name is the name of the SAS data set. For example, in "study.detergents," "study." is the library reference, and "detergents" is the name of the SAS data set.

There are several advantages to storing SAS data sets permanently.

- SAS data sets are self-documenting, so you can easily monitor the information they contain.
- You can easily access the data set and process it with an SAS procedure at a later time. You do not have to re-create the data set.
- You save computer time since the data step is not required to create the data set.

To access the data set, use the data = option in the proc statement and specify the two-level name.

The "%include" is an SAS macro statement. At this point it is sufficient if you understand that the statement points to the location of any other previously written SAS code you might like to use while submitting an SAS program. For the present study, we have defined some formats that readily help us understand the values of some of the variables. These formats are called *user-defined* formats, as they do not correspond to the normal data formats available within SAS. Our user-defined formats are stored in a file called "format.sas." The %include statement makes the format definitions available for the SAS session. The %include statement can be used only once in each SAS session. However, it is included in all our programs.

Presenting the Raw Data

Before using SAS to analyze the data, you need to assemble the raw data in ways that can be read by the SAS system. There are several ways you can do this. You can enter the data in a spreadsheet and directly import into SAS by using the Import Wizard under the File menu. You could even use a comma-delimited file. For this study, the raw data is provided through an ordinary text file called "detergents.txt." When you open the text file, you'll notice that the field values are entered in sequence, exactly as they appear in the questionnaire. There is a space separating each value. If the value is blank, it is depicted by a period (.). SAS treats periods as blank values. For SAS to identify each value separately, variable values must be separated with at least one blank space. In our case we have chosen to present the input raw data as a text file to demonstrate the easy integration of the user-defined variable formats as the data file is read into SAS to create an SAS data set.

Figure D.13 shows the data entry from the detergent questionnaire using a Notepad file. Each questionnaire is serialized. The serial number appears as the very first item followed by the individual coded responses to each item in sequence as they appear in the questionnaire. Each response is separated from the subsequent item by at least one blank space. If a response is missing for any item, it is indicated by a period. In short, the rows represent the several participant questionnaires received in the survey. The columns represent the responses to the individual items in the questionnaires.

Note: The data is available at www.mesharpe.com. Search by author name (Neelankavil) and there will be a link to the data set.

Figure D.13

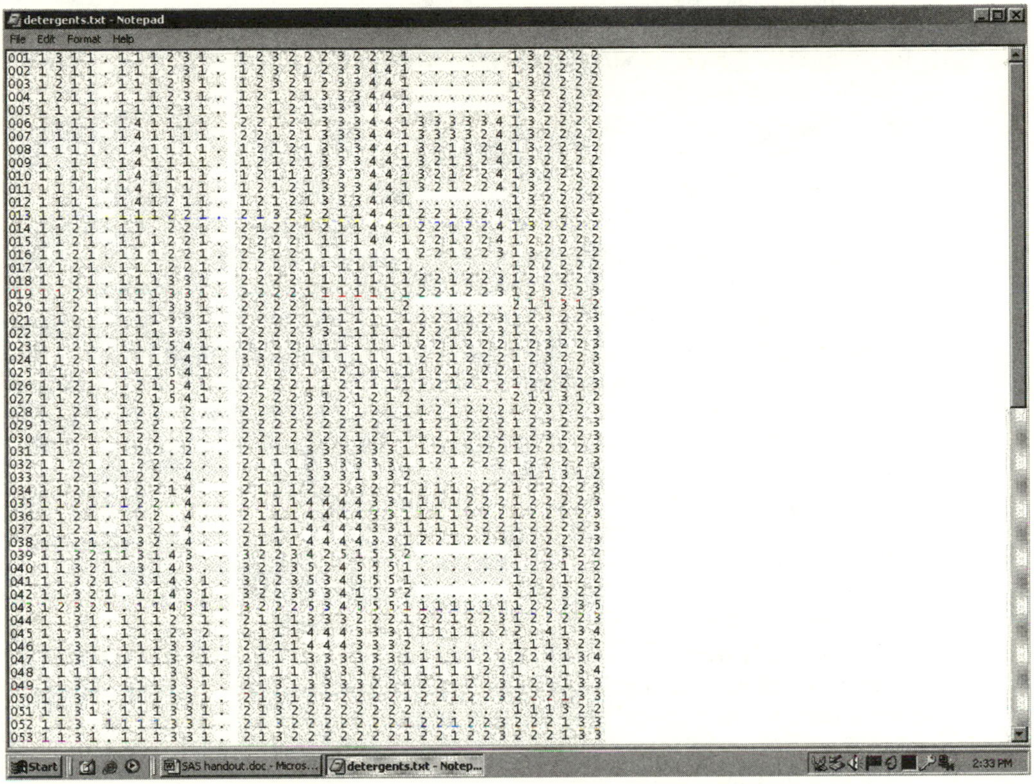

THE DATA STEP

Let us try to gain some understanding of the data step by looking into the code of the "import data.sas" program. You may open this program into the Program Editor.

- The data statement provides a name for the data set being created. The name has two parts. "Study." refers to the library and "detergents" refers to the data set name. The two are separated by a period (.). If you intend to create only a temporary data set, you need not give the library reference.
- The infile statement points to the raw data file being read into SAS. The file and its path are enclosed within quotes.
- The format statement identifies the format to be used for the variables being created in the data step. Formats have a period (.) at the end of their names. The format can be identified once for a group of variables sharing a format. For example, the variables whoDecidesDetergent, OwnWashMachine, UseDetergents, and BuyOtherBrands share a single format called "yes1fmt." The format name is mentioned once at the end of the list of variables using this format.
- The input statement identifies the variables to be read in exactly the sequence they appear in the raw data file. Notice that character strings are identified with a dollar sign ($).

• The run statement executes the data step. All SAS data and proc steps need a run statement at the end.

THE SAS PROCEDURES USED TO ANALYZE THE DETERGENTS DATA

1. Proc Format: Creating User-Defined Formats

It is appropriate to describe proc format at this point, as this is the first procedure we use in the study. You might recall that this step (via format.sas) is included in all the programs with the help of the %include statement described above. The format procedure allows you to create new formats to your own specifications. You can use these user-defined formats as you would any SAS format. Associate them with variables by using a format statement in a data step or a proc step. In our study, all variables have been linked to their respective user-defined format while reading raw data into SAS. As a result, we do not need the format statements in our proc steps. If you wish to change a format, a new format definition within a proc format step and a format statement (within a proc step) to link the new format to a particular variable can be considered.

If you open the file format.sas, you'll notice that the very first statement is the proc statement, which ends in a semicolon. There are a series of value statements, providing a name for each format, the values of the variable, and their decoding—what the variable values mean. All the variable values in the study are numeric. If you need to provide a user-defined format for a string variable, you need to enclose the variable values in quotes, too. As expected, the proc step ends with a run statement. A format is a set of directions that tells the SAS system how to write data values. When SAS prints the values of the variables, the system uses the associated formats specified in the format statement.

You can use the format statement to associate output formats with variables in the data step or a proc step.

The general form for the format statement is as follows. The format name can be user defined or can be in the form of one of the standard SAS formats. Again, notice that the format name ends with a period (.).

format variablename formatname. ;

If you add the format statement to the data step (as in import data.sas), the formats are stored in the SAS data set (this is what was done for the study). If you add the format statement to a proc step, the formats are used only for the duration of that proc step.

2. Proc Contents: Examining the Contents of the Data Set

Since the SAS system automatically documents the contents of SAS data sets, you can easily find out what information is contained within a data set. The contents procedure lists the names of the SAS data sets in the SAS data library and prints the descriptions of the contents. Please see the contents.sas program.

3. Proc Freq: Generating Frequency Crosstabs

The proc freq produces one-way to *n*-way frequency and cross-tabulation tables. For each frequency or cross-tabulation table you want, put a table request in the tables statement. You can insert multiple tables statements in the same proc freq step.

The general form of the tables syntax is

tables requests/options;

where "requests" names the variables for which the frequency tables are to be generated. A one-way frequency table is generated by each variable named. Two-way cross-tabulations are generated by two variables joined with an asterisk. Any number of variables may be joined for a multi-way table.

Three of our programs use the proc freq. You may open the frequencies.sas, cross tabs. sas, and chi square.sas files to understand the syntax. Notice that in the chi square.sas file, the table statement has the chisq option to generate the chi-square statistic.

4. Proc Corr: Generating Correlation Statistics

You can use the SAS procedure corr to generate correlation coefficients. The use of the corr procedure is demonstrated in the correlations.sas program

The procedure generates correlation coefficients for all numeric variables in the data set. To get the coefficients for only a selected few variables, but not for all the numeric variables in the data set, use the var statement to list the variables of interest.

5. Proc Means: Generating Descriptive Statistics

The means procedure produces simple univariate descriptive statistics for numeric variables. The SAS procedure can perform calculations on an entire SAS data set or on groups of observations in the data set. The var statement can be used to generate the descriptive statistics for a selected list of variables. Please open the file means.sas to review the syntax.

Some of the options that can appear in the proc means statement are

n	indicates the number of observations on which the calculations are based
mean	requests the average data value
min	requests the smallest or minimum data value
max	requests the greatest or maximum data value
sum	requests the total or sum of the data values
std	requests the calculation of the standard deviation

6. Proc Univariate: Generating Descriptive Statistics

You can use the univariate procedure to generate more univariate statistics in addition to what is generated by proc means. You can use the usual var statement to list the variables for which you wish to generate the univariate statistics. "Plot normal" after the data set name in the proc statement will generate the normal probability plots, box plots, and stem-and-leaf plots. Please see the file univariate.sas.

7. Proc Factor: Procedure for Factor Analyses and Principal Component Analyses

Proc factor can be used for both factor analyses and principal component analyses. The var statement is used to list the variables to be used for the analysis. The procedure has a rich set of options to customize a study. For more information, refer to the SAS Stat User Guide.

Method	specifies the method to be used in extracting factors or components. "Prin" is used for the principal factors method. There are other methods, which can be looked up in the SAS manuals.
Mineigen	specifies the critical eigenvalue a component must display. For the current study, we have used "Mineigen = 1."
Nfactor	requests the number of factors to be retained and rotated. For factor analysis, we have retained four factors in our program.
Out	directs the data into a permanent or temporary data set. This data set will contain all the statistics generated by the procedure.
Priors	specifies prior communality estimates. "Priors = one" is used for principal component analysis. If priors is set to "smc," then the prior communality estimates are squared multiple correlations.
Reorder	causes the variables of various factor matrices to be reordered on the printout. Variables with the highest absolute loading on the factor are printed first, from the largest to the smallest, followed by the variables with their highest absolute loading on the second factor, and so on.
Rotate	specifies the rotation method to be used. In our study we have requested a promax rotation that results in oblique correlated factors.
Scree	creates a plot that graphically displays the size of the eigenvalue associated with each component. This helps in deciding how many components should be retained.
Simple	requests simple descriptive statistics: the number of usable cases on which the analysis was performed, and the means and standard deviations of the observed variables.

8. Proc Reg: Performing Multiple Regression Analyses

Proc reg invokes the regression procedure. Please see the syntax in the file regression.sas and regression2.sas. While calling the regression procedure, you need to specify the model by using a model statement. More than one model statement can be used under a proc reg. An output statement may be useful in creating a new data set containing regression statistics useful for further analyses. In our programs, the "out =" in the output statement directs the data into a permanent data set. Two variables generated by the regression procedure are included in the permanent data set and are given meaningful names—*p* statistic is renamed "PdtAgeGroup" and *r* statistic is renamed "resid." The general form of the model statement is as follows.

model dependent variable =
independent variable1 independent variable2. . . . . . . /options;

A few options of the reg procedure are listed below.

p	Calculates predicted values from the input data and the estimated model
r	Requests an analysis of the residuals
clm	Prints the 95 percent upper and lower confidence limits for the expected value of the dependent mean for each observation
cli	Requests the 95 percent upper and lower confidence limits for an individual predicted value
vif	Requests the variance inflation factor
dw	Generates the Durbin-Watson test statistic

You can also specify the method for model selection.

The methods of model selection implemented in proc reg are specified with the "selection =" option in the model statement. When no selection option is mentioned, the complete model specified in the model statement is used to fit the model. The different selection options are briefly discussed below.

Forward   This selection starts with no variables in the model and adds variables. The p-values for these F statistics are compared to the "slentry =" value that is specified in the model statement (or to 0.50 if the "slentry =" option is omitted). If no F statistic has a significance level greater than the "slentry =" value, the forward option stops. Otherwise, the forward option adds the variable that has the largest F statistic to the model. The forward option then calculates the F statistic again for the variables still remaining outside the model, and the evaluation process is repeated.

Backward   This selection begins by calculating statistics for a model, including all the independent variables. Then the variables are deleted from the model one by one until all the variables remaining in the model produce an F statistic significant at the "slstay =" level specified in the model statement (or at the 0.10 level if the "slstay =" option is omitted).

Stepwise   As in the forward selection method, variables are added one by one to the model, and the F statistic for a variable to be added must be significant at the "slentry=" level. After a variable is added, the stepwise method looks at all the variables already included in the model and deletes any variable that does not produce an F statistic significant at the "slstay =" level.

Maxr   This method tries to find the best one-variable model, the best two-variable model, and so forth.

rsquare   This method finds subsets of independent variables that best predict a dependent variable by linear regression in the given sample.

NOTE

1. This handout provides limited information. It is designed to help you get started. For full information, consult the SPSS for Windows manual or online help.

The SPSS screen shots were generated using SPSS software. Copyright © 1995–2007 SPSS Inc., Chicago, IL, USA.

2. The screen shots were generated using SAS software, version 8.2 of the SAS System for Microsoft Windows. Copyright © 2002–2007 SAS Institute Inc., Cary, NC, USA. All Rights Reserved. Reproduced with permission of SAS Institute Inc., Cary, NC.

Appendix E. Country Statistics

Country	Population	Capital	Type of Government	Currency (name)	Total GDP	Per Capita GDP	Exchange Rate to US$ (September 2004)
Afghanistan	28,513,677	Kabul	Transitional administration	Afghani (AFA)	$20.0 bil (2003)	$700	43.83
Albania	3,544,808	Tirana	Republic	Lek (ALL)	$16.1 bil (2003)	$4,500	102.10
Algeria	32,129,324	Algiers (El Djazair)	Republic	Dinar (DZD)	$194.3 bil (2000)	$5,900	72.12
Andorra	69,865	Andorra la Vella	Parliamentary coprincipality	Euro (EUR)	$1.3 bil (2000)	$19,000	0.82
Angola	10,978,552	Luanda	Republic	New Kwanza (AON)	$20.6 bil (2003)	$1,900	85.30
Antigua and Barbuda	68,320	Saint John's	Constitutional monarchy with British-style parliament	East Caribbean dollar (XCD)	$750 mil (2002)	$11,000	2.67
Argentina	39,144,753	Buenos Aires	Republic	Peso (ARS)	$432.7 bil (2003)	$11,200	2.99
Armenia	2,991,360	Yerevan	Republic	Dram (AMD)	$11.8 bil (2003)	$3,900	516.54
Australia	19,913,144	Canberra	Democratic, federal state system	Australian dollar (AUD)	$570.3 bil (2003)	$28,900	1.44
Austria	8,174,762	Vienna	Federal republic	Euro (EUR)	$245.5 bil (2003)	$30,000	0.82
Azerbaijan	7,868,385	Baku	Republic	Manat (AZM)	$26.3 bil (2003)	$3,400	4,911.63
The Bahamas	299,697	Nassau	Independent commonwealth	Bahamian dollar (BSD)	$5.1 bil (2003)	$16,800	1.00
Bahrain	677,886	Manama	Constitutional monarchy	Dinar (BHD)	$11.4 bil (2003)	$17,100	0.38
Bangladesh	141,340,476	Dhaka	Parliamentary democracy	Taka (BDT)	$258.8 bil (2003)	$1,900	59.29
Barbados	278,289	Bridgetown	Parliamentary democracy	Barbados dollar (BBD)	$4.5 bil (2003)	$16,200	2.02
Belarus	10,310,520	Minsk	Republic	Ruble (BYR)	$61.9 bil (2003)	$6,000	2,185.31
Belgium	10,348,276	Brussels	Parliamentary democracy under a constitutional monarch	Euro (EUR)	$298.2 bil (2003)	$29,000	0.82
Belize	272,945	Belmopan	Parliamentary democracy	Belize dollar (BZD)	$1.3 bil (2002)	$4,900	1.98

Country	Population	Capital	Government	Currency	GDP	GDP per capita	
Benin	7,250,033	Porto-Novo (constitutional); Cotonou (administrative)	Republic	CFA franc BCEAO (XOF)	$7.7 bil (2003)	$1,100	539.40
Bhutan	2,185,569	Thimphu	Monarchy	Ngultrum (BTN)	$2.7 bil (2002)	$1,300	45.80
Bolivia	8,724,156	La Paz (administrative); Sucre (judicial)	Republic	Boliviano (BOB)	$20.9 bil (2003)	$2,400	7.97
Bosnia and Herzegovina	4,007,608	Sarajevo	Federal republic	Converted marka (BAM)	$24.4 bil (2003)	$6,100	1.61
Botswana	1,561,973	Gaborone	Parliamentary republic	Pula (BWP)	$13.9 bil (2003)	$8,800	4.77
Brazil	184,101,109	Brasilia	Federal republic	Real (BRL)	$1.379 tril (2003)	$7,600	2.91
Brunei	365,251	Bandar Seri Begawan	Independent sultanate	Dollar (BND)	$6.5 bil (2002)	$18,600	1.69
Bulgaria	7,517,973	Sofia	Republic	Lev (BGL)	$57.1 bil (2003)	$7,600	1.60
Burkina Faso	13,574,820	Ouagadougou	Republic	CFA franc BCEAO (XOF)	$14.3 bil (2003)	$1,100	539.40
Burma. See Myanmar							
Burundi	6,231,221	Bujumbura	In transition	Franc (BIF)	$3.8 bil (2003)	$600	1,075.80
Cambodia	13,363,421	Phnom Penh	Constitutional monarchy	Riel (KHR)	$22.8 bil (2003)	$1,700	3,850.00
Cameroon	16,063,678	Yaounde	Republic	CFA franc BEAC (XAF)	$27.6 bil (2003)	$1,800	539.54
Canada	32,507,874	Ottawa	Confederation with parliamentary democracy	Dollar (CAD)	$957.7 bil (2003)	$29,700	1.30
Cape Verde	415,294	Praia	Republic	Escudo (CVE)	$600.0 mil (2002)	$1,400	91.07
Central African Republic	3,742,482	Bangui	In transition	CFA franc BEAC (XAF)	$4.6 bil (2003)	$1,200	539.54
Chad	9,538,544	N'Djamena	Republic	CFA franc BEAC (XAF)	$10.9 bil (2003)	$1,200	539.54
Chile	15,823,957	Santiago	Republic	Peso (CLP)	$154.6 bil (2003)	$9,900	615.37
China	1,298,847,624	Beijing	Communist Party–led state	Yuan renminbi (CNY)	$6.449 tril (2003)	$5,000	8.28
Colombia	42,310,775	Bogota	Republic	Peso (COP)	$262.5 bil (2003)	$6,300	2,537.50
Comoros	651,901	Moroni	In transition	Franc (KMF)	$441.0 mil (2002)	$700	404.79
Congo (formerly Zaire)	58,317,930	Kinshasa	In transition	Franc (CDF)	$35.6 bil (2003)	$600	396.51
Congo Republic	2,998,040	Brazzaville	Republic	CFA franc BEAC (XAF)	$2.2 bil (2003)	$700	539.54
Costa Rica	3,956,507	San Jose	Republic	Colon (CRC)	$35.2 bil (2003)	$9,000	445.96

(continued)

Country	Population	Capital	Type of Government	Currency (name)	Total GDP	Per Capita GDP	Exchange Rate to US$ (September 2004)
Côte d'Ivoire	17,327,724	Yamoussoukro	In transition	CFA franc BCEAO (XOF)	$24.5 bil (2003)	$1,400	539.40
Croatia	4,496,869	Zagreb	Parliamentary democracy	Kuna (HRK)	$47.1 bil (2003)	$10,700	6.07
Cuba	11,308,764	Havana	Communist state	Peso (CUP)	$31.6 bil (2003)	$2,800	21.00
Cyprus	775,927	Nicosia	Republic	Pound (CYP)	Greek area: $8.9 bil; Turkish area: $1.2 bil (2003)	Greek area: $16,000; Turkish area: $5,600	0.47
Czech Republic	10,246,178	Prague	Republic	Koruna (CZK)	$160.5 bil (2003)	$15,700	25.91
Denmark	5,413,392	Copenhagen	Constitutional monarchy	Krone (DKK)	$167.7 bil (2003)	$31,200	6.12
Djibouti	466,900	Djibouti	Republic	Franc (DJF)	$619.0 mil (2002)	$1,300	169.75
Dominican Republic	8,833,634	Santo Domingo	Republic	Peso (DOP)	$52.2 bil (2003)	$6,000	36.25
East Timor	1,019,252	Dili	Republic	U.S. dollar and Indonesian rupiah	$440.0 mil (2001)	$500	9113 (2002)
Ecuador	13,212,742	Quito	Republic	U.S. dollar	$45.5 bil (2003)	$3,300	1.00
Egypt	76,117,421	Cairo	Republic	Pound (EGP)	$294.3 bil (2003)	$3,900	6.23
El Salvador	6,587,541	San Salvador	Republic	Colon (SVC)	$31.0 bil (2003)	$4,800	8.75
Equatorial Guinea	523,051	Malabo	Republic	CFA franc BEAC (XAF)	$1.3 bil (2002)	$2,700	539.54
Eritrea	4,447,307	Asmara	In transition	Nakfa (ERN)	$3.3 bil (2002)	$700	13.50
Estonia	1,341,664	Tallinn	Republic	Kroon (EEK)	$17.4 bil (2003)	$12,300	12.90
Ethiopia	67,851,281	Addis Ababa	Federal republic	Birr (ETB)	$48.5 bil (2003)	$700	8.69
Fiji	880,874	Suva	Republic	Fiji dollar (FJD)	$5.0 bil (2003)	$5,800	1.76
Finland	5,214,512	Helsinki	Constitutional republic	Euro (EUR)	$141.7 bil (2003)	$27,300	0.82
France	60,424,213	Paris	Republic	Euro (EUR)	$1.654 tril (2003)	$27,500	0.82
Gabon	1,355,246	Libreville	Republic	CFA franc BEAC (XAF)	$7.3 bil (2003)	$5,500	539.54
The Gambia	1,546,848	Banjul	Republic	Dalasi (GMD)	$2.6 bil (2003)	$1,700	29.25
Georgia	4,693,892	Tbilisi	Republic	Lari (GEL)	$12.2 (2003)	$2,500	1.92
Germany	82,424,609	Berlin	Federal republic	Euro (EUR)	$2.271 tril (2003)	$27,600	0.82
Ghana	20,757,032	Accra	Republic	Cedi (GHC)	$44.5 bil (2003)	$2,200	9,097.00
Greece	10,647,529	Athens	Parliamentary republic	Euro (EUR)	$212.2 bil (2003)	$19,900	0.82
Grenada	89,357	Saint George's	Parliamentary democracy	East Caribbean dollar (XCD)	$440.0 mil (2002)	$5,000	2.67
Guatemala	14,280,596	Guatemala City	Republic	Quetzal (GTQ)	$56.5 bil (2003)	$4,100	7.89
Guinea	9,246,462	Conakry	Republic	Franc (GNF)	$18.9 bil (2003)	$2,100	2,592.90

Country	Population	Capital	Government	Currency	GDP	GDP per capita	Exchange rate
Guinea-Bissau	1,388,363	Bissau	In transition	CFA franc BCEAO (XOF)	$1.2 bil (2003)	$900	539.40
Guyana	705,803	Georgetown	Republic	Dollar (GYD)	$2.8 bil (2003)	$4,000	178.50
Haiti	7,656,166	Port-au-Prince	In transition	Gourde (HTG)	$12.2 bil (2003)	$1,600	35.00
Honduras	6,823,568	Tegucigalpa	Republic	Lempira (HNL)	$17.5 bil (2003)	$2,600	18.40
Hungary	10,032,375	Budapest	Parliamentary democracy	Forint (HUF)	$139.7 bil (2003)	$13,900	203.56
Iceland	293,966	Reykjavik	Constitutional republic	Krona (ISK)	$8.7 bil (2003)	$30,900	71.98
India	1,065,070,607	New Delhi	Federal republic	Rupee (INR)	$3.022 tril (2003)	$2,900	45.80
Indonesia	238,452,952	Jakarta	Republic	Rupiah (IDR)	$758.1 bil (2003)	$3,200	9,113.54
Iran	67,503,205	Tehran	Islamic republic	Rial (IRR)	$477.8 bil (2003)	$7,000	9,762.01
Iraq	25,374,691	Baghdad	In transition	Dinar (IQD)	$38.8 bil (2003)	$1,600	1,462.45
Ireland	3,969,558	Dublin	Parliamentary republic	Euro (EUR)	$117.0 bil (2003)	$29,800	0.82
Israel	6,199,008	Jerusalem	Republic	New shekel (ILS)	$120.6 bil (2003)	$19,700	4.48
Italy	58,057,477	Rome	Republic	Euro (EUR)	$1.552 tril (2003)	$26,800	0.82
Jamaica	2,713,130	Kingston	Parliamentary democracy	Jamaican dollar (JMD)	$10.2 bil (2003)	$3,800	61.91
Japan	127,333,002	Tokyo	Parliamentary democracy	Yen (JPY)	$3.567 tril (2003)	$28,000	110.34
Jordan	5,611,202	Amman	Constitutional monarchy	Dinar (JOD)	$23.6 bil (2003)	$4,300	0.71
Kazakhstan	15,143,704	Astana	Republic	Tenge (KZT)	$105.3 bil (2003)	$7,000	135.25
Kenya	32,021,856	Nairobi	Republic	Shilling (KES)	$33.1 bil (2003)	$1,000	80.51
Kiribati	100,798	South Tarawa	Republic	Australian dollar (AUD)	$79.0 mil (2001)	$800	1.44
Korea, North	22,697,553	Pyongyang	Communist state	Won (KPW)	$22.9 bil (2003)	$1,000	2.20
Korea, South	48,598,175	Seoul	Republic	Won (KRW)	$855.3 bil (2003)	$17,700	1,147.30
Kuwait	2,257,549	Kuwait City	Constitutional monarchy	Dinar (KWD)	$39.5 bil (2003)	$18,100	0.29
Kyrgyzstan	5,081,429	Bishek	Republic	Som (KGS)	$7.7 bil (2003)	$1,600	42.22
Laos	6,068,117	Vientiane	Communist	Kip (LAK)	$10.3 bil (2003)	$1,700	10,552.00
Latvia	2,306,306	Riga	Republic	Lats (LVL)	$23.8 bil (2003)	$10,100	0.54
Lebanon	3,777,218	Beirut	Republic	Pound (LBP)	$17.8 bil (2003)	$4,800	1,514.00
Lesotho	1,865,040	Maseru	Modified constitutional monarchy	Loti (LSL)	$5.6 bil (2003)	$3,000	6.58
Liberia	3,390,635	Monrovia	In transition	Liberian dollar (LRD)	$3.3 bil (2003)	$1,000	45.00
Libya	5,631,585	Tripoli	Islamic Arabic Socialist "mass state"	Dinar (LYD)	$35.0 bil (2003)	$6,400	1.32

(continued)

Country	Population	Capital	Type of Government	Currency (name)	Total GDP	Per Capita GDP	Exchange Rate to US$ (September 2004)
Liechtenstein	33,436	Vaduz	Hereditary constitutional monarchy	Swiss franc (CHF)	$825.0 mil (1999)	$25,000	1.27
Lithuania	3,607,899	Kaunas	Republic	Litas (LTL)	$40.2 bil (2003)	$11,200	2.85
Luxembourg	462,690	Luxembourg-Ville	Constitutional monarchy	Euro (EUR)	$25.0 bil (20030	$55,100	0.82
Macedonia	2,071,210	Skopje	Republic	Denar (MKD)	$13.8 bil (2003)	$6,700	50.12
Madagascar	17,501,871	Antananarivo	Republic	Malagsy Franc (MGF)	$13.0 bil (2003)	$800	2,021.00
Malawi	11,906,855	Lilongwe	Republic	Kwacha (MWK)	$6.8 bil (2003)	$600	108.05
Malaysia	23,522,482	Kuala Lumpur	Constitutional monarchy	Ringgit (MYR)	$207.2 bil (2003)	$9,000	3.80
Maldives	339,330	Male	Republic	Rufiyaa (MVR)	$1.3 bil (2002)	$3,900	11.77
Mali	11,596,788	Bamako	Republic	CFA franc BCEAO (XOF)	$10.5 bil (2003)	$900	539.40
Malta	396,851	Valletta	Parliamentary democracy	Lira (MTL)	$7.1 bil (2003)	$17,700	0.35
Marshall Islands	55,738	Majuro	Republic	U.S. dollar	$115.0 mil (2001)	$1,600	1.00
Mauritania	2,998,563	Nouakchott	Islamic republic	Ouguiya (MRO)	$5.2 bil (2003)	$1,800	253.52
Mauritius	1,220,481	Port Louis	Republic	Rupee (MUR)	$13.9 bil (2003)	$11,400	28.50
Mexico	104,959,594	Mexico City	Federal republic	Peso (MXN)	$942.2 bil (2003)	$9,000	11.53
Micronesia	108,155	Palikir, on Pohnpei	Republic	U.S. dollar	$277.0 mil (2002)	$2,000	1.00
Moldova	4,446,455	Chisinau	Republic	Leu (MDL)	$7.8 bil (2003)	$1,800	11.99
Monaco	32,270	Monaco-ville	Constitutional monarchy	Euro (EUR)	$870.0 mil (1999)	$27,000	0.82
Mongolia	2,751,314	Ulaanbaatar	Republic	Tugrik (MNT)	$4.9 bil (2003)	$1,800	1,199.00
Morocco	32,209,101	Rabat	Constitutional monarchy	Dirham (MAD)	$128.3 bil (2003)	$4,000	9.05
Mozambique	18,811,731	Maputo	Republic	Metical (MZM)	$21.2 bil (2003)	$1,200	21,845.00
Myanmar (formerly Burma)	42,720,196	Yangon (Rangoon)	Military	Kyat (MMK)	$78.8 bil (2003)	$1,900	6.02
Namibia	1,954,033	Windhoek	Republic	Namibia dollar (NAD)	$13.7 bil (2003)	$7,100	6.57
Nauru	12,809	Nauru	Republic	Australian dollar (AUD)	$60.0 mil (2001)	$5,000	1.44
Nepal	27,070,666	Kathmandu	Constitutional monarchy	Rupee (NPR)	$38.1 bil (2003)	$1,400	75.13
Netherlands	16,318,199	Amsterdam (official); The Hague (administrative)	Parliamentary democracy under a constitutional monarch	Euro (EUR)	$461.4 bil (2003)	$28,600	0.82

Country	Population	Capital	Government	Currency	GDP	GDP per capita	Exchange rate
New Zealand	3,993,817	Wellington	Parliamentary democracy	New Zealand dollar (NZD)	$85.3 bil (2003)	$21,600	1.52
Nicaragua	5,359,759	Managua	Republic	Gold cordoba (NIO)	$11.5 bil (2003)	$2,200	15.96
Niger	11,360,538	Niamey	Republic	CFA franc BCEAO (XOF)	$9.1 bil (2003)	$800	539.40
Nigeria	137,253,133	Abuja	Republic	Naira (NGN)	$110.8 bil (2003)	$800	133.45
Norway	4,574,560	Oslo	Hereditary constitutional monarchy	Kroner (NOK)	$171.6 bil (2003)	$37,700	6.92
Oman	2,903,165	Muscat	Absolute monarchy	Rial (OMR)	$37.5 bil (2003)	$13,400	0.38
Pakistan	159,196,336	Islamabad	Republic with strong military influence	Rupee (PKR)	$317.7 bil (2003)	$2,100	58.89
Palau	20,016	Koror	Republic	U.S. dollar	$174.0 mil (2003)	$9,000	1.00
Panama	3,000,463	Panama City	Republic	Balboa (PAB)	$18.6 bil (2003)	$6,300	1.00
Papua New Guinea	5,420,280	Port Moresby	Parliamentary democracy	Kina (PGK)	$11.4 bil (2003)	$2,200	3.03
Paraguay	6,191,368	Asuncion	Republic	Guarani (PYG)	$28.0 bil (2003)	$4,600	5,914.75
Peru	27,544,305	Lima	Republic	Nuevo sol (PEN)	$146.9 bil (2003)	$5,200	3.35
Philippines	86,241,697	Manila	Republic	Peso (PHP)	$390.7 bil (2003)	$4,600	56.13
Poland	38,626,349	Warsaw	Republic	Zloty (PLN)	$426.7 bil (2003)	$11,000	3.58
Portugal	10,524,145	Lisbon	Republic	Euro (EUR)	$182.3 bil (2003)	$18,000	0.82
Qatar	840,290	Doha	Traditional monarchy	Rial (QAR)	$17.5 bil (2003)	$21,500	3.64
Romania	22,355,551	Bucharest	Republic	Lei (ROL)	$154.4 bil (2003)	$6,900	33,533.55
Russia	143,782,338	Moscow	Federal republic	Ruble (RUB). On January 1, 1998, Russia eliminated 3 digits from the ruble	$1.287 tril	$8,900	29.22
Rwanda	7,954,013	Kigali	Republic	Franc (RWF)	$10.1 bil (2003)	$1,300	561.78
Saint Kitts and Nevis	38,836	Basseterre	Constitutional monarchy	East Caribbean dollar (XCD)	$339.0 mil (2002)	$8,800	2.67
Saint Lucia	164,213	Castries	Parliamentary democracy	East Caribbean dollar (XCD)	$866.0 mil (2002)	$5,400	2.67
Saint Vincent and the Grenadines	117,193	Kingstown	Constitutional monarchy	East Caribbean dollar (XCD)	$339.0 mil (2002)	$2,900	2.67
Samoa (formerly Western Somoa)	177,714	Apia	Constitutional monarchy	Tala (WST)	$1.0 bil (2002)	$5,600	2.86
San Marino	28,503	San Marino	Republic	Euro (EUR)	$940.0 mil (2001)	$34,600	0.82
Sao Tome and Principe	181,565	Sao Tome	Republic	Dobra (STD)	$200.0 mil (2002)	$1,200	8,856.65

(continued)

Country	Population	Capital	Type of Government	Currency (name)	Total GDP	Per Capita GDP	Exchange Rate to US$ (September 2004)
Saudi Arabia	25,795,938	Riyadh	Monarchy with council of ministers	Riyal (SAR)	$286.2 bil (2003)	$11,800	3.75
Senegal	10,852,147	Dakar	Republic	CFA franc BCEAO (XOF)	$16.9 bil (2003)	$1,600	539.40
Serbia and Montenegro (formerly Yugoslavia)	10,825,900	Belgrade	Federal republic	Dinar (YUN)	$24.0 bil (2003)	$2,300	60.94
Seychelles	80,832	Victoria	Republic	Rupee (SCR)	$626.0 mil (2002)	$7,800	5.42
Sierra Leone	5,883,889	Freetown	Republic	Leone (SLL)	$3.1 bil (2003)	$500	2,450.00
Singapore	4,353,893	Singapore	Republic	Singapore dollar (SGD)	$109.1 bil (2003)	$23,700	1.69
Slovakia	5,423,567	Bratislava	Republic	Koruna (SKK)	$72.3 bil (2003)	$13,300	32.89
Slovenia	2,011,473	Ljubljana	Republic	Tolar (SIT)	$36.9 bil (2003)	$18,300	196.07
Solomon Islands	523,617	Honiara	In transition	Dollar (SBD)	$800.0 mil (2001)	$1,700	7.48
Somalia	8,304,601	Mogadishu	In transition	Shilling (SOS)	$4.4 bil (2003)	$500	2,764.95
South Africa	42,718,530	Cape Town (legislative); Pretoria (administrative); Bloemfontein (judicial)	Republic	Rand (ZAR)	$456.7 bil (2003)	$10,700	6.57
Spain	40,280,780	Madrid	Constitutional monarchy	Euro (EUR)	$885.5 bil (2003)	$22,000	0.82
Sri Lanka	19,905,165	Colombo	Republic	Rupee (LKR)	$73.5 bil (2003)	$3,700	103.51
Sudan	39,148,162	Khartoum	Republic with strong military influence	Dinar (SDD)	$70.8 bil (2003)	$1,900	259.54
Suriname	436,935	Paramaribo	Republic	Guilder (SRG)	$1.5 bil (2003)	$3,500	2.73
Swaziland	1,169,241	Mbabane (administrative); Lobamba (legislative)	Constitutional monarchy	Lilangeni (SZL)	$5.7 bil (2003)	$4,900	6.58
Sweden	8,986,400	Stockholm	Constitutional monarchy	Krona (SEK)	$238.1 bil (2003)	$26,800	7.52
Switzerland	7,450,867	Bern (administrative); Lausanne (judicial)	Federal republic	Franc (CHF)	$239.8 bil (2003)	$32,800	1.27
Syria	18,016,874	Damascus	Republic (under military regime)	Pound (SYP)	$58.0 bil (2003)	$3,300	51.60
Taiwan	22,749,838	Taipei	Democracy	Dollar (TWD)	$528.6 bil (2003)	$23,400	33.85
Tajikistan	7,011,556	Dushanbe	Republic	Somoni (TJS)	$7.0 bil (2003)	$1,000	2.79

Country	Population	Capital	Government	Currency	GDP	GDP per capita	Exchange rate
Tanzania	36,588,225	Dodoma	Republic	Shilling (TXS)	$21.6 bil (2003)	$600	1,069.95
Thailand	64,865,523	Bangkok	Constitutional monarchy	Baht (THB)	$475.7 bil (2003)	$7,400	41.25
Togo	5,556,812	Lome	Republic	CFA franc BCEAO (XOF)	$8.2 bil (2003)	$1,500	539.40
Tonga	110,237	Nuku'alofa	Constitutional monarchy	Pa'anga (TOP)	$236.0 mil (2001)	$2,200	2.01
Trinidad and Tobago	1,096,585	Port-of-Spain	Parliamentary democracy	Tobago dollar (TTD)	$10.6 bil (2003)	$9,600	6.29
Tunisia	9,974,722	Tunis	Republic	Dinar (TND)	$68.8 bil (2003)	$6,900	1.27
Turkey	68,893,918	Ankara	Republic	Lira (TRL)	$455.3 bil (2003)	$6,700	1,497,751.13
Turkmenistan	4,863,169	Ashgabat	Republic with authoritarian rule	Manat (TMM)	$27.1 bil (2003)	$5,700	5,200.00
Tuvalu	11,468	Funafuti	Parliamentary democracy	Australian dollar (AUD)		$1,100	1.43
Uganda	26,404,543	Kampala	Republic	Shilling (UGS)	$36.1 bil (2003)	$1,400	1,715.50
Ukraine	47,732,079	Kiev	Republic	Hryvnia (UAH)	$256.5 bil (2003)	$5,300	5.31
United Arab Emirates	2,523,915	Abu Dhabi	Federation of emirates	Dirham (AED)	$57.7 bil (2003)	$23,200	3.67
United Kingdom	60,270,708	London	Constitutional monarchy	Pound (GBP)	$1.664 tril (2003)	$27,700	0.56
United States	293,027,571	Washington DC	Federal republic, strong democratic tradition	U.S. dollar	$10.98 tril (2003)	$37,800	1.00
Uruguay	3,399,237	Montevideo	Republic	Peso (UYP)	$42.9 bil (2003)	$12,600	27.73
Uzbekistan	26,410,416	Tashkent	Republic	Som (UZS)	$44.1 bil (2003)	$1,700	1,031.95
Vanuatu	202,609	Port-Vila	Republic	Vatu (VUV)	$563.0 mil (2002)	$2,900	115.05
Vatican City (The Holy See)	921	Euro (EUR)	0.82				
Venezuela	25,017,387	Caracas	Federal republic	Bolivar (VEB)	$117.9 bil (2003)	$4,800	1,917.60
Vietnam	82,689,518	Hanoi	Communist	Dong (VND)	$203.9 bil (2003)	$2,500	15,744.00
Western Samoa. *See Samoa*							
Yemen	20,024,867	Sana'a	Republic	Rial (YER)	$15.2 bil (2003)	$800	184.20
Yugoslavia. *See Serbia and Montenegro*							
Zaire. *See Congo*							
Zambia	10,462,436	Lusaka	Republic	Kwacha (ZMK)	$8.6 bil (2003)	$800	4,787.50
Zimbabwe	12,671,860	Harare	Republic	Zimbabwe dollar (ZWD)	$24.0 bil (2003)	$1,900	5,549.80

Glossary

After-only experimental design. An experimental design in which postmeasurement of the dependent variable is done after the manipulation of the independent variable.

ANOVA (analysis of variance). Technique used to compare means of two or more populations when the data scale is interval. The statistical technique utilized here analyzes the sample variance in order to test and estimate the means; hence, it is called the analysis of variance.

Area sampling. A form of cluster sampling in which geographic areas serve as the primary sampling units.

Attitude scale. A rating scale constructed to measure dimensions of an individual's attitude toward an object. Likert and semantic differential scales are examples of attitude scales.

Back translation. A procedure used to ensure that a questionnaire translated from one language to another is exactly the same as the original questionnaire. In this approach, a questionnaire is translated from its origin language to another and then translated back to the original by a second individual. Then the two versions are compared to see how similar the translation is.

Balance of payments. A statement that summarizes all economic transactions between a country and the rest of the world for a particular period of time.

Before-after experimental design. An experimental design in which premeasurement is conducted before manipulating the independent variable and postmeasurement is conducted after manipulating the independent variable.

Between-treatment variance. The variance in the response variable for different treatments.

Bivariate analysis. An analysis of the relationship between one or more independent variables and a dependent variable that may help explain the influence of the independent variable.

Causal research. Techniques used to identify the cause-and-effect relationship between two or more variables.

Centralization. An organizational structure in which the decision making is done at headquarters.

Chi-square test. A statistical test of independence between two variables and or a test for goodness of fit, i.e., a test to determine whether a given set of observations corresponds to an expected pattern.

Cluster analysis. Techniques used for separating objects into mutually exclusive groups that have homogeneous characteristics.

Cluster sampling. A probability sampling approach in which the population is first divided into similar groups (clusters) and then the groups become the sampling units.

Coding. The use of numbers to identify responses to enable data entry into computers for statistical analysis.

Coefficient of determination (r^2). A measure of the proportion of the total variation observed in the dependent variable that can be explained by the independent variable(s).

Comparability. Equivalency of results across societies or countries.

Comparative research. Research that compares respondent attitudes, behavior, and values in two or more societies or countries to identify similarities and differences between them.

Confidence interval. The range of values within which a population value is likely to fall.

Conjoint analysis. Techniques used to measure the relative importance of one attribute versus another.

Constant-sum scale. Scale used to identify a respondent's relative preference between objects by dividing a constant sum such as 10 or 100 among the objects.

Construct validity. Understanding why a given measure works on the basis of some underlying theory.

Content analysis. Technique used in studying cultures through a systematic evaluation of media and its content.

Control group. Subjects that are not exposed to the experimental treatment.

Convenience sample. A nonprobability sampling method chosen on the basis of convenience. Personal contacts, employees, and students are examples of commonly used convenience samples.

Correlation. Degree of association between two or more variables. The association could be direct or inverse. The value of correlation is a number between -1 and $+1$.

Country analysis. A process of examining a country's economic, political, and other market-related factors to determine the potential for business opportunities.

Cross-tabulation. A matrix that shows how a given value of one variable is associated with one or more other variables.

Culture. The values, norms, standards, mores, folklore, and other artifacts that distinguish one society from another.

Current account balance. An important account in the balance of payments that measures the difference between total exports and imports of a country.

Database. A collection of data and information that is accessible through computers.

Decentralization. An organizational structure in which decisions are made at the subsidiary level.

Degrees of freedom. The number of unconstrained data used in calculating a statistic.

Dependent variable. A variable whose value is affected by another variable.

Depth interview. An unstructured interview in which the interviewer asks questions based on the respondent's answers and further probes for additional information.

Discriminant analysis. A statistical technique for classifying individuals or objects into two or more categories by using a set of interval-scaled independent variables.

Descriptive research. A type of research that is specific and focuses on obtaining an accurate description of the variables in a research context.

Dummy variable. Used in regression analysis, a variable that can assume either of only two values, 0 or 1, where one value represents the existence of a certain condition and the other value indicates that the condition does not exist.

Economic integration. Formation of group that streamlines economic policies and removes all trade barriers among the countries within the group.

Editing. Steps taken to ensure that the information collected is accurate and readable.

Ethnocentrism. A belief that one's own culture is superior to other cultures.

Exchange rate. The price of one currency vis-à-vis another currency.

Expected value. The estimated value of a decision calculated by adding the product of all payoffs by its probability.

Experiments. A type of research that isolates the cause-and-effect relationship between variables by systematically changing the values of variables to measure the effect on other variables.

Exploratory research. A flexible research design whose aim is to study the underlying factors that influence a situation.

Exponential smoothing. A forecasting technique that uses the weighted average of the previous periods. In exponential smoothing, more recent periods are weighted more heavily than earlier periods.

Factor analysis. Analysis that helps researchers to determine underlying dimensions of a set of data and to determine the relationships among variables. It is commonly used to reduce and simplify a data set.

Factor loadings. Coefficients of factors that link the factors to the variables and help interpret the factors.

First-mover advantage. The economies of scale and familiarity with market benefits achieved by entering the market ahead of the competition.

Focus group. A group interview that attempts to understand the reasons for buying, using, or liking an object through group dynamics. Focus groups use a trained moderator to facilitate the discussion.

Foreign direct investment (FDI). Flows of funds in the form of investments into a foreign country.

Frequency distribution. A summary of responses given by respondents in a survey.

Gap analysis. Analysis that shows why a company's sales are less than its potential for a product in a given market.

Geocentric. An approach that recognizes the needs of both the home country and the host country.

Gross domestic product. The total of all economic activity of a country.

Hypothesis. An educated guess about the outcome of an empirical test that may be used to answer research issues.

Independent variable. A variable that is manipulated by the researcher to observe the effects it has on a dependent variable.

Internal business research. A formalized approach to obtaining information that can be used to make critical business decisions.

Interval estimate. A statistical estimate of an unknown parameter about a population that uses an interval that is likely to include the value of the population parameter.

Interval scale. A scale that uses real numbers and in which the differences between values are meaningful. This scale can be used for most computations including means and variance.

Judgment sampling. A sampling approach in which experts' opinions are used to select a representative sample.

Kurtosis. The shape of a distribution relative to a normal distribution.

Likert scale. A rating scale that requires respondents to indicate whether they agree or disagree with a statement.

Mall-intercept survey. A survey conducted in a shopping mall.

Mean. A measure of central tendency that is obtained by adding all observations and dividing the sum by the number of observations.

Median. Another measure of central tendency. It is the value that falls in the middle when the measurements are arranged in order of magnitude.

Mode. The third of the central tendencies. It is the value that occurs most frequently.

Multidimensional scaling. Any of the techniques used to represent objects on a spatial diagram.

Multiple-choice questions. Questions that require respondents to choose from a set of pre-determined alternative responses.

Multivariate techniques. Statistical techniques used when there are multiple measures of each observation and two or more variables are to be analyzed.

Nominal scale. A scale in which values are assigned arbitrarily. It is used for counting and determining proportions.

Nonprobability sample. A sample selection procedure that relies on personal judgment in selecting sample units.

Null hypothesis. The hypothesis that a proposed result is not true for the population.

Observational method. A research approach that relies on observations to gather information about subjects.

One-tailed test. A hypothesis test in which the alternative hypothesis specifies the direction of anticipated difference between two values (greater or less than).

One-way frequency distribution. The distribution for a single variable.

Open-ended question. A question in which each respondent has the opportunity to freely express his or her views.

Operational definition. A description of the activities a researcher must complete in order to assign a value to the parameter or concept to be measured.

Ordinal scale. A scale in which the values represent the rank order of the responses. It can be used for calculating median and any other measure based on ranking.

Paired comparison test. A method to rank objects by presenting all possible pairs one pair at a time.

Panel. A group of individuals who have agreed to be test subjects.

Parameter. The numerical characteristics of a model.

Pearson correlation coefficient. The degree to which there is a linear association between two interval-scaled variables.

Personal interviews. An approach to gather information through face-to-face interaction.

Political risk. The dynamic and violent shifts in political stability of a country that may result in losses for a company.

Pretest. Testing a questionnaire before it is actually administered to isolate potential problems with the questions or the questionnaire's format.

Primary research. Techniques used in collecting data for a specific project for which there is very little information currently available.

Probability sample. A sampling approach in which each element in a population has a known and equal chance of being selected.

Problem definition. A statement that specifies the type of information that is needed to solve a problem.

Projective technique. A method to gather information from subjects that uses their own experiences and feelings in framing a response.

Purchasing power parity. A mechanism to equate the economic activities of countries that have different rates of consumer buying power.

Qualitative research. Techniques that aid in understanding the underlying reasons for consumer choice process and purchase of goods and services.

Quota sample. A nonprobability sampling approach that ensures that the demographic characteristics of interest are represented in the same proportion as they are in the population.

Random stratified sample. A probability sampling technique that is done in two steps. First, the population is dividend into subsets, and then simple random samples of elements are selected from each subset.

Rating scales. Scales developed to measure various attributes (attitude, feelings of like and dislike, importance, and so on) about an object.

Ratio scale. A scale that has an absolute zero and therefore allows the comparison of the magnitude that is being measured.

Regression analysis. A technique that involves developing a mathematical equation that analyzes the relationship between two or more interval-scaled variables. If one independent and one dependent variable are involved, the technique is called simple regression. If two or more independent variables are involved, the technique is called multiple regression.

Reliability. The extent of variable error in a measurement. In other words, it is the ability to obtain similar results for the same situation in different settings.

Research design/research process. A framework for conducting a research study. It includes defining the problem, identifying the sources of information, outlining the information-gathering process, describing the analytical steps to be taken, and estimating the cost of the study.

Research proposal. A written document that spells out the research design and acts as a guide for the researcher.

Response rate. The number of completed interviews divided by the number of elements in the original sample.

Return on investment (ROI). A ratio of net profits to total investment.

Sample. The number of individuals or objects chosen from the population of interest in a research study.

Sample mean. The arithmetic mean of a variable in a sample.

Sampling distribution. The probability distribution of sample means for all possible samples drawn from a particular population

Sampling frame. A listing of the population that is used to select the sample elements.

Scanner data. Data on items sold in stores obtained through optical character recognition equipment that reads bar codes on packages of the items sold.

Secondary data. Any data that is currently available through any source that was not collected for the problem at hand.

Semantic differential scale. A scale that requires respondents to check which cell between a set of bipolar adjectives best describes their position.

Simple random sample. A probability sampling technique in which single units are drawn from a population by a single-stage procedure.

Snowball sample. A judgment sample that first locates an initial set of respondents with the desired characteristics and then uses this group to locate others with similar characteristics.

Spearman rank-order correlation coefficient. A technique for determining the degree of association between two ordinal or rank-ordered variables.

Standard deviation. The positive square root of the variance of a set of measurements. It measures the dispersion of the measurements.

Standard error of the mean. The standard deviation of a sampling distribution of the mean. It is equal to the population standard deviation divided by the square root of the sample size.

Survey. A method to collect data that uses a questionnaire.

Syndicated research services. Data collected by independent research companies on specific topics that are then sold to companies that subscribe to these reports for a fee.

Tabulation. A procedure used to count the number of cases in each category.

Tariff. A tax levied on imported goods.

Time series analysis. A forecasting technique that has time as the independent variable. There are four effects that are found in a time series. trend, cyclical, seasonal, and random variations.

Tracking studies. A continuing series of surveys that measure the same variable over time.

Two-tailed test. A test of a hypothesis in which the alternative includes both higher and lower values of the parameter.

Type I error. An error caused by accepting the alternative hypothesis when the null hypothesis is true.

Type II error. An error caused by accepting the null hypothesis when the alternative hypothesis is true.

Thematic apperception test (TAT). A projective technique in which respondents are asked to describe the feelings of a person shown in a photograph. It appears that quite often the respondent normally reveals his or her own feelings while describing the feelings of the person in the photograph.

Word association. An instrument containing a list of words to which respondents are asked to respond with the first word that comes to mind.

Name Index

Abrams, B., 144n3, 145
Achenbaum, A.A., 126n1
Agarwal, J., 18, 303
Albaum, G., 58, 224n3
Amin, S.G., 17n12
Anderson, R.E., 365
Angelmar, R., 209n4
Arpan, J.S., 175, 192n9
Arredinido, L., 375
Arsan, M., 226
Assael, H., 241

Bachmann, D., 225n21
Baker, W.H., 376
Bakken, D., 126
Bangert, D.C., 18, 126n8
Banks, S.K., 242
Barabba, V.P., 58
Barnard, P., 225n9
Baron, S., 225n14
Barson, D.C., 18
Bartholomew, D.J., 365
Bartlett, C.A., 39, 39n6
Bartos, R., 31, 191n2
Bartram, P., 17n13
Baumgartner, H., 145
Bausell, B.R., 158
Bean, A.G., 192n11
Becker, E., 17n16
Becker, R., 144n1, 225
Berenson, C., 225n5
Berger, P., 158
Bidkale, S., 102n2
Bijmolt, T.H.A., 365n2
Binder, J.J., 353

Black, J.S., 40
Black, W.C., 365
Blackburn, R., 126
Bradley, N., 86n7
Branon, D., 365
Brislin, R., 191n8
Brock, S.E., 241
Brooks, L., 17n5, 39
Brown, S.J., 158n3
Brown, T.J., 17, 264, 303, 322
Burke, R.R., 225n11
Burns, A.C., 191n5
Bush, R.F., 191n5
Buta, P., 103n9
Butler, E., 225n8

Cantril, A., 202, 209n6
Castleberry, S.B., 86
Chau, L.L-F., 226
Chen, P.Y., 352
Chisnall, P.M., 86
Chonko, L.B., 86n3
Churchill, G.A., 17, 191n4, 264, 303, 322
Clancy, K.J., 126n4
Cobanoglu, C., 225
Cooper, H.R., 226
Craig, C.S., 17, 191n1, 192n10
Creswell, J.W., 58
Crispell, D., 86n4, 86n6
Crowley, A., 225n18
Czinkota, M.R., 18, 39, 86nn1–2

Daft, R.A., 39
Dalbec, B., 126
Dallin, R.F., 126n9

Daniels, K., 17n8
Dansky, K.H., 365
Darlinton, R.B., 353
Dawson, S., 225n4
Day, E., 126n2
De Chernatony, L., 17n8
DeSarbo, W.S., 145n8, 365
deVaus, D.A., 126
Dickinson, D., 225n4
Dillon, W.R., 302n2, 365n1
Ding, A.A., 365
Dochartaigh, N.O., 86
Dodd, J., 226
Douglas, C.J., 365
Douglas, S.P., 17, 191n1, 192n10
Drake, P.D., 103
Draper, P., 39n7
Drozdenko, R.G., 103
Durvasula, S., 145, 209n11

Edmunds, H., 126
Edris, T.A., 145
Elfrink, J., 225n21
Elmer, J.B., 225n10
Eroglu, S., 209n9
Esselmont, D., 18

Farmer, T., 225n19
Feid, N., 226
Fenwick, I., 365
Fowler, F.J., 145
Frank, R.A., 365
Franses, P.H., 365
Frieman, J., 225n8
Frost, F., 225n13
Fryxell, G.E., 191n6
Fu, M.Y.C., 175, 192n9

Gallup, G., Jr., 18, 220, 225n12
Gandz, J., 58
Garner, K.C., 352n1
Garratt, M.CHECKSPELLING???, 158n2
Geissler, B., 225n18
Gendall, P., 18
Ghoshal, S., 39n6
Gillet, R., 241
Glen, J.J., 365
Goldstein, M., 302n2, 365n1
Goold, M., 39n8
Gordon, C.C., 145n4
Gordon, G.L., 145n4
Gorn, G.J., 158
Gould, G.F., 158

Gould, J.L., 158
Govindarajan, V., 39n1
Grecco, C., 225n16
Green, P.E., 17, 58, 365, 366
Greenbaum, T.L., 126
Grunert, K.G., 126
Grunnert, S.C., 126
Gupta, A., 39n1

Hair, J.F., 365
Halliday, J., 103
Han, M.C., 145
Hart, S.J., 17n14
Hasson, L., 86n5
Hausknecht, D.R., 126n9
Hawkins, D.I., 18
Hayajnea, A.F., 17n12
Healey, N.M., 225n14
Hoffer, J.A., 103
Holway, A., 226
Hunt, J.W., 39n5

Illieva, J., 225n14
Irwin, J.R., 353

Jaffe, G., 376
Jain, A.K., 366
James, D., 225n17
Jarillo, C.J., 39
Jobber, D., 226
Johansson, J.K., 18, 145n5, 145n10
Johnson, G., 17n8
Johnson, L.W., 126n9
Jones, G., 39
Jones, M.V., 17n14
Jussaume, R.A., 225n6

Kahle, L.R., 145
Kamakura, W.A., 365
Kamins, M.K., 86
Kanuk, L., 225n5
Kassarjian, H.H., 126
Keen, P., 103n11
Keillor, B., 191n3
Kelly, S., 39n11
Kemsley, E.K., 365
Keon, J., 241
Keown, C.F., 226
Kephart, P., 17n11
Kerlinger, F.N., 126
Khana, T., 39n4
Kjell, G., 241
Klastorin, T.D., 366

Kleiser, S., 18
Knott, M., 365
Kobayashi, K., 39n7
Korzenny, A., 145n9
Korzenny, F., 145n9
Kotabe, M., 103
Krieg, P.C., 126n4
Kuhfeld, W.F., 158n2
Kumar, V., 17

Laird, L.E., 242
Langbourne, R., 144n2
Laudon, J.P., 102n1, 103, 103n10
Laudon, K.C., 102n1, 103, 103n10
Leach, J., 376
Lee, B., 17n2
Lee, B.-W., 145
Leech, T., 375
Leiber, R.B., 126n10
Lemeshaw, S., 241
Lemon, K.W., 86
Levy, P.S., 241
Lewis, P., 58n1
Lewis, P.V., 375
Lichtenstein, D.R., 145, 209n11
Lind, D.A., 264, 322
Loeb, M., 145n6
Low, G.S., 376
Luk, S.T.K., 87
Luyens, S., 302n1
Lynch, J.G., 158

MacElroy, B., 225n18
MacFarlane, P., 242
Macht, J., 18
Malhotra, N.K., 17, 18, 198, 209n2, 225n22, 265, 277,
    302n3, 303, 322, 365
Marchal, W.G., 264, 322
Martin, I.M., 209n9
Martin, J., 103
Martin, W.S., 353
Martinez, J.I., 39
Martinez, Z., 18
Maurer, R., 158
May, W.H., 201, 209n5
McClelland, G.H., 353
McFadden, F.R., 103
Meidan, A., 145
Melamed, L., 158n3
Mendenhall, W., 352
Miller, T.W., 103
Miron, M.S., 209n5
Mitchell, J., 209n3

Mohan, C.N., 18
Mohr, J.J., 376
Monk, D., 224n2
Moody, J., 376
Moreo, P.J., 225
Morgan, D.L., 126
Morrall, K., 102n5
Morris, K., 17n10
Morton, M.S., 39
Muranyi, N.R., 102n8
Murphy, L.H., 102n4, 191n7, 224n1
Murray, I.P., 18, 225n23

Nelson, T.A., 86
Netemeyer, R.G., 145, 209n11
Nevid, J.S., 126n7
Nevin, J.R., 158
Nonaka, I., 18, 145n5, 145n10
Nowlis, S.M., 86

Ocken, V., 102n3
O'Donnell, S.W., 39
Oosterveld, J.P., 39n9
Order, C.K., 209n7
Osgood, C.E., 201, 209n5
Owens, D., 191n3

Padilla, B., 127
Pak, S, 264n1
Palepu, K., 39n4
Peterson, M., 18, 303
Pettijohn, C., 191n3
Pol, L.G., 264n1
Popovich, P.M., 352
Prahalad, C.K., 39n9
Pras, B., 209n4

Quible, J.K., 126n5

Rabianski, J.S., 87
Reily, S., 17n7
Reiter, J.P., 242
Rentz, K.C., 127
Ricks, D., 17n6, 18, 175, 192n9
Ro, K-K., 145
Rogers, T.M., 145n4
Ronkainen, I.A., 18, 39, 86n1
Rose, G., 145
Rosenbaum, P.R., 158
Rosenblum, J., 225n16
Roszkowski, M.J., 192n11
Rummel, R.J., 366
Ryman, Anne, 33

Sabena, P., 126n3
Saunders, J., 226
Schmit, N., 353
Schoenbachler, D.D., 145n4
Sengupta, J., 158
Shapiro, A.C., 352n1
Sharma, S., 207, 209n8, 209n10
Shimp, T., 207, 209n10
Shoham, A., 145
Sincich, T., 352
Siu, W-S., 226
Smith, E.R., 86n3
Smith, S.A., 58n2
Sobel, M., 158
Solomon, M.B., 18
Soutar, G.N., 126n9
Sta Maria, N.L., 126n7
Steekamp, J-B.E.M., 145
Stewart, D.W., 86
Strandskov, J., 224n3
Sudman, S., 145n7, 241
Summers, G.F., 209n1
Sundaram, A.K., 40
Sweeney, J.C., 126n9, 226
Sweet, C., 127
Szenberg, M., 127

Taggart, J.H., 40
Tatham, R.L., 365
Tatterson, D., 17n2
Tenopir, C., 103
Thompson, S.K., 241
Tobia, R.D., 158n2
Toyne, B., 18
Tull, D.S., 17, 18, 58
Turner, J.F., 86n3

Vazzana, G., 225n21
Venkatram, R., 145n8
Vogelstein, F., 87

Wade, K., 127
Walker, J., 242
Wallace, J., 225n15
Warde, B., 225
Warner, F., 17n1
Wathen, S.A., 264, 322
Weathers, D., 209n8
Webb, J.R., 17n14
Webster, L., 241n8
Wedel, M., 365, 365n2
Weible, R., 225n15
Weiner, B., 86n8
Wheeler, D.R., 127, 145n11
Whipple, T.W., 58
Wilk, R.R., 127
Wilson, D.R., 58
Wind, Y., 365, 366
Winters, L.C., 225n7
Wiseman, F., 366
Wisner, S., 103
Wittink, D., 352
Wyner, G.A., 158n1, 241n3, 241n7

Yamada, Y., 225n6
Yavas, U., 241n1
Yoffie, A.J., 103
Young, M.R., 365

Zellner, A., 353
Zhao, T., 17n2
Zikmund, W.G., 18, 265, 303, 322
Zimmerman, A.S., 127

Subject Index

Note: Page numbers in italics refer to figures and tables.

Abstract Business Information (ABI/Inform), 80, 90
ACNielsen, 4, 34, 79, 99, 136, 139
After-only experiment, 149–150
After-only with control experiment, 150, 151–152
Alternative hypothesis, 277, 278, 300
Ambiguous wording, 167–168
Analysis of covariance, 308
Analysis of interdependence, 354–355
Analysis of variance. *See* ANOVA
ANCOVA, 308
ANOVA, 53, 271, 272, 304, 308, 317
   basic steps, 308–311
   between-column variation, 311–312
   between-row variation, 312, *313*
   degrees of freedom (DF), 312–313
   one-way analysis of variance, 308
   SAS and, 320–322
   sums of squares total (SST), 313–316
   two-way analysis of variance, 316
Area knowledge, 19
Area sampling, 233, 235
Arithmetic mean. *See* Mean
Articulation problems, 179
Asian-Pacific countries data sources, 391–392
Association techniques, 107, 119–120
Assumptions in questionnaire design, 169
Audits, 52, 141, 142, 143

Back translation, 132, 174–175
Balance of Payments (BOP), 66, 67, 77, 78, 100
Before-after with control experiment, 150–151

Behavioral measurement. *See* Scale measurements
Between-column variation, 311–312
Between-row variation, 312, *313*
Bias
   cultural bias, 29, 129–130, 143
   in focus group research, 114
   interpretation bias, 140
   interviewer bias, 144, 212, 221, *223,* 224
   observational bias, 138, 140, 142
   order bias, 182
   in questionnaire design, 164, 165, 173, 182, 185
   response bias, 164, 185, 261
   sampling bias, 231, 239, 240, 261–262
   selection bias, 148, 157
Bibliographic databases, 80, 90
Biomedical Computer Programs (BMDP), 274
Bivariate analysis, 300, 354. *See also* Multivariate
    analysis
Bloomberg Terminal, 99, 100
BMDP (Biomedical Computer Programs), 274
BOP (Balance of Payments), 66, 67, 77, 78, 100
Burdensome questions, 169–170
Business knowledge, 19

Calibration equivalence, 131–132, 143
Capital account balance, 67
Categorization, 266, 271
Category equivalence, 131, 143
Causal research, 134–135, 146, 155–157
Causal research designs. *See* Experimental research
Causality, 134, 155–157
Census data, 76, 228
Central limit theorem, 231, 262

Central tendency, 246–248, 251, 273, 300
Centralization, 20, 27–29, *30, 32*
Centralized databases, 96, 102
CETSCALE (consumer ethnocentric scale), 207
Chi-square distribution, 53, 293–296, 300–301, *414*
    contingency table tests and, 296–299, 300
    goodness-of-fit tests and, 293, 304–308, 317
    interpreting results, 299
Chicago Research in Security Prices (CRSP), 99, 100
Citibank database, 99
Civil law, 69
Class intervals, 244
Classification of data
    international research data chart, *50*
    techniques, 272–276
Classification questions, 182
Close-ended questions, 171, 172
Cluster analysis, 355, 360, 363, 364
Cluster sampling, 232, 233, *236,* 240
Coding, 268–271, 300
    codebooks, 270
    coding schemes, 269
    coding sheets, 272
    computerized data entry, 271–272, 274
    open-ended questions, 177, 268, 271
    software programs for, 268–269
    structure questions, 269
    variables in, 270
Coefficient of correlation, 334–335, 342, 433
Coefficient of determination, 235
Common law, 69
Common variance, 357
Communality, 357
Comparability, 9, 113, 129–130, 143
    centralization and, 28
    decentralization and, 31
Comparative research, 45, 132, 133, 202
Competitive environment, 64–65
Competitor information, 11
Completion rate, 260, 261
Completion techniques, 107, 120
Computerized data entry, 271–272, 274
Concept equivalence, 130–131, 143
Conclusive research, 128, 133–134, 143
    causal research, 134–135, 146, 155–157
    descriptive research, 134–135, 143
    experimental research, 52, 146–147, 157
    longitudinal studies, 54, 134, 136, 143, 374
    observational techniques, 134–135
        audits, 52, 141, 142, 143
        benefits of, 142, 144
        bias in, 138, 140, 142
        content analysis, 52, 140–141, 143

Conclusive research
    observational techniques *(continued)*
        contrived/set-up environment observation, 142
        disguised observation, 142
        mechanical observation, 138–139, 143
        natural environment observation, 142
        personal observation, 137–138, 143
        problems with, 143, 144
        structured observation, 141–142
        trace analysis, 52, 139–140, 143
        undisguised observation, 142
        unstructured observation, 142
    surveys, 134, 135–136, 143
    types of, 134
    vs. exploratory research, 105
Concomitant variation, 155
Confidence interval estimator, 256, 262, 294–296
Confidentiality of data, 374
Construct equivalence, 130, 143
Construct validity, 206–207, 208
Consumer ethnocentric scale (CETSCALE), 207
Content analysis, 52, 140–141, 143
Content validity, 206
Context of questions, 179–180
Contingency table tests, 296–299, 300
Contrived environment observation, 142
Control groups, 147, 150–153
Convenience sampling, 230, *236,* 237, 240
Correlation, 323, 342, 372, 433
    coefficient of correlation, 334–335, 342, 433
    correlation matrix, 357
Country risk analysis, 11–12, 14–16, 73
Country selection, 82
Country statistics, 447–457
Covariance, analysis of, 308
Cross-tabulation, 53, *264,* 272, 273–274, *276,* 300
    SAS and, 432–433
    tables, 297
CRSP (Chicago Research in Security Prices), 99, 100
Cultural bias, 29, 129–130, 143
Cultural factors
    business environment and, 70–71
    ethnocentrism, 207
    exploratory research and, 107
    focus groups and, 108, 109, 114
    international databases and, 100–101
    multicountry research and, 9
    primary data collection and, 129–130, 131
    questionnaire design and, 160, 161, 163, 166–167,
        173, 185
    scale measurements and, 199
    translating questionnaires and, 173, 174–175
    translation equivalence and, 132–133, 143

Culture shock, 71
Currency data sources, 77
Current account balance, 67
Customized services, 34–35

Data equivalence, 130–133
Data analysis, 10–11, 52, 53, 266, 299
    categorization, 266–267, 271
    classification of data, 272–276
    coding, 268–271, 300
        codebooks, 270
        coding schemes, 269
        coding sheets, 272
        open-ended questions, 177, 268, 271
        structure questions, 269
        variables in, 270
    computerized data entry, 271–272, 274
    cross-tabulation, 53, *264,* 272, 273–274, *276,* 300
        SAS and, 432–433
        tables, 297
    data matrix, 269–270, 272, *360*
    editing, 53, 267–268, 271, 299
    frequency distribution, 272–273, *275,* 300
    multivariate analysis, 272, 300
    purpose of, 272
    in reports, 368
    simple analysis, 272
    SPSS and, 417–423
    techniques, 272–276
    univariate analysis, 272, 300, 354
    variables in, 266
Data collection. *See* Primary data; Secondary data
Data confidentiality, 374
Data entry, computerized, 271–272, 274
Data matrix, 269–270, 272, *360*
Data mining, 94, *95*
Data quality, 8
Data safety, 374
Data storage and retrieval, 374
Database management systems (DBMS), 94
Databases, 88, 101–102. *See also* Management
        information systems (MIS)
    advantages of, 90–92
    development of, 96, 98–99, 102
    external databases, 89–92, 99–100, 102
    external secondary data, 80
    internal databases, 89, 90–92, 98-99, 102
    internal secondary data and, 73
    international databases, 80
        problems in, 100–101
    numeric data in, 90
    role in MIS, 92
    structures of, 96, 98

Databases *(continued)*
    textual data in, 90
    uses of, 89–90
Datastream International, 99, 100
DBMS (database management systems), 94
Decentralization, 20, 23, 27, 28, 30–32, 101, 102
Deciles, 249
Decision making, , 3, 5, 7 10–11. (*See also* Organizational
        structures)
    financial decisions, 12–13, 84
    marketing decisions, 84
    plant location decisions, 83
    reports and, 54, 367, 375
    in research process, 48–49, 57
Decision support systems (DSS), 95–96, *97*
Degrees of freedom (DF), 312–313
Demographic data, 76
Demographic environment, 70
Dependent variables, 147, 157
Depth interviews, 51, 107, 116–118, 124–125, 238
Description in scales, 194
Descriptive data, 52
Descriptive research, 134–135, 143
Descriptive statistics, 243–244, 262
Design process, questionnaire, *162*
Designs, experimental, 148–154, 157
Detergent questionnaire, 186–191, 377–390
Determination, coefficient of, 235
Determination, sample size, 243–244, 262
Developing countries, 66
    data for, 392
    sampling in, 228, 239
DF, (degrees of freedom), 312–313
Dichotomous questions, 171–172
Differences, tests of, 304, 317. *See also* ANOVA;
        Goodness-of-fit tests
Digital image processing, 96
Direct approaches. *See* Nondisguised approaches
Directory databases, 80
Discriminant analysis, 355, 360–362, 363, *364*
Discriminant validity, 206, 207
Disguised approaches, 107, 118–122, 124, 125
Disguised observation, 142
Dispersion, 248–249, 262
Distance in scales, 194
Distributed databases, 96, 98
Distribution, 253–255, 262, *413*
Divisional structures, 21, *22*
Donnelly demographics database, 80
Double-barreled questions, 168
Drawing conclusions from samples, 262
Drawing samples, 238–239, 240
DRI/McGraw-Hill, 99

Drop-down substitution, 239
DSS (decision support systems), 95–96, *97*
Dun & Bradstreet (D&B), 78, 136

Economic environment, 65–66
Economic factors, 11
Economic data sources, 72, 76–78, 399, 403
Editing, 53, 267–268, 271, 299
Electronic questionnaire distribution, 224
Embarrassing questions, 178
Empirical databases, 80
Entering markets, 82–83
Environmental variables, 64–70
Environments. *See* International business environments
Equivalence of data, 130–133, 143
ESS (executive support system), 95
Estimates in questionnaire design, 170–171
Ethnocentrism, 207. *See also* Cultural bias
Eurobases and Euroscope databases, 80
European countries data sources, 78, 80–81, 392–394
Evaluating countries. *See* Country risk analysis
Exchange rate risks, 12–13, 37, 63, 67–68, 85
Executive summaries, 368, 375
Executive support system (ESS), 95, *97*
Expected value, 231, 253
Expenditure approaches, 66
Experimental research, 52, 146–147, 157
    designs, 148–154, 157
        after-only, 149–150
        after-only with control, 150, 151–152
        before-after with control, 150–151
        factorial, 153, 154, *155*
        pre-post test, 149–150
        pre-post test with control, 150–151
        randomized block, 153
        static group design, 150
        time series, 152–153
    key terms in, 147
    preconditions for conducting, 155–156
    problems in, 156–157
    validity in, 154–155, 157
    variables in, 147, 157
Exploratory research, 104 (*See also* Focus group research)
    advantages of, 112–113, 117, 122, 125
    completion techniques, 107, 120
    depth interviews, 51, 107, 116–118, 124–125, 238
    disadvantages of, 113–115, 117, 122, 125
    disguised approaches, 107, 118–122, 124, 125
    expressive techniques, 119, 121, 125
    new directions in, 123–124, 125
    nondisguised approaches, 107, 124
    projective techniques, 51, 107, 118–122, 125
    sentence completion, 119, 120, 125

Exploratory research (*continued*)
    uses of, 105–106
    vs. conclusive research, 105
    word association, 118, 119–120, 125
Exponential smoothing, 319
Export data sources, 78
Expressive techniques, 119, 121, 125
External data sources, 71, 73–81
External databases, 89–90, 92, 99–100, 99, 102
External environmental variables, 63–64
External secondary data sources, 73–81, 85. *See also* Secondary data
External suppliers. *See* Suppliers
Extraneous (external) variables, 147–148, 157
Eye cameras, 139

Face validity, 206
Factor analysis, 355, 363–364
    considerations in, 355–356
    example, *357*
Factorial experiment, 153, 154, *155*
Failures, international business, 19
FDI (foreign direct investment), 67, 75
Financial databases, 99–100
Financial decisions, 12–13, 84
Financial environment, 67-69, 11
Financial secondary data sources, 72, 77–78, 403-407
Fiscal policies, 68
Focus group research, 107–108, 124
    applications of, 115
    benefits of, 112–113
    bias in, 114
    critical interview factors, 108–110
    key elements in, *116*
    moderators, 109, 114, 124
    planning for, 110–112
    problems with, 113–115
    steps in research, *111*
    variations in, 115–116
Foreign direct investment (FDI), 67, 75
Forrester Research, 34
Frequency distribution
    in data analysis, 272–273, *275,* 300
    as statistical concept, 244–246, *247,* 262
Frost & Sullivan Research Reports Abstracts, 90
Full-service suppliers, 34
Functional knowledge, 19
Functional structures, 21, 25, *25*

Generalizations in questionnaire design, 170–171
Geocentric approaches, 22
Geographic environment, 71
Geographic structures, 21, *24,* 24–25

Global Vantage, 99, 100
Globalization, 4
    scale measurements and, 207
    secondary sources and, 85
    strategy formulation and, 13
Goodness-of-fit tests, 293, 304–308, 317
Government agencies, 73, 75–76, 81
Government data sources, 409–412
Government regulations, 11
Graphic rating scale, 202, *203*
Gross Domestic Product (GDP), 66, 67, 77
Gross National Product (GNP), 62, 63, 66–67, 77

Heterogeneous databases, 98
Hierarchical clustering, 360
History variables, 147, *223*
Homogeneous databases, 98
Human resources data, 72
Hybrid structures. *See* Matrix structures
Hypothesis testing, 53, 276–293
    alternative hypothesis, 277, 278, 300
    elements of, 277–278
    errors in, 279, 300
    nonparametric tests, *277*
    null hypothesis, 277, 278, 300
    one-tailed tests, 283–284, 291
    parametric tests, 276, *277*
    probability value (p Value), 284–289
    steps in, 279–283
    test statistic, 277, 278, 317
    two-tailed tests, 283–284, 287–289, 291, *413*
    unknown standard deviation and, 289–293

IMS Health, 32
Incidence rate, 260, 261, 262
Income approaches, 66
Independent variables, 147, 157
Indirect approaches. *See* Disguised approaches
Industrialized countries, 66–67
    sampling in, 228
Inferential statistics, 243, 244, 262
Inflation, 68
Information Resources Inc. (IRI), 32–33
Information sources. *See* Secondary data
Information systems. *See* Databases; Management
        information systems (MIS)
Infrastructural environment, 12, 69–70
Instrumentation, 148
Intercept, 324
Interdependence techniques, 354–355
Internal control, 270
Internal databases, 89, 90–92, 102
    development of, 98–99

Internal databases *(continued)*
    structures of, 96
Internal secondary data sources, 71–72, 85
    databases and, 73
International business environment, 62
    competitive environment, 64–65
    demographic environment, 70
    difficulties in, 63–64
    economic environment, 65–66
    financial environment, 67–68
    geographic environments, 71
    infrastructural environment, 69–70
    legal environment, 69
    political environment, 68–69
    technological environment, 70
International corporations, world's largest, *5*
International data sources (general), 81, 394–397
International databases, 80
    problems in, 100–101
International Finance Corporation (IFC), 99
International management, 3
International Monetary Fund (IMF), 66, 73, 76, 99, 100
International organizations, 73, 76–78
International research, 3–7, 10–11. *See also* Globalization
    complexity of, 9
    cost of, 7–8, 35–37
    country risk analysis, 11–12, 14–16
    data quality, 8
    evaluating countries, 11–12
    financial decisions, 12–13
    information needs, 19, 37
    issues in, 7–10, 35
    lead time, 9
    location decisions, 13
    market potential, 12
    multicountry research, 9–10
    nature of, 10
    organizing for, 26–37
    overview of, 3–7
    process of, 7, 41
    proposals, 41, *43,* 55–56, 57
    secondary data availability, 8
    strategy formalization, 13–14
    suppliers, 32–35
    time pressures, 8–9
    uses of, 11–14
Internet-based research, 219–222
Internet services, 81, 84
Interpretation bias, 140
Interval estimator, 256, 262, 294–296
Interval scales, 197, *198,* 199, 208, 300
Intervals in scale measurement, 195
Interviewer bias, 144, 212, 221, *223,* 224

Interviews
  bias in, 144, 212, 221, *223,* 224
  depth interviews, 51, 107, 116–118, 124–125, 238
  factors affecting methods, *223*
  in focus groups, 108–110
  internet-based methods, 219–222
  mail interviews, 211–214, 223
  personal interviews, 216–219, 223–224
  in questionnaire administration, 222–223
  technology-driven methods, 219–222
  telephone interviews, 214–217, 223
Investment data sources, 79, 403–407
IPSOS-NPD, 136
Itemized rating scales, 202, 203–204

Japan External Trade Organization (JETRO), 90

Kantar Group, 32
Knowledge work system (KWS), 96, *97*

Latin American countries data sources, 394
Lead questions, 180–182
Leading questions, 166–167
Legal environment, 69
Legitimacy of questions, 179–180
Likert scale, 130, 199–200, 205
Limited-service suppliers, 34
Linear regression, 324, 332, 336
  SAS and, 327–328
Location decisions, 13
Longitudinal studies, 54, 134, 136, 143, 374

Mail interviews, 211–214, 223
Mailing lists, 235
Main body questions, 181–182
Mall intercept interviews, 217
Management, global/international, 3
Management information systems (MIS), 88, 92–93, 101.
    See also Databases
  basic elements, 94
  data collection and, 89
  development of, 89, *90,* 93–94
  model of, *94*
  purpose of, 88–89
  subsystems, 95–96
  uses of, 94–95
Manual data analysis, 53
Market entry, 82–83
Market Facts, 136
Market potential, 12
Marketing data sources, 72, 407–409
Marketing decisions, 84
Matrix structures, 21, 25–27, *26*

Maturation variables, 147–148
MDS (multidimensional scaling), 355, 362–364
Mean, 246–247, 255–257, 259, 262
Measurement, 193. *See also* Scale measurement
Measures of dispersion. *See* Dispersion
Mechanical observation, 138–139, 143
Median, 246, 247–248, 262
Memory problems, 179
MIS. *See* Management information systems (MIS)
Mode, 246, 248, 262
Moderators, 109, 114, 124
Monetary policies, 68
Mortality variables, 148
Multicountry research, 9–10
Multidimensional scaling (MDS), 355, 362–364
Multinominal distribution, 317
Multiple-choice questions, 171–172
Multiple regression analysis, 319, 336–342, 363, *364,*
    434–435
Multivariate analysis, 272, 300, 354–355, 363
  cluster analysis, 355, 360, 363, 364
  discriminant analysis, 355, 360–362, 363, *364*
  factor analysis, 355, 363–364
    considerations in, 355–356
    example of, *357*
    factor loadings, 357, 358
    factor scores, 358, 359–360
    model of, 358–359
    terms used in, 357–358
    uses of, 356–357
  multidimensional scaling (MDS), 355, 362–364
  sample size and, 355

National data sources, 397–399
National Family Opinion Inc., 136
National Trade Data Bank (NTDB), 76
Natural environment observation, 142
Net material product (NMP), 62
Net statistical discrepancy, 67
Nominal scales, 195–196, *198,* 208
Nondisgused approaches, 107
Nonhierarchical clustering, 360
Nonparametric tests, *277,* 300
Nonprobability sampling, 229–231, *236,* 240
Nonverbal stimuli questions, 172
Normal distribution, 253, 262
NTDB (National Trade Data Bank), 76
Null hypothesis, 277, 278, 300
Number system, 195, 196
Numeric data, 90
Numerical measures. *See* Mean; Median; Mode

Objective variables, 194

Observation techniques, 134–143
    audits, 52, 141, 142, 143
    benefits of, 142, 144
    bias in, 138, 140, 142
    content analysis, 52, 140–141, 143
    contrived/set-up environment observation, 142
    disguised observation, 142
    mechanical observation, 138–139, 143
    natural environment observation, 142
    personal observation, 137–138, 143
    problems with, 143, 144
    structured observation, 141–142
    trace analysis, 52, 139–140, 143
    undisguised observation, 142
    unstructured observation, 142
OECD (Organization for Economic Cooperation and Development), 90
Office automation system (OAS), 96
Official reserves account, 67
One group pre-post test experiment, 149-150
One-tailed tests, 283–284, 291
One-way analysis of variance (ANOVA), 308
Open-ended questions
    coding of, 177, 268, 271
    in questionnaires, 52, 160, 171, 172, 177, 185
Opening questions, 180–182
Operations, international, 4–6
Opinion polls, *228*
Oral reports, 167, 370–375
Order bias, 182
Ordinal scales, 196–197, *198, 208*
Organization for Economic Cooperation and Development (OECD), 76, 78, 90
Organizational structures, 19–21
    centralization in, 20, 27–29, *30,* 32
    decentralization in, 20, 23, 27, 28, 30–32, 101, 102
    divisional structures, 21, *22*
    functional structures, 21, 25, *25*
    geographic structures, 21, *24,* 24–25
    matrix structures, 21, 25–27, *26*
    product structures, 21, 22–23, *23*
Origin in scales, 194–195
Oversampling, 239

Paired comparison tests, 291, 292
Panels, 136, 139, 143, 220
Parameter, 227, 255, 256, 257, 259, 262, 278
Parametric tests, 276, 300. *See also* Hypothesis testing
Parralel translation, 132
Pearson coefficient of correlation, 334–335, 342, 433
Percentage scales, 202, 204
Percentiles, 248–249, 262

Personal interviews, 216–219, 223–224
    in questionnaire administration, 210–211, 212
    in questionnaire design, 177, 183
    telephone interviews, 214–217, 223
Personal observation, 137–138, 143
PIMS (Profit Impact of Market Strategies), 99
Plant location decisions, 83
Political data sources, 409–412
Political environment, 11, 68–69
Political risk, 11, 14–15, 356. *See also* Country risk analysis
Polls, *228*
Population, 227
Population, list of. *See* Sampling frame
Population characteristics, 228–229
Population definition, 240
Population growth data, 70, 77
Population standard deviation, 257–258
PowerPoint presentations, 373
PPP (purchasing power parity), 67
Pre-post test experiment, 149–150
Pre-post test with control experiment, 150–151
Preconditions for conducting experiments, 155–156
Predictive validity, 206
Presentations
    audiovisual presentation, 373, 375
    oral reports, 370–373
    questionnaires, 183–184
Pretesting questionnaires, 184, 185
Primary data, 51-53, 56, 57 (*See also* Conclusive research; Exploratory research; Focus group research; Observational research Questionnaires; Surveys)
    comparability of data, 129, 143
    cultural bias, 129–130, 143
    equivalence of data, 130–133, 143
    key influential factors, 129–133
Probability distribution, 253, 262, 305–306, 317
Probability sampling, 229, 231–233, *236,* 240, 263
Probability value (p Value), 284–289
Problem definition, 41, 42, 44–46, 57, 105, 161, 368
Problem identification, *46*
Product knowledge, 19
Product structures, 21, 22–23, *23*
Production approaches, 66
Production data, 72
Profit Impact of Market Strategies (PIMS), 99
Projective techniques, 107, 118–122, 121, 125
    sentence completion, 119, 120, 125
    word association, 118, 119–120, 125
Proportion, 258–259
Proposals, research, 41, *43,* 55–56, 57
Psycho-galvanometers, 139

Pupilometers, 139
Purchasing power parity (PPP), 67
p Value, 284–289

Qualitative research. *See* Exploratory research
Quality of data, 8
Quantitative research. *See* Conclusive research
Quantitative response measurements. *See* Scale
    measurements
Quartiles, 249
Question formats in scales, 198–199
Questionnaire administration, 210
    data collection methods, 210, 224
    factors affecting, *223*
    mail questionnaires, 210
    personal interviews, 210–211, 212
    selecting interviewing approaches, 222–223
    self-administered questionnaires, 210–211
    technology-driven methods, 219–222
    telephone questionnaires, 210
Questionnaires, 159, 160, 184. *See also* Surveys
    bias in, 164, 165, 173, 182, 185
    designing
        arranging questions, 180–182
        basic requirements of, 160–161
        cultural factors in, 160, 161, 163
        design process, *162*
        estimates in, 170–171
        generalizations in, 170–171
        information needs, 163–164
        problem definition, 41, 42, 44–46, 57, 105, 161, 368
        relevancy and accuracy in, 161, 185
        research objectives and, 161–163
        response categories, 172, 175, 176–177, 185, 196
        sample questionnaire, 186–191, 377–390
    lead questions, 180–182
    personal interviews and, 177, 183
    pretesting of, 184, 185
    question development, 164–166, 185
        answers for questions, 175–177
        difficulties for respondents, 178–180
        reworking questions, 177–178
    question structure
        close-ended questions, 171, 172
        dichotomous questions, 171–172
        multiple-choice questions, 171–172
        nonverbal stimuli questions, 172
        open-ended questions, 52, 160, 171, 172, 177, 185
        scaled response questions, 171, 173
    question wording
        to avoid, 166–171
        reevaluation of, 173–174
        to use, 164–166, 173–174, 185

Questionnaires *(continued)*
    structured questionnaires, 159–160
    style and presentation of, 183–184
    translation of, 173, 174–175
    types of, 159–160
    unstructured questionnaires, 160
Quota sampling, 230, *236,* 239, 240

Random sampling, 232–233, *236,* 240
Randomized block experiment, 153
Range, 248, 262
Range of answers, 175–177
Rank order correlation, 195, 196, 197
Rating scales, 202–204
Ratio scales, 197–198, 208, 300
Regression, statistical, 148, 157
Regression analysis, 53, 323–327, 342
    coefficient of correlation, 334–335, 342, 433
    coefficient of determination, 235
    evaluating regression models, 330
    intercept, 324
    multiple regression analysis, 319, 336–342, 363,
        364, 434–435
    SAS and, 328–330, 347–352
    simple linear regression, 324, 332, 336
    slope, 324, 330–332
    standard error of the estimate, 327–328, 336
Regulatory data sources, 78
Rejection region, 277, 278, *283*
Reliability, 8
Reports, 367
    audiovisual presentation, 373, 375
    executive summaries, 368, 375
    oral reports, 167, 370–375
    presenation of, 371–372, 375
    storage and retrieval of, 374
    written reports, 54, 367–370, 375
Resampling, 239
Research. *See* international research
Research industry, 32, 220
Research proposals, 41, *43,* 55–56, 57
Research reports, secondary, 80–81
Research suppliers. *See* Suppliers
Resembling, 239
Respondent identification, 270
Response bias, 164, 185, 261
Response categories, 172, 175, 176–177, 185,
    196
Retrieval, research report, 374
Return on investment (ROI), 251–253

Sample mean. *See* Mean
Sample questionnaire, 186–191, 377–390

Sample size, 240. *See also* Statistical concepts
   adjustments to, 260–261
   determination, 243–244, 259, 262
   estimating, 262
   mean estimates, 255–257, 259
   multivariate analysis and, 355
   proportion estimates and, 258–259
   selecting, 143, 262
Samples, 227
   development of
      defining target population, 233, 234-235, 240
      obtaining an accurate list, 240
      sampling frame selection, 240
Sampling, 227, 240
   bias in, 231, 239, 240, 261–262
   central limit theorem, 231
   distribution, 253, *254,* 262
   drawing conclusions from, 262
   elements in, 228
   equivalence of, 133, 143
   errors in, 240
   population characteristics, 228–229
   process of, 233–234
      choosing a sampling method, 236–237, 240
      defining target population, 233, 234–235, 240
      determining sample size, 237–238
      drawing samples, 238–239, 240
      selecting sampling units, 237
   qualitative and quantitative analysis in, 240
   sampling frames, 228, 233, 235–236, 240
   sampling techniques, 229–230, 239, 240
      cluster sampling, 232, 233, *236,* 240
      comparison of, *236*
      convenience sampling, 230, *236,* 237, 240
      judgment sampling, 230, *236,* 240
      nonprobability sampling, 229–231, *236,* 240
      probability sampling, 229, 231–233, *236,* 240
      quota sampling, 230, *236,* 239, 240
      simple random sampling, 232, *236,* 240
      snowball sampling, 230–231, 239, 240
      stratified random sampling, 232, *236,* 240
      systematic sampling, 233, *236,* 239, 240
   sampling units, 228, 237, 240
   substitution methods, 239
   techniques, comparison of, *236*
SAS, 271, 272, 274, 308, 320–322, 362, 435–447
Scale equivalence, 130, 143
Scale measurements, 193–194
   cultural factors in, 199
   development of, 207
   properties of, 197
   question forms in, 198–199
   reliability in, 204–205

Scale measurements *(continued)*
   types of scales, number system and, 195, 196
   validity in, 206–207
   variables in, 194
Scaled response questions
   in question development, 171, 173
   in scale measurements, 202–204
Scales, 194
   characteristics of, 194–195, *198*
   problems using, 202
   properties of, *198*
   question formats in, 202–204
   types of, 195
      interval scales, 197, *198,* 199, 208, 300
      likert scale, 130, 199–200, 205
      nominal scales, 195–196, *198,* 208
      ordinal scale, 196–197, *198,* 208
      rating scales, 202–204
      ratio scales, 197–198, 208, 300
      semantic differential scale, 200–202, 208
      staple scales, 202, 204
Scanner data, 34
Scanner volume-tracking data, 34
ScanTrack, 79, 99, 136
Searching secondary sources, *74*
Secondary data, 59, 72. *See also* databases; International
      business environments
   advantages of, 60
   application and use of, 81–84
   availability, 8
   census data, 76, 228
   developing countries, 392
   disadvantages of, 60–61
   evaluation of, 61–62
   external data sources, 71, 73–81, 85
      Asian-Pacific countries, 391–392
      census data, 76, 228
      databases and, 80
      developing countries, 392
      economic data, 399–403
      European countries, 78, 80–81, 392–394
      financial data, 403–407
      general international data, 394–397
      government data, 409–412
      Internet services, 81, 84
      investment data, 403–407
      Latin American countries, 394
      major sources, *75*
      marketing data, 407–409
      national data, 397–399
      political data, 409–412
      regulatory data, 78
      research reports, 80–81

Secondary data
external data sources *(continued)*
syndicated services, 78–79
tax regulation data, 78
trade associations, 73, 79–80
internal sources, 71–72, 85
databases and, 73
purpose of, 85
searching, *74*
statistical data, 76–78, 81
types of, 71
uses of, 59–60
Selection bias, 148, 157
Self-administered questionnaires, 210–211
Self-reference criterion, 62
Semantic differential scale, 200–202, 208
Sentence completion, 119, 120, 125
Service organizations, 78
Set-up environment observation, 142
Simple data analysis, 272
Simple language, 185
Simple linear regression, 324, 332, 336
SAS and, 327–328
Simple random sampling, 232, 233, *236,* 240
Simple tabulations, 53. *See also* Frequency distribution
Single-source data, 34
Slope, 324
Snowball sampling, 230–231, 239, 240
Sociocultural environment, 12, 70–71
Software packages
statistical. *See* SAS; SPSS
coding, 268–269
Spearman rank-order correlation. *See* Rank order
correlation
SPSS, 271, 272, 274, 308, 362, 425–434
SST (sums of squares total), 313–316
Standard & Poor's database, 99
Standard deviation, 250–252, 254, 262
of unknown populations, 257–258
Standard error of the estimate, 327–328, 336
Standard error of the mean, 231, 253, 255, 276, 281
Standardized services, 34. *See also* Suppliers
Staple scales, 202, 204
Starch Readership Survey, 34
Stastical Analysis System. *See* SAS
Static group experiment, 150
Statistical analytical approaches, *300*
Statistical concepts
central limit theorem, 262
coefficient of variation (CV), 252–253
confidence interval estimator, 256, 262, 294–296
descriptive statistics, 243–244, 262
dispersion, 248–249, 262

Statistical concepts *(continued)*
distribution, 253–254, 262, *413*
drawing conclusions from samples, 262
inferential statistics, 243, 244, 262
mean, 246–247, 255–257, 259, 262
median, 246, 247–248, 262
methods used for analyzing variables, *364*
mode, 246, 248, 262
percentiles, 248–249, 262
proportion, 258–259
range, 248, 262
standard deviation, 250–252, 254, 257–258, 262
standard error of the estimate, 327–328, 336
standard error of the mean, 231, 253, 255, 276, 281
variability, 248, 250–253, 262
variance, 250, 262
Statistical data sources, 76-78, 81, 412–415
Statistical Package for the Social Sciences. *See* SPSS
Statistical regression, 148, 157
Statistical significance tests, 304, 317. *See also* ANOVA;
Goodness-of-fit tests
Statistical tables, 417–424
Statistical yearbooks and sources, 73, 76–78
Statistics by country, 447–457
Storage, research report, 374
Storytelling research technique, 123
Strategic Planning Institute database, 99
Strategy formalization in research, 13–14
Stratified random sampling, 232–233, *236,* 240
Structured-direct questions. *See* Close-ended questions
Structured observation, 141–142
Structured questionnaires, 159–160
Structured questions, 52, 171
coding of, 269
Subjective research. *See* Scale measurements;
Scales
Subjective variables, 194
Substitution methods, 239
Sums of squares total (SST), 313–316
Suppliers, 32–35
customized services, 34–35
of international databases, 80
standardized services, 34
syndicated services, 34
top ten research companies worldwide, *33*
Surveys, 52, 134, 135–136, 143, 159–160. *See also*
Questionnaires
internet-based surveys, 221
questionnaires and, 159
Syndicated services
as data sources, 78–79
suppliers of, 34
Systematic sampling, 233, *236,* 239, 240

Tabulations. *See* Cross tabulation; Frequency distribution
Tarifs, 78, 85
TAT (thematic apperception tests), 51, 107, 119, 121–122, 125
Tax regulation data, 78
Technological environment, 11, 70
Technology-driven interview methods, 219–222
Telephone interviews, 214–217, 223
Test statistic, 277, 278, 317
Test units, 147, 148
Testing effects, 148
Tests of independence. *See* Chi-square distribution
Tests of statistical significance, 304, 317. *See also* ANOVA; Goodness-of fit tests
Text-based databases, 80
Textual data, 90
Thematic apperception test (TAT), 107, 119, 121–122
Theocratic law, 69
Time code, 270
Time order of occurrence of variables, 155–156
Time series experiment, 152–153
TPS (transaction-processing system), 96
Trace analysis, 52, 139–140, 143
Tracking studies, 54. 374
Trade associations, 73, 79–80
Transaction-processing system (TPS), 96, *97*
Transition questions, 181
Translating questionnaires, 173, 174–175
Translation equivalence, 132–133, 143
Transportation systems, 69
True-life research technique, 123–124
Two-tailed tests, 283–284
    p value for, 284–289
Two-way analysis of variance (ANOVA), 316
Type I error, 279, 300
Type II error, 279, 300

Undisguised observation, 142
United Nations (UN), 66, 73, 76, 244

Univariate analysis, 272, 300, 354
Universal Product Codes (UPCs), 136, 139
Unstructured observation, 142
Unstructured questionnaires, 160
Unstructured questions. *See* Open-ended questions
Unstructured research, 105, 160
UPCs (Universal Product Codes), 136

Validity
    in experiments, 154–155, 157
    hypothesis validity, 317
    in questionnaire administration, 222
    in scale measurements, 206–207
Variables
    in coding, 270
    in data analysis, 266
    in experimental research, 147, 157
    in multivariate analysis, 355
    in statistical methods for analyzing, *364*
    in statistics, 248, 250–253, 262
Variance, 250, 262, 317. *See also* ANOVA
Variation, coefficient of (CV), 252–253
VideoFocus Direct, 107
Virtual interviewing techniques, 220
VNU, 32

Warm-up questions, 181
Wide-Area Telecommunications Service (WATS), 214, 215
Word association, 118, 119–120, 125
Wording in question development
    to avoid, 166–171
    reevaluation of, 173–174
    to use, 164–166, 173–174, 185
World Bank, 73, 76, 77
World Wide Web index sites, 81
Written reports, 54, 367–370, 375

Yankee Group, 34

About the Author

James P. Neelankavil is professor of marketing and international business at Hofstra University. He has had extensive work experience with Firestone Tires, Inc., in India, and has served on the faculties of the Asian Institute of Business in Manila, Philippines, and the Stern School of Business of New York University. Dr. Neelankavil's research interests include cross-cultural management skills, impact of research and development on international profitability, international business corruption and its effect on individual firms, and value drivers in global operations.